What's Cooking America

More than 800 family-tested
recipes from American cooks
of today and yesterday

Linda Stradley & Andra Cook
Illustrated by Ben Anderson

ThreeForks™

© 1997 Linda Stradley and Andra Cook
Illustrated by Ben Anderson

Published by ThreeForks Books, an imprint of Falcon® Publishing, Inc., Helena, Montana
Printed in Canada.
Second edition

1 2 3 4 5 6 7 8 9 0 TP 05 04 03 02 01 00

Cover art by Richard Ferguson, Maxim Graphics.

ISBN: 1-56044-792-3
Library of Congress Catalog number 95-92570

For extra copies of this book and information about other ThreeForks Books, write to Falcon, P.O. Box 1718, Helena, Montana 59624; or call 1-800-582-2665. You can also visit our website at www.Falcon.com or contact us by e-mail at falcon@falcon.com.

What's Cooking
America

Acknowledgments

First and foremost, we thank our wonderful husbands, Bill and Don, for their support, patience, encouragement, and eagerness to sample and taste our recipes as we tested them. Without their love and support, this book would never have been possible.

To our wonderful children, Nancy Hartman, Brenda Weller, Ron Zemp, Derek Cook, and Cyndy Otto, who without knowing it, provided the inspiration for starting this book. Because of their requests for their favorite recipes and our desire to pass our recipes down to them, a cookbook was born. A heartfelt thanks to each for their testing, tasting, comments, and timely advice.

To Linda's mother, Dorothy Hagerman, and sister, Carol Arroyo, our grateful thanks for their time, patience, and advice. We also thank them for the long hours spent reading, proofing, and editing this cookbook. Their help is greatly appreciated.

Thanks to Ben Anderson for the wonderful illustrations. Without Ben's artistic ability, this book would not have taken on such a pleasant life.

To Nancy Ponzi, Heidi Foster, Bob Sherwin, and all our friends and family members who willingly tasted our recipes and encouraged us. We must not forget our favorite coffee shop, Coffee Ala Carte, where we spent hours discussing this book. A million thanks!

Introduction

A prime ingredient of our culture and social fabric has always been the food we have shared. Take good friends and good food spiced with laughter and friendly conversation, and you have a recipe for contentment of body and soul. If you can provide your own good friends, then let us provide some good food recipes that will encourage the laughter and lively conversation.

What's Cooking America is actually the combination of two separate books. Each began as a collection of favorite family recipes, both old and new, written at the request of our children and friends who remembered the satisfying experiences of the food served at our own tables. To these old recipes, we have added many new and exciting delights, all tested and tasted by eager husbands, families, and friends.

Both of us, having lived in various parts of the country, has her own unique collection of regional favorites provided by friends and neighbors. For that reason, we have not directed our efforts to any particular region or cooking style. *What's Cooking America* offers recipes from all over our country.

Because regional recipes often employ phrases or measures not universally familiar throughout America, we have standardized all measures and references. For the new and inexperienced cooks, we have stated things like pan and bowl sizes and have carefully explained steps more experienced cooks would deem self-evident.

Interesting and helpful are the sidebar tips, hints, and historical references on every page, which are especially welcomed by those who wish to perfect their culinary skills.

Neither of us has had professional culinary training, nor have we worked for a famous restaurant, but we both love to cook and to try new and innovative recipes. You will find both simple and gourmet fare here. Our families tell us everything we prepare is gourmet, but we think there must be some self-serving and ulterior motive at work here. You will be the judge of that.

Contents

Appetizers & Beverages

Baked Brie

1 french bread cannonball (round loaf, roughly 6-inches across)
1 (8-ounce) round brie cheese
5 to 6 sundried tomatoes (packed in olive oil), coarsely chopped
5 to 6 fresh basil leaves, chopped
Bread or assorted crackers

Preheat oven to 350 degrees. Cut bread horizontally, approximately halfway up from bottom. Using brie cheese as a size guide, cut and scoop out center of bread so that cheese can fit into bottom half of bread (save chunks of bread to serve with heated loaf). Before placing cheese inside, drizzle a little of the olive oil from jar of sundried tomatoes into the cavity of the bread.

Remove top rind of brie. Place brie cheese into scooped out bread, dot top with sundried tomatoes and basil leaves; drizzle with a little more olive oil. Place upper half of bread on top. Wrap tightly in aluminum foil. Bake 15 to 20 minutes or until brie cheese is soft and thoroughly heated. Remove from oven, unwrap, and remove bread top. Transfer onto a serving tray and serve immediately with additional bread or assorted crackers.

Serves many.

Brie Cheese

Brie originated in France centuries ago. It is named after La Brie, the province in northern France where it was first made. One of the most popular of imported cheeses, brie has been called the "king of all cheeses."

This cheese is made from whole, skim, or partially skim cow's milk. It is described as creamy, smooth, and very delicate.

Brie is generally considered an excellent cheese for any occasion, but especially dessert.

Because brie is perishable, it should be kept refrigerated. Bring to room temperature before serving.

The natural white rind of the brie cheese is edible, so don't discard it when serving brie as an appetizer. If you need to remove the rind, chill the cheese and use a sharp knife to cut off the rind. You can also bring the cheese to room temperature to soften it, then use a spoon to scoop it out of the rind.

TIP: Look for brie cheese rounds that are no more than one-inch thick. If thicker, they can get overripe on the edges before ripening in the center.

Walnut-Glazed Brie

2/3 cup finely chopped walnuts
1/4 cup coffee-flavored liqueur
3 tablespoons firmly packed brown sugar
1/2 teaspoon vanilla extract
1 (12-ounce) round brie cheese
Assorted crackers
Pear slices

Preheat oven to 350 degrees. Spread walnuts onto bottom of an ungreased pie plate. Bake 10 to 12 minutes or until toasted, stirring occasionally. Remove from oven and stir in coffee-flavored liqueur, brown sugar, and vanilla extract; set aside.

Reduce oven temperature to 325 degrees. Remove top rind of brie cheese. Place brie cheese into an ungreased shallow baking dish; top with walnut mixture. Bake, uncovered, 8 to 10 minutes or until brie cheese is soft and thoroughly heated. Remove from oven and serve immediately with assorted crackers and pear slices.

Serves many.

Fondue

The word fondue comes from the French word "fondre," which means "to melt." It is said that the original fondue was developed in Switzerland during the 18th century.

The Swiss people baked bread and made cheese during the summer and fall months, and stockpiled their supply to last through the winter. Before the next summer arrived, the cheese and bread had become hard and difficult to chew. Because of this, someone decided to try melting the cheese and dunking the stale bread into the melted cheese mixture. Presto, the first fondue!

Today, cubes of crusty bread are speared on long-handled forks. Each diner dips his cube of bread into the cheese mixture, swirls it around, and then eats the tasty morsel.

A good chilled, light white wine and a crisp, green salad are perfect accompaniments to fondue.

Tomato & Basil Gouda Fondue

1 (8-ounce) round gouda cheese
2 small roma tomatoes, cored and diced
1 tablespoon finely chopped fresh basil
1 loaf baguette bread, sliced and toasted

Remove coating from gouda cheese and carefully scoop out center, leaving a 1/4-inch thick shell; set shell aside. Coarsely chop scooped-out cheese into small pieces and place in a microwave-safe bowl; mix in tomatoes and basil.

Cook, uncovered, in microwave oven on high for 1 minute. Stir and cook another 2 minutes, stirring every 20 seconds or until cheese is bubbling. Remove from microwave oven; pour cheese mixture into shell, pushing into corners to fill shell. Serve hot with toasted baguette slices.

ALTERNATIVE:
Omit tomatoes and basil. Combine 1 tablespoon chopped green chilies, 1 chopped green onion, and 1/4 teaspoon ground cumin with the chopped cheese. Proceed as above.

Serves many.

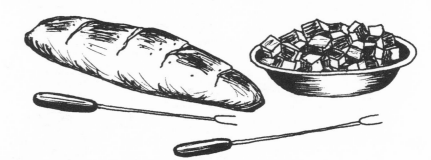

Cheese Fondue

1 cup water
1 cup dry white wine
1 teaspoon garlic powder
1 tablespoon butter or margarine
1/8 teaspoon white pepper
1/8 teaspoon ground nutmeg
1 (2-pound) loaf processed white American cheese, shredded*
Petite rye bread slices

* Found in the deli section of the store.

In the top pan of a double boiler over hot water, combine water, white wine, garlic powder, butter or margarine, white pepper, and nutmeg; bring to a boil. MUST USE A DOUBLE BOILER OR CHEESE WILL BURN. Add white American cheese; stir continuously until cheese melts into a smooth, heavy sauce. Serve with petite rye bread slices for dipping.

Serves many.

Shrimp Cheese Ball

This is also excellent as a sandwich spread.

2 (8-ounce) packages cream cheese, room temperature
1 (6-ounce) can shrimp, drained and rinsed
1 (6-ounce) can black olives, drained and chopped
Seasoning salt to taste
Lemon juice to taste
3 small green onions, finely chopped
Chopped nuts
Chopped fresh parsley
Assorted crackers

In a large bowl, mash cream cheese with a fork. Add shrimp, black olives, seasoning salt, lemon juice, and green onions; stir until well blended. With your hands, form cheese mixture into a large ball.

In a small bowl, combine nuts and parsley; roll cheese ball in nut mixture to coat completely. Cover with plastic wrap and refrigerate until ready to serve. Serve with assorted crackers.

Yields 1 ball.

Roquefort Cream Mousse

This mousse makes a wonderful first impression.

2 (8-ounce) packages cream cheese, room temperature
1/2 cup crumbled roquefort or blue cheese, room temperature
1 tablespoon minced onion
1/8 teaspoon worcestershire sauce
1 package unflavored gelatin
1 tablespoon dry sherry
1/3 cup whipping cream
Assorted crackers

Line a 3-cup decorative mold with clear plastic wrap. In a large bowl, combine cream cheese and roquefort or blue cheese; stir until well blended. Stir in onion and worcestershire sauce until very smooth.

In a small saucepan, sprinkle gelatin over sherry; let soften 5 minutes. Over low heat, cook and stir until gelatin dissolves. Remove from heat.

In a small saucepan over medium-low heat, heat whipping cream just until hot (do not boil). Remove from heat and add to gelatin mixture; cool to room temperature. Add cooled gelatin mixture to cheese mixture; stir until well blended. Pour into prepared mold. Cover and chill at least 8 hours or overnight. Unmold onto a lettuce-lined plate. Serve with assorted crackers.

Serves many.

Salmon-Shrimp Starter

This recipe makes a fast and delicious appetizer.

8 pieces of lox (smoked salmon)
8 large shrimp, cleaned, deveined, and cooked
Cream cheese

Assemble by placing shrimp on top of lox and topping the shrimp with a teaspoonful of cream cheese.

Roll shrimp and cream cheese inside the lox. Secure with a toothpick if necessary to hold closed.

Goat Cheese Torta

When this torta is sliced, it reveals colorful distinct layers.

2 (8-ounce) packages cream cheese, room temperature
8 ounces goat cheese, room temperature
2 cloves garlic, minced
4 teaspoons chopped fresh oregano or 1 1/4 teaspoons dried oregano, crushed
1/8 teaspoon pepper
1/4 cup prepared pesto
1/2 cup sundried tomatoes (packed in olive oil)
1 to 2 tablespoons toasted slivered almonds
Fresh oregano or parsley sprig
Stone-ground wheat crackers or thinly sliced baguette bread

Line a 9x5-inch loaf pan, souffle pan, or decorative gelatin mold with clear plastic wrap. In a food processor or a large bowl, combine cream cheese, goat cheese, garlic, oregano, and pepper; stir until well blended.

Spread 1/3 of the cheese mixture onto the bottom of prepared pan. Top with pesto, spreading evenly. Layer with another 1/3 of the cheese mixture. Drain sundried tomatoes, reserving one tomato for garnish. Cut remaining sundried tomatoes into small pieces; spread evenly over cheese mixture in pan. Top with remaining cheese mixture. Cover with plastic wrap and press gently to pack cheese. Refrigerate several hours or overnight.

Uncover and invert onto a serving plate. Cut reserved sundried tomato into thin slices. Garnish torta with tomato, almonds, and oregano or parsley. Serve with crackers or baguette bread.

NOTE: This can be made 5 days in advance and refrigerated, or it can be frozen up to 2 months.

Makes 12 to 16 servings.

Goat Cheese

Goat cheese (chevre cheese) can be found in many varieties, packed in various shapes and sizes, and varying in texture and taste.

Fresh goat cheese should look moist. Reject if air-bloated, moldy, or leaking whey.

In the refrigerator, protect cheese from air with original wrappings, plastic wrap, or wax paper. Discard any cheese that develops an off-odor, strange colors, or more than a touch of mold.

WAYS TO ENJOY SOFT GOAT CHEESE:

- *Spread on toast or bagels.*
- *Substitute for cream cheese in dips.*
- *Swirl or layer with pesto to spread on crackers.*
- *Top green salads with crumbled cheese, or with slices briefly warmed in the oven.*
- *Crumble over pizza.*
- *Stuff into seeded fresh chilies; broil until golden.*
- *Stir into vegetable soups.*

Wisconsin Herb Cheese

Much better than the store-bought ones.

1/2 cup butter, room temperature
2 (8-ounce) packages cream cheese, room temperature
3/4 teaspoon dried thyme, crushed
1/2 teaspoon dried marjoram, crushed
1/8 teaspoon dried sage, crushed
2 teaspoons dried chives, crushed
1 teaspoon finely chopped green onions
1/8 teaspoon Beau Monde seasoning
1/16 teaspoon garlic powder
Assorted crackers

In a large bowl, combine butter and cream cheese; stir until well blended. Mix in thyme, marjoram, sage, chives, green onions, Beau Monde seasoning, and garlic powder. With your hands, mold cheese mixture into desired shape and cover with plastic wrap; refrigerate for 24 hours. Remove cheese from refrigerator, unwrap, and serve at room temperature with assorted crackers.

Serves many.

Deluxe Fajita Nachos

A new twist on everyone's favorite dish.

2 1/2 cups cooked and shredded chicken
1 package fajita seasoning mix
1/3 cup water
1 1/4 cups shredded cheddar cheese
1 cup shredded monterey jack cheese
1 cup corn chips
1 large tomato, finely diced
1 (2 1/4-ounce) can sliced black olives, drained
1/4 cup sliced green onions
Tomato salsa
Corn chips

Preheat broiler. In a large frying pan over medium-high heat, combine chicken, fajita seasoning mix, and water. Bring to a boil; reduce heat to low and simmer 3 minutes. On a large ungreased shallow ovenproof platter, layer chicken, cheddar cheese, and monterey jack cheese. Arrange corn chips around the edge. Broil to melt cheese. Remove from oven and top with tomato, black olives, green onions, and desired amount of tomato salsa. Serve with additional corn chips.

NOTE: 1 1/4 pounds cooked ground beef can be used in place of shredded chicken. Can also top with guacamole and sour cream.

Serves many.

Cyndy's Taco Nacho Salad

1 head lettuce, chopped
Sour Cream Mixture
1 (12-ounce) bottle hot salsa sauce
Jalapeño chile peppers (optional)
1 green bell pepper, cored, seeded, and finely chopped
1 red bell pepper, cored, seeded, and finely chopped
1 large tomato, finely diced
Scallions or green onions to taste, finely chopped
1 pound cheddar cheese, shredded
1 package taco chips

In the center of a large serving platter, make a bed of lettuce. Place Sour Cream Mixture onto the middle, forming a bowl shape; indent with spoon. Place salsa sauce into indentation. Top mixture with jalapeño peppers, green bell pepper, red bell pepper, tomato, scallions or green onions, and cheddar cheese. Arrange taco chips around lettuce.

Serves many.

SOUR CREAM MIXTURE:
1 cup sour cream
1 (8-ounce) package cream cheese, room temperature
1 package taco seasoning mix

In a large bowl, combine sour cream, cream cheese, and taco seasoning mix; stir until well blended.

Grating Cheese

1/4 pound of cheese equals 1 cup of grated or shredded cheese.

Cheeses like swiss, cheddar, and monterey jack are easier to shred by hand or in the food processor if they're cold. Before grating cheese, put it in the freezer for about forty minutes. The cheese won't be as sticky and will grate much easier.

Hard cheeses like parmesan and romano cheese should be at room temperature to grate.

Both hard and semi-hard cheeses can be grated ahead of time and stored in a plastic bag until ready to use.

TIPS: Don't throw out your dried-out cheese (without mold). Save it for when you need grated cheese in your cooking.

Rub the grater with a little vegetable oil to prevent cheese from sticking to it.

Guacamole

There seem to be more versions of guacamole than there are avocados in this world.

The recipe on this page follows traditional precepts; the mixture must be chunky (never a puree), have a bite from fresh chilies (if fresh chilies are unavailable, use canned chilies), and be perfumed with fresh cilantro.

Good guacamole requires good avocados. This recipe is best made with California-type avocados (Haas), those with rough, dark-green skins.

Guacamole does not keep well, so make it at the last moment before serving.

Guacamole Dip With Cilantro

In the cuisine of the Southwest, guacamole is used as a cocktail dip, or one of the toppings and/or fillings of enchiladas, tacos, tostadas, or burritos. It is also wonderful as a cold sauce for grilled meats or fish.

1 large tomato, diced
2 tablespoons finely chopped onion
1 green chile pepper, cored, seeded, and finely chopped
2 tablespoons lime juice
1 ripe Haas avocado, peeled and seeded
1/2 teaspoon cumin seeds, toasted
1/4 cup firmly packed chopped fresh cilantro
Salt to taste
Coarsely ground pepper to taste
Corn chips

In a medium bowl, combine tomato, onion, chile pepper, and lime juice; set aside.

In a medium bowl, mash avocado with a fork until smooth. Add cumin seeds, cilantro, salt, and pepper. Add tomato mixture to avocado mixture; stir until well blended. Let set at least 15 minutes for the flavors to blend before serving. Serve with corn chips.

Serves many.

Brenda's Salsa

Salsa is a delicious uncooked chunky tomato sauce. You can develop a real passion for salsa, since it is low in calories and very flavorful. There are no hard-and-fast rules in making salsa. Add or delete ingredients according to your taste. Serve with corn chips (if you eat too many corn chips, then it is not low in calories!)

6 to 7 medium tomatoes, diced
1 large onion, diced
1 bunch fresh cilantro, finely chopped
6 cloves garlic, minced
1/2 teaspoon red (cayenne) pepper or to taste
Salt to taste
1/8 teaspoon hot pepper sauce or to taste
Corn chips

In a large bowl, combine tomatoes, onion, cilantro, and garlic. Add cayenne pepper, salt, and hot pepper sauce. Refrigerate at least 2 hours or overnight before serving. Serve with corn chips.

NOTE: Chile peppers may be substituted for cayenne pepper and hot pepper sauce. How hot you make your salsa depends on the kind of chilies and the amount you use.

Serves many.

Texas Layered Bean Dip

Serve this layered dip with tortilla or corn chips. Watch your guests dig in.

FIRST LAYER:
1 (15-ounce) can black beans, drained
1 tablespoon minced onion
1 to 2 jalapeño chile peppers, cored, seeded, and
   finely chopped
1 cup shredded sharp cheddar cheese
1/8 teaspoon hot pepper sauce or to taste
Salt to taste
2 tablespoons vegetable oil

In a medium bowl, mash the black beans. Add onion, chile peppers, cheddar cheese, hot pepper sauce, and salt; stir until well blended.

In a medium frying pan over medium heat, heat vegetable oil; add the bean mixture, stirring until the cheese is melted and the mixture is bubbling. Remove from heat and set aside.

SECOND LAYER:
2 medium Haas avocados, peeled and seeded
2 tablespoons lemon juice
1/2 teaspoon salt
1/2 teaspoon coarsely ground pepper

In a medium bowl, combine avocados, lemon juice, salt, and pepper; mash together until well blended; set aside.

THIRD LAYER:
1 cup sour cream
1/2 cup mayonnaise
1/2 teaspoon red (cayenne) pepper

In a small bowl, combine sour cream, mayonnaise, and cayenne pepper; set aside.

FOURTH LAYER:
1 (7-ounce) can olives, drained and chopped
3 medium tomatoes, peeled and coarsely chopped
1 cup chopped green onions

In a medium bowl, combine olives, tomatoes, and chopped green onions; set aside.

TO ASSEMBLE:
Spread half of the bean mixture onto a large shallow serving platter. Top with half of the second layer. Spread with half of the third layer and half of the fourth layer. Repeat with the balance of each of the four mixtures, ending with the tomato mixture on top. Serve immediately.

Makes 6 to 8 servings.

Fresh Green Chile Peppers

Fresh green chilies, such as jalapeños, serranos, or poblanos, are becoming easier to find. If a recipe calls for fresh chilies, the canned versions are not a good substitute.

If the chilies are too hot or spicy for a recipe, soak them in salted water for about one hour. Chop and add as a substitute for canned chilies.

Make Your Own Tortilla Chips

Buy packaged fresh corn or flour tortillas from your supermarket. Remove from package and stack tortillas, cut stack into six wedges.

TO FRY: In a large heavy saucepan, heat one-half inch of vegetable oil. Fry the tortilla wedges, a few at a time (approximately one minute for corn tortillas or forty-five seconds for flour tortillas) until they are crisp and lightly browned. Drain well on paper towels.

TO BAKE: Preheat oven to 500 degrees. Bake tortillas five minutes; turn and bake another one to two minutes. Remove from oven.

If desired, sprinkle the chips lightly with salt.

Easy Street Crab Meat Dip

This is fantastic looking and tastes wonderful. Your guests will rave about this one. This recipe can be made up to two days in advance.

1/2 pound cooked crab meat
1 (8-ounce) package cream cheese, cut into chunks
1 (10 3/4-ounce) can cream of mushroom soup, undiluted
1 package unflavored gelatin
1/2 cup mayonnaise
1/2 cup sliced green onions
1/2 cup chopped celery
Assorted crackers

Lightly oil a 4-cup mold and set aside. Carefully clean the crab meat of any shells or cartilage.

In a medium saucepan over medium-low heat, combine cream cheese and mushroom soup; stir until well blended. Sprinkle gelatin over mixture; stir until well blended. Stir in mayonnaise until well blended (do not let mixture boil). Remove from heat and carefully blend in crab meat, green onions, and celery.

Pour crab mixture into prepared mold and refrigerate at least 6 hours or overnight. To unmold, briefly dip mold in hot water, being careful not to let water run into the mold. Invert onto a serving platter and serve with assorted crackers.

Makes 10 servings.

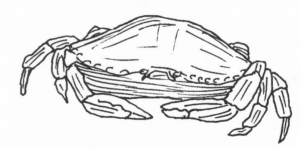

Types of Crab

There are several varieties of crabs in the United States. The Pacific states have their Dungeness crab and Alaskan King crab. The Eastern states have the Blue crab which inhabits Atlantic and Gulf waters.

The Dungeness crab is a Pacific crab found in waters from Alaska to Baja, California. It takes its name from a small town on the Olympic Peninsula in Washington, where it was first commercially caught. By law, only adult males at least 6 1/4-inches across can be harvested.

The Dungeness crab is in its prime season during the winter. It is sweeter than that of the Blue crab and makes larger flakes (this makes Dungeness crab meat especially good for salads, cocktails, and creamed dishes).

Hot Dungeness Crab Appetizer

1/2 pound cooked crab meat or 1 (6-ounce) can Dungeness crab meat, drained and rinsed
2/3 cup mayonnaise
1/2 cup marinated artichoke hearts, drained and chopped
1 teaspoon lemon juice
1/2 cup freshly grated parmesan cheese
1/4 cup diced onion
Baguette bread

Preheat oven to 350 degrees. If using fresh crab meat, carefully clean the crab meat of any shells or cartilage.

In an ungreased small 2-cup baking dish, combine crab meat, mayonnaise, artichoke hearts, lemon juice, parmesan cheese, and onion. Bake, uncovered, 15 to 20 minutes or until thoroughly heated. Remove from oven and serve immediately with warm sliced baguette bread.

Makes 10 servings.

Crab-Almond Delight

1/2 pound cooked crab meat
1 (8-ounce) package cream cheese, room temperature
1/3 cup mayonnaise
1/4 cup chopped onion
1 1/2 tablespoons white wine
1 tablespoon milk
1 tablespoon chopped fresh parsley
1 tablespoon lemon juice
1 teaspoon prepared horseradish
1 teaspoon prepared mustard
1/2 teaspoon seasoned salt
1/2 teaspoon garlic salt
1/2 teaspoon worcestershire sauce
Slivered almonds
Assorted crackers

Preheat oven to 350 degrees. Carefully clean the crab meat of any shells or cartilage. In an ungreased 1 1/2-quart casserole dish, combine crab meat and cream cheese; stirring until well blended. Stir in mayonnaise, onion, white wine, milk, and parsley. Add lemon juice, prepared horseradish, prepared mustard, seasoned salt, garlic salt, and worcestershire sauce, stirring until well blended. Sprinkle top generously with almonds.

Bake, uncovered, 20 minutes. Remove from oven and transfer into a chafing dish to keep warm. Serve warm with assorted crackers.

Makes 10 servings.

Crab Cocktail Cakes

1 pound cooked crab meat or 2 (6-ounce) cans crab meat, drained and rinsed
2 egg whites, lightly beaten
1 1/4 cups sour cream, divided
1 cup chopped green onions, divided
1 tablespoon dried basil
1 1/2 teaspoons Old Bay Seasoning
1 tablespoon chopped fresh cilantro
1 tablespoon lemon juice
1 cup bread crumbs
2 teaspoons minced fresh dill or 1 teaspoon dried dill weed, crushed
1 lemon, cut into wedges

Preheat oven to 375 degrees. If using fresh crab, carefully clean the crab meat of any shells or cartilage. In a large bowl, combine crab meat, egg whites, 1/4 cup sour cream, 1/2 cup green onions, basil, Old Bay Seasoning, cilantro, and lemon juice. Form mixture into 1-inch diameter patties.

In a small bowl, combine bread crumbs and dill; roll crab patties in crumb mixture. Place onto a large nonstick baking sheet; bake, uncovered, 10 to 15 minutes or until lightly browned. Remove from oven and transfer onto a serving platter.

In a small bowl, combine 1 cup sour cream and 1/2 cup green onions. Serve crab cakes with lemon wedges and sour cream mixture.

Makes 12 to 15 servings.

Crab

When you buy canned or fresh crab meat, finger through meat carefully to remove the bits of shell or cartilage that may be there.

Soak canned crab meat for a short time in cold water to remove the "tinny" flavor. Crab meat that is soaked this way tastes fresher.

Refrigerate leftover crab meat no longer than two days.

Horseradish

Native to eastern Europe; now grown mainly in northern Europe, Britain, and the United States.

Grated horseradish is best fresh, prepared just before serving, but it may be refrigerated in a tightly covered jar. It's much more potent than store-bought; even the fumes are very strong.

When you handle the peeled or grated root, be sure not to rub your eyes. When you peel it, remove any tinge of green, which will cause a very bitter taste.

If possible, do not choose horseradish roots with soft or wrinkled ends, which are signs of age. The cut root will keep for months, unpeeled, if refrigerated in a sealed plastic bag.

HOMEMADE HORSERADISH:
1 horseradish root
2 tablespoons white vinegar
1/2 teaspoon salt
1/2 teaspoon sugar

Peel horseradish and cut enough root into 1/2-inch pieces to make 2/3 cup. In a food processor, chop pieces until finely minced, approximately 90 seconds, scraping bowl down as needed. Add vinegar, salt, and sugar; whirl 20 seconds.

HORSERADISH CREAM: Whip 1/2 cup whipping cream until soft peaks form. Fold in horseradish until desired taste is obtained.

Pat's Hot Clam Dip

3 tablespoons butter or margarine
4 tablespoons all-purpose flour
2 (6 1/2-ounce) cans minced clams, drained and reserving juice
3/4 cup milk
2 egg yolks, beaten
2 tablespoons chopped fresh chives
1/4 teaspoon hot pepper sauce
1 tablespoon prepared horseradish
1/8 teaspoon salt
1/4 cup bread crumbs
1/2 cup shredded cheddar cheese
Butter or margarine
Assorted crackers

Preheat oven to 350 degrees. Lightly grease a 1 1/2-quart baking dish. In a medium saucepan over medium heat, melt butter or margarine. Add flour, 1/2 cup of reserved clam juice, and milk, stirring continuously until mixture just starts to boil. Remove from heat; stir in egg yolks, chives, clams, hot pepper sauce, prepared horseradish, and salt.

Pour mixture into prepared baking dish. Top with bread crumbs and cheddar cheese. Dot with butter or margarine. Bake, uncovered, 45 minutes. Remove from oven and serve with assorted crackers.

Makes 6 to 8 servings.

Dill Dip for Vegetables

2/3 cup sour cream
2/3 cup mayonnaise
3/4 teaspoon dried dill weed, crushed
1 teaspoon dried parsley, crushed
2 teaspoons dried onion flakes, crushed
2 teaspoons Beau Monde seasoning
Assorted cold vegetables

In a large bowl, combine sour cream and mayonnaise. Mix in dill weed, parsley, onion flakes, and Beau Monde seasoning. Cover and refrigerate at least 1 hour or overnight. Transfer into a serving bowl and serve with assorted cold vegetables.

Serves many.

Mo's Green Bean Pâté

This unusual pâté will be a big hit at your next party. Everyone will ask for this recipe, so be prepared.

1/2 pound fresh green beans, ends trimmed
3 large onions, peeled and sliced
1/4 cup vegetable broth
3 hard-cooked egg whites
1 cup walnut pieces
1/2 teaspoon salt
1/2 teaspoon coarsely ground pepper
Assorted crackers

In a large saucepan over medium-high heat, cook green beans in water for 12 minutes. Remove from heat and drain. In a medium frying pan over medium heat, sauté onions in vegetable broth 30 minutes or until onions are well done, stirring frequently. Remove from heat.

In a food processor, place green beans, onions, hard-cooked egg whites, walnuts, salt, and pepper; whirl until a pâté-like consistency is reached. Transfer into a serving bowl and serve with assorted crackers.

Yields 2 cups.

Spinach Dip

This dip is also excellent substituted for the clam dip in the Stuffed French Bread recipe on page 16.

1 cup sour cream
1 cup mayonnaise
1 (10-ounce) package frozen chopped spinach, thawed and drained
1 small onion, finely chopped
1 (8-ounce) can chopped water chestnuts
1 envelope dry vegetable soup mix
Assorted crackers

In a medium bowl, combine sour cream and mayonnaise. Stir in spinach, onion, water chestnuts, and vegetable soup mix; stir until well blended. Cover and refrigerate at least 1 hour or overnight. Transfer into a serving bowl and serve with assorted crackers.

Serves many.

"Skinny" Dips

Reducing calories and fat doesn't mean doing without dips. It means "lightening up" on the ingredients used to make them.

TIPS: Instead of all sour cream, mix three parts lowfat plain yogurt with one part dairy sour cream.

To reduce calories and fat, use nonfat sour cream instead of regular sour cream.

Cottage cheese can be used in place of sour cream. Just place it in the blender until it is creamed.

When your recipe calls for mayonnaise, use a half-and-half combination of regular mayonnaise and a reduced or nonfat mayonnaise.

Dipper Ideas

Arrange one or more of the following dippers around your bowl of dip or spread; guests fix their own, with the help of toothpicks:

- *Tomato wedges*
- *Pineapple sticks*
- *Radishes*
- *Green-pepper strips*
- *Green onions*
- *Cauliflower flowerets*
- *Cucumber strips*
- *Carrot or celery sticks*
- *Apple chunks*
- *Broccoli flowerets*

Festive Wings

3/4 cup (about 18 crackers) Ritz crackers, finely crushed
1/3 cup freshly grated parmesan cheese
1 teaspoon dried oregano, crushed
1/2 teaspoon garlic powder
1/2 teaspoon paprika
1/8 teaspoon coarsely ground pepper
1/3 cup Dijon mustard
2 pounds chicken wings, split and tips removed

Preheat oven to 350 degrees. Grease a large baking sheet. In a shallow bowl, combine cracker crumbs, parmesan cheese, oregano, garlic powder, paprika, and pepper; set aside.

In a small bowl, place Dijon mustard and coat chicken pieces; then roll in crumb mixture and place onto prepared baking sheet.

Bake, uncovered, 35 to 40 minutes or until golden brown, turning chicken pieces over halfway through baking time. Remove from oven and serve warm.

Makes 12 servings.

Paprika

Paprika is the ground, dried pod of a variety of capsicum. Its growth habits are similar to those of the bell pepper, to which it is closely related.

It is native to Central America, where it was found by the early Spanish and Portuguese explorers. It is now grown in central and southern Europe, as well as in southern California.

In cooking, paprika is traditionally used to give color, as well as a sweet pepper flavor to pale soups and cream sauces.

Paprika loses its flavor and aroma quickly, becoming brown and stale-tasting if kept too long. Store in an airtight container in a cool, dark place.

TIP: Buy the best quality of sweet paprika available. It is worthwhile for the superior flavor.

Barbecued Ribs, Meatballs or Chicken Wings

PORK RIBS: In a large saucepan, boil ribs, covered with water, for 20 minutes or until pork is cooked.

MEATBALLS: Preheat oven to 350 degrees. In a medium bowl, combine 1 pound lean ground beef, 1 egg, and 1/4 cup bread crumbs; mix until well blended. Form into walnut-sized balls. Place onto an ungreased baking sheet and bake 20 minutes.

CHICKEN WINGS: Cut tips from wings. In a small bowl, roll wings in flour. In a medium frying pan over medium heat, heat vegetable oil until hot; add chicken wings and fry until fully cooked and tender. Drain on paper towels.

CHILI SAUCE:
2 1/4 cups or 1 (18-ounce) jar grape jelly
1 1/2 cups or 1 (12-ounce) jar chili sauce
1/4 teaspoon red (cayenne) pepper

In a crockpot, combine grape jelly, chili sauce, and cayenne pepper. After you have prepared either the ribs, meatballs or chicken wings, put them into the Chili Sauce.

NOTE: You may want to add a little water to keep sauce from becoming too thick. Cook, covered, on low heat in crockpot 3 hours before serving.

Serves many.

Roasted Garlic

Garlic becomes very mellow and spreadable after cooking.

Whole garlic heads
Olive oil
Salt and pepper to taste
Freshly grated parmesan cheese
Baguette bread
Cream cheese, room temperature

Preheat oven to 275 degrees. Peel the outer skin of the garlic only; leave garlic whole. Cut off the tips (so that when you pour the olive oil over, it will get into the cloves of garlic).

Place garlic heads into a small baking dish; pour olive oil over the tops to a depth of about 1/2-inch. Sprinkle with salt and pepper. Cover and bake 1 hour. Remove from oven and uncover. Sprinkle with parmesan cheese. Cover and bake another 1 hour. Remove from oven and cool before serving.

To serve, spread baguette bread with cream cheese, squeeze clove onto the bread, and spread.

Serves many.

Garlic Dip With Garlic Cheese Bread

1 1/4 cups whipping cream
1 clove garlic, minced
1/4 teaspoon dried thyme, crushed
1/3 cup crumbled gorgonzola cheese
Garlic Cheese Bread

In a small saucepan over medium-high heat, combine whipping cream, garlic, and thyme; bring to a boil. Stir in gorgonzola cheese until melted. Reduce heat to low, stirring occasionally, and simmer slowly until sauce is reduced by half (the sauce will thicken as it reduces). Transfer into a serving bowl and serve warm with Garlic Cheese Bread.

GARLIC CHEESE BREAD:
1/2 cup butter or margarine, room temperature
6 cloves garlic, minced
3/4 teaspoon dried basil, crushed
3/4 teaspoon dried oregano, crushed
1/2 cup freshly grated parmesan cheese
1 loaf french bread, split in half lengthwise

Preheat broiler. In a small bowl, combine butter or margarine, garlic, basil, oregano, and parmesan cheese; spread over each half loaf of bread. Cut into serving pieces and broil 3 to 5 minutes or until golden brown. Remove from oven.

Yields about 64 strips.

Serving Roasted Garlic

Roasted garlic is excellent used in your baking. It is milder than raw garlic. In fact, raw garlic is two to four times stronger in flavor.

Roast (bake) whole heads and serve with crunchy bread and cream cheese. After it is baked, just squeeze the soft garlic out of the skin and spread it like butter over the bread.

ADDITIONAL USES FOR ROASTED GARLIC ARE:

SOUPS: The cloves are so soft that they melt into pureed soups with only a little bit of stirring.

SAUCES: In a small bowl, blend one tablespoon of roasted garlic with one tablespoon of butter and mix into the pan juice of any roast.

MAYONNAISE: Mix a few roasted garlic cloves into plain mayonnaise.

Garlic

1 medium clove garlic equals 1/2 teaspoon minced garlic, or 1/8 teaspoon garlic powder, or 1/4 teaspoon garlic juice, or 1/2 teaspoon garlic salt.

TIP: When selecting garlic, it should be plump and firm, with its paper-like covering intact, not spongy, soft, or shriveled.

Worcestershire Sauce

This spicy sauce is based on a recipe from India. The sauce was first manufactured in Worcestershire, England; hence the name.

Worcestershire sauce is made from a combination of vinegar, molasses, anchovies, shallots, sugar, tamarind, and spices. The exact proportions of the ingredients remain the manufacturer's secret.

Use it sparingly so it doesn't overwhelm natural flavors.

Seasoned Oyster Crackers

1 (1-ounce) package ranch-style salad dressing mix
3/4 cup vegetable oil
1/2 teaspoon dried dill weed, crushed
1/2 teaspoon lemon pepper
1/4 teaspoon garlic powder
1 tablespoon freshly grated parmesan cheese
2 cups oyster crackers

Preheat oven to 350 degrees. In a small bowl, combine salad dressing mix, vegetable oil, dill weed, lemon pepper, garlic powder, and parmesan cheese.

Place crackers into a large bowl and pour in salad dressing; toss to coat thoroughly. Place onto an ungreased cookie sheet. Bake, uncovered, 10 minutes (stir crackers 2 or 3 times while baking). Remove from oven and cool on a wire rack. Transfer into a serving bowl.

Stuffed French Bread

This looks so decorative and festive.

2 round loaves french bread

Preheat oven to 250 degrees. Cut off top of one loaf of bread; hollow out bottom part and fill with Clam Dip. Place lid back on, wrap loaf in aluminum foil, and bake 3 hours. Remove from oven and transfer onto a serving plate. Cut second loaf into large cubes for dipping. Serve with wooden skewers or toothpicks.

TO DECORATE: Choose a wide ribbon, set lid off to the side a little, and hook bow down with a straight pin.

Serves many.

CLAM DIP:
2 (8-ounce) packages cream cheese, room temperature
3 (6 1/2-ounce) cans chopped clams, drained
2 tablespoons lemon juice
1/2 cup chopped fresh parsley
1/2 cup minced green onions
1/2 teaspoon salt
1 tablespoon worcestershire sauce
1/2 teaspoon hot pepper sauce

In a medium bowl, combine cream cheese, clams, lemon juice, and parsley. Add green onions, salt, worcestershire sauce, and hot pepper sauce; stir until well blended.

BLT Cherry Tomatoes

2 pints cherry tomatoes
1 1/2 pounds bacon
Mayonnaise

Cut a small portion off the bottoms of the cherry tomatoes so they will sit on a tray without rolling. Slice off the tops of tomatoes and scoop out centers with the small end of a melon scoop; discard centers. Invert tomatoes onto damp paper towels and cover with plastic wrap. Refrigerate until ready to fill.

In a large frying pan over medium-high heat, fry bacon until crisp; drain and crumble into bits. In a small bowl, combine bacon bits and mayonnaise; stir to moisten. Fill tomatoes with bacon mixture; refrigerate at least 1 hour or overnight before serving.

Serves many!

Hot Garlic-Parmesan Soufflé

This hot appetizer is not really a soufflé, but a delectable and delicate dip for bread. The taste will surprise you.

15 cloves garlic, peeled
2 cups chicken broth
2 (8-ounce) packages cream cheese, room temperature
1 cup freshly grated parmesan cheese
1 (10.5-ounce) can cream of mushroom soup, undiluted
2 egg yolks, beaten
1 loaf Baguette bread, thinly sliced

Preheat oven to 350 degrees. In a medium saucepan over medium-high heat, combine garlic cloves and chicken broth; bring to a boil and poach 15 minutes or until garlic is soft.

Remove garlic cloves to a small bowl and allow them to cool. When cool, mash with a fork.

Cook and reduce chicken broth to a glaze; remove from heat and set aside.

In a large bowl, combine cream cheese, parmesan cheese, mushroom soup, garlic-chicken glaze, and egg yolks; stir until well blended. Transfer into a shallow ungreased 1 1/2-quart souffle dish. Bake, uncovered, 45 to 50 minutes or until golden brown. Remove from oven and serve with bread.

Serves many!

Cherry Tomatoes

25 to 30 cherry tomatoes equals 2 cups chopped tomatoes.

Cherry tomatoes are the midgets of the cherry family, small but packed with flavor. They should be thin skinned and, for best flavor, locally grown.

They can be added whole to salads, skewered for kabobs, hollowed out and stuffed, and used for appetizers.

Unless they are completely ripe, store them at room temperature.

TIPS: Turn cherry tomatoes upside down and use the bottom for the top when stuffing. This keeps them standing straight.

To seed cherry tomatoes, cut off the tops of the tomatoes and scoop out the centers with the small end of a melon scoop.

Mushrooms

1 pound mushrooms equals 5 to 6 cups sliced uncooked mushrooms or 2 cups cooked mushrooms.

The ancient Greeks claimed mushrooms were the food of the gods. The Egyptians thought the common man so unworthy of them that only the Pharaohs were permitted to eat them.

Choose firm, white caps, closed at the stem (gills should not be showing). Stems should be relatively short. No dark spots, bruises, or mold.

Trim bottoms of stems. Just before cooking, wash quickly in cold water; drain well.

Mushrooms last longer and keep better when they are refrigerated, but they should be used within two or three days of purchase.

TIPS: If you desire to keep the mushrooms white, add a small amount of lemon juice or vinegar to the rinse water. Never immerse mushrooms in water when cleaning them because they will absorb too much water.

To keep mushrooms white and firm when sautéing them, add a teaspoon of lemon juice to each quarter-pound of melted butter.

Use an egg slicer to slice fresh mushrooms quickly and uniformly.

My Favorite Stuffed Mushrooms

1 pound medium mushrooms, washed and dried
3 tablespoons butter or margarine
1 small onion, chopped
1/2 cup chopped cooked chicken, ham, shrimp, or bacon
1/2 cup bread crumbs
Salt and pepper to taste
Dried crushed oregano to taste
2 tablespoons milk, sherry, or wine

Preheat oven to 325 degrees. Break stems from mushrooms and finely chop. In a large frying pan over medium heat, melt butter or margarine. Add onion and mushroom stems; sauté until onions are soft. Add chicken, ham, shrimp, or bacon, bread crumbs, salt, pepper, and oregano; stir until well blended. Gradually add milk, sherry, or wine; stir until well blended. Remove from heat.

Stuff mixture into mushroom caps. Place onto an ungreased baking sheet or microwave-proof dish; bake, uncovered, 15 to 20 minutes in an oven or 3 to 4 minutes in a microwave on high heat. Remove from oven or microwave, place onto a serving platter, and serve immediately.

NOTE: A thin slice of your favorite cheese can be added on top before heating.

Serves many.

Stuffed Pennsylvania Mushrooms

1 pound medium mushrooms, washed and dried
1 (16-ounce) jar Italian salad dressing
Onion
Butter or margarine
Caraway cheese or hot pepper cheese

Break stems from mushrooms; reserve stems. In a medium bowl, pour salad dressing over mushroom caps; refrigerate and marinade at least 6 hours or overnight.

Preheat oven to 300 degrees. Chop mushroom stems and an equal amount of onion. In a medium frying pan over medium heat, melt butter or margarine. Add mushroom stems and onion; sauté until onions are soft.

Remove mushroom caps from marinade; fill with hot onion mixture. Top with a slice of caraway or hot pepper cheese. Place onto an ungreased baking sheet and bake, uncovered, 15 minutes or until cheese is melted. Remove from oven, transfer onto a serving platter, and serve immediately.

Serves many.

Mushrooms Stuffed With Spinach

3 tablespoons butter or margarine
1 or 2 cloves garlic, minced
12 large mushrooms, washed, dried, and stems removed
1 (10-ounce) package frozen chopped spinach
5 tablespoons freshly grated parmesan cheese, divided
3 tablespoons mayonnaise
1/2 teaspoon seasoned salt
1/2 teaspoon worcestershire sauce

Preheat oven to 350 degrees. In a small saucepan over medium heat, melt butter or margarine. Add garlic and sauté until golden brown; dip mushroom caps into the butter. Remove from heat and arrange mushroom caps, smooth side down, on a large ungreased baking sheet.

Cook spinach according to package directions; drain well in colander, pressing back of a spoon against spinach to force out excess moisture.

In a medium bowl, combine spinach, 3 tablespoons parmesan cheese, mayonnaise, seasoned salt, and worcestershire sauce. Spoon mixture into mushroom caps.

Bake, uncovered, 20 minutes. Remove from oven and sprinkle with 2 tablespoons parmesan cheese. Transfer onto a serving platter, and serve immediately.

Makes 6 servings.

Burgundy Mushrooms

These mushrooms are also great on a grilled steak.

1 2/3 cups burgundy wine
1 cup beef broth
1/2 cup butter or margarine
2 teaspoons worcestershire sauce
3/4 teaspoon salt
1/2 teaspoon dill seeds
1/2 teaspoon pepper
3 or 4 cloves garlic, minced
2 pounds medium mushrooms, washed and dried

In a large pan or dutch oven over medium-high heat, combine burgundy wine, beef broth, butter or margarine, worcestershire sauce, salt, dill seeds, pepper, and garlic; bring to a boil. Reduce heat to low; add mushrooms and simmer, covered, 1 hour. Uncover and simmer another 1/2 hour or until only a small amount of liquid remains. Remove from heat and transfer into a chafing dish to serve. Serve hot.

Makes 4 cups.

Stuffed Mushrooms

When you microwave mushrooms, arrange the mushroom caps in a circle on a plate suitable for microwave ovens.

Microwave at high heat three to four minutes, rotating plate one-half turn after two minutes. If mushroom size is not uniform, smaller caps will cook in less time.

Stuffed mushrooms can be prepared ahead of time. Cover and refrigerate until just before serving, then bake.

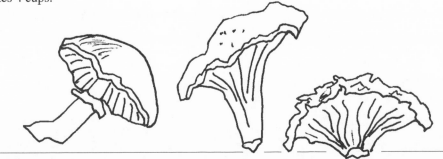

Wontons

Wonton literally means "swallowing a cloud" in Chinese.

Wontons are a very popular Chinese delicacy. They are small shapes of very thinly rolled dough, filled with sweet or savory mixtures. The size and shape of wontons, and the type of filling used, vary according to the different culinary traditions in each region of China.

When using wrappers, avoid undue exposure to air. Cover them with a damp cloth to prevent drying. They are usually found fresh in one-pound packages. They freeze well.

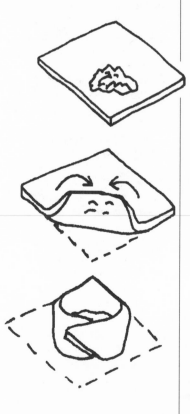

Sweet & Sour Marinated Vegetables

1 bunch fresh broccoli
1 1/2 cups cauliflower flowerets
1/2 pound mushrooms, washed, dried, and cut in half
1/2 cup sugar
1/2 cup vegetable oil
2 tablespoons cider vinegar
1 teaspoon celery seeds
3/4 teaspoon salt
1 teaspoon paprika
2 tablespoons finely chopped green onions
Garlic powder to taste

Trim off broccoli leaves; remove tough ends of lower stalk and wash thoroughly. Cut flowerets and stems into bite-sized pieces. In an ungreased shallow serving dish, place broccoli, cauliflower, and mushrooms.

In a jar with a lid, combine sugar, vegetable oil, cider vinegar, celery seeds, salt, paprika, green onions, and garlic powder; cover securely and shake vigorously. Pour marinade over vegetables. Cover vegetables and refrigerate at least 3 hours or overnight before serving.

Makes 12 servings.

Fried Wontons

This Cantonese recipe uses a basic wonton dough to make little fried dumplings, which may be served as an appetizer or as a main course.

1/2 pound ground pork
1 tablespoon chopped green onions
2 teaspoons salt
1 tablespoon soy sauce
2 tablespoons sesame oil
40 wonton wrappers*
Vegetable oil

* Found in Chinese food stores.

Preheat oven to 300 degrees. In a large bowl, combine ground pork, green onions, salt, soy sauce, and sesame oil; stir until well blended.

For each wonton, place one wonton skin on a flat surface with one corner toward you. Spoon a rounded teaspoon of filling just below the center of wonton skin. Fold the corner closest to you over the filling and tuck in under the filling. Roll up, leaving one inch unrolled at the top. Moisten the right corner with water. Grasp right and left corners and bring them over the filling, lapping the right corner over the left corner. Press firmly to seal.

In a large heavy saucepan or deep-fat fryer over medium-high heat, heat 2 inches of vegetable oil. Fry the wontons, a few at a time, for 2 to 3 minutes or until golden brown. Drain on paper towels. Keep wontons warm in oven while frying the remainder. Transfer onto a serving platter and serve.

Yields 40 wontons.

Egg Rolls

1/2 pound ground beef
1/2 pound ground pork
1 head of cabbage, finely chopped
2 (7.75-ounce) packages bean threads (cook until clear and drain)*
1 bunch scallions, chopped
Salt and pepper to taste
Soy sauce to taste
2 eggs
Pastry wrappers*
Vegetable oil

* Found in Chinese food stores.

Line a cookie sheet with aluminum foil. In a large bowl, combine ground beef, ground pork, cabbage, bean threads, scallions, salt, pepper, soy sauce, and eggs; stir until well blended.

Separate pastry wrappers and place a wet paper towel over those not being used to keep moist. Place one pastry wrapper on a flat surface and place a scoop of beef mixture on one end of circle. Roll part way. Wet end of sides and fold over to middle. Continue rolling up and wet ends to seal. Place side by side onto prepared cookie sheet.

In a large frying pan over medium heat, heat vegetable oil. Fry a few egg rolls at a time, turning to brown on all sides. Remove from pan and drain on paper towels. Transfer onto a serving platter and serve.

NOTE: Egg rolls can be frozen before frying by placing in an airtight container. When ready to use, simply remove from freezer 1 hour before frying.

Yields 24 egg rolls.

Potato Skins

12 medium baking potatoes
1/2 cup butter or margarine, melted
2 cups shredded cheddar or monterey jack cheese
Garlic or seasoned salt (optional)
Prepared salsa sauce
Sliced green onions

Preheat oven to 425 degrees. Wash and scrub potatoes; prick potatoes with a fork. On an ungreased baking sheet or the oven rack, bake potatoes 40 to 50 minutes or until tender. Remove from oven and cut in half lengthwise. Scoop out the insides (reserve for another use), leaving 1/2-inch thick shells. Brush both sides of potato skins with butter or margarine. Place, cut side up, onto a large ungreased baking sheet.

Bake, uncovered, 10 to 15 minutes or until crisp. Sprinkle with cheese, and if desired, garlic or seasoned salt. Bake another 2 minutes or until cheese melts. Remove from oven and serve with salsa and green onions.

Yields 24.

Quickie Appetizer Ideas

Mix chive cream cheese with a few orange-section bits. Serve with your favorite crackers.

Place one (8-ounce) package cream cheese on a serving dish. Top with one of the following and serve with crackers:
- *Jalapeño pepper jelly*
- *Fruit chutney*
- *Chili sauce and small shrimp*
- *Chili sauce and crab meat*

Set out soft round brie cheese, petite rye bread, and apple slices.

CAESAR MUSHROOMS: Drain juice from canned whole mushrooms; pour bottled Caesar dressing into the can to cover the mushrooms. Refrigerate at least two hours. Drain and serve with toothpicks.

Mexican Chocolate

Forbidden to women and reserved for men of superior rank, chocolate was the royal drink of Mexico during the Aztec time. Modern Mexico is still a land of chocolate lovers.

The Spanish were the first Europeans to discover the cacao bean; that was one of the perks of conquering Mexico. They learned to make hot chocolate from the Aztecs.

Lemons & Limes

1 medium lemon equals about 3 tablespoons of juice and about 1 tablespoon of zest.

1 medium lime equals about 1 1/2 tablespoons of juice and about 1/2 tablespoon of zest.

TIPS: Microwaving the lemon or lime for a few seconds before squeezing will help extract more juice. Don't overdo it. You don't want to boil the juice.

When using lemons or limes for juice, don't waste the flavorful rind. Grated lemon and lime zest can add a nice flourish to a simple green salad. Freeze the zest until ready to use. Always thoroughly wash lemons and limes to remove insecticide before using their peel for zest.

If sprinkled with water and refrigerated in plastic bags, lemons and limes will last a month or more.

Mexican Hot Chocolate

Sweet chocolate drink with an almond and cinnamon flavor.

2 wedges for each cup of Ibarra Chocolate*
1 cup of milk per person

In the top of a double boiler over hot water, heat milk until very hot. Break up chocolate into small wedges that are already marked off; place in blender or food processor. Whirl chocolate pieces until finely ground; add to hot milk. Heat, stirring occasionally, until chocolate is melted. Serve hot.

* Mexican sweet chocolate can be found in the Mexican section of the grocery store.

Real Old-Fashioned Lemonade

Juice of 6 lemons (1 cup)
3/4 cup sugar or to taste
4 cups cold water
1 lemon, sliced
Ice cubes

In a large pitcher, combine lemon juice and sugar; stir to dissolve sugar. Add water, lemon slices, and ice cubes; stir until well blended. Serve in tall glasses over ice.

VARIATION: To make limeade, substitute fresh lime juice for lemon juice.

Yields approximately 6 cups.

Fresh Lemon-Limeade

1 cup plus 2 tablespoons sugar
5 1/2 cups water, divided
3/4 cup fresh lemon juice
3/4 cup fresh lime juice
Lemon and lime slices

In a medium saucepan over medium-high heat, combine sugar and 1 1/2 cups water; heat and stir to dissolve sugar. Just before mixture comes to a boil, remove from heat. Stir in 4 cups cold water; pour into a pitcher. Stir in lemon juice and lime juice; refrigerate until cold. Serve in tall glasses over ice, garnished with lemon and lime slices.

Makes 4 servings.

Cyndy's Party Punch

1 quart cranberry juice
1 quart pineapple juice
1 1/2 cups sugar
1 teaspoon almond extract
1 (liter-size) bottle ginger ale

In a large container, combine cranberry juice, pineapple juice, sugar, and almond extract. (Can be put into containers and frozen 2 or 3 days ahead of time. When ready to serve, thaw 3 to 4 hours ahead.)

To serve, pour punch mixture into a punch bowl and mix with ginger ale.

Christmas Punch

2 (6-ounce) packages cherry-flavored gelatin
2 cups boiling water
6 cups cold water
1 (12-ounce) can frozen orange juice
1 (12-ounce) can frozen lemonade
1 (12 ounce) can frozen pineapple juice
2 (liter-size) bottles ginger ale

In a large bowl, combine gelatin and boiling water; stir to dissolve gelatin. Add cold water, orange juice, lemonade, and pineapple juice; stir until well blended. Store in refrigerator until ready to serve.

To serve, pour punch mixture into a punch bowl over crushed ice and ginger ale.

Peppermint Float Punch

This punch is always a hit at gatherings. It's like drinking a peppermint float.

1 gallon vanilla ice cream, room temperature
Peppermint extract to taste
Green food coloring
3 to 4 (liter-size) bottles 7-Up

To serve, mix ice cream with peppermint extract and green food coloring in a punch bowl. (Very carefully add peppermint extract, one drop at a time – a little goes a long way.) Add 7-Up to ice cream mixture.

NOTE: You can keep adding 7-Up to the punch if you need more volume.

Party Punch

TIPS: Dilution from melting ice can be a problem with cold punches, but this can be minimized in several ways. Mix all punch ingredients together in advance except perishable items such as liquor and carbonated mixers; then refrigerate.

Make the ice out of the same fruit juice used in the punch recipe. Use your favorite gelatin mold to make a pretty shaped block. You can even freeze strawberries, cherries, or grapes in the mold for a special visual effect.

It is always desirable to blend punch at least one hour in advance to let the flavors mix thoroughly.

All ingredients for cold punches should be well chilled before preparation begins.

When you are gauging how much punch to make, figure at least two (4-ounce) servings per person.

Fresh Apple Cider

Fresh sweet cider is the natural liquid that is released or expressed by pressing the apple. Although apples are the most common fruit from which cider is made, pears and sweet cherries are often pressed for cider as well. The liquid is considered fresh cider as long as it remains in its natural state and is not sweetened, preserved, or otherwise altered.

Apple cider ferments very rapidly and sometimes even violently at temperatures over fifty degrees. The process is more leisurely and the results much smoother when the temperature is around forty degrees or less. As fermentation converts the sugar into alcohol and the solid particles slowly settle, the sweetness begins to subside and the cider appears clearer and lighter in color.

Our forefathers were proud of their cider production and they eagerly anticipated a good annual supply. The mildly alcoholic beverage was not only a pleasure to drink, but also a most convenient and easy means of preserving the usually bountiful apple harvest.

Slush Punch

Very refreshing and tasty.

6 cups water
4 cups sugar or 2 cups honey
5 large bananas
Juice of 2 lemons
1 (12-ounce) can frozen orange juice
1 (36-ounce) can pineapple juice
4 (liter-size) bottles 7-Up (2 bottles chilled and 2 bottles at room temperature)

In a large saucepan over medium heat, bring water and sugar or honey to a boil; cool and set aside.

In a medium bowl or blender, blend together bananas, lemon juice, orange juice, and pineapple juice; add to boiled mixture. Freeze until firm.

To serve, pour 2 bottles chilled 7-Up and 2 bottles room temperature 7-Up over frozen mixture in a punch bowl.

Tequila Cider

This will really warm you up on a cold day. Use fresh, unpasteurized apple cider, not apple juice, for the fullest flavor.

2 quarts fresh apple cider
1 cup tequila
1/3 cup orange liqueur
3 tablespoons fresh lemon juice
2 tablespoons sugar (optional)

In a large saucepan over medium-low heat, combine apple cider, tequila, orange liqueur, lemon juice, and, sugar (if desired). Heat until hot. Remove from heat and serve in mugs.

Coffee Liqueur (Kahlua)

4 cups sugar
2 cups boiling water
3/4 cup powdered instant coffee (not freeze dried)
2 cups vodka (any proof)
1 vanilla bean, split and chopped into four pieces

In a large saucepan over medium heat, combine sugar, boiling water, and instant coffee; stir until sugar and coffee are dissolved; remove from heat and let cool. Put in a covered container and let set at room temperature for 3 days. Then add vodka and vanilla bean, cover, and let set for 30 days.

Our Favorite Tom & Jerry Batter

This is a wonderful recipe. Make it your Christmas tradition.

6 eggs, separated and room temperature
2 1/4 cups superfine sugar, divided
Salt to taste
1 teaspoon vanilla extract
1 cup powdered milk
Boiling water
Rum, brandy or whiskey
Nutmeg

In a small bowl, beat egg yolks until thick. In a large bowl, beat egg whites until stiff peaks form. Fold 1/2 cup sugar slowly into whites; fold into egg yolks. Add 1 3/4 cups sugar, salt, and vanilla extract. Gradually beat in powdered milk. Store, covered, in refrigerator, and use as needed.

To serve, place 1 heaping tablespoon of batter into a cup or mug, add boiling water and liquor (use either rum, brandy or whiskey); stir until well blended. Sprinkle with nutmeg.

Grand Orange-Cognac (Grand Marnier)

1/3 cup grated orange zest
1/2 cup sugar
2 cups cognac or French brandy
1/2 teaspoon glycerin

In a small bowl, mash and combine orange zest and sugar (use the back of a wooden spoon or a pestle). Continue mashing until sugar is absorbed into the orange zest and is no longer distinct. Place sugar mixture and cognac or French brandy into a storage container with a lid; stir, cover, and let age in a cool dark place 2 to 3 months, shaking monthly.

After initial aging, pour through fine-mesh strainer placed over a medium bowl. Rinse out aging container. Pour glycerin into aging container; place cloth bag or coffee filter inside strainer. Pour liqueur back into aging container through the cloth bag or filter. Stir with a wooden spoon to combine. Cover and age another 3 months before serving.

Powdered Sugar

1 pound powdered sugar equals 4 cups unsifted or 4 1/2 cups sifted.

SUBSTITUTION: 1 3/4 cups powdered sugar equals 1 cup granulated sugar.

Powdered sugar is called "icing sugar" in Britain and "sucre glace" in France.

TIPS: Break up lumps in powdered sugar by whirling it in a food processor fitted with a metal blade.

Never sprinkle powdered sugar over a moist cake, pudding, or other dessert until just before serving. The moisture will liquefy the sugar and turn it an unappealing gray color.

Superfine Sugar

1 pound superfine sugar equals 2 1/3 cups.

Superfine sugar is also known as bar sugar or castor sugar. It is very similar to granulated sugar except that it has very tiny crystals. Since it dissolves quickly and completely, leaving no grainy texture, it is the perfect choice for caramel, drinks, meringues, cold desserts, and fine-textured cakes.

TIP: Create your own superfine sugar by processing granulated sugar in the food processor for one minute or until almost powdery. But watch it carefully, you don't want powdered sugar.

Cranberry Blossom

Chilled orange juice
Chilled club soda, 7-Up,
*   or seltzer*
Cranberry Juice Cocktail

Fill a tall (12-ounce) glass
1/3 full with orange juice.
Pour in club soda, 7-Up, or
seltzer from freshly opened
bottle, filling glass to 2/3 full.
Since the mixture will foam
up, quickly top glass off with
cranberry juice cocktail.

NOTE: Champagne or
sparkling white wine may be
substituted for the club soda,
7-Up or seltzer.

Makes 1 serving.

Hot Buttered Rum Mix

1 cup butter, room temperature
1 2/3 cups powdered sugar
1 cup firmly packed brown sugar
1/2 teaspoon ground nutmeg
1 pint vanilla ice cream, softened
Boiling water
Rum to taste
1 teaspoon ground cinnamon

In a large bowl, combine butter, powdered sugar, brown sugar, and nutmeg; mix in ice cream. Freeze until ready to serve.

To serve, place 1 heaping tablespoon of mix into a cup or mug, add boiling water and rum; stir until well blended. Sprinkle with cinnamon.

Egg Nog Punch

Very good egg nog recipe for a large crowd during the holidays.

2 quarts vanilla ice cream, softened
4 cups hot coffee
2 (liter-size) bottles 7-Up
4 cups whiskey
1 cup light rum
7 cups commercial egg nog mix
Ground nutmeg

In a punch bowl, combine vanilla ice cream and coffee, blending until ice cream is melted. Add 7-Up, whiskey, rum, and egg nog mix; stir until lightly blended. Sprinkle with nutmeg. NOTE: More 7-Up can be added.

Do-Ahead Bloody Marys for a Crowd

2 (46-ounce) cans tomato juice
1/4 cup lemon juice
1/8 teaspoon worcestershire sauce
1/2 teaspoon hot pepper sauce
1 teaspoon salt
1/2 teaspoon pepper
1 fifth vodka
Lemon slices, lime slices, or celery stalk

In a large container, combine tomato juice, lemon juice, worcestershire sauce, and hot pepper sauce. Add salt and pepper; stir until well blended. To serve: Add vodka and garnish with a slice of lemon, lime, or celery stalk.

Yields 1 gallon.

Breads & Sandwiches

Scholls Squash-Date Bread

A very hearty and delicious bread.

1 2/3 cups all-purpose flour
1 1/2 cups sugar
1/4 teaspoon baking powder
1 teaspoon baking soda
1 teaspoon ground nutmeg
1 teaspoon ground cloves
1 teaspoon ground cinnamon
1/2 cup vegetable shortening
1 (8-ounce) can crushed pineapple, drained
1/2 cup cooked and mashed squash (butternut or delicata squash)
2 eggs, beaten
1 cup chopped dates
1 cup chopped walnuts

Preheat oven to 375 degrees. Grease a 9x5-inch loaf pan. In a large bowl, sift together flour, sugar, baking powder, baking soda, nutmeg, cloves, and cinnamon. In a medium bowl, combine vegetable shortening, pineapple, squash, and eggs; mix until blended. Add squash mixture to the dry ingredients; stir until blended. Fold dates and walnuts into the batter.

Pour batter into prepared pan and bake 50 minutes. Reduce oven temperature to 350 degrees and bake another 15 to 20 minutes or until a toothpick inserted in center comes out clean. Remove from oven and cool on a wire rack 10 minutes; remove from pan. Cool completely before slicing.

Yields 1 loaf.

Banana Pumpkin Bread

1/2 cup vegetable shortening
1 cup sugar
2 eggs
1 very ripe banana, mashed
1/4 cup solid-packed pumpkin
1 1/4 cups all-purpose flour
3/4 teaspoon baking soda
1/4 teaspoon salt
1 teaspoon ground cinnamon
1/2 cup chopped nuts

Preheat oven to 350 degrees. Grease a 9x5-inch loaf pan. In a large bowl, cream vegetable shortening and sugar until light and fluffy. Add eggs, one at a time, beating well after each addition. Stir in banana and pumpkin. Sift in flour, baking soda, salt, and cinnamon; stir until dry ingredients are moistened. Stir in nuts.

Pour batter into prepared loaf pan and bake 45 to 50 minutes or until a toothpick inserted in center comes out clean. Remove from oven and cool on a wire rack 10 minutes; remove from pan. Cool completely before slicing.

Yields 1 loaf.

Quick Breads

As the name implies, quick breads can be made quickly and easily. Because the leavening agent is either baking powder, baking soda, or steam, there is no rising time required.

IMPORTANT: When working with baking powder or baking soda, DO NOT BEAT THE BATTER; stir only enough to just moisten the dry ingredients. There may still be lumps remaining in the dough, but this is okay. The more you mix a quick-bread batter, the more you develop the flour's gluten, and the tougher the resulting bread.

A baked quick bread will generally have a gently rounded top that is slightly bumpy. Don't worry about a crack on top of the quick bread loaves; it's normal.

TIPS: Because glass bakeware retains heat better than metal bakeware, reduce the temperaure of your oven by twenty-five degrees when using glass pans.

If you find that your bread is beginning to brown too fast, cover it with a tent of aluminum foil.

Cool quick breads in the loaf pan for ten minutes; then remove from pan and allow to cool completely before slicing.

Nuts

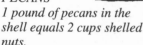

ALMONDS
1 pound of almonds in the shell equals 1 cup shelled nuts.

BRAZIL NUTS
1 pound of Brazil nuts in the shell (about 40 nuts) equals 1 1/2 cups shelled nuts.

HAZELNUTS
1 pound of hazelnuts in the shell equals 1 1/2 cups shelled nuts.

PECANS
1 pound of pecans in the shell equals 2 cups shelled nuts.

WALNUTS
1 pound of walnuts in the shell equals 2 cups shelled nuts.

PEANUTS
1 pound of peanuts in the shell equals 2 cups shelled nuts.

TIPS: *When shelling a large quantity of nuts, some shells may become mixed with the nut meat. To separate the pieces of shell, put the nuts in a bowl of water. The nuts will sink and the shells will float to the surface and can easily be lifted from the water. Place nuts on a paper towel until thoroughly dry.*

Carrot-Pineapple Bread

3 eggs, beaten
1 cup vegetable oil
1 1/2 cups sugar
3 cups sifted all-purpose flour
1 1/4 teaspoons baking soda
1 teaspoon cinnamon
1 teaspoon salt
2 cups grated carrots
1 (8-ounce) can crushed pineapple, undrained
1 teaspoon vanilla extract
1 cup chopped nuts

Preheat oven to 350 degrees. Grease and lightly flour two 9x5-inch loaf pans. In a large bowl, combine eggs, vegetable oil, and sugar; stir until well blended. Sift in flour, baking soda, cinnamon, and salt; stir until blended. Add carrots, pineapple, vanilla extract, and nuts; stir just until combined.

Pour batter into prepared loaf pans. Bake 55 to 60 minutes or until a toothpick inserted in center comes out clean. Remove from oven and cool on a wire rack 10 minutes; remove from pan. Cool completely before slicing.

Yields 2 loaves.

Lemon Tea Bread

This bread is excellent served for an afternoon tea or for dessert in the evening.

2 cups sugar
3/4 cup butter or margarine, room temperature
4 eggs
1 cup milk
3 cups all-purpose flour
2 teaspoons baking powder
1 cup chopped nuts
Grated zest of 2 large lemons
1 teaspoon lemon extract
Lemon Icing

Preheat oven to 350 degrees. Grease and lightly flour two 9x5-inch loaf pans. In a large bowl, cream sugar and butter or margarine until light and fluffy. Add eggs, one at a time, beating well after each addition. Stir in milk, flour, baking powder, nuts, lemon zest, and lemon extract; stir until dry ingredients are moistened.

Divide batter among prepared loaf pans and bake 50 to 55 minutes or until a toothpick inserted in center comes out clean. Remove from oven and place on wire racks. Spoon Lemon Icing over bread as soon as it is removed from oven. Leave bread in pans until completely cooled. Use spatula and patience to remove from pans.

Yields 2 loaves.

LEMON ICING:
Juice of 2 lemons
1 1/2 cups sugar

In a small bowl, combine lemon juice and sugar; stir until well blended.

Banana Nut Bread

1 cup butter or margarine, room temperature
2 cups sugar
4 eggs
4 cups all-purpose flour
2 teaspoons baking powder
2 teaspoons baking soda
1/4 teaspoon salt
6 very ripe bananas, mashed
1 cup finely chopped pecans

Preheat oven to 350 degrees. Grease two 9x5-inch loaf pans. In a large bowl, cream butter or margarine and sugar until light and fluffy. Add eggs, one at a time, beating well after each addition. Sift in flour, baking powder, baking soda, and salt; stir until dry ingredients are moistened. Fold in bananas and pecans.

Pour batter into prepared loaf pans and bake 55 to 60 minutes or until a toothpick inserted in center comes out clean. Remove from oven and cool on a wire rack 10 minutes; remove from pans. Cool completely before slicing.

Yields 2 loaves.

Sugarless Banana Bread

2 eggs, beaten
1 cup buttermilk
3 very ripe bananas, mashed
2 tablespoons (9 individual packets) artificial sweetener
1/2 cup vegetable oil
1 1/4 cups quick-cooking oats
1 1/4 cups whole wheat flour
1 teaspoon baking soda

Preheat oven to 350 degrees. Grease a 9x5-inch loaf pan. In a large bowl, combine eggs, buttermilk, and bananas. Add artificial sweetener, vegetable oil, oats, flour, and baking soda; stir until dry ingredients are moistened.

Pour batter into prepared loaf pan and bake 55 to 60 minutes or until a toothpick inserted in center comes out clean. Remove from oven and cool on a wire rack 10 minutes; remove from pan. Cool completely before slicing.

Yields 1 loaf.

Quick Breads

Don't increase the quantity of baking powder called for in a particular recipe, for too much leaves a distinctive and unpleasant taste.

Don't substitute self-rising or cake flour for all-purpose flour, unless you are confident of being able to calculate exactly how much to reduce the quantity of baking powder or baking soda to compensate.

Bake all quick breads as soon as the ingredients are assembled. Since high temperatures are often called for, it is best to bake them in the center of the oven, as the heat in the top third of the oven will be too intense.

If your oven tends to overheat, reduce the oven temperature by twenty-five degrees and increase the cooking time by five minutes.

Breads that contain fruit, nuts, or butter may be stored for two or three days, well wrapped in plastic wrap or aluminum foil.

Nearly all quick breads freeze well, but if kept for over a month they tend to become dry. After thawing frozen breads, reheat them in a 400-degree oven for a few minutes before serving.

Quick Breads

Measuring Correctly

When measuring liquids, use a glass measuring cup. The glass permits you to see the level of the liquid being measured. The cup for liquids should have additional space above the one-cup line, so that a full cup can be accurately measured without spilling. Check the measurement at eye level.

To measure dry ingredients, use standard individual cups. Lightly spoon dry ingredients into correct cup size, heap up, and level off with edge of spatula by cutting across the top. Use measuring spoons in this way too.

Flour need not be sifted before measuring unless recipe specifies it. Sifting flour onto a sheet of wax paper instead of into a bowl cuts down on dishwashing.

Measure brown sugar by packing it firmly into a measuring cup or into a measuring spoon.

Cranberry Bread

2 oranges
Boiling water
1/4 cup vegetable oil
2 cups sugar
3 egg whites
2 cups whole wheat flour
2 cups all-purpose flour
1 teaspoon baking powder
1 teaspoon baking soda
1/2 cup chopped nuts
2 cups ground or sliced cranberries

Preheat oven to 350 degrees. Lightly grease two 9x5-inch loaf pans. Grate zest off the oranges; set aside. Cut oranges in half and squeeze out juice; add enough boiling water to make 1 1/2 cups of liquid. Combine orange juice with orange zest; set aside.

In a large bowl, combine vegetable oil, sugar, and egg whites; stir until well blended. Stir in orange juice. Sift in whole wheat flour, all-purpose flour, baking powder, and baking soda; stir until dry ingredients are moistened. Fold in nuts and cranberries.

Pour batter into prepared loaf pans and bake 55 to 60 minutes or until a toothpick inserted in center comes out clean. Remove from oven and cool on a wire rack 10 minutes; remove from pans. Cool completely before slicing.

Yields 2 loaves.

Mincemeat Nut Bread

1 1/2 cups all-purpose flour
3/4 cup sugar
2 1/2 teaspoons baking powder
1/2 teaspoon salt
2 eggs, lightly beaten
3 tablespoons vegetable shortening, melted and cooled
1 teaspoon vanilla extract
1 1/3 cups prepared mincemeat
1/2 cup chopped walnuts
Powdered sugar

Preheat oven to 350 degrees. Grease a 9x5-inch loaf pan. In a large bowl, sift together flour, sugar, baking powder, and salt. In a medium bowl, cream eggs, vegetable shortening, and vanilla extract until light and fluffy. Fold in mincemeat and walnuts. Pour egg mixture into flour mixture; stir until dry ingredients are moistened.

Pour batter into prepared loaf pan and bake 55 to 60 minutes or until a toothpick inserted in center comes out clean. Remove from oven and cool on a wire rack 10 minutes; remove from pan. Cool completely before slicing. Sprinkle top with powdered sugar.

Yields 1 loaf.

Grandma Myers' Holiday Orange Nut Bread

2 1/4 cups all-purpose flour
3/4 cup sugar
1 tablespoon grated orange zest
2 1/4 teaspoons baking powder
1/2 teaspoon salt
1/4 teaspoon baking soda
1 cup Orange Peel Preserves, finely chopped
1/2 cup mixed candied fruit (optional)
2 tablespoons vegetable shortening
1 egg
3/4 cup fresh orange juice
1 cup chopped nuts

Preheat oven to 350 degrees. Grease a 9x5-inch loaf pan. In a large bowl, combine flour, sugar, orange zest, baking powder, salt, and baking soda. Add Orange Peel Preserves and candied fruit; toss to coat fruit. Add vegetable shortening, egg, and orange juice; stir until dry ingredients are moistened. Fold in nuts.

Pour batter into prepared loaf pan and bake 55 to 60 minutes or until a toothpick inserted in center comes out clean. Remove from oven and cool on a wire rack 10 minutes; remove from pan. Let stand 24 hours before serving.

Yields 1 loaf.

ORANGE PEEL PRESERVES:
4 large oranges
4 cups water, divided
2 cups sugar
1 tablespoon vegetable shortening

Peel oranges, removing most of the white, and cut peel into thin slivers. In a medium saucepan over medium heat, place orange peel; add 2 cups water to cover the orange peel. Bring to boil and boil 5 minutes. Remove from heat and drain.

Return to heat; add 2 cups water and sugar. Bring to a boil; boil slowly another 30 to 45 minutes over medium-high heat until a candy thermometer reaches 242 degrees or until syrup spins a 6- to 8-inch thread (when the consistency of the liquid is correct, a fine thread will be formed when dripped from the edge of a wooden spoon). Stir in vegetable shortening until melted. Remove from heat and refrigerate until ready to use.

Yields 2 cups preserves.

Zest

Zest is the outer colored portion of the citrus peel. Freshly grated orange or lemon zest packs a flavor wallop no bottled dried zest can match.

Use a citrus zester (available in kitchen specialty shops) to obtain long, thin strands of citrus zest. A zester has five tiny cutting holes that create threadlike strips of peel.

Press firmly as you draw the zester down along the skin of the fruit. For continuous strips of zest, begin at one end of the fruit, and cut in a spiral around and down.

If you do not have a zester, use a vegetable peeler or a small, sharp knife. You will also note that many recipes call for grated zest or peel. In this case, use a cheese grater to remove the peel.

When removing the skin from oranges or other citrus fruits, be sure to take only the thin outer zest or colored portion. The white pith will give your dish a bitter undertaste.

Zucchini

1 pound zucchini equals approximately 3 medium zucchini or 2 1/2 cups chopped uncooked zucchini.

Baking Powder

Baking powders are believed to have been first manufactured in Boston in 1885 under the name of "yeast powders."

Baking powder is a leavener that consists of a combination of baking soda, cream of tartar, and a moisture absorber (like cornstarch). Most baking powders are double acting, which releases some of its gas when it becomes wet and the rest when exposed to heat.

IMPORTANT:
When purchasing a new can of baking powder from the store, always check the date on the bottom of the can to be sure it isn't outdated.

To test the potency of your baking powder, combine one teaspoon with one-third cup hot water. If it bubbles, it's fine.

Zucchini Bread

3 eggs
2 cups sugar
1 cup vegetable oil
3 cups all-purpose flour
1 teaspoon salt
1 teaspoon ground cinnamon
1 teaspoon baking powder
1 teaspoon baking soda
1 teaspoon ground cloves
2 cups shredded unpeeled zucchini
1 cup chopped nuts
1 teaspoon vanilla extract

Preheat oven to 350 degrees. Lightly grease and flour two 9x5-inch loaf pans. In a large bowl, cream eggs, sugar, and vegetable oil until light and fluffy. Mix in flour, salt, cinnamon, baking powder, and baking soda. Add cloves, zucchini, nuts, and vanilla extract; stir until well blended.

Pour batter into prepared loaf pans and bake 55 to 60 minutes or until a toothpick inserted in center comes out clean. Remove from oven and cool on wire racks 10 minutes; remove from pans. Cool completely before slicing.

Yields 2 loaves.

Spicy Pineapple-Zucchini Bread

3 eggs
1 cup vegetable oil
2 cups sugar
1 teaspoon vanilla extract
2 cups shredded unpeeled zucchini
1 (20-ounce) can crushed pineapple, drained
3 cups all-purpose flour
2 teaspoons baking soda
1 teaspoon salt
1/2 teaspoon baking powder
1 1/2 teaspoons ground cinnamon
3/4 teaspoon ground nutmeg
1 cup finely chopped nuts
1 cup raisins

Preheat oven to 350 degrees. Grease and flour two 9x5-inch loaf pans. In a large bowl, combine eggs, vegetable oil, sugar, and vanilla extract; beat until thick and foamy. Stir in zucchini and pineapple. Add flour, baking soda, salt, baking powder, cinnamon, nutmeg, nuts, and raisins; stir until well blended.

Pour batter into prepared loaf pans and bake 55 to 60 minutes or until a toothpick inserted in center comes out clean. Remove from oven and cool on wire racks 10 minutes; remove from pans. Cool completely before slicing.

Yields 2 loaves.

Orange Poppy Seed Bread

This bread is wonderful. It's almost like cake. This is excellent served at an afternoon tea.

3 cups all-purpose flour
2 1/4 cups sugar
2 tablespoons poppy seeds, toasted
1 1/2 teaspoons baking powder
1/2 teaspoon salt
3 eggs
1 1/2 cups milk
1 cup vegetable oil
3 tablespoons grated orange zest
1 teaspoon vanilla extract
1/2 teaspoon almond extract
Orange Glaze

Preheat oven to 350 degrees. Grease two 9x5-inch loaf pans. In a large bowl, combine flour, sugar, poppy seeds, baking powder, and salt. Add eggs, milk, vegetable oil, orange zest, vanilla extract, and almond extract; stir until dry ingredients are moistened.

Pour batter into prepared loaf pans. Bake 55 to 60 minutes or until a toothpick inserted in center comes out clean. Remove from oven and place on wire racks.

While still hot, using a long-tined fork, poke holes into the top of baked loaves. Pour Orange Glaze over loaves. Cool in pans for 10 minutes; remove from pans. Cool completely before slicing.

Yields 2 loaves.

ORANGE GLAZE:
3/4 cup sifted powdered sugar
1/4 cup fresh orange juice
1/2 teaspoon vanilla extract
1/2 teaspoon almond extract

In a medium bowl, combine powdered sugar, orange juice, vanilla extract, and almond extract; stir until well blended.

Poppy Seeds

Did you know that it takes nearly a million tiny poppy seeds to make a pound?

The opium poppy, from which the seeds are cultivated, is among the oldest cultivated plants. Greeks grew the plant specifically for its seeds which, among other uses, were mixed into cakes with honey and taken by Olympic athletes to provide an immediate burst of energy.

Poppy seeds have none of the narcotic qualities of the opium drug.

Store poppy seeds in an airtight container in the refrigerator for up to six months.

The poppy seeds you buy are raw; you must toast them for full flavor before using them in your recipes. This process will take care of itself when you sprinkle the seeds on dough to be baked.

TOASTING POPPY SEEDS:
Toast poppy seeds in a 350-degree oven or in a dry frying pan over medium heat. Stir occasionally, toasting only until seeds begin to brown.

Quick Breads

Cornmeal

There are two types of cornmeal: steel-ground and stone-ground.

STEEL-GROUND:
The husk and germ have been almost completely removed. Because of this, it can be stored almost indefinitely in an airtight container in a cool, dark place.

STONE-GROUND:
It retains some of the corn's hull and germ. Because of the fat in the germ, it is more perishable. Store in an airtight container in the refrigerator for up to four months.

Cornbread

Cornbread can be wrapped in foil for up to one day. Reheat in a 350-degree oven for about ten to fifteen minutes or until warm.

Quick Hush Puppies

Fishermen in the South used to cook these finger-shaped concoctions over their campfire, along with their fish catch. It is rumored that they threw a large number to their barking dogs saying, "Hush, puppy!"

1 cup self-rising cornmeal
3/4 cup water or buttermilk
1 teaspoon sugar
1 tablespoon all-purpose flour
1 teaspoon minced onion
1 tablespoon vegetable oil
1 egg
Vegetable oil

In a medium bowl, combine cornmeal, water or buttermilk, sugar, flour, onion, vegetable oil, and egg; stir until well blended.

In a large frying pan over medium-high heat, heat vegetable oil; drop batter from end of spoon into oil. Brown all sides; remove with a slotted spoon and drain on paper towels. Transfer to a serving platter and serve warm.

Makes 6 to 8 servings.

Indiana Cornbread

1 cup yellow or white stone-ground cornmeal
1 cup all-purpose flour
2 teaspoons baking powder
1/2 teaspoon baking soda
4 teaspoons sugar
1/2 teaspoon salt
2 eggs
2/3 cup buttermilk
2/3 cup milk
2 tablespoons unsalted butter, melted

Preheat oven to 425 degrees. Grease a 9-inch square baking pan with unsalted butter. In a large bowl, combine cornmeal, flour, baking powder, baking soda, sugar, and salt. Make a well in cornmeal mixture; add eggs, stirring lightly. Add buttermilk and milk; stir quickly just until combined. Add melted butter; stir until well blended.

Pour batter into prepared pan. Bake 25 minutes or until top is golden brown, lightly cracked, and edges have pulled away from sides of pan. Remove from oven and cool on a wire rack 10 minutes. Cut cornbread into squares and serve warm.

Makes 9 servings.

Quick Spicy Coffee Ring

2 tablespoons butter or margarine
1/3 cup firmly packed brown sugar
1 teaspoon ground cinnamon
Walnut halves
1 (10-biscuit) package refrigerated biscuits
2 tablespoons raisins

Preheat oven to 425 degrees. Grease an 8-inch round baking pan. In a small saucepan over low heat, melt butter or margarine.

In a small bowl, combine brown sugar and cinnamon. Place a ring of walnut halves onto bottom of prepared pan. Dip biscuits in melted butter or margarine, then in mixture of brown sugar and cinnamon. Place biscuits onto ring of walnut halves, overlapping slightly. Tuck raisins between biscuits. Bake 13 to 15 minutes or until golden brown. Remove from oven and serve warm.

Makes 10 servings.

Easy Cinnamon Rolls

1 (1-pound) loaf frozen bread dough, thawed
1 tablespoon butter or margarine, melted
1 tablespoon sugar
1 teaspoon ground cinnamon
Orange Glaze

Spray a large baking pan with vegetable-oil cooking spray. On a lightly floured surface, roll dough into a 12x8-inch rectangle. (If the dough is difficult to roll out, let it rest for a short time and roll again. Repeat as necessary.) Brush dough with butter or margarine; sprinkle evenly with sugar and cinnamon. Roll up dough, beginning from one of the long sides; seal seam with your fingers. Slice into twelve 1-inch pieces.

Place rolls onto prepared pan with one cut side down. Cover and let rise in a warm place (85 degrees), free from drafts, about 30 minutes or until nearly double in bulk.

Preheat oven to 375 degrees. Bake 20 to 25 minutes or until golden brown. Remove from oven and cool on a wire rack 10 minutes; remove from pan. Drizzle Orange Glaze over warm rolls. Serve warm or at room temperature.

Yields 12 rolls.

ORANGE GLAZE:
1/2 cup powdered sugar
1/4 teaspoon grated orange zest
2 to 3 teaspoons fresh orange juice

In a small bowl, combine powdered sugar, orange zest, and enough orange juice to make a thin glaze.

Processing Nuts

Did you know that you can also process or can nuts?

Place shelled nuts in sterilized canning jars and seal tightly. Bake in a 250-degree oven for about forty-five minutes. (Do not try to tighten jar lids after baking.) Nuts processed this way will keep for two to three years.

Cream Cheese

1 (3-ounce) package of cream cheese equals 6 tablespoons.

1 (8-ounce) package of cream cheese equals 16 tablespoons or 1 cup.

Cream cheese is the simplest and mildest form of cheese. It is prepared by souring the milk, draining the curds, and seasoning them.

Always store cream cheese in its original wrapping in the coldest part of the refrigerator. After opening, rewrap airtight.

If mold shows up on cream cheese, THROW IT AWAY! There is no way that it can be safely salvaged.

TIP: Cream cheese can be softened in the microwave oven for ease in spreading or blending. Remove the cream cheese from its foil wrapper and place on a microwave-safe plate. Microwave eight ounces of cream cheese on medium for one to one and one-half minutes or until it has softened.

Caramel Pull-Aparts

Simple and delicious.

18 frozen bread dough rolls
1/2 cup butter or margarine, melted
1/2 cup firmly packed brown sugar
1 (4-serving size) package butterscotch or vanilla pudding and pie filling
1/2 cup chopped walnuts

Grease an 8-inch round baking pan. Place frozen rolls into prepared pan. Pour butter or margarine over rolls and sprinkle with brown sugar and dry pudding mix. Top with walnuts. Cover and let rise in a warm place (85 degrees), free from drafts, about 1 to 1 1/2 hours until doubled in bulk, or overnight in the refrigerator.

Preheat oven to 350 degrees. Bake 30 minutes or until golden brown. Remove from oven and serve warm.

Yields 18 rolls.

Easy Cheese Danish

2 (8-roll) packages refrigerated crescent rolls
2 (8-ounce) packages cream cheese, room temperature
1 cup sugar
1 egg
1 teaspoon vanilla extract
Butter Frosting

Preheat oven to 350 degrees. Grease a 13x9-inch baking dish. Unroll one can of crescent rolls and press onto bottom of dish, pressing perforations together to form a flat sheet of dough. Ease edges of dough slightly up sides of dish.

In a large bowl, combine cream cheese, sugar, egg, and vanilla extract; spread over crescent roll dough. Unroll remaining can of crescent rolls and place them over the cream cheese mixture, pinching perforations together; press edges together to seal.

Bake 30 minutes or until golden brown. Remove from oven and cool on a wire rack. While still warm, spread Butter Frosting evenly over the top and cut into rectangles to serve. Serve warm or at room temperature.

Makes 16 servings.

BUTTER FROSTING:
1/2 cup butter or margarine, melted
1/2 cup sugar
1 teaspoon ground cinnamon
1 cup chopped nuts

In a medium bowl, combine melted butter or margarine, sugar, cinnamon, and nuts; stir until well blended.

Date Drop Scones

Scones are the Scottish cousins of biscuits, but noticeably richer because they include eggs and cream.

2 cups all-purpose flour
1/4 cup sugar
2 1/2 teaspoons baking powder
3/4 teaspoon salt
1/2 teaspoon baking soda
1/2 teaspoon ground nutmeg
1/2 cup chilled unsalted butter, cut into 1/4-inch pieces
1/2 cup chopped dates
1 egg, beaten
2/3 cup buttermilk

Preheat oven to 425 degrees. Lightly grease a large baking sheet. In a large bowl, sift together flour, sugar, baking powder, salt, baking soda, and nutmeg. With a pastry blender or two knives, cut butter into flour mixture until particles are the size of small peas; stir in dates. Add egg and buttermilk; stir just until mixed.

Drop by heaping tablespoonfuls onto prepared baking sheet, 2 inches apart to allow for spreading, making 10 mounds. Bake 15 to 18 minutes or until golden brown. Remove from oven and serve warm.

Yields 10 scones.

Cherry Scones

2 cups all-purpose flour
1/3 cup plus 2 tablespoons sugar, divided
2 teaspoons baking powder
1/8 teaspoon salt
1/3 cup chilled unsalted butter, cut into 1/4-inch pieces
1 egg, beaten
1 teaspoon vanilla extract
1/2 cup whipping cream
1/2 cup fresh or frozen pitted sour cherries, drained
1 egg, beaten

Preheat oven to 375 degrees. Lightly grease a large baking sheet. In a large bowl, combine flour, 1/3 cup sugar, baking powder, and salt. With a pastry blender or two knives, cut butter into flour mixture until particles are the size of small peas. Add 1 egg, vanilla extract, and whipping cream; stir just until mixed.

On a lightly floured surface, knead dough gently. Pat or roll out the dough into a circle 1/2-inch thick. To make wedge-shaped scones, cut into eight pieces. Use an 1 1/2-inch diameter cookie cutter to cut out center of circle; separate each section. Place wedges 1 1/2 inches apart onto prepared baking sheet. Make a small indentation in the center of each scone. Place approximately 1 tablespoon cherries in the indentation. Brush scones, except for the cherries, with 1 egg; sprinkle with 2 tablespoons sugar. Bake 15 to 18 minutes or until golden brown. Remove from oven and serve warm.

Yields 8 scones.

All-Purpose Flour

1 pound all-purpose flour equals 3 1/2 to 4 cups flour.

Wheat flour has actually been whitened for centuries. The popular demand has traditionally been for whiter bread, since white has always been associated with purity. In the Middle Ages, all the richer people bought "white" bread, and so it became linked with quality. In fact, the bakers whitened the grain with chalk, alum, and in some cases, arsenic powder or ground-up bones from the graveyard.

All-purpose flour is made from a blend of high-gluten hard wheat and low-gluten soft wheat. It is a fine-textured flour milled from the inner part of the wheat kernel and contains neither the germ (the sprouting section) nor the bran (the outer husk).

By law, in the United States, all flours not containing wheat germ must have niacin, riboflavin, and thiamin added. Most all-purpose and bread flours are labeled "enriched," indicating that these nutrients have been added. All-purpose flour comes bleached and unbleached, and they can be used interchangeably.

Raisins

1 pound raisins equals approximately 3 cups raisins.

The term refers to a special grape which has been sundried or commercially dried. Raisins should be plump and soft, not hard or dry.

Store raisins on the shelf in a cool place or in the refrigerator.

TIPS: If raisins clump together, put them in a strainer and spray hot, running water over them. You can also put them in the microwave oven and heat at high for about ten to twenty seconds.

Before adding raisins or currants to a cake, bread, or cookie batter, toss with some of the flour called for in the recipe, separating the raisins with your fingers. This will keep the raisins from sinking to the bottom of the batter.

To plump raisins for bread or muffin recipes, pour boiling water over them to cover, let stand for a minute or two, then drain, and dry on paper towels.

Wonderful Scones

3 cups all-purpose flour
3 tablespoons sugar
1 tablespoon baking powder
1/4 teaspoon salt
1/2 cup chilled unsalted butter, cut into 1/4-inch pieces
1 cup raisins
3 eggs, divided
1 cup plus 1 tablespoon milk, divided

Preheat oven to 450 degrees. Spray a large baking sheet with vegetable-oil cooking spray. In a large bowl, combine flour, sugar, baking powder, and salt. With a pastry blender or two knives, cut butter into flour mixture until particles are the size of small peas; stir in raisins. In a medium bowl, beat 2 eggs lightly with 1 cup milk. Add to flour mixture; stir just until mixed.

On a lightly floured surface, knead dough gently. Pat or roll out the dough into a circle 1/2-inch thick. Using a lightly greased and floured 3-inch biscuit cutter, cut into rounds, cutting close together to generate as few scraps as possible. Dip cutter into flour as often as necessary to keep dough from sticking. Push scraps of dough together so that edges join; firmly pinch edges with fingertips to make a partial seal. Pat this remaining dough to 1/2-inch thick; continue to cut 3-inch rounds. Space 1-inch apart onto prepared baking sheet.

In a small bowl, combine 1 egg and 1 tablespoon milk; brush onto scones. Bake 15 to 18 minutes or until golden brown. Remove from oven and serve warm.

Yields 12 to 14 scones.

Strawberry-Raisin Scone Bake

2 cups all-purpose flour
4 tablespoons sugar, divided
1 tablespoon baking powder
1/4 teaspoon salt
1/2 cup chilled unsalted butter, cut into 1/4-inch pieces
1/2 cup milk
2 eggs, beaten
3/4 cup raisins
1 tablespoon unsalted butter, melted
1/2 cup thick strawberry jam

Preheat oven to 425 degrees. Grease an 8-inch round cake pan. In a large bowl, combine flour, 2 tablespoons sugar, baking powder and salt. With a pastry blender or two knives, cut 1/2 cup butter into flour mixture until particles are the size of small peas. Stir in milk, eggs, and raisins.

With floured hands, pat half of dough onto bottom of prepared pan; press dough 1/4 inch up sides of pan; spread strawberry jam over top. Top with remaining dough. With a sharp knife, score dough into 8 wedges. Brush top lightly with 1 tablespoon butter and sprinkle with 2 tablespoons sugar. Bake 20 to 25 minutes or until golden brown. Remove from oven, cut into wedges, and serve warm.

Yields 8 scones.

Orange-Currant Scones

3 cups all-purpose flour
3/4 cup sugar
1/2 teaspoon baking powder
1 teaspoon baking soda
2 teaspoons grated orange zest
1/2 cup chilled butter, cut into 1/4-inch pieces
3/4 cup currants
3/4 cup buttermilk
Orange Butter

Preheat oven to 400 degrees. Lightly grease a large baking sheet. In a large bowl, combine flour, sugar, baking powder, baking soda, and orange zest. With a pastry blender or two knives, cut butter into flour mixture until particles are the size of small peas. Stir in currants. Add buttermilk; stir just until mixed and evenly moistened.

TO MAKE ROUND SCONES: On a lightly floured surface, knead dough gently 10 times. Pat or roll out the dough into a circle 1/2-inch thick. Use a lightly greased and floured 3-inch biscuit cutter, cut into rounds, cutting close together to generate as few scraps as possible. Dip cutter into flour as often as necessary to keep dough from sticking. Push scraps of dough together so that edges join; firmly pinch edges with fingertips to make a partial seal. Pat this remaining dough to 1/2-inch thick; continue to cut 3-inch rounds. Space scones 1-inch apart onto prepared baking sheet. Bake 15 to 18 minutes or until golden brown. Remove from oven and serve warm with Orange Butter.

TO MAKE WEDGE-SHAPED SCONES: On a lightly floured surface, knead dough gently. Pat or roll out the dough into a circle 1/2-inch thick and cut into eight pieces. Use a 1 1/2-inch diameter cookie cutter to cut out center of circle; separate each section. Place wedges 1 1/2 inches apart onto prepared baking sheet. Bake 15 to 18 minutes or until golden brown. Remove from oven and serve warm with Orange Butter.

Yields 8 scones.

ORANGE BUTTER:
1/2 cup butter
1 teaspoon grated orange zest
1 tablespoon powdered sugar

In a small bowl, cream butter, orange zest, and powdered sugar until well blended.

3 INCH BISCUIT CUTTER

Scones

> WHEN MAKING SCONES, WORK THE DOUGH QUICKLY AND DO NOT OVERMIX. *Place the dough rounds into the heated oven as soon as possible.*
>
> *It is said that the process, from mixing to pulling the finished scones out of the oven, shouldn't take more than twenty minutes.*

Scones are best served warm and fresh, split open, and topped with thick homemade jam and clotted cream (Devonshire cream) or crème fraîche.

When they are cool, wrap airtight and hold at room temperature for up to one day or freeze to store longer.

To reheat, unwrap scones (thaw wrapped, if frozen) and place onto a baking sheet. Bake in a 350-degree oven eight to ten minutes or until warm.

1½ INCH BISCUIT CUTTER

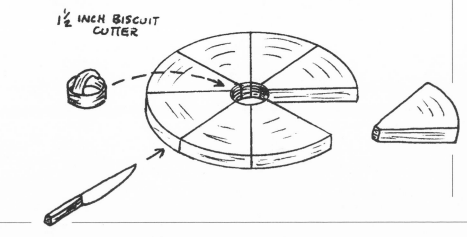

Popovers

What Makes Popovers Pop?

It is usually the baking, rather than the preparation. Since they pop because of steam caused by the high heat into which they are put, the heat of the oven is of prime importance. The oven should be preheated to 450 degrees.

Pour popover batter into HOT muffin pans rather than cold ones. They should be heated in the oven sufficiently so that they sizzle when buttered.

The batter must then be poured into the pan quickly and be put instantly into the oven, where they are baked for twenty minutes without the oven door being opened, no matter how curious the cook may be! Drafts can easily collapse popovers.

The oven heat is then reduced to 350 degrees and the popovers baked until they are done.

Yorkshire Pudding

First cousin to the popover, this is a traditional English accompaniment to roast beef.

The batter for Yorkshire Pudding is exactly the same as a popover batter, but it is baked in roast beef drippings and becomes a main course "pudding." It may be cooked in one large dish or in muffin tins as small individual puddings.

Sesame Popovers

1 cup sifted all-purpose flour
2 tablespoons toasted sesame seeds
1/4 teaspoon salt
1 cup milk, room temperature
2 extra-large eggs, room temperature
1 tablespoon unsalted butter, melted

Preheat oven to 450 degrees. Adjust oven rack to lowest position. Place empty muffin or popover pan in oven to heat while making batter.

In a medium bowl, combine flour, sesame seeds, and salt. In a small bowl, lightly whisk milk, eggs, and butter; pour into flour mixture all at once; whisk just until blended.

Remove hot muffin pan or popover pan from oven; using butter or margarine, generously grease interior of each cup and pan rim. Fill each cup 1/2 full with batter. Place in oven and bake, without opening oven door, for 20 minutes. Lower heat to 350 degrees and bake another 15 to 20 minutes or until popovers are golden brown. Remove from oven and serve warm.

NOTE: If it is necessary to hold popovers for any length of time, reduce heat to 250 degrees. They will stay puffed and crisp for another 20 minutes.

Yields 12 popovers.

Yorkshire Pudding

USE POPOVER RECIPE LISTED ABOVE (deleting sesame seeds).

1/4 cup (12 teaspoons) drippings from the roasting pan (supplement the drippings with vegetable oil if necessary)

Preheat oven to 450 degrees. Remove beef roast from the oven 25 minutes before it is to be served. Using a bulb baster or a spoon, pour 1 teaspoon of the beef drippings into each cup of 12 large ungreased muffin cups or 1/4 cup beef drippings into an ungreased 9-inch square baking pan.

Place baking pan or muffins cups into the oven to reheat beef drippings while you prepare the popover batter. When the drippings are very hot, pour the popover batter into the baking pan or muffin cups. Return the baking pan or muffins cups to the oven and bake 10 minutes. Reduce heat to 375 degrees and bake another 15 minutes. Remove from oven, cut into squares or remove from muffin cups, and serve immediately.

NOTE: If it is necessary to hold Yorkshire Pudding for any length of time, reduce heat to 250 degrees. It will stay puffed and crisp for another 20 minutes.

Makes 12 servings.

Banana Berry Popover

This tasty, versatile popover can be served for dessert, breakfast, or brunch.

2/3 cup sifted all-purpose flour
1/3 cup sifted cake flour
1/2 cup sugar
1/4 teaspoon salt
1 cup milk
2 eggs, lightly beaten
1 teaspoon vanilla extract
1/4 teaspoon ground nutmeg
1/2 cup fresh or frozen blueberries, blackberries, or raspberries (sprinkled with
    sugar if tart)
1 small banana, halved lengthwise, then sliced into 1/4-inch pieces
1 1/2 tablespoons firmly packed brown sugar
1/4 teaspoon ground cinnamon
Devonshire Cream (see page 156)

Preheat oven to 450 degrees. Adjust oven rack to lowest position. Place empty 9-inch metal pie plate or shallow baking dish in oven to heat while making batter.

In a medium bowl, combine flour, cake flour, sugar, and salt. In a small bowl, lightly whisk milk, eggs, and vanilla extract. Make a well in flour mixture and add milk mixture; whisk just until blended. Gently stir nutmeg into batter.

Remove hot pie plate or baking dish from oven; using butter or margarine, generously grease, including the rim. Distribute berries and banana evenly onto bottom of hot pie plate or dish, leaving a 1-inch border around the edge. Gently pour batter into the pan over berries and banana. In a small bowl, mix together brown sugar and cinnamon; sprinkle over batter.

Bake, without opening oven door, for 20 minutes. Lower heat to 350 degrees and continue to bake another 15 to 20 minutes or until popover is puffed and golden. Remove from oven, cut into wedges, garnish with Devonshire cream, and serve immediately.

Makes 6 servings.

Popovers

Always bring the milk and eggs to room temperature before mixing into popover batter.

Popovers always double in size when baked. Allow for this expansion when pouring batter (a little less than one-half full is safe).

Popover batter can be prepared ahead and refrigerated for up to four days. If you're making the batter ahead, bring batter to room temperature and stir well before pouring it into a hot pan.

Popovers can also be frozen in airtight plastic bags. When ready to serve, place in a 325-degree oven five to ten minutes or until thoroughly heated.

Almond Paste

This homemade almond paste is far better than most you can buy. In European countries, almond paste is molded into small fruits and dipped in chocolate to be eaten as a candy.

2 cups blanched almonds, thoroughly dry but not toasted
1 1/2 cups sifted powdered sugar
2 egg whites
1 teaspoon almond extract

Whirl almonds in the food processor until finely ground. Using your hands, blend the ground nuts with powdered sugar, egg whites, and almond extract. Form into a ball, wrap in plastic wrap, and place in an airtight container. Age in the refrigerator for five to eight days before using.

Raspberry Surprise Muffins

1/2 cup butter or margarine, room temperature
3/4 cup sugar
2 eggs
1 teaspoon baking powder
1/2 teaspoon baking soda
1 teaspoon almond extract
2 cups all-purpose flour, divided
1 cup plain yogurt
1/4 cup raspberry jam
Almond Paste

Preheat oven to 350 degrees. Lightly grease a muffin pan. In a large bowl, cream butter or margarine and sugar until well blended. Beat in eggs, one at a time; beat well after each addition. Add baking powder, baking soda, and almond extract; stir until well blended. With a rubber spatula, fold in 1 cup flour. Fold in yogurt and then fold in remaining 1 cup flour, stirring just until moistened.

Spoon 2 tablespoons of batter into each prepared muffin cup and smooth surface with your fingers. Top with a level teaspoon of raspberry jam; add a small amount of almond paste. Top each muffin with another 2 tablespoons of batter. Bake 25 to 30 minutes or until golden brown. Remove from oven and immediately remove from pan. Serve warm or at room temperature.

Yields 16 muffins.

Best Blueberry Muffins

2 cups sifted all-purpose flour
2 1/2 teaspoons baking powder
2 tablespoons sugar
3/4 teaspoon salt
1/2 cup chilled butter or margarine, cut into 1/4-inch pieces
1 egg, well beaten
3/4 cup milk
1 teaspoon grated orange zest
1 1/2 cups fresh or frozen blueberries

Preheat oven to 400 degrees. Lightly grease a muffin pan. In a large bowl, combine flour, baking powder, sugar, and salt. With a pastry blender or two knives, cut in butter or margarine until particles are the size of small peas; make a well in the center. In a small bowl, combine egg and milk; add all at once to the well in flour mixture, stirring just until moistened. Fold in orange zest and blueberries.

Fill prepared muffin cups 2/3 full. Bake 25 to 30 minutes or until golden brown. Remove from oven and immediately remove from pan. Serve warm or at room temperature.

NOTE:
If using fresh blueberries, dust them lightly with flour; this helps prevent the blueberries from "bleeding" into the muffins.

If using frozen blueberries, add them frozen to the batter; this will help prevent them from "bleeding" out their juices.

Yields 12 muffins.

Chocolate Chip-Orange Muffins

1 3/4 cups all-purpose flour
1/2 cup sugar
2 teaspoons baking powder
1/2 teaspoon salt
1 egg, beaten
1 cup milk
1/4 cup vegetable oil
1 cup semisweet chocolate chips
1 tablespoon grated orange zest
Powdered sugar

Preheat oven to 375 degrees. Lightly grease a muffin pan. In a large bowl, combine flour, sugar, baking powder, and salt; make a well in the center. In a small bowl, combine egg, milk, and vegetable oil; add all at once to flour mixture, stirring just until moistened. Stir in chocolate chips and orange zest.

Fill prepared muffin cups 2/3 full. Bake 25 to 30 minutes or until golden brown. Remove from oven and immediately remove from pan. Sprinkle with powdered sugar. Serve warm or at room temperature.

Yields 12 muffins.

Lemon-Poppy Seed Muffins

1/4 cup vegetable oil
1 cup milk
2 eggs
1 (4-serving size) package lemon instant pudding and pie filling
2 cups baking mix (Bisquick)
1/4 cup poppy seeds, toasted
1/4 teaspoon grated lemon zest
Lemon Glaze

Preheat oven to 375 degrees. Grease bottoms only of muffin cups. In a large bowl, combine vegetable oil, milk, eggs, and pudding; stir with a fork until well blended. Add baking mix, poppy seeds, and lemon zest, stirring just until moistened.

Fill prepared muffin cups 2/3 full. Bake 25 to 30 minutes or until golden brown. Remove from oven and immediately remove from pan. Cool 10 minutes and then drizzle Lemon Glaze over muffins. Serve warm or at room temperature.

Yields 12 muffins.

LEMON GLAZE:
2/3 cup powdered sugar
3 to 4 teaspoons fresh lemon juice

In a small bowl, combine powdered sugar and lemon juice; stir until well blended.

Muffins

Use vegetable shortening or vegetable-oil cooking spray when greasing the muffin cups.

Do not grease muffin cups that won't be used, but fill with a little water to keep the pan from burning.

IMPORTANT: Muffin batter should not be beaten too long, or the muffins will be coarse. STIR ONLY UNTIL ALL THE DRY INGREDIENTS ARE MOISTENED. Don't worry about the lumps, they will disappear during baking.

Remember that even in putting the batter into the muffin pan, too much manipulation causes a tough muffin.

To keep muffins warm for a few minutes after they are baked, slightly tilt each one in the pan and return to the turned-off oven with the door ajar.

Muffins can be reheated by loosely wrapping in aluminum foil and baking in a 325-degree oven for about ten minutes, or microwave at high for fifteen to thirty seconds.

Orange Blossom Muffins

2 cups baking mix (Bisquick)
1/4 cup sugar
1 egg, beaten
1/2 cup orange juice
2 tablespoons vegetable oil
1/2 cup orange marmalade
1/2 cup chopped hazelnuts
Spice Topping

Preheat oven to 375 degrees. Lightly grease a muffin pan. In a large bowl, combine baking mix and sugar; make a well in the center. In a small bowl, combine egg, orange juice, and vegetable oil; pour into well in dry ingredients, stirring just until moistened. Stir in marmalade and hazelnuts.

Fill prepared muffin cups 2/3 full. Sprinkle Spice Topping over each muffin. Bake 20 to 25 minutes or until golden brown. Remove from oven and immediately remove from pan. Serve warm or at room temperature.

Yields 12 muffins.

SPICE TOPPING:
1/4 cup sugar
4 teaspoons all-purpose flour
1/2 teaspoon ground cinnamon
1/4 teaspoon ground nutmeg
3 tablespoons chilled butter or margarine, cut into 1/4-inch pieces

In a small bowl, combine sugar, flour, cinnamon and nutmeg. With a pastry blender or two knives, cut in butter or margarine until particles are the size of small peas.

History of Baking Mix

An executive of General Mills was traveling by train. When he went into the dining car just before closing to eat, he was surprised to find freshly baked biscuits with his meal. He wondered how fresh biscuits could be served so late in the day. He asked the chef for his secret. Simple, explained the chef; he mixed the ingredients for biscuits together and stored them on ice.

The executive thereupon took the concept of Bisquick back to his company.

Sour Cherry Muffins

1 1/2 cups fresh or frozen pitted sour cherries, drained
1 1/2 cups all-purpose flour
1/2 cup sugar
1/2 teaspoon salt
1/2 teaspoon ground cinnamon
1 teaspoon baking powder
2 eggs, beaten
1/2 cup milk
1/2 cup butter or margarine, melted
1/2 teaspoon vanilla extract
1/4 teaspoon almond extract

Preheat oven to 375 degrees. Lightly grease a muffin pan. Chop cherries into small pieces. In a large bowl, sift together flour, sugar, salt, cinnamon, and baking powder. In a small bowl, combine eggs, milk, butter or margarine, vanilla extract, and almond extract; add to the flour mixture and stir just until moistened. Fold in the cherries.

Fill prepared muffin cups 2/3 full. Bake 20 to 25 minutes or until golden brown. Remove from oven and immediately remove from pan. Serve warm or at room temperature.

Yields 12 muffins.

French Breakfast Cakes

1 1/2 cups all-purpose flour
1 1/2 teaspoons baking powder
1/2 teaspoon salt
1/4 teaspoon ground mace
1/3 cup vegetable shortening
1/2 cup sugar
1 egg
1/2 cup milk
3 ounces cream cheese, cut into 8 pieces
1/4 cup butter or margarine, melted
Cinnamon Topping

Preheat oven to 375 degrees. Lightly grease a muffin pan. In a medium bowl, combine flour, baking powder, salt, and mace. In a large bowl, cream vegetable shortening, sugar, and egg until light and fluffy; add flour mixture alternately with milk, stirring just until combined.

Fill prepared muffin cups 1/3 full. Add a piece of cream cheese in each muffin cup. Top with remaining batter, filling muffin cups 2/3 full. Bake 20 to 25 minutes or until golden brown. Remove from oven and immediately remove from pan. Roll muffins in butter or margarine and then in Cinnamon Topping; covering entire muffin. Serve warm.

Yields 8 cakes.

CINNAMON TOPPING:
1 cup sugar
2 teaspoons ground cinnamon

In a small bowl, combine sugar and cinnamon.

Orange-Blueberry Tea Muffins

1/4 cup vegetable shortening
2 eggs, well beaten
2 cups all-purpose flour
1 tablespoon baking powder
1/4 cup sugar
2 tablespoons grated orange zest
1/4 teaspoon orange extract
1/2 cup milk
1/2 cup fresh orange juice
1 cup fresh or frozen blueberries

Preheat oven to 375 degrees. Lightly grease a muffin pan. In a large bowl, combine vegetable shortening and eggs; stir until well blended. Add flour, baking powder, sugar, orange zest, and orange extract, stirring just until moistened. Add milk and orange juice, stirring just until moistened (batter will be stiff). Fold in blueberries.

Fill each prepared muffin cup 2/3 full and bake 25 minutes or until golden brown. Remove from oven and immediately remove from pan. Serve warm or at room temperature.

Yields 12 muffins.

Blueberries

1 pint blueberries equals 2 cups blueberries.

1 (10-ounce) package of frozen blueberries equals 1 1/2 cups.

TIP: If blueberries are frozen, do not defrost before adding to batter. Always add them frozen to the batter and they will not bleed out their juice.

Biscuits

Did you know that biscuits helped win the West? They were so liked by cowboys in cow camps that they gave their cooks the nickname "biscuit shooter."

> **IMPORTANT:**
> For tender and flaky biscuits, have the fat (butter, margarine, or shortening) chilled. Cut the fat into the dry ingredients only until particles are the size of small peas.
>
> Excess handling causes tough biscuits. Do not reroll the dough.
>
> Always bake biscuits on pans without sides. The heat will circulate more evenly than on pans with sides.

Buttermilk Powder

Buttermilk powder is wonderful for those who don't have a carton of buttermilk sitting in the refrigerator. You can make more versatile use of dry buttermilk than of liquid. It has the same flavorful tang and lightness as its fresh buttermilk counterpart, but without the hassle of liquid leftovers.

TIP: If you find yourself short of buttermilk for your recipe, you can make your own by adding one tablespoon of vinegar to one cup of whole milk.

Sweet Potato Biscuits

1 cup all-purpose flour
3 teaspoons baking powder
1/2 teaspoon salt
3 tablespoons chilled vegetable shortening
1 cup cooked mashed sweet potatoes
About 1/4 cup milk

Preheat oven to 450 degrees and position rack in center of oven. In a large bowl, sift flour, baking powder, and salt together. With a pastry blender or two knives, cut in vegetable shortening until particles are the size of small peas. Add mashed sweet potatoes; stir until well blended. Gradually add enough milk to make a soft dough.

On a lightly floured surface, knead dough gently about 20 times. Gently roll dough 1/4-inch thick. Cut with a floured 3-inch biscuit cutter and place onto an ungreased baking sheet.

Bake 12 to 15 minutes or until golden brown. Remove from oven and immediately remove from baking sheet. Serve warm.

Yields 12 biscuits.

Old-Fashioned Biscuits

4 cups all-purpose flour
1 teaspoon baking powder
1/2 teaspoon baking soda
1 teaspoon salt
1 cup chilled vegetable shortening
2 cups buttermilk

Preheat oven to 450 degrees. In a large bowl, combine flour, baking powder, baking soda, and salt. With a pastry blender or two knives, cut in vegetable shortening until particles are the size of small peas; make a well in the center. Pour buttermilk into the well; stir just until the dough sticks together and forms into a ball.

On a lightly floured surface, knead dough gently about 20 times. Gently roll dough to 1/2-inch thickness. Cut with a floured 3-inch biscuit cutter and place onto an ungreased baking sheet, close together for soft-sided biscuits or 1 inch apart for crisp-sided ones. Prick biscuits with a fork.

Bake 5 minutes; reduce oven to 400 degrees and bake another 8 to 10 minutes or until golden brown. Remove from oven and immediately remove from baking sheet. Serve warm.

Yields 20 biscuits.

Alaskan Sourdough Biscuits

1 1/2 cups all-purpose flour
2 teaspoons baking powder
1/4 teaspoon baking soda
1/2 teaspoon salt
1/4 cup chilled butter or margarine, cut into 1/4-inch pieces
1 cup sourdough starter, room temperature (see page 56)
Melted butter

Preheat oven to 425 degrees. Grease a baking sheet. In a large bowl, sift together flour, baking powder, baking soda, and salt. With a pastry blender or two knives, cut in butter or margarine until particles are the size of small peas. Mix in sourdough starter.

On a lightly floured surface, knead dough gently about 20 times. Gently roll dough to a 1/2-inch thickness. Cut with a floured 2-inch biscuit cutter and place onto prepared pan. Brush with butter. Cover and let rise in a warm place (85 degrees), free from drafts, about 1 hour. Bake 20 minutes or until golden brown. Remove from oven and immediately remove from baking sheet. Serve warm.

Yields 10 biscuits.

Mom's Biscuits & Gravy

When I asked my husband, Don, what was his favorite meal that his mother used to make, he said: "Biscuits and gravy. We must get Mom's recipe for her biscuits and gravy." So here it is:

2 cups all-purpose flour
1/2 teaspoon salt
1 tablespoon baking powder
6 tablespoons chilled vegetable shortening
2/3 cup milk

Preheat oven to 450 degrees. In a large bowl, sift together flour, salt, and baking powder. With a pastry blender or two knives, cut in vegetable shortening until particles are the size of small peas; make a well in the center. Add milk, all at once, into the well; stir just until dough sticks together.

On a lightly floured surface, knead dough gently about 20 times. Gently roll dough to 1/2-inch thickness. Cut with a floured 2-inch biscuit cutter. Place onto an ungreased baking sheet. Bake 12 to 15 minutes or until golden brown. Remove from oven and immediately remove from baking sheet. Split biscuits and top with the Milk Gravy. Serve warm.

Yields 16 biscuits.

MILK GRAVY:
1/4 cup bacon drippings
1/4 cup all-purpose flour
2 cups milk
Salt to taste

In a medium frying pan over medium-high heat, combine bacon drippings and flour; brown flour, stirring constantly. Add milk and cook until thick. Season with salt.

Sourdough History

In our frontier days, a sourdough starter was the most important personal possession, something to be guarded at the expense of everything else.

The American pioneers jealously guarded their starters, as freshly baked bread, biscuits, and pancakes often provided the only variety in the wilderness diet. They usually carried their starters in wooden pails, which became permeated with the culture and which would retain the life of the yeast even if the starter spilled.

The prospectors of the Yukon during the Alaskan Gold Rush of the 1890s were nicknamed "sourdoughs" because of the sourdough starters that they usually had hidden under their jackets to keep warm.

In addition, there was the alcoholic by-product called "hooch," the clear liquid which rises to the top of the starter and had its own uses!

Yeast Breads

Yeast

Yeast is available in active dry and in compressed forms.

1 package of active dry yeast is equal to 1 cake of compressed yeast.

1 package of active dry yeast is equal to about 1 tablespoon.

Yeast is a one-celled plant or organism (fungus) that requires definite conditions of temperature, food, and moisture for its growth.

It feeds upon sugar and starch. The temperature that is best suited to the multiplication of yeast cells and consequent leavening and lightening of the dough in which it is used is between 70 and 90 degrees. Yeast is destroyed by heat at a temperature of 132 degrees and also by cold at approximately 40 degrees.

TESTING YEAST: Add one-half teaspoon of sugar to the yeast when stirring it into the water to dissolve. If it foams and bubbles within ten minutes, you know the yeast is alive and active.

Hot Cross Buns

Hot Cross Buns go back to the Greek and Roman times. They served as a symbol of the sun, bisected by a cross into four seasons. Later in history, these buns became associated with Easter and were sold only on Good Friday. Now you can enjoy them anytime.

4 to 4 1/2 cups all-purpose flour, divided
2 packages active dry yeast
3/4 teaspoon ground cinnamon
3/4 cup milk
1/2 cup vegetable oil
1/3 cup sugar
3/4 teaspoon salt
3 eggs, room temperature
1 cup raisins
1 egg white, room temperature and slightly beaten
Vanilla Frosting

In a large bowl, combine 2 cups flour, yeast, and cinnamon; set aside. In a small saucepan over medium heat, scald milk; stir in vegetable oil, sugar, and salt. Remove from heat and let cool to lukewarm (105 to 115 degrees). Gradually add milk mixture to flour mixture, beating at low speed of electric mixer. Add eggs; beat 3 minutes at high speed. Stir in raisins and enough remaining flour to make a soft dough.

Place dough into a well-greased bowl, turning to grease top. Cover and let rise in a warm place (85 degrees), free from drafts, about 1 1/2 hours or until doubled in bulk. Punch down dough; cover, and let rest another 10 minutes.

Grease a large baking sheet. Divide dough into 18 pieces; shape into balls, and place 2 inches apart on prepared baking sheet. Cover and let rise in a warm place (85 degrees), free from drafts, about 1 hour or until doubled in bulk.

Preheat oven to 375 degrees. Using a sharp knife, cut a shallow cross on top of each bun; brush each with egg white. Bake 15 to 20 minutes or until golden brown. Remove from oven and cool on a wire rack 5 minutes; spread Vanilla Frosting into cross-shaped indentations of each bun while still warm.

Yields 18 rolls.

VANILLA FROSTING:
1 cup powdered sugar
1 tablespoon milk
1/2 teaspoon vanilla extract

In a medium bowl, combine powdered sugar, milk, and vanilla extract, stir until well blended.

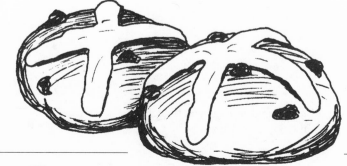

Heavenly Cinnamon Rolls

4 packages active dry yeast
2 cups milk, scalded and cooled to lukewarm (105 to 115 degrees)
1 cup sugar, divided
1 cup sour cream, room temperature
1 1/2 cups butter, room temperature
1 1/2 teaspoons salt
6 egg yolks, room temperature
3 whole eggs, room temperature
8 to 10 cups all-purpose flour
2/3 cup butter, melted and divided
4 tablespoons ground cinnamon, divided
1 1/2 cups sugar, divided
1 cup raisins, divided
Cloud Frosting

In a small bowl, combine yeast and milk; stir until yeast is dissolved. Add 1/2 cup sugar and sour cream; set aside.

In a large bowl, cream 1 1/2 cups butter, 1/2 cup sugar, and salt; cream until light and fluffy. Add egg yolks and eggs, one at a time, beating well after each addition. Stir in yeast mixture. Mix in flour, one cup at a time (add just enough so that dough can be handled without sticking).

On a lightly floured surface, knead dough, adding a little flour at a time, as needed, until dough is smooth and not sticky. (Add additional flour carefully. You can always add more flour, but once you've added too much, the result will be a dry product.) Place dough into a well-greased bowl, turning to grease top. Cover and let rise in a warm place (85 degrees), free from drafts, about 2 hours.

Punch down the dough, and on a lightly floured surface knead dough for about 5 minutes. Cover and let rise in a warm place (85 degrees), free from drafts until doubled in bulk, about 1 hour.

Grease two large baking sheets. Divide dough in half. On a lightly floured surface, roll each half into a rectangle about 1/4-inch thick; spread each with 1/3 cup butter, 2 tablespoons cinnamon, 3/4 cup sugar, and 1/2 cup raisins. Starting from the wide end, roll up into a tight roll; cut into 1 1/2-inch slices. Place onto prepared baking sheets; cover and let rise in a warm place (85 degrees), free from drafts, about 1 hour.

Preheat oven to 350 degrees. Bake 30 to 40 minutes or until golden brown. Remove from oven and cool on a wire rack for 10 minutes; spread Cloud Frosting over the cinnamon rolls while still warm.

Yields 2 dozen large cinnamon rolls.

CLOUD FROSTING:
2 cups powdered sugar
2 teaspoons vanilla extract
4 tablespoons hot water

In a medium bowl, combine powdered sugar and vanilla extract. Add hot water gradually, stirring just enough to give it a thick spreading consistency.

Yeast Bread Rising

When you add ingredients at room temperature to yeast doughs, their rising and baking times are shortened.

Yeast doughs need a warm place in which to rise. Begin by covering the bowl containing the dough with a slightly damp towel to retain the natural moisture.

Yeast dough should rise to double its original bulk. To test it after the first rise, poke two fingers into the dough. Don't be timid – jab them in a good one-half inch. If the indentations stay, the dough is ready. The finger-poke method is only good for the first rise.

After the dough is shaped into loaves and has risen for the second time, you don't want to ruin the bread by poking holes in the center. Instead, simply look to see whether or not the dough has doubled in bulk.

TIPS:
• *Dough rises nicely inside a gas oven warmed only by the pilot light, or an electric oven that's been heated at 200 degrees for one minute and then turned off.*

• *Set your dough over a pan of hot water on the bottom shelf of a closed oven.*

• *Bring two cups of water to a boil in your microwave oven to create a warm, moist atmosphere. Turn off the power; set the dough inside and close the door.*

Yeast Breads

Using Flour in Bread Making

Always remember that no bread recipe can specify exactly how much flour will be required. It depends on the brand and type of flour used and the weather.

So always start with a slightly lesser amount of flour and then add as needed. You can always add more flour if needed, but you cannot remove it if too much has been used.

Bowl Covers

TIP: When you need a container cover for yeast dough rising and need "head room" for the dough to expand, how about using an inexpensive plastic shower cap. The elastic will maintain a reasonably tight closure while allowing the dough to extend above the top of the container. The cap can be washed and reused.

Angel Buns

You will have to look long and hard to find a lighter, better biscuit than Angel Buns, which is an old Southern favorite. This is a quick version using baking mix.

1 package active dry yeast
1/4 cup lukewarm water (105 to 115 degrees)
1 tablespoon sugar
2 cups baking mix (Bisquick)
1/4 cup milk

Grease a large baking sheet. In a large bowl, combine yeast and water; stir until yeast is dissolved. Stir in sugar. Add baking mix and milk; stir until well mixed. On a lightly floured surface, knead dough about 10 times. Gently roll or pat out the dough into a circle 1/2-inch thick. Cut with a floured 2-inch biscuit cutter. Place onto prepared baking sheet. Cover and let rise in warm place (85 degrees), free from drafts, until soft and puffed, about 30 minutes.

Preheat oven to 425 degrees. Bake 6 to 8 minutes or until golden brown. Remove from oven and cool on a wire rack.

Yields 9 to 11 buns.

Super Simple Refrigerator Bread

This is the easiest way to make bread if you don't have an automatic bread machine. There's no kneading, and it can wait in the refrigerator for as long as 24 hours.

1/3 cup plus 1 teaspoon sugar, divided
1/3 cup vegetable shortening
1 tablespoon salt
2 cups boiling water
2 packages active dry yeast
1/4 cup lukewarm water (105 to 115 degrees)
2 eggs, well beaten
7 1/2 to 8 cups all-purpose flour, divided

In a large bowl, combine 1/3 cup sugar, vegetable shortening, salt, and boiling water; let cool to lukewarm (105 to 115 degrees).

In a small bowl, mix together yeast, 1 teaspoon sugar, and lukewarm water; let stand in a warm place (80 degrees) until bubbly, about 15 minutes. Combine yeast mixture with sugar mixture; stir in eggs.

Stir in 4 cups of flour. Gradually stir in as much of the remaining flour as dough will absorb, mixing well. (Add additional flour carefully. You can always add more flour, but once you've added too much, the result will be a dry product.) Place dough into a well-greased bowl, turning to grease top. Cover and refrigerate for at least 3 hours or up to 24 hours.

Grease two 9x5-inch loaf pans. Divide dough in half. With greased hands, shape each half into a smooth loaf. Place dough into prepared pans; cover and let rise in a warm place (85 degrees), free from drafts until almost doubled, about 2 hours.

Preheat oven to 350 degrees. Bake 30 to 35 minutes or until loaves sound hollow when tapped. Remove from oven. Let bread cool in pans on wire racks for 10 minutes, then turn bread onto racks to cool completely.

Yields 2 loaves.

Mom's Refrigerator Rolls

My mother received this recipe from my grandmother, who got this recipe from her elderly neighbor in the 1930s. We figure this recipe is approximately 100 years old. Don't worry – it has been tested in today's kitchen. In our family, these rolls are always made for the holidays. They are wonderful and so easy to make.

1/4 cup sugar
3 tablespoons vegetable shortening
1 1/2 teaspoons salt
1 cup milk
1 package active dry yeast
3/4 cup lukewarm water (105 to 115 degrees)
1 egg, beaten
4 to 4 1/2 cups all-purpose flour, divided
Butter, melted

In a large bowl, combine sugar, vegetable shortening, and salt; stir until well blended. In a small saucepan, scald milk; pour over sugar mixture. Cool to lukewarm (105 to 115 degrees).

In a small bowl, combine yeast and water; stir until yeast is dissolved. Mix in egg until well blended; stir into milk mixture.

Add 2 cups flour. Gradually stir in as much of the remaining flour as dough will absorb, mixing well. (Add additional flour carefully. You can always add more flour, but once you've added too much, the result will be a dry product.) Place dough into a well-greased bowl, turning to grease top. Cover bowl and dough with wax paper and a towel, held in place with a rubber band. Refrigerate at least 8 hours but no longer than 5 days.

Grease a baking pan or muffin cups. To bake, shape into desired rolls (cloverleaf rolls, Parker House rolls, or crescent-shaped rolls) and place onto prepared baking pan or into prepared muffin cups. Cover and let rise in a warm place (85 degrees), free from drafts, until double in bulk, about 1 hour.

Preheat oven to 400 degrees. Bake 15 to 20 minutes or until golden brown. Remove from oven and remove from pans.

Yields 18 to 24 rolls.

Cloverleaf Rolls

Form dough into one-inch balls. Place three balls into each greased muffin cup. Brush with melted butter.

Parker House Rolls

Roll dough into an oblong shape, about one-fourth inch thick. Cut into three-inch circles and brush with melted butter.

Make a crease across each circle; fold so top half overlaps slightly. Press edges together. Place close together onto greased baking pan. Brush with butter.

Crescent-Shaped Rolls

Roll dough into a twelve-inch circle, about one-fourth-inch thick. Spread with melted butter.

Cut into sixteen wedges. Roll up, beginning at rounded edge. Place rolls, with point underneath, onto greased baking sheet, curving slightly. Brush with butter.

Quick Yeast Baking

You can speed up standard yeast bread recipes by changing the yeast in the recipe.

Substitute one package fast-acting dry yeast for one package regular active dry yeast. Quick yeast is more finely ground and thus absorbs moisture faster, rapidly converting starch and sugars to carbon dioxide, the tiny bubbles that make the dough expand and stretch.

Quick Yeast Bread & Rolls

3 packages active dry yeast
2 cups lukewarm water (105 to 115 degrees)
1/4 cup sugar, honey, brown sugar, or molasses
2 teaspoons salt
3 tablespoons vegetable shortening
6 cups all-purpose flour, divided
Butter

In a large bowl, combine yeast and water; stir until yeast is dissolved. Stir in sugar, honey, brown sugar, or molasses. Add salt and vegetable shortening; mix thoroughly. Mix in 3 1/2 cups flour, one cup at a time (add just enough so that dough can be handled without sticking).

On a lightly floured surface, knead dough, adding a little flour at a time, as needed, until dough is smooth and not sticky. (Add additional flour carefully. You can always add more, but once you've added too much, the result will be a dry product.) Form dough into loaves or rolls and place into well-greased baking pans or muffin cups. Cover and let rise in a warm place (85 degrees), free from drafts until doubled in size (loaves take about 20 minutes, rolls about 15 minutes).

Preheat oven to 350 degrees. Bake loaves 45 minutes or until loaves sound hollow when tapped. Bake rolls 25 to 30 minutes or until golden brown. Remove from oven, remove from pans, and place onto a wire rack. For soft top crust, butter the tops well and let cool uncovered.

Yields 2 large loaves or 1 loaf and 1 1/2 dozen rolls.

CINNAMON ROLLS:
Brown sugar
1/2 of the dough in above recipe
2 tablespoons butter or margarine, softened
1 1/2 teaspoons cinnamon
1/2 cup firmly packed brown sugar
2/3 cup raisins
Quick Frosting

Preheat oven to 350 degrees. Grease a large baking sheet and sprinkle lightly with brown sugar; set aside.

On a lightly floured surface, roll dough into a rectangle about 1/4-inch thick. Spread with butter or margarine. Sprinkle with cinnamon, brown sugar, and raisins. Starting from the wide end, roll up in a tight roll; cut into 1 1/2-inch slices. Place onto prepared baking sheet. Cover and let rise in a warm place (85 degrees) until doubled, about 20 minutes.

Bake 25 to 30 minutes or until golden brown. Remove from oven and place onto a wire rack. Spread Quick Frosting over the rolls while still warm.

Yields 20 to 24 cinnamon rolls.

QUICK FROSTING:
1/2 cup powdered sugar
2 tablespoons milk
1/8 teaspoon salt
1/2 teaspoon vanilla extract

In a small bowl, combine powdered sugar, milk, salt, and vanilla extract.

German Pancake — Dutch Baby

Scrumptious! Bring this spectacular dutch baby to the table as soon as it comes out of the oven for a lot of oohs and aahs.

1 cup milk, room temperature
6 eggs, room temperature
1 cup all-purpose flour
1 drop vanilla extract
1/4 teaspoon ground cinnamon
6 tablespoons butter or margarine

Preheat oven to 450 degrees. In a large bowl, using lowest speed on electric mixer, combine milk, eggs, flour, vanilla extract, and cinnamon; mix until well blended.

In a 13x9-inch glass dish, melt butter or margarine in oven until hot and sizzling. Pour batter into hot dish and bake 15 to 20 minutes or until puffed and golden brown (it may puff irregularly in the center). Remove from oven. Working quickly, cut into serving-sized pieces and transfer to individual serving plates. Top with your favorite topping and serve immediately.

TOPPING IDEAS:
- Sifted powdered sugar
- Fresh applesauce with a dash of cinnamon
- Crushed pineapple, drained
- Whipped cream and sliced fresh strawberries
- Syrups – maple syrup, your favorite fruit syrup, or honey
- Canned pie filling, cold or warm

Makes 4 to 6 servings.

Apple Pancake

The smell of the apples cooking will drive you wild, let alone the taste of the pancake after it is baked.

1/4 cup sugar
2 teaspoons ground cinnamon
3 eggs, beaten and room temperature
1/2 teaspoon salt
1/2 cup all-purpose flour
1/2 cup milk, room temperature
7 tablespoons butter or margarine
1 to 2 green tart cooking apples, thinly sliced

Preheat oven to 400 degrees. In a small bowl, combine sugar and cinnamon; set aside. In a large bowl, combine eggs, salt, flour, and milk; Beat until batter is smooth.

In a large heavy ovenproof frying pan or a cast-iron skillet over medium heat, melt butter or margarine, turning pan to cover sides. Add apples and sprinkle with sugar and cinnamon mixture. Stir and let cook for 5 minutes.

Pour batter over apples into pan and bake 25 minutes or until puffed above sides of the pan and lightly browned. Remove by flipping upside down onto a serving platter (apples and cinnamon will be on top). Serve immediately.

Makes 2 servings.

Storage of Flour

Flour does not have an indefinite shelf life. White flour, the most highly refined type, may be stored in a cool place for up to six months before any loss of quality.

Whole wheat flour has a shorter storage time, about two months.

Stone-ground, whole wheat flour, which is milled so as to keep the germ intact, is best stored in the refrigerator or a cool, dry place and should be used within a few weeks.

Flour may also be stored in the freezer for longer storage. Always bring chilled flours to room temperature before using in recipes for baked goods.

Pancakes

Sourdough Starter

Sourdough starter will keep for years if it is fed monthly and kept properly covered in the refrigerator. Try to use the starter at least once a week.

To use in recipes, stir sourdough starter well before use. Pour out required amount called for in recipe and use as directed. Always use the starter at room temperature in your baking.

You may freeze the starter if it is not to be used for several weeks. Allow at least twenty-four hours for the frozen starter to become active again at room temperature before using.

To avoid spoilage, wash the starter crock about once a week with a detergent and warm water. Rinse well and dry carefully before returning the starter to the crock.

TO REPLENISH STARTER: Discard all but one cup of the starter, because any excess, unless reactivated, may become rancid.

ADD ONE CUP OF STARTER TO:
- *1 cup all-purpose flour*
- *1 cup lukewarm water (105 to 115 degrees)*

Let stand overnight until fermented and bubbling, then use or refrigerate.

Sourdough Starter

1 package active dry yeast
1/2 cup lukewarm water (105 to 115 degrees)
2 cups all-purpose flour
1 tablespoon salt
1 tablespoon sugar
1 1/2 cups chilled water

In a small bowl, combine yeast and 1/2 cup lukewarm water; stir until yeast is dissolved (stir with a wooden spoon; never use metal).

In a large bowl, combine flour, salt, sugar, and 1 1/2 cups chilled water; stir in the yeast mixture. Cover with plastic wrap and place in a warm place (80 to 90 degrees) for 3 to 4 days or until it bubbles and emits a good sour odor. Stir the starter down daily. If a crust develops, stir it down also.

Pour the starter into a jar, allowing room for expansion, and cover with plastic wrap or wax paper before securing lid. Store in the refrigerator.

Yields 7 to 8 cups.

Sourdough Pancakes

1 cup sourdough starter, room temperature
2 cups all-purpose flour
2 cups warm milk (90 degrees)
1 teaspoon salt
2 teaspoons baking soda
2 eggs
3 tablespoons butter or margarine, melted
2 tablespoons sugar

In a large bowl, combine sourdough starter with flour, milk, and salt. For the sourest flavor, cover and let stand in a warm place (85 degrees) 12 to 24 hours or until bubbly and sour smelling.

Just before baking, remove 1 cup batter to replenish sourdough starter in jar. To the remaining batter in the bowl, add baking soda, eggs, butter or margarine, and sugar; stir until well blended.

Preheat a griddle or large frying pan over medium heat. Grease lightly, just enough to prevent pancakes from sticking. Spoon 1/4 cup batter per pancake onto frying pan or griddle; cook 3 minutes or until most of the bubbles on top of pancakes pop and bottom is brown. Turn pancakes over; cook 1 minute or until brown on bottom. Remove from heat and transfer onto a warm serving platter.

Yields 12 to 15 pancakes.

Best Buttermilk Waffles

The secret to great waffles is a thick batter, so don't expect to pour this one.

1 cup all-purpose flour
1 tablespoon cornmeal (optional)
1/2 teaspoon salt
1 teaspoon baking soda
1 egg, separated
3/4 cup plus 2 tablespoons buttermilk
2 tablespoons unsalted butter, melted

Preheat waffle iron. In a medium bowl, combine flour, cornmeal, salt, and baking soda. Add egg yolk, buttermilk, and butter; stir until batter is blended but still lumpy.

In a medium bowl, beat egg white until stiff; gently fold egg white into batter.

Spread batter onto waffle iron. Cook 2 to 5 minutes or until golden brown. Remove from waffle iron, transfer onto a serving platter, and serve immediately. To keep waffles warm, put onto a wire rack in a 200-degree oven for up to 5 minutes.

NOTE: Make toaster waffles out of leftover batter – undercook the waffles a bit, cool on a wire rack, wrap in plastic wrap, and freeze. Pop them in the toaster for a quick breakfast.

Yields 3 to 4 waffles.

Overnight Waffles

1 package active dry yeast
5 cups all-purpose flour
1/3 cup sugar
3/4 teaspoon salt
2 teaspoons baking soda
4 cups buttermilk
3/4 cup butter or margarine, melted
4 eggs
3/4 cup finely chopped blanched almonds (optional)

In a large bowl, sift together yeast, flour, sugar, salt, and baking soda. Stir in buttermilk and butter or margarine. Add eggs and stir until batter is blended but still lumpy. Stir in almonds, if desired. Cover bowl and let rise in a warm place (85 degrees), free from drafts, until bubbly, about 30 minutes, or refrigerate overnight.

Preheat waffle iron. Bake, using a little less batter than usual, as these expand more than regular waffles. To keep waffles warm, place in a single layer, directly onto racks in a 200-degree oven for at least 5 minutes or until serving time.

NOTE: You may also cool waffles completely on racks, wrap in aluminum foil and freeze up to one month. Reheat (without thawing) in a toaster.

Yields 12 waffles.

Cooking Pancakes and Waffles

*Grease a waffle iron **only** the first time you use it. You should brush it with unsalted fat, then bake one waffle until it is good and brown. Throw that waffle out. From then on, wipe the waffle iron out after use. Brush out crumbs, then wipe with a dry soft cloth or paper towel. Let the waffle iron cool with the top up. NEVER WASH IT.*

A pancake griddle and waffle iron should be very hot. To test it, drop a few drops of cold water on the griddle. When the water begins to sizzle and jump about, the heat is just right. If the water evaporates instantly, the griddle is too hot.

IMPORTANT: Never open a waffle iron during baking or the waffle is likely to break apart. They are done when the lid rises slightly, the steaming has stopped, and the sides are golden brown. If the top resists when trying to lift it, the waffle is not done.

Overmixing pancake batter will make pancakes "tough." STOP MIXING BEFORE ALL THE LUMPS DISAPPEAR AND REFRIGERATE THE BATTER. The lumps will dissolve by themselves, and the smooth batter will yield a tender texture and even browning when cooked.

Homemade Maple-Flavored Syrup

You'll never purchase syrup again after trying this simple recipe. This recipe is thinner than most commercially prepared syrup. Refrigerate any leftovers; it keeps for as long as a month. If crystals form, place the jar of syrup in a pan of hot water; this will melt the crystallized sugar.

2 cups sugar
1 cup water
3 tablespoons light corn
  syrup
1/2 teaspoon maple
  flavoring

In a small pan over medium-high heat, combine sugar, water, and corn syrup. Bring to a boil; boil for 3 minutes. Remove from heat and stir in maple flavoring. Let cool.

Makes about 1 1/2 cups.

Special Weekend French Toast

Very rich and decadent version of an old favorite.

2/3 cup orange juice
1/3 cup orange-flavored liqueur
1/3 cup milk
1/2 teaspoon vanilla extract
1/4 teaspoon salt
1/4 cup sugar
6 eggs, beaten
12 slices thick-sliced french bread
2 tablespoons butter or margarine, divided
Powdered sugar

In a large shallow dish, combine orange juice, liqueur, milk, vanilla extract, salt, and sugar; stir in eggs until well blended. Place thick slices of french bread into the batter, turning bread once. Cover and refrigerate overnight.

Preheat a griddle or large frying pan over medium heat; melt 1 tablespoon butter or margarine. Add a few slices of the bread and cook 6 to 8 minutes on each side or until golden brown; remove from heat and place onto a warm platter in a 200-degree oven to keep warm. Cook remaining bread slices in 1 tablespoon of butter; remove from heat and transfer onto warm platter. Dust with powdered sugar and serve immediately.

Makes 6 servings.

Aloha French Toast

Elegant but easy.

4 eggs
2 teaspoons vanilla extract
1 tablespoon maple syrup
1 tablespoon plain yogurt
1 tablespoon sugar
1 (8-ounce) can crushed pineapple, drained
1/4 cup milk
8 slices thick-sliced french bread
4 tablespoons butter or margarine, divided
Powdered sugar
Shredded coconut

In a food processor or blender, combine eggs, vanilla extract, maple syrup, yogurt, sugar, pineapple, and milk; whirl until smooth. Place bread slices into a large shallow dish; pour egg mixture over them, turning bread once. Allow mixture to saturate.

Preheat a griddle or large frying pan over medium heat; add 1 tablespoon butter or margarine and melt. Add a few slices of the bread and cook 6 to 8 minutes on each side or until golden brown. Place onto a warm platter in a 200-degree oven to keep warm. Cook remaining slices in 1 tablespoon of butter. Dust with powdered sugar and shredded coconut. Serve immediately.

Makes 4 servings.

Avocado Tea Sandwiches

SLICED:
On one side of fresh bread, first spread with butter and then mayonnaise; place thin slices of avocado over top and sprinkle with salt and pepper.

Carefully cut the crusts from sandwich with a long, sharp knife. Cut in half diagonally, then cut in half again.

MASH AND SPREAD:
1 or 2 ripe avocados, peeled and seeded
Lemon juice
Salt and pepper to taste

In a small bowl, combine avocado, lemon juice, salt, and pepper; mash with a fork until well blended. On one side of fresh bread, first spread with butter and then mayonnaise; spread mashed avocados on top.

Carefully cut the crusts from the sandwich with a sharp knife. Cut in half diagonally, then cut in half again.

Tomato Tea Sandwiches

On one side of fresh pumpernickel rounds, spread mayonnaise. Place thin slices of cherry tomato or very thinly sliced tomatoes over the mayonnaise. Sprinkle with salt and pepper; sprinkle fresh basil leaves onto top. Chill.

Putting on the Ritz Egg Salad Sandwiches

8 hard-cooked eggs
1/2 cup mayonnaise
Salt and pepper to taste
1 tablespoon finely chopped fresh dill
6 tablespoons unsalted butter, room temperature
20 slices best-quality white bread

Peel eggs and place into a medium bowl. Slice eggs and then coarsely mash them with the back of a fork. Add mayonnaise, salt, pepper, and dill; stir until well blended. (Can be refrigerated, covered, up to 2 days.)

Spread butter onto one side of each slice of bread. Spread the buttered side of 10 slices of bread with 2 tablespoons egg mixture. Top with remaining slices of bread, buttered side down.

Carefully cut the crusts from sandwich with a sharp knife. Cut in half diagonally, then cut in half again.

Yields 10 whole sandwiches or 20 halves or 40 fourths.

Tea Sandwiches

Allow 4 to 6 cut sandwich servings for each person.

Choose the best-quality white or wheat bread as possible. Never serve end slices. (Freezing the bread before cutting and then spreading makes for easier handling.)

Bread slices should be lightly buttered no matter what the filling. Unsalted butter should always be used. Butter should be at room temperature before spreading.

Sandwiches will not become limp and soggy as readily if you spread the butter to the edge of the bread.

When using cucumber and tomatoes, cut them and allow to drain well on paper towels before putting them in the sandwiches.

Cut the crusts off the bread with a long, sharp knife after the sandwiches are filled. This keeps everything neater.

Since tea sandwiches should be delicate, cut each sandwich in half on the diagonal or into thirds or fourths before serving. Decorative shapes can be made with cookie cutters.

Perfect Pot of Tea

Bring water to a boil, then pour into the teapot to rinse and warm it. Discard water.

Place a heaping teaspoon of loose tea leaves for each person and one more "for the pot" into the teapot.

Bring more water to boil and pour into the teapot.

Put the lid on the teapot and allow to brew for three to six minutes, depending on the type of tea you are using.

Stir the pot just a little, then pour through a tiny strainer into cups.

Serve with milk, if you desire. (Do not use cream, as it may curdle). Pour the milk in first, then add the tea.

If you are brewing just one cup of tea, you can put leaves into a tea ball (a pierced stainless steel ball with a lid and chain). Place the tea ball into the cup and pour boiling water directly into the cup.

Cucumber Tea Sandwiches

1/2 seedless cucumber, peeled and very thinly sliced (about 32 slices)
1/2 cup unsalted butter, room temperature
1/2 cup coarsely chopped watercress leaves
16 slices best-quality white bread
Salt to taste
1/2 cup alfalfa sprouts

Place cucumbers slices between layers of paper towels to remove excess moisture.

In a small bowl, combine butter and watercress; spread on one side of each slice of bread. Lay cucumber slices onto the buttered side of 8 slices of bread. Sprinkle with salt. Cover each with 1 tablespoon alfalfa sprouts and top with the remaining slices of bread, buttered side down.

Carefully cut the crusts from each sandwich with a sharp knife. Cut the sandwiches in half diagonally and then cut in half again.

Yields 8 whole sandwiches or 16 halves or 32 fourths.

Cucumber-Shrimp Sandwiches

1 (8-ounce) package cream cheese, divided and room temperature
3 tablespoons finely chopped cucumber
2 teaspoons finely chopped onion
1 (4 1/2-ounce) can shrimp, drained
1 teaspoon finely chopped fresh watercress or parsley
2 teaspoons lemon juice
1/4 teaspoon ground red (cayenne) pepper
1/8 teaspoon salt
16 slices best-quality wheat bread
1/2 cup unsalted butter, room temperature
3/4 cup finely chopped fresh watercress or parsley

In a food processor, place cream cheese and whirl 8 to 10 seconds or until smooth. Add cucumber, onion, shrimp, 1 teaspoon watercress or parsley, and lemon juice; whirl until smooth. Add cayenne pepper and salt; whirl until blended. Reserve 1/4 of cream cheese mixture; set aside.

Spread one side of each piece of bread lightly with butter. Top the buttered side of 8 slices of bread with remaining cream cheese mixture; top with remaining bread slices, buttered side down.

Carefully cut the crusts from each sandwich with a sharp knife. Cut the sandwiches in half diagonally and then cut in half again. Spread the outer edges of sandwiches with reserved cream cheese mixture; roll edges in 3/4 cup watercress or parsley to coat. Cover and refrigerate.

Yields 8 whole sandwiches or 16 halves or 32 fourths.

Chicken Curry Tea Sandwiches

2 cooked whole chicken breasts, finely chopped
1/4 cup finely chopped nuts
4 celery stalks, finely chopped
Salt to taste
Mayonnaise (enough to moisten)
Curry powder or paste to taste
16 slices best-quality wheat bread
1/2 cup unsalted butter, room temperature

In a large bowl, combine chicken, nuts, celery, salt, and mayonnaise; stir until well blended. Add curry powder or paste (A LITTLE GOES A LONG WAY – BE CAREFUL).

Spread one side of each piece of bread lightly with butter. Top the buttered side of 8 slices of bread with some of the chicken mixture and top with the remaining bread slices, buttered side down.

Carefully cut the crusts from each sandwich with a sharp knife. Cut the sandwiches in half diagonally and then cut in half again.

Yields 8 whole sandwiches or 16 halves or 32 fourths.

Walnut Tea Sandwiches

1 1/2 (8-ounce) packages cream cheese, room temperature
1/2 cup ground toasted walnuts
2 tablespoons finely minced fresh parsley
1 tablespoon finely minced green bell pepper
1 tablespoon finely minced onion
1 teaspoon fresh lemon juice
1/4 teaspoon grated fresh nutmeg (or more to taste)
Salt and white pepper to taste
24 slices of best-quality white bread
1/2 cup unsalted butter, room temperature

In a large bowl, combine cream cheese, walnuts, parsley, and bell pepper. Add onion, lemon juice, nutmeg, salt, and pepper; stir until well blended.

Spread one side of each piece of bread lightly with butter. Top the buttered side of 12 slices of bread with some of the cream cheese mixture; top with the remaining bread slices, buttered side down.

Carefully cut the crusts from each sandwich with a sharp knife. Cut into triangle or long finger sandwiches.

Yields 12 whole sandwiches or 24 halves or 48 fourths.

Making Sandwiches Ahead of Time

If you need to make tea sandwiches in advance and need to keep them from drying out, cover them loosely with a sheet of wax paper and then place a damp kitchen towel over the wax paper. (Never place a damp towel directly on top of the bread because the sandwiches will become soggy.) Refrigerate.

To serve, remove from refrigerator. Uncover sandwiches just before serving.

Date & Nut Cream Cheese Tea Sandwiches

1 (8-ounce) package cream cheese, room temperature
1/4 cup finely diced pitted dates
2 tablespoons finely chopped walnuts, almonds, or hazelnuts
2 tablespoons finely grated carrot
16 slices best-quality wheat bread
1/2 cup unsalted butter, room temperature

In a small bowl, combine cream cheese, dates, nuts, and carrot. Spread one side of each piece of bread lightly with butter. Top the buttered side of 8 slices of bread with some of the cream cheese mixture, and top with the remaining bread slices, buttered side down.

Carefully cut the crusts from each sandwich with a sharp knife. Cut the sandwiches in half diagonally and then in half again.

Yields 8 whole sandwiches or 16 halves or 32 fourths.

Flavored Butters

These tasty spreads are ideal for tea breads, muffins, and pancakes.

In a medium bowl, whip 1/2 cup unsalted butter (room temperature) until fluffy and add one of the following combinations, using a food processor if desired:

RAISIN NUT BUTTER
1/2 cup finely chopped toasted walnuts
1/4 cup finely chopped raisins
1 tablespoon fresh orange juice
1 tablespoon sugar
1 teaspoon ground cinnamon

HONEY FRUIT BUTTER
1/4 cup honey
2 tablespoons fresh orange juice
1 small banana

MARMALADE BUTTER
1/2 cup marmalade (lemon, orange, or grapefruit)

SWEET CITRUS BUTTER
1/4 cup honey
2 teaspoons grated orange or lemon zest
1 tablespoon fresh orange or lemon juice
2 tablespoons sugar
2 teaspoons ground cinnamon

Candies & Cookies

Brenda's Toffee Candy

1/2 cup coarsely chopped pecans
1/2 cup butter
3/4 cup firmly packed brown sugar
1/2 cup semisweet chocolate chips

Butter an 8-inch square pan. Spread pecans over bottom of prepared pan. In a large saucepan over low heat, melt butter. Stir in brown sugar and bring to a boil; boil 7 minutes, stirring constantly. Remove from heat and immediately spread mixture over pecans in prepared pan. Let stand 2 to 3 minutes.

Sprinkle chocolate chips over hot mixture; let stand 1 to 2 minutes or until chocolate chips are melted. With a knife, spread chocolate over candy. Refrigerate until firm; break into pieces.

Yields 3 dozen candies.

Peanut Butter Cups

Very rich and peanut buttery. You can't help but love these.

1 cup butter, melted
1 1/2 cups graham cracker crumbs
2 cups powdered sugar
2 cups peanut butter, room temperature and divided
1 (12-ounce) package semisweet chocolate chips

In a large bowl, combine butter, graham cracker crumbs, powdered sugar, and 1 cup peanut butter; stir until well blended. Spread into an ungreased 13x9-inch baking pan. In a large saucepan over medium-low heat, melt chocolate chips and 1 cup peanut butter. Remove from heat and spread evenly over crumb mixture. Refrigerate until firm. Cut into bars. Store, covered, in the refrigerator.

Yields 96 small bars or 48 medium bars.

Peanut Butter Candy Balls

2 1/3 cups powdered sugar
1 1/2 cups graham cracker crumbs
1 cup shredded coconut
1 cup chopped nuts
1 cup crunchy peanut butter, room temperature
1 cup butter, melted
1 (12-ounce) package semisweet chocolate chips
1/2 block (2-ounce) paraffin wax

In a large bowl, combine powdered sugar, graham cracker crumbs, coconut, nuts, peanut butter, and butter; form into balls (approximately walnut size) and place onto wax paper.

In the top of a double boiler over hot water, melt chocolate chips and paraffin wax. Using a toothpick to hold balls, dip each ball into chocolate mixture to coat; place onto wax paper to harden.

Yields 4 dozen balls.

Candy

When you first begin the candy-making process, gather and measure out all the ingredients needed in the recipe.

NEVER DOUBLE A CANDY RECIPE. It will affect the cooking time and affect the quality of the candy.

Use a saucepan large enough to allow space for candy to bubble up when boiling. Too large or too small a saucepan may also affect the cooking time.

During humid weather or rainy days, cook candy one or two degrees higher than you would on a normal day.

TIPS: When a candy recipe calls for water (unless cold water is specified), always use hot water and your candy will be clearer.

When beating candy, use a large wooden spoon and never a rotary beater unless it is specified. Tilt the pan and beat vigorously.

Always remove, with a dampened brush or swab, any drops of syrup from the sides of the saucepan while the candy is cooking, or it will cause crystallization.

Candy Temperatures

If you don't have a candy thermometer, use the following cold water tests. If candy does not pass the cold water test, continue cooking.

FUDGE, FONDANT, CREAMS PENUCHE, MAPLE, ETC:
234° to 240° – Soft Ball
When a small amount of sugar syrup is dropped into very cold water, it forms a ball that does not hold its shape when pressed.

CARAMELS & DIVINITY:
246° to 248° – Firm Ball
When a small amount of sugar syrup is dropped into very cold water, it forms a ball that holds its shape when pressed.

TAFFY:
250° to 268° – Hard Ball
When a small amount of sugar syrup is dropped into very cold water, it forms a ball that holds its shape but is pliable.

BUTTERSCOTCH & TOFFEE:
270° to 290° – Soft Crack
When a small amount of sugar syrup is dropped into very cold water, it separates into hard but not brittle threads.

PEANUT BRITTLE:
300° to 310° – Hard Crack
When a small amount of sugar syrup is dropped into very cold water, it separates into hard brittle threads.

Grand Betty's Crunch Bars

1 (4-ounce) package saltine crackers
1 cup butter
1 cup firmly packed brown sugar
1 (12-ounce) package semisweet chocolate chips
Chopped nuts

Preheat oven to 400 degrees. Line a baking sheet with sides with aluminum foil. Crush saltine crackers; spread onto bottom of prepared baking sheet. In a medium saucepan over medium heat, melt butter. Add brown sugar and bring to a boil; boil 3 minutes, stirring occasionally. Remove from heat and pour mixture over crackers, coating evenly. Bake 6 minutes; remove from oven.

Sprinkle chocolate chips over warm cracker mixture. Sprinkle nuts over chocolate. Refrigerate until firm; break into pieces.

Yields 20 pieces.

Microwave Peanut Brittle

1 cup sugar
1/4 cup corn syrup
1 cup raw peanuts
1/4 teaspoon salt
1 tablespoon butter
1 teaspoon vanilla extract
1 teaspoon baking soda

Butter a baking sheet. In an ungreased 2-quart microwave-safe dish, combine sugar, corn syrup, peanuts, and salt. Microwave on high power for 8 minutes. Add butter and vanilla extract; stir until well blended. Microwave at high power another 2 minutes. Stir in baking soda (as quickly as possible).

Remove from microwave and quickly pour onto prepared baking sheet. Refrigerate until firm; break into pieces.

Yields lots!

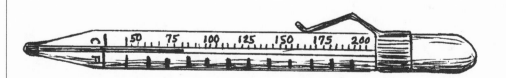

Presto Pralines

1 cup sugar
1 cup firmly packed dark brown sugar
1/2 cup evaporated milk
1 cup pecan halves

In a large saucepan over medium-high heat, combine sugar, brown sugar, and milk; cook, stirring constantly with wooden spoon, until candy thermometer reaches 236 degrees (soft ball). Immediately remove thermometer and remove from heat; set in a large pan of cold water to cool.

When candy has almost cooled, beat with a spoon 1 minute or until it begins to lose its gloss. Immediately stir in pecans and drop by tablespoonfuls onto wax paper. Refrigerate until candies are firm and no longer glossy.

Yields 18 small pralines.

Aplets

1 cup grated Delicious apples
2 cups sugar
2 tablespoons unflavored gelatin
5 tablespoons cold water
1/8 teaspoon rose culinary essence*
1 cup finely chopped walnuts
Powdered sugar

* Culinary essence can be found in Indian stores. NOTE: If necessary, substitute 1 tablespoon lemon juice.

Grease an 8-inch square pan. In a large saucepan over medium heat, combine apples and sugar. Bring to a boil; boil 1 minute, stirring constantly. Turn heat to low and simmer another 30 minutes. Remove from heat. In a small bowl, combine gelatin and water; add to sugar mixture, stirring constantly until dissolved. Add culinary essence and walnuts; stir until well blended. Pour into prepared pan; cool at least 2 hours. Cut into 1-inch squares and then roll in powdered sugar. Store, covered, in refrigerator.

Yields 64 candy squares.

Porcupine Candy

2 (12-ounce) packages butterscotch chips
1 (8.2-ounce) can chow mein noodles
1 (16-ounce) can salted cocktail peanuts

In the top of a double boiler over hot water, melt butterscotch chips. Add chow mein noodles and cocktail peanuts, stirring until blended. Drop by teaspoonfuls onto wax paper. Refrigerate until firm.

NOTE: Semisweet chocolate chips can be substituted.

Yields 4 cups.

Paraffin Wax

Paraffin wax is used in many candy recipes and in making jams and jellies. It is packaged in one pound boxes (four blocks in each pound). Check your recipe carefully for the amount needed.

Candy Thermometer

> BUY A GOOD CANDY THERMOMETER!
>
> *It is important, for best results when making candy, that you use a dependable candy thermometer.*

Stand the thermometer in candy mixture before you start to cook and leave it in during cooking. The bulb must be completely covered with boiling syrup, yet must not rest on the bottom of the pan.

To read the temperature on the thermometer, your eyes should be on a level with the mercury. When mixture is ready to be removed from heat, take out thermometer and lay it where it can cool before washing; otherwise, it may break.

Candy

"Soup to Nuts"

In earlier, more formal times, the arrival of salted nuts on the table meant that the meal was ended.

Because formal meals started with soup, the expression "soup to nuts" came to signify the completeness or the full treatment.

Chocolate Fudge

TIP: To improve the texture of your fudge, try adding a teaspoon of cornstarch when you first start mixing.

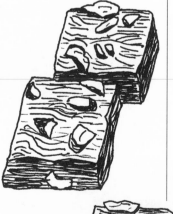

Coated Pecans

2 egg whites, room temperature
1 3/4 cups firmly packed brown sugar
4 to 5 cups pecan halves

Preheat oven to 250 degrees. In a large bowl, beat egg whites until stiff peaks form; fold in brown sugar and pecans. Place coated pecans onto an ungreased baking sheet. Bake 5 minutes. Remove from heat and transfer pecans onto wax paper to cool.

Yields 4 to 5 cups.

Sugared Walnuts

I warn you – they're addictive.

1/4 teaspoon salt
1 cup sugar
1/4 cup light corn syrup
1/4 cup water
1/2 teaspoon ground cinnamon
3 cups walnut halves
1/2 teaspoon baking powder
1 teaspoon vanilla extract

In a large saucepan over medium-high heat, combine salt, sugar, corn syrup, water, and cinnamon: bring to a boil and cook until candy thermometer reaches 240 degrees (soft ball). Immediately remove thermometer and remove pan from heat. Fold walnuts into hot mixture; let stand a few minutes to slightly cool. Add baking powder and vanilla extract; stir until well blended. Quickly separate sugared walnuts and place onto wax paper to cool.

Yields 3 cups.

Never Fail Fudge

This fudge recipe is guaranteed not to be sugary, just creamy rich.

2 cups sugar
3/4 cup evaporated milk
2 tablespoons butter
1 (8-ounce) jar marshmallow cream
1 (12-ounce) package semisweet chocolate chips
1/2 cup chopped nuts
1/2 teaspoon vanilla extract

Butter a 9-inch square baking pan. In a large saucepan over medium heat, combine sugar, evaporated milk, and butter; bring to a boil and cook until candy thermometer reaches 240 degrees (soft ball). Immediately remove thermometer and remove pan from heat. Add marshmallow cream, chocolate chips, nuts, and vanilla extract; stir, but do not beat, until blended. Pour into prepared pan. When partly cooled, mark into squares, cutting apart when cool.

Yields 3 dozen squares.

Chocolate Fondue

This is a delightful way to serve dessert. Use skewers or toothpicks to dip the fruit.

2 (1-ounce) squares unsweetened chocolate, broken into pieces
1 tablespoon butter or margarine
1 cup sugar
1 (5 3/8-ounce) can evaporated milk
1 tablespoon Kahlua, Tia Maria, or rum
Fruits for dipping, cut into bite-sized pieces (see below)

In the top of a double boiler over hot water, melt chocolate and butter or margarine. Add sugar, evaporated milk, and Kahlua, Tia Maria, or rum; stir until sugar is dissolved and mixture is smooth. Remove from heat and transfer to a fondue pot or a chafing dish. Serve with assorted fruits for dipping.

Yields 1 1/2 cups.

FRUITS FOR DIPPING:
Bananas
Apples
Cherries
Grapes
Mandarin orange sections
Strawberries
Pineapple

Coconut

Coconuts are the stones of the fruits borne by the coconut palm, which originated in Malaya and now grows freely in all the tropical regions of the world.

To store packaged coconut, reseal the bag as tightly as possible and refrigerate. Can be stored ten days to two weeks.

Most people tend to think of coconut with sweets, candies, cakes, custards, and pies. It is also used in curries of India and the stews of Latin America and the Caribbean.

Chocolate Cherry Balls

4 tablespoons butter, room temperature
2 cups powdered sugar
24 maraschino cherries, chopped
2/3 cup peanut butter, room temperature
1/2 cup chopped walnuts
1 cup shredded coconut
1/2 teaspoon salt
1 (12-ounce) package semisweet chocolate chips
1/4 bar (1-ounce) paraffin wax

In a large bowl, combine butter, powdered sugar, maraschino cherries, peanut butter, walnuts, coconut, and salt; shape into 1-inch balls.

In the top of a double boiler over hot water, melt chocolate chips and paraffin wax. Insert a toothpick into each ball; dip into chocolate mixture to coat exterior. Place onto wax paper to set. Use another toothpick to push ball from inserted toothpick. If a hole remains where toothpick was inserted, add a small amount of chocolate coating to cover.

Yields 3 dozen balls.

Dipping Chocolate

All chocolate used for dipping should be melted in the top of a double boiler over hot, never boiling, water; too high a temperature changes the flavor and color.

TIP: If chocolate thickens while dipping, add additional water in the lower part of the double boiler; NEVER ADD WATER TO THE CHOCOLATE.

Millionaires

1/2 cup butter
1 (14-ounce) package caramels
2 cups pecans, chopped
8 (1.55-ounce) chocolate candy bars
1/4 bar (1-ounce) paraffin wax, grated

In the top of a double boiler over hot water, melt butter; add caramels, cover, and stir occasionally. (Butter will be hard to get mixed in with caramel, but do not give up!) Stir in pecans; drop by teaspoonfuls onto greased wax paper. Refrigerate until firm. In the top of a double boiler over hot water, melt chocolate bars and paraffin wax. Use toothpicks to dip cooled candies into chocolate mixture. Place onto wax paper to cool.

Turtles

1 (8-ounce) package caramels or 1/2 recipe of Vanilla Caramels
2 tablespoons heavy cream
1 cup pecan halves
16 (1-ounce) squares semisweet chocolate

In the top of a double boiler over hot water, melt caramels in heavy cream. Arrange pecans in groups of five (head and four legs) on greased wax paper. Spoon caramel into a small mound in the middle of the nuts to make the body. (The caramel should partially cover the nuts to keep them in place.) Let stand until hard.

In the top of a double boiler over hot water, melt chocolate; stir with spoon until melted. With a spoon, coat body, head and legs with dipping chocolate, leaving ends of pecans uncovered. Refrigerate 30 minutes or until chocolate is firm.

Vanilla Caramels

2 cups sugar
1 cup light corn syrup
2 cups heavy cream, lukewarm (105 to 115 degrees)
1/2 cup butter, cut into 1/2-inch pieces
1 teaspoon vanilla extract
2 teaspoons grated paraffin wax

Lightly oil a large baking pan; set aside. Lightly oil a 3-quart saucepan and then add sugar and corn syrup; cook over low heat, stirring constantly, until sugar is completely dissolved and mixture comes to a boil. Cook, stirring occasionally, until candy thermometer registers 250 degrees (firm ball). Very slowly add cream so mixture never stops boiling. Cook until temperature again reaches 250 degrees. Add butter, a little at a time, so mixture never stops boiling. Stir a little to blend; let mixture cook to 250 degrees again.

Remove from heat. Add vanilla extract and paraffin wax; stir until blended. Pour in steady stream into prepared baking pan (do not scrape excess from saucepan). Score in 1-inch squares, but do not cut all the way through. After caramel has cooled completely, cut into marked squares. Wrap individual pieces immediately in plastic wrap or wax paper; store in an airtight container.

Yields 81 (1-inch) pieces.

Caramels

Many candy-makers have been discouraged from making caramels by the long and tedious process described in old cookbooks.

This recipe is very simple and easy to make. It uses a simple shortcut of adding the butter and cream after the syrup has reached the firm ball stage. Making caramels in stages cuts the cooking down to a reasonable time and also makes a better-tasting candy.

Popcorn Balls

Once used for Halloween treats, these popcorn balls are great all year long.

3 quarts unsalted popped corn
1 cup sugar
1/3 cup light corn syrup
1/3 cup water
1/4 cup butter or margarine
3/4 teaspoon salt
3/4 teaspoon vanilla extract

In a large bowl, place popped corn (make sure that all unpopped kernels are removed). In a large saucepan over medium-high heat, combine sugar, corn syrup, water, butter or margarine, and salt; cook until candy thermometer reaches 270 degrees (soft crack). Immediately remove thermometer and remove saucepan from heat. Add vanilla extract; stir only enough to mix. Pour over popped corn; mix together with a wooden spoon until corn is well coated.

When corn is cool enough to handle, with lightly buttered fingers, press into balls. Place onto wax paper; cool completely. Wrap individually in plastic wrap or place in plastic bags.

Yields 12 balls.

Oven Caramel Corn

3 3/4 quarts unsalted popped corn
3 cups walnut halves, pecan halves, peanuts,
    or whole almonds
1 cup firmly packed brown sugar
1/2 cup butter or margarine
1/4 cup light corn syrup
1/2 teaspoon salt
1/2 teaspoon baking soda
2 teaspoons vanilla extract

Preheat oven to 200 degrees. Divide popped corn and nuts between two ungreased 13x9-inch baking pans.

In a large saucepan over medium-high heat, combine brown sugar, butter or margarine, corn syrup, and salt; cook, stirring occasionally, until bubbly around the edges. Continue cooking another 5 minutes.

Remove pan from heat and stir in baking soda and vanilla extract until foamy; pour over popped corn and nuts, stirring until popcorn is well coated. Bake 1 hour, stirring every 15 minutes. Remove from oven and cool on a wire rack for 10 minutes; loosen mixture from baking pan with spatula. Let stand at room temperature 1 hour to harden. Store in airtight containers.

Yields 15 (1-cup) servings.

Popcorn

1/2 cup unpopped popcorn equals about 1 quart when popped.

Unpopped popcorn can be stored at room temperature for about one year. It will retain its natural moisture better if it is kept in an airtight container in the refrigerator or freezer. Popcorn that keeps its moisture produces larger popped kernels.

Popcorn that is packaged with oil in its own "pan" should be stored no longer than three months at room temperature. Longer than that and you risk having the oil turn rancid.

Store leftover, unbuttered popcorn in an airtight container or plastic bag at room temperature for up to two weeks. Refrigerate buttered popcorn.

TIP: To make popcorn pop like crazy, pour the kernels into a strainer, wash in cold water, drain well, and pour into the popper. WATCH IT POP!

Refrigerator or Icebox Cookies

The refrigerator cookie is ideal if you wish to have freshly baked cookies on hand at all times. The rolls of dough may be made up in advance and stored. Cookies can easily be cut and baked as needed. The dough can also be frozen to store for longer periods.

Form the dough into cylinders that are from one to two inches in diameter, depending on the size cookie desired. Wrap the cylinders in parchment or wax paper and refrigerate at least overnight.

TIP: Use scissors to cut down the length of a cardboard tube, such as the core of a roll of paper towels. Line the inside of the tube with wax paper.

Pack the cookie dough into the tube. When the tube is full, close it, wrap a rubber band around each end, and refrigerate.

After the dough is chilled, unwrap and slice for baking. The dough will be perfectly shaped.

Grandma Myers' Refrigerator Cookies

During the late 1920s and 1930s in Vernonia, Oregon, Grandma Myers baked these cookies in the oven of her wood stove. My mother tells me that they used to test the heat by sticking their hand in the oven. If the temperature felt right, then they put the cookies in. These cookies have been adapted for use in our modern kitchens.

1/2 cup vegetable shortening
1/4 cup butter, room temperature
1/2 cup sugar
1/2 cup firmly packed brown sugar
2 eggs, well beaten
1 teaspoon vanilla extract
2 1/2 cups all-purpose flour
1/2 teaspoon salt
1/2 teaspoon baking soda
1/2 cup chopped dates
1/2 cup chopped nuts

In a large bowl, cream vegetable shortening, butter, sugar, and brown sugar until light and fluffy; stir in eggs and vanilla extract. Add flour, salt, and baking soda; stir until well blended. In a small bowl, combine dates and nuts until dates are coated with nuts; stir into cookie dough. Shape cookie dough into a log, wrap in wax paper, and refrigerate overnight.

Preheat oven to 350 degrees. Lightly grease cookie sheets. Cut cookie dough into 1/8-inch slices; place onto prepared cookie sheets. Bake 10 minutes or until light brown. Remove from oven and cool on wire racks.

Yields 5 dozen cookies.

Peanut Butter Cookies

A recipe book wouldn't be complete without most children's favorite cookie.

1/2 cup butter or margarine, room temperature
1/2 cup sugar
1/2 cup firmly packed brown sugar
1/2 cup peanut butter, room temperature
1 egg
1 cup all-purpose flour
1 teaspoon baking soda

Preheat oven to 350 degrees. Lightly grease cookie sheets. In a large bowl, cream butter or margarine, sugar, brown sugar, and peanut butter until light and fluffy. Stir in egg, flour, and baking soda.

Using your hands, roll dough by teaspoonfuls into small balls; place onto prepared cookie sheets. Flatten into a crisscross pattern with a fork that has been dipped in water. Bake 10 to 12 minutes or until light brown. Remove from oven and cool on wire racks.

Yields 3 dozen cookies.

Peppermint Rounds

Now you, too, can make cookies that look professional.

1 cup butter or margarine, room temperature
1/2 cup sugar
2 eggs
1 teaspoon vanilla extract
2 3/4 cups all-purpose flour
1 1/2 teaspoons baking powder
1/2 teaspoon salt
1 cup old-fashioned rolled oats
1/3 cup hard peppermint candy, crushed
Powdered sugar
Peppermint Frosting

In a large bowl, cream butter or margarine, sugar, eggs, and vanilla extract until light and fluffy. Mix in flour, baking powder, and salt. Stir in rolled oats and peppermint candy; stir until well blended. Cover and refrigerate at least 1 hour.

Preheat oven to 350 degrees. Lightly grease cookie sheets. Divide dough in half; roll each to 1/8-inch thickness on a surface dusted with powdered sugar. Cut with a 2 1/2-inch round cookie cutter and place onto prepared cookie sheets. Bake 10 to 12 minutes or until light brown. Remove from oven and cool on wire racks.

Spread cookies with white Peppermint Frosting. Before frosting sets, drizzle lines of pink Peppermint Frosting across each cookie. With a toothpick, draw lines back and forth across the pink frosting for a scalloped pattern.

Yields 4 dozen cookies.

PEPPERMINT FROSTING:
4 cups sifted powdered sugar
1/4 to 1/2 cup half and half cream
1/8 teaspoon salt
1 teaspoon peppermint extract
Red food coloring

In a large bowl, combine powdered sugar, 1/4 cup cream, salt, and peppermint extract, stirring until smooth (add additional cream for desired consistency).

In a small bowl, place 1/4 cup of the frosting and stir in 1 to 2 drops red food coloring for pink frosting.

Yields 1 1/2 cups frosting.

Crisp or Rolled Cookies

Crisp or rolled cookies are made from a stiff dough which is rolled and cut with sharp cookie cutters, a knife, or a pastry wheel. They should be thin and crisp.

It is usually best to work with a small amount of dough at a time. Chill the dough if it is too soft to handle easily.

For the most tender cookies, use as little flour as possible when rolling out. Save all the dough trimmings and roll at one time (these cookies will be less tender).

TIP: Crisp or rolled cookies should be stored in a container with a tight-fitting cover.

Cookies

Cookie Sheets

Cookie sheets with little or no sides will allow the cookies to bake quickly and evenly.

Grease cookie sheets with either vegetable shortening or unsalted butter. Don't use vegetable oil for greasing. The oil between cookies will burn during baking; this is very difficult to clean.

If cookie dough has a large amount of vegetable shortening or butter, it is not necessary to grease the pan. Most cookie doughs can be baked on ungreased pans.

Avoid placing one sheet above another in the oven, as this causes uneven baking. Cookies should be baked in the center of the oven.

TIPS: If you flour a cookie sheet after it is greased, there will be less tendency for the cookies to thin out and spread too much during baking. A greased and floured sheet is also preferred for any dough containing chocolate chips (the chocolate which comes in contact with the sheet is less likely to stick and burn while baking).

Russian Teacakes

This favorite holiday cookie is known by many different names, such as Mexican Wedding Cakes or Swedish Tea Cakes. These cookies always seem to be a favorite of men.

1 cup butter, room temperature
1/2 cup sifted powdered sugar
2 teaspoons vanilla extract
2 1/4 cups all-purpose flour
1/4 teaspoon salt
3/4 cup finely chopped nuts
Powdered sugar

In a large bowl, cream butter, powdered sugar, and vanilla extract until light and fluffy. Sift in flour and salt; stir until well mixed. Mix in nuts. Refrigerate 1 hour.

Preheat oven to 400 degrees. Roll dough into 1-inch balls. Place onto ungreased cookie sheets. Bake 10 to 12 minutes or until set but not brown. Remove from oven and cool on wire racks. While still warm, roll cookies in powdered sugar. Roll in powdered sugar again.

VARIATION: Substitute 1 cup miniature semisweet chocolate chips for the nuts.

Yields 4 dozen cookies.

Peanut Butter – Chocolate Kiss Cookies

What better place to put a chocolate kiss than in the center of a delicious peanut butter cookie.

1/2 cup vegetable shortening
1/2 cup smooth peanut butter, room temperature
1/2 cup sugar
1/2 cup firmly packed brown sugar
1 egg
1 tablespoon milk
1 teaspoon vanilla extract
1 3/4 cups all-purpose flour
1 teaspoon baking soda
1/2 teaspoon salt
1/4 cup sugar
48 chocolate kiss candies

Preheat oven to 375 degrees. Lightly grease cookie sheets. In a large bowl, cream vegetable shortening and peanut butter until light and fluffy. Gradually add 1/2 cup sugar and brown sugar; beating until light and fluffy. Add egg, milk, and vanilla extract; beat well. Add flour, baking soda, and salt; stir into creamed mixture until well mixed.

Roll cookie dough into 1-inch balls; roll in 1/4 cup sugar. Place balls 2 inches apart onto prepared cookie sheets. Bake 8 minutes. Remove from oven; press a chocolate kiss candy into the center of each cookie. Return to oven and bake another 2 minutes or until light brown. Remove from oven and cool on wire racks.

Yields 4 dozen cookies.

Snickerdoodles

The name of this favorite cookie, which originated in New England, is just a 19th-century nonsense word for quick-made cookies.

1/2 cup vegetable shortening
1/2 cup butter, room temperature
1 1/2 cups sugar
2 eggs
2 3/4 cups all-purpose flour
2 teaspoons cream of tartar
1 teaspoon baking soda
1/4 teaspoon salt
2 tablespoons sugar
2 teaspoons ground cinnamon

Preheat oven to 400 degrees. In a large bowl, cream vegetable shortening, butter, 1 1/2 cups sugar, and eggs until light and fluffy. Add flour, cream of tartar, baking soda, and salt; stir until well blended.

In a small bowl, combine 2 tablespoons sugar and cinnamon. Roll dough into balls the size of small walnuts; roll in sugar and cinnamon mixture. Place 2 inches apart onto ungreased cookie sheets. Bake 8 to 10 minutes or until light brown. Remove from oven and cool on wire racks. NOTE: Cookies puff when they begin to bake and then flatten out with crinkled tops.

Yields 8 dozen cookies.

Coconut Macaroons

These coconut macaroons are a delicious, chewy version of the classic macaroon cookie. They are also very easy to prepare.

2 egg whites, room temperature
1/8 teaspoon cream of tartar
1 cup powdered sugar
1 cup shredded coconut
2 cups corn flakes cereal
1/2 teaspoon salt
1 teaspoon vanilla extract

Preheat oven to 325 degrees. Heavily grease cookie sheets. In a large bowl, beat egg whites and cream of tartar until stiff peaks form. Fold in powdered sugar, coconut, corn flakes cereal, salt, and vanilla extract.

Drop by small teaspoonfuls onto prepared cookie sheets, about 2 inches apart. Bake 12 to 15 minutes or until light brown. Remove from oven and cool on wire racks.

Yields 2 dozen cookies.

Cookies

Cookies should be of a uniform thickness and size so they will bake in the same amount of time.

A baking sheet should be either cool or at room temperature when the cookie dough is placed on it; otherwise, the dough will start to melt, adversely affecting the cookies' shape and texture.

Bake one cookie sheet at a time, and be sure that the sheet fits in the oven with at least one inch of space around its edges for the proper heat circulation.

Unless the recipe directs otherwise, remove baked cookies from cookie sheet to wire rack immediately to prevent further baking.

Store soft cookies and crisp cookies separately. Store cookies in an airtight box or tin to keep them crisp. Separate layers with sheets of wax paper or aluminum foil.

Macaroon Cookies

Macaroons originated in an Italian Monastery around 1790. They were baked by the Carmelite nuns who followed the principle: "Almonds are good for girls who do not eat meat."

During the Revolution, two nuns who hid in the town called Nancy, made and sold macaroons. They became known as the "Macaroon Sisters."

Most macaroon and meringue cookies are fragile and need special handling. Keep them small and they will hold together better.

Some of the meringues, heavy in nuts, keep well if stored in a tightly covered container.

TIP: Should they harden on the pan, return the cookie sheet to the warm oven for a minute before trying to remove them.

Hazelnut Macaroons

These macaroons are absolutely delicious.

3 egg whites, room temperature
1/8 teaspoon cream of tartar
2 cups powdered sugar
2 teaspoons lemon juice
2 cups finely ground hazelnuts
Whole hazelnuts

Preheat oven to 325 degrees. Heavily grease cookie sheets. In a large bowl, beat egg whites and cream of tartar until stiff peaks form. Gradually beat in powdered sugar; continue beating until glossy. Stir in lemon juice. In a small bowl, reserve 3 tablespoons of mixture; set aside. Into the remaining mixture, fold ground hazelnuts.

Drop by small teaspoonfuls onto prepared cookie sheets about 2 inches apart; put a small dab of reserved mixture onto each cookie and press a whole hazelnut in the middle. Bake 20 minutes or until light brown. Remove from oven and cool on wire racks.

Yields 3 dozen cookies.

Spritz Cookies

Crisp, fragile, and buttery tasting. Great for Christmas goodies. A Norwegian tradition is to make them in shapes of S's and O's. The name comes from "spritzen," which is German for "to squirt or spray."

2 cups butter, room temperature
1 cup sugar
1 egg, well beaten
1 teaspoon vanilla extract
4 cups sifted all-purpose flour

Preheat oven to 400 degrees. In a large bowl, mix butter until creamy. Gradually add sugar; cream until light and fluffy. Add egg and beat well; stir in vanilla extract. Gradually add flour to mixture, beating well after each addition.

Press cookie dough through a cookie press, forming desired shapes, onto ungreased cookie sheets. Bake 6 to 9 minutes or until light brown. Remove from oven and cool on wire racks.

Yields 6 dozen cookies.

VARIATIONS:
CHOCOLATE SPRITZ – Add 2 ounces melted unsweetened chocolate to powdered sugar mixture.

ORANGE SPRITZ – Add 1 tablespoon grated orange zest with dry ingredients.

High Tea Lemon Cookies

An old-fashioned cookie that is very rich and delicate. Be prepared – all your friends will want this recipe after they taste these delicious cookies.

2 cups butter, room temperature*
2/3 cup powdered sugar
1 teaspoon grated lemon zest
1/2 teaspoon vanilla extract
2 cups all-purpose flour
1 1/2 cups cornstarch
Lemon Frosting

* Very important that you use room temperature butter (not softened or melted).

Preheat oven to 350 degrees. In a large bowl, beat butter until creamy. Add powdered sugar; cream until light and fluffy. Add lemon zest and vanilla extract; beat well. Sift flour and cornstarch into butter mixture and beat well until well mixed.

Roll cookie dough into 1-inch balls. Place onto ungreased cookie sheets and bake 15 minutes or until bottoms are light brown. Carefully remove from oven and cool on wire racks (when warm, the cookies are delicate). When cool, spread Lemon Frosting onto top of cookies.

Yields 6 dozen cookies.

LEMON FROSTING:
This recipe makes enough for a double batch of cookies.

1/3 cup butter, room temperature
1 teaspoon grated lemon zest
1/3 cup fresh lemon juice
4 cups powdered sugar

In a medium bowl, combine butter, lemon zest, lemon juice, and powdered sugar; stir until well mixed.

Date Balls (Sugar Balls)

Great for Christmas cookie exchanges.

1 cup chopped nuts
1 cup shredded coconut
1/2 cup butter
1 cup sugar
2 eggs
1 1/4 cups chopped dates
3 cups Rice Krispies cereal
Nuts
Shredded coconut

In a small bowl, combine nuts and coconut; set aside. In a large saucepan over medium heat, add butter, sugar, eggs, and dates; cook 7 minutes. Add Rice Krispies cereal; stirring to blend. Remove from heat and roll dough mixture into 1-inch balls; roll in nuts and coconut. Place onto wax paper to cool.

Yields 2 dozen cookies.

Cookie Exchanges

This tradition has been around for many years. The Christmas holiday season is a favorite time to have these parties. They are a lot of fun, plus you take home some wonderful cookies.

Each person invited bakes a batch of their favorite cookies and brings them to the gathering. After coffee and cookies (of course) are served, each person gets to take home an assortment of cookies.

Chocolate Melted in Liquid

To melt chocolate in a liquid such as milk, cream, water, syrup, or any combination of these liquids, first place the liquid in a double boiler over hot water and then add the chocolate (the chocolate will melt quicker and easier if it is first cut into small pieces). To get a smooth and perfect blend, beat with a rotary egg beater.

A smoother blend of chocolate and liquid is obtained by adding the chocolate to cold milk and melting it slowly, rather than by adding it to hot milk and melting it rapidly.

Occasionally chocolate is melted in water, as in making hot chocolate. Cold water is added to the chocolate; the mixture is placed over direct heat, and stirred constantly until thick and smooth. This method is generally used when cocoa is substituted for chocolate, except in mixtures such as batters, in which the cocoa may be more conveniently added by sifting it with the flour.

Chocolate Aggies

These are wonderful – a chocolate lover's delight.

4 tablespoons butter
4 (1-ounce) squares unsweetened chocolate
2 cups sugar
4 extra-large eggs
2 cups sifted all-purpose flour
2 teaspoons baking powder
1/4 teaspoon salt
1/2 cup chopped walnuts
1 cup powdered sugar

In a large, heavy saucepan over low heat, melt butter and chocolate. Cook, stirring occasionally, until smooth; remove from heat. With a heavy wooden spoon, stir sugar into warm chocolate mixture. Stir in eggs, one at a time, beating well after each addition. Sift in flour, baking powder, and salt; stir until smooth. Stir in walnuts.

NOTE: This will be a soft dough and must be refrigerated. It may be left in saucepan or transferred to a bowl. Either way, cover and refrigerate, preferably for 1 1/2 hours; dough may be refrigerated longer or overnight, if you wish.

Preheat oven to 300 degrees. Adjust two racks to divide oven into thirds. Line cookie sheets with aluminum foil.

In a small bowl, place powdered sugar. Sugar palms of your hands with some of the powdered sugar. Roll dough into 1 1/2-inch balls. Roll balls around in powdered sugar and place 2 inches apart onto prepared cookie sheets.

Bake 20 to 22 minutes or until tops of cookies are barely semi-firm to touch. Reverse position of sheets top to bottom and front to back once during baking to ensure even baking. Remove from oven and cool on wire racks.

DO NOT OVERBAKE – these should be slightly soft in the centers. (If you bake only one sheet at a time, bake high in oven.)

Yields 2 1/2 dozen cookies.

Oatmeal Scotch Chippers

1 1/4 cups butter or margarine, room temperature
1 1/2 cups firmly packed brown sugar
1 cup sugar
3 eggs
1 1/4 cups peanut butter, room temperature
2 teaspoons baking soda
4 1/2 cups old-fashioned rolled oats
1 cup semisweet chocolate chips
1 cup butterscotch chips
1 cup chopped walnuts

Preheat oven to 350 degrees. In a large bowl, cream butter or margarine, brown sugar, and sugar until light and fluffy; stir in eggs. Add peanut butter and baking soda; stir until well blended. Stir in rolled oats. Stir in chocolate chips, butterscotch chips, and walnuts; mix until well blended.

Drop by rounded teaspoonfuls of dough 2 inches apart onto an ungreased baking sheet. Bake 12 to 14 minutes or until lightly browned. Remove from oven and cool 2 minutes on baking sheet. Remove from baking sheet and cool on wire racks.

Yields 6 dozen cookies.

Nancy's Rocky Mountain Bars

2 cups sugar
1/2 cup butter or margarine
1/2 cup milk
4 tablespoons cocoa
1/4 teaspoon salt
1/2 cup peanut butter, room temperature
3 cups old-fashioned rolled oats
2 teaspoons vanilla extract

In a large saucepan, combine sugar, butter or margarine, milk, cocoa, and salt; bring to a boil. Boil 7 minutes or until candy thermometer registers 225 degrees; remove from heat. Add peanut butter, rolled oats, and vanilla extract; stir until well blended. Drop by tablespoonfuls onto wax paper; cool until set.

Yields 2 dozen bars.

Drop Cookies

Almost any cookie dough can be baked as a drop cookie if additional liquid is added to the batter.

Drop cookie doughs vary in texture. Some fall easily from the spoon and flatten into wafers in baking. Stiffer doughs need a push with a finger or the use of a second spoon to release them.

To make uniform soft drops, use a measuring teaspoon. When chilled, these doughs may be formed into balls and flattened between palms. First dust your hands with flour or powdered sugar. If the cookies are dark or chocolate, use cocoa for dusting.

Melting Chocolate in the Microwave

Melt chocolate in the microwave by heating dark chocolate on medium heat (50 percent power) and milk or white chocolate, which contain heat-sensitive milk solids, on low (30 percent power).

Stir the chocolate every fifteen seconds, heating the chocolate just until it is melted.

Rolled Cookies

Cookie dough should be chilled for fifteen to thirty minutes before rolling. This will prevent the dough from sticking to the rolling pin.

When using plastic cookie cutters, they should be dipped in warm vegetable oil while you are working. You will get a cleaner, more defined edge on the patterns.

TIP: Sugar cookies will not get stiff or tough if you roll them in sugar instead of flour.

Merry Christmas Cookies

Christmas would hardly seem like Christmas without fancifully shaped and decorated cookies. Decorated cookies are thought to have originated in pre-Christian times as offerings to various gods. You and your children will love these cookies. The honey in this recipe makes these cookies melt in your mouth.

1/3 cup vegetable shortening
1/3 cup sugar
1 egg
2/3 cup honey
1 teaspoon lemon extract
2 3/4 cups all-purpose flour
1 teaspoon baking soda
1 teaspoon salt

In a large bowl, cream vegetable shortening, sugar, egg, honey, and lemon extract until light and fluffy. Sift in flour, baking soda, and salt; stir until well blended. Refrigerate dough at least 1 hour or overnight.

Preheat oven to 375 degrees. Lightly grease cookie sheets. On a lightly floured board, roll dough to 1/4-inch thick; cut into desired shapes with cookie cutters. Place 1 inch apart onto prepared cookie sheets.

Bake 8 to 10 minutes or until edges are light brown. Remove from oven and cool on wire racks. When cool, frost with Milk Frosting and decorate as desired.

Yields 5 dozen cookies.

MILK FROSTING:
1 cup powdered sugar
1/2 teaspoon lemon extract
1 to 1 1/2 tablespoons milk

In a small bowl, combine powdered sugar, lemon extract, and enough milk to make frosting easy to spread. Tint, if desired, with a few drops of food coloring.

Grandma's Crispy Cookies

Ben, our illustrator, says that whenever he visited his grandma's house, she'd have a big tin of these cookies ready for him. When he would leave, she would send some along with him in the car – it made the long trip seem shorter.

1 1/2 cups sugar
1 cup vegetable shortening
2 eggs
1 teaspoon vanilla extract or almond extract
2 1/4 cups all-purpose flour
1 teaspoon salt
1 cup coarsely chopped walnuts

Preheat oven to 375 degrees. In a large bowl, cream sugar, vegetable shortening, eggs, and vanilla or almond extract until light and fluffy; gradually add flour and salt. Mix in walnuts. Spoon onto ungreased cookie sheets and slightly flatten with your hand. Bake 10 minutes or until edges are light brown. Remove from oven and cool on wire racks.

Yields 5 dozen cookies.

Flavored Sugars

The simplest way to decorate cookies is to sprinkle them with colored or flavored sugars. Use these flavored sugars to sprinkle over cookies either before or after baking.

CINNAMON SUGAR: Combine one tablespoon cinnamon and one cup granulated sugar. This will keep indefinitely if stored in a covered jar.

LEMON SUGAR: Grate the thin outer rind (zest) of six large lemons. Do not use the white part, as it is bitter. Add the zest to one cup of granulated sugar and stir. Store in the refrigerator. This will keep for months.

ORANGE SUGAR: Follow recipe for Lemon Sugar, using four large oranges. This will keep refrigerated for many months.

VANILLA SUGAR: Sift one pound powdered sugar into a canister. Take three vanilla beans and cut them in half lengthwise; bury the pieces in the sugar. This will keep indefinitely.

Sugar Cookies

These cookies will bring back a lot of nice childhood memories. For really good sugar cookies, quality ingredients are a must. It is especially important to use butter or a good margarine.

1/2 cup butter or margarine, room temperature
1 cup sugar
2 eggs, beaten
1 tablespoon milk
1 teaspoon vanilla extract
2 1/4 cups sifted all-purpose flour
1 1/2 teaspoons baking powder
1/2 teaspoon ground nutmeg
Sugar

Preheat oven to 425 degrees. In a large bowl, cream butter or margarine and 1 cup sugar until light and fluffy. Add eggs, milk, and vanilla extract; stir until well blended. Sift in flour, baking powder, and nutmeg; stir until well blended.

On a lightly floured board, roll cookie dough out 1/4-inch thick and cut into desired shapes with cookie cutters; sprinkle with sugar. Place onto ungreased cookie sheets and bake 7 minutes or until edges are light brown. Remove from oven and cool on wire racks.

NOTE: Crisp sugar cookies are better than ever when a few anise seeds are rolled into the dough. (Children love the licorice flavor of these seeds.)

Yields 5 dozen cookies.

History of Cookies

The first historic record of cookies was their use as test cakes. A small amount of cake batter was baked to test the oven temperature. The name cookie is derived from the Dutch word "koekje," meaning "little cake."

The first American cookie was originally brought to this country by the English, Scotch, and Dutch immigrants. Our simple "butter cookies" strongly resemble the English tea cakes and the Scotch shortbread.

The Southern colonial housewife took great pride in her cookies, almost always called simply "tea cakes." These were often flavored with nothing more than the finest butter, sometimes with the addition of a few drops of rose water.

In earlier American cookbooks, cookies were given no space of their own but were listed at the end of the cake chapter. They were called by such names as "Jumbles," "Plunkets," and "Cry Babies." The names were extremely puzzling and whimsical.

There are hundreds upon hundreds of cookie recipes in the United States. No one book could hold the recipes for all of the various types of cookies.

Beacon Hill Cookies

1 cup semisweet chocolate chips
2 egg whites, room temperature
1/4 teaspoon salt
1/2 cup sugar
1/2 teaspoon vanilla extract
1/2 teaspoon cider vinegar
3/4 cup chopped pecans

Preheat oven to 350 degrees. Lightly grease cookie sheets. In the top of a double boiler over hot water, melt chocolate chips. In a medium bowl, beat egg whites and salt until foamy; gradually beat in sugar and keep beating until stiff peaks form. Beat in vanilla extract and vinegar. Fold in melted chocolate and pecans. Drop by small teaspoonfuls onto prepared cookie sheets. Bake 10 minutes or until lightly browned. Remove from oven and cool on wire racks.

Yields 3 dozen cookies.

Moravian Cookies

Moravia once was part of Czechoslovakia. Persecuted for their religious beliefs, they found refuge first in Germany and then in the United States. Although many settled in Pennsylvania, a contingent traveled to Winston-Salem, North Carolina.

3/4 cup vegetable shortening
1 1/4 cups firmly packed brown sugar
2 cups molasses
1 tablespoon baking soda
1 tablespoon ground cinnamon
1 tablespoon ground ginger
1 tablespoon ground cloves
1/2 teaspoon salt
4 1/2 cups all-purpose flour

In a large saucepan over medium heat, combine vegetable shortening, brown sugar, molasses, baking soda, cinnamon, ginger, cloves, and salt; heat until warm, mashing out any lumps. Remove from heat; while still warm, stir in flour. Cover and refrigerate overnight.

Preheat oven to 375 degrees. Lightly grease cookie sheets. When ready to bake, take what you need out of the refrigerator. (Unused dough may be stored in the refrigerator as long as a month – in fact, cookies are better if dough has "mellowed" for awhile.) Roll dough on a lightly floured surface, using as little flour as possible. Also flour rolling pin. Roll dough out paper thin and cut into desired shapes with cookie cutters. Place onto prepared cookie sheets.

Bake 5 to 6 minutes or until light brown. After removing cookies from oven, with a clean soft cloth lightly brush off any excess flour. Let cool on cookie sheet and remove when you can handle them comfortably. Store in airtight containers.

Yields many!

Grandma Hagerman's Fruit Cake Cookies

These cookies are simply great. They are lovely to look at, easy to make, fabulous eating, and expensive to make. They are like a fruit cake. The longer you store them, the better they taste.

2 1/2 cups dates, cut into small pieces
3 tablespoons rum
3/4 cup candied cherries
3/4 cup white raisins
2 slices candied pineapple, coarsely chopped
2 cups coarsely chopped toasted walnuts
2 cups coarsely chopped toasted almonds
2 cups coarsely chopped toasted pecans
1/4 cup all-purpose flour
1/2 cup butter, room temperature
3/4 cup firmly packed brown sugar
1 egg, well beaten
1 cup cake flour
1/2 teaspoon baking soda
1/2 teaspoon baking powder
1/4 teaspoon salt
1/2 teaspoon ground cinnamon
1/2 teaspoon ground mace
Grated zest of 1 orange
Grated zest of 1 lemon
1 teaspoon vanilla extract
1/4 teaspoon almond extract

In the top of a double boiler over hot water, combine dates and rum; let steep 2 to 3 hours.

Preheat oven to 300 degrees. In a large bowl, combine candied cherries, white raisins, candied pineapple, walnuts, almonds, and pecans. Sift 1/4 cup flour over the fruit and nut mixture; stir until well blended. Set aside.

In a medium bowl, cream butter and brown sugar until light and fluffy; add egg and continue to cream until light and fluffy. Sift cake flour, baking soda, baking powder, salt, cinnamon, and mace into butter mixture; stir until well blended. Add steeped dates, orange zest, lemon zest, vanilla extract, and almond extract to batter; stir until well blended. Add fruit and nut mixture; stir until well blended.

Drop by teaspoonfuls onto ungreased cookie sheets. Bake 15 to 20 minutes or until golden brown (be careful not to overbake). Remove from oven and cool on wire racks. Store cookies in an airtight container.

NOTE: You can use any combination of nuts or fruits in the recipe that you wish. Whatever you have on hand in the pantry.

Yields 5 dozen cookies.

Toasting Nuts or Seeds

FRYING PAN:
Toast nuts or seeds in an ungreased frying pan over medium heat, stirring frequently, until golden brown.

MICROWAVE:
Nuts and seeds toasted in the microwave oven will barely change color, but they will taste toasted. Place one cup seeds or chopped nuts on a paper plate. Microwave on high for three to four minutes, or until nuts smell toasted. Rotate plate a half-turn after two minutes.

OVEN:
On an ungreased baking sheet, toast them in a 350-degree oven, stirring occasionally, for about ten minutes or until golden brown.

Cookies

Mailing Cookies

When mailing cookies, choose cookies that are hardy so they can stand the trip. Soft cookies generally are the best travelers.

Use a strong cardboard box or metal container; line with either wax paper or aluminum foil. Then place a cushion of crumpled wax paper, plastic wrap, or cellophane straw on the bottom.

Wrap cookies in pairs, back to back, with wax paper between them. A moisture-proof material, such as plastic wrap, safely holds the flavor while the cookies bounce around.

Pack snugly in rows with heavy cookies at the bottom. Tuck popcorn, puffed cereal, or crushed wax paper into the holes to prevent jiggling. Cover each layer with a cushion of wax paper or paper towels.

Tape the box shut, print address on box (if paper should become torn enroute, the address will not be destroyed with it) and wrap in heavy brown paper. Tie or tape securely.

Print name and address plainly on front of package and label "FRAGILE, HANDLE WITH CARE."

Big & Little Chocolate Chip Cookies

What could be more American than chocolate chip cookies? Everyone loves them. Did you know that chocolate chip cookies were created by a Massachusetts housewife in 1929? These cookies are also called "Toll House Cookies."

1 cup butter, room temperature
3/4 cup sugar
3/4 cup firmly packed brown sugar
1 teaspoon vanilla extract
2 eggs
2 1/4 cups all-purpose flour
1 teaspoon baking soda
1 teaspoon salt
1 (12-ounce) package semisweet chocolate chips
1 cup nuts, chopped

Preheat oven to 375 degrees. Lightly grease cookie sheets. In a large bowl, cream butter, sugar, brown sugar, and vanilla extract until light and fluffy. Stir in eggs until light and fluffy. Sift in flour, baking soda, and salt; stir until well blended. Stir in chocolate chips and nuts.

Drop by rounded teaspoonfuls onto prepared cookie sheets. Bake 8 to 10 minutes or until light brown. Remove from oven and cool on wire racks.

Yields 5 dozen cookies.

BIG COOKIES:
Preheat oven to 325 degrees. Lightly grease cookie sheets. After you have made the above basic batter, use a large tablespoon for portioning the dough (to get a more uniform cookie, roll in palm of hand). Place dough 2 inches apart onto prepared cookie sheets; wet your hand with water, and pat the dough ball out into a 3-inch round. Repeat with remaining dough.

Bake, on middle rack, 15 to 17 minutes or until light brown. Remove from oven and cool on cookie sheets for 5 minutes. Remove from cookie sheets and cool on wire racks.

Yields 2 dozen cookies.

Brenda's Chocolate Chip Cookies

The addition of powdered rolled oats makes these exceptional chocolate chip cookies. They'll probably become your favorite.

5 cups old-fashioned rolled oats
4 cups all-purpose flour
1 teaspoon salt
2 teaspoons baking powder
2 teaspoons baking soda
2 cups butter, room temperature
2 cups sugar
2 cups firmly packed brown sugar
4 eggs
2 teaspoons vanilla extract
1 (24-ounce) package semisweet chocolate chips
3 cups chopped nuts

Preheat oven to 375 degrees. Lightly grease cookie sheets. Make a powder out of the rolled oats by putting small amounts into the blender at one time.

In a large bowl, combine powdered rolled oats, flour, salt, baking powder, and baking soda. In a large bowl, blend butter, sugar, and brown sugar until light and creamy; stir in eggs and vanilla extract. Add the flour mixture; stir until well blended. Stir in chocolate chips and nuts. Roll into golf-ball-sized cookies. Place 2 inches apart onto prepared cookie sheets. Bake 15 minutes or until light brown. Remove from oven and cool on wire racks.

Yields 8 1/2 dozen cookies.

Carol's Gingersnaps

Gingersnaps have been popular with children for generations, and today's children have seldom tasted a true gingersnap cookie. This excellent recipe makes cookies that really snap.

3/4 cup vegetable shortening
1 cup firmly packed brown sugar
1 egg
1/4 cup molasses
2 1/4 cups all-purpose flour
2 teaspoons baking soda
1 teaspoon ground cinnamon
1 teaspoon ground ginger
1/2 teaspoon ground cloves
1/4 teaspoon salt
Sugar

In a large bowl, cream vegetable shortening, brown sugar, egg, and molasses until light and fluffy. Gradually add flour, baking soda, cinnamon, ginger, cloves, and salt; stir until well blended. Refrigerate at least 1 hour or overnight.

Preheat oven to 375 degrees. Lightly grease cookie sheets. Shape dough by rounded teaspoonfuls into balls; dip tops in sugar. Place dough, sugared side up, 3 inches apart onto prepared cookie sheets. Bake 10 to 12 minutes or until light brown. Remove from oven and cool on wire racks.

Yields 3 dozen cookies.

Oats

OLD-FASHIONED (ROLLED) OATS: Oats that have been steamed and then flattened into flakes.

QUICK-COOKING OATS: Oats that have been cut into several pieces before being steamed and flattened.

INSTANT OATS: Oats that have been cut into very small pieces, precooked, and dried so that they need no real cooking. This process makes them unsuitable as a substitution in recipes for old-fashioned (rolled) or quick-cooking oats.

Bars and Squares

Bars and squares are a softer type of cookie. They are more like cake.

Bake bars and squares in greased pans that are at least one and one-half inches deep and have sides.

> IMPORTANT:
> Do observe all pan sizes indicated in your recipes, because the texture is affected by the thickness. A pan smaller than indicated in the recipes will give a cake-like result, not a chewy one. A pan too large will give a dry, brittle result.

Bars and squares are done when the sides shrink from the pan, or the top springs back when lightly touched with the finger.

Bars and squares should be stored in a tightly covered container or right in the baking pan, covered with plastic wrap or aluminum foil.

Citron

Citron is a semitropical citrus fruit like a lemon, but larger and less acidic. It is grown for its thick peel and usually candied.

The candied citron should be moist and slightly sticky; if it is hard and crystallized, it has been kept too long and has dried out.

German Lebkuchen Squares

A wonderful German Christmas treat. Make these cookies at least one month in advance, for they improve with age. They will keep for six months in an airtight container.

5 cups sifted all-purpose flour
1 1/2 teaspoons salt
1 1/2 teaspoons baking soda
1 teaspoon ground cloves
1 teaspoon ground cinnamon
2 cups finely chopped almonds
1/4 cup chopped candied citron
1/4 cup chopped candied orange peel
2 cups honey
2 cups sugar
4 tablespoons whiskey
3 eggs, well beaten
Milk Frosting

Preheat oven to 375 degrees. Lightly grease a 15x10-inch rimmed pan. In a large bowl, combine flour, salt, baking soda, cloves, cinnamon, almonds, candied citron, and candied orange peel; set aside.

In the top of a double boiler over hot water, combine honey, sugar, and whiskey; stir until sugar is dissolved. Remove from heat and let mixture cool a little. Add eggs, one at a time, beating well after each addition; add to flour mixture and mix until well blended.

Spread batter onto prepared baking pan. Bake 15 to 20 minutes or until light brown. Remove from oven and place on a wire rack. While still hot, spread the Milk Frosting onto the top of the baked Lebkuchen with a spatula or a pastry brush. Cool, cut into bars, and remove from pan. Store to mellow.

Yields 5 dozen squares.

MILK FROSTING:
1 cup powdered sugar
1 to 1 1/2 tablespoons milk

In a small bowl, combine powdered sugar and enough milk to make frosting easy to spread.

Lemon Bars Deluxe

These delicious cookies are wonderful for luncheons and teas. They taste like a lemon meringue pie.

FIRST LAYER:
2 cups all-purpose flour
1/2 cup powdered sugar
1 cup chilled butter, cut into 1/4-inch pieces

Preheat oven to 350 degrees. In a large bowl, combine flour and powdered sugar. With a pastry blender or two knives, cut butter into flour mixture until particles are the size of small peas. Press into an ungreased 13x9-inch baking pan. Bake 20 minutes. Remove from oven and cool on a wire rack.

SECOND LAYER:
4 eggs
2 cups sugar
1/3 cup lemon juice
1/4 cup all-purpose flour
1 teaspoon baking powder
Powdered sugar

Reduce oven temperature to 325 degrees. In a large bowl, beat eggs; stir in sugar and lemon juice. Add flour and baking powder to egg mixture; stir until well blended. Spread over first layer. Bake 30 minutes. Remove from oven and cool on a wire rack. Sprinkle with powdered sugar. Cut into bars and remove from pan. Store, covered, in refrigerator.

Yields 2 dozen bars.

Congo Squares

2/3 cup butter or margarine
2 1/3 cups firmly packed brown sugar
3 eggs
2 3/4 cups all-purpose flour
2 1/2 teaspoons baking powder
1/2 teaspoon salt
1 cup chopped pecans or walnuts
1 (12-ounce) package semisweet chocolate chips

Preheat oven to 350 degrees. Lightly grease a 13x9-inch baking pan. In a large saucepan over medium heat, melt butter or margarine. Add brown sugar; stir until well blended. Allow to cool slightly. Add eggs, one at a time, beating well after each addition. Sift in flour, baking powder, and salt; stir until well blended. Mix in pecans or walnuts and chocolate chips. Pour into prepared pan.

Bake 25 minutes or until light brown (do not overcook). Remove from oven and cool on a wire rack; when almost cool, cut into squares and remove from pan.

Yields 3 to 4 dozen squares.

Brown Sugar

1 pound box brown sugar equals 2 1/4 cups firmly packed brown sugar.

The darker the brown sugar, the more cane molasses it contains, and the "deeper" the flavor.

TIPS: Store brown sugar in a thick plastic bag in a cool, dry place.

Brown sugar won't harden if an apple slice is placed in the container.

A slice of bread placed in the package of hardened brown sugar will soften it again in a couple of hours.

The easiest way to soften brown sugar in a hurry is to just zap it, box and all, in the microwave oven for a few seconds. You'll immediately have brown sugar that's warm, soft, and ready to use.

Rocky Road S'mores Bars

1/2 cup butter or margarine, room temperature
1/2 cup firmly packed brown sugar
1 cup all-purpose flour
1/2 cup graham cracker crumbs
2 cups miniature marshmallows
1 cup semisweet chocolate chips
1/2 cup chopped walnuts

Preheat oven to 375 degrees. Lightly grease a 9-inch square pan. In a large bowl, cream butter or margarine and brown sugar until light and fluffy. Add flour and graham cracker crumbs; stir until well blended. Press onto bottom of prepared pan. Sprinkle with marshmallows, chocolate chips, and walnuts.

Bake 15 to 20 minutes or until golden brown. Remove from oven and cool on a wire rack. Cut into bars and remove from pan.

Yields 3 dozen bars.

Ten Plus Brownies

Cut into tiny squares – they are very gooey and rich. Another delicious way to serve them is to microwave them for thirty seconds and top with vanilla ice cream. Either way you serve them, they are sure to be a family favorite.

Brownies

For a little variety in your brownies, bars, or squares, use a different type of pan. Use a muffin tin for individual servings with ice cream, or pie pans to make a more festive dessert.

TIP: To store brownies, wrap bars in the pan they are baked in. If storing for prolonged periods, wrap each square in aluminum foil after they have cooled.

4 (1-ounce) squares unsweetened chocolate
1 cup butter or margarine
2 cups sugar
1 cup all-purpose flour
4 eggs, beaten
2 teaspoons coffee liqueur
1 cup semisweet chocolate chips
1 cup chopped nuts

Preheat oven to 325 degrees. Grease a 13x9-inch baking pan. In a small saucepan over low heat, melt chocolate and butter, stirring constantly. Remove from heat.

In a large bowl, combine sugar and flour. Add chocolate mixture, eggs, and coffee liqueur; stir until well blended. Stir in chocolate chips and nuts.

Spread batter into prepared pan. Bake 35 minutes or until edges are firm (center will be soft). Remove from oven and cool 30 to 60 minutes on a wire rack before cutting. Refrigerate at least 2 hours before serving.

Makes 3 dozen bars.

Missouri Waltz Marbled Brownies

Rich, tasty, and out of this world.

6 ounces cream cheese, room temperature
5 tablespoons butter or margarine, room temperature
1/3 cup sugar
2 eggs
2 tablespoons all-purpose flour
3/4 teaspoon vanilla extract
1 (family-size) package brownie mix
Milk Chocolate Frosting

Preheat oven to 350 degrees. Lightly grease a 13x9-inch baking pan. In a large bowl, combine cream cheese and butter or margarine. Add sugar, eggs, flour, and vanilla extract; cream until light and fluffy.

Prepare the brownie mix as directed on package. Pour half of the brownie batter onto bottom of prepared pan. Pour cream cheese mixture over the brownie layer. Spoon the remaining brownie batter in spots over the top. Swirl the top two layers together with a knife or spatula.

Bake 35 to 40 minutes or until golden brown. Remove from oven and cool on a wire rack; frost with Milk Chocolate Frosting. Cut into bars and remove from pan.

Yields 2 dozen bars.

MILK CHOCOLATE FROSTING:
3 tablespoons butter or margarine
2 tablespoons cocoa
1 1/2 cups powdered sugar
2 tablespoons milk
1 teaspoon vanilla extract

In a medium saucepan over medium heat, melt butter or margarine. Stir in cocoa until dissolved. Add powdered sugar, milk, and vanilla extract; stir until smooth. NOTE: If necessary, add more milk to make a soft spreading consistency. Remove from heat.

Secrets for Perfect Cookies and Bars

Some simple secrets to remember are:

• *Always measure correctly and accurately, using standard equipment.*

• *Have all ingredients at room temperature for more glamorous, perfect cookies.*

• *Shortening should hold its shape when turned out of the measuring cup. The same applies to brown sugar.*

• *Dry ingredients are lightly spooned into the measuring utensil. A level measurement is obtained by running a spatula or knife across the top of the utensil.*

CUTTING BAR COOKIES:
To prevent jagged edges that often occur when cutting bars and squares, use a sharp knife to score the bars as soon as the pan comes out of the oven. Then cut the cooled bars along the scored lines.

Peanut Butter Bars

1/2 cup butter or margarine, room temperature
1/2 cup sugar
1/2 cup firmly packed brown sugar
1/2 cup creamy peanut butter, room temperature
1 egg, beaten
1 teaspoon vanilla extract
1 cup all-purpose flour
1/2 cup quick-cooking oats
1 teaspoon baking soda
1/4 teaspoon salt
1 1/4 cups semisweet chocolate chips

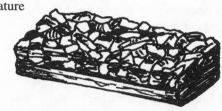

Preheat oven to 350 degrees. Grease a 13x9-inch baking pan. In a large bowl, cream butter or margarine, sugar, brown sugar, and peanut butter until light and fluffy. Add egg and vanilla extract; stir until well blended. Add flour, oats, baking soda, and salt; stir until well blended.

Spread mixture into prepared baking pan. Sprinkle with chocolate chips. Bake 20 to 25 minutes or until lightly browned. Remove from oven and cool on a wire rack for 10 minutes. Drizzle with Peanut Icing while still warm. When cool, cut into bars and remove from the baking pan.

Yields 3 to 4 dozen bars.

PEANUT ICING:
3/4 cup powdered sugar
2 tablespoons creamy peanut butter, room temperature
2 tablespoons milk

In a small bowl, combine powdered sugar, peanut butter, and milk; stir until well blended.

Freezing Cookies & Cookie Dough

Cookie dough and baked cookies can be frozen and stored for up to six months.

Freeze baked cookies in an airtight container, separating layers with plastic wrap or aluminum foil. Thaw cookies at room temperature for about ten minutes.

Wrap cookie dough in aluminum foil or a double layer of plastic wrap before freezing. Thaw dough just until soft enough to use.

Freeze bar-cookie dough in the pan in which it is to be baked; cover with plastic wrap, then aluminum foil. Before baking, partially thaw.

Walnut & Date Squares

Attention date lovers! You'll absolutely love these squares.

1 cup chopped dates
1 cup chopped walnuts
3 tablespoons all-purpose flour
1 teaspoon baking powder
1 cup sugar
3 eggs, beaten
Powdered sugar, sifted

Heat oven to 350 degrees. Grease a 9-inch square baking pan. In a large bowl combine dates, walnuts, flour, baking powder, sugar, and eggs.

Spread onto bottom of prepared pan. Bake 35 minutes. Remove from oven and cool on a wire rack for 15 minutes. Cut into squares. When cool, roll in powdered sugar.

Yields 1 dozen bars.

Dieters Beware Brownies

This recipe screams with calories. Very rich, very good, and very fattening.

FIRST LAYER:
1 (1-ounce) square unsweetened chocolate
1/4 cup butter
1 egg
1/2 cup sugar
1/4 cup all-purpose flour
1 cup chopped nuts

Preheat oven to 350 degrees. Lightly butter a 9-inch square pan. In the top of a double boiler over hot water, combine chocolate with butter; stir until melted. In a small bowl, beat egg and sugar; slowly beat into chocolate mixture. Stir in flour and nuts. Remove from heat and spread onto bottom of prepared pan.

Bake 20 minutes, remove from oven, and cool on a wire rack.

SECOND LAYER:
1/4 cup butter, room temperature
2 cups powdered sugar
1/2 teaspoon vanilla extract
3 to 4 tablespoons whipping cream

In a medium bowl, cream butter and powdered sugar until light and fluffy. Stir in vanilla extract and enough cream to make mixture spreadable. Spread evenly onto top of first layer.

THIRD LAYER:
1 (1-ounce) square unsweetened chocolate
1/4 cup butter

In the top of a double boiler over hot water, melt chocolate and butter. Remove from heat and drizzle onto top of second layer, tilting pan so that chocolate covers the white cream layer completely and evenly. Refrigerate 30 minutes or until chocolate is hardened. Cut into 2-inch squares and remove from pan.

Yields 2 dozen bars.

Cocoa

Unsweetened chocolate powder is often used in baking. Most of the cocoa available is "Dutch-processed cocoa," which means it has been treated to darken its color and allow it to dissolve more easily in liquid.

Dutch-processed cocoa has a little less chocolate flavor than untreated cocoa.

Store powdered cocoa in a cool, dry place away from sunlight.

Flouring Cookie Pans

When greasing and flouring a pan before baking a chocolate cake or brownies, use cocoa to "flour" the pan. This will prevent the white residue that usually forms on the outside.

Bars

Chocolate Facts

Did you know that the Aztecs considered all chocolate an aphrodisiac? Because of this, all foods made with chocolate were strictly forbidden to women.

The Spanish general, Hernando Cortes, landed in Mexico in 1519. The Aztecs believed he was the reincarnation of one of their lost gods. They honored him by serving him an unusual drink, presented in a cup of pure gold. This unusual drink was called "chocolatl" by the Aztecs.

When Cortes returned to Spain, he took the cocoa bean with him and there it was mixed with sugar and vanilla. This sweet drink became fashionable and soon there were chocolate houses in all the capitals of Europe.

A delicate tree, cacao is only grown in rain forests in the tropics, usually on large plantations, where it must be protected from wind and intense sunlight. The tree is harvested twice a year.

Milk chocolate was invented in 1876 by a Swiss chocolatier, Daniel Pieter. Today, the finest chocolate is still made in Switzerland, and the consumption of milk chocolate far outweighs that of plain chocolate.

Touchdown Chocolate Bars

1 3/4 cups all-purpose flour
1 cup sugar
1/4 cup cocoa
1/2 cup chilled butter or margarine, cut into 1/4-inch pieces
1 egg, beaten
1 (14-ounce) can sweetened condensed milk
1 (12-ounce) package semisweet chocolate chips, divided
1 cup chopped nuts

Preheat oven to 350 degrees. Lightly grease a 13x9-inch baking pan. In a large bowl, combine flour, sugar and cocoa. With a pastry blender or two knives, cut butter or margarine into flour mixture until particles resemble coarse crumbs. Add egg; stir until well blended. In a small bowl, reserve 1 1/2 cups flour mixture and set aside. Press remainder evenly onto bottom of prepared pan. Bake 10 minutes and remove from oven.

In a medium saucepan over low heat, combine sweetened condensed milk and 1/2 package of chocolate chips; cook and stir until chocolate chips are melted and mixture is smooth. Remove from heat and spread evenly onto top of baked crust.

Add nuts and remaining chocolate chips to reserved flour mixture; sprinkle evenly onto top of chocolate layer. Bake 25 minutes. Remove from oven and cool on a wire rack. Cut into bars and remove from pan. Store, covered, at room temperature.

Yields 2 to 3 dozen bars.

Caramel-Chocolate Squares

1 (14-ounce) package light caramels
2/3 cup evaporated milk, divided
1 package German chocolate cake mix
3/4 cup butter or margarine, melted
1 cup chopped nuts
1 cup semisweet chocolate chips

Preheat oven to 350 degrees. Lightly grease and lightly flour a 13x9-inch baking pan. In a large heavy saucepan over low heat, combine caramels and 1/3 cup evaporated milk; stir constantly until caramels are melted. Remove from heat and set aside.

In a large bowl, combine dry cake mix, butter or margarine, 1/3 cup evaporated milk, and nuts; stir until mixture holds together. In a medium bowl, reserve half of cake mixture and set aside. Press half of cake mixture onto bottom of prepared pan. Bake 6 minutes and remove from oven.

Sprinkle chocolate chips over baked crust; spread caramel mixture over chocolate pieces. Crumble reserved cake mixture over caramel mixture. Return to oven and bake another 18 minutes. Remove from oven and cool on a wire rack. Cut into small squares and remove from pan.

Yields 2 dozen squares.

Chocolate-Mint Squares

You'll enjoy this refreshing combination of chocolate and mint.

FIRST LAYER
2 (1-ounce) squares unsweetened chocolate
1/2 cup butter
2 eggs, beaten
1 cup sugar
1/2 cup sifted all-purpose flour

Preheat oven to 350 degrees. Lightly grease an 8-inch square pan. In the top of a double boiler over hot water, melt chocolate and butter. Remove from heat and let cool slightly. Add eggs and sugar; stir until well blended. Mix in flour until well blended.

Pour into prepared pan and bake 20 minutes. Turn oven off and leave in oven 5 minutes. Remove from oven and cool on a wire rack.

SECOND LAYER
1 1/2 cups powdered sugar
3 tablespoons butter, room temperature
2 tablespoons heavy cream
1 teaspoon peppermint extract
1 to 2 drops green food coloring (optional)

In a large bowl, cream powdered sugar, butter, and cream until light and fluffy. Blend in peppermint extract and food coloring. Spread on top of first layer. Refrigerate until chilled.

THIRD LAYER
3 (1-ounce) squares unsweetened chocolate
3 tablespoons butter

In a small, heavy saucepan over low heat, melt chocolate and butter; spread onto top of second layer. Refrigerate until chilled. Cut into small squares and remove from pan.

Yields 2 dozen squares.

Chocolate Glossary

UNSWEETENED CHOCOLATE:
It is also called baking chocolate, bitter chocolate, or plain chocolate. This is the most common type used in baking.

SEMISWEET CHOCOLATE:
Slightly sweetened during processing, and most often used in frostings, sauces, fillings, and mousses. They are interchangeable in most recipes.

MILK CHOCOLATE or SWEET CHOCOLATE:
Chocolate to which whole and/or skim milk powder has been added. Rarely used in cooking because the protein in the added milk solids interferes with the texture of the baked product.

WHITE CHOCOLATE:
Not really a chocolate at all, but sweetened cocoa butter mixed with milk solids, sometimes with vanilla added. Best used only in small amounts, as it is extremely sweet.

CONVERTURE:
A term generally used to describe high-quality chocolate used by professional bakers in confectionery and baked products. It's specially formulated for dipping and coating.

High-Altitude Baking – Cookies and Bars

In altitudes up to 3,500 feet, simple cookies usually need no adjustment. For cookies rich in chocolate, nuts, or dates, a reduction of about one-half the baking powder or soda may be advisable.

At very high altitudes, a slight reduction in sugar may help, but the soda should not be reduced beyond one-half teaspoon for each cup of milk or cream used.

Cranberry-Pineapple Bars

1 cup fresh cranberries
3 tablespoons firmly packed brown sugar
1 1/2 teaspoons cornstarch
1 (8-ounce) can crushed pineapple in juice, undrained
3/4 cup all-purpose flour
3/4 cup quick-cooking oats
1/4 cup firmly packed brown sugar
1/4 teaspoon ground ginger
1/4 teaspoon ground cinnamon
5 tablespoons chilled butter or margarine, cut into 1/4-inch pieces
1 egg white, lightly beaten
3 tablespoons chopped pecans

Preheat oven to 350 degrees. Spray an 8-inch square pan with vegetable-oil cooking spray. In a medium saucepan over medium heat, combine cranberries, brown sugar, cornstarch, and pineapple; bring to a boil and cook 1 minute. Cover, reduce heat to low, and simmer another 10 minutes or until cranberry skins pop and mixture thickens, stirring occasionally. Remove from heat and set aside.

In a large bowl, combine flour, oats, brown sugar, ginger, and cinnamon. With a pastry blender or two knives, cut butter or margarine into flour mixture until particles resemble coarse crumbs. In a small bowl, reserve 1/2 cup oat mixture and set aside. To the remaining oat mixture, add egg white; stir until well blended. Press oat mixture onto bottom of prepared pan. Bake 10 minutes. Remove from oven.

Spread hot cranberry mixture over baked crust. Combine reserved oat mixture and pecans; sprinkle over cranberry mixture. Bake another 25 to 30 minutes or until light brown. Remove from oven and cool completely in pan on a wire rack. Cut into squares and remove from pan.

Yields 2 dozen bars.

Chewy Noels

2 tablespoons butter
2 eggs
1 cup firmly packed brown sugar
5 tablespoons all-purpose flour
1/8 teaspoon baking soda
1 cup chopped nuts
1 teaspoon vanilla extract
Powdered sugar

Preheat oven to 350 degrees. Place butter into a 9-inch square baking pan and melt in the oven; remove from oven. In a small bowl, beat eggs slightly. Add brown sugar, flour, baking soda, and nuts; stir until well blended. Stir in vanilla extract. Pour mixture over butter in baking pan; do not stir. Bake 25 minutes. Remove from oven and cool completely on a wire rack. Cut into oblong shapes and then roll in powdered sugar.

Yields 2 dozen bars.

Apricot Gems

Everyone goes for these gems of a dessert.

2/3 cup dried apricots
1/2 cup butter, room temperature
1/4 cup sugar
1 1/2 cups sifted all-purpose flour, divided
1 teaspoon baking powder
1/4 teaspoon salt
1 cup firmly packed brown sugar
2 eggs, beaten
1/2 teaspoon vanilla extract
1/2 cup chopped nuts
Powdered sugar

Preheat oven to 350 degrees. Grease an 8-inch square pan. In a small saucepan over medium high heat, place apricots; cover with water and slowly boil 10 minutes. Remove from heat, drain, and cool. When cool, chop into small pieces; set aside.

In a food processor, mix butter, sugar, and 1 cup flour until crumbly. Spread mixture onto bottom of prepared pan. Bake 25 minutes or until light brown; remove from oven.

In a medium bowl, combine 1/2 cup flour, baking powder, and salt. In a small bowl, gradually beat brown sugar into eggs; add to flour mixture and stir until well combined. Mix in vanilla extract, nuts, and apricots; spread onto top of baked layer.

Bake 30 minutes or until lightly browned; cool completely in baking pan on a wire rack. Cut into bars and then roll in sifted powdered sugar.

Yields 2 dozen bars.

Coconut Delight Squares

2 tablespoons butter, melted
1 cup graham cracker crumbs
1 cup butterscotch chips
1 cup semisweet chocolate chips
1 1/2 cups shredded coconut
1 (14-ounce) can sweetened condensed milk
1 cup chopped nuts

Preheat oven to 325 degrees. Pour butter onto bottom of a 9-inch square baking pan. Sprinkle graham cracker crumbs over butter. Place butterscotch chips and chocolate chips over the top; cover with coconut. Slowly pour sweetened condensed milk over the top of the coconut, covering all ingredients. Sprinkle with nuts.

Bake 35 to 40 minutes. Remove from oven and cool completely on a wire rack before cutting into small squares.

Yields 1 1/2 dozen bars.

Butter

1 pound of butter equals 4 sticks or cubes of butter or 2 cups of butter.

1 stick or cube of butter equals 1/2 cup or 8 tablespoons of butter.

TIPS: Grating a stick of butter softens it quickly. A quick way to cut in butter is to first grate it, using the large holes of your cheese grater. Grate frozen butter into the bowl containing the flour and other dry ingredients, then finish cutting in the butter with knives or a pastry blender.

Dipping the spoon or cup into hot water before measuring shortening or butter will cause it to slip out easily without sticking to the spoon or cup.

Use vegetable shortening or unsalted butter to grease baking pans and cookie sheets. Salted butter may cause baked goods to stick to the pan and it will cause over-browning at oven temperatures over 400 degrees.

Biscotti

Biscotti

Biscotti means "twice cooked." The dough is formed into logs and baked until golden brown. The logs are then sliced, and the individual biscotti are baked again to give them their characteristic dryness.

Turn the dough out of the mixing bowl while it's still crumbly and knead in the last bit of flour by hand.

Once the dough is mixed, it will be a little tacky. To shape the dough into a log, lightly sprinkle flour on the work surface, on top of the dough, and on your hands. Use just enough flour to form the logs and to prevent sticking; you don't want the logs to be covered thickly with flour.

You can't judge the cooking by the color. They shouldn't change color during the second baking, so poke them to tell if they're done. They should feel dry and offer some resistance.

Chocolate Biscotti

These biscotti are as pretty as they are delicious tasting. Excellent served with a cup of coffee. But on special occasions or after dinner, serve them with a sparkling wine or a sweet dessert wine for a wonderful treat.

3 cups all-purpose flour
3/4 cup sugar
1/2 cup firmly packed brown sugar
1 teaspoon baking powder
3/4 teaspoon salt
3 (1-ounce) squares unsweetened chocolate
3 eggs
1/3 cup olive oil
1 tablespoon grated orange zest
2 tablespoons fresh orange juice
2 tablespoons rum
1 teaspoon vanilla extract
1 cup semisweet chocolate chips
1 cup chopped pecans, walnuts, or almonds

Preheat oven to 350 degrees. Lightly grease three baking sheets. In a large bowl, combine flour, sugar, brown sugar, baking powder, and salt.

In the top of a double boiler over hot water, melt chocolate; remove from heat and cool. Combine melted chocolate, eggs, olive oil, orange zest, orange juice, rum, and vanilla extract; stir into flour mixture. Add chocolate chips and pecans, walnuts, or almonds; mix until dough is well blended.

Divide dough into six equal pieces. With your hands, pat and shape each piece into a loaf approximately 3 inches wide, 7 inches long, and 3/4-inch high. Place two rolls onto each prepared baking sheet with 3 to 4 inches of space between them. Bake 25 minutes or until dough pops back up when lightly pressed with a finger. (After dough has baked 10 minutes, reverse cookie sheets from front to back and move from the top rack to the bottom one. Repeat this again after another 10 minutes). Remove from oven, and cool 10 minutes on a wire rack.

Reduce oven to 275 degrees. Using a long serrated knife, cut logs diagonally into 1/2-inch thick slices. Turn the slices over, onto their sides; return slices, on baking sheets, to oven. Bake another 15 minutes. Remove from oven and cool completely on wire racks. Store in an airtight container.

Yields about 6 dozen biscotti.

Honeyed Apricot Biscotti

3 eggs
1/2 cup honey
3 cups all-purpose flour, sifted
3/4 teaspoon baking powder
3/4 teaspoon baking soda
1/4 teaspoon salt
1/2 cup plus 2 tablespoons sugar
1 1/2 teaspoons ground anise seeds
1 cup dried apricots, chopped

Preheat oven to 300 degrees. Lightly grease a baking sheet. In a small bowl, whisk together eggs and honey until well blended; set aside.

In a large bowl, combine flour, baking powder, baking soda, salt, and sugar. Stir in anise seeds. Make a well in the center and add egg mixture; stir until dry ingredients are completely moistened. Stir in apricots.

Divide dough into two equal pieces. With your hands, pat and shape each piece into a loaf approximately 3 inches wide, 7 inches long, and 3/4-inch high. Place rolls onto prepared baking sheet with 3 to 4 inches of space between them. Bake 25 to 28 minutes or until dough pops back up when lightly pressed with a finger. (After dough has baked 10 minutes, reverse cookie sheet from front to back and move from the top rack to the bottom one. Reverse this process after another 10 minutes.) Remove from oven and cool 10 minutes on a wire rack.

Reduce oven to 275 degrees. Using a long serrated knife, cut each log diagonally into 1/2-inch thick slices. Turn the slices over, onto their sides. Return slices, on baking sheets, to oven. Bake another 10 to 15 minutes. Remove from oven and cool completely on wire racks. Store in an airtight container.

Yields about 3 dozen biscotti.

Anise Seeds

The black licorice sticks of childhood are brought to mind by this flavor. Anise is especially popular with German cooks.

The Romans thought that anise removed all bad odors from the mouth if chewed in the morning. This is still recommended today. They also believed that the herb helped to maintain a youthful appearance and would also prevent bad dreams if kept near the bed at night. Because of the value of anise, it became one of the spices used by the Romans to pay taxes.

Anise seeds can be used whole or ground in cooking. If buying fresh, the leaves can also be used. Chop them and add to salads or use whole as a garnish.

TIP: Substitute anise seeds for caraway seeds in bread.

Bob's Toffee Delight Biscotti

2 cups all-purpose flour
1/2 teaspoon baking soda
1/2 teaspoon baking powder
1/8 teaspoon salt
1 cup minus 2 tablespoons sugar
1 cup toffee bits (Skor candy bits)
1 cup semisweet chocolate chips
3 eggs
1 teaspoon vanilla extract

Preheat oven to 350 degrees. Lightly grease a baking sheet.

In a large bowl, sift flour, baking soda, baking powder, and salt. Add sugar; stir until well blended. In a food processor, place 1/2 cup of flour mixture and 1/2 cup toffee bits. Whirl for 45 seconds or until toffee bits are quite small and some have turned to powder; pour mixture back into bowl with remaining flour mixture. Stir in remaining toffee bits and chocolate chips.

In a small bowl, combine eggs and vanilla extract; add to dry ingredients and stir until well blended.

Divide dough into two equal pieces. With your hands, pat and shape each piece into a loaf approximately 4 inches wide, 6 inches long, and 3/4-inch high. Place rolls onto prepared baking sheet with 3 to 4 inches of space between them.

Bake 25 to 28 minutes or until dough pops back up when lightly pressed with a finger. (After dough has baked 10 minutes, reverse cookie sheet from front to back and move from the top rack to the bottom one. Reverse this process after another 10 minutes.) Remove from oven and cool 20 minutes on a wire rack.

Reduce oven to 275 degrees. Using a long serrated knife, cut each log diagonally into 1/2-inch thick slices. Turn the slices over, onto their sides. Return slices, on baking sheet, to oven. Bake another 10 to 15 minutes. Remove from oven and cool completely on wire racks. Store in an airtight container.

Yields about 3 dozen biscotti.

Desserts

Orange Poppy Seed Cake

An old-fashioned cake – ideal for a quiet afternoon with a cup of coffee or tea.

2 tablespoons poppy seeds
1/4 cup milk, room temperature
3 cups cake flour
2 1/2 teaspoons baking powder
1/4 teaspoon salt
1 1/4 cups unsalted butter, room temperature
1 3/4 cups sugar
4 eggs, room temperature
1 tablespoon grated orange zest
2 teaspoons vanilla extract
3/4 cup fresh orange juice
Orange Glaze

In a small bowl, soak poppy seeds in milk for 2 hours.

Preheat oven to 325 degrees. Generously grease and flour a 12-cup bundt pan. In a large bowl, combine flour, baking powder, and salt; set aside.

In a large bowl, cream butter until smooth, gradually stir in sugar until light and fluffy. Add eggs, one at a time, beating well after each addition. Beat in orange zest, vanilla extract, and poppy seed mixture. Stir in flour mixture and orange juice alternately in three additions, beginning and ending with flour. Pour batter into prepared pan.

Bake 50 to 60 minutes or until a toothpick inserted in center comes out clean. Remove from oven and cool 15 minutes on a wire rack; remove from pan and invert onto a cake plate. Spoon Orange Glaze over warm cake.

Makes 16 servings.

ORANGE GLAZE:
1 cup powdered sugar
1 teaspoon grated orange zest
2 to 3 tablespoons fresh orange juice

In a small bowl, combine sugar and orange zest. Stir in orange juice until smooth.

Cake Flour

Cake flour is very finely ground wheat used to make tender, fine-textured cakes. It is bleached with chlorine gas which, besides whitening the flour, also makes it slightly acidic. This acidity makes cakes set faster and have a finer texture.

Cake flour and all-purpose flour cannot generally be substituted for one another in baking.

TIP: Many boxed cake flours are self-rising and contain baking powder. Since most cake recipes don't call for self-rising flour, don't substitute this for the regular unless you delete the baking powder called for in the recipe.

Mississippi Mud Cake

This old Southern dessert is a chocolate lover's delight.

1 cup butter or margarine, room temperature
1/2 cup cocoa
1/4 teaspoon salt
2 cups sugar
4 eggs, room temperature and beaten
1 1/2 cups all-purpose flour
1 1/2 cups chopped pecans
1 (16-ounce) jar marshmallow cream
Mud Icing

Preheat oven to 350 degrees. Grease a 13x9-inch baking pan. In a large saucepan over medium-low heat, melt butter or margarine. Stir in cocoa, salt, sugar, eggs, flour, and pecans.

Pour into prepared pan and bake 30 minutes or until a toothpick inserted in center comes out clean. Remove from oven and place onto a wire rack.

While cake is still hot, spread marshmallow cream over top. Pour Mud Icing over marshmallow cream and spread evenly. Leave in pan until cool; cut into squares.

Makes 10 to 12 servings.

MUD ICING:
1/2 cup butter or margarine
1/3 cup cocoa
1 tablespoon vanilla extract
1/3 cup milk
1 (16-ounce) box powdered sugar

In a medium saucepan over medium-low heat, melt butter or margarine. Add cocoa, vanilla extract, milk, and powdered sugar; stir until well blended. Cook until thickened; remove from heat and cool slightly.

Dump Cake

This cake usually shows up at every potluck. It is definitely very easy to make.

1 (20-ounce) can crushed pineapple, undrained
1 (20-ounce) can cherry pie filling
1 (18 1/4-ounce) package white or yellow cake mix
1 cup chopped nuts (walnuts or pecans)
1 cup butter or margarine

Preheat oven to 350 degrees. Dump crushed pineapple into an ungreased 13x9-inch baking pan. Dump cherry pie filling over the top of pineapple. Dump the cake mix over the top of cherry pie filling. Sprinkle chopped nuts over the cake mix. Slice the butter or margarine into small pieces and place on top.

Bake 1 hour or until a toothpick inserted in center comes out clean. Remove from oven and cool on a wire rack. Leave in pan and cut into squares.

Makes 18 servings.

Rum Cake

1 cup chopped pecans or walnuts
1 (18 1/4-ounce) package yellow cake mix (with or without pudding in cake mix)
1 (4-serving size) package vanilla instant pudding mix
1/2 cup dark rum, 80 proof
4 eggs, room temperature
1/2 cup water
1/2 cup vegetable oil
Rum Glaze

Preheat oven to 325 degrees. Grease and lightly flour a 10-inch tube pan or a 12-cup bundt pan. Sprinkle chopped pecans or walnuts onto bottom of prepared pan.

In a large bowl, combine cake mix, vanilla pudding mix, rum, eggs, water, and vegetable oil; stir until well blended. Pour batter into prepared pan over nuts. Bake 50 to 55 minutes or until a toothpick inserted in center comes out clean. Remove from oven and cool on a wire rack.

Invert cake onto a cake plate. Prick holes in top of cake and drizzle Rum Glaze evenly over top and sides; allow cake to absorb glaze. Repeat until glaze is all used.

Makes 8 to 10 servings.

RUM GLAZE:
1/2 cup unsalted butter
1/4 cup water
1 cup sugar
1/2 cup dark rum

In a medium saucepan over medium-low heat, melt butter; stir in water and sugar. Bring to a boil and cook 5 minutes, stirring constantly. Remove from heat. Add rum and stir until blended.

Date Crumble

Another date lover's delight. A very rich dessert – delicious.

1 cup chopped dates
1 cup chopped nuts (walnuts, pecans, or hazelnuts)
1 cup sugar
2 eggs, room temperature
1 teaspoon baking powder
1 tablespoon all-purpose flour
Prepared whipped topping

Preheat oven to 350 degrees. Grease a 9-inch square baking pan. In a large bowl, combine dates, nuts, sugar, eggs, baking powder, and flour; spread into prepared pan.

Bake 25 to 30 minutes or until a toothpick inserted in center comes out clean. Remove from oven and cool on a wire rack. Leave in pan and cut into squares. Serve with prepared whipped topping.

Makes 8 servings.

Dates

8 ounces of pitted dates equals about 60 whole dates or 1 1/2 cups chopped dates.

One of the earliest fruits known to man, dates were grown in Mesopotamia (now Iraq) and in Egypt more than 5,000 years ago. Called "the candy that grows on trees," they served as food for camel caravans making treks across the desert.

Dried dates keep much longer than fresh dates. All dates keep well in a tightly closed container at room temperature. For longer storage, store them in the refrigerator.

TIPS: Chill dates in the freezer before cutting or chopping. Do not try to chop dates too fine; you will end up with a gooey date mess instead.

When dates stick together, put them in a warm oven for a few minutes. This way you will not risk tearing the skins when you separate them.

If dates become dried out, heat them in a 350-degree oven for a few minutes, or place in a jar and sprinkle a little water over them, and then place in the refrigerator for a short time.

Before adding dates to cake batter, toss them in flour used in the recipe. Coating with flour will prevent them from sinking to the bottom during baking.

Flambé

The word "flambé" describes any food enveloped in flame from spirits of high alcoholic content. Cognac, rum, vodka, and even whiskey are used.

IMPORTANT: When you flambé for the first time, it is advisable to rehearse privately before attempting a flambé display for guests. It is also desirable to have all necessary equipment and food assembled on serving table or cart, well removed from drafts, curtains, and other possible hazards.

Allow two to four ounces of spirits for recipes designed to serve six people.

Ice Cream

To prevent ice cream from forming a waxlike film on top of a previously opened carton, press a piece of wax paper against the surface and reseal. If you wrap your ice cream container very tightly in aluminum foil, you will prevent ice crystals from forming when you freeze it.

Baked Alaska

Baked Alaska is a spectacular-looking dessert, invariably causing exclamations of wonder at how an ice cream-filled cake can be baked without melting.

4 egg whites, room temperature
1/4 teaspoon cream of tartar
1/4 teaspoon salt
1/2 teaspoon lemon juice
1 cup powdered sugar
1 (1-pound) loaf of pound or sponge cake (already made)
2 pints brick ice cream (any flavor may be used)
1 cup brandy (optional)

In a large bowl, make a meringue by beating egg whites, cream of tartar, and salt until frothy; add lemon juice and continue to beat until egg whites form soft peaks. Gradually fold in powdered sugar and beat until glossy and stiff peaks form; set aside.

Cut a 3/4-inch slice horizontally from bottom of cake and place onto an ovenproof plate or dish. Cover cake slice with ice cream, trying to shape like a loaf cake. Slice remaining cake into three thin layers. Place one layer onto top of ice cream. Cut second layer to fit sides and third layer to fit ends. Completely enclose ice cream with cake, trimming ends to fit neatly. Spread cake completely with 1-inch layer of meringue. Put into freezer until serving time.

Preheat oven to 425 degrees. Bake 6 to 8 minutes or until golden brown. Remove from oven and pour brandy over cake and flambé (optional).

Makes 8 servings.

War Cake

This is a World War II cake that was made when eggs, milk, and butter were rationed and in short supply.

1 cup firmly packed brown sugar
1 1/4 cups water
1 cup raisins
1 cup nuts
1/2 cup candied citron, chopped fine
1/3 cup vegetable shortening
1/2 teaspoon salt
1 teaspoon ground nutmeg
1 teaspoon ground cinnamon
2 cups all-purpose flour
5 teaspoons baking powder
Prepared whipped topping

Preheat oven to 350 degrees. Grease an 8-inch square baking pan. In a large saucepan over medium heat, combine brown sugar and water. Add raisins, nuts, candied citron, vegetable shortening, salt, nutmeg, and cinnamon; bring to a boil and boil 3 minutes. Remove from heat and cool. Sift in flour and baking powder; stir until well blended. Pour into prepared pan and bake 45 minutes or until a toothpick inserted in center comes out clean. Remove from oven and cool on a wire rack. Leave in pan and cut into squares. Serve with prepared whipped topping.

Makes 8 servings.

Original German Sweet Chocolate Cake

4 (1-ounce) squares German sweet chocolate
1 cup butter or margarine, room temperature
2 cups sugar
4 eggs, separated and room temperature
1 teaspoon vanilla extract
2 cups all-purpose flour
1 teaspoon baking soda
1/2 teaspoon salt
1 cup buttermilk, room temperature
Coconut-Pecan Frosting

Preheat oven to 350 degrees. Prepare three 9-inch cake pans by greasing, lining bottoms with wax paper, greasing wax paper, and lightly flouring.

Melt chocolate in the top of a double boiler over hot water; remove from heat and cool. In a medium bowl, cream butter or margarine and sugar until light and fluffy. Beat in egg yolks, vanilla extract, and chocolate; set aside.

In a large bowl, combine flour, baking soda, and salt; beat in chocolate mixture alternately with buttermilk. In a medium bowl, beat egg whites until stiff peaks form; fold into batter. Pour batter into prepared pans.

Bake 30 minutes or until a toothpick inserted in center comes out clean. Remove from oven and cool on wire racks 15 minutes; remove from pans and remove wax paper. Invert onto a cake plate and spread Coconut-Pecan Frosting between layers and over top of cake.

Makes 16 servings.

COCONUT-PECAN FROSTING:
1 (12-ounce) can evaporated milk
1 cup sugar
3 egg yolks, slightly beaten
1/2 cup butter or margarine
1 teaspoon vanilla extract
1 1/3 cups shredded coconut
1 cup chopped pecans

In a large saucepan over medium heat, combine evaporated milk, sugar, egg yolks, butter or margarine, and vanilla extract; cook and stir until thickened. Remove from heat. Stir in coconut and pecans. Cool until of spreading consistency.

Frosting a Cake

TIPS: To prevent frosting from becoming dry and cracked, add one-half teaspoon of baking powder to each cup of powdered sugar called for in the recipe.

Completely cool cake layers before frosting them and brush off all loose crumbs from the sides and bottom of each layer. If you refrigerate the cake for at least one-half hour before frosting, it becomes even more crumb resistant.

To keep your cake plate clean, cut triangles of wax paper and arrange them, overlapping slightly, to form a circle on top of the plate. Place the cake on this. When you have finished frosting the cake, pull the pieces of paper out, one by one, from under the cake. You will be left with a perfectly clean plate and a professional-looking job.

To give your cake that professional decorated look, use a hair dryer to "blow-dry" the frosted surfaces of the cake. The hot air of the hair dryer slightly melts the frosting which gives it that smooth and lustrous appearance.

Cakes

Melting Chocolate

Melt chocolate in the top of a double boiler over hot, not boiling, water.

Speed up melting by first cutting the chocolate into small pieces, so that more surface area is exposed to the heat. Stir chocolate constantly while melting to keep the temperature consistent throughout.

Be careful not to drip any water into the chocolate. One drop of moisture in the chocolate makes it tighten and become unsatisfactory for dipping.

TIPS: Make sure the melting pan does not touch the water in the bottom pan or it will become too hot.

If chocolate starts to harden after melting, add enough vegetable oil to liquefy.

Belle's 8-Layer Chocolate Torte

A truly spectacular-looking and -tasting cake for that very special occasion.

6 eggs, separated and room temperature
1 1/4 cups sugar
2 tablespoons lemon juice, divided
1/4 cup cornstarch
3/4 cup all-purpose flour
1/2 teaspoon salt
Chocolate Frosting
Chopped nuts

MAKE CAKE RECIPE TWICE.

Preheat oven to 375 degrees. Line two 15x10-inch rimmed pans with wax paper. Grease wax paper with butter or margarine.

In a large bowl, beat egg yolks until thick and creamy. Gradually beat in sugar and 1 tablespoon lemon juice. In a small bowl, sift cornstarch, flour, and salt together; add to egg mixture. Add remaining lemon juice and beat until smooth. In a medium bowl, beat egg whites until stiff peaks form; fold into batter mixture.

Spread batter evenly onto prepared baking sheets. Bake 10 to 15 minutes and remove from oven. Remove from baking sheets immediately and remove wax paper. Cool on wire racks.

To assemble, cut each layer in half widthwise. NOTE: After making this recipe twice, you will end up with a total of 8 layers. Place onto a cake plate and frost each layer with Chocolate Frosting; frost top layer and sprinkle with chopped nuts.

Makes 16 servings.

CHOCOLATE FROSTING:
3 (1-ounce) squares unsweetened chocolate
3 (1-ounce) squares semisweet chocolate
6 egg yolks
1 cup sugar
3/4 cup heavy cream
1 3/4 cups butter or margarine, room temperature

Melt chocolate in the top of a double boiler over hot water. In a medium bowl, combine egg yolks and sugar. Stir in heavy cream; add to chocolate. Cook, stirring until thickened; cool.

In a medium bowl, cream butter or margarine until light and fluffy; beat into chocolate mixture, 1 tablespoon at a time. Chill until of spreading consistency.

Orange Crunch Cake

Beautiful cake and good too. Great to bring to a gathering.

1 cup graham cracker crumbs
1/2 cup firmly packed brown sugar
1/2 cup chopped walnuts
1/2 cup butter or margarine, melted
1 (18 1/4-ounce) package yellow cake mix (with pudding included)
1/2 cup water
1/2 cup grated orange zest
2 tablespoons fresh orange juice
1/3 cup vegetable oil
3 eggs, room temperature
Vanilla Frosting
1 (11-ounce) can mandarin oranges, drained or 1 orange, sectioned and drained
Mint leaves, if desired.

Preheat oven to 350 degrees. Grease and lightly flour two 9-inch round cake pans. In a small bowl, combine graham cracker crumbs, brown sugar, walnuts, and butter or margarine; mix until crumbly. Press half of crunch mixture onto bottom of each prepared pan.

In a large bowl, combine cake mix, water, orange zest, orange juice, vegetable oil, and eggs at low speed of electric mixer until moistened; beat another 2 minutes at high speed. Pour batter evenly over crunch layer. Bake 30 to 35 minutes or until a toothpick inserted in center comes out clean. Remove from oven and cool 15 minutes on wire racks; remove from pans.

Place one layer, crunch-side-up, onto a cake plate; spread with 1/4 of the Vanilla Frosting. Top with remaining layer, crunch-side-up. Spread top and sides with remaining frosting. Arrange orange sections on top. Garnish with mint leaves. Store in the refrigerator.

Makes 16 servings.

VANILLA FROSTING:
1 (12-ounce) can prepared vanilla frosting
1 cup prepared whipped topping
3 tablespoons grated orange zest
1 teaspoon grated lemon zest

In a medium bowl, beat prepared frosting until fluffy. Add whipped topping and continue beating until light and fluffy. Fold in orange and lemon zest.

Oranges

1 medium orange equals about 1 to 2 tablespoons zest or 1/4 to 1/3 cup juice.

Select a smooth-skinned orange that's compact, fairly round, and heavy for its size. To determine if an orange is sweet, examine the navel. Choose the ones with the biggest holes. Store oranges in a cool place.

TIP: Put oranges in a hot oven a few minutes before peeling them. No white membrane will be left on the oranges. They can also be warmed in the oven or the microwave for a few minutes to yield more juice.

Creaming

Creaming incorporates air into the butter, margarine, or vegetable shortening to give the cake a light, fine-grained texture.

When creaming butter and sugar together, beat sugar gradually into room temperature butter or margarine to be sure it is absorbed.

If you use an electric mixer to cream, use medium speed. Excessive speed can damage the air bubbles and melt the butter, resulting in a loss of volume and a cake that's too dense. Then beat on high speed until mixture is light and fluffy, contains no lumps, and is almost white in color. Be sure to scrape down the sides of the bowl.

Quick & Easy Dessert Pancakes

Do you need a last-minute, elegant-looking dessert for company? This recipe is so easy, you'll wonder why you didn't think of it yourself.

1 (18 1/4-ounce) package chocolate cake mix
Prepared whipped topping

Prepare chocolate cake according to package directions. Heat a large nonstick frying pan or griddle until hot. (To test, sprinkle with a few drops of water. If bubbles skitter around, heat is just right.)

Pour cake batter into hot frying pan as in making a 4 1/2-inch pancake. Cook until puffed and dry around edges. Turn and cook other side.

Layer the pancakes, four to a stack, alternating with the whipped topping to serve.

Fabulous Lemon Cake

1 (18 1/4-ounce) package lemon cake mix (with or without pudding in cake mix)
1 (4-serving size) lemon instant pudding mix
1/4 cup fresh lemon juice
Water
4 eggs, room temperature and slightly beaten
1/2 teaspoon lemon extract
2/3 cup vegetable oil
Lemon Glaze

Preheat oven to 350 degrees. Lightly oil a 12-cup bundt pan. In a medium bowl, combine cake mix and pudding mix. In a measuring cup, place lemon juice and enough cold water to make 2/3 cup; add to cake mixture and stir until blended. Add eggs, lemon extract, and vegetable oil; with an electric mixer, beat at medium speed for 6 minutes or until smooth.

Pour batter into prepared pan and bake 45 minutes or until the top is golden brown and the cake is springy to the touch. Remove from oven and cool for 15 minutes on a wire rack. Invert and unmold cake onto a cake plate. Prick holes in top of cake and drizzle Lemon Glaze over top and sides; allow cake to absorb glaze.

Makes 8 servings.

LEMON GLAZE:
1 teaspoon grated lemon zest
1/4 cup fresh lemon juice
1/2 teaspoon lemon extract
1 cup powdered sugar

In a small bowl, combine lemon zest, lemon juice, lemon extract, and powdered sugar.

Hazel's Yummy Dessert

1 cup unsalted butter, melted
2 cups all-purpose flour
2 1/2 tablespoons sugar
1 tablespoon cider vinegar
4 teaspoons vanilla extract, divided
2 (8-ounce) packages cream cheese, room temperature
2 cups sugar, divided
2 tablespoons lemon juice
2 cups chilled whipping cream
2 (8-ounce) cans crushed pineapple, well drained

Preheat oven to 350 degrees. Grease a 13x9-inch baking pan. In a medium bowl, combine butter, flour, 2 1/2 tablespoons sugar, vinegar, and 2 teaspoons vanilla extract; spread onto bottom of prepared baking pan. Bake 7 to 10 minutes or until light golden brown. Remove from oven and cool on a wire rack.

In a medium bowl, combine cream cheese, 1 cup sugar, and lemon juice; stir until well blended. Spread evenly over top of first layer. In a medium bowl, beat whipping cream, 1 cup sugar, and 2 teaspoons vanilla extract until stiff. Spread over top of second layer. Spread crushed pineapple over the top. Refrigerate. Leave in pan and cut into squares.

Makes 8 to 10 servings.

Chocolate Chip Ice Cream Cake

This cake makes a beautiful presentation – lots of calories, but who cares?

42 chocolate chip cookies, divided
1/3 cup butter or margarine, melted
1 cup chocolate fudge topping, divided
2 quarts ice cream (any combination of flavors), softened and divided
Prepared whipped topping
Fresh strawberries or chopped mixed nuts

In a food processor or blender, whirl 30 of the cookies to fine crumbs. Add butter or margarine; whirl 5 to 10 seconds more. Press 2/3 of crumb mixture onto bottom of an ungreased 9-inch springform pan. Stand remaining 12 cookies around edge of pan. Spread 3/4 cup fudge topping over crumb mixture. Freeze 15 minutes or until firm.

Spread 1 quart ice cream over fudge layer. Sprinkle remaining crumb mixture over ice cream. Scoop remaining ice cream into balls; arrange over crumb layer. Freeze 4 hours or overnight or until firm.

To serve, slide a small knife around edge of pan to loosen it and remove sides of the springform pan; transfer onto a cake plate. Garnish with prepared whipped topping, remaining fudge topping, and fresh strawberries or chopped mixed nuts. Serve immediately.

Makes 12 servings.

High-Altitude Baking – Cakes

Above 3,000 feet, a cake is likely to fall and become coarse-textured unless you alter the recipe. Because each cake recipe differs in the proportions of its ingredients, there can be no set rules for modifying sea-level cake recipes to suit high elevations. You'll need to experiment, but the general guidelines are as follows:

- *At 3,000 to 5,000 feet, reduce the baking powder by 1/8 teaspoon for each teaspoon used, reduce sugar by 2 tablespoons for each cup used, and increase each cup of liquid by 2 to 4 tablespoons.*

- *At 5,000 to 7,000 feet, reduce the baking powder by 1/4 teaspoon for each teaspoon used, reduce sugar by 2 tablespoons for each cup used, and increase each cup of liquid by 2 to 4 tablespoons.*

- *At 7,000 to 10,000 feet, reduce the baking powder by 1/4 teaspoon for each teaspoon used, reduce the sugar by 1 to 3 tablespoons for each cup used, and increase each cup of liquid by 3 to 4 tablespoons.*

- *Above 10,000 feet, reduce each teaspoon of baking powder by 1/4 to 1/2 teaspoon, reduce each cup of sugar by 2 to 3 tablespoons, increase each cup of liquid by 3 to 4 tablespoons, add an extra egg to the batter, and increase each cup of flour by 1 to 2 tablespoons.*

Cakes

Upside-Down Cake

Use your old cast-iron frying pan. The heavy pan keeps the butter from burning, and the handle makes it easy to flip the cake upside down when it is done.

How to Season a New Cast-Iron Pan

The surfaces of a new cast-iron pan are porous and have microscopic jagged peaks. You season a pan by rubbing it with oil, heating it for thirty to sixty minutes in a 300-degree oven, and then letting it cool to room temperature.

The oil fills the cavities and becomes entrenched in them, as well as rounding off the peaks. By seasoning a new pan, the cooking surface develops a nonstick quality because the formerly jagged and pitted surface becomes smooth. Also, because the pores are permeated with oil, water cannot seep in and create rust that would give food an off-flavor.

IMPORTANT:
Unless you use your cast-iron pans daily, they should be washed briefly with a little soapy water and then rinsed and thoroughly dried in order to rid them of excess surface oil. If you do not do this, the surplus oil will become rancid within a couple of days.

Traditional Pineapple Upside-Down Cake

The upside-down cake, which was so popular in the '50s and '60s, is again gaining in popularity. No wonder – it's still wonderful.

TOPPING:
1/4 cup butter or margarine
2/3 cup firmly packed brown sugar
1 (1-pound, 4-ounce) can sliced pineapple
Maraschino cherries
1/4 to 1/2 cup chopped nuts

Preheat oven to 350 degrees. In a 10-inch cast-iron frying pan or a 9x2-inch cake pan over low heat, melt butter or margarine. Stir in brown sugar until blended. Remove from heat. Drain pineapple, reserving 2 tablespoons syrup. Arrange pineapple slices onto top of sugar mixture. Place a maraschino cherry in center of each slice. Sprinkle with chopped nuts.

CAKE:
1 cup all-purpose flour
3/4 cup sugar
1 1/2 teaspoons baking powder
1/4 teaspoon salt
1 egg, room temperature
1/2 cup milk
1/4 cup vegetable shortening
1/4 teaspoon grated lemon zest
1 teaspoon fresh lemon juice
1 teaspoon vanilla extract

In a large bowl, combine flour, sugar, baking powder, and salt. Add egg, milk, and vegetable shortening; beat 2 minutes. Add reserved pineapple syrup, lemon zest, lemon juice, and vanilla extract; beat 2 minutes. Pour over pineapple slices in frying pan, spreading evenly. Bake 40 to 50 minutes or until a toothpick inserted in center comes out clean. Remove from oven and cool 5 minutes on a wire rack. Run knife around edge of pan to loosen; cover with a cake plate and invert. Serve warm.

Makes 8 servings.

Banana-Pecan Upside-Down Cake

Follow the recipe for Traditional Pineapple Upside-Down Cake, substituting 2 tablespoons maple syrup for the pineapple syrup. Make the following changes in the topping:

TOPPING:
1/4 cup butter
1 cup firmly packed brown sugar
3 tablespoons genuine Vermont maple syrup
1/4 cup coarsely chopped toasted pecans
4 large ripe bananas, peeled and cut diagonally into 1/4-inch thick slices

Preheat oven to 350 degrees. In a 10-inch cast-iron frying pan or 9x2-inch cake pan over low heat, melt butter or margarine. Stir in brown sugar until blended. Remove from heat. Pour maple syrup over mixture. Sprinkle pecans evenly over the top; place banana slices in circles onto top of pecans, overlapping slightly and covering bottom.

Amaretto-Irish Cream Cheesecake

CRUST:
1 1/2 cups vanilla wafer cookie crumbs
1/2 cup toasted whole almonds, finely chopped
1/4 cup butter or margarine, melted
2 tablespoons sugar
1 tablespoon Amaretto liqueur

Preheat oven to 375 degrees and position rack in center of oven. Lightly grease a 9-inch springform pan. In a large bowl, combine cookie crumbs, almonds, butter or margarine, sugar, and Amaretto liqueur; stir until well blended. Press mixture onto bottom of prepared pan. Bake 7 minutes or until edges are light brown. Remove from oven and cool crust completely on a wire rack. Reduce oven temperature to 350 degrees.

FILLING:
3 (8-ounce) packages cream cheese, room temperature
1 cup sugar
4 eggs, room temperature
1/3 cup whipping cream
1/3 cup ground blanched almonds
1/4 cup Irish cream liqueur
1/4 cup Amaretto liqueur

In a large bowl, combine cream cheese and sugar; cream until light and fluffy. Add eggs, one at a time, beating well after each addition. Add whipping cream, almonds, Irish cream liqueur, and Amaretto liqueur; stir until well blended. Pour filling into prepared crust.

Place cheesecake in center of middle oven rack. Position a baking pan, filled halfway with hot water, on lower rack. Bake 1 hour or until edges are light brown and center is almost set. Turn oven off. Let cake stand in oven, with door ajar, 30 minutes or until center is completely set. Remove from oven and cool completely on a wire rack.

TOPPING:
1 1/2 cups sour cream
1 tablespoon sugar
1/2 teaspoon vanilla extract
1/3 cup sliced almonds, lightly toasted

Preheat oven to 350 degrees. In a small bowl, blend sour cream, sugar, and vanilla extract until smooth; spread over baked cheesecake. Bake 10 minutes. Remove from oven and sprinkle with almonds.

Cover with plastic wrap and refrigerate at least 8 hours or overnight. To serve, slide a small knife around edge of cake to loosen it and remove sides of the springform pan; transfer onto a cake plate.

Makes 10 to 12 servings.

Secrets for Perfect Cheesecakes

• *Make the cheesecake twenty-four to thirty-six hours before serving. This will allow the cheesecake to cool and firm up completely. It also allows flavors to blend and mellow. Cool cheesecake to room temperature and then store, covered, in the refrigerator or freezer.*

• *Before mixing, have eggs and cream cheese at room temperature. Then beat the cream cheese until light and fluffy before blending in the other ingredients.*

• *Use an electric mixer or food processor to beat the filling. Beat at medium speed just until smooth. If you overbeat or mix at high speeds, it can cause cracks to form in the cheesecake as it bakes.*

Cheesecakes

What is a Springform Pan?

A springform pan not only has sides that can be removed but the bottom comes out too. Used mostly in baking, this unusual pan has a fastener on the side that can be opened to remove the rim after the cake is cool.

They are available in a number of sizes, 9- and 10-inch diameter being the most common.

Cheesecakes or tortes baked in this type of pan can be served easily once the side of the pan is removed.

Cracks in Cheesecake

Don't worry! No one needs to know! Disguise cracks with a variety of toppings.

Some suggested toppings are:
- *Whipped cream*
- *Sour cream*
- *Fresh berries*
- *Your favorite jam*

Sweet Potato Cheesecake

A wonderful cheesecake with a light sweet potato taste.

CRUST:
1 1/4 cups graham cracker crumbs
1/4 cup sugar
1/4 cup butter or margarine, room temperature

Preheat oven to 350 degrees and position rack in center of oven. Lightly grease a 9-inch springform pan. In a large bowl, mix graham cracker crumbs, sugar, and butter or margarine until well blended. Press mixture onto bottom of prepared pan. Bake 7 minutes or until edges are light brown. Remove from oven and cool crust completely on a wire rack. Reduce oven temperature to 325 degrees.

FILLING:
2 pounds sweet potatoes
3 (8-ounce) packages cream cheese, room temperature
3/4 cup plus 2 tablespoons sugar
1/3 cup sour cream
1/4 cup whipping cream
3 eggs, room temperature

Bake sweet potatoes 1 hour or until knife inserted in centers goes through easily. Cool potatoes slightly, peel, and purée in blender or food processor. Transfer 1 1/2 cups puree to a large bowl. Add cream cheese, sugar, sour cream, and whipping cream; beat until smooth. Add eggs, one at a time, beating well after each addition. Pour sweet potato filling into prepared graham cracker crust, using the back of a spoon to spread evenly over the crust.

Place cheesecake in center of middle oven rack. Position a baking pan filled halfway with hot water on lower rack. Bake 1 1/4 hours or until edges are light brown and center is almost set. Turn oven off. Let cake stand in oven, with door ajar, 30 minutes or until center is completely set. Remove from oven and cool completely on a wire rack.

TOPPING:
3/4 cup firmly packed brown sugar
1/4 cup butter or margarine
1/4 cup whipping cream
1 cup chopped toasted pecans

In a small heavy saucepan over low heat, combine brown sugar and butter or margarine; stir until sugar dissolves. Increase heat to medium-high and bring to a boil; remove from heat and mix in whipping cream and pecans. Pour hot topping over baked cheesecake.

Cool completely on a wire rack; cover with plastic wrap and refrigerate at least 8 hours or overnight. To serve, slide a small knife around edge of cake to loosen it and remove sides of the springform pan; transfer onto a cake plate.

Makes 10 to 12 servings.

Lean Chocolate Cookie Cheesecake

A low-calorie version of a high-calorie dessert.

CRUST:
1 (9-ounce) package dark chocolate wafer cookies
1 egg white

Preheat oven to 300 degrees. Lightly spray the bottom and sides of a 9-inch springform pan with vegetable-oil cooking spray.

In a blender or food processor, whirl cookies to make fine crumbs (you should have about 2 1/2 cups). In a small bowl, stir egg white slightly with a fork; add to crumbs and whirl or mix just until evenly moistened. Press crumbs onto bottom and halfway up sides of prepared pan. Bake 20 minutes. Remove from oven and cool crust completely on a wire rack. Maintain oven temperature.

FILLING:
2 cups nonfat large or small curd cottage cheese
2 (8-ounce) packages light cream cheese, room temperature and cut into chunks
6 egg whites, room temperature
1/2 cup all-purpose flour
2 teaspoons vanilla extract
1/2 to 3/4 cup sugar
1 (5 1/2-ounce) package chocolate sandwich cookies, or
    14 dark chocolate wafer cookies

In a blender or food processor, purée cottage cheese, cream cheese, egg whites, flour, vanilla extract, and sugar until smooth. Pour 2/3 of the cheese mixture into prepared crust. Break cookies in half and scatter over mixture (overlapping cookies, if needed). Pour remaining cheese mixture over and around cookies.

Set pan with cheesecake on a large baking sheet. Bake 25 to 30 minutes. Cool completely on a wire rack; cover with plastic wrap and refrigerate at least 8 hours or overnight. To serve, slide a small knife around edge of cake to loosen it and remove sides of the springform pan; transfer onto a cake plate.

Makes 16 to 23 servings.

Baking a Perfect Cheesecake

• *Cheesecakes are egg based, and they need low heat. Place a shallow pan full of water on the lower rack in the oven. The water will also help minimize cracking in the top of the cheesecake.*

• *Do not open the oven door during the first thirty minutes of baking. Drafts can cause a cheesecake to fall or crack.*

• *Let the cheesecake "rest" after baking. Unless other directions are specified in the recipe, when the cheesecake is done, turn off the oven and open the door.*

• *DO NOT JAR THE CHEESECAKE WHILE IT IS BAKING OR COOLING.*

• *Expect a slight shrinkage as it cools. If there is great shrinkage, you have baked it at too high a heat.*

• *The cheesecake is done when center is almost set, but jiggles slightly when gently shaken. Cheesecakes always need to be well chilled before serving, preferably eight hours or overnight.*

113

Cheesecakes

Cinnamon

Did you know that cinnamon was one of the spices that started world exploration? It was once considered a gift fit for a monarch. It was thought in ancient times to inspire love, and a love potion was concocted from it.

The Old Testament mentions cinnamon as an incense ingredient; this spice is still widely used in cathedrals today.

Romans burned it to gain favor with Mercury, their God of Commerce. Ancient Jews anointed the vessels of the tabernacle with cinnamon-perfumed oils. Oriental women once perfumed their beds with this fragrance.

When the Dutch were in control of the world spice market, they burned cinnamon when its price went too low to suit them.

Pumpkin Cheesecake

Never again make a pumpkin pie for the holidays – this cheesecake is absolutely wonderful. Let your family be the judge.

CRUST:
1 cup graham cracker crumbs
1/3 cup ground toasted hazelnuts
1/4 cup sugar
1/4 cup butter or margarine, melted

Preheat oven to 350 degrees and position rack in center of oven. Lightly grease a 9-inch springform pan. In a small bowl, combine graham cracker crumbs, hazelnuts, sugar, and butter or margarine. Mix well and press firmly onto bottom of prepared pan. Bake 7 minutes or until edges are light brown. Remove from oven and cool crust completely on a wire rack. Maintain oven temperature.

FILLING:
2 (8-ounce) packages cream cheese, room temperature
1 cup sugar
1 1/2 teaspoons vanilla extract
1/4 cup sour cream
1/4 cup whipping cream
3/4 teaspoon ground cinnamon
1/3 teaspoon ground ginger
1/3 teaspoon ground nutmeg
1/8 teaspoon ground cloves
1/8 cup all-purpose flour
4 eggs, room temperature
1 1/2 cups canned solid-packed pumpkin

In a large bowl, combine cream cheese, sugar, and vanilla extract. Add sour cream and whipping cream; stir until well blended. Mix in cinnamon, ginger, nutmeg, cloves, and flour. Add eggs, one at a time, beating well after each addition; beat in pumpkin. Pour pumpkin mixture into prepared graham cracker crust.

Place cheesecake in center of middle oven rack. Position a baking pan filled halfway with hot water on lower rack. Bake 15 minutes, then lower oven temperature to 300 degrees and bake another 70 minutes or until edges are light brown and center is almost set. Turn oven off. Let cake stand in oven, with door ajar, 30 minutes or until center is completely set. Remove from oven and cool completely on a wire rack. Cover with plastic wrap and refrigerate at least 8 hours or overnight.

To serve, slide a small knife around edge of cake to loosen it and remove sides of the springform pan; transfer onto a cake plate.

NOTE: If a crack should appear, simply blend together some sour cream, powdered sugar, and vanilla extract; spread over the top when ready to serve.

Makes 10 to 12 servings.

Chocolate Fudge Cheesecake

This cheesecake is absolutely wonderful.

CRUST:
1 1/2 cups (about 22 cookies) cream-filled chocolate cookie crumbs, including
   the filling
3 tablespoons butter, melted

Preheat oven to 350 degrees and position rack in center of oven. Lightly grease a
9-inch springform pan. In a food processor, whirl cookie crumbs to fine crumbs. Add
butter; whirl 5 to 10 seconds more. Put crumb mixture onto bottom of prepared pan,
being careful not to get crumbs on sides of pan. Press crumb mixture firmly and
evenly over the bottom. Bake 10 minutes. Remove from oven and cool crust
completely on a wire rack. Maintain oven temperature.

FILLING:
4 (8-ounce) packages cream cheese, room temperature
1 1/2 cups sugar
5 eggs, room temperature
1/4 cup all-purpose flour
1/2 teaspoon salt
1/4 cup whipping cream
1 tablespoon vanilla extract
3 (1-ounce) squares semisweet chocolate, melted and cooled
1/2 cup semisweet chocolate chips

In a large bowl, combine cream cheese and sugar; cream until light and fluffy. Add
eggs, one at a time, beating well after each addition. Beat in flour, salt, whipping
cream, and vanilla extract; set aside. In a medium bowl, place 1 1/2 cups of the
cream cheese mixture. Gradually add melted chocolate, stirring constantly; stir until
well combined. Stir in chocolate chips; set aside.

Pour all but 2 cups of remaining cream cheese mixture over prepared crust. Spoon
chocolate filling in a 2-inch wide ring onto the cream cheese mixture, approximately
1 1/2 inches from the edge of pan. Using the back of a spoon, carefully press
chocolate mixture down until top is level. Spoon reserved cream cheese mixture
evenly over all; smooth top with the back of a spoon.

Place cheesecake in center of middle oven rack. Position a baking pan filled halfway
with hot water on lower rack. Bake 15 minutes. Reduce heat to 300 degrees. Bake
another 1 hour or until edges are light brown and center is almost set. Turn oven off.
Let cake stand in oven, with door ajar, 30 minutes or until center is completely set.
Remove from oven and cool completely on a wire rack.

CHOCOLATE SOUR CREAM TOPPING:
3 tablespoons powdered sugar
2 teaspoons unsweetened cocoa powder
1 cup sour cream
1 teaspoon vanilla extract
2 (1-ounce) squares semisweet chocolate, grated

In a medium bowl, combine powdered sugar, cocoa, sour cream, and vanilla extract;
spread over top of baked cheesecake. Sprinkle grated chocolate in a 2-inch band
around the outer edge of top. Cover with plastic wrap and refrigerate at least 8 hours
or overnight. To serve, slide a small knife around edge of cake to loosen it and
remove sides of the springform pan; transfer onto a cake plate.

Makes 10 to 12 servings.

Cutting a Cheesecake

*Cut cheesecakes using a
wet knife or a piece of
dental floss. Dip the knife in
water before each cut. To
use dental floss, stretch it
tightly between your hands
and press firmly through
the cheesecake.*

Crumb Crusts

*16 squares graham
crackers equals 1 cup
crumbs.*

*24 (2-inch) vanilla
wafers equals 1 cup
crumbs.*

*18 (2-inch) chocolate
wafers equals 1 cup
crumbs.*

*28 squares saltine
crackers equals 1 cup
crumbs.*

*Crushed graham crackers,
chocolate and vanilla
wafers, gingersnap cookies,
and nuts can become quick
and delicious crusts for
cheesecakes or cream
fillings. Simply break the
crackers or cookies into
pieces, place them in a
plastic bag, and crush with
a rolling pin. Or put pieces
into a food processor and
whirl to make fine crumbs.*

Fruit Cakes

Fruit cakes are basically butter cakes with just enough batter to bind the fruit.

Fruit cakes will remain moist if you wrap them with a damp towel when storing.

To store for a long period of time, wrap in brandy- or wine-soaked towels, and then wrap in aluminum foil.

For very long storage, bury the liquor-soaked cake in powdered sugar and place in a tightly covered tin in a cool place (fruit cakes can be enjoyed as long as twenty-five years this way).

TIP: Coat candied fruit and nuts being used in a recipe with a little flour from the recipe to prevent them from falling to the bottom when baking.

Regal Fruit Cake

1 1/2 cups candied yellow pineapple, chopped
1 1/2 cups candied red cherries, chopped
1 cup raisins
3/4 cup currants
2 cups chopped pecans or walnuts
1/2 cup white grape juice
1 cup butter or margarine, room temperature
2 cups firmly packed light brown sugar
5 eggs, room temperature
2 1/4 cups all-purpose flour
1/4 teaspoon baking soda
1/2 teaspoon ground cinnamon
1/2 teaspoon ground mace
1 teaspoon almond extract
Brandy

Grease a 10-inch tube or bundt pan; line with wax paper and grease well. In a large bowl, combine candied pineapple, candied cherries, raisins, currants, and pecans or walnuts. Add grape juice; stir until well blended. Let stand 1 hour.

Preheat oven to 275 degrees. In a large bowl, cream butter or margarine. Gradually add brown sugar, stirring until light and fluffy. Add eggs, one at a time, beating well after each addition.

In another large bowl, combine flour, baking soda, cinnamon, and mace; gradually add to butter mixture. Add almond extract and fruit mixture; stir until well blended. Spoon into prepared pan. Bake 3 hours and 20 minutes or until a toothpick inserted into the cake comes out clean. Remove from oven and cool on a wire rack for 30 minutes. Remove from pan, peel paper liner from cake, and cool completely. Wrap in a brandy-soaked cheesecloth; store in an airtight container for one week. After one week, store in the refrigerator.

Makes 1 large cake.

No-Bake Fruit Cake

1 (16-ounce) package miniature marshmallows
1 (14-ounce) can sweetened condensed milk
4 cups graham crackers crumbs
1 1/2 cups raisins
1 1/2 cups red and green candied cherries, chopped
1 1/4 cups dates, cut into small pieces
4 cups chopped pecans

Spray a 9-inch square baking pan with vegetable-oil cooking spray. In a large saucepan over low heat, combine marshmallows and sweetened condensed milk; heat until marshmallows are melted and well blended.

In a large bowl, combine graham cracker crumbs, raisins, candied cherries (reserve a few candied cherries for garnish), dates, and pecans. Pour marshmallow mixture into graham cracker mixture; stir until well blended (using your hands if necessary). Press mixture into prepared baking pan, packing firmly. Garnish with reserved cherries. Refrigerate 8 hours or overnight before serving. Store in the refrigerator.

Makes 1 cake.

Panforte Di Siena

An Italian confection that is a cross between fruit cake, candy, and honey cakes called Lebkuchen (lasting cakes). It is a wonderful confection and so easy to make.

BREAD CRUMB PAN LINING:
1 tablespoon cake flour
1 tablespoon bread crumbs
2 tablespoons ground almonds

Preheat oven to 300 degrees and adjust oven rack to center position. Brush an 8-inch cake pan or an 8-inch springform pan with butter. Cut a disk of parchment or wax paper to fit pan bottom. Brush paper with butter and fit into pan bottom. In a small bowl, combine cake flour, bread crumbs, and almonds; evenly scatter over sides and bottom; pat gently into place.

CAKE:
1/2 cup plus 2 tablespoons cake flour, divided
1 1/2 teaspoons ground cinnamon, divided
1/4 teaspoon ground coriander
1/4 teaspoon ground cloves
1/4 teaspoon ground nutmeg
1/2 cup honey
1/2 cup sugar
1/2 cup candied citron or candied melon, cut into small pieces
1/2 cup candied orange peel, cut into small pieces
1 cup almonds, toasted and coarsely chopped
Powdered sugar

In a small bowl, combine 1/2 cup cake flour, 1 teaspoon cinnamon, coriander, cloves, and nutmeg; set aside. In another small bowl, combine the remaining 2 tablespoons of cake flour and 1/2 teaspoon cinnamon; set mixture aside and save for the top.

In a medium saucepan over low heat, combine honey and sugar. Cook, stirring occasionally to prevent scorching, until mixture comes to a full boil; remove from heat. Stir in candied fruit and almonds. Sift in flour mixture; stir until well blended. Pour batter into prepared pan. Smooth top with the slightly wet palm of your hand. Sift reserved cinnamon-flour mixture over the top. Place cake in center of middle oven rack. Bake 30 minutes or until panforte just starts to simmer around edge of pan. Remove from oven; cool completely on a wire rack.

Loosen from pan by running a small knife around perimeter (if using a springform pan, remove sides of springform pan). Invert onto a wire rack, letting excess cinnamon flour fall away. Use knife to peel away parchment or wax paper. Invert panforte again and transfer onto a wire rack. Dust top with powdered sugar. When cool, it can be wrapped in several layers of plastic wrap and a layer of aluminum foil and stored in an airtight container for several weeks, or frozen for up to six months. Serve at room temperature. Cut into small wedges to serve.

Makes 16 servings.

VARIATION: To make a chocolate panforte, follow recipe for Panforte Di Siena, making the following changes: Add 4 ounces chopped semisweet chocolate to honey and sugar mixture *after* it is removed from the heat. Cover and let stand 2 minutes or until chocolate melts. Add 1/4 teaspoon salt to the flour and spices.

VARIATION: To make date panforte, follow recipe for Panforte Di Siena. Substitute 1/2 cup chopped dates for 1/2 cup candied citron or melon.

ITALY

Parchment Paper

Parchment paper is available in a roll in a handy dispenser box with a serrated metal cutting edge, or in sheets.

It is used to line a cake or bread pan before baking. A delicate cake or bread will slip right out without sticking. After removing the cake from the pan, simply peel off the paper.

To line the removable bottom of a tart pan, trace the bottom onto a piece of parchment paper and cut out the parchment piece. Place it into the pan and grease lightly.

Pudding Cakes

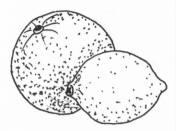

Lemons

1 medium lemon equals about 1 tablespoon of zest and 2 tablespoons of juice.

One of the most common fruit trees. Both savory and sweet dishes benefit from the tangy, refreshing flavor of lemons. The zest, the juice, and the fruit (sliced or quartered) can be used. Lemon juice poured over other fruits prevents discoloration of the flesh when exposed to air. The juice can be used as a substitute for vinegar if a lighter-flavored vinaigrette is desired.

Choose smooth-skinned lemons that are heavy for their size. Store in the refrigerator.

TIPS: If you need only a few drops of juice, prick one end with a fork and squeeze the desired amount. Return the lemon to the refrigerator and it will be as good as new.

If you are using a lemon for zest and juice, grate the zest first and then squeeze the juice.

Lemon Pudding Cake

2 tablespoons unsalted butter, room temperature
1/2 cup plus 2 tablespoons sugar
1/8 teaspoon salt
3 egg yolks, room temperature
3 tablespoons all-purpose flour
2 to 3 teaspoons grated lemon zest
1/4 cup fresh lemon juice, strained
1 cup milk
4 egg whites, room temperature

Preheat oven to 325 degrees. Adjust oven rack to center position. Lightly butter baking pan or custard cups of your choice. Bring several quarts of water to boil for water bath.

In a large bowl, combine butter, sugar, and salt; beat until crumbly. Beat in egg yolks and flour, mixing until smooth. Slowly beat in lemon zest and juice; stir in milk.

In a large bowl, beat egg whites until stiff peaks form. Gently whisk whites into batter just until no large lumps remain. Immediately ladle batter into prepared baking pan or custard cups. Do not pour; otherwise, the first cups get all the froth and the later cups get all the batter.

Set a roasting pan onto oven rack. Lay folded dish towel onto bottom of roasting pan; set custard cups or baking pan on top of towel. Pour enough boiling water into roasting pan to come halfway up sides of baking pan or custard cups.

Bake 25 minutes or until pudding cake center is set and springs back when gently touched. Remove roasting pan from oven and set on a wire rack. Let pan or cups continue to stand in water bath for 10 minutes. Serve at room temperature or chilled.

Makes 4 to 6 servings.

Orange Pudding Cake

Follow the recipe for Lemon Pudding Cake, making the following changes: Substitute the zest and juice (1/4 cup) from 1 medium orange for the lemon zest and juice. Add 2 tablespoons lemon juice along with the orange juice.

Chocolate Pudding Cake

Follow the recipe for Lemon Pudding Cake, making the following changes: In a medium bowl, make a thick cocoa paste by slowly stirring 1/2 cup boiling water into 1/3 cup unsweetened cocoa. Cool the paste slightly, then stir in 1 tablespoon dark rum. Substitute cocoa paste for lemon zest and juice. Decrease flour from 3 tablespoons to 2 tablespoons.

Bourbon Pudding Cake

This sauce is sinful – it is so rich and wonderful.

Follow the recipe for Lemon Pudding Cake, making the following changes:
Decrease flour from 3 to 2 tablespoons, substitute 1 tablespoon vanilla extract and
1 tablespoon bourbon whiskey for lemon zest and juice, and increase milk from 1 to
1 1/3 cups.

To serve, spoon Bourbon Butter Sauce over each pudding cake. Pass leftover sauce
separately.

Makes 6 servings.

BOURBON BUTTER SAUCE:
1/2 cup butter
2/3 cup sugar
2 tablespoons bourbon
1/2 teaspoon freshly grated nutmeg
2 tablespoons water
1 egg, beaten

In a small saucepan over medium-low heat, combine butter, sugar, bourbon, nutmeg,
and water; stirring occasionally, until bubbly around the edges. Remove from heat.
Blend beaten egg into hot butter mixture. Return to heat; bring to a boil over
medium-low heat, stirring constantly. Cook 1 to 2 minutes or until thickened.
Remove from heat.

Pudding Cakes

*Pudding cakes are
basically egg custards,
but with two improvements.
Unlike ordinary egg
custards, pudding cakes
contain a little flour and
beaten egg whites.*

*During baking, the beaten
egg whites will float to the
top, forming a spongy,
cake-like cap. Meanwhile,
the remainder of the batter
settles to the bottom to
make a pudding-like layer.*

English Trifle

1 (18 1/4-ounce) package yellow cake mix
1 cup raspberry jam, divided
1 (29-ounce) can sliced peaches, drained (reserve juice)
1/2 cup dry or medium sherry, divided
1 (8-serving size) vanilla pudding mix (not instant)
3 cups milk
2 cups sweetened whipped cream
Sliced toasted almonds

Prepare the yellow cake according to package directions using a 9-inch cake pan (reserve one layer for another use). Slice one cake layer horizontally into two equal layers.

Place one sliced layer into a trifle dish or a large glass bowl with straight sides; cover with 1/2 cup raspberry jam and half of the sliced peaches. Pour approximately half of the reserved peach juice over the cake or until it is moist but not sloppy. Pour 1/4 cup sherry over the top, as evenly as possible. Place the second sliced cake layer on top and cover with remaining jam and peaches; pour remaining peach juice and sherry over the top.

Prepare the vanilla pudding according to package directions, using the 3 cups of milk. Pour hot pudding over cake. When cool, spread with whipped cream. Decorate with toasted sliced almonds. Cover with plastic wrap and refrigerate overnight.

Makes 10 to 12 servings.

Chocolate-Almond Trifle

A delicious new version of a classic dessert.

1 (8-serving size) chocolate pudding mix (not instant)
3 cups milk
1/4 teaspoon almond extract
1/2 cup apricot jam
3/4 cup brandy, divided
1 (6-inch) angel food cake (already made)
1 cup sweetened whipped cream
2/3 cup roasted diced almonds

Prepare the pudding according to package directions, using the 3 cups of milk; stir in almond extract and refrigerate until well chilled.

In a small saucepan over very low heat, combine apricot jam and 6 tablespoons brandy; simmer for 15 minutes. Set aside to cool slightly.

Cut cake into 1-inch squares. In a trifle dish or a large glass bowl with straight sides, place one-third of the cake squares. Sprinkle with 2 tablespoons of brandy. Spread first layer with one-third of the apricot mixture. Spread one-third of the whipped cream over top and sprinkle with one-third of the almonds. Repeat the above steps with the remaining two layers.

Pour the chocolate pudding over the top; sprinkle remaining almonds on top. Cover with plastic wrap and refrigerate overnight.

Makes 8 to 10 servings.

Trifle

What is an English trifle? It is a cake well soaked with sherry and served with a boiled custard poured over it. The English call this cake a "Tipsy Pudding."

George Washington is said to have preferred trifle over all other desserts.

It is very good made a day ahead, but it can be served the day it is prepared too. If you don't have a true trifle bowl, use any straight-sided round glass bowl – the layers look beautiful from the side.

NOTE: The recipe versions in this book call for sherry, cherry-flavored liqueur, and brandy; however, you can omit these ingredients and still have a fabulous dessert.

Tennessee Trifle

1 (18 1/4-ounce) package chocolate cake mix
1 (4-serving size) package vanilla instant pudding mix
2 1/2 cups milk
2 cups apricot preserves, divided
1/4 cup cherry-flavored liqueur
1 (15 1/2-ounce) can pitted dark cherries, drained and divided
1 cup sweetened whipped cream
1/2 cup sliced toasted almonds

Prepare the chocolate cake according to package directions using a 9-inch cake pan (reserving one layer for another use); slice cake layer horizontally into two equal layers.

Prepare the pudding according to package directions, using the 2 1/2 cups of milk. Refrigerate 30 minutes or until slightly thickened.

In a medium bowl, combine apricot preserves and cherry liqueur. Spread one layer of cake with 1 cup of the preserve mixture; place the other layer onto top. Cut the cake into 2-inch squares.

Spoon one-third of the pudding into the bottom of a trifle dish or a large glass bowl with straight sides; top with half of the cake squares, pressing them down slightly. Spread half of the cherries and 1/2 cup of preserve mixture over the top. Repeat the steps with the next layer. Top with remaining pudding.

Spread the whipped cream onto top of trifle. Sprinkle with toasted almonds. Cover with plastic wrap and refrigerate overnight.

Makes 6 to 8 servings.

Fruit Trifle

1 (4-serving size) instant vanilla pudding mix
2 1/2 cups milk
1 (1-pound) loaf pound cake (already made)
3 tablespoons cream sherry or brandy, divided
1/4 cup strawberry preserves or currant jelly, divided
2 cups sliced and peeled fresh peaches, fresh kiwi fruit,
    fresh strawberries, fresh raspberries, or fresh blueberries, divided
2 tablespoons toasted sliced almonds, divided
Prepared whipped topping

Prepare pudding according to package directions, using the 2 1/2 cups of milk. Cut pound cake into 1-inch squares.

In a trifle dish or a large glass bowl with straight sides, layer half of the cake squares. Sprinkle with half of the sherry or brandy, dot with half of the preserves or jelly, top with half of the fruit, and half of the almonds. Pour half of the pudding over all. Repeat the steps with the next layer. Cover with plastic wrap and refrigerate overnight. To serve, top with prepared whipped topping.

Makes 8 to 10 servings.

Kiwis (Kiwi fruit)

Did you know that you can eat the skin? Firmly grasp the kiwi, open wide, and bite right in. What a taste sensation!

Kiwi fruit is a native of China. It was introduced into New Zealand in 1906 and has been commercially cultivated there ever since. It is now being grown in Oregon. Since kiwi is really a Chinese gooseberry and the name is rather unenchanting, they decided to rename the fruit "kiwi." This name not only identifies New Zealand, but also describes the appearance of a New Zealand native, the tiny Kiwi bird.

Choose kiwi fruit that is plump and unbruised. When ripe, kiwi fruit yields to gentle pressure. With the right conditions, kiwi fruit will stay firm for six months. At home, store the fruit in the refrigerator to maintain its firmness.

Firm fruit could take from one to four weeks to become soft. To hasten ripening, place kiwi fruit in a plastic bag with an apple or banana, at room temperature. The fruit will ripen in a few days. It is ready to eat when slightly soft to touch.

The simplest way to eat the fruit is to cut in half widthwise and scoop out the moist, refreshing flesh with a teaspoon.

Perfect Pie Crust

8- OR 9-INCH ONE-CRUST PIE
1/3 cup plus 1 tablespoon chilled vegetable shortening
1 cup all-purpose flour
1/2 teaspoon salt
2 to 3 tablespoons chilled water

8- OR 9-INCH TWO-CRUST PIE
2/3 cup plus 2 tablespoons chilled vegetable shortening
2 cups all-purpose flour
1 teaspoon salt
4 to 6 tablespoons chilled water

In a large bowl with a pastry blender or two knives, cut shortening into flour and salt until particles are the size of small peas. Sprinkle in water, 1 tablespoon at a time, tossing with fork until all flour is moistened and pastry dough almost cleans side of bowl (1 to 2 teaspoons additional water can be added if necessary).

On a lightly floured surface, form pastry into a ball; shape into a flattened round. (For two-crust pie, divide pastry into halves and shape into two rounds.) Roll pastry 2 inches larger than an inverted pie plate with a floured rolling pin. Fold pastry into quarter folds and ease into plate, pressing firmly against bottom and side.

FOR ONE-CRUST PIE: Trim overhanging edge of pastry 1 inch from rim of pie plate. Fold and roll pastry under, even with pie plate; flute. Fill and bake as directed in recipe.

FOR TWO-CRUST PIE: Turn desired filling into pastry-lined pie plate. Trim overhanging edge of pastry 1/2 inch from rim of plate. Roll other round of pastry. Fold into quarters. Place over filling and unfold. Trim overhanging edge of pastry 1 inch from rim of plate. Fold and roll top edge under lower edge, pressing on rim to seal; flute. Cut slits so steam can escape. Cover edge with strip of aluminum foil to prevent excessive browning; remove foil during last 15 minutes of baking. Bake as directed in recipe.

FOR BAKED PIE SHELL: Prick bottom and sides thoroughly with a fork. Bake in oven at 475 degrees 8 to 10 minutes or until light brown; cool.

Apple Flan

Flan Crust
2 green tart cooking apples, peeled, cored, and sliced
1 (8-ounce) package cream cheese, room temperature
1/2 cup sugar
2 tablespoons lemon juice
2 eggs

Preheat oven to 375 degrees. Prepare Flan Crust. Arrange apples on prepared flan crust. In a medium bowl, mix together cream cheese, sugar, lemon juice, and eggs. Pour mixture over apples and bake 40 to 50 minutes or until crust is golden brown and apples are tender. Remove from oven and cool on a wire rack before cutting and serving.

Makes 6 to 8 servings.

FLAN CRUST:
1 1/2 cups all-purpose flour
1/4 cup powdered sugar
1/2 cup chilled butter or margarine
1 egg

In a food processor, combine flour, powdered sugar, and butter or margarine; whirl until particles are the size of small peas. Add egg and whirl until blended. Form pastry into a ball, wrap in plastic wrap, and refrigerate 1 hour.

On a lightly floured surface, roll pastry 1/8-inch thick. Place dough over mold and gently ease it into the flan ring, being careful not to stretch or tear dough. Pass rolling pin over top to remove excess pastry.

Oregon Apple Pie

Pastry for 9-inch two-crust pie (see page 122)
3/4 cup sugar
1/2 teaspoon ground cinnamon
1/8 teaspoon ground nutmeg
1/8 teaspoon ground cloves
5 to 6 medium (2 pounds) green tart cooking apples
2 tablespoons butter or margarine, cut into small pieces
1 tablespoon sugar

Preheat oven to 400 degrees. Prepare pie pastry. In a large bowl, combine sugar, cinnamon, nutmeg, and cloves. Peel, core, and slice apples 1/4-inch thick. Toss apple slices in sugar mixture until well coated. Spoon apple filling into pastry-lined plate and dot with butter or margarine. Cover with remaining pastry and flute. Cut slits in pastry so steam can escape. Sprinkle 1 tablespoon sugar onto top of pie crust.

Bake 45 to 50 minutes or until crust is golden brown and apples are tender. Remove from oven and cool on a wire rack before cutting and serving. Serve warm or at room temperature.

Makes 8 servings.

Fruit Flan

Fruit flan is an European dessert. Its sweet pastry has a tender, crumbly consistency, because of the eggs.

A flan is nothing more than a tart baked in a special metal form that has no bottom or top. The shell is made by fitting rolled-out pastry dough into the flan ring; since the form has no bottom, the tart must be baked on a baking sheet. After baking, you slip the filled or unfilled pastry shell out of the flan ring onto a plate.

Instead of a flan ring, a 9-inch round cake pan can be used.

To make, place flan form on baking sheet. Roll pastry 1/8-inch thick. Place dough over mold and gently ease it into the ring, being careful not to stretch or tear dough. Pass rolling pin over top to remove excess pastry. Bake blind (see tip on page 130), or fill and bake.

After baking, the form can easily be removed, since the pastry shrinks.

Freezing Whole Apples

Freeze whole apples for baking, or for use in pies and puddings. The tartness of a summer apple seems to give a better apple flavor throughout the winter if frozen.

Wash firm apples without blemishes, then place six to ten in a freezer bag and freeze.

To prepare frozen apples for cooking, run cold water over each frozen apple for three to five minutes, then peel, core or slice. Work fast! Apples that are allowed to thaw before being peeled darken quickly. Peel, then cut.

To bake them, peel, prepare according to recipe and bake, even if the apple is not completely thawed.

Apple Strudel Pie

Pastry for 9-inch one-crust pie (see page 122)
6 or 7 green tart cooking apples
Juice of 1/2 lemon
3/4 cup sugar
1/4 cup firmly packed light brown sugar
1/4 cup raisins
1 tablespoon all-purpose flour
1 teaspoon ground cinnamon
1/2 teaspoon ground nutmeg
2 tablespoons chilled water
1 tablespoon butter or margarine, melted and cooled
Strudel Topping
Lemon Glaze

Preheat oven to 425 degrees. Prepare pie pastry. Peel and slice enough apples 1/4-inch thick to make 6 cups. Place in a large bowl and toss with lemon juice. Add sugar, brown sugar, raisins, flour, cinnamon, and nutmeg; toss lightly to distribute evenly. Add water and butter or margarine and toss. Place mixture evenly into a pastry-lined plate.

Spread Strudel Topping lightly over apples, covering top completely. Bake 10 minutes. Reduce heat to 325 degrees and bake another hour or until crust is golden brown and apples are tender. Remove from oven and cool slightly on a wire rack. Drizzle Lemon Glaze over warm pie; cool completely on a wire rack before cutting and serving.

Makes 8 to 10 servings.

STRUDEL TOPPING:
6 tablespoons butter or margarine, room temperature
1/4 cup all-purpose flour
1/4 cup sugar
1/4 cup firmly packed light brown sugar
1/2 teaspoon ground cinnamon
1/4 teaspoon ground nutmeg

In a medium bowl, using pastry blender or two knives, cut butter or margarine into flour until mixture is crumbly. Mix in sugar, brown sugar, cinnamon, and nutmeg.

LEMON GLAZE:
1/2 cup powdered sugar
1 to 2 tablespoons fresh lemon juice

In a small bowl, combine powdered sugar and lemon juice; mix until smooth.

Cherry Pie

Pastry for 9-inch two-crust pie (see page 122)
1 1/3 cups sugar
4 tablespoons quick-cooking tapioca
6 cups fresh or frozen pitted sour cherries
1/4 teaspoon almond extract
2 tablespoons butter or margarine

Preheat oven to 400 degrees. Prepare pie pastry. In a large bowl, combine sugar and tapioca. Add cherries; stir until well blended. Pour into pastry-lined plate; sprinkle with almond extract and dot with butter or margarine. Cover with remaining pastry and flute. Cut slits in pastry so steam can escape. Cover edge with aluminum foil to prevent excessive browning.

Place pie on a baking sheet. Bake 45 to 50 minutes or until crust is golden brown and juice begins to bubble through slits on crust. Remove aluminum foil during last 15 minutes of baking. Remove from oven and cool on a wire rack before cutting and serving. Serve warm or at room temperature.

Makes 8 to 10 servings.

Luscious Cranberry & Blueberry Pie

Pastry for 9-inch two-crust pie (see page 122)
1 (16-ounce) can whole berry cranberry sauce
1/3 cup firmly packed brown sugar
1/4 cup sugar
2 tablespoons all-purpose flour
2 tablespoons cornstarch
1/2 teaspoon grated orange zest
2 tablespoons fresh orange juice
1/8 teaspoon salt
2 cups fresh or frozen blueberries

Preheat oven to 425 degrees. Prepare pie pastry. In a large bowl, combine cranberry sauce, brown sugar, sugar, flour, cornstarch, orange zest, orange juice, and salt. Fold in blueberries. Spoon into pastry-lined plate. Cover with remaining pastry and flute. Cut slits in pastry so steam can escape. Cover edge with aluminum foil to prevent excessive browning.

Bake 35 to 40 minutes or until crust is golden brown and juice begins to bubble through slits in crust. Remove aluminum foil during last 15 minutes of baking. Remove from oven and cool on a wire rack before cutting and serving.

Makes 8 to 10 servings.

Pie Making

TIPS: Avoid messy spills in the oven by setting the pie plate on a baking sheet lined with aluminum foil. The pan catches any juice if the pie bubbles over. This makes for a fast and easy cleanup!

Glaze the top crust of double-crust pies to make them look and taste special. Brush the unbaked top crust with milk, water, or melted butter; then sprinkle lightly with sugar.

Use a glass pie plate or a dull metal pie plate for making pies. The shiny metal pans keep the crust from browning properly.

Cool baked pies on a wire rack set on the counter. The rack allows air to circulate under the pie, preventing it from becoming soggy from the steam remaining in it.

To prevent a pie crust from browning too much, cut out the center of a disposable aluminum pie tin and save the resulting ring. Lay this aluminum ring on top of your crust during cooking if the edges are becoming too brown.

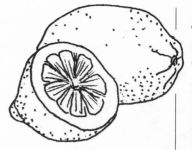

Fantastic Lemon Meringue Pie

This lemon meringue pie is exceptional. Try serving it with your favorite seafood dish.

Pastry for 9-inch one-crust pie (see page 122)
1/2 cup graham cracker crumbs
1 cup sugar
1/4 cup cornstarch
1/8 teaspoon salt
1 1/2 cups water
6 egg yolks, slightly beaten
1 tablespoon grated lemon zest
1/2 cup fresh lemon juice
2 tablespoons butter
Meringue Topping

Preheat oven to 400 degrees. Prepare pie pastry; dust lightly with flour, wrap in plastic wrap, and refrigerate 30 minutes before rolling.

Sprinkle work area with 2 tablespoons graham cracker crumbs. Roll pastry with floured rolling pin, sprinkling additional crumbs underneath and on top to heavily coat dough. Roll pastry 2 inches larger than an inverted 9-inch pie pan. Fold pastry into quarter-folds and ease into pan, pressing firmly against bottom and side; flute edges. Prick crust at 1/2-inch intervals before baking. Bake 15 minutes; reduce oven to 350 degrees and bake another 10 minutes or until crust is golden brown. Remove from oven and cool on a wire rack. Reduce oven to 325 degrees.

In a large saucepan over low heat, combine sugar, cornstarch, salt, and water; simmer until translucent. Whisk in egg yolks gradually. Whisk in lemon zest, lemon juice, and butter. Remove from heat and pour into baked pie shell.

Spread Meringue Topping over pie filling, being careful to spread to edge of pastry to prevent shrinkage during baking. Bake 20 minutes or until meringue is golden brown. Remove from oven and cool completely on a wire rack before cutting and serving.

Makes 8 servings.

MERINGUE TOPPING
1 tablespoon cornstarch
1/3 cup water
4 egg whites, room temperature
1/2 teaspoon vanilla extract
1/4 teaspoon cream of tartar
1/2 cup sugar

In a small saucepan over low heat, combine cornstarch and water; bring to simmer, stirring until mixture thickens and turns translucent. Remove from heat and cool.

In a large bowl, beat egg whites and vanilla extract until frothy. In a small bowl, combine cream of tartar and sugar; add to egg whites, 1 tablespoon at a time, beating until soft peaks form. Slowly add cornstarch mixture, 1 tablespoon at a time; continue to beat until stiff peaks form.

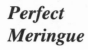

Perfect Meringue

Meringue recipes work better with eggs that are at least three or four days old.

Cold eggs separate more easily than those at room temperature because the whites hold together better.

When separating eggs, if a speck of egg yolk falls into the egg whites, lift it out with an empty eggshell half. Do not try to fish it out with your fingers; the oil on your skin will prevent the egg whites from expanding.

After separating, bring egg whites to room temperature to ensure volume when beating.

When beating egg whites and the recipe calls for sugar, add the sugar at the very end when the whites have formed soft peaks. As a general rule, add one-fourth cup of sugar for each egg white.

To cut baked meringue into serving pieces, use a knife dipped in cold water.

Florida Key Lime Pie

Key limes are a variety of limes that were once grown extensively on the Florida Keys. This lime is very popular in Florida. You'll love this delightful and easy-to-make pie.

1 (9-inch) prepared graham cracker pie crust
1 (14-ounce) can sweetened condensed milk
Grated zest from 1 key lime (optional)
1/4 cup key lime juice
2 eggs, separated
1 egg, room temperature
4 tablespoons sugar

Refrigerate graham cracker crust until well chilled.

Preheat oven to 350 degrees. In a medium bowl, combine condensed milk, key lime zest, and key lime juice. Add egg yolks and egg; stir until well blended. Pour into chilled graham cracker crust.

In a medium bowl, beat egg whites until stiff peaks form; gradually fold in sugar. Spread meringue over key lime mixture, being careful to spread to edge of pastry to prevent shrinkage during baking. Bake 20 minutes or until meringue is golden brown. Remove from oven and cool completely on a wire rack. Refrigerate before serving.

Makes 6 servings.

Basic Oregon Blackberry Pie

This pie is worth the scratches and stained hands you get when picking your own fresh blackberries.

Pastry for 9-inch two-crust pie (see page 122)
1 quart fresh blackberries
1 cup sugar (or to taste)
3 tablespoons quick-cooking tapioca
1/2 teaspoon ground cinnamon
1/4 teaspoon lemon juice

Preheat oven to 400 degrees. Prepare pie pastry. In a large bowl, combine blackberries, sugar, tapioca, cinnamon, and lemon juice. Spoon into pastry-lined plate. Cover with remaining pastry and flute. Cut slits in pastry so steam can escape. Cover edge with aluminum foil to prevent excessive browning.

Bake 10 minutes; reduce heat to 375 degrees and bake another 45 minutes. Remove aluminum foil during last 15 minutes of baking. Remove from oven and cool on a wire rack before cutting and serving. Serve warm or at room temperature.

Makes 8 servings.

Sweetened Condensed Milk

1 (14.5-ounce) can equals 1 1/4 cups.

Condensed milk is defined as milk which has been reduced by evaporation until the water content has been reduced by as much as 60 percent. It also contains a large amount of sugar, as much as one-half cup in a 14.5-ounce can.

HOMEMADE SWEETENED CONDENSED MILK:
1 1/2 cups nonfat powdered milk
1/2 cup milk (2 percent)
2/3 cup sugar
1 teaspoon vanilla extract

Whisk powdered milk and milk in a saucepan until it is very smooth, about one minute. Whisk in sugar and vanilla extract; cook over low heat, continuing to whisk constantly until the sugar and powdered milk dissolve, about five minutes. Cool before using, then whisk again to be sure that no graininess remains. This can be covered and refrigerated for up to one week.

Yields 14 ounces.

Pecans

1 pound of pecans in the shell equals approximately 2 cups shelled nuts.

Pecans, native American nuts, were used by Indians for food before Columbus arrived.

Pecans are considered a Southern tradition and are a favorite confection in the form of praline candies.

To remove pecans whole from the shell, soak the unshelled nuts in salted water for several hours before you crack them.

Nuts in the shell may be kept at room temperature if you are planning to use them within two months.

If you plan to keep them longer, they should be treated like fresh fruits. Once a can, jar, or bag of shelled nuts has been opened, refrigerate the contents, well covered, or freeze.

Unlike most other foods, nuts can be refrozen and do not have to be thawed before you use them in cooking.

Chocolate Chip Pecan Pie

Pastry for 9-inch one-crust pie (see page 122)
4 eggs, beaten
1 cup sugar
1 cup light corn syrup
3 tablespoons butter or margarine, room temperature
1 teaspoon vanilla extract
1/4 teaspoon salt
2 cups pecan halves
1/2 cup semisweet chocolate chips
1 tablespoon plus 1 1/2 teaspoons bourbon (optional)

Preheat oven to 375 degrees. Prepare pie pastry. In a large bowl, combine eggs, sugar, corn syrup, butter or margarine, vanilla extract, and salt; stir until well blended. Stir in pecans, chocolate chips, and bourbon.

Pour into pastry-lined plate. Bake 40 to 50 minutes or until the pie center has a slight jiggle to it when shaken. Remove from oven and cool completely on a wire rack before cutting and serving.

Makes 8 to 10 servings.

D.K.'s Pecan Pie

The only way this pie could be better tasting is to serve it warm and top with a big scoop of vanilla ice cream.

Pastry for 9-inch one-crust pie (see page 122)
1/3 cup butter or margarine, room temperature
3/4 cup firmly packed brown sugar
3 eggs
1 cup light corn syrup
1 cup coarsely chopped pecans
1/8 teaspoon salt
1 teaspoon vanilla extract
1/3 cup raisins

Preheat oven to 375 degrees. Prepare pie pastry. In a large bowl, cream butter or margarine until light and fluffy; gradually add brown sugar. Beat in eggs, one at a time, beating well after each addition. Add corn syrup, pecans, salt, and vanilla extract; stir until well blended. Stir in raisins. Pour into pastry-lined plate.

Bake 40 to 50 minutes or until the pie center has a slight jiggle to it when shaken. Remove from oven and cool completely on a wire rack before cutting and serving.

Makes 8 servings.

Pumpkin Pecan Pie

Pastry for 9-inch one-crust pie (see page 122)
4 eggs, slightly beaten
1 (16-ounce) can solid-packed pumpkin
1 cup sugar
1/2 cup dark corn syrup
1 teaspoon vanilla extract
1/2 teaspoon ground cinnamon
1/4 teaspoon salt
1 cup chopped pecans

Preheat oven to 375 degrees. Prepare pie pastry. In a large bowl, combine eggs, pumpkin, sugar, corn syrup, vanilla extract, cinnamon, and salt. Pour into pastry-lined plate and top with pecans. Bake 40 to 50 minutes or until the pie center has a slight jiggle to it when shaken. Remove from oven and cool completely on a wire rack before cutting and serving.

Makes 8 to 10 servings.

Pecan-Almond Tart

Pastry for 9-inch one-crust pie (see page 122)
1/2 cup sugar
3/4 cups light corn syrup
3 tablespoons butter, cut into 1/4-inch pieces
3 eggs, lightly beaten
1 teaspoon vanilla extract
1 cup chopped pecans
1/4 cup sliced toasted almonds
Butterscotch-Bourbon Sauce

Preheat oven to 350 degrees. Prepare pie pastry. On a lightly floured surface, form pastry into a ball and flatten. Roll pastry to fit into an ungreased 10-inch tart pan or 10-inch round cake pan; cut edge flush with top.

In a medium saucepan over medium-high heat, add sugar and corn syrup; bring to a boil and boil 2 minutes. Remove from heat and stir in butter. Add the eggs and vanilla extract, stirring constantly. When the butter has completely melted, pour the mixture into prepared pastry crust. Spread a layer of pecans over the top and then a layer of almonds. Bake 30 to 35 minutes or until edges are set but pie center still jiggles slightly when shaken. Remove from oven and cool completely on a wire rack. Serve with Butterscotch-Bourbon Sauce.

Makes 8 to 10 servings.

BUTTERSCOTCH-BOURBON SAUCE:
1/3 cup light corn syrup
3/4 cup firmly packed brown sugar
2 tablespoons butter
1/3 cup heavy cream
2 tablespoons bourbon whiskey

In a small saucepan over medium-high heat, combine corn syrup, brown sugar, and butter. Cook, stirring constantly, 6 minutes. Remove from heat and stir in cream. Cool 20 minutes and then stir in the bourbon. Serve at room temperature.

Corn Syrup

Corn syrup is produced when starch granules from corn are processed with acids or enzymes. This thick, sweet syrup comes in light and dark forms. Light corn syrup has been clarified to remove all color and cloudiness. The more strongly flavored dark corn syrup is a mixture of corn syrup and refiners' syrup.

SUBSTITUTION FOR 1 CUP DARK CORN SYRUP:
3/4 cup light corn syrup plus 1/4 cup light molasses, or 1 1/4 cups firmly packed brown sugar plus 1/4 cup water.

SUBSTITUTION FOR 1 CUP LIGHT CORN SYRUP:
1 1/4 cups sugar plus 1/4 cup water.

Baked goods made with corn syrup retain their moisture and stay fresh longer.

Hazelnuts or Filberts

1 pound of hazelnuts in the shell equals about 1 1/2 cups shelled nuts.

Hazelnuts (shelled or unshelled) can be stored in the refrigerator or freezer for two years, if packaged in sealed plastic containers or bags. After storage, allow nuts to warm up in an unopened plastic container or bag.

ROASTING OR TOASTING HAZELNUTS: Spread shelled hazelnuts in a shallow pan and roast in a 275-degree oven for twenty to thirty minutes or until skins crack. To remove skins, rub nuts while warm with a rough cloth or between your hands.

What is Baking Blind?

Baking blind is the technique used for baking an unfilled pastry shell. The pastry shell is first pricked with a fork to prevent puffing, covered with aluminum foil or parchment paper, and then weighted with rice or beans.

The pastry shell is then baked for a short period of time, about ten to fifteen minutes, to set.

After baking, the rice or beans and the aluminum foil are then removed, and the shell is baked as needed or until lightly browned.

Chocolate-Hazelnut Tart

A very rich and wonderful dessert.

Pastry for 9-inch one-crust pie (see page 122)
3/4 cup firmly packed brown sugar
1/2 cup butter, room temperature
3 eggs
2/3 cup dark corn syrup
3 tablespoons molasses
2 tablespoons hazelnut liqueur
2 teaspoons vanilla extract
1 3/4 cups roasted hazelnuts
5 (1-ounce) squares bittersweet chocolate, cut into 1/2-inch chunks
3 tablespoons all-purpose flour

Preheat oven to 450 degrees. Prepare pie pastry. On a lightly floured surface, form pastry into a ball and flatten. Roll pastry to fit into an ungreased 10-inch tart pan or 10-inch round cake pan; cut edge flush with top. Bake blind by covering dough with aluminum foil, filling with raw dried beans, and baking 20 minutes. Remove beans and foil; bake another 10 minutes.

Reduce oven temperature to 325 degrees. In a large bowl, cream brown sugar and butter until light and fluffy. Add eggs, one at a time, beating well after each addition. Add corn syrup, molasses, hazelnut liqueur, and vanilla extract; stir until well blended. In a small bowl, combine hazelnuts, chocolate, and flour; stir into batter until well blended.

Pour chocolate-hazelnut mixture into pastry crust; bake 20 minutes or until a deep golden brown. Make a tent with aluminum foil, supporting foil on either side of dish with an empty can.

Bake another 40 to 45 minutes or until edges are set but pie center still jiggles slightly when shaken. Remove from oven and cool completely on a wire rack. Cover and refrigerate at least 4 hours or overnight before cutting and serving.

Makes 12 servings.

Praline Pumpkin Pie

Pastry for 9-inch one-crust pie (see page 122)
2 tablespoons apricot jam
1 (15-ounce) can solid-packed pumpkin
1 cup sugar
3 eggs
1 teaspoon ground cinnamon
1/4 teaspoon ground ginger
1/4 teaspoon ground cloves
1 1/2 cups half and half or light cream
2 tablespoons bourbon
1 cup firmly packed brown sugar
1 cup chopped pecans
1/4 cup butter, melted
Whipped cream

Preheat oven to 400 degrees. Prepare pie pastry; brush bottom of pie shell with apricot jam. Place on a cookie sheet.

In a large bowl, combine pumpkin, sugar, eggs, cinnamon, ginger, and cloves; stir until well blended. Add half and half or light cream and bourbon; stir until well blended. Pour into pastry-lined plate. Bake 20 minutes; reduce oven temperature to 350 degrees and bake another 35 minutes or until the pie center has a slight jiggle to it when shaken. Remove from oven and cool on a wire rack.

In a medium bowl, combine brown sugar, pecans, and butter; stir until well blended. Sprinkle sugar mixture over the pie and carefully broil until bubbling (be careful not to burn the praline). Serve at room temperature with a dollop of whipped cream.

Makes 8 servings.

D.K.'s Pumpkin Pie

Pastry for 9-inch one-crust pie (see page 122)
1 cup sugar
1/2 teaspoon cornstarch
1/2 teaspoon salt
1/2 teaspoon ground cinnamon
1/2 teaspoon ground ginger
1/2 teaspoon ground nutmeg
1 (15-ounce) can solid-packed pumpkin
2 eggs, beaten
1 1/2 tablespoons butter or margarine, melted
1/8 cup sorghum molasses
1 1/2 cups milk

Preheat oven to 450 degrees. Prepare pie pastry. In a large bowl, sift together sugar, cornstarch, salt, cinnamon, ginger, and nutmeg. Add pumpkin; stir until well blended. Stir in eggs, butter or margarine, molasses, and milk; pour into pastry-lined plate. Bake 15 minutes; reduce oven temperature to 350 degrees and bake another 45 minutes or until the pie center has a slight jiggle to it when shaken. Remove from oven and cool completely on a wire rack before cutting and serving.

Makes 8 servings.

Custard Pies

Since unbaked custard pie fillings are very thin mixtures, rub the unbaked pie crust with butter or margarine before adding the filling to prevent it from becoming soggy.

To check for doneness after baking for the correct time, insert a knife off-center; if it comes out clean with no custard filling clinging to it, the pie is done.

Or, gently shake the pie. If the area that appears to be liquid is less than the size of a quarter, the pie is done.

After the custard pie cools to room temperature, cover and refrigerate if it is not to be served immediately.

Sorghum

Sorghum is different from molasses, although many people use the terms interchangeably. Molasses comes from the juice of the sugar cane stalk, and sorghum is made from the juice of the sweet-sorghum cane stalk.

Molasses is darker and can be bitter, because much of the sugar is removed in the refining process. Sorghum has no sugar removed and thus is significantly sweeter.

Rhubarb

"Pie plant" is the old name for rhubarb. Rhubarb is actually a vegetable. Only the stalks can be used. The leaves contain a large amount of oxalic acid, making them poisonous.

Fresh rhubarb is at its peak in May and June. Keep picked rhubarb cold. It can be stored in the refrigerator for up to five days.

To freeze rhubarb, wash stalks and remove all leaves. Cut stalks into one-inch pieces and seal in a plastic storage bag. They keep well for ten to twelve months.

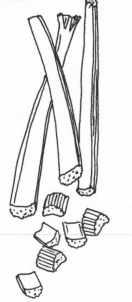

Ice Cream Pies

TIP: Frozen ice cream pies taste and serve better if they're removed from the freezer and allowed to soften for ten to fifteen minutes before serving.

Rhubarb Custard Pie

Pastry for 9-inch one-crust pie (see page 122)
1 tablespoon all-purpose flour
3 1/2 cups coarsely chopped fresh rhubarb
1 1/2 cups sugar
3 eggs, lightly beaten
1/4 cup half and half cream
1/2 teaspoon freshly grated nutmeg
1/8 teaspoon salt

Preheat oven to 375 degrees. Prepare pie pastry; sprinkle flour over bottom. In a large bowl, combine rhubarb, sugar, eggs, half and half cream, nutmeg, and salt; pour into pastry-lined plate. Bake in lower third of oven 1 hour or until a knife inserted in the center comes out clean. Remove from oven and cool completely on a wire rack before cutting and serving.

Makes 8 servings.

Grasshopper Pie

18 chocolate sandwich cookies, frozen
1/4 cup butter, melted
24 marshmallows
1/2 cup milk
1 cup whipping cream
4 tablespoons creme de menthe liqueur
2 tablespoons creme de cacao liqueur
3 drops of green food coloring

In a food processor, whirl cookies to fine crumbs, reserving 2 tablespoons of crumbs for top. Add butter; whirl 5 to 10 seconds more. Press crumb mixture firmly and evenly into a 9-inch pie plate. In a large saucepan over low heat, melt marshmallows in milk; cool. Beat whipping cream until stiff. Add liqueurs to cooled marshmallow mixture, add green food coloring, and then fold in whipped cream; pour into pastry-lined plate. Sprinkle reserved crumb mixture over the top. Place in freezer at least 4 hours or overnight. Serve frozen.

Makes 8 servings.

Mud Pie

1/2 package Nabisco Chocolate Wafers
1/4 cup butter or margarine, melted
1 gallon coffee ice cream, softened
1 1/2 cups chilled fudge sauce
Prepared whipped topping

In a food processor, whirl chocolate wafers to fine crumbs. Add butter; whirl another 5 to 10 seconds. Press crumb mixture firmly and evenly into a 9-inch pie plate. Spread ice cream over the pastry-lined plate. Freeze until ice cream is firm. Top with fudge sauce (it helps to place fudge sauce in freezer for a time to make spreading easier). Place in freezer approximately 10 hours. Serve frozen. Slice into eight portions and serve on chilled dessert plates with chilled forks. Top with prepared whipped topping.

Makes 8 servings.

Chocolate Banana Pudding Pie

4 (1-ounce) squares semisweet chocolate
2 tablespoons milk
1 tablespoon butter or margarine
1 (9-inch) prepared graham cracker crust
2 medium bananas, sliced
2 3/4 cups milk
2 (4-serving size) packages vanilla or banana cream flavor instant
    pudding and pie filling
1 1/2 cups prepared whipped topping

In a small glass bowl, microwave chocolate, milk, and butter or margarine on high heat 1 to 1 1/2 minutes; stirring every 30 seconds. Stir until chocolate is completely melted. Spread evenly into prepared graham cracker crust. Refrigerate 30 minutes or until chocolate is firm.

Arrange banana slices over chocolate mixture. In a large bowl, combine milk and pudding mixes; beat with wire whisk 1 minute. Let stand 5 minutes. Spoon over bananas in crust. Spread with prepared whipped topping. Refrigerate 4 hours or until set.

Makes 8 servings.

Chocolate Mousse Pie

So rich it will make your cheeks flush. Great with a good red wine.

Pastry for 9-inch one-crust pie (see page 122)
1 (12-ounce) package semisweet chocolate chips
1/2 cup prepared coffee
2 egg yolks
1/2 cup chilled whipping cream
1/8 cup sugar
4 egg whites, room temperature
1/8 teaspoon salt
Prepared whipped topping

Preheat oven to 400 degrees. Bake pie crust 15 minutes or until golden brown.

Melt chocolate chips in double boiler over hot water, stirring occasionally. Add coffee and stir until well blended; cool to room temperature. Add egg yolks, one at a time, beating thoroughly after each addition.

In a medium bowl, beat whipping cream until thickened; gradually beat in sugar until stiff. In a separate medium bowl, beat egg whites and salt until stiff peaks form. Gently fold egg whites into whipped cream.

Pour chocolate mixture into a large bowl. Combine one-third of the whipped cream and egg mixture into chocolate mixture; stir until well blended. Gently fold remaining cream and egg mixture into chocolate mixture. Pour into baked pie crust. Refrigerate 2 hours or until set. Serve with prepared whipped topping.

Makes 6 servings.

Pie Crust Cinnamon Rolls

Children (and adults) look forward to these cinnamon rolls made out of the leftover pie crust dough. Better yet, purposely make extra pie dough so as to make these cinnamon rolls.

*DIRECTIONS:
Roll out the leftover pie crust to a 1/8-inch thickness, brush with melted butter or margarine, and sprinkle generously with ground cinnamon and sugar. Roll into a long cylinder roll. Bake in the oven with your pie until golden brown. Slice and enjoy!*

Apples

1 pound (3 medium) apples equals 3 cups sliced apples.

Did you know that the apple tree is a member of the rose family? Also that there are about 7,500 varieties of apples in the world, but only twenty are grown commercially in this country? In fact, eight varieties of apples account for 80 percent of American apple production. They are Granny Smith, Golden Delicious, Red Delicious, McIntosh, Rome Beauty, Jonathan, York, and Stayman.

TIPS: Toss freshly cut apples in lemon juice and they won't darken.

To avoid wrinkled skins on apples when baking, cut a few slits in the skin to allow for expansion.

Apples will store for a longer period if they do not touch one another.

Fruit Etiquette

It is considered proper etiquette in England and on the Continent today, to eat peaches, pears, and bananas with a knife and a fork. They say only peasants, picknickers, and "Americans" pick up a piece of fruit and bite into it.

Country Apple Bake

1 (8-ounce) can refrigerated crescent rolls, divided into 8 triangles
Unsalted butter, melted
2 medium green tart cooking apples, halved, peeled, and cored
1 tablespoon sugar
1 teaspoon ground cinnamon
Apricot Sauce or Almond Sauce

Preheat oven to 400 degrees. For each dumpling, place 2 triangles of dough onto an ungreased jelly-roll pan or cookie sheet, with short sides touching; brush with some of the butter. Place an apple half, flat-side down, in center of buttered triangles of dough.

In a small bowl, combine sugar and cinnamon; sprinkle 1/4 of mixture over apple. Fold end of one triangle over apple; fold end of other triangle over apple, in same way, so a bit of apple peeks out of center. Repeat with the remaining apple halves and dough, making four dumplings in all.

Bake, uncovered, 20 to 30 minutes or until apples are tender and the pastry is lightly browned. Remove from oven and brush with remaining butter. Serve dumplings warm with hot Apricot or Almond Sauce spooned over the top.

Makes 8 servings.

APRICOT SAUCE:
1/4 cup apricot jam
3 tablespoons water
1 tablespoon butter
1/4 teaspoon ground nutmeg

In a small saucepan over low heat, combine apricot jam, water, butter, and nutmeg; stir and heat until hot.

ALMOND SAUCE:
1/2 cup sugar
1/2 cup whipping cream
1 egg
1 tablespoon Amaretto liqueur
1/2 cup sliced almonds

In a small bowl, using a wire whisk, combine sugar, whipping cream, egg, Amaretto liqueur, and almonds.

Deluxe Apple Dumplings

4 (6-inch) squares of puff pastry dough (phyllo)
4 tablespoons sugar, divided
4 tablespoons raisins, divided
4 medium green tart cooking apples, peeled and cored
2 eggs, lightly beaten
1 pint vanilla ice cream

Preheat the oven to 375 degrees. Using a floured rolling pin, on a lightly floured work surface, roll out a square of the puff pastry so that it is large enough to wrap around one of the apples.

Sprinkle the center of each puff pastry square with 1 tablespoon sugar; sprinkle 1 tablespoon of raisins over the sugar. Place an apple on top of the raisins. Brush some of the beaten eggs over the surrounding dough. Bring up all the sides so that the apple is covered and press the sides together at the top.

Place the pastry-covered apple upside down onto an ungreased baking sheet. Brush the outside of the dumpling with the beaten egg. Repeat the process with the remaining apples. Bake, uncovered, 20 to 30 minutes or until apples are tender and the pastry is lightly browned.

In a medium saucepan over low heat, melt the ice cream to create a sauce. Serve the baked apple dumplings on top of pools of the sauce.

Makes 4 servings.

Danish Apple Delight

This cake is almost like a pudding. Ben, our illustrator, says that as a child in the 1940s, one of his fondest memories was visiting his grandparents' farm. After dinner, Grandma would serve this wonderful cool dessert with fresh whipped cream.

2 teaspoons ground cinnamon
3 cups bread crumbs
2 tablespoons sugar
1/2 cup butter
3 cups sweetened applesauce
1 tablespoon vanilla extract
Prepared whipped topping
Cinnamon
1 large apple, cored, peeled, and sliced

In a medium saucepan over medium heat, combine cinnamon, bread crumbs, sugar, and butter and cook until browned; stir constantly, as it will burn easily. Remove from heat and transfer into a large bowl to stop the cooking process. Add applesauce and vanilla extract to cooked mixture.

Transfer into an ungreased 8-inch square dish and refrigerate until firm. When ready to serve, garnish with a dollop of prepared whipped topping, a sprinkle of cinnamon, and a couple of apple slices on each serving.

Makes 6 servings.

Phyllo Pastry

The most important thing to remember when working with phyllo is to keep it covered; otherwise, it will dry out and become brittle.

Have everything ready before you unwrap the phyllo. Place a stack of pastry sheets on a large piece of wax paper. Keep it covered with another sheet of wax paper and a damp cloth at all times. Don't let the damp cloth touch the phyllo itself. Remove one sheet of phyllo at a time.

Phyllo keeps for months in a refrigerator without spoiling if tightly wrapped.

TIP: Do not thaw frozen phyllo at room temperature. This will make the outside sheets sticky and leave the inner ones still unthawed. For best results, place the phyllo in the refrigerator for five hours or overnight.

Banana Desserts

Bananas

1 pound bananas equals 3 medium or 4 small bananas.

1 pound bananas equals 2 cups sliced or 1 1/2 cups mashed.

The banana was probably one of the first plants to be cultivated. The earliest historical reference to the fruit was 327 B.C., when Alexander the Great found them flourishing in India. Traders in the Indian Ocean carried the banana to the eastern coast of Africa, and Chinese traders introduced the banana to the Polynesians before the second century A.D.

The banana is harvested green, even for local consumption. It is the one fruit which, if left to ripen on the plant, never develops its best flavor. After they are picked, the sugar content increases from 2 percent to 20 percent. The yellower the skin, the sweeter the fruit will be.

After bananas have ripened, store in the refrigerator to help slow down ripening. The skin will turn dark brown, but this does not damage the fruit inside. If bananas become too ripe, freeze in their skins for later use in your banana breads.

Bananas Foster

This dish was created in the early 1950s at Brennan's Restaurant in New Orleans as part of a Breakfast at Brennan's promotion that has since become a city tradition. It was named after one of their regular customers.

1 large ripe banana
3 tablespoons firmly packed brown sugar
3 tablespoons butter
1 tablespoon lemon juice
1/8 teaspoon ground cinnamon
2 tablespoons banana liqueur (any flavored liqueur will work)
2 ounces white rum
Vanilla ice cream
Sweetened whipped cream or prepared whipped topping

Peel banana and slice in half lengthwise. In a large frying pan, simmer the banana halves gently in brown sugar and butter until golden brown and tender. Sprinkle with lemon juice and dust with cinnamon. Remove pan from heat.

In a small saucepan over medium heat, warm liqueur and rum; pour over banana mixture. (Optional: Set aflame, basting banana until the flame dies out.) Serve over ice cream with whipped cream or prepared whipped topping on top.

Makes 2 servings.

Bananas Baked in Orange Juice

6 to 8 medium bananas
1 medium orange, peeled and cut in chunks
2 tablespoons orange juice
1 tablespoon lemon juice
1/3 cup sugar
Ground cinnamon to taste
Ground nutmeg to taste
1/4 cup chopped nuts

Preheat oven to 325 degrees. Peel bananas; place bananas and oranges into an ungreased 13x9-inch baking dish.

In a small bowl, combine orange juice, lemon juice, sugar, cinnamon, nutmeg, and nuts; pour over bananas and oranges. Bake, uncovered, 25 to 30 minutes or until bananas are golden brown and tender. Remove from heat. Serve hot or cold.

Makes 6 to 8 servings.

Blueberry Coffee Cake

This is berry, berry, berry good.

2 cups all-purpose flour
3/4 cup sugar
2 1/2 teaspoons baking powder
3/4 teaspoon salt
1/4 cup vegetable oil
3/4 cup milk
1 egg
2 cups fresh or frozen blueberries
Sugar Topping

Preheat oven to 375 degrees. In a large bowl, combine flour, sugar, baking powder, salt, vegetable oil, milk, and egg. Fold in blueberries.

Pour into an ungreased 8-inch square baking dish. Sprinkle Sugar Topping onto top of cake batter. Bake, uncovered, 50 minutes or until a toothpick inserted in center comes out clean.

Makes 8 servings.

SUGAR TOPPING:
1/4 cup butter, room temperature.
1/2 cup sugar
1/3 cup all-purpose flour
1/2 teaspoon ground cinnamon

In a medium bowl with a pastry blender or two knives, cut butter into sugar, flour, and cinnamon until well blended.

Blueberries

1 pint fresh blueberries equals 2 cups.

1 (10-ounce) package frozen blueberries equals 1 1/2 cups.

The early American Indians valued the wild blueberries. They called them "star berries" because at the blossom end of each berry, the calyx forms a perfect five-pointed star. Their legends tell of a time when children were dying of hunger during a famine and the Great Spirit sent "star berries" to feed them.

Unwashed blueberries will stay fresh for up to two weeks in the refrigerator if kept dry.

FREEZING BLUEBERRIES: Place dry, unwashed, and unsweetened berries in freezing containers or plastic bags. Seal and freeze. The berries will freeze individually and pour out like marbles.

TIP: When using frozen blueberries in your baking, do not thaw them. Always add them frozen so they will not "bleed" in your baked goods.

Berry Desserts

Berries

When buying berries, shop with your nose. Always pick the plumpest and most fragrant berries. They should be firm, bright, and fresh looking with no mold or bruises. If possible, buy locally grown berries. They're likely to be sweeter and juicier than those that are bred for shipment.

Select berries that are in dry, unstained containers. (Stained containers may indicate oversoft berries that are not freshly picked.) Mold on berries spreads quickly. Never leave a moldy berry next to a good one.

Do not wash or hull berries until you're ready to use them, and refrigerate unwashed berries as soon as possible.

Store them in a colander in the refrigerator. This allows the cold air to circulate around them.

TIP: Remove berries from refrigerator one to two hours before serving. Berries are at their fullest flavor at room temperature.

Dumplings

To cook dumplings so that the bottoms don't get soggy, place them on top of the fruit mixture when it is bubbling hot. They will bake faster and be lighter. This will also work for cobblers.

Blueberry Kuchen

1 cup all-purpose flour
2 tablespoons sugar
1/4 teaspoon salt
1/2 cup chilled butter or margarine
1 tablespoon cider vinegar
2 tablespoons all-purpose flour
1 cup sugar
1/8 teaspoon ground cinnamon
3 cups fresh or frozen blueberries, divided
Powdered sugar

Preheat oven to 400 degrees. In a large bowl, combine 1 cup flour, 2 tablespoons sugar, and salt. With a pastry blender or two knives, cut in butter or margarine until particles are the size of small peas. Sprinkle vinegar evenly over surface; stir with a fork until all dry ingredients are moistened. Press pastry onto bottom and 1 inch up sides of an ungreased 9-inch springform pan.

In a medium bowl, combine 2 tablespoons flour, 1 cup sugar, and cinnamon. Stir in 2 cups blueberries; spread evenly over pastry. Bake, uncovered, 45 minutes. Remove from oven, and sprinkle remaining 1 cup blueberries evenly over top.

Cool in refrigerator until well chilled. To serve, slide a small knife around edge of kuchen to loosen it and remove sides of the springform pan; transfer onto a cake plate. Sprinkle with powdered sugar.

Makes 6 servings.

Blueberry Grunt

2 (15-ounce) cans blueberries
1/2 cup sugar
2 cups all-purpose flour
4 teaspoons baking powder
2 teaspoons grated orange zest
1/4 teaspoon ground nutmeg
1/4 teaspoon salt
1/2 cup chilled butter or margarine, cut into 1/2-inch cubes
3/4 cup milk

In a 10-inch cast-iron frying pan over medium heat, mix together blueberries, their juices, and sugar. Cook blueberries 15 to 20 minutes or until hot and bubbly.

In a large bowl, combine flour, baking powder, orange zest, nutmeg, and salt. With a pastry blender or two knives, cut in butter or margarine until particles are the size of small peas. Stir in milk until dry particles are just moistened. Drop dough by large spoonfuls onto top of hot blueberries.

Reduce heat to medium low. Cover frying pan and simmer 15 to 20 minutes or until topping is lightly browned. Remove from heat, remove cover, and cool on a wire rack for at least 10 minutes before serving.

Makes 8 servings.

Old-Fashioned Strawberry Shortcake

Nothing could be a more typical, totally American, dessert than strawberry shortcake.

5 cups fresh strawberries
2 to 3 tablespoons sugar
Shortcake
3 cups chilled whipping cream
Sugar to taste

Wash and hull strawberries; drain. In a large bowl, place strawberries and sprinkle with sugar; cover and refrigerate. Prepare shortcake.

In a medium bowl, beat the whipping cream until stiff peaks form; fold in sugar.

To serve, split baked shortcakes into halves. Ladle strawberries onto top of shortcake and top with a dollop of whipped cream.

NOTE: Best served when shortcake is warm. Shortcake can be reheated. The berries will be juicier if you crush a few before sugaring and let them sit for an hour before using.

Makes 8 servings.

SHORTCAKE:
4 cups all-purpose flour
1/2 cup sugar
2 tablespoons baking powder
1/4 teaspoon salt
1/2 cup chilled butter or margarine
1 egg, beaten
1 1/4 cups milk

Preheat oven to 400 degrees. Grease two large baking sheets. In a large bowl, combine flour, sugar, baking powder, and salt. With a pastry blender or two knives, cut in butter or margarine until particles are the size of small peas; stir in egg and milk.

On a lightly floured surface, using 1/2 cup dough per biscuit, pat dough into eight (4-inch rounds). Bake 15 to 17 minutes or until golden brown.

Strawberries

1 pint of fresh strawberries equals about 3 1/4 cups whole berries, or 2 1/4 cups sliced berries, or 1 2/3 cups puréed berries.

Did you know that the American Indians were actually cultivating strawberries in 1643?

By the 1800s, commercial strawberries had been cultivated. Strawberries are the leading small fruit crop in the United States today. They are farmed from Florida to Alaska, with the largest strawberry-growing centers located in California, Washington, Oregon, Louisiana, Michigan, and Tennessee.

Before using, sort through the strawberries and separate the soft ones from the firm, fully ripe berries. Discard any mushy or spoiled berries.

Remove caps from strawberries only after washing. The caps protect the flavor and texture of the fruit. Wash the berries just before you plan to use them. Use as soon as possible; strawberries ripen no further once picked.

Whipping Cream

1 cup whipping cream equals 2 cups whipped cream.

Fat content has a lot to do with how well cream whips. When you whip cream, you incorporate air into the mixture in the form of tiny bubbles. These air pockets are what gives the whipped cream its light, fluffy texture. Cream with a fat content of 30 percent or more can be whipped into a foam.

FOR BEST RESULTS IN WHIPPING CREAM, OBSERVE THESE GUIDELINES:

Whipping cream and all equipment should be well chilled. Place the bowl and beaters in the refrigerator for a short time.

Do not sweeten until the cream is whipped. Sugar decreases stability and makes the cream harder to whip. Use powdered sugar instead of granulated sugar for best stability.

Do not overwhip. Stop beating when the cream forms stiff peaks. If it is whipped longer, it first becomes granular and then turns into butter and whey.

Cream that is to be folded into other ingredients should be underbeaten, since the action of folding it in, whips it more and may overwhip it.

Strawberry Romanoff

VERSION 1:
2 pints fresh strawberries
1/3 cup sugar
1/3 cup Grand Marnier liqueur
1 orange
Sweetened whipped cream

Wash and hull berries; drain. In a medium bowl, combine strawberries, sugar, and Grand Marnier liqueur.

From the orange, using a paring knife, vegetable peeler, or zester, remove 1-inch piece of peel; cut into thin strips (do not cut into the white pulp). Add peel to strawberries and fold together gently. (Save orange for another use.) Cover bowl and refrigerate until ready to serve. To serve, top the strawberries with a dollop of whipped cream.

Makes 8 servings.

VERSION 2:
2 pints fresh strawberries
1/3 cup sugar
1 pint vanilla ice cream, room temperature
Sweetened whipped cream
Juice of 1 lemon
1/2 cup Cointreau liqueur

Wash and hull berries; drain. In a medium bowl, combine strawberries and sugar. In a medium bowl, whip ice cream slightly; fold in whipped cream. Add lemon juice and Cointreau liqueur; pour over strawberries and serve.

Makes 8 servings.

Amaretto Strawberries

1 pint fresh strawberries
1/4 cup Amaretto liqueur
Vanilla ice cream
Slivered almonds

Wash and hull strawberries; drain. In a large bowl, marinate strawberries in Amaretto liqueur overnight. Serve over ice cream and sprinkle with slivered almonds.

Makes 4 servings.

Strawberry Sundae With Syrup

This makes a very colorful dessert. It tastes as good as it looks.

1 quart fresh strawberries
1/3 cup sugar
2 tablespoons fresh lemon juice
1 quart best-quality vanilla ice cream, softened
Strawberry Syrup

Wash and hull berries; drain. In a food processor or blender, whirl the strawberries, sugar, and lemon juice into a smooth purée.

In a large bowl, combine strawberry purée and vanilla ice cream; stir until well blended. Freeze, covered, at least 8 hours or overnight until firm.

To serve, place scoops of the ice cream mixture into 4 to 6 large parfait glasses. Spoon Strawberry Syrup on top. Repeat layers.

Makes 4 to 6 servings.

STRAWBERRY SYRUP:
3/4 cup sugar
1 cinnamon stick
1 whole clove
2 peppercorns, cracked
1/4 teaspoon ground nutmeg
1/4 cup water
1 3/4 cups red wine
2 cups sliced fresh strawberries (1/4-inch thick)

In a large saucepan over medium-high heat, combine sugar, cinnamon stick, clove, peppercorns, nutmeg, and water; stir 6 to 8 minutes or until sugar is deep amber. Remove from heat; stir in wine. Return to heat and boil another 8 to 10 minutes, stirring often, or until volume is reduced to 1 cup.

Add strawberries. Reduce heat to low and simmer an additional 15 to 20 minutes, stirring occasionally, until mixture is reduced to 1 1/4 cups. Remove cinnamon stick and clove. Serve warm.

To Crack Peppercorns

Place peppercorns in a small plastic bag and seal tightly. Lay bag on a cutting board and hit with back of a spoon several times until they are cracked.

Gelatin

1 (1 1/4-ounce) envelope powdered gelatin equals 1 tablespoon powdered gelatin.

1 (1 1/4-ounce) envelope powdered gelatin will gel 2 cups of liquid.

Always soak gelatin in cold liquid (whatever recipe directs) for three to five minutes before dissolving it. This softens and swells the gelatin granules so that they will dissolve smoothly when heated.

To speed the setting of a gelatin mixture, place the bowl containing the mixture in a larger bowl of ice water. Stir constantly until mixture is cool and has reached the consistency desired. You can also speed the setting by starting the mold in the freezer for twenty to thirty minutes, then transfer to the refrigerator. Set a timer so you won't end up with a frozen dish.

A gelatin mixture that has set too fast can be saved and resoftened by placing the bowl containing the mixture in a larger bowl of warm water and stirring until mixture is desired consistency.

TIP: Never let a gelatin mixture boil. You'll destroy its setting capabilities.

Chocolate-Strawberry Cheesecake Mousse

This is a splendid dessert to serve for the finest occasion.

1 cup (24 cookies) vanilla wafer crumbs
1/3 cup butter or margarine, melted
1/2 cup finely chopped hazelnuts (any type of nut may be substituted)
3 packages unflavored gelatin
1/2 cup water
1 cup whipping cream
2 (8-ounce) packages cream cheese, room temperature
1/2 cup sugar
1 teaspoon vanilla extract
2 (10-ounce) packages frozen sliced strawberries in syrup, defrosted and undrained
4 (1-ounce) squares semisweet chocolate, grated (save some for garnish)
5 to 6 fresh strawberries, sliced

Preheat oven to 350 degrees. Lightly butter a 10-inch springform pan. In a food processor, whirl cookie crumbs to fine crumbs. Add butter and hazelnuts; whirl 5 to 10 seconds more. Press crumb mixture onto bottom and 1 inch up the sides of prepared pan. Bake 10 minutes. Remove from oven and cool crust completely on a wire rack.

In a small bowl, combine gelatin and water; let stand 4 to 5 minutes or until softened; set aside.

In a large bowl, beat whipping cream until stiff peaks form; set aside. In another large bowl combine cream cheese, sugar, and vanilla extract; beat until cream cheese is smooth and fluffy. Add gelatin mixture; stir until well blended. Fold in whipped cream, strawberries, and chocolate until well blended.

Pour mousse into the prepared crust. Cover with plastic wrap and refrigerate overnight. To serve, slide a small knife around edge of mousse to loosen it and remove sides of the springform pan; transfer onto a cake plate. Garnish with reserved grated chocolate and sliced strawberries.

NOTE: Frozen raspberries may be substituted for the strawberries.

Makes 8 to 10 servings.

Simply Strawberries

A very simple and elegant way to serve strawberries. It will remind you of cheesecake.

Fresh strawberries, washed, hulled, and dried
1 cup sour cream
1 cup firmly packed brown sugar

Place strawberries, sour cream, and brown sugar in separate bowls. To serve, let each guest dip a strawberry into sour cream and then into brown sugar. ENJOY!

Fresh Strawberries Dipped in Chocolate

During strawberry season, these are served as a finale to dinner. They also make attractive decorations for cakes.

1 (12-ounce) package semisweet chocolate chips
3/4 cup half and half cream
1 to 2 tablespoons brandy, your favorite liqueur, or 2 teaspoons prepared coffee
60 large fresh strawberries, rinsed, with stems left intact

In the top of a double boiler over hot water, melt chocolate; add cream, stirring until smooth. Remove from heat and blend in brandy, liqueur, or coffee.

Holding each berry by the stem, swirl in chocolate to partially cover; place onto wax paper-lined cookie sheet. Place into refrigerator until chocolate is set; transfer fruit onto a serving platter to serve.

Raspberry Brownie Delight

Absolutely the best dessert for summer.

1 (20-ounce) package light fudge-brownie mix
4 cups lowfat vanilla ice cream, softened
1/2 cup chocolate wafer crumbs (about 10 cookies)
2 cups fresh or frozen raspberries
1/4 cup sugar

Preheat oven to 350 degrees. Spray a 13x9-inch baking pan with vegetable-oil cooking spray. Prepare brownie mix according to package directions. Pour into prepared pan and bake 20 minutes. Remove from oven and cool completely on a wire rack.

Spread ice cream evenly over cooled brownies; sprinkle wafer cookies over the top. Cover and freeze 5 hours or overnight. In a medium bowl, combine raspberries and sugar. To serve, cut brownies into bars; top each bar with 2 tablespoons raspberries.

Makes 16 servings.

Raspberries

1 pint fresh raspberries equals about 2 cups raspberries (depending on the size).

Raspberries are at their very best when eaten fresh with a little sugar and perhaps some cream.

Raspberries should be picked in the early morning hours. They should easily fall from their caps when picked. Attached hulls are a sign that the berries were picked too early and will be tart.

Fresh raspberries can be stored, unwashed, in the refrigerator for two days.

FREEZING RASPBERRIES: To freeze, lay the berries onto a cookie sheet and freeze for three to four hours or until firm. Then transfer into plastic bags or containers. (By freezing this way, they will separate easily for later use.)

DO NOT WASH THE BERRIES BEFORE FREEZING. Thaw frozen raspberries in the refrigerator.

Blackberries

1 pint fresh blackberries equals 1 1/2 to 2 cups blackberries (depending on size).

Select plump, well-colored blackberries. They should not have stem caps attached. If hulls are still attached, the berries are immature and were picked too early. Avoid berries showing any signs of decay.

Pick through berries and discard any that are bruised or decaying; cover with plastic wrap and refrigerate for up to two days. Do not wash until shortly before using.

Blackberry Cobbler

This old-fashioned cobbler is absolutely wonderful.

1 1/2 cups sugar
1/2 cup all-purpose flour
8 cups fresh or frozen blackberries
3 tablespoons lemon juice
3 tablespoons butter or margarine
Biscuit Topping
Vanilla ice cream

Preheat oven to 400 degrees. In a large bowl, combine sugar, flour, blackberries, and lemon juice. Pour into an ungreased 13x9-inch baking dish; dot with butter or margarine.

Bake, uncovered, 15 to 20 minutes or until hot and bubbly. When blackberry mixture is hot, spoon Biscuit Topping mixture onto the top in 10 or 12 large spoonfuls. Return to oven and bake another 20 minutes or until biscuits are lightly browned. Remove from oven and cool on a wire rack for a least 10 minutes before serving. To serve, top with vanilla ice cream.

Makes 12 servings.

BISCUIT TOPPING:
2 cups all-purpose flour
4 teaspoons baking powder
3 tablespoons sugar
1 teaspoon salt
1/2 cup chilled butter or margarine, cut into 1/4-inch pieces
2/3 cup milk
1 egg, slightly beaten

In a large bowl, sift together flour, baking powder, sugar, and salt. With a pastry blender or two knives, cut in butter or margarine until particles are the size of small peas. Add milk and egg; stir with a fork just until blended.

Tortillas Fantastics

2 cups cherry pie filling
4 flour tortillas
Slivered almonds
Vegetable oil
Powdered sugar

Reserve 1/4 cup cherry filling for topping. Spoon remainder onto centers of flour tortillas. Sprinkle 1 to 2 tablespoons almonds onto center of each. Fold in half and roll tortillas around filling.

In a large frying pan over medium-high heat, heat vegetable oil. (To test temperature of oil, dip edge of tortilla into oil. If it sizzles, oil is hot enough.) Place 2 tortillas seam-side down in frying pan; fry 1 minute on each side or until light golden brown and crispy. Drain briefly on paper towels. Fry remaining tortillas.

To serve, place onto individual serving plates. Sift powdered sugar over each. Top with remaining cherry pie filling and slivered almonds. Serve hot.

Makes 4 servings.

Quick Cherry Dessert

1 cup butter or margarine, room temperature
1 1/2 cups sugar
4 eggs
1 teaspoon almond extract
2 cups all-purpose flour
2 teaspoons baking powder
1 (21-ounce) can cherry pie filling
Powdered sugar
Prepared whipped topping

Preheat oven to 350 degrees. Grease a 13x9-inch baking pan. In a large bowl, combine butter or margarine and sugar until well blended. Add eggs and beat until blended. Stir in almond extract. Stir in flour and baking powder. Spread mixture into prepared pan; spoon pie filling, in 16 even spots, onto top.

Bake, uncovered, 45 to 50 minutes or until a toothpick inserted in center comes out clean (filling will sink into cake while baking). Remove from oven.

Cover with a serving platter and invert. Dust with powdered sugar. To serve, spoon prepared whipped topping onto top.

Makes 16 servings.

Tart or Sour Cherries

1 pound fresh cherries equals 2 1/2 to 3 cups pitted cherries.

Montmorency is the most popular of the sour cherry varieties and may be eaten fresh. They are harvested in July and are light to dark red.

TIP: For an even sweeter sour cherry, leave the cherries on the trees until just before you think they will rot. The sugar content is the highest then.

Fresh sour cherries are not usually sold in the markets, just canned. You'll need to find a farmers' market to purchase them fresh.

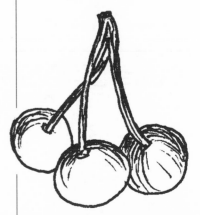

Unsalted Butter

Unsalted butter is preferred for cooking and baking because it allows the cook to adjust the seasoning.

Because unsalted butter contains absolutely no salt, it's more perishable than salted butter. It should be stored in the refrigerator for no more than two weeks. It can be placed in a plastic bag and frozen for up to six months.

TIP: If you do not have unsalted butter and the recipe calls for it, use regular butter. Since regular butter has salt, leave the salt out of the recipe.

Cherry Delight

Very rich and wonderful tasting. Serve this to your guests.

1 cup all-purpose flour
1 1/4 cups sugar
1 teaspoon baking soda
1 teaspoon ground cinnamon
1/2 teaspoon salt
1 tablespoon butter or margarine, melted
1 egg, beaten
2 cups fresh or frozen pitted sour cherries, drained (reserve 1 cup juice)
1/2 teaspoon almond extract
1/2 cup chopped nuts (walnuts, pecans, or hazelnuts)
Cherry Sauce
Prepared whipped topping

Preheat oven to 350 degrees. In a large bowl, sift together flour, sugar, baking soda, cinnamon, and salt. In a medium bowl, combine butter or margarine, egg, sour cherries, almond extract, and nuts; add to flour mixture.

Bake, uncovered, in an ungreased 9-inch square pan 40 to 45 minutes or until a toothpick inserted in center comes out clean. Remove from oven and cut into squares. Serve with hot Cherry Sauce and prepared whipped topping.

Makes 8 servings.

CHERRY SAUCE:
1 cup cherry juice
1 tablespoon cornstarch
1/2 cup sugar
1/4 teaspoon almond extract
1 tablespoon butter or margarine

In a small saucepan over medium-high heat, combine cherry juice, cornstarch, sugar, almond extract, and butter or margarine; cook for 10 minutes; stirring constantly.

Cherry Biscuit Cobbler

1 3/4 cups sugar
1 1/2 tablespoons cornstarch
1 tablespoon quick-cooking tapioca
1 1/2 (6 cups) pounds fresh or frozen pitted sour cherries
1 teaspoon almond extract
Biscuit Dough
1 tablespoon unsalted butter, melted
1 tablespoon sugar

Preheat oven to 450 degrees and line the oven floor with aluminum foil to catch any drips.

In a large bowl, combine 1 3/4 cups sugar with cornstarch and tapioca; fold in cherries and almond extract. Pour cherry mixture into an ungreased 3-quart baking dish or a 10-inch glass pie plate.

Make a lattice top over the cobbler with the Biscuit Dough. Brush the lattice top with butter; sprinkle 1 tablespoon sugar over the butter.

Bake, uncovered, 20 minutes or until the top is beginning to brown. Lower oven temperature to 350 degrees and bake another 30 minutes (if the edge is browning too quickly, cover it with aluminum foil). Remove from oven and cool on a wire rack at least 30 minutes. Serve warm or at room temperature.

NOTE: If at all possible, use fresh sour cherries in this recipe. If you must use canned cherries, cut the sugar back to 3/4 cup.

Makes 6 to 8 servings.

BISCUIT DOUGH:
2 cups all-purpose flour
1 tablespoon baking powder
1/2 teaspoon salt
1/2 cup chilled unsalted butter, cut into 1/2-inch cubes
3/4 cup chilled milk

In a food processor, whirl the flour, baking powder and salt until mixed. Add the butter and whirl until particles are the size of small peas. Drizzle milk evenly over the dry ingredients and whirl a few times, just until dough forms small clumps.

On a lightly floured surface, roll out dough 1/8-inch thick and at least as large as the baking dish you are using. Lift the dough frequently as you roll and lightly reflour the surface to prevent the dough from sticking. Using a fluted pastry wheel, cut the dough into 1 1/2-inch wide strips.

Lattice Crusts

To weave, place half of the dough strips from left to right over cobbler, about 3/4-inch apart. Fold back every other strip halfway.

Place a strip across the unfolded strips from front to back. Unfold the strips. Fold back the alternates. Place the next strip 3/4-inch from the last. Continue until half of the cobbler is latticed. Then repeat the process, beginning on the other side of the center line.

Trim the overhanging dough flush with the edge of the baking dish.

Papaya & Peach Desserts

Papayas

Papayas are also known as pawpaw, the medicine tree, and the melon tree.

Papayas that are fully ripe are golden yellow in color. Look for smooth-skinned papayas with as little green as possible on the skin. Ripe fruit is slightly soft when pressed.

Keep at room temperature until fully ripe; then store in a plastic bag in the refrigerator for up to one week.

Peaches

1 pound fresh peaches (4 to 5 medium peaches) equals 2 1/2 cups sliced or 2 1/4 cups chopped peaches.

When purchasing peaches, the best thing to remember is that they must look good to be good. Buy peaches which are fairly firm or just becoming a trifle soft. Don't buy peaches with large bruises, or they will not ripen properly.

Ripe peaches can be stored in a plastic bag in the refrigerator for up to five days.

PEELING PEACHES: Peaches can be peeled easily by dipping them in boiling water for twenty to thirty seconds and then plunging them immediately into ice water. The skins will then slip off readily.

Baked Papaya

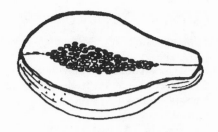

1/4 cup butter or margarine
1 teaspoon ground ginger
1 teaspoon ground coriander
1/4 teaspoon curry powder
3 teaspoons honey
3 teaspoons lime juice
2 papayas, cut in half and seeded

Preheat oven to 325 degrees. In a small saucepan over low heat, melt butter or margarine. Add ginger, coriander, curry powder, honey, and lime juice, stir until well blended. Place papaya halves into an ungreased baking dish, cut side up. Brush with butter mixture.

Bake, uncovered, 25 minutes. Baste occasionally with the butter mixture until papayas are fork-tender. Remove from oven and cool on a wire rack at least 10 minutes before serving.

Makes 4 servings.

Peach Cream Freeze

A great dessert that can be made ahead of time. No last-minute hassle with this dessert.

1 (29-ounce) can peach halves, drained and cut into cubes
1 (14-ounce) can sweetened condensed milk
1 (8-ounce) can crushed pineapple, drained
1/4 cup lemon juice
1/4 teaspoon almond extract
1 cup chilled whipping cream
Chopped nuts

In a large bowl, combine peach halves, sweetened condensed milk, pineapple, lemon juice, and almond extract.

In a chilled medium bowl, beat whipping cream until stiff peaks form; fold into peach mixture (reserving some whipped cream for garnish). Spoon mixture into an ungreased 9x5-inch loaf pan. Freeze until firm.

To serve, unmold and slice. Garnish each serving with reserved whipped cream and chopped nuts. Serve immediately.

Makes 8 servings.

Gingered Pineapple

1 fresh pineapple (with green leaves)
1/4 cup dark rum
1 teaspoon ground ginger
1/2 cup shredded coconut
Sliced strawberries
Mint leaves

Cut pineapple in half lengthwise through green top; cut each half into halves. Cut core from each quarter and cut along curved edges of fruit with knife. Cut fruit widthwise into 3/4-inch slices; then cut lengthwise down center of slices, leaving cut fruit in the shell.

In a small bowl, combine rum and ginger; spoon over pineapple. Cover and refrigerate at least 4 hours but no longer than 24 hours.

Preheat oven to 350 degrees. Bake coconut, uncovered, in an ungreased baking pan 8 to 10 minutes, stirring occasionally, or until golden brown. Remove from oven and cool on a wire rack. To serve, sprinkle coconut, strawberries, and mint leaves over the tops of the fruit-filled pineapple quarters.

Makes 4 servings.

Spiced Pear Halves

1/4 cup prepared mincemeat
3 tablespoons water
1 orange
1 tablespoon butter or margarine
2 fresh pears, peeled, cored and cut in half
1/4 cup white port wine or apple juice, divided

In a 1-cup glass measuring cup, combine mincemeat and water. In a microwave, cook on high 2 to 2 1/2 minutes, stirring once, or until water is absorbed.

From an orange, using a paring knife, a vegetable peeler, or a zester, remove an 1-inch piece of peel; cut into thin strips (do not cut into the white pulp) and set aside for garnish. Grate remaining orange peel to yield 1/2 teaspoon of zest; stir grated zest and butter into mincemeat. (Reserve remaining orange for another use.)

Place pear halves, cut side up, into an ungreased 8-inch square baking dish. Over each pear half, pour 1 tablespoon wine or apple juice; spoon 1 1/2 tablespoons mincemeat mixture into each half. Cover with wax paper; cook in microwave on high 4 to 6 minutes or until pears are fork-tender. Remove from microwave and let stand 1 minute before serving.

Makes 4 servings.

Pineapples

Best March through June. Buy pineapples as large and heavy as available. Leaves at top should be deep green. Do not buy if they have soft spots.

TIP: Do not use fresh pineapples in gelatin desserts. They contain an enzyme that prevents gelatin from setting.

Pears

Summer pears turn yellow or crimson as they mature. Most varieties you'll find in the winter remain brown or green. To tell if a pear is ready to eat, see if it gives slightly near the stem when pressed. If the fruit's base is soft, the pear is overripe.

Pears should be fully ripe for "fresh" use, such as eating out of hand, salads, or shortcakes. If they are hard and unyielding to the touch at time of purchase, allow them to stand at room temperature until the flesh responds readily to a gentle pressure of the hand.

TIPS: Pears ripen quickly by placing them in a brown paper bag along with a ripe apple. Place in a cool spot and make certain a few holes are punched into the bag. This trick has the same effect on peaches and tomatoes.

For baking and other cooking purposes, pears are best when they are still firm and slightly under-ripe.

Fruit Pizza

A beautiful dessert for brunch or any special occasion. It will not keep well, so plan on using it up. You may also use your own sugar cookie recipe in place of the refrigerated cookie dough.

1 (18-ounce) package refrigerated cookie dough
1 (8-ounce) package cream cheese, room temperature
1/3 cup sugar
1/2 teaspoon vanilla extract or other flavoring (almond, orange, or lemon)
Fresh blueberries, banana slices, mandarin orange sections, seedless grapes,
    strawberry halves, kiwi fruit (or any other fruit you want), well drained
1/2 cup orange, peach, or apricot preserves
1 tablespoon water

Preheat oven to 375 degrees. Line an ungreased 14-inch pizza pan with cookie dough cut in 1/8-inch slices, overlapping slightly. Bake 12 minutes or until light brown; remove from oven and cool on a wire rack.

In a medium bowl, combine cream cheese, sugar, and vanilla extract or other flavoring; spread over cookie crust. Arrange fruit over cream cheese layer in any design you want (use your imagination).

In a small saucepan over very low heat, make a glaze by heating preserves and water. Brush glaze over fruit, making sure to cover the fruit that will turn dark. Refrigerate until ready to serve.

Makes 8 to 10 servings.

Ambrosia

A traditional Christmas dish in many Southern homes, where the dessert is served in the best cut-glass bowl from the sideboard.

Ambrosia has been around a long time. As a matter of fact, in the ancient days, the gods ate ambrosia because they thought it was a magical substance and kept them immortal. Without it, a god became weak. A human who ate it became strong and immortal.

Heavenly Ambrosia

2 firm medium bananas, peeled and sliced
1 (8 1/4-ounce) can crushed pineapple, drained
1 cup miniature marshmallows
1 cup shredded coconut, divided
1 cup seedless grapes
1/2 cup coarsely chopped walnuts
1/2 cup whipping cream
1/2 teaspoon grated lime zest
1 tablespoon fresh lime juice
2 teaspoons sugar
1 (11-ounce) can mandarin oranges, drained

In a large bowl, combine bananas, pineapple, marshmallows, 1/2 cup coconut, grapes, and walnuts.

In a medium bowl, beat whipping cream, lime zest, lime juice, and sugar until stiff; fold into banana mixture. Fold in mandarin oranges. Spoon onto dessert plates or into tall glasses. To serve, sprinkle each serving with remaining coconut.

Makes 4 to 6 servings.

Vermont Maple Treats

MAPLE SAUCE:
3/4 cup genuine Vermont maple syrup
1/2 cup butter
3/4 cup firmly packed brown sugar
1/2 cup chopped nuts

In a small saucepan over low heat, combine maple syrup and butter; cook until butter is melted. Stir in brown sugar until it is dissolved and well blended. Stir in chopped nuts. Divide mixture into two ungreased 9-inch pie plates; set aside.

COCONUT FILLING:
1 (8-ounce) package cream cheese, room temperature
3 tablespoons butter or margarine, room temperature
1/4 cup powdered sugar
1/2 cup shredded coconut

In a large bowl, combine cream cheese and butter or margarine; cream until well blended. Sift powdered sugar into cream cheese mixture; stir until well blended. Stir in coconut; set aside.

BUTTERMILK BISCUITS:
Old-Fashioned Biscuits (see page 48)

Preheat oven to 350 degrees. Prepare biscuit dough. Gently roll dough to 1/4-inch thickness. Cut with a floured 3-inch biscuit cutter into twenty round biscuits. Flatten each circle with your hand to form a 4-inch round.

Place 1 teaspoon of Coconut Filling onto center of dough; wrap dough around the filling; pinching edges to seal. Set biscuits into pie pans onto top of Maple Sauce, sealed edges up. Bake, uncovered, 20 minutes or until biscuits are light brown. Remove from oven and cool on a wire rack at least 10 minutes before serving.

Yields 20.

Maple Parfait

4 egg yolks, beaten
1 cup pure genuine Vermont maple syrup
2 cups chilled whipping cream

In the top of a double boiler over hot water, combine eggs and maple syrup; cook until mixture coats a metal spoon. Remove from heat and refrigerate.

In a large bowl, beat whipping cream until stiff; fold in maple mixture. Cover with aluminum foil and let freeze until firm. To serve, spoon into glass serving dishes.

Makes 8 servings.

Maple Syrup

Maple syrup is a native American product. It is now considered a delicacy, but in colonial days it was used extensively as an ordinary sweetener.

PURE MAPLE SYRUP: Pure maple syrup is sap that has been boiled until much of the water has evaporated. It has a more subtle flavor and is not as sweet as artificial maple syrups. It is graded according to color and flavor. The higher the grade, the lighter the color, and more delicate the flavor.

Pure maple syrup should always be refrigerated after opening to keep mold from forming. Maple syrup can be refrigerated for up to one year.

MAPLE-FLAVORED SYRUP: It is a mixture of low-cost syrup, such as corn syrup, and a small amount of pure maple syrup.

PANCAKE SYRUP: It is nothing more than corn syrup flavored with artificial maple extract.

Vanilla Extract

Vanilla is the bean of a delicate climbing pale yellow orchid which grows in clusters of a dozen or so blooms, but which only flowers one by one for a day.

The vanilla bean originated in southern Mexico, and to this day, the best vanilla comes from the state of Veracruz in Mexico.

Store liquid vanilla extract in an airtight container in a cool, dark place, or it can be refrigerated. Store whole vanilla beans in glass jars with tightly fitting lids in a cool, dark place.

Vanilla beans can be reused to flavor a dish if immediately washed and dried. Vanilla sugar is another way of storing the bean. Just store a vanilla bean in a jar of granulated sugar.

VANILLA EXTRACT: Place six long vanilla beans, split open and cut into pieces, into one quart of good-quality vodka. Cap tightly and place in a cool, dark place. Leave for four to six weeks, shaking the bottle occasionally.

Before using, pour through a strainer lined with cheesecloth (or use a coffee filter), rinse the bottle to remove residue, and pour back into the bottle. Add one whole vanilla bean and cap tightly until used.

Baked Custard

3 eggs, slightly beaten
1/3 cup sugar
1 teaspoon vanilla extract
1/8 teaspoon salt
2 1/2 cups milk, scalded
Ground nutmeg

Preheat oven to 350 degrees. In a large bowl, combine eggs, sugar, vanilla extract, and salt. Gradually stir in milk. Pour into six (6-ounce) custard cups; sprinkle with nutmeg. Place cups into a rectangular pan on oven rack. Pour very hot water into pan, within 1/2 inch of tops of cups.

Bake, uncovered, 45 minutes or until a knife inserted halfway between center and edge comes out clean. Remove from oven and remove custard cups from water. Serve warm or chilled.

Makes 6 servings.

New Orleans Bread Pudding

3 tablespoons butter or margarine, melted
1 loaf french bread
4 cups milk
3 eggs
2 cups sugar
2 tablespoons vanilla extract
1 cup raisins
Whiskey Sauce

Preheat oven to 350 degrees. Pour butter into a 13x9-inch baking pan. In a large bowl, soak bread in milk; crush with your hands until well mixed. Stir in eggs, sugar, vanilla extract, and raisins.

Pour mixture into prepared pan. Bake, uncovered, 1 to 1 1/2 hours or until very firm. Remove from oven and cool on a wire rack. To serve, cut into squares and put into individual serving dishes. Serve warm with Whiskey Sauce.

Makes 6 servings.

WHISKEY SAUCE:
1 cup sugar
1 egg
1/2 cup butter or margarine, melted
Whiskey to taste

In a medium saucepan over medium heat, combine sugar and egg; stir until well blended. Add butter or margarine; stir until sugar is dissolved. Stir in whiskey.

Tapioca Pudding

4 eggs, separated and room temperature
3 3/4 cups milk
6 tablespoons quick-cooking tapioca
10 tablespoons sugar, divided
1/4 teaspoon salt
2 teaspoons vanilla extract
Zest of 1 lemon

In a large saucepan, slightly beat egg yolks; stir in milk, tapioca, 6 tablespoons sugar, and salt; let stand 5 minutes. Bring to a full boil over medium heat, stirring constantly; remove from heat.

In a large bowl, beat egg whites until frothy; add 4 tablespoons sugar and continue beating until stiff peaks form. Add egg whites, vanilla extract, and lemon zest to hot milk mixture; stir until well blended. Pour into serving dishes and refrigerate.

Makes 8 servings.

Tapioca

If you are out of instant or quick-cooking tapioca and have only pearl tapioca in your pantry, just place it in a spice grinder, blender, or food processor and grind away. You now have instant tapioca.

Overstirring a tapioca mixture while cooling it produces a sticky, gelatinous texture.

TIP: Store tapioca in an airtight container in a cool, dry place; it will keep indefinitely.

Quick Chocolate Pots de Crème

A chocolate lover's delight. This is a very rich and delicious dessert.

2/3 cup light cream
1 cup semisweet chocolate chips
3 tablespoons very strong prepared coffee
2 tablespoons coffee liqueur or brandy
2 eggs
Sweetened whipped cream
Chocolate curls
Chopped nuts

In a small, heavy saucepan over medium-low heat, heat light cream just to boiling; remove from heat. In a food processor or blender, combine chocolate chips, coffee, coffee liqueur or brandy, eggs, and cream; cover and blend at high speed for about 3 minutes.

Pour into six demitasse cups or small custard cups. Refrigerate at least 4 hours or overnight. To serve, top with whipped cream; garnish with chocolate curls and nuts.

Makes 6 servings.

Perfect Crème Brûlée

Very few desserts are more delicious to eat and to look at. Translated from the French, this popular dessert means "burnt cream," referring to the caramelized finish. A classic finale to a meal, crème brûlée can be served slightly warm or chilled.

6 egg yolks, chilled
6 tablespoons sugar
1 1/2 cups whipping cream, chilled
4 tablespoons firmly packed dark brown sugar

Preheat oven to 275 degrees. Adjust oven rack to center position. Butter six (6-ounce) custard cups and set them into a glass baking dish.

In a medium bowl, beat egg yolks until slightly thickened. Add sugar and mix until dissolved; mix in cream, then pour mixture into prepared custard cups. Set baking dish on oven rack and pour warm water into dish to come halfway up the custard cups.

Bake, uncovered, 45 minutes or until custards are just barely set. Remove baking dish from oven, leaving custard cups in the hot water; cool on a wire rack to room temperature. Remove each custard cup from water and cover with plastic wrap; refrigerate at least 2 hours or overnight.

While custards are cooling, spread brown sugar in a small baking pan; set in turned-off (but still warm) oven 20 minutes or until sugar dries. Transfer sugar to a small zipper-lock freezer bag; seal bag and crush sugar fine with a rolling pin. Store sugar in an airtight container until ready to top custards.

When ready to top custards, adjust oven rack to the next-to-the-highest position and heat broiler. Remove chilled custard cups from refrigerator and uncover; sprinkle 2 teaspoons brown sugar on top of each. Set custard cups in a baking dish. Broil 2 to 3 minutes or until toppings are golden brown, watching constantly and rotating pan for even caramelization. Remove from oven and refrigerate 30 minutes. Serve within 1 hour, as topping will deteriorate.

Makes 6 servings.

Crème Caramel Topping Shortcuts

Instead of coating the bottom of each cup mold with caramelized sugar, use a tablespoon of real maple syrup.

Another shortcut is to pack a tablespoon of brown sugar into the bottom of each cup. It melts during baking and provides a lovely brown "caramel sauce."

TIP: This is a tip used by many chefs. Use a mini blowtorch to caramelize tops (they are available in hardware stores). They caramelize sugar on top of desserts and tarts very efficiently.

Chocolate-Rum Flan

1 cup sugar
1 (14-ounce) can sweetened condensed milk
1 (12-ounce) can evaporated milk
2 eggs
6 egg yolks
1/4 cup chocolate syrup
2 tablespoons rum

Preheat oven to 375 degrees. Adjust oven rack to center position. Set six (6-ounce) custard cups into a glass baking dish.

In a medium saucepan over medium heat, add sugar, stirring constantly, 10 minutes or until the sugar has melted and is a light amber color. Remove from heat and pour caramel sugar into individual custard cups.

In a food processor or blender, combine sweetened condensed milk, evaporated milk, eggs, egg yolks, chocolate syrup, and rum; whirl until smooth. Pour flan mixture over the caramel sugar. Set baking dish on oven rack and pour warm water into dish to come halfway up the custard cups.

Bake, uncovered, 15 minutes. Reduce heat to 350 degrees and bake another 30 minutes or until custards are just barely set. Remove baking dish from oven, leaving custard cups in the hot water; cool on a wire rack to room temperature. Remove each custard cup from water and cover with plastic wrap; refrigerate at least 2 hours or overnight. To serve, run a knife around the inside edges of the custard cups and invert the flans onto individual serving plates.

Makes 6 servings.

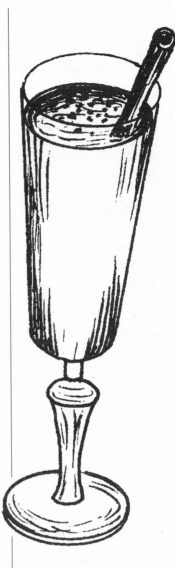

Cappuccino Cream

1 envelope unflavored gelatin
1/4 cup plus 2 tablespoons sugar
2 cups skim milk
2 eggs, separated and room temperature
1 teaspoon powdered instant espresso coffee
2 teaspoons coffee-flavored liqueur
2 tablespoons semisweet chocolate chips, pulverized in a food processor
3 tablespoons finely chopped walnuts
7 cinnamon sticks for garnish, optional
Grated unsweetened chocolate for garnish, optional

In a large saucepan, combine the gelatin and sugar; set aside. In a large bowl, beat milk, egg yolks, and coffee until frothy. Stir into gelatin mixture; cook mixture over low heat, stirring constantly, 7 minutes or until thickened very slightly. Remove from heat and transfer back into the bowl. Stir in coffee-flavored liqueur; chill 1 1/2 to 2 hours until the mixture mounds when dropped from a spoon. (If the coffee mixture has jelled, beat it to make it smooth.) Stir in the pulverized chocolate chips.

In a small bowl, beat egg whites until stiff; fold into coffee mixture. Divide the cappuccino cream among seven champagne glasses; sprinkle with walnuts, and refrigerate at least 2 to 3 hours or overnight. To serve, garnish with a cinnamon stick and grated chocolate.

Makes 7 servings.

Instant Espresso Coffee

1 teaspoon powdered instant espresso coffee can be substituted for 2 teaspoons granulated instant coffee.

Instant espresso coffee can be found with the instant coffee in large stores and in gourmet-coffee shops.

Creams

Devonshire Cream

The real Devonshire cream is made by allowing milk to stand for six to twenty-three hours or until the cream rises to the top.

Next, the pan is set over very low heat until the milk is quite hot, though it must never be allowed to boil. The more slowly this process can be done, the better will be the results.

As soon as the milk is hot, it should be put in a cool place for twenty-four hours. The thick cream is then skimmed off and stored in jars. It is usually served with fresh fruit.

Devonshire Cream

Also called Mock Devonshire Cream. Excellent on hot scones or with fresh strawberries.

3 ounces cream cheese, room temperature
1 tablespoon sugar
1/8 teaspoon salt
1 cup whipping cream

In a large bowl, combine cream cheese, sugar, and salt; stir until well blended. Stir in whipping cream. With an electric mixer, beat mixture until stiff. Store in refrigerator.

Crème Fraîche

Crème Fraîche is widely used in France, where the cream is unpasteurized and contains the "friendly" bacteria necessary to thicken it naturally.

Commercial crème fraîche is quite expensive, so this homemade version is a life saver.

Since crème fraîche doesn't curdle when boiled, it's the ideal thickener for many sauces and soups.

Vegetables (particularly potatoes) benefit from a dollop of it. It's also delicious on fresh fruit, cakes, cobblers, and puddings.

Crème Fraîche

1 cup whipping cream, room temperature
1 tablespoon buttermilk or 1/2 cup sour cream, room temperature

In a jar with a lid, place whipping cream and buttermilk or sour cream; cover securely and shake 15 seconds. Set aside at room temperature for 24 hours or until very thick. Stir once or twice during that time. Cream will thicken faster if the room is warm.

Stir thickened crème fraîche well. Refrigerate at least 6 hours before serving. Cover tightly and store in refrigerator for up to 2 weeks.

WHIPPED CRÈME FRAÎCHE: Beat crème fraîche until soft peaks form (it won't become stiff).

SWEETENED CRÈME FRAÎCHE: Add 1 to 2 tablespoons powdered sugar before shaking the cream.

VANILLA-FLAVORED CRÈME FRAÎCHE: Stir 1 to 1 1/2 teaspoons vanilla extract into crème fraîche just before refrigerating.

Cappuccino Cream Topping

Excellent over cakes, bread puddings, and mousses.

1 cup whipping cream
1 tablespoon instant espresso coffee powder or 1 1/2 tablespoons instant coffee
   granules
1 teaspoon vanilla extract
1/4 cup powdered sugar
2 tablespoons coffee-flavored liqueur

In a large bowl, combine whipping cream and instant coffee; stir until coffee dissolves. Beat the cream mixture at high speed until it is the consistency of thick pudding. Add vanilla extract and powdered sugar; beat until soft peaks form. With mixer running, gradually drizzle in coffee-flavored liqueur, beating until cream is desired consistency.

Yields 2 cups.

Burnt Caramel Cream

Excellent served on pound cakes and over fresh fruit.

1/2 cup sugar
2 tablespoons water
1/8 teaspoon salt
1 teaspoon vanilla extract
1 cup heavy whipping cream

In a small saucepan over medium heat, combine sugar, water, and salt; let sit until well blended. Cook, without stirring, until mixture turns a golden brown. Immediately remove from heat.

Stirring constantly with a wooden spoon, very gradually add whipping cream (mixture will clump and harden). Return to medium heat, stirring constantly, until mixture is smooth.

In a medium bowl, place caramel cream. Cover and chill until very cold (about 1 1/2 hours in the freezer or 3 hours in the refrigerator). May be refrigerated for up to 3 days.

Up to 6 hours before serving, beat the caramel cream until stiff peaks form. Cover and refrigerate until ready to use.

Yields 1 1/2 cups.

Cream

Refrigerate cream in the coldest part of the refrigerator. Most creams will keep up to one week past the pull date on the carton.

You can freeze cream as long as there is at least 1/2 inch of airspace at the top of the cardboard container. Double wrap the container in a freezer-proof plastic bag. Defrost in the refrigerator overnight; shake well before using.

> *SUBSTITUTION FOR LIGHT CREAM IN COOKING OR BAKING:*
> *7/8 cup of whole milk and 3 tablespoons of butter.*

If you think cream has just begun to sour, whisk in one-eight teaspoon baking soda. Taste the cream before using to make sure the flavor is acceptable.

Lemon Curd

A British teatime favorite. This sweet, yet tart, velvety spread is heavenly on freshly baked scones, muffins, and tea breads.

Fruit Dips

Fruits make a wonderful and light refreshing snack or appetizer. Try some of these fruits with your favorite fruit dip:

- *Apple wedges*
- *Pear wedges*
- *Banana slices*
- *Orange wedges*
- *Dark sweet cherries*
- *Strawberries*
- *Cantaloupe chunks*
- *Honeydew melon chunks*
- *Peach slices*

Lemon Curd

3 to 4 tablespoons lemon zest
1/2 cup fresh lemon juice (4 to 6 lemons)
1 1/2 cups sugar
6 tablespoons butter
3 eggs, lightly beaten

In a medium saucepan over medium-high heat, combine lemon zest, lemon juice, and sugar. Bring to a boil; reduce heat to medium-low and simmer 5 minutes. Add butter and stir until it has melted.

Remove from the heat and cool to room temperature. Beat eggs into lemon-sugar mixture until well blended. Cook, stirring constantly, 10 to 15 minutes or until mixture thickens and coats spoon. Store in the refrigerator.

Fluffy Fruit Dip

1/3 cup apricot preserves or orange marmalade
1 cup sour cream
1/4 cup finely chopped walnuts
2 to 3 tablespoons milk
Assorted fruit dippers
Assorted cheeses, cut up

Remove large pieces of fruit from apricot preserves or orange marmalade; cut into smaller sizes. Place preserves or marmalade and fruit pieces into a small bowl. Stir in sour cream and walnuts. Add enough milk to make of dipping consistency. Cover and chill in the refrigerator at least 1 hour or overnight to allow flavors to blend. Serve with fruit and cheese.

Yields 1 1/2 cups.

Coconut-Honey Fruit Dip

2 cups cottage cheese
1/4 cup plain yogurt
1/4 cup honey
1/4 cup shredded coconut
1 teaspoon grated orange zest (optional)
Assorted seasonal fruit

In a blender or food processor, place cottage cheese; cover and whirl at low speed until the cottage cheese is smooth, stopping 2 or 3 times to scrape down sides with a rubber spatula. Transfer into a medium bowl. Add yogurt, honey, coconut, and orange zest; stir until well blended. Cover and refrigerate 1 hour or until chilled.

Transfer the dip into a small glass serving bowl. Place the dip in the center of a large serving plate and arrange an assortment of seasonal fruits of your choice, cut up into bite-sized pieces or whole, around the dip.

Meatless Meals

Broccoli-Cheese Pie

The wonderful smell of the potato crust as it bakes will set your taste buds alive. That is just the beginning – this whole pie is absolutely fantastic.

Potato Crust
3 tablespoons butter
1 cup chopped onion
1 medium clove garlic, minced
1/2 teaspoon salt
1/2 teaspoon pepper
1/8 teaspoon dried thyme, crushed
1/2 teaspoon dried basil, crushed
1 1/2 cups broccoli flowerets
1 1/2 cups shredded cheddar cheese, divided
2 eggs
1/4 cup milk
Paprika to taste

Make Potato Crust and bake while preparing broccoli mixture.

In a large frying pan, over medium-high heat, melt butter. Sauté onion and garlic until onion is soft. Add salt, pepper, thyme, basil, and broccoli; cover and cook 10 minutes, stirring occasionally.

Place half of the cheddar cheese into the baked Potato Crust; pour the broccoli mixture onto top of cheese. Sprinkle the remainder of the cheddar cheese evenly onto top.

In a small bowl, combine eggs and milk; stir until well blended. Pour egg mixture onto top of the broccoli mixture; sprinkle with paprika. Bake 30 to 40 minutes or until a knife inserted halfway between center and edge comes out clean. Remove from oven and serve immediately.

Makes 4 servings.

POTATO CRUST:
2 firmly packed cups grated raw potatoes
1/2 teaspoon salt
1 egg, beaten
1/4 cup grated onion
Vegetable oil

Preheat oven to 400 degrees. Oil a 9-inch pie pan. Place raw potatoes in a colander. Salt potatoes and let set for 10 minutes. Squeeze out the excess water.

In a medium bowl combine potatoes, egg, and onion. Pat potato mixture into prepared pie pan, building up the sides of the crust with lightly floured fingers.

Bake 35 to 40 minutes or until golden brown (after the first 20 minutes brush the crust with vegetable oil to crispen it). Remove from oven. Reduce oven temperature to 375 degrees.

Eggs

Because eggs are so porous, they are best stored in the carton they come in; not on the door or in egg trays. Always store eggs large end up. This keeps them fresher and helps keep the yolk centered. Never place them near foods like onions because they easily absorb odors right through their shells.

TIPS: To tell if an egg is fresh, place it in a bowl of salted, cool water. If it sinks, it's fresh – if it floats, throw it out!

If you only need half an egg in your recipe, lightly beat one whole egg and then measure out one and one-half tablespoons.

EGG-BUYING TIPS: Most recipes are calibrated on large eggs; using other egg sizes may throw the recipe off kilter. When in doubt, use large eggs.

Open the carton and examine each egg closely to see that it is uncracked and clean. Cracked or soiled eggs may contain harmful bacteria.

Quiche

A quiche is an open-faced pie or tart having an egg filling and a variety of other ingredients. It is thought to have originated in the French province of Lorraine.

Bread dough was traditionally used, but in modern times, pie pastry and occasionally puff pastry is commonly substituted.

Today, all kinds of ingredients are used in making a quiche, from shellfish and smoked salmon to asparagus tips and corn. While this is a long way from the classic quiche, it makes good culinary sense and eating.

Mushroom Quiche

Pastry for 9-inch deep-dish one-crust pie (see page 122)
1 (10-ounce) package frozen chopped spinach
1 (8-ounce) can sliced mushrooms, drained
1 cup shredded swiss cheese
4 eggs
1 (12-ounce) can evaporated milk
1/4 teaspoon salt
1/8 teaspoon pepper
1 tablespoon chopped chives, optional
Red (cayenne) pepper to taste

Preheat oven to 400 degrees. Prepare pie pastry. Prick pie shell with a fork and bake 10 to 15 minutes or until lightly browned; remove from oven and cool on a wire rack.

Reduce oven temperature to 350 degrees. Cook spinach according to package directions; drain and squeeze out as much water as possible (reserve half of spinach for another use). Separate remaining spinach with a fork and arrange onto bottom of baked pie shell; sprinkle mushrooms and cheese over top of spinach.

In a large bowl, beat eggs until creamy. Add evaporated milk, salt, pepper, chives, and cayenne pepper; stir until well blended.

Place pie shell onto oven rack (partly pulled out). Carefully pour in egg mixture and slide into the oven. Bake, uncovered, 40 to 45 minutes or until a knife inserted halfway between center and edge comes out clean. Remove from oven and cool on a wire rack 10 minutes before cutting and serving.

Makes 4 to 6 servings.

Roquefort Quiche

Pastry for 9-inch deep-dish one-crust pie (see page 122)
3/4 cup crumbled roquefort cheese
3 egg yolks
2 eggs
2/3 cup light cream
1/4 cup shredded swiss cheese
1/2 teaspoon salt
1/8 teaspoon nutmeg

Preheat oven to 375 degrees. Prepare pie pastry. Prick pie shell with a fork and bake 10 to 15 minutes or until lightly browned; remove from oven and cool on a wire rack. Sprinkle roquefort cheese into cooled pie shell.

In a large bowl, combine egg yolks, eggs, light cream, swiss cheese, salt, and nutmeg; stir until well blended. Pour egg mixture over the roquefort cheese. Bake 15 minutes; reduce heat to 350 degrees and bake another 15 minutes or until a knife inserted halfway between center and edge comes out clean. Remove from oven and cool on a wire rack 10 minutes before cutting and serving.

Makes 6 servings.

Huevos Rancheros

Huevos Rancheros is a term for eggs and tortillas. A Southwestern favorite – popular for brunch or supper. Egg dishes such as this one were served in Mexico at "almuezo," a second breakfast served to ranch hands and farm workers after their early-morning chores.

12 corn tortillas
1 to 2 tablespoons butter or margarine
12 eggs
1/4 cup water
1/2 teaspoon salt

ACCOMPANIMENTS:
Medium hot sauce
Avocado slices
Fresh cilantro
Chopped green onions
Shredded monterey jack or mild cheddar cheese
Tomato salsa

CORN TORTILLAS:
To toast, moisten your hands lightly with water; rub over tortillas, one at a time. Place tortilla flat into an ungreased heavy frying pan or onto a griddle over medium heat; turn frequently until soft and pliable, approximately 30 seconds. Remove from heat and stack hot tortillas in a covered dish or wrap in aluminum foil. Keep hot for up to 2 hours on an electric warming tray or in a 150-degree oven.

SCRAMBLED EGGS:
In a large frying pan over medium-low heat, melt butter or margarine. In a large bowl, blend together eggs with water and salt; pour eggs into frying pan. As eggs begin to set, push cooked portions aside with a spatula to let uncooked egg flow underneath. Repeat until eggs are cooked.

TO SERVE:
For each serving, place 2 tortillas on a plate; top with a serving of scrambled eggs and garnish with accompaniments.

Makes 6 servings.

Frequently Asked Questions about Eggs

(1) IS THERE ANY DIFFERENCE IN BROWN AND WHITE EGGS?

The color of the eggshell is determined by the breed of the chicken and has nothing to do with flavor, freshness, or quality.

(2) DO BLOOD SPOTS IN EGGS MAKE THEM UNFIT TO USE?

Usually the candling of eggs for quality eliminates those with blood spots, but if very small spots escape detection, they in no way affect the desirability of the egg for cooking.

(3) WHAT DO CERTAIN EGG TERMS MEAN?

*LIGHTLY BEATEN:
Use a fork or whisk to beat eggs just until yolks and whites are blended.*

*WELL BEATEN:
Use an electric mixer or rotary beater and beat eggs until light, frothy, and well blended.*

*FOLDING:
When combining whites with heavier mixtures, they must be handled carefully or the air beaten into the whites will be lost. The best method is to first stir in a small amount of the egg whites. This thins the basic mixture so that the balance of the egg whites can be incorporated more easily. Use a large metal spoon and a down, under, and up motion.*

Cheese & Eggs

Soufflé

Soufflé is taken from the French word "souffler" meaning to blow or puff up.

TIPS: Spoon the soufflé mixture gently into the soufflé dish. Do not let the mixture drop into the dish from a height or all the air will be expelled. The more air there is in the mixture, the more the soufflé will rise.

Always bake a soufflé in the lower third of the oven. This way, the soufflé will get a concentrated blast of heat that gives it the upward push it needs to help it rise.

Scrambled Eggs

The secret to successfully scrambling eggs is slow cooking. A rubber spatula does a good job of moving the eggs. Don't worry about melting the rubber – the heat is (or should be) too low to damage it.

Always remove scrambled eggs from the heat when they are almost set but still appear shiny and a bit underdone.

TIP: After removing the pan with the scrambled eggs from the heat, add one teaspoon cold light cream or milk for each four eggs and stir fast for a second. This is to stop the cooking, which would otherwise continue for a few minutes by the internal heat retained by the eggs. Without this last step, the eggs would be overcooked and dry.

Do-Ahead Brunch Soufflé

This do-ahead soufflé is always a big hit with guests. This easy recipe lets the cook out of the kitchen to visit with the guests or (even better) sleep a little longer in the morning. Serve with cooked fresh or frozen green peas and a slice of tomato.

12 slices of white bread (crusts removed)
1/2 pound shredded sharp cheddar cheese
8 eggs, room temperature
3 cups milk
6 tablespoons butter, melted

Grease a 13x9-inch casserole dish. Place 6 slices of bread onto bottom of prepared dish; cover with half of cheddar cheese. Layer with remaining bread slices and cover with remainder of cheddar cheese; set aside. In a medium bowl, combine eggs and milk. Add melted butter; stir until well blended. Pour egg and milk mixture over bread and cheese. Cover with aluminum foil and refrigerate overnight.

Preheat oven to 325 degrees. Bake, covered with aluminum foil, 35 to 40 minutes. Uncover and bake another 35 to 40 minutes. Remove from oven and serve immediately.

Makes 6 large servings.

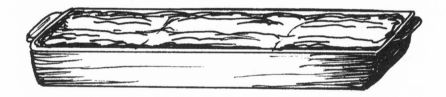

Melt-in-Your-Mouth Scrambled Eggs

Very hearty and tasty.

2 tablespoons butter or margarine, divided
2 tablespoons all-purpose flour
1/2 cup sour cream
12 eggs
1/4 teaspoon salt
1/8 teaspoon white pepper
Green onion tops

In a small saucepan over medium heat, melt 1 tablespoon butter or margarine; stir in the flour and cook until bubbly. Remove from heat and stir in sour cream. Return to heat and cook until bubbly and smooth; remove from heat and set aside.

In a medium bowl, combine eggs, salt, and pepper; stir until well blended. In a large frying pan over medium heat, melt 1 tablespoon butter or margarine. Pour in eggs; cook gently, stirring often until eggs are soft set. Remove from heat and stir in sour cream mixture. Transfer onto a serving platter and garnish with onion tops.

Makes 6 servings.

Baked Eggs & Cheese

1/2 cup butter or margarine
1/4 cup all-purpose flour
Salt and pepper to taste
1 1/2 teaspoons prepared mustard
2 cups milk
1 1/3 cups (1/3 pound) shredded processed American cheese
8 eggs

Preheat oven to 325 degrees. Generously butter four custard cups and set onto an ungreased baking sheet.

In the top of a double boiler over hot water, melt butter or margarine. Stir in flour, salt, pepper, and prepared mustard; stir until well blended. Slowly stir in milk until well blended and creamy. Add American cheese; stir until cheese melts. Remove from heat. Pour half of cheese sauce into prepared custard cups.

Into a cup, break eggs, one by one; pour two eggs onto top of sauce in each custard cup. Spoon on remaining cheese sauce, covering all except the center of each egg yolk.

Bake, uncovered, 15 to 20 minutes or until egg whites are opaque and yolks are softly set. (Do not overcook, as eggs will continue to cook after being removed from oven.) Remove from oven and serve immediately.

Makes 4 servings.

Welsh Rarebit

Welsh Rarebit is a traditional British dish.

1 tablespoon all-purpose flour
2 cups shredded sharp cheddar cheese
1/4 cup beer
1 teaspoon worcestershire sauce
1 teaspoon Dijon mustard
3 drops hot pepper sauce
1 egg yolk, beaten
Salt and pepper to taste
4 slices freshly-toasted rye or white bread

Preheat broiler. In a large saucepan over medium heat, combine flour and cheddar cheese; stir until well blended. Add beer, worcestershire sauce, Dijon mustard, and hot pepper sauce; stir constantly until the cheese has melted and mixture is smooth. Remove from heat; beat in egg yolk and season with salt and pepper.

Arrange toast in individual heatproof serving dishes. Pour the rarebit over the toast and place under broiler 2 minutes or until light brown and bubbly. Remove from oven and serve immediately.

Makes 4 servings.

Processed Cheeses

1 pound of processed cheese equals 4 to 5 cups shredded.

Processed cheeses are artificial cheeses made to look and smell like natural cheese. Unlike naturally aged cheese, processed cheeses undergo a manufacturing process.

They are made from a range of chemical and organic materials, including vegetable oils. They contain less fat than natural cheese, but a similar amount of calories, protein, vitamins, minerals, and moisture content.

Processed cheeses can be stored much longer than natural cheese. For example, imitation mozzarella will keep for a year, compared to three months for natural mozzarella.

They generally have a rubbery texture and are lacking in flavor compared to natural cheese.

Poaching Eggs

The best eggs for poaching are the freshest eggs you can find. If eggs are more than a week old, the whites thin out. Whites of fresh eggs will gather compactly around the yolk, making a rounder, neater shape.

Poaching Eggs for a Crowd

To poach eggs for a crowd, cook eggs ahead of time, slightly undercooking them. Slide them into a large bowl of cold water. When ready to be served, reheat in simmering water.

If you are making eggs only a short while ahead, slide all of them, as they are cooked, into a large bowl of hot (not boiling) water. Don't worry about them sticking together. Top with more hot water from time to time to keep them warm. The eggs will be soft, warm, and ready to eat when you are ready to serve them.

TIP: When you poach eggs, try adding a little vinegar and salt to the water. This will set the eggs and keep them in shape.

Eggs Florentine

Eggs can be poached and the hollandaise sauce prepared ahead of time for this easy and wonderful brunch dish.

1 (10-ounce) package frozen chopped spinach
3 English muffins, halved
6 eggs
Hollandaise Sauce
Paprika for garnish

Prepare spinach according to package directions; drain and squeeze out as much liquid as possible. Toast muffin halves and place 1 to 2 muffin halves on each serving plate.

In a large frying pan over high heat, bring water (1 1/2 to 2 inches) to a boil; reduce to low and let water come to a simmer. Break each egg into measuring cup or saucer; holding cup or saucer close to water's surface, slip one egg at a time into water. Cook 3 to 5 minutes or until desired doneness. NOTE: If poached the day before, reheat in a bowl of very hot water for 5 to 10 minutes.

To serve, cover each muffin half with drained spinach. Lift eggs from hot water with slotted spoon, drain well, and place 1 egg onto each spinach-topped muffin. Spoon approximately 2 tablespoons Hollandaise Sauce over each egg; sprinkle with paprika.

Makes 3 to 6 servings.

HOLLANDAISE SAUCE:
1 whole egg or 3 egg yolks
1 teaspoon prepared mustard
1 tablespoon lemon juice or white wine vinegar
1/2 cup butter or margarine

In blender or food processor, whirl egg or egg yolks, prepared mustard, and lemon juice or white wine vinegar until well blended.

In a small saucepan over medium heat, melt butter or margarine just to a boil, but do not brown. With motor of food processor or blender on high, add butter or margarine to egg mixture, a few drops at a time in the beginning, but increasing to a slow, steady stream as mixture begins to thicken (should take about 30 seconds). Serve immediately or keep warm.

NOTE: If sauce is not being used immediately, pour into a small thermos jug to keep hot.

Makes 1 to 1 1/2 cups.

Basic Deviled Eggs

12 eggs, hard cooked, peeled and sliced in half
1/4 cup mayonnaise
Salt and pepper to taste
1 teaspoon ground mustard or 1/4 teaspoon prepared mustard
2 to 3 teaspoons sweet pickle juice
Paprika for garnish

Remove yolks from eggs. In a medium bowl, mash yolks with a fork; add mayonnaise, salt, pepper, ground mustard or prepared mustard, and pickle juice; mix thoroughly. Spoon into egg halves or load into a pastry bag and pipe into whites. Sprinkle with paprika.

Makes 24 deviled egg halves.

CHEESE DEVILED EGGS:

12 eggs, hard cooked, peeled and sliced in half
1/4 cup mayonnaise
Salt and pepper to taste
Worcestershire sauce to taste
1 tablespoon minced onion
1 tablespoon minced celery
1/4 teaspoon prepared mustard
1/4 cup shredded cheddar cheese

Remove yolks from eggs. In a medium bowl, mash yolks with a fork; add mayonnaise, salt, pepper, and worcestershire sauce; mix until well blended. Add onion, celery, prepared mustard, and cheddar cheese; mix thoroughly and spoon into egg halves.

Makes 24 deviled egg halves.

WATERCRESS-STUFFED EGGS:

12 eggs, hard cooked, peeled and sliced in half
1/2 cup unsalted butter, room temperature
1/2 cup finely chopped onion
1 1/2 teaspoons fresh lemon juice
1 cup chopped watercress
Red (cayenne) pepper to taste
Salt and pepper to taste
Thinly sliced black olives for garnish

Remove yolks from eggs. In a medium bowl mash yolks with a fork; add butter; stir until well blended. Add onion, lemon juice, watercress, cayenne pepper, salt and pepper; blend until watercress is just incorporated, do not overmix. Spoon into egg halves. Garnish with sliced olives.

Makes 24 deviled egg halves.

Hard-Cooked Eggs

To hard-cook eggs, place the eggs in a pan with cold water to cover them. Bring to a boil, remove from heat, cover tightly, and allow to stay in the water for twenty minutes. Then place under running, cold water to cool quickly. This way of cooking is also known as "coddling." It does not toughen the whites as boiling does.

TIPS: To tell if an egg is hard cooked or raw, place the egg on its side and spin it evenly on a level surface; if it wobbles, it is raw.

You cannot hard cook eggs in a microwave (they'll explode), but if you find after peeling an egg that it is not quite done at the center, pierce it once or twice with a fork, set microwave to medium power and cook the egg for ten to twenty seconds. Let stand twenty seconds before checking for doneness.

Deviled Eggs

Deviled or stuffed eggs can be covered with plastic wrap and refrigerated three days.

TIP: After boiling and peeling eggs, slice off a nickel-sized piece of egg from each end to make them stable when sitting. Halve the eggs widthwise, not lengthwise – this makes them easier to eat gracefully.

Eggplant

Eggplant is available year-round, with the peak season during the months of August and September.

Choose a firm, smooth-skinned eggplant that is heavy for its size; avoid those with soft or brown spots. Gently push with your thumb or forefinger. If the flesh gives slightly but then bounces back, it is ripe. If the indentation remains, it is overripe and the insides will be mushy. If there is no give, the eggplant was picked too early. Also make sure an eggplant isn't dry inside, knock on it with your knuckles. If you hear a hollow sound, don't buy it.

Eggplants are very perishable and become bitter with age. They should be stored in a cool, dry place and used within a day or two of purchase.

When young, the skin of most eggplants are edible; older eggplants should be peeled. Since the flesh discolors rapidly, an eggplant should be cut just before using.

TIP: The fewer seeds in an eggplant, the less bitter it tastes. When picking an eggplant for the fewest seeds, check the bottom (the end opposite the stem). On the bottom you will find a greyish scar or indentation about the size of a dime. If the scar is oval or oblong, the eggplant will be loaded with seeds. Choose the one with the round scar and you will have an eggplant with far fewer seeds.

Meatless (Eggplant) Moussaka

Moussaka is a savory dish which originated in the Balkans, but is now one of the best known of all Greek dishes. It is known as the shepherd's pie of Greece. The dish traditionally contains eggplant and mutton, but this meatless recipe has been widely adapted.

1 tablespoon vegetable oil
1 large eggplant, peeled and sliced
Salt and pepper to taste
2 tablespoons butter or margarine
1 clove garlic, minced
1 large onion, finely chopped
1 1/2 cups cooked long-grain brown rice
3 tablespoons tomato paste
1/2 cup red wine
1/2 cup frozen peas
1/4 cup chopped fresh parsley
1/8 teaspoon ground cinnamon
1/2 cup chopped walnuts
1/2 cup bread crumbs
1/2 cup freshly grated parmesan cheese
Custard Sauce

Preheat oven to 375 degrees. In a large frying pan over medium heat, heat vegetable oil. Add eggplant and cook until light brown; season with salt and pepper. Remove from pan and set aside. In same frying pan, melt butter or margarine. Add garlic and onion; sauté until golden brown. Stir in brown rice, tomato paste, red wine, and peas. Add parsley, cinnamon, salt, and pepper; stir until well blended. Remove from heat.

In an ungreased 13x9-inch casserole dish, layer eggplant and rice mixture; sprinkle walnuts, bread crumbs, and parmesan cheese over the top.

Pour Custard Sauce over the top. Bake, uncovered, 45 minutes or until top is golden brown and a knife inserted in the center comes out clean. Remove from oven and cool on a wire rack 20 minutes before serving. Cut into squares.

NOTE: Flavor is improved by standing one day. Reheat before serving.

Makes 6 servings.

CUSTARD SAUCE:
1/4 cup butter or margarine
3 tablespoons whole-wheat flour
2 cups milk
2 eggs, beaten
1 cup ricotta or cottage cheese
Ground nutmeg to taste

In a medium saucepan over low heat, melt butter or margarine. Stir in flour with a wire whisk until well blended; add milk, stirring until thick and smooth. Remove from heat; cool slightly. Add eggs, ricotta or cottage cheese, and nutmeg; stir until well blended.

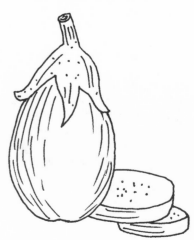

Eggplant Parmesan Supreme

Italian Sauce
1 medium eggplant
2 eggs
1/4 cup water
1/3 cup all-purpose flour
1 cup bread crumbs
Vegetable oil
8 ounces mozzarella cheese, sliced
1/4 cup freshly grated parmesan cheese

Preheat oven to 350 degrees. Prepare Italian Sauce; set aside. Cut unpeeled eggplant lengthwise into 1/4-inch slices. In a medium bowl, combine eggs and water. In a shallow pie plate, place the flour. In another shallow pie plate, place the bread crumbs. Coat eggplant slices with flour, dip in egg mixture, then coat with bread crumbs.

In a large frying pan over medium heat, heat vegetable oil (add as needed to fry eggplant slices). Add eggplant slices and cook until lightly browned, turning once. Remove from heat and drain on paper towels.

In a 9-inch square baking dish, spread 1/2 cup Italian Sauce. Layer half of the eggplant slices, half of the mozzarella cheese, and half of the remaining Italian Sauce. Repeat the steps with the next layer. Sprinkle with parmesan cheese.

Bake, uncovered, 20 to 30 minutes or until thoroughly heated. Remove from oven and serve immediately.

Makes 4 servings.

ITALIAN SAUCE:
1 tablespoon olive oil
1 medium onion, sliced
1 1/2 cups sliced fresh mushrooms
1 (14 1/2-ounce) can stewed tomatoes, undrained
1 (8-ounce) can tomato sauce
1 (6-ounce) can tomato paste
2 tablespoons dry red wine
1 clove garlic, minced
2 teaspoons dried oregano, crushed
1/4 teaspoon salt

In a large frying pan over medium heat, heat olive oil. Add onion and mushrooms; sauté until tender, but not brown. Stir in tomatoes, tomato sauce, tomato paste, and wine. Add garlic, oregano and salt; stir until well blended. Bring to a boil. Reduce heat to low; simmer 30 minutes. Remove from heat.

Tomato Paste

1/2 cup tomato paste plus 1/2 cup water equals 1 cup canned tomatoes (solid pack).

TIPS: When a recipe calls for only a little tomato paste, don't throw away the rest of the can. Use the following ideas:

Measure what is left by the tablespoonful onto wax paper and freeze the sheet. When hard, remove from the paper and put into a container. This way, you'll always have it, already measured, on hand.

Remove from can by removing both ends of the can. Use the lid at one end to push the paste out onto a sheet of plastic wrap. Wrap tomato paste in plastic wrap and place in the freezer. When paste has frozen, cut off only as much as is needed, then return the frozen log to the freezer.

Tomato Sauce

1 (8-ounce) can tomato sauce equals 1 pound fresh tomatoes.

1 (8-ounce) can tomato sauce plus 1/4 cup water equals 1 (10 3/4-ounce) can condensed undiluted tomato soup.

Tomato sauce is little more than seasoned tomato pureé. Usually tomato sauce contains onion, sweet pepper, herbs, spices, sugar, and salt, in addition to tomatoes.

Eggplant

Mozzarella Cheese

Fresh mozzarella cheese is an Italian specialty that has moved into the American culinary mainstream. Home cooks have discovered that the sweet, milky flavor and soft texture of this fresh cheese is radically different from the rubbery, processed product most of us associate with pizza.

Mozzarella dates back to the 15th century, and its name comes from the Italian verb "mozzare," which means "to cut off" or "chop up." Probably a reference to cheese curds that were chopped by hand.

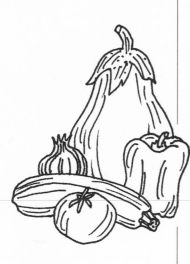

What is Ratatouille?

It is a Mediterranean vegetable stew, using eggplant, tomatoes, zucchini, onions, green bell peppers, and garlic. Ratatouille is good hot or cold.

Baked Eggplant Slices

1 large eggplant, peeled and sliced 1/4-inch thick
3 to 4 tablespoons olive oil, divided
1/2 cup mayonnaise
3/4 cup crushed saltine crackers
3/4 cup freshly grated parmesan cheese
1/2 cup chopped fresh basil, divided
Salt and pepper to taste
1 large or 2 medium tomatoes, thickly sliced
4 ounces mozzarella cheese, sliced

Preheat oven to 375 degrees. Lightly brush a large baking sheet with olive oil. Coat both sides of eggplant slices lightly with mayonnaise.

In a shallow bowl, combine cracker crumbs and parmesan cheese; dip eggplant slices into mixture. Place eggplant slices onto prepared baking sheet; sprinkle with 1/4 cup basil, salt, and pepper. Arrange tomato slices on top of each eggplant slice; sprinkle with 1/4 cup basil. Top with mozzarella cheese and another light brushing of olive oil.

Bake, uncovered, 15 to 20 minutes or until eggplant is tender and cheese is bubbling and golden. Remove from oven, transfer onto a serving platter, and serve immediately.

Makes 4 servings.

Garden Ratatouille

The vegetable amounts and kinds can be varied according to what is in season or in abundance in your garden. The flavor in this dish is even better if prepared the day before serving.

2 tablespoons olive oil
1 medium onion, thinly sliced
1 clove garlic, minced
1 pound zucchini squash, sliced
2 or 3 small tomatoes, peeled and sliced
1 small eggplant, diced
1 green bell pepper, cored, seeded, and cut into thin strips
1 tablespoon chopped fresh oregano or 1 1/2 teaspoons dried oregano, crushed
Salt and coarsely ground pepper to taste
Chopped fresh parsley, for garnish

In a large saucepan over medium-high heat, heat olive oil. Add onion and garlic; sauté 5 minutes or until onion is lightly browned. Stir in zucchini, tomatoes, eggplant, and bell pepper. Sprinkle with oregano, salt, and pepper; stir gently. Reduce heat to low, cover, and simmer 10 to 15 minutes or until vegetables are tender but hold their shapes. Remove from heat and cool on a wire rack to room temperature before serving.

NOTE: Can refrigerate up to 24 hours. Bring to room temperature before serving. To serve, sprinkle with chopped parsley.

Makes 4 servings.

Gluten — Meat Substitute

DOUGH:
8 cups all-purpose flour (the cheapest and most unrefined contains the most gluten)
3 cups water
Vegetable Broth

In a large bowl, combine flour and water; knead 5 minutes or until smooth. Cover dough with cold water and soak for 45 minutes or overnight. Place bowl into the sink with cold running water as you knead and wash dough. Change water frequently until almost clear (the flour will make the water milky in color – if water is completely clear, the gluten tends to be tough).

Form dough into a long cylinder on a cutting board. Slice into 1/2-inch pieces or pull apart into thin patty-sized pieces, approximately 4-inch diameter. Place pieces into boiling Vegetable Broth and cook for 45 to 60 minutes. Refrigerate until ready to fry or use in another recipe.

VEGETABLE BROTH:
(Use your favorite vegetable broth or the following recipe)
3 quarts water
1 to 2 dried bay leaves
1 onion, sliced
1 clove garlic, minced
6 tablespoons soy sauce
2 tablespoons firmly packed brown sugar
4 to 5 stalks celery with leaves, chopped
Salt and pepper to taste

In a large pot over medium-high heat, bring water, bay leaves, onion, garlic, soy sauce, brown sugar, celery, salt, and pepper to a boil. Simmer 30 minutes to blend flavors.

Tofu Sidekick

Extra-firm tofu holds up better when frying, but less firm varieties will also do.

2 to 3 tablespoons peanut oil
1 (14-ounce) package-extra firm tofu, cut into 1/2- to 1-inch cubes
1 large onion, cut into fourths and sliced
2 (11-ounce) cans tomato bisque soup, undiluted
1/2 teaspoon Five-Spice Seasoning*
Salt and pepper to taste
Cooked Rice

In a large frying pan over high heat, heat peanut oil. Add tofu cubes and fry until lightly browned; stir frequently to keep from sticking and to brown sides evenly. Reduce heat to medium and add onion; fry until onion is cooked but not browned. Stir in tomato bisque soup, Five-Spice Seasoning, salt, and pepper. Remove from heat and serve over cooked rice or as a side dish by itself.

* Five-Spice Seasoning can be found in Asian food stores.

Makes 4 servings.

Gluten

This is a healthy, nutritious meat substitute that can be made from the gluten in wheat. It has the texture of some meats and can be used in many recipes in place of meat. It must be seasoned, just as you must season most meats before eating.

Gluten may be made ahead and kept in the refrigerator or freezer to be added to dishes as needed. It can also be ground like ground beef or fried whole in a breading.

TIPS: If you don't want to go to the trouble of making your own gluten, similar products made from soy can be purchased in most large grocery stores or health food stores.

Substitute two cups ground gluten for one pound ground meat in recipes. Great to use in chili, lasagna, tacos, meatballs, or meat loaf.

Five-Spice Seasoning

To make your own Five-Spice Seasoning:

2 teaspoons anise seeds
2 teaspoons fennel seeds
2 teaspoons peppercorns
2 teaspoons whole cloves
1 stick of cinnamon

In a blender or electric grinder, grind all the above ingredients until mixture is a powder. Store in an airtight container.

Yields 1/4 cup.

Legumes (Beans)

1 pound dried beans equals 2 1/2 to 3 cups uncooked beans, or 5 1/2 to 6 1/2 cups cooked beans.

1 cup dried beans equals 2 to 2 1/2 cups canned beans.

Legumes are described as plants that have pods which divide in halves, such as beans and peas. They can be grown in every climate. They are also high in protein and low in cost. They make wonderful cholesterol-free dishes that are delicious, high in fiber, and rich in iron, calcium, potassium, and B vitamins.

Most legumes, other than lentils and split peas, require soaking overnight to shorten cooking time. Cooking in a pressure cooker will also shorten the time.

For quick soaking, cover legumes with water and boil for two minutes. Remove from heat and let stand for about one hour. Drain and rinse before cooking.

Legumes cook very well in crockpots or other slow cookers.

TIP: Always discard the soaking water and cook your legumes in fresh water.

Lentil & Hazelnut Patties

This is a delicious patty. Can be served with catsup or used as a garden burger on a bun with all the regular trimmings. It's even good as a cold sandwich the next day. They can also be reheated.

3 cups dry lentils
1 medium onion, chopped
1 cup bread crumbs
1 tablespoon chopped fresh parsley
3 eggs
1 cup finely chopped roasted hazelnuts or walnuts
1/2 teaspoon dried thyme, crushed
1 teaspoon dried basil, crushed
1 1/2 teaspoons salt
Pepper to taste
1 to 2 tablespoons vegetable oil

Cook lentils according to package directions; drain and cool. Combine lentils, onion, bread crumbs, parsley, eggs, and hazelnuts or walnuts. Stir in thyme, basil, salt, and pepper. Mold into 16 burger-sized patties.

In a large frying pan over medium-high heat, heat vegetable oil. Add four patties at a time and brown. For best results, wipe out frying pan and add new oil for each new batch. Remove from heat and drain on paper towels. Transfer onto a serving platter to serve.

Yields 16 patties.

Bean Casserole

Excellent potluck dish.

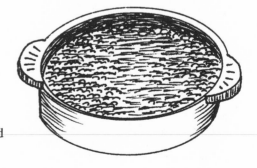

1 (16-ounce) can kidney beans, drained
1 (16-ounce) can wax beans, drained
1 (16-ounce) can green beans, drained
1 (16-ounce) can baked beans, undrained
1 teaspoon ground mustard
1 tablespoon worcestershire sauce
1 1/2 teaspoons salt
2 tablespoons white vinegar
1/2 cup catsup
1/2 cup firmly packed brown sugar
1 small onion, chopped

Preheat oven to 350 degrees. In a large bowl, combine kidney beans, wax beans, green beans, and baked beans; set aside.

In a small bowl, combine ground mustard, worcestershire sauce, salt, white vinegar, catsup, brown sugar, and onion; stir until well blended. Pour sauce over beans; stir until well blended. Into an ungreased 13x9-inch baking dish, pour bean mixture. Bake, uncovered, 45 to 60 minutes. Remove from oven and serve.

Makes 8 to 10 servings.

Vegetarian Meatballs

1 quart tomato juice
1 large onion, chopped
1 tablespoon sugar
1/2 teaspoon pepper
1 tablespoon soy sauce
1/8 teaspoon ground cumin
4 cups crushed saltine crackers
1/2 pound shredded cheddar cheese
1 large onion, chopped
1 cup chopped walnuts
6 eggs, well beaten
1 to 2 tablespoons vegetable oil

In a large saucepan over medium heat, combine tomato juice, onion, sugar, pepper, soy sauce, and cumin; stir until heated and well blended. Set aside.

In a large bowl, combine cracker crumbs, cheddar cheese, onion, and walnuts; stir until well blended. Add eggs and continue mixing until well blended. Form into 1-inch balls (they will puff up when cooked).

In a large frying pan over medium-high heat, heat vegetable oil. Add meatballs and fry until brown. Remove from heat and drain on paper towels. When all the meatballs have been browned, add to tomato sauce, return to heat, and simmer 1 hour. Remove from heat, transfer onto a serving platter, and serve.

Makes 10 to 12 servings.

Tabouli

1 cup bulgur wheat
1 1/2 cups boiling water
1 1/2 teaspoons salt
1/4 cup fresh lemon or lime juice
1 clove garlic, minced
1/4 cup olive oil
1/2 teaspoon dried mint, crushed
Coarsely ground pepper to taste
1/2 cup chopped scallions (including greens)
2 medium tomatoes, diced
1 cup firmly packed chopped fresh parsley
Feta cheese
Olives

In a medium bowl, combine bulgur wheat, boiling water, and salt. Cover and let stand 15 to 20 minutes or until bulgur is chewable. Add lemon or lime juice, garlic, olive oil, mint, and pepper; stir until well blended. Refrigerate 2 to 3 hours or overnight. Just before serving add scallions, tomatoes, parsley and one or all of the optional vegetables listed below. Garnish with feta cheese and olives.

OPTIONAL VEGETABLES:
1/2 cup cooked chickpeas, 1 chopped green pepper, 1/2 cup coarsely grated carrot, or 1 chopped cucumber or summer squash

Makes 6 to 8 servings.

Walnuts

1 pound of walnuts in the shell equals 2 cups shelled nuts.

One of the most valuable of nuts. There are two main varieties, English and black walnut. The English walnut is grown in California and Oregon, while the black walnut is grown in the eastern part of the United States.

Walnuts in the shell will last well for about six months. Shelled walnuts will keep well at room temperature for about a month or in the refrigerator for about three months. They will freeze indefinitely.

TIP: Walnuts will be easier to crack if you cover them with water, then bring to a boil. Remove from heat, cover and set aside for at least fifteen minutes, or until cool. Blot the nuts dry and crack end to end.

Wild Rice

Wild rice, so called because of its appearance, is not really rice at all but an aquatic grass grown in the wetlands of the Great Lakes states. It was first discovered growing wild by Indians, and it is still hand harvested from waters that belong to surviving tribes. Today, most wild rice on the market is a commercially cultivated hybrid that ripens quickly, but lacks the intense nutty flavor of the true wild kind.

Arborio Rice

Arborio rice was virtually synonymous with risotto for many years. It is the best known of the top-grade varieties of Italian rice. When purchasing arborio rice, the only precaution is to check the label to be sure it is not precooked.

Risotto Etiquette

In Italy, risotto is served mounded, steaming hot, in the center of warmed individual shallow bowls. Using a fork or a spoon, push the grains of cooked rice out slightly toward the edge of the bowl, eating only from the pulled out ring of rice. Continue spreading from the center and eating around the edges in a circle. This will keep the risotto hot as you enjoy your risotto.

Lemon Wild Rice Risotto

Add a bottle of wine, a fresh green salad, and warm sourdough bread for a wonderful and delicious meal.

1 cup wild rice
3 tablespoons butter or margarine
1/2 cup finely chopped onion
1 1/2 cups chicken broth
1/4 teaspoon saffron
1/4 teaspoon dried basil, crushed
1/4 teaspoon dried marjoram, crushed
1/4 teaspoon dried thyme, crushed
1/4 teaspoon dried oregano, crushed
1/4 teaspoon red (cayenne) pepper
1/3 cup dry sherry
3 cups chicken broth
1 cup arborio rice
1 teaspoon grated lemon zest
3 tablespoons fresh lemon juice
2 tablespoons butter or margarine, cubed
Salt and coarsely ground pepper to taste
5 Roma tomatoes, chopped
3 green onions, chopped
1/2 cup freshly grated parmesan cheese

Wash wild rice carefully and drain. In a large paella pan or large frying pan over medium heat, melt 3 tablespoons butter or margarine. Add onion; sauté until soft. Add 1 1/2 cups chicken broth and bring to a boil. Add saffron and stir to dissolve.

Reduce heat to low. Add wild rice, basil, marjoram, thyme, oregano, and cayenne pepper; simmer 20 to 25 minutes or until most of the liquid is absorbed. Add sherry and simmer, covered, another 30 minutes or until most of the sherry is absorbed.

Add 3 cups chicken broth, arborio rice, lemon zest, and lemon juice. Simmer, stirring frequently, 20 minutes or until arborio rice is just tender but still firm to bite and mixture is creamy.

Remove from heat. Add 2 tablespoons butter or margarine, salt, pepper, tomatoes, onions, and parmesan cheese. Stir until butter or margarine is melted. Serve immediately.

Makes 4 to 6 servings.

Lemon Risotto

1 tablespoon olive oil
1/2 cup chopped onion
1 cup arborio rice or medium-grain white rice
3 cups beef broth
3 tablespoons fresh lemon juice
2 teaspoons grated lemon zest
1 tablespoon butter
1/4 cup freshly grated parmesan cheese
Salt and pepper to taste
1 tablespoon chopped fresh parsley

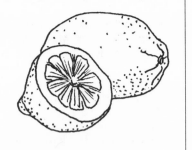

In a large frying pan over medium-high heat, heat olive oil. Add onion; sauté
4 minutes or until soft. Add rice; stir 1 minute. Add beef broth, lemon juice, and
lemon zest. Reduce heat to medium-low. Simmer, stirring frequently, 20 minutes or
until rice is just tender but still firm to bite and mixture is creamy.

Remove from heat. Add butter; stir until melted. Stir in parmesan cheese, salt, and
pepper. Transfer onto individual serving plates and garnish with parsley. Serve
immediately.

Makes 2 servings.

Vegetable Risotto

2 tablespoons vegetable oil
2 large onions, sliced
1 clove garlic, minced
1 pound tomatoes, peeled, sliced, divided
1 cup arborio rice or medium-grain white rice
2 1/2 cups water
2 large carrots, diced or grated
1/4 cup fresh or frozen peas
Salt and pepper to taste
4 ounces mushrooms, sliced
2 tablespoons chopped fresh parsley, divided
2 cups shredded cheddar cheese, divided

In a large frying pan over medium heat, heat vegetable oil. Add onions and garlic;
sauté until onions are soft. Remove some of the onion rings and set aside. Stir in
half of tomato slices, arborio rice, and water; bring to a boil. Stir in carrots and peas;
simmer 10 minutes.

Reduce heat to low. Add salt, pepper, remaining tomato slices, mushrooms, and
remaining onion rings. Cook another 10 minutes or until rice is just tender but still
firm to bite and mixture is creamy.

Remove from heat. Add 1 tablespoon of parsley and 1 cup of cheddar cheese; stir
until blended. Transfer into a serving bowl; sprinkle with 1 tablespoon parsley, 1 cup
cheddar cheese, and serve immediately.

Makes 4 to 6 servings.

Risotto

*The dish was invented in
the late 16th century in
Milan when their great
cathedral was under
construction. It is said that
the master glassworker on
the job, who was known for
using saffron to enhance his
paint pigments, added
saffron to a pot of rice
at a wedding party. The
response of the guests was
"Risus optimus," Latin for
"excellent rice." It was
later shortened to risotto.*

*Risotto should only be
prepared with Italian short-
grain rice (arborio rice).
This is because it is highly
glutinous, a quality that
enables the rice to absorb
the flavors of the other
ingredients with which it is
cooked. It also allows the
rice to combine with the
cooking liquid to create a
thick, creamy-smooth
consistency that the Italians
call all'onda, meaning
"with waves."*

FOUR RULES FOR PERFECT RISOTTO:

*(1) Do not add too
much liquid at once.*

*(2) Do not add more
liquid until the
previous addition
has been adsorbed.*

(3) Stir, stir, and stir.

*(4) Immediately serve
because the mixture
thickens as it stands.*

Nuts, Legumes, & Grains

How to Cook Rice

Bring two cups of salted water to a boil. Add one cup rice. Cover. Reduce heat to low. Cook twenty minutes. DO NOT OPEN LID. Fluff and serve. Makes three cups cooked rice.

TIPS: To keep rice white while cooking, add a few drops of lemon juice to the water.

A few minutes before your rice is done, place a doubled paper towel just under the lid and finish cooking. The rice will come out fluffier and drier.

To obtain the right amount of water to cook rice without measuring, place a quantity of rice in a pot, shake the pot to smooth out and settle the rice, then place your index finger lightly on top of the rice (do not make a dent), add water until your first knuckle is covered (about one inch above the surface of the rice).

To tenderize brown rice, allow rice to soak for one or two hours before cooking.

Garden Fried Rice

1 to 2 tablespoons vegetable oil
2 cups long-grain white rice, cooked
3 tablespoons soy sauce
1/2 cup chopped green onions
1/2 cup grated carrots
1/2 cup fresh or frozen peas, cooked and drained
1 egg

In a large frying pan over medium-high heat, heat vegetable oil. Add rice and cook until brown. Pour soy sauce over rice; stir until well blended. Stir in green onions, carrots, and peas. Remove pan from heat.

Break egg over rice; stir until well blended. Transfer onto a serving platter and serve immediately.

Makes 4 servings.

Mexican Rice

3 tablespoons butter or margarine
1 small onion, finely chopped
1 cup long-grain white rice
1 clove garlic, minced
2 medium-size tomatoes, peeled, seeded, and chopped
1 1/2 cups vegetable broth
1 or 2 green chilies, chopped
Salt and pepper to taste
2 tablespoons chopped fresh cilantro
1/2 cup sliced pimiento-stuffed green olives

In a large saucepan over medium heat, melt butter or margarine. Add onion and sauté until soft. Add rice and garlic; cook 5 minutes, stirring occasionally, until rice is golden. Add tomatoes, vegetable broth, chilies, salt, and pepper; cover and bring to a boil. Reduce heat to low and simmer another 20 minutes or until rice is tender and all liquid is absorbed.

Turn off heat and stir in cilantro and green olives. Let stand, covered, for 10 minutes. Transfer into a serving bowl and serve immediately.

Makes 4 to 6 servings.

Arkansas Rice With Pine Nuts

1 1/2 cups long-grain brown rice
3 cups water
2 tablespoons butter or margarine
1 onion, chopped
1 tablespoon ground cumin
Salt and pepper to taste
1 tablespoon chopped fresh parsley
1/4 cup pine nuts

In a large bowl, soak rice in water at least 1 hour or overnight.

In a large heavy frying pan over medium-high heat, melt butter or margarine. Add onion and sauté until golden brown. Add rice with soaking water, cumin, salt, and pepper; bring to a boil.

Reduce heat to low, cover, and simmer 20 minutes or until rice is tender and water is absorbed. Remove from heat and transfer into a serving dish. To serve, sprinkle parsley and pine nuts onto top.

Makes 4 servings.

Rice Facts

1 pound uncooked rice equals 2 to 2 1/2 cups uncooked rice.

1 cup uncooked rice equals 3 cups cooked rice.

Rice has been a staple part of the diet for thousands of years in Asia, China, Africa, South America, Spain, and Italy.

It is now estimated that more rice is eaten than any other grain.

Did you know that 50 percent of all the world's rice is eaten within eight miles of where it is grown?

Peanut Butter-Carrot Loaf

This makes a good sandwich after it has been in the refrigerator. Serve with fresh lettuce and mayonnaise on a slice of your favorite bread.

1 tablespoon vegetable oil
1 large onion, chopped
2 ribs celery, finely chopped
2 cups grated carrots
2 cups tomato juice
2/3 cup peanut butter
2 eggs, beaten
1 cup bread crumbs
1/2 cup old-fashioned rolled oats
1/2 teaspoon salt
1/4 teaspoon pepper

Preheat oven to 375 degrees. Grease a 8-inch square baking dish or a small loaf pan.

In a large frying pan over medium heat, heat vegetable oil. Add onion, celery, and carrots; sauté 5 to 10 minutes or until crisp-tender. Remove from heat and add tomato juice, peanut butter, eggs, bread crumbs, rolled oats, salt, and pepper; stir until well blended.

Pour into prepared baking dish and bake, uncovered, 30 to 40 minutes or until knife inserted in center comes out clean. Remove from oven and serve.

Makes 8 to 10 servings.

Peanut Sauce

For a delicious and nutritious sauce to pour over rice, dilute as much peanut butter as desired with a little cream or canned milk. Heat in the microwave or on the stove top until hot. DO NOT BOIL. Serve in a small pitcher or ladle onto rice.

Pasta

Cooking Perfect Pasta

One pound of dry pasta or freshly made pasta will serve 6 as an appetizer or 4 as a main course.

Use at least one quart of water for every four ounces of dry pasta. Bring water to a fast boil.

IMPORTANT:
Pasta added to water before it starts to boil gets a head start on mushiness. Pasta quickly begins to break down in tepid water as the starch dissolves. You need the intense heat of boiling water to "set" the outside of the pasta, which prevents the pasta from sticking together.

That's why the fast boil is so important; the water temperature drops when you add the pasta, but if you have a fast boil, the water will still be hot enough for the pasta to cook properly.

Test dry pasta for doneness after about five minutes by tasting it. Pasta should be tender but still firm when you eat it, what the Italians call al dente. Freshly made pasta will cook in about two to three minutes, so check it carefully to be sure it does not overcook. When pasta is done, drain immediately. Do not rinse unless the recipe says to do so.

Fettuccine Piccata

You'll be pleasantly surprised at the wonderful taste of this pasta.

1 (16-ounce) package uncooked fettuccine pasta
1/3 cup olive oil
1/4 cup capers, drained
1/4 cup white wine
1/2 cup prepared pesto
2 cloves garlic, minced
1/2 cup sliced black olives
1 tablespoon lemon juice
1/2 cup cottage cheese
Salt and coarsely ground pepper to taste
Freshly grated parmesan cheese

Cook pasta according to package directions; drain and return to pan to keep warm.

In a small saucepan over medium-high heat, heat olive oil, capers, white wine, pesto, and garlic 1 minute or until aromatic; stir in black olives, lemon juice, and cottage cheese. Remove from heat and pour over pasta; toss to coat thoroughly. Season with salt and pepper. Transfer onto individual serving plates and garnish with parmesan cheese.

Makes 4 servings.

Orange-Poppy Seed Pasta

An excellent side dish – very refreshing and light.

1 (16-ounce) package uncooked linguine pasta
1/4 cup fresh orange juice
1 teaspoon cider vinegar
1/2 cup butter or margarine, cut into 6 pieces, at room temperature
1/4 teaspoon freshly grated nutmeg
2 tablespoons toasted poppy seeds
Salt and coarsely ground pepper to taste
2 tablespoons grated orange zest

Cook pasta according to package directions; drain and return to pan to keep warm.

In a small saucepan over medium-high heat, cook orange juice and vinegar until reduced to 2 tablespoons. Add butter or margarine and nutmeg; whisk until melted. Remove from heat.

Add butter mixture, poppy seeds, salt, and pepper to pasta in pan; toss to coat thoroughly. Transfer onto individual serving plates and garnish with orange zest.

Makes 4 servings.

Lemon Noodles

Serve as a side dish instead of potatoes.

1 (16-ounce) package uncooked spaghetti pasta
1/2 cup butter or margarine
2 cups sour cream
1 teaspoon grated lemon zest
3 tablespoons fresh lemon juice
Coarsely ground pepper to taste
1/4 cup minced fresh parsley
Freshly grated parmesan cheese

Preheat oven to 400 degrees. Cook pasta according to package directions; drain and place into a large ungreased baking dish.

In a small saucepan over low heat, melt butter or margarine; remove from heat. Stir in sour cream, lemon zest, and lemon juice; pour over pasta and toss to coat thoroughly.

Bake, uncovered, 20 to 25 minutes. Remove from oven. Sprinkle with pepper, parsley and parmesan cheese; toss to coat thoroughly. Transfer onto individual serving plates.

Makes 4 servings.

Linguine With Tomatoes & Basil

This is the perfect recipe for those hot summer days when your garden is plentiful with fresh tomatoes and basil.

6 very ripe large tomatoes, peeled, seeded, and cut into bite-sized pieces
1 cup extra-virgin olive oil
1 cup fresh basil leaves, cut into strips
1 cup freshly grated parmesan cheese
3/4 cup sliced black olives
1/2 cup sliced pimiento-stuffed green olives
4 cloves garlic, minced
1 tablespoon salt
1 teaspoon coarsely ground pepper
1 (16-ounce) package uncooked linguine pasta
Freshly grated parmesan cheese

In a large bowl, combine tomatoes, olive oil, basil, parmesan cheese, black olives, green olives, garlic, salt, and pepper; stir until blended. Cover and let stand at room temperature 2 hours.

Cook pasta according to package directions; drain and return to pan. Add tomato mixture and toss to coat thoroughly. Transfer onto individual serving plates and garnish with additional parmesan cheese.

Makes 4 servings.

History of Pasta

It is said that Marco Polo introduced pasta to Italy after his journeys in China. Perhaps this is due to the similarity between pasta and noodles, as the Chinese had perfected the long, thin noodle many centuries before.

There is another legend that an Italian sailor persuaded his Chinese mistress to show him how to make noodles. Then with Italian flair, he rolled the dough into bigger and wider rolls, and pasta was born.

Spaghetti's popularity in the United States dates back only fifty years. It arrived here in the 1920s with the immigration from southern Italy. It is said that this dish was greatly assisted by Prohibition. This is because the only place where a glass of wine could be drunk, more or less legally, were the Italian speakeasies that all served spaghetti.

There are about 150 major varieties of pasta, cut in every imaginable shape.

Olive Oil

Olive oil is one of the oldest culinary oils. In ancient Athens, the olive was a symbol of the city's prosperity, and its oil was used both in cooking and as fuel for oil-burning lamps.

Buying oil in small sizes, or splitting larger bottles with friends, is a practical way to buy expensive oils. Oil purchased in bulk should always be poured into smaller containers, preferably in a can or a dark-colored bottle.

Air, heat, and light will cause olive oil to turn rancid, so it should be stored in a cool place in an airtight container. When chilled, or in cold weather, the oil may turn cloudy and even solidify. Such oil will clear again as it warms, so cloudiness should not be taken as an indication that the oil is past its prime. Be sure bottles are tightly sealed. Never store olive oil in the refrigerator.

Creamy Spinach & Tortellini

1 (16-ounce) package fresh or frozen uncooked cheese tortellini
2 tablespoons olive oil
1/2 cup chopped onion
3 cloves garlic, minced
1 (9-ounce) package frozen chopped spinach, thawed
1 large tomato, cubed
1/4 cup chopped fresh basil
1/2 teaspoon salt
1/2 teaspoon pepper
1 cup whipping cream
1/4 cup freshly grated parmesan cheese

Cook tortellini according to package directions; drain and return to pan to keep warm.

In a large frying pan over medium heat, heat olive oil. Add onion and garlic; sauté 4 minutes or until lightly browned. Stir in spinach, tomato, basil, salt, and pepper; cook another 5 minutes, stirring occasionally. Stir in whipping cream and parmesan cheese. Cook until mixture just comes to a boil. Reduce heat to low and mix in tortellini; cook an additional 4 minutes or until thoroughly heated. Remove from heat, transfer onto individual serving plates, and serve with additional parmesan cheese.

Makes 4 servings.

Penne a la Vodka

1 (16-ounce) package uncooked penne pasta noodles
1 tablespoon butter or margarine
2 tablespoons olive oil
1 medium onion, chopped
4 cloves garlic, minced
24 mushrooms, sliced
20 small tomatoes, peeled and seeded
2 bunches fresh basil
1/4 cup vodka
1/8 teaspoon red (cayenne) pepper
Salt and pepper to taste
1/3 cup light cream
Additional fresh basil leaves for garnish
Freshly grated parmesan cheese

Cook pasta according to package directions; drain and return to pan to keep warm.

In a large frying pan over medium heat, heat butter or margarine and olive oil. Add onion and garlic; cook 5 minutes or until vegetables are tender. Add mushrooms; cook another 5 minutes. Add tomatoes, basil, vodka, cayenne pepper, salt, and pepper; reduce heat to low and simmer an additional 20 minutes. Remove from heat and set aside to cool slightly.

In a food processor or a blender, whirl the mixture until it is almost smooth; add light cream and whirl just until combined. Pour sauce over cooked pasta. Transfer onto individual serving plates; garnish with basil leaves and parmesan cheese.

Makes 4 servings.

Avocado Linguine

1 large avocado
2 tablespoons lemon juice
1 (16-ounce) package uncooked linguine pasta
1/4 cup white wine
1/3 cup chicken or vegetable broth
4 ounces gorgonzola or cambozola cheese, crumbled
4 or 5 fresh basil leaves, minced
Salt and coarsely ground pepper to taste
1/4 cup toasted pine nuts

Peel, pit, and slice avocado into 1/2-inch thick wedges. Place wedges onto a plate and coat with lemon juice; set aside.

Cook pasta according to package directions; drain and return to pan and set on low heat.

In a small saucepan over high heat, combine white wine and chicken or vegetable broth; bring to a boil. Reduce heat to medium and simmer until liquid is reduced to 1/3 cup.

Add gorgonzola or cambozola cheese, basil, and broth mixture to pasta; toss until cheese melts and most of the liquid is absorbed. Season with salt and pepper. Remove from heat, transfer onto individual serving plates, and arrange avocado slices onto top of pasta. Garnish with pine nuts.

Makes 4 servings.

Spinach & Goat Cheese Pasta

1 (16-ounce) package uncooked spinach fettuccine noodles
1 1/2 pounds fresh spinach, washed, dried, stemmed, and shredded
2/3 cup vegetable broth
1/2 pound soft goat cheese, crumbled
2 cups cherry tomatoes, cut in half
Salt and pepper to taste

Cook pasta according to package directions; drain and return to pan to keep warm.

In a large saucepan over medium-high heat, cook spinach in water 30 to 45 seconds or until wilted; remove from heat and drain. Add spinach to pasta; toss until blended and set aside.

In large saucepan over medium-high heat, bring vegetable broth to a boil. Stir in goat cheese until melted; remove from heat. Add cheese mixture to pasta; toss to coat thoroughly. Transfer onto individual serving plates. Scatter tomatoes over top; season with salt and pepper.

Makes 4 servings.

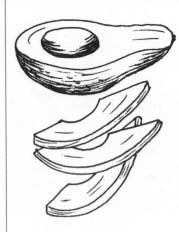

Types of Olive Oil

Olive oil is made only from green olives. Nearly the entire production of green olives in Italy is converted into olive oil.

EXTRA-VIRGIN OLIVE OIL:
It is made from slightly under-ripe olives and is produced by stone crushing and cold pressing. This oil has the lowest acidity (1 percent) and the most flavor of the olive oils and is excellent for salads. It should be thick, green-gold, and richly flavored.

VIRGIN OLIVE OIL:
It is made from olives that are slightly riper than those used for extra-virgin oil and is produced in exactly the same manner. This oil has a slightly higher level of acidity (1 1/2 percent).

PURE OLIVE OIL:
It is solvent-extracted from olive pulp, skins, and pits; then refined. It is lighter in color and blander than virgin olive oil. It is a more general-purpose olive oil.

Pasta

Sundried Tomatoes

Drying tomatoes in the sun is an age-old process of preservation. It gives them an intensely rich and sweet flavor. Most commercial sundried tomatoes, especially those produced in the United States, are not dried in the sun; they're dehydrated by oven heat.

When home drying tomatoes, use plum tomatoes (also called Roma tomatoes) because their water content is lower than that of other varieties. The amount of liquid in beefsteak tomatoes is so high that there's little left after drying but skin.

Choose tomatoes that are similar in size for drying. If you seed the tomatoes, they will dry faster.

The best way to store sundried tomatoes is in olive oil. After the tomatoes are gone, you have a wonderfully flavored oil to use in salad dressings, in cooking, or simply to drizzle over thick slices of French bread.

Spinach Fettuccine

1/4 cup pine nuts
1 (8-ounce) package uncooked fettuccine noodles
2 tablespoons olive oil
2 cloves garlic, coarsely chopped
1 small bunch fresh spinach, washed, dried, stemmed, and shredded
1 teaspoon balsamic vinegar
1/4 cup finely chopped sundried tomatoes
1/2 cup crumbled feta cheese
Freshly grated nutmeg to taste
Salt and coarsely ground pepper to taste

In a large ungreased frying pan over medium-high heat, toast pine nuts until golden brown. Remove from heat and transfer onto a plate; set aside to cool. Cook pasta according to package directions; drain and return to pan to keep warm.

In the same frying pan over medium-high heat, combine olive oil and garlic; cook 2 to 3 minutes or until garlic is soft. Add spinach and cook until slightly wilted. Sprinkle balsamic vinegar over spinach; toss to combine.

Add spinach mixture (including any excess oil in frying pans), sundried tomatoes, and feta cheese to the pasta; toss to combine thoroughly. Remove from heat and transfer onto individual serving plates. Season with nutmeg, salt, and pepper.

Makes 2 to 4 servings.

Macaroni & Cheese

1 (16-ounce) package uncooked macaroni noodles
2 tablespoons butter or margarine
2 tablespoons all-purpose flour
1/2 teaspoon salt
1/8 teaspoon pepper
1 cup milk
1 cup shredded cheddar cheese
1/2 cup bread crumbs
1 tablespoon butter or margarine

Preheat oven to 350 degrees. Cook pasta according to package directions; drain and return to pan to keep warm.

In a large saucepan over medium heat, melt butter or margarine. Add flour, salt, and pepper; stirring until smooth. Add milk slowly, stirring constantly; cook until smooth and thick. Stir in cheddar cheese. Pour over pasta; stirring to mix well. Pour pasta mixture into an ungreased 3-quart casserole dish.

In a small bowl, combine bread crumbs and butter or margarine; spread onto top of casserole. Bake, uncovered, 15 minutes or until top is browned. Remove from oven and serve.

Makes 4 servings.

Garden Fresh Pasta

1 (16-ounce) package uncooked egg noodles
2 tablespoons olive oil
1 red bell pepper, cored, seeded, and cut into thin strips
2 to 4 cloves garlic, minced
1 medium yellow summer squash, halved lengthwise and cut into 1/2-inch pieces
2 cups sugar snap peas or snow pea pods
2 cups vegetable broth
1/3 cup snipped or chopped assorted fresh herbs (tarragon, thyme, dill, and basil)
Salt and coarsely ground pepper to taste
Crumbled feta cheese

Cook pasta according to package directions; drain and return to pan to keep warm.

In a large saucepan over medium-high heat, heat olive oil. Add bell pepper, garlic, squash, sugar peas or pea pods, and vegetable broth; bring to a boil. Reduce heat to low and simmer, stirring occasionally, 4 to 5 minutes or until vegetables are crisp and tender. Stir in herbs of your choice; season with salt and pepper. Remove from heat and pour over pasta; toss to coat evenly. Transfer onto individual serving plates. Garnish with feta cheese.

Makes 6 servings.

Feta Cheese

Feta cheese was originally made from ewe's milk by shepherds in the mountains near Athens. The demand for it is now so great that it is often made with goat's milk or a combination of goat's milk and cow's milk.

The smell is like cider vinegar and the taste is tangy and salty.

Garbanzo Pasta Quick Dish

1 (16-ounce) package uncooked extra-wide egg noodles
1 (15 1/2-ounce) can garbanzo beans, drained
3/4 cup chicken broth
2 tablespoons butter or margarine
1 large onion, chopped
1 clove garlic, minced
1 (4-ounce) can sliced mushrooms, undrained
1 (10 3/4-ounce) cans cream of mushroom soup, undiluted
1/2 cup sour cream
1/2 teaspoon dried red peppers, crushed
1 teaspoon dried tarragon, crushed
Salt and coarsely ground pepper to taste
1/4 cup freshly grated parmesan cheese

Prepare pasta according to package directions; drain and return to pan to keep warm.

In a food processor or a blender, add garbanzo beans and chicken broth; whirl until smooth. Set aside.

In a large frying pan over medium heat, melt butter or margarine. Add onion and garlic; cook 2 to 3 minutes or until onion is soft. Add garbanzo bean mixture, mushrooms, mushroom soup, sour cream, red peppers, tarragon, salt, and pepper; stir until well blended. Remove from heat and pour over pasta; toss to coat evenly. Transfer onto individual serving plates and sprinkle with parmesan cheese.

Makes 6 servings.

Garbanzo Beans

Garbanzo beans are also called chick peas, Bengal gram, Egyptian pea, and ceci.

They are used a great deal in Mexican cooking. The dried garbanzo beans require a lot of cooking to soften; add one-half teaspoon of baking soda to the water when boiling. They are delicious puréed and particularly good in salads.

Lasagna Al la Gluten

1 (16-ounce) package uncooked lasagna noodles
1 tablespoon olive oil
1 tablespoon soy sauce
2 cups gluten, washed, drained and chopped in food processor (see page 171)
1 onion, chopped
1 (30-ounce) jar spaghetti sauce
1 (32-ounce) container ricotta cheese
1 (12-ounce) package shredded mozzarella cheese
2 eggs
1/4 cup freshly grated parmesan cheese
1 teaspoon salt
1/4 teaspoon pepper
1/2 cup chopped fresh parsley or 2 tablespoons dried parsley
1/2 teaspoon dried oregano, crushed

Preheat oven to 350 degrees. Prepare lasagna noodles according to package directions; rinse and drain. Place each noodle separately on wax paper or aluminum foil to cool while preparing the sauce.

In a large frying pan over medium-high heat, heat olive oil and soy sauce. Add gluten and sauté until golden brown, stirring constantly. Add onion and continue browning until onion is cooked. Add spaghetti sauce; when heated, remove from heat.

In a large bowl, combine ricotta cheese, mozzarella cheese (save enough to sprinkle on top of dish), eggs, and parmesan cheese. Mix in salt, pepper, parsley, and oregano.

Cover bottom of a 13x9-inch glass baking dish with a third of the spaghetti sauce. Alternate layers of lasagna, spaghetti sauce, and cheese mixture. Top with remaining spaghetti sauce, and cheese mixture. Sprinkle with additional parmesan cheese if desired.

Bake, covered, 1 hour or until hot and bubbly. Remove cover and bake another 10 minutes or until top is lightly browned. Remove from oven and cool on a wire rack for 10 minutes before cutting and serving.

VARIATION: For spinach lasagna, prepare one (10-ounce) package frozen chopped spinach according to package directions and drain. Add to different layers while preparing dish.

Makes 8 to 10 servings.

Pasta Etiquette

It is considered proper, in Italy, to eat pasta with only a fork, not a fork and a spoon. If possible, serve warm pasta in warm, shallow bowls instead of on dinner plates. The sides of the bowl aids in turning spaghetti on the fork.

Broccoli Pasta in Sweet Tomato Sauce

1 (8-ounce) package uncooked spaghetti or linguine pasta
1 medium head broccoli flowerets
Sweet Tomato Sauce
2 tablespoons minced fresh parsley
Freshly grated parmesan cheese

Prepare pasta according to package directions; drain well and return to pan to keep warm.

In a large saucepan over medium-high heat, cook broccoli in boiling water 2 to 3 minutes or just until tender. Remove from heat and rinse under cold running water; drain.

Add the cooked broccoli to the warm Sweet Tomato Sauce; mix together thoroughly. Pour mixture over the pasta; toss to coat evenly. Transfer onto individual serving plates and sprinkle with parsley and parmesan cheese to serve.

Makes 4 servings.

SWEET TOMATO SAUCE
1 tablespoon olive oil
2 cloves garlic, minced
4 large tomatoes, peeled, cored, and chopped or 1 large (28-ounce) can whole
    tomatoes, chopped, with their juice
1 (6-ounce) can tomato paste
2 tablespoons golden raisins, chopped
1/8 teaspoon red (cayenne) pepper
Salt to taste
1 1/2 tablespoons whole pine nuts or chopped almonds

In a large saucepan over medium heat, heat olive oil. Add garlic and cook 3 minutes or until golden brown. Add the tomatoes, tomato paste, raisins, cayenne pepper, and salt; reduce heat to low and simmer another 15 minutes. Add the pine nuts or almonds; simmer an additional 5 minutes. Remove from heat.

Making Pasta Ahead

Cook the pasta as usual, being particularly careful to cook it only until al dente (tender, but still firm to the bite). Drain, rinse under cold running water to stop the cooking, and again drain thoroughly.

Let pasta cool completely, then toss with a couple of teaspoons of oil so it won't stick together. Pasta can be stored in a plastic bag or in a covered bowl in the refrigerator for up to three days.

Reheating Pasta

Microwave the pasta in the storage container on HIGH for one to three minutes, tossing the pasta halfway through. The length of time in the microwave depends on how much pasta you have.

You can also reheat the pasta by putting it in a colander and running very hot water over it. Be sure to drain the pasta well before putting sauce over it.

Pizza

Quick Pizza Dough

1 1/2 cups all-purpose flour
1 teaspoon salt
1/2 package of Rapid-Rise
   yeast
1 tablespoon vegetable oil
1/2 cup lukewarm water
   (105 to 115 degrees)

Preheat oven to 425 degrees. Lightly grease a pizza pan or baking sheet. In a large bowl, combine flour, salt and yeast. Stir in vegetable oil and lukewarm water. Mix to a soft dough, then knead for five minutes or until smooth. Pat and stretch dough to a ten-inch circle and place onto a greased baking sheet.

Spread your favorite pizza toppings and cheese over the pizza dough; cook until cheese is melted or topping warm.

Pizza Dough

TIP: Do not handle pizza dough more than is needed to prepare it. Pat into ball and flatten with your hand. Stretch out into wheel. Start in the center of wheel and pat with fingers to stretch. DO NOT ROLL.

California-Style Pizza

1 (12-inch) unbaked refrigerated pizza crust
1 (15 1/2-ounce) jar spaghetti sauce
1 (6-ounce) jar marinated artichoke hearts, drained and cut in half
1/2 cup sliced black olives
1 cup (4-ounces) shredded monterey jack cheese

Place pizza crust onto a lightly oiled pizza pan or baking sheet. Spread spaghetti sauce over crust to within one inch of edge. Top with artichoke hearts and black olives.

Bake according to directions on pizza crust package. Sprinkle with cheese and bake another 5 minutes or until cheese melts. Remove from oven and cut into wedges to serve.

OPTIONAL TOPPING IDEAS:
Let your imagination run wild in making pizza. Use your own favorite ingredients.

CHEESES:
Goat cheese, crumbled
Feta cheese, crumbled
Mozzarella cheese, shredded
Swiss cheese, shredded
Cheddar cheese, shredded
Monterey jack cheese, shredded

VEGETABLES:
Sundried tomatoes, chopped
Sliced onions
Green peppers, chopped or sliced
Fresh tomato slices
Fresh or canned mushrooms, sliced
Cooked broccoli flowerets
Canned beans, drained
Avocado slices

POPULAR EXTRAS:
Black or green olives, sliced
Crushed dried hot red chilies
Minced garlic
Fresh herbs, chopped (such as basil, dill, oregano, rosemary, mint, or sage)

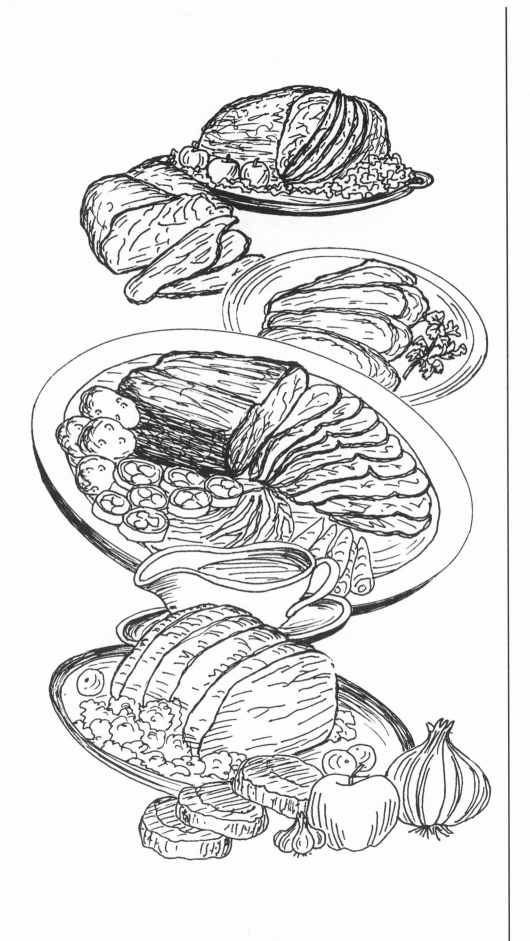

Meats

Beef Cooking Techniques

Chateaubriand

Rub the chateaubriand well with butter, then season with salt and pepper. Place roast onto a rack in a shallow baking pan. After broiling or baking, remove from oven and transfer onto a cutting board; let stand 15 minutes before carving. The thicker portion will be medium-rare, and the smaller end will be medium-well done (with variations in between). Transfer onto a serving platter and serve immediately.

BROILED: 2-POUND ROAST – Makes 4 to 6 servings.
Preheat broiler. Broil 18 to 20 minutes, approximately 3 inches from broiling unit, basting frequently with additional butter.

BAKED: 2-POUND ROAST – Makes 4 to 6 servings.
Preheat oven to 400 degrees. Bake 35 to 40 minutes for a medium-rare center.

BAKED: 4-POUND ROAST – Makes 8 to 12 servings.
Preheat oven to 400 degrees. Bake 45 to 50 minutes for a medium-rare center.

London Broil

This mini-roast needs to be broiled or grilled. For medium-rare, it will take 15 to 20 minutes per side (depending on the thickness) on a grill over medium heat. You should turn the London Broil more often than you would a steak.

Remove from oven or grill and transfer onto a cutting board; let stand 15 minutes before carving. It should be cut in very thin slices against the grain. Transfer onto a serving platter and serve immediately. Each London Broil will normally serve two people, depending on the size.

Prime Rib Roast

6-POUND AND 12-POUND
Preheat oven to 325 degrees. Place roast, fat side up, onto a rack in a shallow baking pan. Rub with coarsely ground pepper. If you wish, rub with a little dried rosemary, thyme, marjoram, or minced garlic. Bake, uncovered, to an internal temperature of:
    115 to 120 degrees for rare
    125 to 130 degrees for medium-rare

For a medium-rare roast, bake the 6-pound roast 2 hours, and the 12-pound roast 3 1/2 hours. Remove from oven and transfer onto a cutting board; let stand 15 minutes before carving. Transfer onto a serving platter and serve immediately.

The 6-pound roast makes 6 to 8 servings, and the 12-pound roast makes 12 to 16 servings.

Beef

When buying beef, choose bright red meat that is well marbled. The flesh should be firm and the fat a rich, creamy color. Leaner cuts won't have the even marbling, but they are lower in calories.

An efficient way to marinate meat is to place it, with the marinade liquid, in a heavy resealable plastic bag. Seal it tightly, eliminating as much air as possible. This easy technique requires less marinade and also takes less space in your refrigerator.

IMPORTANT:
Never cook a roast that is cold or right out of the refrigerator. Let stand at least one hour at room temperature before roasting.

When roasting meat, it should be placed onto a rack instead of onto the pan's flat surface. This is because as the meat roasts, it releases juices that collect at the bottom of the roasting pan. If the meat rests on the bottom of the pan, its underside will cook in the liquid and will be cooked by moist, rather than dry heat (this is because moist heat cooks faster than dry).

Wine in Cooking

Never cook with any wine or spirit you WOULD NOT DRINK! Cooking and the process of reducing a sauce will bring out the worst in an inferior potable.

A small quantity of wine will enhance the flavor of the dish. The alcohol in the wine evaporates while the food is cooking, and only the flavor remains.

Wine should never be added to a dish just before serving. It should simmer with the food or in the sauce while it is being cooked; as the wine cooks, it reduces and becomes an extract which flavors. Wine added too late in the preparation will give a harsh quality to the dish.

Peppered Chutney Tenderloin

The best tenderloin roast ever.

1 (3- to 4-pound) beef tenderloin roast
Port Marinade
2 teaspoons coarsely ground pepper
4 or 5 bacon slices
1/3 cup chutney (use your favorite chutney)

Place roast in a large resealable plastic bag and set into a shallow dish. Pour Port Marinade over roast and close bag. Marinate in the refrigerate several hours or overnight; turning roast occasionally to distribute marinade. Remove roast from refrigerator and let stand at room temperature for 1 hour; drain, reserving marinade.

Preheat oven to 425 degrees. Rub roast with pepper. Wrap bacon slices around roast, securing with toothpicks. Place roast onto a rack in a shallow baking pan, tucking the thin end under to make it as thick as the rest of the roast. Insert a meat thermometer into thickest part of roast.

Bake, uncovered, 30 to 45 minutes or until thermometer registers 135 degrees. Baste roast twice during baking with reserved marinade.

Remove from oven, remove bacon, and spoon chutney evenly over roast. Return to oven and bake another 5 to 10 minutes or until thermometer registers 140 degrees.

Remove from oven and transfer onto a cutting board; let stand 15 minutes before carving. Transfer onto a serving platter and serve immediately.

Makes 6 to 8 servings.

PORT MARINADE:
1 (6-ounce) can unsweetened pineapple juice
1/2 cup steak sauce
1/3 cup worcestershire sauce
1/3 cup port wine
1/3 cup olive oil
1/4 cup lemon juice
2 teaspoons seasoned salt
1 teaspoon pepper
1 teaspoon lemon-pepper seasoning
1 teaspoon ground mustard

In a medium bowl, combine pineapple juice, steak sauce, worcestershire sauce, port wine, olive oil, lemon juice, seasoned salt, pepper, lemon-pepper seasoning, and ground mustard; stir until well blended.

Tenderloin With Pepper Marinade

The next-best tenderloin.

1 (4 to 6-pound) beef tenderloin roast
Pepper Marinade
6 to 10 bacon slices

Place roast in a large resealable plastic bag set into a shallow dish. Pour Pepper Marinade over roast and close bag. Marinate in the refrigerator for several hours or overnight; turning roast occasionally to distribute marinade. Remove roast from refrigerator and let stand at room temperature for 1 hour; drain, discarding marinade.

Preheat oven to 425 degrees. Wrap bacon slices around roast, securing with toothpicks. Place roast onto a rack in a shallow baking pan, tucking the thin end under to make it as thick as the rest of the roast. Insert a meat thermometer into thickest part of the roast.

Bake, uncovered, 60 minutes or until thermometer registers 140 degrees. Remove from oven and transfer onto a cutting board; let stand 15 minutes before carving. Transfer onto a serving platter and serve immediately.

Makes 8 to 12 servings.

PEPPER MARINADE:
1 cup port wine
3/4 cup soy sauce
1/3 cup olive oil
1 teaspoon coarsely ground pepper
2 or 3 cloves garlic, minced
1 dried bay leaf
Hot pepper sauce to taste

In a small bowl, combine port wine, soy sauce, olive oil, pepper, garlic, bay leaf, and hot pepper sauce; stir until well blended.

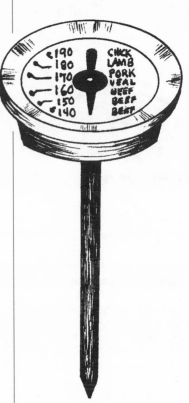

Prime Rib Supreme

1/3 cup beef broth
1/4 cup garlic salt
2 tablespoons curry powder
1 tablespoon coarsely ground pepper
1 (5 to 6-pound) standing rib roast (at least 3 ribs)

Preheat oven to 500 degrees. Combine beef broth, garlic salt, curry powder, and pepper to form a paste. Apply paste to both ends and fat side of roast, pressing to adhere as much as possible.

Insert a meat thermometer into thickest part of roast and place, rib side down, onto a rack in a shallow baking pan. Bake, uncovered, 20 minutes. DO NOT OPEN DOOR. Decrease temperature to 350 degrees and continue to bake another 1 to 1 2/3 hours. Watch thermometer and remove at desired doneness.

Remove from oven and transfer onto a cutting board; let stand 15 minutes before carving. Transfer onto a serving platter and serve immediately.

Makes 8 servings.

Meat Thermometer

To use a meat thermometer, insert it through the fat side of the meat, being careful not to touch bone. Bone conducts heat faster, and you'll get a false reading of the meat's temperature.

TESTING A MEAT THERMOMETER:
Hold the stem of the meat thermometer in boiling water for fifteen seconds. Assuming you are at sea level, the thermometer should register 212 degrees.

If your thermometer does not register 212 degrees, twist the small nut beneath the thermometer face with pliers until the temperature is correct.

Degreasing

*SPOONING AWAY
SHALLOW FAT:*
*Place the tip of a large
spoon into the liquid. Tilt
the bowl enough to allow
the fat to flow into the
spoon, without draining off
any of the juices. Repeat
the procedure as often as
necessary.*

*LADLING OFF A
DEEP FAT LAYER:*
*Tilt the side of a large ladle,
preferably a basting ladle,
downward into the juices.
Let the fat flow into the ladle
until its bowl is about half
full. Empty the fat into a
bowl. Repeat the procedure
as often as necessary.*

BLOTTING UP FAT:
*Fold several thicknesses
of paper towels together.
Holding the towels by the
edges, lay the center section
over the surface of the
liquid briefly. Lift up the
towels the instant they
become saturated. Repeat
the procedure, as necessary,
using fresh paper towels
every time.*

*LIFTING
SOLIDIFIED FAT:*
*Slide one edge of a metal
spoon under the bottom of
the layer of chilled, solid
fat. Carefully lift it up and
remove.*

Peppered Rib Eye of Beef

1 (5-pound) beef rib eye roast, trimmed of fat
1/2 cup coarsely ground pepper
1/2 teaspoon ground cardamom seeds
Tomato Marinade
1 cup water

Place roast into a large baking dish. In a small bowl, combine pepper and cardamom seeds. Firmly press pepper mixture onto roast. Pour Tomato Marinade over roast. Cover and refrigerate at least 6 hours or overnight, basting occasionally. Remove roast from refrigerator and let stand at room temperature for 1 hour; drain, discarding marinade.

Preheat oven to 300 degrees. Wrap the marinated roast in heavy-duty aluminum foil. Transfer roast into a shallow pan. Bake 1 1/2 to 2 hours for medium-rare or until thermometer registers 140 degrees. Remove from oven and transfer onto a cutting board; let stand 15 minutes before carving. Remove aluminum foil from roast.

Degrease drippings. In a small saucepan over medium-high heat, combine 1 cup drippings with 1 cup water; bring to a boil. Remove from heat and transfer into a serving bowl.

Carve roast, transfer onto a serving platter, and serve immediately; passing sauce separately.

Makes 8 to 10 servings.

TOMATO MARINADE:
1 tablespoon tomato paste
1 teaspoon paprika
1/2 teaspoon garlic powder
1 cup soy sauce
3/4 cup red wine vinegar

In a medium bowl, combine tomato paste, paprika, and garlic powder. Stir in soy sauce and wine vinegar; stir until well blended.

Rare Roast Beef

This is a basic and infallible recipe for obtaining a rare roast.

Preheat oven to 500 degrees. Place beef roast (preferably a beef rib eye or round roast), uncovered, in preheated oven; no seasonings are necessary.

Cook at 500 degrees • 5 minutes for each pound.
Example: 3-pound roast x 5 minutes = 15 minutes total baking time.

Turn oven off and let roast remain inside 2 hours. DO NOT OPEN OVEN DOOR.

Remove from oven and transfer onto a cutting board; let stand 15 minutes before carving. Transfer onto a serving platter and serve immediately.

Garlic-Seasoned Roast Beef

3 large cloves garlic, minced
1 1/2 tablespoons salt
1/2 teaspoon paprika
1/2 teaspoon ground turmeric
1/2 teaspoon ground thyme
1/2 teaspoon pepper
1 (7-pound) beef rib roast
2 tablespoons vegetable oil
Pan Gravy

In a small bowl, combine garlic, salt, paprika, turmeric, thyme, and pepper. Wipe roast dry with paper towels; rub all sides with vegetable oil. Rub the garlic mixture over sides and top of roast. Transfer roast into a shallow pan. Cover loosely with aluminum foil. Refrigerate overnight. Remove roast from refrigerator and let stand at room temperature for 1 hour.

Preheat oven to 450 degrees. Position oven rack in lower third of oven. Bake, uncovered, 30 minutes to sear; then reduce oven temperature to 325 degrees. Bake another hour or until thermometer inserted straight down from top center reads 140 degrees.

Remove from oven and transfer onto a cutting board; let stand 15 minutes before carving. Carve roast into 1/2-inch slices. Transfer onto a serving platter and serve immediately with Pan Gravy.

Makes 10 servings.

PAN GRAVY:
1/4 cup beef drippings
1/4 cup all-purpose flour
2 cups water
Salt and pepper to taste

In a large glass measuring container, pour beef drippings; leaving brown particles in the pan. Let fat rise to top of drippings; skim off fat, reserving 1/4 cup of beef juice.

Return reserved juice to baking pan; stir in flour. Cook over low heat, stirring constantly, until mixture is thickened and bubbly; remove from heat. Stir in water; return to heat and bring to boil, stirring constantly. Boil and stir 1 to 2 minutes. Season with salt and pepper. Remove from heat and transfer into a serving bowl.

Cooking Beef

For cooking meat to perfection, A MEAT THERMOMETER IS A MUST.

Remove meat from the oven when the internal temperature measures five to ten degrees below the desired temperature.

Once outside the oven, food will continue to cook those last degrees before serving. This is called the "carry-over cooking time," and it can make the difference between perfection and a near miss.

Allow roasts and other large cuts of meat to rest for fifteen minutes after they're cooked. This sets the juices and makes the meat easier to carve.

Keeping Meat Warm

When you remove cooked meats from the oven to prevent overcooking but need to keep the meat warm until serving, use a tent of aluminum foil. Use a piece of aluminum foil large enough to loosely cover the platter of meat. Make a tent by placing aluminum foil (shiny side down to reflect heat downward) over the food. (Don't tuck foil edges under the platter; this would cause condensation of steam that could drip onto the meat.)

Onions

1 large onion equals about 1 cup chopped onion.

1 medium onion equals about 3/4 cup chopped onion.

When choosing onions, be sure that the skins are shiny and dry. They should have absolutely NO SMELL whatever. If they do, they are probably bruised somewhere under the skin and are on their way out.

Don't buy onions that are beginning to sprout unless you just want to watch them turn into a green bouquet. Young onions are sweeter than old ones.

Pressure Cooking

You can cook vegetables, beans, sauces, and even risotto in the pressure cooker, and in a lot shorter time than you can in a pan on top of the stove.

Pressure cooking cooks food faster because the water used in cooking can be heated to a higher temperature under pressure than it can in an ordinary pan.

Before using any pressure cooker, read and follow the manufacturer's instructions.

Peppered Tenderloin With Coriander Sauce

1 (5-pound) beef tenderloin roast with some surface fat
2 tablespoons coarsely ground pepper
Coriander Sauce

Preheat oven to 450 degrees. For a compact and even shape, tie roast snugly with cotton string at about 2-inch intervals. Place roast onto a rack in a shallow baking pan and firmly pat pepper all over it. Lightly brush some of the Coriander Sauce onto roast.

Insert a meat thermometer into the thickest part of the roast. Bake, uncovered, 30 to 45 minutes or until thermometer registers 140 degrees. Baste roast twice during baking with Coriander Sauce. Remove from oven and transfer onto a cutting board; let stand 15 minutes before carving. Transfer onto a serving platter and spoon hot Coriander Sauce over roast before serving.

Makes 8 to 10 servings.

CORIANDER SAUCE:
3/4 cup dry white wine
1/4 cup butter or margarine
1 tablespoon coriander seeds, crushed
1/2 tablespoon soy sauce
1/2 tablespoon Dijon mustard
1/2 cup diagonally sliced green onions (including tops)

In a large saucepan over medium-high heat, combine white wine, butter or margarine, coriander seeds, soy sauce, and Dijon mustard; stir until well blended. Reduce heat to low and bring to a simmer; remove from heat. Before serving, stir in green onions.

Mac's Roast Beef

If you are not afraid of pressure cookers – this is your recipe.

1 tablespoon vegetable oil
1 (3-pound) beef sirloin steak or beef round roast
6 beef-flavored bouillon cubes
3 cups hot water
3 dried bay leaves
1 medium onion, minced
1/2 teaspoon dried sage, crushed

In a large frying pan over medium-high heat, heat vegetable oil. Add steak or roast and brown on all sides; remove and transfer into a pressure cooker. In same pan, dissolve bouillon cubes in hot water; place bouillon liquid, bay leaves, onion, and sage in the pressure cooker.

Heat pressure cooker to low temperature (according to manufacturer's directions), just enough to keep pressure release moving. Cook 40 minutes. Turn off heat and let stand for 15 minutes. Remove steak or roast from pressure cooker and transfer onto a cutting board. Carve, transfer onto a serving platter, and serve with drippings from roast.

Makes 6 servings.

King of Meats – Beef Rouladens

This is a traditional German dish. It should be made ahead and reheated in the gravy when ready to serve (the taste is better if this is done).

2 pounds beef sirloin steak or beef round steak
All-purpose flour
Salt and pepper to taste
1 large onion, chopped
4 to 6 bacon slices
Vegetable oil
1/2 cup dry white wine
Water

Cut steaks into strips measuring 3 to 4 inches. On a floured surface, coat steak strips with flour and, using a meat mallet, pound until thin. Season each steak strip with salt and pepper. Put a little chopped onion and 1/4 bacon slice onto the top of each steak strip. To make rouladens, roll up and tie well with string.

In a large frying pan over medium-high heat, heat vegetable oil. Add rouladens and brown thoroughly. Remove rouladens from frying pan and transfer onto a large plate; add white wine to drippings in pan and let simmer 1 minute.

In a large heavy baking pot or dutch oven, place rouladens and cover with wine mixture; add water to cover the rouladens. Simmer gently 2 hours or until tender. Remove rouladens, discard strings, and transfer onto a serving platter; set aside.

To make gravy, skim the fat from the pan juices. Add enough flour to thicken. Cook over medium heat, stirring constantly, until the mixture is thickened and bubbly, about 10 minutes. Season with additional salt and pepper, if desired. Remove from heat and transfer into a serving bowl. Serve with rouladens.

Makes 4 to 6 servings.

Grilled New York Sirloin Steaks

Seasoned pepper
6 beef New York steaks, cut 1 1/2-inch thick
6 cloves garlic, minced
2 cups soy sauce
1/2 cup worcestershire sauce

Generously sprinkle seasoned pepper over steaks. Spread 1 clove of the minced garlic over the surface of each steak; press garlic into meat. In a large baking dish, arrange steaks in a single layer. Pour soy sauce and worcestershire sauce over steaks. Cover and marinate in the refrigerator at least 1 hour or overnight; turning steaks occasionally.

Preheat barbecue grill. Drain steaks, reserving marinade. Place steaks onto hot grill. Spoon 2 tablespoons of the reserved marinade onto each steak. Cover barbecue with lid, open any vents, and cook 9 to 11 minutes for medium-rare or 10 to 12 minutes for medium, turning steaks and spooning additional marinade on steaks. Remove from grill and transfer onto a serving platter.

Makes 6 servings.

Deglazing

One of the delights of shallow frying or even pan roasting is that you are left with delicious meat juices in the pan. With very little effort, these can be made into a really delicious sauce or gravy to pour over the meat when serving.

With a process called deglazing, you can take advantage of this resource of flavor by diluting the residue with liquid over heat to make a sauce or even a gravy.

Wine is used as a frequent deglazing liquid, and it lends its flavor to a pan sauce, gravy, or braising liquid. Be sure to boil a wine-based mixture for a few minutes to evaporate the alcohol.

Barbecuing or Grilling

To keep food from sticking to the grill, brush the hot grill with vegetable oil before cooking or spray with vegetable-oil cooking spray.

To avoid flare-ups and charred food when grilling, remove visible fat from meat.

Bill's Great Steaks

This is the perfect recipe when the men decide to cook – easy and very good!

Preheat barbecue grill. Sprinkle steaks with garlic salt and worcestershire sauce. Poke holes with a fork so juices can run into steak. Place onto heated grill and cook to your preference.

Rubs and Pastes

For the best flavor, use the best-quality ingredients you can find. Always use fresh herbs and spices when you can.

Pastes and rubs on rubbed on meats before cooking. They will add even more flavor if left on at least thirty minutes.

Remove meat from the refrigerator at least thirty minutes, but preferably one hour, before grilling to bring it closer to room temperature; it will cook quicker.

TIP: Electric coffee grinders make excellent spice grinders and are particularly useful when preparing rubs.

Korean-Style Barbecued Beef

This is traditionally barbecued but can be prepared on the stove top. Excellent served over rice.

2 pounds beef sirloin steak
5 tablespoons soy sauce
5 tablespoons sugar
7 tablespoons sesame oil, divided
5 tablespoons rice wine or sherry
1 tablespoon sesame seeds
2 tablespoons chopped green onions
6 cloves garlic, minced
1/2 teaspoon pepper
1/2 teaspoon red (cayenne) pepper

Freeze steak 2 hours; remove from freezer and cut across the grain into thin, diagonal slices.

In a large bowl, combine soy sauce, sugar, 5 tablespoons sesame oil, and rice wine or sherry. Add sesame seeds, green onions, garlic, pepper, and cayenne pepper; stir until well blended. Add steak strips and marinate at least 1 hour or overnight.

In a large frying pan over high heat, heat 2 tablespoons sesame oil. Remove steak strips from marinade and drain; sauté until brown on both sides. Remove from heat, transfer onto a serving platter, and serve.

Makes 5 servings.

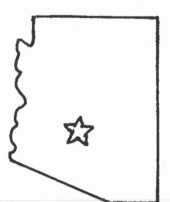

Grilled Arizona Beef

3 tablespoons firmly packed brown sugar
1 tablespoon black peppercorns
1 tablespoon mustard seeds
1 tablespoon whole coriander seeds
4 cloves garlic
2 pounds beef top round steak or beef London broil (about 1 1/2-inch thick)
Salt to taste

In a food processor or blender, place brown sugar, peppercorns, mustard seeds, coriander seeds, and garlic; whirl until seeds and garlic are crushed. Pat spice mixture onto beef. Season generously with salt.

Preheat barbecue grill. Oil hot grill to help prevent sticking. Place steak onto hot grill. Cover barbecue with lid, open any vents, and cook 12 to 15 minutes for medium doneness, turning once. Remove from grill and transfer onto a cutting board. Let stand 5 minutes before carving. To serve, cut across the grain into thin, diagonal slices. Transfer onto a serving platter and serve immediately.

Makes 6 servings.

Grilled Persian Kabobs

1 cup plain yogurt
1 small onion, chopped
1/3 cup olive oil
1/2 teaspoon saffron threads or 1 tablespoon ground Mexican saffron
1 pound beef sirloin steak, cut into 1 1/2-inch pieces
Hot cooked rice

In a large shallow bowl, combine yogurt, onion, olive oil, and saffron; stir until well blended. Add steak pieces; stir until well coated. Refrigerate at least 2 hours or overnight.

Preheat barbecue grill. Remove steak pieces from yogurt mixture and thread onto metal skewers – DON'T WIPE OFF THE YOGURT. Place kabobs onto hot grill and cook until done to your preference. Remove from grill and serve over hot cooked rice.

Makes 2 servings.

Grilled Beef Shish Kabobs

2 pounds beef sirloin steak, cut into 1 1/2-inch pieces
Teriyaki sauce
Small whole boiling onions
Green peppers
Mushrooms
Cherry tomatoes
Zucchini
Hot cooked rice

In a large shallow bowl, combine steak pieces and teriyaki sauce; stir until well coated. Refrigerate at least 2 hours or overnight.

Preheat barbecue grill. Remove steak pieces from marinade with a slotted spoon; drain. Thread steak pieces onto metal skewers; alternate with the different vegetables. Place onto hot grill and cook until done to your preference, basting with the teriyaki sauce. Remove from grill and serve over hot cooked rice.

Makes 4 servings.

Sirloin Tip

When you're in the mood for beef kabobs or Stroganoff, or when you want a couple of good tender steaks without taking out a loan, look for a sirloin tip roast. This roast is boneless and very easy to cut into the serving-sized pieces you need.

It is one of the more versatile cuts of beef in your butcher's meat case, and one that offers real money-saving potential.

Shish Kabobs

Shish Kebab was the invention of nomadic sheep herdsmen in the Near East, who found they could conveniently roast lamb or mutton over their campfires by cutting the meat into small pieces and threading onto skewers.

Through the years, the term shish kebab (or kabob, as it is commonly spelled) has been extended to the combination of any meats and vegetables cooked on a skewer.

TIPS: Partially precook all the vegetables except the tomatoes. Otherwise, the vegetables will not be done the same time as the beef cubes.

If using wooden skewers, soak in water before adding meat. Wrap end of skewer in foil to prevent wood from burning.

Beef

Pot Roasting

In pot roasting, the size of the pan is important. It should hold the roast snugly but with ample room for the vegetables. If it is too large, the food will dry out. If too small, the meat will not cook evenly.

IMPORTANT:
When browning beef, never crowd the pan or you will create steam and the meat will turn gray instead of brown. SEAR A FEW PIECES AT A TIME, removing them as you go along and draining them on paper towels.

Be sure the meat is very dry, unless you are dredging the pieces first in seasoned flour, as some recipes suggest.

Baked Round Steak

4 tablespoons vegetable oil, divided
4 pounds beef round steak, cut into individual portions
Salt and pepper to taste
2 tablespoons all-purpose flour
1 cup water
1 cup catsup
3 onions, thinly sliced
2 carrots, grated
1/2 teaspoon hot pepper sauce

Preheat oven to 300 degrees. In a large frying pan over medium-high heat, heat 2 tablespoons vegetable oil; add steak pieces and brown, turning to brown on all sides. Remove from pan and place into an ungreased 13x9-inch baking dish; season with salt and pepper.

Make a sauce by adding an additional 2 tablespoons vegetable oil to frying pan; stir in flour until smooth. Stir in water, catsup, onions, carrots, and hot pepper sauce; cook 5 minutes. Pour sauce over steak pieces; cover, and bake 1 1/2 to 2 hours or until meat is tender (add more water, if needed, to keep steak pieces moist). Remove from oven and serve immediately.

Makes 6 to 8 servings.

Burgundy Pot Roast

1/2 cup all-purpose flour
1 tablespoon paprika
1 (5-pound) boneless beef chuck roast or eye of round roast
2 tablespoons olive oil
1 cup burgundy wine
2 cups beef broth
6 cloves garlic, halved
3 medium onions, thinly sliced
1 dried bay leaf
8 small red potatoes, cleaned and quartered
8 carrots, cut lengthwise

In a small bowl, combine flour and paprika; pat onto all sides of roast. In a large pot or dutch oven, heat olive oil. Add the roast and brown, turning to brown on all sides. Remove roast from pot and place onto a plate; set aside.

Add burgundy wine and beef broth; scraping up the brown bits clinging to the bottom of the pot. Add garlic, onions, and bay leaf; bring to a boil.

Reduce heat to low and return roast to the pot. Simmer, covered, 2 1/2 to 3 hours or until fork-tender. Add potatoes and carrots. Simmer, covered, another 35 to 45 minutes or until potatoes and carrots are tender. Remove from heat, transfer onto a serving platter, and serve immediately.

Makes 8 servings.

Connecticut Yankee Pot Roast Dijon

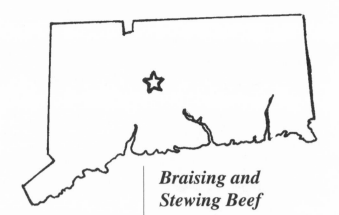

1 (3-pound) boneless beef chuck roast
1 teaspoon celery salt
1 teaspoon lemon-pepper seasoning
1 teaspoon garlic powder
2 tablespoons vegetable oil
1 1/3 cups water
1/2 cup port wine
1/3 cup chopped onion
1/4 cup tomato sauce
2 tablespoons Dijon mustard
1 teaspoon worcestershire sauce
Wine Gravy

Trim excess fat from roast. Sprinkle roast with celery salt, lemon-pepper seasoning, and garlic powder. Rub seasonings into roast with fingertips.

In a large pot or dutch oven over medium-high heat, heat vegetable oil; add roast and brown, turning to brown all sides. Add water, port wine, onion, tomato sauce, Dijon mustard, and worcestershire sauce. Reduce heat to low, cover, and simmer 2 to 2 1/2 hours or until fork-tender. Remove from heat and transfer onto a serving platter. Serve with Wine Gravy.

Makes 6 servings.

WINE GRAVY:
1/2 cup cold water
1/4 cup all-purpose flour

In a large glass measuring container, pour juices from the baking pan; skim off fat. Measure 1 1/2 cups of juice. Return juice to baking pan. In a small bowl, stir water into flour until smooth; stir into pan juices. Cook and stir over medium-low heat until mixture is thickened and bubbly. Remove from heat and transfer into a serving bowl.

Braising and Stewing Beef

The more economical cuts of meat (such as rump, shank, brisket, chuck, and short ribs) which would be tough if open roasted, can be turned into tender dishes by stewing or braising. They require moist heat to transform them from tough to succulent. The technique called "braising" or "stewing" is basically long, slow cooking in a liquid in a tightly covered dutch oven or a heavy baking pot (either on top of the stove or in the oven).

Dutch Oven

A dutch oven is a heavy covered skillet used in home cooking for almost any slow cooking. This handy cooking pot is generally made of cast iron and is very heavy.

When Lewis and Clark made their journey to the Northwest in 1805, they listed the dutch oven as one of their most valued pieces of equipment. Many families still own and use dutch ovens that made the trip west by covered wagon.

Beef

Gravy Tips

If you brown the flour well before adding the liquid when making gravy, you will avoid pale or lumpy gravy.

You can also make dark gravy with unbrowned flour by making a dark roux. A roux is a thickener made from equal amounts of fat and flour. Heat the fat, add the flour, and cook over medium heat, stirring constantly until the roux becomes a deep brown. When making gravy with the roux, it will not thicken as well, so you will need more of it.

If all the above tips fail in getting your gravy to brown to a rich color or you just want a quick and easy solution, add one-eighth teaspoon instant coffee granules and stir to blend.

Thin gravy can be easily thickened by adding a mixture of either flour and water or cornstarch and water, which has been mixed to a smooth paste. Add gradually, stirring constantly, while bringing to a boil.

1-1-1 Formula

When making sauces and gravies and want to get the right consistency without trial and error, just remember this easy 1-1-1 Formula.

To thicken one cup of stock, use one tablespoon butter and one tablespoon flour.

The Best Pot Roast & Gravy

Serve the sliced pot roast on a warmed platter and pass the gravy.

1 (4-pound) boneless beef chuck roast
Salt and pepper to taste
1 to 2 tablespoons olive oil, divided
1 medium onion, finely chopped
2 cloves garlic, minced
2 (10 3/4-ounce) cans tomato soup, undiluted
1/2 cup red wine
1 teaspoon worcestershire sauce
2 cups water
1 tablespoon dried thyme, crushed
1 package sazon seasoning*
6 carrots, cut into large pieces
6 potatoes, cut into quarters
8 to 10 small onions
Cornstarch Gravy

* Sazon seasoning can be found in Spanish stores or large supermarkets. (If you cannot find sazon seasoning, use chili powder to taste.)

Sprinkle roast lightly with salt and pepper. In a large pot or dutch oven over medium-high heat, add 1 tablespoon olive oil; brown roast, turning to brown all sides. Remove roast to a large plate; set aside.

Add remaining 1 tablespoon of olive oil, if necessary, and sauté onion until lightly browned. Add garlic and continue to sauté until soft. Add tomato soup, red wine, worcestershire sauce, water, thyme, and sazon seasoning. Bring liquid to a boil. Reduce heat to low.

Place roast back into the baking pan, cover, and simmer 2 to 2 1/2 hours or until meat is almost done. Add carrots, potatoes, and onions. Simmer another 35 to 40 minutes or until roast is fork-tender and vegetables are cooked. Remove from heat and transfer onto a serving platter. Serve with Cornstarch Gravy.

CORNSTARCH GRAVY:
1/4 cup cornstarch
1/3 cup cold water
Water
Salt and pepper to taste

In a small bowl, dissolve cornstarch in water. Skim the fat from pan juices and add cornstarch mixture; cook over low heat, stirring constantly, 10 minutes or until mixture is thickened and bubbly (add more water if mixture is too thick). Season with salt and pepper. Remove from heat and transfer into a serving bowl.

Makes 6 servings.

Taco Pie

1 pound lean ground beef
1 package taco seasoning mix
1/2 cup chopped onion
1/2 cup sliced black olives
1 cup torn fresh corn tortillas
Taco sauce to taste
1 cup shredded cheddar cheese
1 1/4 cups milk
3/4 cup baking mix (Bisquick)
3 eggs

Preheat oven to 400 degrees. In a large frying pan over medium-high heat, add ground beef and sauté until brown; drain. Stir in taco seasoning mix; remove from heat and spread into an ungreased 9-inch pie plate. Top with onion, black olives, corn tortillas, taco sauce, and cheddar cheese (in order given).

In a blender on high speed, whirl milk, baking mix, and eggs 5 seconds or until smooth; pour into pie plate over the other ingredients. Bake, uncovered, 25 to 30 minutes or until knife inserted between center and edge comes out clean. Remove from oven and cool on a wire rack 5 minutes before cutting and serving.

Makes 4 servings.

Football Night Nachos

1 pound extra-lean ground beef
1 package taco seasoning mix
1 (16-ounce) can refried beans
1 large onion, chopped
2 cups shredded cheddar cheese
Corn chips
1 head lettuce, chopped
Avocado slices
Sour cream
Chopped tomatoes
Taco sauce

In a large frying pan over medium-high heat, add ground beef and taco seasoning mix; sauté until brown. Drain and remove from heat. On individual serving plates or a large ovenproof platter, spread refried beans, ground beef, onion, and cheddar cheese. Arrange corn chips around sides of dish.

In a microwave or oven, heat just until cheese melts. Remove from oven. To serve, top with lettuce and toppings of your choice such as avocado slices, sour cream, tomatoes, or taco sauce.

Makes 4 servings.

Frijoles Refritos (Refried Beans)

Did you know that you can make your own refried beans? It's very easy. Just follow the easy recipe listed below:

3 bacon slices, coarsely chopped
2 medium onions, chopped
2 cloves garlic, minced
2 (15-ounce) cans black beans
2 tablespoons white vinegar
Salt and pepper to taste

In a large nonstick frying pan over medium heat, cook bacon 4 minutes, stirring often, or until it begins to brown. Discard all but 1 tablespoon of the bacon drippings.

Add onions and garlic to pan; cook 7 minutes, stirring often, or until onions are limp and bacon is browned.

Drain canned beans, reserving 1/2 cup liquid. To pan, add beans, reserved liquid, and white vinegar. With the back of a spoon, coarsely mash beans; season to taste with more vinegar (if needed), salt, and pepper. Remove from heat.

If making ahead, cover and chill up to 1 day.

Makes 3 1/4 cups.

Beef

Ground Beef or Hamburger History

According to history, the hamburger began as a dish of raw chopped beef first prepared by the Tartar people in Baltic Russia.

It wasn't until ships from the German port of Hamburg began calling on Russian ports that the recipe for what we call "Tartar Steak" was transported to Hamburg, Germany.

German immigrants brought it to the United States in the 19th century. In America, the chopped meat cooked Hamburg-style became known as the "hamburger."

It is considered a fact that Americans consume more ground beef than any other nation.

The Whole Enchilada

1 tablespoon vegetable oil
1/2 cup chopped onion
1 (4-ounce) can chopped green chilies
2 jalapeño chile peppers, cored, seeded, and finely chopped
1 clove garlic, minced
2 1/2 pounds lean ground beef
1/2 cup beef broth or water
1 1/2 teaspoons chili powder
1/2 teaspoon ground cumin
1/8 teaspoon red (cayenne) pepper
1/2 teaspoon salt
8 flour tortillas
1 (16-ounce) jar taco sauce
1 cup shredded cheddar cheese
Sour cream for garnish
Finely chopped green onions for garnish

Preheat oven to 375 degrees. In a large pot or dutch oven over medium heat, heat vegetable oil. Add onion, green chilies, jalapeño peppers, and garlic; cook 2 minutes, stirring frequently. Add ground beef and beef broth or water; sprinkle with chili powder, cumin, cayenne pepper, and salt. Reduce heat to low; cover and simmer until ground beef is cooked. Remove from heat.

Divide beef mixture evenly among tortillas; roll tortillas up. In an ungreased 13x9-inch baking dish, spread a small amount of taco sauce evenly onto the bottom. Place rolled tortillas on top of the taco sauce; top tortillas with remaining taco sauce and sprinkle with cheddar cheese. Bake, uncovered, 20 minutes or until hot. Remove from oven; garnish with sour cream and green onions.

Makes 8 servings.

Easy Grilled Hamburger

1 pound lean ground beef
1 teaspoon salt
1 teaspoon worcestershire sauce
1/4 cup seasoned bread crumbs
1 egg

Preheat barbecue grill. In a large bowl, combine ground beef, salt, worcestershire sauce, bread crumbs, and egg; stir until well blended. Form into 4-inch patties. Place patties onto hot grill. Cover barbecue with lid, open any vents, and cook 7 to 10 minutes; turn patties over and cook another 7 to 10 minutes. Remove from grill and transfer onto a serving platter.

Makes 4 servings.

Spinach Lasagna

This is not your ordinary lasagna. The spinach filling gives it a very flavorful taste.

1 (8-ounce) package uncooked lasagna noodles
1 medium onion, chopped
1 clove garlic, minced
2 tablespoons butter
1 pound lean ground beef
1 (4-ounce) can mushrooms, undrained
1 (8-ounce) can tomato sauce
1 (6-ounce) can tomato paste
1 dried bay leaf, crumbled
2 teaspoons salt, divided
1 teaspoon dried oregano, crushed
2 eggs
1 package frozen chopped spinach, thawed and drained
1 tablespoon olive oil
1/2 cup chopped fresh parsley
1 cup (8-ounces) ricotta cheese
1/4 cup freshly grated parmesan cheese
1 teaspoon dried basil, crushed

Heat oven to 350 degrees. Prepare lasagna noodles according to package directions; rinse and drain. Return to pan to keep warm.

In a large saucepan, lightly brown onion and garlic in butter. Add ground beef and cook until brown. Stir in mushrooms and liquid, tomato sauce, tomato paste, bay leaf, 1 teaspoon salt, and oregano; simmer 15 minutes.

In a medium bowl, beat 1 egg; pour over noodles, stirring well to coat noodles. In the same bowl, beat second egg; add spinach, olive oil, parsley, ricotta cheese, parmesan cheese, 1 teaspoon salt, and basil; stir until well blended.

Pour half of the meat mixture into an ungreased 13x9-inch baking dish. Layer half of the noodles over the sauce; spread with spinach-cheese mixture. Repeat noodle layer and top with the remainder of meat mixture.

Bake, uncovered, 45 minutes. Remove from oven and cool for 5 minutes before serving.

Makes 4 servings.

Ground Beef

When you purchase commercially ground beef, the key to quality is fat content. The lighter the color of ground meat, the more fat it contains and the more your hamburgers or meat loaves will shrink in cooking.

When seasoning ground beef, use your fingers to lightly toss the ground beef together with whatever seasonings you are using.

TIP: When shaping into patties, shape them gently. A loosely formed hamburger cooks more evenly than a compact patty.

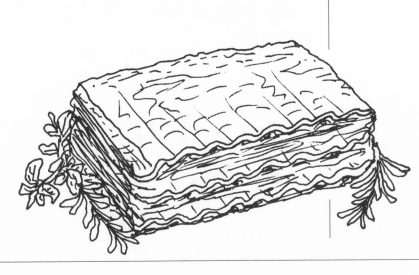

Meat Grinder

The meat grinder is one of the best money-saving gadgets that you'll find in any kitchen but not found in many modern kitchens today.

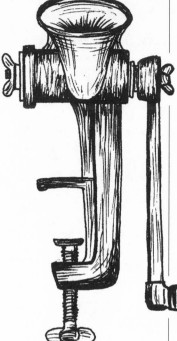

Back in the days when Great Grandma was a girl, they were as common as butter churns and used as often. But today, if you find one at all, it will very likely be buried at the back of the bottom cupboard and seldom ever used.

TIP: When chuck roast is on special in your local grocery store, buy a couple, bone them out, make a good rich soup from the bones, and grind the meat a couple of times through your old-fashioned meat grinder for the best ground chuck you've ever tasted.

Avocado Ground Beef

Comfort-type meal – very hearty.

1 1/2 pounds extra-lean ground beef
1 medium onion, chopped
1/2 teaspoon salt
1 clove garlic, minced
1 teaspoon pepper
1 (10 3/4-ounce) can cream of mushroom soup, undiluted
1 cup plain yogurt or sour cream
1 medium avocado, peeled, seeded, and cubed
3 cups cooked rice
Avocado slices
Lemon juice

In a large frying pan over medium-high heat, add ground beef and sauté until brown; drain. Add onion, salt, garlic, and pepper. Reduce heat to low, cover, and simmer 30 minutes. Blend in soup; cook another 5 minutes (add water if mixture is too thick).

Fold in yogurt or sour cream and avocado; cook until the mixture is thoroughly heated. Remove from heat and serve immediately over hot cooked rice. Garnish with avocado slices dipped in lemon juice.

Makes 4 to 6 servings.

Meat Loaf Surprise

What a surprise when you serve this classic favorite with the eggs in the center. It makes a wonderful presentation.

1 pound ground beef
1 teaspoon salt
1 teaspoon worcestershire sauce
1 egg
1/4 cup seasoned bread crumbs
2 hard-cooked eggs, peeled

Preheat oven to 350 degrees. In a large bowl, combine ground beef, salt, worcestershire sauce, egg, and bread crumbs; form into a loaf and place onto rack of a shallow baking pan.

Place hard-cooked eggs in the middle of loaf, making sure the eggs are buried inside. Bake, uncovered, 45 minutes or until ground beef is cooked. Remove from oven and serve immediately.

Makes 2 servings.

Swedish Meatballs

Excellent served over cooked rice or egg noodles.

1 pound ground beef
1/3 cup chopped onion
1/4 cup seasoned bread crumbs
1 egg
1 teaspoon worcestershire sauce
4 tablespoons all-purpose flour
1 tablespoon paprika
1 1/2 teaspoons salt
1 1/8 teaspoons pepper
2 cups boiling water

In a large bowl, combine ground beef, onion, bread crumbs, egg, and worcestershire sauce; form into walnut-sized meatballs. In a large frying pan over medium heat, add meatballs; brown and cook 15 minutes. Remove from pan and set aside.

Make a gravy by stirring flour into hot pan with meat juices; stir until smooth. Add paprika, salt, and pepper; cook and stir until flour is browned. Slowly add water and stir until smooth. Reduce heat to low; add meatballs and simmer, covered, 5 minutes. Remove from heat and transfer into a serving bowl.

Makes 4 servings.

Meatballs

Meatballs originate from the Middle East. They are usually made from beef or lamb, but are also made from a combination of beef, lamb, pork, and veal. Whatever meat is used, it needs to be fairly lean.

Meatballs are often served highly spiced. This is due to their Middle Eastern heritage, where spices are used abundantly.

Cincinnati Chili

1 large onion, chopped
1 1/2 pounds lean ground beef
1 clove garlic, minced
1 tablespoon chili powder
1 teaspoon ground allspice
1 teaspoon ground cinnamon
1 teaspoon ground cumin
1/2 teaspoon red (cayenne) pepper
1/2 teaspoon salt
1 (15-ounce) can tomato sauce
1 tablespoon worcestershire sauce
1 tablespoon cider vinegar
1/2 cup water
Spaghetti noodles
Chopped onion
Shredded cheddar cheese
Refried beans

In a large frying pan over medium-high heat, add onion, ground beef, garlic, and chili powder; sauté until ground beef is slightly cooked. Add allspice, cinnamon, cumin, cayenne pepper, salt, tomato sauce, worcestershire sauce, cider vinegar, and water. Reduce heat to low and simmer, uncovered, 1 1/2 hours. Remove from heat.

Cook spaghetti noodles according to package directions and transfer onto individual serving plates. Ladle chili over noodles and top with onion, cheddar cheese, and refried beans.

Makes 4 servings.

Cincinnati Chili

Outside of San Antonio, Texas, Cincinnati, Ohio is the most chili-crazed city in the United States.

Cincinnatians enjoy their chili spooned over freshly made pasta and topped with a combination of the toppings of chopped onions, shredded cheddar cheese, refried beans or kidney beans, and crushed oyster crackers.

If you choose "the works," you are eating what they call "Five-Way Chili." Make sure to pile on the toppings – that's what sets it apart from any other chili dish.

Stew

The French word "etuver" is used for this kind of procedure. The word is usually translated as "stew," but this may be misleading. More precisely, it means "to cook or steam in its own juices" or "to sweat."

Always cook stews at low temperatures; the surface of the liquid should barely move. When you simmer very gently, the fat melts out of rich meats and mingles with the liquid. The dish can then be chilled, and the fat easily skimmed off.

Parsley

More legends and folk tales surround this herb than most others. It is said to thrive in the garden only if the woman is the boss of the household.

Did you know that parsley has a high chlorophyll content that makes it a natural breath sweetener? It is said that the Romans used it at orgies to cover up the smell of alcohol on their breath.

TIP: Parsley can be stored by placing it, stem ends down, in a tall glass filled with enough cold water to cover one inch of the stem. Cover and top with a plastic bag, securing it to the glass with a rubber band. Store in the refrigerator. Change the water every two days.

Brunswick Stew

This is an excellent dish to use small portions of meats.

1/2 pound beef round steak, cut into 1-inch pieces
1 chicken breast, boneless and skinless, cut into 1-inch pieces
1 large pork chop, cut into 1-inch pieces
1 small veal chop, cut into 1-inch pieces
1 1/2 teaspoons salt
Water
2 (14 1/2-ounce) cans stewed tomatoes
1 (15 1/4-ounce) can whole kernel corn, undrained
1 cup coarsely chopped potatoes
1 (10-ounce) package frozen lima beans
1/2 cup chopped onion
1 teaspoon salt
1/4 teaspoon pepper
Red (cayenne) pepper to taste

In a large pot or a dutch oven over medium-high heat, place steak pieces, chicken pieces, pork pieces, veal pieces, and 1 1/2 teaspoons salt. Add just enough water to cover; bring just to a gentle boil. Reduce heat to low and simmer 2 hours or until meats are tender (add more water as necessary).

Add tomatoes, corn, potatoes, lima beans, and onion; stir gently. Add 1 teaspoon salt, pepper and cayenne pepper. Simmer another 2 hours or until soup is thick and well blended. Remove from heat and transfer into individual serving bowls.

Makes 8 to 10 servings.

Cyndy's Autumn Stew

1/4 cup olive oil
1/2 cup chopped onion
4 cloves garlic, minced
1 pound boneless beef chuck steak or roast, cut into 1-inch pieces
1/2 cup sliced celery
1 cup sliced carrots, cut into 1-inch pieces
3 cups chicken stock
1 medium potato, cubed
2 dried bay leaves
Chopped fresh parsley
Salt and pepper to taste

In a large pot or dutch oven over medium-high heat, heat olive oil. Add onion and garlic and sauté until soft; add beef pieces and lightly brown on all sides. Add celery and carrots and lightly sauté. Add chicken stock, potato, bay leaves, parsley, salt, and pepper; bring just to a gentle boil. Reduce heat to low and simmer 1 hour or until potatoes are tender. Remove from heat and transfer into individual serving bowls.

Makes 4 servings.

Old Time Beef Stew

2 tablespoons vegetable oil
2 pounds boneless beef chuck, cut into 1-inch pieces
1 clove garlic, minced
1 medium onion, sliced
4 cups boiling water
1 tablespoon lemon juice
1 teaspoon worcestershire sauce
2 dried bay leaves
Salt and pepper to taste
1 teaspoon sugar
1/8 teaspoon ground allspice or ground cloves
1/2 teaspoon paprika
6 carrots, sliced
1 pound small white onions
6 potatoes, cubed

In a large pot or a dutch oven over medium-high heat, heat vegetable oil. Add beef pieces and sauté until brown; remove beef pieces to a plate. Add garlic and onion; sauté until soft. Stir in water, lemon juice, worcestershire sauce, bay leaves, salt, pepper, sugar, allspice or cloves, and paprika; add beef pieces. Reduce heat to low, cover, and simmer 2 hours, stirring occasionally. Remove bay leaves; add carrots, onions, and potatoes. Cover and simmer another 30 minutes or until meat and vegetables are tender. Remove from heat and transfer into individual serving bowls.

Makes 6 to 8 servings.

Beef Ragout

1/4 cup all-purpose flour
2 teaspoons salt
1/4 teaspoon pepper
2 pounds beef sirloin steak, cut into 1-inch pieces
2 tablespoons vegetable oil
2 medium onions, sliced
1 cup burgundy wine or dry red wine
1/2 cup water
1 beef-flavored bouillon cube or 1 teaspoon beef-flavored instant bouillon
1 dried bay leaf
2 cinnamon sticks
4 medium carrots, sliced
2 stalks celery, chopped
1 (4-ounce) can mushrooms, pieces and stems, undrained

In a large plastic bag, combine flour, salt, and pepper; add steak pieces and shake to coat. In a large pot or a dutch oven over medium-high heat, heat vegetable oil. Add steak pieces and onions; sauté until brown. Add burgundy or red wine, water, beef bouillon, bay leaf, and cinnamon sticks; bring to a boil. Reduce heat to low, cover, and simmer 1 1/2 hours. (For milder cinnamon flavor, remove cinnamon stick after 1/2 to 1 hour.)

Stir in carrots, celery, and mushrooms. Cook another 30 minutes or until meat and vegetables are tender. Remove cinnamon sticks and bay leaf. Remove from heat and transfer into individual serving bowls.

Makes 6 servings.

Beef Stew

Choose flavorful cuts of meat, such as chuck and round, that benefit from long, slow, moist cooking and won't fall apart.

BROWNING STEW MEAT:
Don't try to rush when you're browning meat for a stew. It's a very important step that will take at least ten to fifteen minutes.

Make sure that you dry the meat thoroughly on paper towels before browning, and don't crowd the pan. Damp meat won't brown, nor will pieces that are too close together in the pan.

Brown in very hot oil. The light flour coating on the meat thickens the sauce slightly; otherwise, the sauce may be thickened later with a small amount of flour and water or boiled down to the desired consistency.

Brisket

Brisket is available "fresh" or "corned." Usually the bones have been removed, and it is sold as a boneless brisket.

Brisket is an inexpensive cut of beef that is tough and coarse of grain. It is both economical and delicious when cooked long and slow.

To tenderize the meat, slow simmering is necessary, and the meat should be carved into thin slices across the grain. Note: If you cut with the grain, long meat fibers give a stringy texture to the slice.

Southern-Style Brisket Dinner

1 (4-pound) fresh brisket of beef
Water to cover
1 teaspoon salt
1 teaspoon pepper
4 yellow onions, halved
1 pound Italian sweet sausage links
6 carrots, cut into 1-inch pieces
1 clove garlic, minced
6 large potatoes, peeled and halved
2 green bell peppers, cored, seeded, and cut into quarters
1 (15 1/4-ounce) can corn kernels, drained
1 (38-ounce) can whole tomatoes, undrained
1 head green cabbage, cut into 6 wedges
1 (15 1/2-ounce) can garbanzo beans or chick peas, drained
Salt and pepper to taste

In a large pot or dutch oven over medium-high heat, place brisket of beef and cover with water. Add 1 teaspoon salt, 1 teaspoon pepper, onions, and Italian sausage; cover and bring to a boil. Reduce heat to low and simmer 2 to 2 1/2 hours or until brisket is fork-tender.

Add carrots, garlic, potatoes, bell peppers, corn, tomatoes, cabbage, and garbanzo beans or chick peas; simmer another 30 to 40 minutes or until vegetables are tender.

Remove from heat; drain off broth and pour into a tureen. Season with salt and pepper. Transfer brisket and sausage onto a cutting board; slice and transfer onto a serving platter. Place vegetables onto a serving platter. Serve the broth in small soup bowls.

Makes 6 servings.

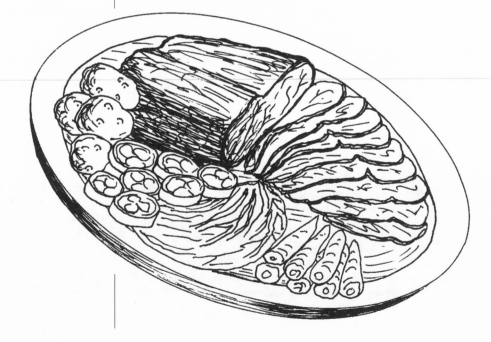

New Mexican Spicy Beef Stew

1 cup dried pinto beans, sorted, rinsed, and drained
1 (3-pound) boneless chuck roast, well trimmed and cut into 1 1/2-inch pieces
Salt and coarsely ground pepper to taste
Santa Fe Seasoning (see recipe below)
3 tablespoons all-purpose flour
6 tablespoons vegetable oil, divided
2 large onions, cut into 1/2-inch pieces
8 cloves garlic, minced
1 jalapeño chile pepper, minced with seeds
3 tablespoons tomato paste
1 1/2 cups red wine
2 cups each of beef stock and chicken stock
1 (28-ounce) can Italian plum tomatoes, undrained
1 smoked ham hock
1/2 teaspoon red (cayenne) pepper
11 ounces smoked kielbasa sausage, cut into 1-inch pieces
2 red and/or yellow bell peppers, cored, seeded, and cut into 1 1/2-inch triangles
2 poblano chilies, ** cored, seeded, and cut into 1 1/2-inch triangles
3 zucchini, cut into 1-inch thick rounds
Minced fresh cilantro

In a large pot over medium-high heat; place beans and cover with water. Bring just to a boil; remove from heat, cover, and let stand 1 hour. Drain and rinse beans; set aside. Place beef pieces in a large bowl; season with salt and pepper. Add 2 teaspoons Santa Fe Seasoning; toss well. Add flour and toss to coat.

In a large pot or a dutch oven over medium-high heat, heat 4 tablespoons vegetable oil. Add beef pieces in batches and brown well; using a slotted spoon, transfer to a bowl. Add 2 tablespoons vegetable oil; reduce heat to medium. Add onions and all but 2 teaspoons Santa Fe Seasoning; toss to coat. Add garlic, jalapeño pepper, and tomato paste; stir 1 minute. Add red wine and bring to a boil, scraping up browned bits. Add beef and chicken stocks, tomatoes, ham hock, and cayenne pepper; reduce heat to low and bring to simmer. Add beef pieces; cover partially and simmer 30 minutes, stirring occasionally.

Add beans, cover partially, and simmer another 1 hour. Uncover, add remaining Santa Fe Seasoning, and simmer an additional 45 minutes or until beef pieces and beans are tender, stirring occasionally. Degrease stew if necessary. Remove ham hock; trim off fat. Cut ham into 1/2-inch pieces.

In a large frying pan over medium heat, add kielbasa sausage and cook 2 minutes per side. Transfer to a plate. Add bell peppers, poblano chilies, and zucchini; sauté another 5 minutes or until crisp-tender. Mix sausage and vegetables into stew; simmer 5 minutes longer or until just tender. Sprinkle with cilantro. Ladle into bowls and serve with bread.

Makes 4 to 6 servings.

SANTA FE SEASONING:
1 tablespoon plus 1/2 teaspoon ground cumin
2 1/2 teaspoons each of ground coriander and chili powder
2 teaspoons each of dried oregano and dried thyme, crushed
1/4 teaspoon each of ground allspice, ground cloves, and ground cinnamon

In a small bowl, combine cumin, coriander, chili powder, oregano, thyme, allspice, cloves, and cinnamon.

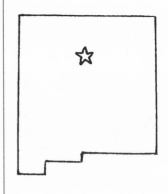

Kielbasa Sausage

Kielbasa is a Polish word meaning sausage, but it can also be found in the culinary heritage of Austria, Germany, and Italy.

Kielbasa is a garlicky, smoky sausage usually made of pork and/or beef. Sold fully cooked, it gets juicier when browned or grilled. Kielbasa is a classic pea soup garnish.

** A fresh green chile, sometimes called a fresh pasilla, is available at Latin American markets and some supermarkets.

Beef

Pasties

This recipe originally was developed in Cornwall, England and were called "Oggies" by the miners. The Cornish people who immigrated to Michigan's Upper Peninsula to work in the mines made them and called them "pasties." The miners reheated the pasties on shovels held over the candles worn on their hats.

The identifying feature of the Cornish Pasty is really the pastry and its crimping. The solid ridge of pastry hand crimped along the top of the pasty was so designed that the miner could grasp the pasty for eating and then throw the crust away. By doing this, he did not run the risk of germs and contamination from dirty hands. Of course, the modern "handle" is delicious and is always eaten.

Cabbage Rolls

For perfect leaves in making stuffed cabbage, immerse the entire head of cabbage into boiling water. Leave the cabbage in the water for three to four minutes or until the leaves have softened and wilted slightly. Remove from water and strip the head of cabbage, one leaf at a time. No further blanching is needed.

Michigan Pasties

Pasty Crust
2 large potatoes, cut into 1/4-inch pieces
2 cups chopped onion
1/2 cup chopped fresh parsley
1 pound beef sirloin steak, cut into 1/4-inch pieces
Salt and pepper to taste
1 tablespoon butter or margarine

Preheat oven to 400 degrees. Make Pasty Crust. In a large bowl, combine potatoes, onion, and parsley. Place 1/4 of mixture on one half of each rolled pastry, keeping it within one inch from the edge; add 1/4 of beef pieces to each. Season with salt and pepper and dot with butter or margarine. Fold the other half of pastry over filling, crimping edges together and slitting tops of each.

Place pasties onto a large ungreased baking sheet. Bake, uncovered, 30 minutes; reduce heat to 350 degrees and bake another 30 minutes. Remove from heat. (May be frozen after baking.)

Makes 4 servings.

PASTY CRUST:
3 cups all-purpose flour
1 teaspoon baking powder
1/2 teaspoon salt
1 cup chilled vegetable shortening
1/2 cup chilled water

In a large bowl, sift together flour, baking powder, and salt. With a pastry blender or two knives, cut vegetable shortening into flour mixture until particles are the size of small peas. Add water, mixing well. Divide dough into quarters. On a lightly floured surface, roll out each section so that it is thin, round, and the size of a pie plate.

Stuffed Cabbage Rolls

8 large cabbage leaves
1 (10 3/4-ounce) can tomato soup, undiluted and divided
1 pound lean ground beef
1 cup cooked rice
1/4 cup chopped onion
1 egg, slightly beaten
1 teaspoon salt
1/4 teaspoon pepper

In a large saucepan over medium heat, cook cabbage in salted water a few minutes to soften; remove from pan and drain. In a medium bowl, combine 2 tablespoons tomato soup, ground beef, rice, onion, egg, salt, and pepper. Divide meat mixture evenly among cabbage leaves; fold in sides and roll up (secure with toothpicks, if necessary).

In a large frying pan over medium heat, place cabbage rolls, seam side down; pour remaining tomato soup over rolls. Cover and cook over low heat 40 minutes, stirring occasionally and spooning sauce over rolls. Remove from heat and transfer onto a serving platter.

Makes 4 servings.

Beef Stroganoff

When this celebrated Russian dish is made very quickly in an open frying pan, you must use a good-quality beef.

1 (16-ounce) package uncooked egg noodles
1 tablespoon vegetable oil
1 pound beef sirloin steak, cut into 1/4-inch strips
1 medium onion, chopped
1 clove garlic, minced
1 (10 3/4-ounce) can cream of mushroom soup, undiluted
1 cup sliced fresh mushrooms
1 tablespoon dried tarragon, crushed
1 teaspoon worcestershire sauce
Salt and pepper to taste
1 cup sour cream

Cook egg noodles according to package directions; drain and return to pan to keep warm. In a large frying pan over medium-high heat, heat vegetable oil. Add steak strips and sauté until medium-rare; transfer onto a warm platter. Reduce heat to low, add onion and garlic; sauté until soft. Stir in mushroom soup, mushrooms, tarragon, worcestershire sauce, salt, and pepper; simmer until mushrooms are cooked. Add sour cream and the steak strips; stir until well blended. Remove from heat and serve over cooked noodles.

Makes 4 servings.

Spaghetti Sauce Supreme

1 pound lean ground beef
1 large onion, chopped
1 small green bell pepper, cored, seeded, and chopped
1 cup sliced mushrooms
4 cloves garlic, minced
1 teaspoon salt
1 teaspoon dried basil, crushed
1 teaspoon dried oregano, crushed
1/2 teaspoon dried rosemary, crushed
1/2 teaspoon dried thyme, crushed
1 dried bay leaf
1 tablespoon molasses or to taste
1 (14 1/2-ounce) can whole tomatoes, undrained
1 (6-ounce) can tomato paste
1 cup water
1 cup dry red wine
Hot cooked spaghetti noodles

In a large pot or a dutch oven over medium-high heat, combine ground beef, onion, bell pepper, mushrooms, and garlic; sauté and stir occasionally until meat is well browned. Add salt, basil, oregano, rosemary, thyme, and bay leaf; stir until well blended. Stir in molasses, tomatoes, tomato paste, water, and red wine; bring to a boil. Reduce heat to low, cover, and simmer at least 1 hour. Add additional water if necessary. To serve, ladle hot sauce over hot spaghetti noodles.

Makes approximately 9 cups.

Spaghetti Sauce

The secret ingredient in this spaghetti sauce recipe is molasses – it gives it that little something extra that says, "I DON'T HAVE TO SLAVE OVER THE STOVE ALL DAY, BUT IT TASTES LIKE I DID!"

Molasses also helps achieve the brownish-red look of a long-cooked sauce and adds a hint of caramel flavor.

The longer spaghetti sauce is allowed to cook, the better it is. If you put all the ingredients into a crockpot after you have browned the ground beef, you can then let it cook all afternoon on low heat.

Pork

Braising

To cook, covered, in a small quantity of liquid. Meats are usually browned in the presence of some fat and then braised.

Unbrowned braised dishes may be called fricassees or blond stews. Pot roasting and swissing are examples of braising.

Sauerkraut

Sauerkraut is made by placing salt between layers of finely shredded cabbage and then subjecting it to pressure, which bruises the cabbage and squeezes out its juices. It then ferments.

When using canned sauerkraut, to reduce its briny flavor, place into a colander and rinse well under cold, running water. Drain well before using.

If it is still too salty for your taste, soak the sauerkraut fifteen to thirty minutes in cold water. Drain well before using.

TIP: Sauerkraut is also delicious cooked with one or two tart apples which have been peeled, cored, and chopped into small pieces. Cook only until it is thoroughly heated; the apples should remain crisp.

Pork Chops Braised in Milk

4 pork loin or rib chops (1/2-inch thick)
2 tablespoons all-purpose flour
1/2 teaspoon salt
1/4 to 1/2 teaspoon pepper
1 1/2 cups milk, divided
1 teaspoon butter or margarine

Trim fat from pork chops. Combine flour, salt, and pepper in a large resealable plastic bag; add pork chops, seal bag, and shake to coat with flour mixture. Remove pork chops from bag and place flour mixture into a small bowl; gradually add 1/2 cup milk, stirring until well blended with a wire whisk.

In a large frying pan over medium-high heat, melt butter or margarine. Add pork chops; cook 3 minutes on each side or until browned. Add milk mixture; cover, reduce heat to low, and cook another 20 minutes, stirring occasionally. Turn the pork chops over. Add remaining 1 cup milk; cover and cook an additional 20 minutes, stirring occasionally.

Uncover frying pan and cook pork chops 15 minutes longer or until the liquid is reduced to 1/4 cup (the gravy will be very thick – if too thick, more milk can be added). Remove from heat, spoon gravy over pork chops, and serve.

Makes 4 servings.

German Pork Chops

Smells good, looks good, and tastes good.

2 (14-ounce) cans sauerkraut, drained and rinsed
2 teaspoons caraway seeds
4 pork loin chops (1/2-inch thick)
Pepper to taste
2 cooking apples, peeled, cored, and sliced
2 tablespoons raisins
4 teaspoons firmly packed brown sugar
4 tablespoons apple juice or water

Preheat oven to 375 degrees. Grease shiny side of four sheets of heavy-duty aluminum foil. Place sauerkraut into a colander; press out excess liquid.

Place 1/4 of the sauerkraut onto the center of each sheet of aluminum foil; sprinkle caraway seeds over the top. Place pork chops onto top of sauerkraut and season with pepper. Arrange apple slices and raisins evenly over pork chops. Sprinkle each portion with 1 teaspoon brown sugar. Over each portion, spoon 1 tablespoon apple juice or water.

To wrap, bring two opposite ends of aluminum foil up and over, making a double fold to seal tightly. Close both ends; seal tightly. Place packets onto a baking sheet and bake 1 hour or until thoroughly cooked; remove from oven. Carefully open packets and transfer pork mixture onto individual serving plates.

Makes 4 servings.

Grilled Honey Pork Chops

1/4 cup lemon juice
1/4 cup honey
2 tablespoons soy sauce
1 tablespoon dry sherry
1 clove garlic, minced
4 pork loin chops (1/2-inch thick)

In a heavy resealable plastic bag, combine lemon juice, honey, soy sauce, sherry, and garlic; add pork chops and seal. Refrigerate at least 4 hours or overnight. Remove pork chops from marinade; reserving marinade.

Preheat barbecue grill. Place pork chops onto hot grill. Spoon marinade onto each pork chop. Cover barbecue with lid, open any vents, and cook 8 to 10 minutes per side or until whitish-pink in the center, turning once, and spooning additional marinade over pork chops. Remove from grill and transfer onto a serving platter.

Makes 4 servings.

Pork Chops in Walnut Butter

1 orange
4 boneless pork loin chops (1/2-inch thick)
Salt and pepper to taste
Walnut Butter

Preheat oven to 350 degrees. Grate the zest off of one orange; set aside to use in preparing Walnut Butter. Cut orange into thin slices; set aside.

Sprinkle pork chops with salt and pepper; place them into an ungreased shallow baking dish. Spread half of the Walnut Butter over one side of each pork chop. Bake, uncovered, 20 minutes. Baste pork chops with remaining Walnut Butter, and bake another 20 minutes or until whitish-pink in the center. Remove from heat. Serve immediately with orange slices.

Makes 4 servings.

WALNUT BUTTER:
Grated zest of 1 orange
3 tablespoons fresh orange juice
4 tablespoons butter, room temperature
1 tablespoon snipped fresh chives
1/2 cup finely chopped walnuts
Salt and pepper to taste

In a small bowl, combine orange zest, orange juice, butter, chives, walnuts, salt, and pepper; stir until well blended.

Garlic Facts and Myths

Did you know that one clove of garlic is ten times stronger pushed through a garlic press than one clove minced fine with a sharp knife?

Did you know that the Roman historian, Pliny, lists no less than sixty-one medicinal uses for garlic? A few are:

- *Vampires flee from it.*
- *Will cure a cold.*
- *Will cure warts.*
- *Will stop fainting spells.*
- *Improves the circulation.*
- *Wards off the evil eye.*
- *Will grow hair.*
- *A restorative for failing masculine powers.*
- *Alleviates high blood pressure.*

Barbecuing with Aluminum Foil

Heavy-duty aluminum foil has many uses at the barbecue, both in sheets and in preformed shallow pans. Here are a few tips for its use:

•   Corn, potatoes, and onions can be cooked directly in the hot coals if tightly wrapped in aluminum foil.

•   Lining the bottom of the grill with aluminum foil before building the fire will promote even distribution of heat during cooking. The aluminum foil can then be used to wrap up the ashes for disposal.

•   A aluminum pan placed under the grill will catch drippings and prevent flare-ups.

•   Disposable aluminum foil pans in small sizes are useful for cooking cut-up vegetables or warming sauces or bread around the edge of the barbecue grill.

•   You can avoid charring the wings and legs of poultry by wrapping the tip ends in foil.

Easy Baked Pork Chops

If you are in a hurry and want an easy dish, this is it.

4 pork loin or rib chops (1/2-inch thick)
1 (10 3/4-ounce) can cream of mushroom soup, undiluted
1 tablespoon lemon juice
Fresh or dried herbs of your choice (tarragon, basil, or oregano)

Preheat oven to 350 degrees. Place pork chops into an ungreased baking dish. In a medium bowl, combine mushroom soup, lemon juice, and herbs; spread on top of pork chops.

Bake, uncovered, 50 to 60 minutes or until whitish-pink in the center. Remove from oven and serve immediately.

VARIATION: Add green salsa to taste instead of herbs.

Makes 4 servings.

Minnesota Grilled Pork Chops

Another easy pork chop recipe. Pork chops will not dry out as much with this coating. Great served with garlic mashed potatoes and green beans.

1/4 cup Italian seasoned bread crumbs
1/4 cup freshly grated parmesan cheese
4 pork loin or rib chops (1-inch thick)

Preheat barbecue grill. In a shallow pie plate, combine bread crumbs and parmesan cheese; coat pork chops with the crumb mixture.

Place pork chops onto hot grill. Cover barbecue with lid, open any vents, and cook 25 to 35 minutes or until whitish-pink in the center; turn after 15 minutes. Remove from grill and transfer onto a serving platter.

Makes 4 servings.

Orange Pork Chops

1 cup orange juice
3 tablespoons orange marmalade
2 tablespoons firmly packed brown sugar
1 teaspoon cider vinegar
1 tablespoon butter or margarine
4 pork loin or rib chops (1/2-inch thick)
1/4 cup water

In a medium bowl, combine orange juice, orange marmalade, brown sugar, and cider vinegar.

In a large frying pan over medium heat, melt butter or margarine. Add pork chops and brown on both sides. Pour orange mixture over the pork chops. Reduce heat to low; simmer, covered, 20 to 30 minutes or until whitish-pink in the center. (If needed, add 1/4 cup water during cooking to keep sauce from getting too thick.) Remove from heat and transfer onto a serving platter.

Makes 4 servings.

Pork

Though available year round, fresh pork is more plentiful and the prices are lower from October to February.

Look for pork that is pale pink with a small amount of marbling and white (not yellow) fat. The darker pink the flesh, the older the animal.

IMPORTANT:
Thanks to improved feeding techniques, trichinosis in fresh pork is rarely an issue. Normal precautions should still be taken, such as washing everything that comes in contact with raw pork and never tasting uncooked pork.

It is recommended to cook pork until it reaches an internal temperature of from 150 to 170 degrees, which will still produce juicy, tender results.

Barbecued Pork Chops

These pork chops have been a "comfort food" for many years. This process works equally well with chicken breasts.

4 pork loin or rib chops (1/2-inch thick)
All-purpose flour
1/4 cup butter or margarine
Barbecue Sauce

Preheat oven to 350 degrees. Coat pork chops with flour. In a large baking pan, melt butter or margarine in oven. Place pork chops into the baking pan in a single layer. Bake, uncovered, 20 minutes. Pour off butter or margarine and turn. Spoon hot Barbecue Sauce over pork chops; bake, covered, another 20 to 30 minutes or until whitish-pink in the center. Remove from oven and serve.

Makes 4 servings.

BARBECUE SAUCE:
1 cup tomato purée or catsup
1/4 cup butter or margarine
1/2 cup hot water
1/3 cup lemon juice
1 tablespoon worcestershire sauce
1 teaspoon salt
1/2 teaspoon pepper
1 tablespoon paprika
1 teaspoon sugar
1 medium onion, finely chopped

In a large sauce pan over medium heat, combine tomato purée or catsup, butter or margarine, hot water, lemon juice, and worcestershire sauce; stir until well blended. Add salt, pepper, paprika, sugar, and onion. Heat to boiling; remove from heat and set aside.

Fennel Seeds

Fennel is an aromatic herb that belongs to the parsley family. It looks a lot like celery and the taste and aroma of anise or licorice. Fennel is grown worldwide, mainly for its fragrant feathery leaves which are used as herbs and also for seeds.

In medieval times, people kept a stash of fennel seeds handy to nibble on through long church services and on fasting days. The seeds were considered to be an appetite suppressant.

During the colonial period, sugar-coated fennel seeds were eaten as a candy.

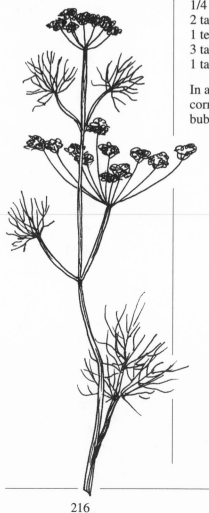

Petite Pork Roast

This is a favorite pork roast. Great for dinner parties.

1 (2-pound) pork tenderloin roast
2 tablespoons soy sauce
1/4 teaspoon ground mustard
2 tablespoons fennel seeds
2 tablespoons caraway seeds
Savory Mustard Sauce

Trim fat from pork roast. In a small bowl, combine soy sauce and ground mustard. Using your fingers, rub the soy mixture onto the roast. On a piece of wax paper, combine fennel seeds and caraway seeds; roll roast in seeds to coat evenly. Wrap tightly in plastic wrap and refrigerate 2 hours or overnight.

Preheat oven to 325 degrees. Unwrap roast. Place fat side up onto a rack in a shallow baking pan. Insert a meat thermometer into thickest part of the roast. Bake, uncovered, 1 1/2 to 1 3/4 hours or until thermometer registers 160 degrees.

Remove from oven and transfer onto a cutting board; let roast stand 15 minutes before carving. Transfer onto a serving platter and serve with Savory Mustard Sauce.

Makes 4 servings.

SAVORY MUSTARD SAUCE:
1/4 cup water
2 tablespoons ground mustard
1 teaspoon cornstarch
3 tablespoons light corn syrup
1 tablespoon cider vinegar

In a small saucepan over medium heat, combine water, ground mustard, and cornstarch. Stir in corn syrup and cider vinegar; cook and stir until thickened and bubbly. Cook and stir another 2 minutes. Remove from heat.

Orange-Pepper Pork Tenderloin

1 (2-pound) pork tenderloin roast
1/4 cup all-purpose flour
Salt and pepper to taste
2 to 3 tablespoons butter or margarine
1 tablespoon vegetable oil
Orange-Pepper Sauce

Cut pork roast widthwise into slices about 1/2-inch thick. Pound pork slices thin by placing one slice at a time between two pieces of plastic wrap. Working from the center to the edges, pound lightly with a meat mallet to 1/4-inch thick.

In a shallow pie plate, combine flour, salt, and pepper. Roll pork slices in flour mixture to coat all sides.

In a large frying pan over medium-high heat, heat 2 tablespoons butter or margarine and vegetable oil. Cook pork slices in a single layer 3 to 5 minutes or until lightly browned on both sides, adding more butter or margarine if needed. Pour Orange-Pepper Sauce over top of pork slices. Simmer a few minutes longer. Remove pork slices from heat and transfer onto a serving platter.

Reduce liquid left in frying pan by boiling 2 or 3 minutes; pour over the pork slices and serve immediately.

Makes 4 to 6 servings.

ORANGE-PEPPER SAUCE:
1/4 cup chopped shallots
3/4 teaspoon coarsely ground pepper
1/3 cup dry white wine
1 tablespoon grated orange zest
2/3 cup fresh orange juice

In a medium frying pan over medium-high heat, combine shallots, pepper, and white wine; stir until shallots are limp. Add orange zest and orange juice; cook until thoroughly heated. Remove from heat.

Shallots

1 plump shallot equals about 1 tablespoon chopped shallot.

With a flavor more subtle than that of the onion and less pungent than that of garlic, the shallot is the most refined member of the onion family. They look more like garlic than onions.

Shallots add a distinctive flavor to many dishes. They can be served as a vegetable in their own right, cooked gently in a little stock and glazed.

Choose shallots that are plump and firm with dry skins. Avoid those that are wrinkled or sprouting. Store them in a cool, dry, well-ventilated place for up to one month.

Carving Roasts

When you are carving a roast, carve the whole roast first, before you start piling it onto the platter. Save out the prettiest center slices and set them aside. Arrange the least attractive end pieces on the platter first and then cover them with the pretty ones.

This way, not only are the best slices offered first, but the less-attractive slices are saved for seconds or another family meal on another day.

Pork

Common Seasoning Ingredients

SALT: Salt has always been a highly prized commodity. It was once taxed as alcohol and tobacco are taxed today. The English word "salary" is derived from the Latin "salarium," or "salt money."

The role of salt is threefold: It seasons food, it preserves food, and it provides sodium and chlorine, which are nutrients necessary to the body's fluid balance and to muscle and nerve activity.

> *IMPORTANT:*
> *Don't use too much salt. Remember that you can always add more, but you can't take it out!*

PEPPER: Pepper is known as the king of spices. Like salt, it was a precious spice. The Arabs grew rich furnishing the Romans with pepper. Pepper probably changed the course of history, being the single most important factor in the European search and exploration for sea routes to the East.

Pepper comes in three forms: white, black, and green. They are from the same berry but processed differently. Black pepper is picked unripe, white is ripened and the hull is removed, and green peppercorns are picked unripe and are preserved before their color darkens.

Grilled Ginger Tenderloin

This ginger-flavored pork tenderloin makes for a wonderful taste sensation.

1 (2-pound) pork tenderloin roast
2 cloves garlic, minced
1 teaspoon freshly grated ginger
1/3 cup soy sauce
2 tablespoons sugar
2 tablespoons water
1 tablespoon vegetable oil

Trim fat from pork roast. Place roast in a large resealable plastic bag and set into a shallow dish. In a small bowl, combine garlic, ginger, soy sauce, sugar, water, and vegetable oil; pour mixture over roast and close bag. Marinate in the refrigerator several hours or overnight; turning roast occasionally to distribute marinade. Drain, reserving marinade.

Preheat barbecue grill. Place roast onto hot grill. Grill, turning frequently and brushing with reserved marinade every 5 to 10 minutes, 30 to 45 minutes or until a meat thermometer inserted into thickest part of the roast registers 160 degrees. Remove from grill and transfer onto a cutting board; let roast stand 15 minutes before carving. Transfer onto a serving platter.

Makes 4 servings.

Roast Loin of Pork

Delicious served with warm applesauce.

1 (2-pound) pork tenderloin roast
1/4 cup Dijon mustard
Coarsely ground pepper
10 bacon slices

Preheat oven to 325 degrees. Trim fat from pork roast. Brush the roast heavily with Dijon mustard and sprinkle pepper evenly over mustard. Wrap bacon slices around roast, securing with toothpicks. Place roast, fat side up, onto a rack in a shallow baking pan. Insert a meat thermometer into thickest part of the roast.

Bake, uncovered, 1 to 1 1/2 hours or until thermometer registers 160 degrees. Remove from oven and transfer onto a cutting board; let roast stand 15 minutes before carving. Transfer onto a serving platter.

Makes 4 to 6 servings.

Pork With Apple & Onion

1 tablespoon coarsely ground pepper
1 (1-pound) pork tenderloin roast, cut into 1-inch slices
1 teaspoon dried thyme, crushed
1 teaspoon vegetable oil
1 teaspoon soy sauce
Apple and Onion Compote

Generously pepper both sides of pork slices and sprinkle with thyme. In a large frying pan over medium-high heat, heat vegetable oil; drag seasoned pork pieces through vegetable oil to avoid sticking. Cook, uncovered, 20 to 30 minutes or until whitish-pink in the center. Add soy sauce and stir to mix. Remove from heat.

To serve, divide Apple and Onion Compote among individual serving plates; top with pork slices.

Makes 4 servings.

APPLE & ONION COMPOTE:
1 cup chopped onion
1 cup peeled, cored and thinly sliced apple
1 clove garlic, minced
2 tablespoons firmly packed dark brown sugar
1 teaspoon soy sauce
1 teaspoon dried thyme, crushed
1 tablespoon cider vinegar
1 tablespoon apple juice

Coat a large frying pan with vegetable-oil cooking spray. Over medium heat, sauté onion 4 minutes or until soft. Add apple slices and garlic; saute another 4 minutes. Sprinkle brown sugar over apple mixture. Add soy sauce, thyme, cider vinegar, and apple juice; sauté an additional 2 minutes. Remove compote from heat and set aside, keeping warm.

Soy Sauce

Soy Sauce was developed over a thousand years ago in China as a way of preserving food. It is derived from fermented soy beans.

ALL-PURPOSE SOY SAUCE or JAPANESE SOY SAUCE: Japanese-style soy sauce, such as Kikkoman, is suitable for most uses.

CHINESE SOY SAUCE: The Chinese use both light (thin) and dark (heavy) soy sauces. Dark soys are fermented longer, with molasses added during the process. They go best with spicy dishes and red meats. The light soys are used in dipping sauces or vegetable and seafood dishes.

HOISIN SAUCE: A mixture of soybeans, garlic, chile peppers, anise seeds, and other seasonings. It is a paste and is used in Chinese barbecue sauces.

REDUCED-SODIUM SOY SAUCE: Now available in both Chinese and Japanese versions, reduced-sodium sauces usually contain one-third to one-half of the sodium of the regular versions. If you're watching salt, they're a good choice, but the flavor is milder.

TAMARI: A dark soy sauce brewed without wheat. In the United States, "tamari" refers to a Japanese-style light soy sauce with a slightly smoky flavor.

Olives

Green olives have been produced for centuries in the Mediterranean countries. California, alone in the world, produces ripe canned black olives. They were brought into California from Mexico by the Padres, being planted first at the San Diego Mission in 1769. It was in 1901 that American experts discovered that the ripe olive (black) could be canned.

Green olives are picked green, cured, brined, and packed in brine. They are a true pickle.

TIPS: After opening a jar of olives, you can extend the storage life by floating a thin layer of vegetable oil on the surface of the brine.

If the brine gets discarded when removing olives from the can, but you need to store some leftovers, add 1/2 teaspoon salt per cup of water.

Don't store olives in the refrigerator. They're not as good to eat when cold. Keep them at room temperature in their brine, covered with oil. Keep wrinkled, dry black olives in a tightly closed jar in a cool cupboard.

NOTE:
Did you know that it is considered proper etiquette to eat olives with your fingers and not with a fork?

Regina's Penil (Pork Roast)

This is a delicious Puerto Rican pork roast that makes a wonderful change for the holidays.

1 large onion, finely chopped
1 green bell pepper, cored, seeded, and finely chopped
3/4 teaspoon dried oregano, crushed
Green olives with pimientos
1/2 teaspoon garlic powder or garlic salt
1/2 teaspoon dried basil, crushed
1 1/4 teaspoons recaito*
1/2 package sazon seasoning*
2 to 3 tablespoons drained capers
1 teaspoon sofrito*
White vinegar
1 (10-pound) pork shoulder roast with bone
1 teaspoon paprika
Olive oil

In a medium bowl, combine onion, bell pepper, oregano, green olives, garlic powder or garlic salt, basil, recaito, sazon seasoning, capers, and sofrito; add enough white vinegar to cover the ingredients; mix and crush together until well blended. Cut 1-inch slits on all sides of the pork roast. Stuff the seasoning mixture into each slit. Place roast into a large dish or pan. Pour any extra seasoning mixture over the roast, cover with aluminum foil, and refrigerate overnight.

Preheat oven to 325 degrees. Place roast onto a rack in a shallow baking pan. Mix paprika with a little olive oil; rub over the roast. Insert meat thermometer into the thickest part of the roast, being careful not to touch the bone. Bake, uncovered, 4 to 5 hours or until thermometer registers 160 degrees; baste with juice every 30 minutes (if roast starts to get too brown during baking, cover with aluminum foil). Remove from heat and transfer onto a cutting board; let stand 15 minutes before carving. Transfer onto a serving platter.

Serves a large family gathering.

* Recaito, sazon seasoning, and sofrito can be found in Spanish stores or large supermarkets. See below for sofrito.

Sofrito

Sofrito is the basis of many Cuban and Puerto Rican dishes.

2 pounds yellow or white onions, peeled and quartered
4 green bell peppers (1 1/2 pounds), cored, seeded, and quartered
1 whole head of garlic, separated into cloves and peeled
1/2 cup olive oil

In a food processor, whirl onions and bell peppers in batches until very finely chopped; set aside. Process garlic separately or mince by hand; set aside. In a large pot or dutch oven over medium heat, place olive oil, onions, and bell peppers; cook, stirring occasionally, 15 minutes or until vegetables release their juices. Add garlic and cook, stirring occasionally, another 15 minutes or until mixture is dry and onions begin to caramelize. Remove from heat and cool to room temperature. Store in airtight containers in the refrigerator up to one week or freeze up to three months.

Yields 5 cups.

Pork Stir-Fry With Apple

1 (1-pound) pork tenderloin roast
Teriyaki Sauce
2 medium red apples, peeled, cored, and chopped
1 tablespoon lemon juice
1 to 2 tablespoons vegetable oil
1 small onion, cut into thin wedges
3 cups hot cooked rice
1 or 2 medium oranges, peeled and sliced widthwise
Mint sprigs

Trim fat from pork roast. Slice lengthwise across the grain into 1/8-inch thick strips about 2 inches long. In a small bowl, combine meat with Teriyaki Sauce; cover and refrigerate at least 30 minutes or overnight.

In a medium bowl, combine apples and lemon juice; set aside. Place a wok or a large frying pan over high heat. When hot, add vegetable oil and onion; stir-fry until onion is soft. Add apples and lemon juice; stir-fry 1 minute or until hot. Spoon mixture into a bowl; set aside.

With a slotted spoon, lift half the pork strips into the wok or frying pan. Stir-fry 2 to 3 minutes or until lightly browned; add cooked pork strips to fruit. Repeat with remaining pork strips, adding more vegetable oil if needed. Return cooked pork strips and fruit to wok or frying pan; add Teriyaki Sauce, stirring until it just comes to a boil. Remove from heat.

Mound rice onto a large serving platter and pour pork mixture over rice; garnish with orange slices and mint sprigs.

Makes 4 servings.

TERIYAKI SAUCE:
1/2 cup orange juice
1/4 cup minced fresh mint leaves
2 tablespoons soy sauce
1 tablespoon freshly grated ginger
1 clove garlic, minced

In a medium saucepan over high heat, combine orange juice, mint, soy sauce, ginger, and garlic; bring to a boil and boil 4 to 5 minutes or until reduced to 1/2 cup.

Wok

Because of the shape of the traditional wok pan, it has three main advantages:

- *The traditional iron wok keeps a steady and intense heat. This decreases cooking time.*

- *After stirring the ingredients, they always return to the center of the wok.*

- *A smaller amount of oil is needed to cook in a wok than a frying pan.*

TIP: For effective browning, it is very important to heat the wok thoroughly before adding ingredients, especially meat, poultry, and seafood. If it is not hot enough, the food will stew.

SEASONING A NEW WOK: A new wok should be seasoned before using it for the first time. This process helps prevent food from sticking. Wash it in hot soapy water, then dry by placing it over medium heat. When dry, add one to two tablespoons vegetable oil. Carefully rotate and tilt the hot wok to distribute the oil. Leave on the heat approximately five minutes. Turn off heat; leave wok to cool. When it is cool, wipe excess oil from it with paper towels.

CLEANING A WOK: Do not scrub your wok with abrasive cleaners. Wash in warm water and wipe dry, then wipe over with a lightly oiled cloth. This will prevent the wok from rusting.

Eggplant

By slicing and liberally sprinkling the eggplants with salt (preferably Kosher salt), then placing them between layers of paper towels in a colander, with a weight on top, you remove any bitterness and the eggplant will absorb less oil in cooking. Rinse and blot dry before cooking.

Thai Spiced Pork

It's very hard to describe the wonderful taste of this dish. Try it; you'll like it.

2 cups water
Salt
1 cup long-grain white rice
1 small eggplant
4 teaspoons cornstarch
1 cup chicken broth
2 tablespoons soy sauce
1 tablespoon freshly grated ginger
3/4 pound ground lean pork
2 tablespoons sliced green onions
Salt and pepper to taste
Peanut Sauce

In a medium saucepan over medium-high heat, bring 2 cups of salted water to a boil; add rice. Cover, reduce heat to low, and cook for 20 minutes (do not open lid). Remove from heat.

While rice is cooking, peel and finely chop eggplant; set 2 cups aside for recipe (save remaining eggplant for another recipe).

In a small bowl, combine cornstarch and chicken broth; stir until well blended. Add soy sauce and ginger; set aside.

In a large frying pan over medium-high heat, cook and stir ground pork until crumbly and well browned; drain off fat. Add the cornstarch mixture; stir until boiling. Mix in chopped eggplant and cook 10 minutes or until eggplant is soft; season with salt and pepper. Remove from heat.

To serve, transfer cooked rice to a serving platter. Pour pork mixture over the rice and sprinkle with green onions. Serve with Peanut Sauce.

Makes 6 servings.

PEANUT SAUCE:
1/4 cup creamy peanut butter
3 tablespoons chicken broth
1/2 teaspoon sesame oil
2 tablespoons berry jelly (your favorite)
2 tablespoons rice vinegar
1 teaspoon soy sauce
1/2 teaspoon freshly grated ginger
1/8 teaspoon dried crushed chile peppers

In a small saucepan over low heat, combine peanut butter, chicken broth, sesame oil, berry jelly, rice vinegar, soy sauce, ginger, and chile peppers; heat until well mixed. Remove from heat and let cool.

Hawaiian Spareribs

5 pounds pork spareribs
1 1/2 teaspoons salt
Orange-Pineapple Sauce

Preheat oven to 350 degrees. Bake spareribs whole or cut into 4-rib portions. Arrange ribs, meat-side up, onto a rack in a shallow baking pan; sprinkle with salt. Bake, covered with aluminum foil, 1 hour; uncover and bake another 30 minutes.

Remove ribs from oven, drain off drippings, and spoon Orange-Pineapple Sauce over ribs. Return ribs to oven and bake an additional 20 to 25 minutes or until cooked through, or place onto a preheated barbecue grill and grill an additional 20 to 25 minutes or until cooked through. Remove from oven or grill and transfer onto a serving platter.

Makes 4 to 6 servings.

ORANGE-PINEAPPLE SAUCE:
2/3 cup thick orange marmalade
1 (8-ounce) can crushed pineapple, undrained
2 tablespoons cornstarch
2 tablespoons soy sauce
1/2 teaspoon freshly grated ginger
2 cloves garlic, minced
3 tablespoons lemon juice

In a medium saucepan over medium heat, combine orange marmalade, pineapple, cornstarch, soy sauce, ginger, garlic, and lemon juice. Bring to a boil and cook, stirring constantly, until thickened. Remove from heat.

Breakfast Sausage Casserole

Make this casserole for a traditional Christmas brunch. What a special treat for a special day.

1 pound ground pork sausage
6 slices bread, crust removed and cut into 1-inch cubes
6 eggs, well beaten
1 cup shredded cheddar cheese
1 teaspoon ground mustard
1 teaspoon salt
2 cups milk

Preheat oven to 350 degrees. Grease a 9-inch square baking dish. In a large frying pan over medium-high heat, brown ground pork sausage; remove from heat, drain thoroughly, let cool, and crumble.

In a large bowl, combine bread cubes, eggs, cheddar cheese, ground mustard, salt, milk, and pork sausage; mix well. Pat into prepared baking dish. Bake, uncovered, 30 minutes or until a knife inserted halfway between center and edge comes out clean. Remove from oven and serve immediately.

Makes 6 to 8 servings.

Spareribs

Spareribs require long, slow cooking to make them tender and juicy. If baked, they require just a bit of watching. Cover the ribs with aluminum foil during the first period of cooking to guarantee juicy, tender pork.

You can also cook the ribs and sauce a day ahead. Bake the ribs the first one and one-half hours as the recipe directs. Prepare sauce and store ribs and sauce separately in the refrigerator. When ready to prepare, bake the ribs an additional fifteen minutes before glazing. Then finish the baking.

Pork

Hogs, Pigs, and Hams

The hog is believed to be the first domesticated animal. Primitive man began to adapt the wild hog to his needs between 7000 and 3000 B.C.

The explorer De Soto brought thirteen hogs on board his ship that landed in Florida. Columbus is said to have brought eight pigs with him on his second voyage to the New World. Pork was a staple of the Pilgrims' diet. Hogs also went west with the covered wagons.

The hams are the back legs of the pig. In other animals, a leg is called a leg; in a pig, the hind leg is called a ham.

The expression "high on the hog" comes from the way meat was once portioned out in the British Army. The tender cuts "high on the hog" went to officers.

Lowfat Breakfast Casserole

6 slices bread, crust removed and cut into 1-inch cubes
3/4 cup diced cooked ham
2 tablespoons diced red bell pepper
1 cup shredded, reduced-fat sharp cheddar cheese
1 1/3 cups skim milk
3/4 cup egg substitute
1/4 teaspoon ground mustard
1/4 teaspoon onion powder
1/4 teaspoon white pepper
Paprika

Place bread cubes evenly onto the bottom of an ungreased 8-inch square baking dish. Coat with vegetable-oil cooking spray. Layer ham, red bell pepper, and cheddar cheese over bread; set aside. In a large bowl, combine milk, egg substitute, ground mustard, onion powder, and white pepper; pour over cheese. Cover and refrigerate at least 8 hours or overnight.

Preheat oven to 350 degrees. Remove baking dish from refrigerator and let stand 30 minutes. Bake, uncovered, 30 minutes or until a knife inserted halfway between center and edge comes out clean. Remove from oven and sprinkle with paprika. Serve immediately.

Makes 6 servings.

Virginia Holiday Ham

The cola adds a delicious caramel coating to the ham as it cooks.

1 (6- to 7-pound) fully cooked boneless ham
1 (12-ounce) can cola
Cream Cheese Spread

Preheat oven to 300 degrees. Place ham, fat side up, onto a rack in a shallow baking pan. Pour cola over ham. Insert a meat thermometer into the thickest part of the ham. Bake, uncovered, 1 1/2 to 2 1/4 hours or until thermometer registers 140 degrees. Remove from oven and transfer onto a serving platter. To serve, spread Cream Cheese Spread onto top of ham.

Makes 10 to 14 servings.

CREAM CHEESE SPREAD:
2 (8-ounce) packages cream cheese, room temperature
1 teaspoon prepared horseradish
1/4 teaspoon white pepper

In a small bowl, combine cream cheese, prepared horseradish, and white pepper; stir until well blended.

Candied Bacon

Excellent to serve for a brunch or special-occasion breakfast.

1/2 cup firmly packed brown sugar
2 tablespoons prepared mustard
1 pound thick-cut pork bacon

In a small bowl, combine sugar and prepared mustard; set aside.

In a large frying pan over medium-high heat, slowly cook bacon until crisp (you'll probably have to do this in batches); drain the fat each time. Remove from pan and place cooked bacon onto paper towels. After draining fat for the last time, reduce heat to low, and put all the bacon back into frying pan. Drizzle sugar and mustard mixture over bacon, tossing with a fork to coat. Remove from heat and transfer onto a serving platter.

NOTE: If the bacon slices touch each other on the serving platter, they will stick together.

Makes 6 to 8 servings.

Bacon

Standard bacon, as we know it in America, is the cured belly of the hog. It consists of alternating layers of lean and fat, and may also have an attached rind.

Unopened bacon that has been vacuum wrapped should keep several weeks in the refrigerator. Once opened, it is very perishable and starts to lose flavor and freshness within four to seven days, even when tightly sealed in plastic wrap and refrigerated. Bacon does not freeze well.

Bacon Quiche Biscuit Cups

A new and interesting brunch dish that is easy to make.

1 (8-ounce) package cream cheese, room temperature
2 tablespoons milk
2 eggs
1/2 cup shredded swiss cheese
2 tablespoons chopped green onions
1 (10-roll) can refrigerated flaky biscuits
5 bacon slices, crisply cooked and finely crumbled

Preheat oven to 375 degrees. Grease 10 muffin cups. In a medium bowl, beat cream cheese, milk, and eggs on low speed of electric mixer until smooth. Stir in swiss cheese and green onions; set aside.

Separate dough into 10 biscuits. Place one biscuit into each muffin cup; firmly press on bottom and up sides forming an 1/4-inch rim. Spoon 2 tablespoonfuls cheese mixture into each biscuit cup; sprinkle bacon over the top.

Bake, uncovered, 20 to 25 minutes or until filling is set and edges of biscuits are golden brown. Remove from oven. Remove from muffin pan and serve immediately.

Makes 10 servings.

TIPS: A quick way to separate bacon is to roll the package into a tube shape and hold for a few minutes.

No "curly" bacon for breakfast when you dip it into cold water before frying.

Sausage

Sausages, in the shape and form we know them, were developed by the ancient Romans to use up scraps of fresh pork. These could not be eaten at once and, therefore, had to be preserved. They became very popular with everyone almost immediately.

Most sausages are of European origin, and nearly every country is represented. Today, thanks to the immigrants who brought their recipes and preferences to America, we can be thought of as the sausage capital of the world.

Generally defined, sausage is one or a combination of meats, chopped or ground, blended with seasonings, stuffed into casings, and cured. It is the casing which gives the sausage its shape.

Nearly all sausage and smoked meat products are cured. Curing is an essential process in the manufacture of sausage. The very word sausage is derived from the Latin word "salsus," meaning salted or preserved meat.

Before refrigeration, heavy salting was a means of preserving meat for the months when fresh meat was not available.

Italian Sausage & Spinach Pie

Pastry for 9-inch one-crust pie (see page 122)
1/2 cup sour cream
1/4 cup freshly grated parmesan cheese
1/4 teaspoon salt, if desired
1 (9-ounce) package frozen chopped spinach, thawed and drained
1 egg
1 pound sweet or hot Italian pork sausage
1 (8-ounce) can tomato sauce
1 cup shredded mozzarella cheese
Topping Mixture

Preheat oven to 375 degrees. Prepare pie pastry. Prick pie shell with fork and bake 10 to 15 minutes or until lightly browned; remove from oven and cool on a wire rack.

In a medium bowl, combine sour cream, parmesan cheese, salt, spinach, and egg; set aside.

If pork sausage comes in casing, remove casing and break sausage into pieces. In a large frying pan over medium-high heat, brown sausage; drain. Reduce heat to low, stir in tomato sauce and simmer 10 minutes, stirring occasionally.

Spread spinach mixture onto bottom of baked pie crust. Sprinkle with mozzarella cheese. Spoon sausage mixture over cheese. Bake, uncovered, 35 to 40 minutes or until crust is a deep golden brown. Remove from oven.

Prepare Topping Mixture; spread evenly over top of pie, covering completely. Cover edge of pie crust with strips of aluminum foil. Bake another 10 minutes or until cheese is melted. Remove from oven and let stand 5 to 10 minutes before serving.

Makes 6 to 8 servings.

TOPPING MIXTURE:
2 teaspoons vegetable oil
1/2 cup chopped onion
1/2 cup sour cream
1/4 cup freshly grated parmesan cheese
2 tablespoons chopped fresh parsley
1 cup shredded mozzarella cheese

In small frying pan over medium heat, heat vegetable oil. Add onion and sauté until soft; stirring occasionally. Remove from heat; stir in sour cream, parmesan cheese, parsley, and mozzarella cheese.

Lamb With Port Sauce

You'll look for an excuse to make this delicious lamb again. Smells good, looks good, and is good.

1 (4 to 5-pound) boneless leg of lamb, rolled, tied, and trimmed of excess fat
4 to 6 cloves garlic, cut in half
4 to 5 sprigs fresh rosemary
Salt to taste
1/4 teaspoon coarsely ground pepper
1 cup ruby port wine
Port Sauce
Fresh rosemary sprigs for garnish

To prepare leg of lamb, cut 1-inch slits on all sides of the lamb. Insert garlic halves into the slits and weave rosemary sprigs in the string used to tie the lamb (some butchers may use a mesh-like material). Sprinkle with salt and pepper. Place lamb into a deep baking pan; pour port wine over lamb. Cover and refrigerate at least 1 hour or overnight.

Preheat oven to 325 degrees. Remove lamb from marinade and place onto a rack in a shallow baking pan; place in the lower half of oven. Insert a meat thermometer into the thickest part of the roast. Bake, uncovered, 2 hours or until thermometer registers 145 degrees; basting with marinade every 15 minutes.

Remove from oven and transfer onto a cutting board; let stand 15 minutes before carving. Transfer lamb onto a serving platter and drizzle Port Sauce over meat. Garnish with fresh sprigs of rosemary.

Makes 8 to 10 servings.

PORT SAUCE:
1 cup ruby port wine
1 tablespoon butter

Add wine to drippings in baking pan and heat over medium-high heat, scraping loose browned bits on the bottom of baking pan. Bring to a boil, stirring frequently until sauce is reduced to the consistency of heavy cream. (If it is reduced too much, use more port wine to make sauce the desired consistency.) Remove from heat. Just before serving, whisk in butter until blended.

Lamb

The term lamb refers to a sheep less than one year old. Baby lamb and spring lamb are both milk fed.

When purchasing lamb, let color be the guide. In general, the darker the color, the older the animal. Baby lamb will be pale pink, regular lamb pinkish red.

No matter the grade or type, always choose lamb that is nicely marbled.

Refrigerate ground lamb and small lamb cuts loosely wrapped for up to three days. Roasts can be stored up to five days.

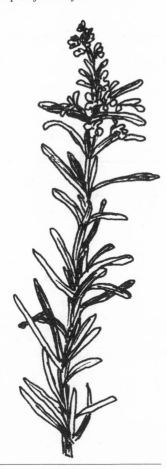

Lamb

Allspice

SUBSTITUTION:
1/2 teaspon ground cloves, 1/4 teaspoon ground cinnamon, and 1/4 teaspoon ground nutmeg is equal to 1 teaspoon of allspice.

Allspice is the ground dried fruit of the evergreen pimento tree (not the pepper pimiento) and is the only major spice grown exclusively in the Western Hemisphere. The best allspice berries come from Jamaica, which produces most of the world's supply.

The cultivated trees grow in what the Jamaicans call an "allspice walk." When they are flowering, the air is filled with perfume from the aromatic bark, leaves, flowers, and later the berries.

The name "allspice" describes its flavor. It tastes like a combination of nutmeg, cinnamon, and cloves, with slight peppery overtones.

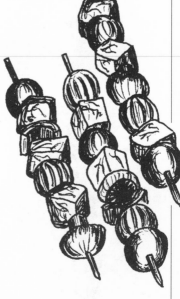

Rack of Lamb With Mustard Crust

1 (2-pound) rack of lamb (8 to 10 chops)
1/4 cup Dijon mustard
3 tablespoons soy sauce
2 tablespoons olive oil
1 tablespoon snipped fresh rosemary or 1 teaspoon dried rosemary, crushed
1/2 teaspoon red (cayenne) pepper
2 cloves garlic, minced

Trim all visible fat from rack of lamb. In a small bowl, combine Dijon mustard, soy sauce, and olive oil; mix in rosemary, cayenne pepper, and garlic to make a paste. Spread onto outside of lamb. If desired, for maximum flavor, lamb may be marinated for up to 2 days in the refrigerator.

Preheat oven to 400 degrees. Place lamb onto a rack in a shallow baking pan (rib side down). Insert a meat thermometer into the thickest part of the lamb. Bake, uncovered, 20 to 25 minutes or until thermometer registers desired doneness.
    Medium – 140 to 145 degrees
    Medium rare – 125 to 135 degrees
    Rare – 115 to 125 degrees

Remove from oven and transfer lamb to a cutting board; let stand 15 minutes before carving. Transfer onto a serving platter and serve immediately.

Makes 4 servings.

Lamb Shish Kabobs

Three days of marinating makes this extra flavorful and tender.

3 to 4 cloves garlic, minced
1 1/2 teaspoons salt
1 dried bay leaf
1/2 teaspoon pepper
1/2 teaspoon ground cloves
1/2 teaspoon ground allspice
1/2 teaspoon ground ginger
1 cup sour cream
1 (6-pound) leg of lamb or lamb roast, cut into 1-inch cubes
Small onions, peeled
Green bell pepper, cored, seeded, and cut into large pieces
Cherry tomatoes
Large mushrooms

In a large bowl, combine garlic, salt, bay leaf, pepper, cloves, allspice, ginger, and sour cream; stir in lamb cubes and marinate, covered, 3 days in the refrigerator.

Preheat barbecue grill. Thread lamb cubes and prepared vegetables alternately onto skewers. Place onto hot grill and cook until lamb is browned on the outside and pink in the middle and vegetables are cooked. Remove from grill and transfer onto a serving platter.

Makes 8 to 12 servings.

Grilled Yogurt Lamb Kabobs

2 pounds lamb sirloins or roast, cut into 1 1/2-inch cubes
Yogurt Marinade
3 onions, peeled and each cut into 6 wedges
3 large red bell peppers, cored, seeded, and each cut into 18 pieces
18 slices lemon, 1/2-inch thick
9 artichoke hearts, cut in half

Prepare Yogurt Marinade; add lamb cubes and marinate, covered, 3 days in the refrigerator.

Preheat barbecue grill. Starting with the first skewer, thread on a piece of onion, a piece of red bell pepper, a slice of lemon, a piece of lamb, and a piece of artichoke. Repeat this sequence twice so that three of everything is on the skewer. Squeeze everything up tightly so that everything fits on the skewer. Repeat with the remaining skewers.

Place onto hot grill and cook 10 minutes or until lamb is browned and pink in the middle and the vegetables are cooked. Remove from grill and transfer onto a serving platter.

Makes 6 servings.

YOGURT MARINADE:
1 cup plain yogurt
3 cloves garlic, finely chopped
1 teaspoon ground coriander
1/2 teaspoon ground cumin
1/2 teaspoon pepper

In a large bowl, combine yogurt, garlic, coriander, cumin, and pepper.

Minted Lamb Chops

4 shoulder blade lamb chops, each 3/4-inch thick
1/2 teaspoon garlic salt
1/4 teaspoon pepper
Mint Sauce

Preheat broiler. Place lamb chops onto a rack in a broiling pan. Sprinkle with garlic salt and pepper. Spoon half of Mint Sauce over lamb chops. Broil 10 minutes for medium-rare or until they are browned on the outside and pink in the middle; remove from oven. To serve, arrange lamb chops onto a warm serving platter; drizzle remaining Mint Sauce over top.

Makes 2 to 4 servings.

MINT SAUCE:
3 tablespoons mint jelly
1 teaspoon dried parsley flakes or 1 tablespoon chopped fresh parsley

In a small saucepan, over low heat, combine mint jelly and dried or fresh parsley until jelly melts.

Garlic Salt

1/2 teaspoon garlic salt equals 1 clove garlic. (Omit 1/2 teaspoon salt from recipe.)

Garlic salt can be bought or made in a mortar by pounding a garlic clove with a few tablespoons of salt.

Some suggested uses for garlic salt:

• Sprinkle over bread, pasta, or meat sandwiches.

• Blend into softened butter for a quick sandwich spread.

• Combine with chopped fresh herbs and cream cheese for a delicious spread.

Mint

Peppermint and spearmint came to the New World with the colonists, who also used them medicinally. They drank mint tea for headaches, heartburn, indigestion, gas, and to help them sleep. They also drank mint tea for pure pleasure, especially since it wasn't taxed.

Peppermint is the premier mint for flavoring candy, gum, and other sweets. Commercially prepared oil or extract are better for these uses than anything you can concoct at home from the fresh herb. For most culinary purposes, garden peppermint is a bit strong. When you do use it, harvest only the young leaves. The older leaves and the stems tend to be bitter.

Spearmint and curly mint are more versatile for culinary uses. Milder than peppermint, they enhance all sorts of meat, fish, or vegetable dishes.

Grilled Minty Lamb Chops

4 shoulder blade lamb chops
1 large clove garlic, minced
1 teaspoon freshly grated ginger
10 coriander seeds, crushed
1/3 cup plain yogurt
Salt and pepper to taste
1 tablespoon olive oil
Mint Sauce

Place lamb chops onto a flat dish or tray. In a small bowl, pound or crush the garlic, ginger, and coriander seeds together. Add yogurt, salt, and pepper; stir until well blended. Spread over lamb chops and marinate in the refrigerator, covered, at least 2 hours or overnight; turn meat occasionally to distribute marinade.

Preheat barbecue grill. Remove lamb chops from refrigerator and scrape off the marinade; wipe dry, brush with olive oil, and sprinkle with salt and pepper. Place lamb chops onto hot grill and cook until they are browned on the outside and pink in the middle. Remove from grill and transfer onto a serving platter. Serve with Mint Sauce.

Makes 4 servings.

MINT SAUCE:
1 tablespoon olive oil
1 teaspoon walnut or sesame oil
1/3 cup plain yogurt
1 tablespoon orange juice
2 tablespoons chopped fresh mint leaves
Salt and pepper to taste

In a small bowl, combine olive oil, walnut or sesame oil, and yogurt, orange juice, mint, salt, and pepper; stir until well blended (add a little water if it is too thick).

New Zealand Mint Sauce

This recipe is from New Zealand – excellent on lamb.

1 cup white vinegar
3/4 cup sugar
1 cup finely chopped mint leaves

In a small saucepan over medium-high heat, combine white vinegar and sugar; bring to a boil and remove from heat. Add mint and stir well. When required, thin down with boiling water.

NOTE: This sauce will keep for a year or more.

Country-Fried Venison & Gravy

This is absolutely the best and only way to cook fresh venison.

Venison Steaks
All-purpose flour
Salt and pepper to taste
Vegetable oil
Milk

Trim fat from venison steaks and thinly slice. Pound venison slices with meat mallet until thin; shake in a plastic bag containing flour, salt, and pepper to coat well. In a large frying pan over medium-high heat, heat vegetable oil. Add venison slices and fry until cooked. Transfer onto a plate and keep warm in a 200-degree oven.

Make a gravy by adding several tablespoons flour to drippings, and brown. Add milk to desired consistency; bring to a boil and simmer at least 15 minutes.

Serve the venison slices with mashed or boiled potatoes and the gravy.

Elsie's Mincemeat

Elsie was a wonderful woman who went to our church. She made the most delicious mincemeat and would sell it during the Christmas season at a bazaar she held.

3 pounds green tomatoes, chopped and drained
1 cup cider vinegar
3 pounds tart apples, chopped
4 pounds brown sugar
2 teaspoons cloves
1 teaspoon nutmeg
1 cup ground suet*
1 pound ground beef or venison
2 pounds raisins
2 teaspoons salt
2 teaspoons cinnamon
1/2 cup margarine
Rum or brandy to taste

* Suet is the fat of beef. Ask the butcher at your favorite meat market for some.

In a large pot over medium-high heat, cover tomatoes with cold water; bring to a boil for 5 minutes. Drain.

Reduce heat to low. Add cider vinegar, apples, brown sugar, cloves, nutmeg, suet, ground beef or venison, raisins, salt, cinnamon, and margarine; simmer 30 to 45 minutes. Remove from heat; add rum or brandy to taste.

Refrigerate or pack in hot sterile jars and seal (see page 232).

Mincemeat

Mincemeat developed as a way of preserving meat without salting or smoking some 500 years ago in England, where mince pies are still considered an essential accompaniment to holiday dinners just like the traditional plum pudding.

It is, very simply, a mixture of fruits and spices that are cooked with or without minced meat and generally doused with brandy, rum, or whiskey. It improves and becomes more moist as the weeks pass, so allow it to mature for at least four weeks before using.

Mincemeat should be checked during storage to prevent dryness. If it looks dry after it has been stirred, add one to two peeled, cored, and grated apples, or one-fourth cup dry sherry or brandy.

Mincemeat Pie

Make pie pastry for a two-crust pie. Fill bottom pie crust with the prepared mincemeat (adding more brandy to your taste). Arrange crust over the top. Seal and flute the edges. Cut vents in the top crust. Bake in a 425-degree oven for thirty-five to forty minutes.

Canning – Boiling Water Bath

Wash jars, lids, and screw bands; leave the jars in hot water. Place the lids and bands in a pan of water; bring to a boil and then remove from heat. Before using, drain the jars on a towel. Fill each jar, and then run a nonmetallic utensil around the inside of the jar to expel air.

Wipe the top and sides of the jar rim clean (food particles will interfere with sealing). Fit hot lid onto top of the jar.

Fit a screw band snugly over the jar rim and lid. Do not force a tight fit (air must escape in processing). Process the jars according to your recipe. Popping sounds from the jars indicate that seals are forming.

When cooled jars have sealed, the lids are concave. Press each lid (it should remain concave). If not, either reprocess the jars with new lids or refrigerate them and use the contents within a few days.

High-Altitude Canning

When processing at high altitudes, use the following formula:

If the processing time is twenty minutes or less, add one minute for each 1,000 feet of altitude above sea level. For longer processing times, add two minutes for each 1,000 feet.

Grandma Myers' Mincemeat

During the Depression in the 1930s, my grandfather used to call venison "land salmon" because the deer that he killed were out of season. He hunted deer all year long to feed his family. My mother said that he always shared it with his neighbors.

4 pounds venison or lean beef
Water
2 1/2 cups suet, finely chopped
7 1/2 cups chopped tart apples
3 cups liquid which beef or venison was cooked in
5 cups sugar
3 cups apple cider
1 cup molasses
1/2 cup cider vinegar
3 cups raisins
2 tablespoons ground cinnamon
1 tablespoon ground cloves
2 tablespoons ground allspice
2 tablespoons ground nutmeg
Juice of 2 lemons
Juice of 2 oranges
1 cup brandy or sherry

* Suet is the fat of beef. Ask the butcher at your favorite meat market for some.

Trim fat from venison. In a large heavy pan over medium heat, place venison or beef; cover with water and simmer until meat is tender. Remove from heat and refrigerate venison or beef in cooking liquid overnight. Remove from refrigerator and remove venison or beef from liquid. Remove all fat from top of liquid; reserve liquid. Separate venison or beef from bones; discard bones. Chop cooked venison or beef into small cubes.

In a large pot, combine venison or beef cubes, suet, apples, reserved liquid, sugar, apple cider, molasses, cider vinegar, raisins, cinnamon, cloves, allspice, nutmeg, lemon juice, and orange juice; simmer for 2 hours. Remove from heat. Add brandy or sherry and mix together.

Refrigerate or pack in hot sterile jars and seal.

Poultry

Chicken & Cashew Bake

Makes a great dinner. Serve this wonderful chicken dish over cooked rice.

2 tablespoons butter or margarine
1 cup sliced celery
1/4 cup chopped onion
3 cups cubed cooked chicken
1/2 cup chopped cashews
1/4 cup water or chicken broth
1 (10 3/4-ounce) can cream of chicken soup, undiluted
1 1/2 cups frozen peas, thawed and drained
1 (2-ounce) jar sliced pimiento, drained
Salt to taste
1/2 cup chow mein noodles
1/4 cup whole cashews

Heat oven to 350 degrees. In a large frying pan over medium-high heat, melt butter or margarine. Add celery and onion; sauté until soft. Stir in chicken, cashews, water or chicken broth, chicken soup, peas, pimiento, and salt; heat thoroughly. Pour into an ungreased 2-quart casserole dish. Bake, uncovered, 25 minutes.

In a small bowl, combine chow mein noodles and cashews; sprinkle topping evenly over casserole. Bake another 5 minutes or until topping is warm. Remove from oven and serve immediately.

Makes 4 servings.

Chicken Piccata

Once you've tried this chicken, it will be your favorite. Excellent for a dinner party.

4 chicken breast halves, boneless and skinless
1/2 cup all-purpose flour
Salt and coarsely ground pepper to taste
2 tablespoons butter
1 tablespoon vegetable oil
1/4 cup lemon juice
1/4 cup white wine
3 tablespoons drained capers

Pound chicken thin by placing one chicken breast at a time between two pieces of plastic wrap. Working from the center to the edges, pound lightly with a meat mallet to 1/4-inch thick.

In a shallow pie plate, combine flour, salt, and pepper. Roll chicken in flour mixture to coat all sides.

In a large nonstick frying pan over medium heat, heat butter and vegetable oil. Add chicken and cook 3 to 5 minutes per side or until fully cooked and tender. Pour lemon juice and white wine over top of chicken. Add capers and simmer another 2 to 3 minutes longer. Remove from heat and transfer chicken onto a serving platter.

Reduce liquid left in frying pan by boiling an additional 2 to 3 minutes; pour over the chicken and serve immediately.

Makes 4 servings.

To Test for Doneness

Poultry is considered cooked or done when it reaches a temperature of 185 degrees. In using a meat thermometer, it is placed in the deepest part of the thigh or breast.

Doneness can also be tested by the following pressure tests.

CHICKEN PIECES: Cut into thickest part of chicken or test with a fork. Chicken should cut easily, be fork-tender, and show no pink at bone.

WHOLE CHICKEN: Drumsticks and wing joints should move easily, and thickest part of chicken should yield easily to pressure from a fork.

TURKEY: Grasp the end of the drumstick. If it moves up and down and twists easily out of thigh joint, and if fleshy part of drumstick feels very soft when pressed with fingers, turkey is done.

Honey

1 pound of honey equals 1 1/3 cups honey.

1 tablespoon honey is equal to 5 tablespoons of sugar.

Honey is the only natural sweetener that doesn't have to be refined. Therefore, nothing is added or taken away, making it the world's only perfect sweetener.

Do you know what accounts for the difference in flavor, aroma, and color in honey? The answer is the flowers from which the bees have gathered their nectar.

More than half of all honey produced in the United States is clover honey. As a rule, the darker the honey, the stronger and heavier it will be. There are also lots of exotic, often expensive, imported honeys.

Breast of Chicken With Honey

Definitely good enough for company.

4 chicken breast halves, boneless and skinless
Seasoning salt and pepper to taste
1/4 cup vegetable oil
1/4 cup honey
1/4 cup white wine tarragon vinegar
1/2 cup chili sauce
1 tablespoon worcestershire sauce
1/2 envelope dry onion soup mix

Preheat oven to 350 degrees. Place chicken into an ungreased 13x9-inch baking dish; season with seasoning salt and pepper.

In a jar with a lid, combine vegetable oil, honey, wine vinegar, chili sauce, worcestershire sauce, and onion soup mix; cover securely and shake vigorously. Pour honey mixture over chicken.

Bake, uncovered, 30 to 40 minutes or until chicken is fully cooked. Remove from oven, transfer onto a serving platter, and serve immediately.

Makes 4 servings.

Lemon-Honey Chicken

4 chicken breast halves, boneless and skinless
Salt and coarsely ground pepper
Lemon-Honey Sauce

Preheat oven to 350 degrees. Sprinkle chicken breasts with salt and pepper; place into an ungreased 13x9-inch baking dish. Pour Lemon-Honey Sauce over chicken.

Bake, uncovered, 30 to 40 minutes or until chicken is fully cooked, turning and basting while cooking. Remove from oven and transfer onto a serving platter. Pour remaining sauce over chicken and serve immediately.

Makes 4 servings.

LEMON-HONEY SAUCE:
1/4 cup vegetable oil
1/4 cup honey
1 egg yolk, slightly beaten
1 tablespoon lemon juice
1 tablespoon soy sauce
1/4 teaspoon ground nutmeg
1 teaspoon paprika

In a medium bowl, combine vegetable oil, honey, egg yolk, and lemon juice. Stir in soy sauce, nutmeg, and paprika; stir until well blended.

Orange-Chicken Risotto

This dish will truly surprise you with its refreshing and delicious taste. It's definitely a recipe you will make many times.

1 tablespoon olive oil
1 cup arborio rice or medium-grain white rice
3 cups chicken broth
4 chicken breast halves, boneless and skinless
3 tablespoons butter
1/2 pound sliced fresh mushrooms
1/2 cup orange juice
1 tablespoon drained capers
1 cup drained artichoke hearts, cut into bite-sized pieces
Salt and pepper to taste
1/4 cup freshly grated parmesan cheese

In a large paella pan or a large frying pan over medium-high heat, heat olive oil. Add rice; stir 1 minute. Add chicken broth; reduce heat to medium-low and simmer, stirring frequently, 20 minutes or until rice is just tender but still firm to bite and mixture is creamy.

Cut chicken into bite-sized pieces. In a large frying pan over medium heat, melt butter. Add chicken and mushrooms; sauté until chicken is fully cooked and tender. Remove chicken and mushrooms with a slotted spoon to a plate; set aside.

Increase heat to high; add orange juice to frying pan. Simmer until liquid is reduced to approximately 1/2 cup. Add capers and simmer 1 to 2 minutes. Add artichoke hearts, chicken and mushroom mixture, salt, and pepper; stir and simmer until thoroughly heated.

Remove from heat and pour over cooked rice; stir just until blended. Sprinkle with parmesan cheese and serve immediately.

Makes 4 servings.

Capers

Capers are the unopened green flower buds of the Capparis Spinosa, a wild and cultivated bush grown mainly in Mediterranean countries, notably southern France, Italy, and Algeria; also California.

Manual labor is required to gather capers, for the buds must be picked each morning just as they reach the proper size. After the buds are picked, they are usually sundried, then pickled in a vinegar brine.

Capers can range in size from that of a tiny peppercorn (the petite variety from southern France, considered the finest) to some as large as the tip of your little finger (from Italy).

Capers generally come in brine but can also be found salted and sold in bulk. Either way, rinse before using to flush away as much salt as possible.

Capers can lend piquancy to many sauces and condiments; they can also be used as a garnish for meat and vegetable dishes.

Dried Herbs

For over 5,000 years, herbs have been grown and used for medicinal, aromatic, and culinary purposes. The Ancient Romans planted herb gardens in the Middle Ages.

To use dried herbs instead of fresh ones, substitute 1 teaspoon of dried herbs for every 1 tablespoon of fresh herbs.

Dried herbs will last longer if you buy the leaf variety instead of the ground or powdered.

You can intensify the flavor of dried herbs by crushing them between your fingers, the warmth of your hands will activate the aromatic oils in the herbs.

If you have an electric blender, food processor, or small coffee grinder, buy seeds such as dill, cumin, coriander, cardamom, and caraway. You will be very surprised at how much more flavorful freshly ground seeds are than the commercially pulverized ones.

Herb Chicken

4 chicken breast halves, boneless and skinless
1/2 cup olive oil
1/2 cup lemon juice
1/2 cup water
1 clove garlic, minced
1 teaspoon paprika
1 tablespoon assorted chopped fresh herbs (basil, oregano, parsley, cilantro)
Coarsely ground pepper to taste

Preheat oven to 350 degrees. Roll up chicken breasts jelly-roll style; secure with wooden toothpicks. Place into an ungreased 13x9-inch baking dish.

In a jar with a lid, combine olive oil, lemon juice, and water. Add garlic, paprika, herbs, and pepper; cover securely and shake vigorously. Pour mixture over rolled chicken breasts.

Bake, uncovered, 30 to 40 minutes or until chicken is fully cooked. Remove from oven and serve immediately.

Makes 4 servings.

Chicken & Rice

This is one of those recipes that you can make at the last minute when you haven't planned dinner ahead. This recipe is very easy to make and is always a favorite with men.

#1 VERSION:
1 cup long-grain rice
1 package dry onion soup mix
4 chicken breast halves, boneless and skinless
1 (10 3/4-ounce) can cream of mushroom soup, undiluted
1 1/2 cups water or milk

#2 VERSION:
1 (6-ounce) package long-grain and wild rice with seasonings
1 tablespoon soy sauce
4 chicken breast halves, boneless and skinless
1 (10 3/4-ounce) can cream of chicken soup, undiluted
1 soup can of water

Preheat oven to 350 degrees. In an ungreased large casserole dish, place rice. Stir onion soup mix (version 1) or seasoning package from rice mix, and soy sauce (version 2) into rice. Place chicken onto top of rice mixture.

In a medium bowl, combine mushroom or chicken soup with milk or water; spread mixture over chicken.

Bake, covered, 45 to 60 minutes or until chicken is fully cooked. Remove cover to brown chicken during the last 20 minutes. Remove from oven and serve immediately.

Makes 4 servings.

Creamy Baked Chicken

4 chicken breast halves, boneless and skinless
4 swiss cheese slices
1 (10 3/4-ounce) can cream of chicken or mushroom soup, undiluted
1/4 cup dry white wine
Seasoned bread crumbs
1/4 cup butter or margarine, melted

Preheat oven to 350 degrees. Roll up chicken breasts jelly-roll style; secure with wooden toothpicks. Place into an ungreased 13x9-inch baking dish. Place one slice of swiss cheese on top of each chicken breast.

In a small bowl, combine chicken or mushroom soup and white wine; spread evenly over chicken. Sprinkle top with seasoned bread crumbs; evenly drizzle with butter or margarine.

Bake, uncovered, 30 to 40 minutes or until chicken is fully cooked. Remove from oven and serve immediately.

Makes 4 servings.

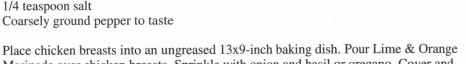

Lime & Orange Chicken

A delicious lowfat way of enjoying chicken.

4 chicken breast halves, boneless and skinless
Lime & Orange Marinade
1 tablespoon minced onion
1/2 teaspoon dried basil or oregano, crushed
1/4 teaspoon salt
Coarsely ground pepper to taste

Place chicken breasts into an ungreased 13x9-inch baking dish. Pour Lime & Orange Marinade over chicken breasts. Sprinkle with onion and basil or oregano. Cover and marinate at room temperature for 20 minutes or refrigerate to marinate longer.

Preheat oven to 350 degrees. Remove chicken from marinade and place onto a rack in a shallow baking pan; reserve marinade for basting. Sprinkle with salt and pepper. Bake, uncovered, 30 to 40 minutes or until chicken is fully cooked; basting once during cooking. Remove from oven and serve immediately.

Makes 4 servings.

LIME & ORANGE MARINADE:
2 tablespoons lime juice
2 tablespoons orange juice
1 tablespoon olive oil

In a small bowl, combine lime juice, orange juice, and olive oil; stir until well blended.

Poultry Safety

It's important to store and handle chicken properly.

• *Always wash your hands, countertops, and utensils in hot soapy water after handling raw chicken.*

• *Never transfer cooked chicken to a plate or bowl that has held raw chicken, unless it has been thoroughly cleaned.*

• *Defrost chicken in the refrigerator or in a microwave, not on the counter. To thaw more quickly, place chicken in a watertight plastic bag and place in cold water; changing water frequently.*

Freezing Fresh Herb Leaves

Rinse herbs and let drain until dry. Lay in a single layer on baking sheets, keeping pieces slightly apart. Freeze on baking sheets just until herbs are rigid, about one hour. Place frozen herbs into small freezer plastic bags, press out air, seal, and return to the freezer.

To use, take herbs you need out of the bags, reseal, and immediately return the rest to the freezer. Frozen herbs will retain flavor up to one year.

Evaporated Milk

1 (6-ounce) can equals 3/4 cup.

1 (14.5-ounce) can equals 1 2/3 cups.

Evaporated milk is fresh whole milk that has had 60 percent of the water removed and then homogenized. It is then vacuum-packed in small cans.

Evaporated milk can be used in any recipe that calls for milk. This includes virtually every recipe category. It is about twice as rich as whole milk and slightly less rich than light cream.

It can be whipped and substituted for whipped cream, both as a dessert topping and as an ingredient in almost any mousse, pudding, chiffon pie, or gelatin salad calling for whipped cream. Also, substituting evaporated milk, you will cut the calories more than half of whipping cream.

Once a can of evaporated milk is opened, it should be put into the refrigerator immediately. Transfer it to a jar with a tight-fitting lid. Store in refrigerator five to seven days.

East-West Chicken

An excellent recipe for the novice cook as well as the experienced.

1/2 cup evaporated milk
1 tablespoon soy sauce
1 cup bread crumbs or corn flake crumbs
1 teaspoon salt
1/8 teaspoon pepper
4 chicken breast halves, boneless and skinless

Lightly grease a 13x9-inch baking dish. In a shallow pie plate, combine evaporated milk and soy sauce. In another shallow pie plate, combine bread crumbs or corn flake crumbs, salt, and pepper. Dip chicken into evaporated milk mixture and then roll in the seasoned crumb mixture.

Place chicken into prepared baking dish; cover with wax paper or plastic wrap. Cook in microwave oven on high 10 minutes; turn dish and bake another 8 to 10 minutes. Remove from microwave and let stand 3 to 5 minutes before serving.

Makes 4 servings.

Pollo Verde

Pollo Verde means "green chicken" in Spanish.

2 medium avocados, peeled and seeded
2 tablespoons lemon juice
1/4 teaspoon garlic salt
1/4 teaspoon red (cayenne) pepper
Coarsely ground pepper to taste
2 tablespoons butter or margarine
4 chicken breast halves, boneless and skinless
3 teaspoons fresh dill or 1 1/4 teaspoons dried dill weed, crushed
4 thick tomato slices
4 (1/4-inch) thick slices cheddar cheese
2 tablespoons diced green chilies
2 bacon slices, cooked and crumbled

In a medium bowl, combine avocados, lemon juice, garlic salt, and cayenne pepper. Mash with fork until slightly chunky. Season with pepper.

Preheat broiler. In a large frying pan over medium heat, melt butter or margarine. Add chicken (in batches if necessary – but do not crowd). Sprinkle with dill. Cook 15 minutes; turn chicken over and cook another 15 to 20 minutes or until chicken is fully cooked. Transfer chicken into an ungreased 13x9-inch baking dish.

Mound avocado mixture on top of each chicken breast. Top each with a tomato slice and cover each with a cheese slice; trimming to fit. Sprinkle with green chilies. Broil just until cheese melts. Remove chicken from oven. To serve, sprinkle with bacon and serve immediately.

Makes 4 servings.

Taco Chicken

4 chicken breast halves, boneless and skinless
Taco Marinade

Place chicken breasts into an ungreased 13x9-inch baking dish. Pour Taco Marinade over chicken breasts. Cover and marinate at room temperature 15 minutes or refrigerate and marinate up to 8 hours.

Preheat oven to 350 degrees. Bake, uncovered, 30 to 40 minutes or until chicken is fully cooked. Remove from oven and serve immediately.

Makes 4 servings.

TACO MARINADE:
1/2 cup green taco sauce
1 (10 3/4-ounce) can cream of mushroom soup, undiluted
Chopped fresh cilantro to taste
5 teaspoons fresh lime or lemon juice
2 teaspoons olive oil
1 clove garlic, minced

In a medium bowl, combine taco sauce, soup, cilantro, lime or lemon juice, olive oil, and garlic; stir until well blended.

Speedy Chicken

4 chicken breast halves, boneless and skinless
1/2 cup plain yogurt
1/2 cup sour cream
3 ounces crumbled blue cheese
1 tablespoon butter or margarine, room temperature
2 teaspoons dried tarragon, crushed and divided

Preheat oven to 350 degrees. Place chicken breasts into an ungreased 13x9-inch baking dish.

In a small bowl, combine yogurt, sour cream, blue cheese, butter or margarine, and 1 teaspoon of tarragon; stir until well blended. Spoon mixture over chicken breasts, covering each piece. Sprinkle remaining 1 teaspoon tarragon on top and bake, uncovered, 30 to 40 minutes or until chicken is fully cooked. Remove from oven and serve immediately.

VARIATION: For additional color and sweetness, spoon 1/4 cup green or red jalapeño jelly over the chicken before baking. Proceed as directed.

Makes 4 servings.

Blue-Veined Cheeses

Blue-veined cheeses are cheeses that have blue-green mold running through them (created by the injection of a mold that spreads throughout the cheese).

In the United States, this cheese is called blue cheese. Nearly every country has its own distinctive type of blue-veined cheese. The most popular are the French bleus, the roquefort, the Italian gorgonzola, the English stilton, and the Danish blue.

Improvising an Oven-Proof Pan

If you don't own an ovenproof pan but want to make a recipe that calls for one, simply wrap your pan's handle in several layers of aluminum foil. This will protect the handle from the intense oven heat.

History of Chicken

Chicken has been around for a long time (since sometime around 1,000 B.C.). Our primitive ancestors, in the jungles of India, first plucked, then impaled on a stick, and then roasted over hot coals, the forefather of the bird we find in today's supermarket.

It used to be that you could tell a lot about a bird by its plumage. You could easily tell a him from a her by the color and by the shape of the tail. You could tell how old a rooster was by the size of his comb and the spurs on his feet. You could tell if he was still a rooster or had been turned into a capon, not only by his behavior in the hen house, but also by the size and shape of his head.

Today, the only plumage you are likely to find on any chicken is some clear plastic wrap. No longer do you have to scald, pluck, and singe to rid the bird of his plumage. Today, simply peel off the plastic wrap and he's plucked.

Light & Easy Italian Chicken

6 chicken breast halves, boneless and skinless
Water
1/2 cup reduced-calorie Italian salad dressing
1/4 teaspoon coarsely ground pepper
1 tablespoon snipped fresh tarragon or basil or 1/2 teaspoon dried tarragon
    or basil, crushed
1/3 cup freshly grated parmesan cheese

Preheat oven to 350 degrees. Place chicken into an ungreased 13x9-inch baking dish. Fill dish with approximately 1/4-inch water. Pour Italian dressing over chicken. Sprinkle with pepper, tarragon or basil, and parmesan cheese.

Bake, uncovered, 30 to 40 minutes or until chicken is fully cooked. Remove from oven and serve immediately.

Makes 6 servings.

Tarragon Chicken

Tarragon Sauce
4 chicken breast halves, boneless and skinless

Preheat oven to 350 degrees. Spoon a little of the Tarragon Sauce on each chicken breast. Roll up chicken breasts jelly-roll style; secure with wooden toothpicks. Place into an ungreased 13x9-inch baking dish. Pour remaining sauce over chicken.

Baked, covered, 30 to 40 minutes or until chicken is fully cooked. Remove from oven and serve immediately.

Makes 4 servings.

TARRAGON SAUCE:
1 (10 3/4-ounce) can cream of mushroom soup, undiluted
1/2 cup sour cream
1/4 cup dry white wine
1/4 cup lemon juice
1 tablespoon dried tarragon, crushed
Salt and pepper to taste
1 clove garlic, minced
1 cup sliced fresh mushrooms

In a medium bowl, combine mushroom soup, sour cream, white wine, and lemon juice; stir until well blended. Add tarragon, salt, pepper, garlic, and mushrooms; stir until well blended.

Southwestern Chicken

8 chicken breasts halves, boneless and skinless
Yogurt Salsa

Preheat oven to 350 degrees. Pierce chicken liberally on both sides with a fork. In a large bowl, place 1/3 cup Yogurt Salsa; add chicken, turning to coat both sides. Place chicken into an ungreased 13x9-inch baking dish. Cover and marinate at room temperature for 15 minutes or refrigerate to marinate longer. Before baking, pour remaining Yogurt Salsa over chicken.

Bake, covered, 30 to 40 minutes or until chicken is fully cooked. Remove from oven and serve immediately.

Makes 8 servings.

YOGURT SALSA:
1 cup plain yogurt
1 tablespoon mayonnaise
1 (4-ounce) can sliced mild green chilies, drained
1/4 cup minced green onions
1 teaspoon ground cumin
1 teaspoon salt

In a medium bowl, combine yogurt and mayonnaise. Add green chilies, green onions, cumin, and salt; stir until well blended.

Grilled Chicken & Mango Kabobs

4 whole chicken breasts, boneless and skinless
1 large mango, peeled and cut into 1-inch chunks
1 large green bell pepper, cored, seeded, and cut into 1-inch squares
Cilantro-Lime Sauce

Preheat barbecue grill. Cut chicken into 1-inch cubes. Thread chicken, mango, and bell pepper alternately onto eight skewers. Place skewers onto hot grill; cook 12 to 15 minutes or until chicken is fully cooked, turning and brushing with Cilantro-Lime Sauce often. Remove from grill and transfer onto a serving platter. Serve with remaining sauce.

Makes 8 servings.

CILANTRO-LIME SAUCE:
3 tablespoons honey
1 teaspoon grated lime zest
3 tablespoons fresh lime juice
2 tablespoons butter or margarine
2 tablespoons chopped fresh cilantro or 2 teaspoons dried cilantro, crushed

In a small saucepan over medium heat, combine honey, lime zest, lime juice, butter or margarine, and cilantro; stir until well blended. Simmer 5 minutes. Keep warm.

Skewers

Skewers make some foods much easier to handle on the grill while barbecuing. It is much easier to control small pieces of food. Threaded onto skewers, the pieces become a single unit to lift and turn.

When loading skewers, keep in mind that meat, poultry, firm-textured fish (swordfish and shellfish) shrink as they cook, tightening their hold on the skewer. Vegetables and fruits get softer or more fragile.

Chutney

The basic definition of chutney is a condiment made from fruits cooked slowly with vinegar, sugar, and spice. But there are as many different versions as there are cooks. Chutneys originated in India, where their Hindu name is "chatni," which means "strongly spiced."

Chutney can vary in taste and texture from sweet to peppery. It was made fresh each day but is now prepared as a preserve.

Chutney is often served as a side dish to curries, but it also makes an excellent condiment for cold meats, cheeses, etc. A chutney can be just the spark needed to pull together a simple broiled dinner or can become the secret ingredient of a recipe.

North Carolina Grilled Chicken

Summer barbecues in North Carolina wouldn't be right without a good barbecue chicken sauce. This is a very good one.

Barbecue Sauce
2 whole chickens, cut into quarters

Prepare Barbecue Sauce. Place chicken quarters directly into a large pot with sauce. Marinate for 2 to 3 hours.

Preheat barbecue grill. Place chicken onto hot grill. Cover barbecue with lid, open any vents, and cook 30 minutes or until chicken is fully cooked; turning and basting several times. Remove from grill, transfer onto a serving platter, and serve immediately.

Makes 4 servings.

BARBECUE SAUCE:
1/2 cup cider vinegar
1/2 cup water
1 cup butter or margarine
1/8 teaspoon salt
1/2 teaspoon pepper
1/8 teaspoon red (cayenne) pepper
1 tablespoon sugar

In a large saucepan over medium-high heat, combine cider vinegar, water, and butter or margarine. Add salt, pepper, cayenne pepper, and sugar; reduce heat to low and simmer 5 to 10 minutes. Remove from heat.

Grilled Chutney Chicken

6 pieces chicken, such as breast halves, legs, or thighs
Chutney Sauce

Preheat barbecue grill (spray grill with vegetable-oil cooking spray). Place chicken onto hot grill and brush generously with Chutney Sauce. Cover barbecue with lid, open any vents, and cook 20 to 30 minutes or until chicken is fully cooked; turning and basting several times. Remove from grill, transfer onto a serving platter, and serve immediately.

Makes 6 servings.

CHUTNEY SAUCE:
1/2 cup of your favorite chutney
2 cloves garlic, minced
1 teaspoon freshly grated ginger
1 teaspoon red (cayenne) pepper

In a small bowl, combine chutney, garlic, ginger, and cayenne pepper; stir until well blended.

Honey-Mustard Chicken Legs

This dish is equally delicious at room temperature, and it's great for picnics.

Honey-Mustard Sauce
1 cup bread crumbs
4 whole chicken legs with thighs
4 teaspoons vegetable oil

Spray a large baking sheet with vegetable-oil cooking spray. In a shallow pie plate, pour bread crumbs. Dip chicken in Honey-Mustard Sauce and then in bread crumbs; place onto prepared baking sheet. Cover with aluminum foil and refrigerate 1 hour.

Preheat oven to 350 degrees. Remove aluminum foil; drizzle vegetable oil over chicken. Bake, uncovered, 30 to 40 minutes or until chicken is fully cooked. Remove from oven and transfer onto a serving platter. Serve with additional Honey-Mustard Sauce.

Makes 4 servings.

HONEY-MUSTARD SAUCE:
1/4 cup Dijon mustard
2 tablespoons honey
3 1/2 teaspoons lemon juice
1/2 teaspoon dried oregano, crushed
1/8 teaspoon ground cloves

In a shallow pie plate, combine mustard, honey, and lemon juice. Add oregano and cloves; stir until well blended.

Dijon Mustard

"Dijon" is the general term of a style of mustard produced in Dijon, France, and only mustard made there may label itself as such. Grey Poupon mustard is the only exception. They have been licensed to produce it in the United States.

Dijon and Dijon-style mustard is made from husked and ground mustard seeds, white wine, vinegar, and spices.

Easy-Bake Chicken Cordon Bleu

This is an excellent recipe for new brides or for the working woman. It makes you feel like a gourmet cook. Serve it with cooked rice.

8 chicken breast halves, boneless and skinless
8 slices baked ham
8 slices swiss cheese
1 (10 3/4-ounce) can cream of chicken soup, undiluted
1/4 cup dry white wine
1 cup herb bread stuffing mix, crushed
1/4 cup butter or margarine

Preheat oven to 350 degrees. Grease a 13x9-inch baking dish. Place chicken into prepared dish; top each with a slice of ham and a slice of swiss cheese.

In a small bowl, combine chicken soup and white wine; spoon onto the top of the chicken. Sprinkle with stuffing mix. Drizzle butter or margarine over stuffing. Bake, uncovered, 30 to 40 minutes or until chicken is fully cooked. Remove from oven and serve immediately.

Makes 8 servings.

Cordon Bleu

Cordon Bleu is a French word that means "an exceptional cook."

There is a cooking school in Paris, established in 1895, called the Cordon Bleu. The "Grand Diplome" of the Cordon Bleu Cooking School is the highest credential a chef can have.

Yogurt

Recipes that most often call for yogurt are East Indian, Balkan, Russian, and Middle Eastern in origin. Cooks in those areas employ yogurt in marinades and sauces.

Because of its acidity, yogurt can be used to marinate and tenderize meats (as it often is used in India and the Middle East). Yogurt can also be used to bind ingredients loosely together, as in a sauce or salad dressing.

Yogurt also makes a wonderful low-calorie substitute for sour cream or mayonnaise in cole slaws, tuna and chicken salads, Stroganoffs, and fruit soups or purées.

Yogurts made in the United States are made of cow's milk. Those of India and the Middle East are more likely to be of the richer goat, sheep, or yak milk.

Store, tightly covered, in the coldest part of the refrigerator for five to seven days.

TIPS: Do not allow any mixture containing yogurt to boil, or it will curdle.

Always bring yogurt to room temperature before adding to a hot mixture. This will prevent the mixture from separating.

Oven-Baked Chicken

This recipe is truly wonderful and is low fat and low calorie. WHAT MORE CAN YOU ASK FOR?

The secret to the success of this recipe is to make sure that both the chicken and the yogurt are very cold (hence, soaking the chicken in the ice water). The preliminary soaking will help the breading adhere and produce a crisp coating much like that of fried chicken.

12 chicken drumsticks, skinless
3 1/2 cups ice water
1 cup plain yogurt
Breading Mixture

Preheat oven to 350 degrees. Spray a large baking sheet heavily with vegetable-oil cooking spray. In a large bowl with ice water, place chicken pieces; set aside.

In a medium bowl, place yogurt. Remove one piece of chicken at a time from ice water. Roll each piece in yogurt. Place one chicken piece into a plastic bag with Breading Mixture, reseal, and shake to coat thoroughly. Transfer breaded chicken to prepared baking sheet. Repeat process until all chicken pieces are breaded. Spray chicken lightly with vegetable-oil spray.

Place baking sheet onto bottom shelf of oven and bake, uncovered, 1 hour or until chicken is fully cooked, turning the chicken pieces every 20 minutes to allow even browning. Remove from oven and transfer onto a serving platter. Serve hot or at room temperature.

Makes 6 to 8 servings.

BREADING MIXTURE:
1 cup seasoned bread crumbs
1 cup all-purpose flour
1 tablespoon creole seasoning
1/2 teaspoon garlic powder
1/8 teaspoon coarsely ground pepper
Red (cayenne) pepper to taste
1/2 teaspoon dried thyme, crushed
1/2 teaspoon dried basil, crushed
1/2 teaspoon dried oregano, crushed

In a large resealable plastic bag, combine bread crumbs, flour, creole seasoning, garlic powder, pepper, cayenne pepper, thyme, basil, and oregano. Seal and shake well to mix.

Southern Fried Chicken

Serve with mashed potatoes and buttermilk biscuits.

1 egg
1 cup all-purpose flour
1 (3-pound) frying chicken, cut into pieces
Vegetable oil
Milk Gravy

In a shallow bowl, beat egg lightly. In another shallow bowl, place flour. Dip chicken pieces, one at a time, into egg until evenly moistened; then roll in the flour; shaking off excess. Place onto a large ungreased baking sheet and refrigerate for 1 hour.

In a large frying pan over medium-high heat, pour enough vegetable oil to reach a depth of 1/4 inch. Remove chicken from refrigerator and coat with flour again; shaking off excess. When oil is hot, add chicken pieces, skin side down in a single layer. Allow enough space between pieces for oil to bubble and sizzle (this assures even cooking and browning).

NOTE: To test temperature of oil, drop a pinch of flour into pan; flour should float and sizzle on hot oil. If flour sinks to bottom of pan and disperses, oil is not hot enough for frying.

Cook chicken pieces 15 minutes. With tongs, turn pieces over and cook another 15 to 20 minutes or until meat is fully cooked. When chicken is done, remove from pan and let drain on paper towels. Serve with Milk Gravy.

Makes 4 servings.

MILK GRAVY:
5 tablespoons of pan drippings
1/4 cup all-purpose flour
2 1/2 cups milk
Salt and pepper to taste

Maintain medium-high heat. Pour off and reserve drippings from frying pan, leaving browned particles on bottom of pan. Return 5 tablespoons of drippings to pan (discard remaining); scrape browned particles free. Return to heat and blend in flour; stirring until mixture becomes bubbly. Gradually pour in milk and continue cooking and stirring until sauce boils and thickens. Season with salt and pepper. Remove from heat and transfer to a serving bowl.

Frying Chicken

Two methods of frying chicken are sautéeing and deep frying. Sautéeing is done in shallow fat, browning and cooking it well by turning. This methods takes about twenty minutes. A ten-minute finish in a moderate (350 degrees) oven improves the product.

The best-known method of frying chicken is Southern Fried Chicken. It is lightly coated with seasoned flour and deep fried until tender. If served with a cream gravy and corn fritters, it becomes Maryland Fried Chicken.

TIPS: For an especially light and delicate crust on coated fried foods, add three-fourths teaspoon of baking powder to the batter and use club soda for the liquid.

After flouring chicken, chill for one hour. The coating will adhere better during frying.

Safety First Frying

Hot fat or oil, even in small amounts, needs to be handled with great care. A frying pan that is allowed to overheat, or spilled fat, can catch fire very readily.

Clay-Pot Cooking

The clay pot, one of the oldest cooking containers, is now enjoying a revival.

IMPORTANT: Always immerse both the top and bottom of a clay cooker in cold water for fifteen minutes before using.

Clay pot cooking should always begin in a COLD oven; set the heat after the dish is in the oven.

When removing the dish from a hot oven, always set it on a rack, pad, towel, or a wooden board. Never set the pot on a burner or warming tray. Also, do not add very cold liquids once the clay pot has been heated up.

To clean, soak pot in hot water and scrub with a stiff brush to remove encrusted food. A little detergent or baking soda is all right, but do not use cleansers; they clog the clay's pores.

Chicken in Clay Pot

1 (2- to 3-pound) whole chicken
Salt and pepper to taste
1 clove garlic, minced
3/4 teaspoon dried thyme, crushed
2 tablespoons butter or margarine
1/4 teaspoon paprika
1 tablespoon lemon juice
1/3 cup dry white wine

Soak the top and bottom of the clay cooking pot in cold water for at least 15 minutes or until you are ready to put the chicken into the pot.

Pat chicken dry inside and out. Sprinkle inside with salt, pepper, garlic, and thyme. Let stand 10 minutes. Place chicken into the clay pot, top with butter or margarine; sprinkle with paprika, lemon juice, and white wine. Cover and place into a COLD oven. Turn oven temperature to 450 degrees and bake 1 hour. Remove lid and bake another 10 minutes if you like the skin crisp. Remove from the oven and serve immediately.

NOTE: You may add new potatoes, carrots, and small onions to clay pot and they will come out tender and flavored with the wonderful juices.

Makes 3 to 4 servings.

Sesame Chicken

8 chicken drumsticks or thighs
1 teaspoon sesame oil
1 tablespoon dry sherry
1/4 teaspoon Five Spice Seasoning*
1/4 teaspoon white pepper
1 clove garlic, minced
1 teaspoon freshly grated ginger
4 tablespoons soy sauce
2 tablespoons sesame seeds
Cooked rice

• Five Spice Seasoning can be found in Asian food stores or see page 171.

Make 2 or 3 slits into the meat on each chicken piece; place into a large dish. In a small bowl, combine sesame oil, sherry, Five Spice Seasoning, white pepper, garlic, ginger, and soy sauce; pour mixture over the chicken pieces. Cover and refrigerate for at least 5 hours or overnight.

Soak top and bottom of the clay cooking pot in cold water for at least 15 minutes. Remove chicken from the marinade and place into the soaked clay pot with all the marinating juices. Sprinkle sesame seeds over the chicken. Cover the pot and place into a COLD oven. Turn oven temperature to 475 degrees and bake 35 minutes; uncover and cook another 15 minutes. Remove from oven. Serve chicken with cooked rice.

Makes 4 servings.

Kentucky Oven-Fried Chicken

3 to 3 1/2 pounds chicken breasts, boneless and skinless
2 cups buttermilk
1 cup bread crumbs
1 teaspoon paprika
1/2 teaspoon garlic powder
1/2 teaspoon salt
1/4 teaspoon dried thyme, crushed
1/4 teaspoon pepper

Cut chicken into large pieces. In a large bowl, place chicken pieces. Pour buttermilk over chicken, turn chicken to coat evenly. Cover and refrigerate several hours or overnight.

Preheat oven to 350 degrees. Spray a large baking sheet with vegetable-oil cooking spray; set aside. Drain buttermilk from chicken by placing chicken on rack placed over sink or large bowl.

In a shallow pie plate, combine bread crumbs, paprika, garlic powder, salt, thyme, and pepper; roll chicken breasts in bread crumb mixture to coat evenly. Place in a single layer onto prepared baking sheet.

Bake, uncovered, 20 minutes. Carefully slide broad spatula under pieces to loosen from pan without tearing coating; turn chicken. Bake another 15 minutes or until chicken is fully cooked. Remove from oven, transfer onto a serving platter, and serve immediately.

Makes 4 servings.

Roasted Lemon Chicken

A very easy and delicious way to roast a chicken. It produces very moist and tender chicken meat.

1 (3- to 4-pound) whole chicken
Salt and coarsely ground pepper
2 small thin-skinned lemons, washed well and dried

Preheat oven to 350 degrees. Thoroughly wash the chicken inside and out in cold water. Remove any bits of loose fat. Pat dry all over. Sprinkle the chicken generously inside and out with salt and pepper; rub in the seasonings.

Set the lemons on a counter and roll them back and forth, pressing with your palm. Puncture each lemon in at least 20 places, using a fork or the tip of a small knife. Place both lemons in the cavity of the chicken. Seal the openings with toothpicks.

Place chicken onto rack of shallow baking pan. Bake, uncovered, 1 1/2 hours or until chicken is fully cooked. Remove from oven and transfer onto a serving platter. Serve immediately.

Makes 4 servings.

NOTE: This is a self-basting chicken. Do not be tempted to add cooking fat of any kind. Try not to puncture the skin at any time during cooking. If it is kept intact, the chicken swells like a balloon, which makes for a wonderful presentation. If it does fail to swell, the flavor will not be affected.

Making Bread Crumbs

1 pound fresh bread equals 9 cups of soft crumbs.

1 slice fresh bread equals 1/2 cup soft bread crumbs.

1 slice dried bread equals 1/3 cup bread crumbs.

Dry bread slices in the oven by placing in a single layer on a baking sheet and baking at 300 degrees until completely dry and lightly browned. Cool completely before breaking into pieces and processing. Crumble the bread and rub through a coarse strainer or crush in the food processor. Use quick on/off pulses until the crumbs are evenly chopped. You can also put the dry bread slices into a heavyweight plastic bag, seal, then crush the slices with a rolling pin.

Add dried herbs, seasonings, or grated cheese for seasoned crumbs that are ready to use.

Store in tightly sealed jars. If refrigerated, they will keep their flavor for several months.

Alabama Chicken Supreme

1 teaspoon salt
1/4 teaspoon pepper
1/2 cup all-purpose flour
6 to 8 chicken breast halves, boneless and skinless
1/2 cup butter or margarine
2 (10 3/4-ounce) cans cream of chicken soup, undiluted
1/2 cup sherry
1 hard-cooked egg, peeled and sliced
1 teaspoon paprika

Preheat oven to 400 degrees. In a shallow pie plate, combine salt, pepper, and flour; roll chicken breasts in mixture to coat evenly. In a 13x9-inch baking dish, melt butter or margarine; place chicken into baking dish. Bake, uncovered, 30 minutes or until golden brown.

In a medium saucepan over medium heat, heat chicken soup, sherry, hard-cooked egg, and paprika; remove from heat. Turn chicken and cover with soup mixture. Reduce heat to 350 degrees; bake, covered, another 20 to 30 minutes or until chicken is fully cooked. Remove from oven and serve immediately.

Makes 6 to 8 servings.

Chicken Parmesan

4 chicken breast halves, boneless and skinless
1 egg
2 teaspoons water
1/3 cup freshly grated parmesan cheese
1/3 cup seasoned bread crumbs
1/4 cup vegetable oil
2 tablespoons butter or margarine
1 onion, finely chopped
1 (6-ounce) can tomato paste
1 (28-ounce) can stewed tomatoes, undrained
1 teaspoon salt
1/2 teaspoon dried marjoram, crushed
1/2 pound shredded mozzarella cheese

Preheat oven to 350 degrees. Pound chicken thin by placing one chicken breast at a time between two pieces of plastic wrap. Working from the center to the edges, pound lightly with a meat mallet to about 1/4-inch thick. In a shallow pie plate, beat egg with water. In another shallow plate, combine parmesan cheese and bread crumbs. Dip chicken in egg mixture and then roll in cheese mixture.

In a large frying pan over medium heat, heat vegetable oil. Add chicken and cook until golden brown; remove from heat and drain on paper towels. Place chicken into an ungreased 13x9-inch baking dish. In the same frying pan, add butter or margarine and melt; add onion and sauté until soft. Add tomato paste, tomatoes, salt, and marjoram. Bring to a boil; boil 2 to 3 minutes, scrapping up browned bits from bottom of pan. Pour 3/4 of sauce over chicken. Top with mozzarella cheese and then with remaining sauce.

Bake, uncovered, 30 minutes or until thoroughly heated. Remove from oven and serve immediately.

Makes 4 servings.

East Indian Chicken Curry

Curries are as important to Asian cooking as casseroles and stews are to European cuisine. Recipes for curries were first sent home to England when the British Raj was in control in India. British travelers took the curry recipes to other countries, and these spicy dishes became known as far away from India as the United States.

Curry Accompaniments
3 to 4 cups cooked rice
3 tablespoons butter or margarine
1/4 cup minced onion
3 tablespoons all-purpose flour
1 1/2 teaspoons curry powder
3/4 teaspoon salt
3/4 teaspoon sugar
1/8 teaspoon ground ginger
1 cup chicken broth (or 1 chicken bouillon cube dissolved in 1 cup hot water)
1 cup milk
2 cups diced cooked chicken
1/2 teaspoon lemon juice

Prepare Curry Accompaniments and place in individual dishes while the rice is cooking so everything will be ready at once.

In a large frying pan over medium heat, melt butter or margarine; add onion and sauté until soft. Blend in flour, curry powder, salt, sugar, and ginger; cook until mixture is smooth and bubbly.

Remove from heat. Stir in chicken broth and milk. Return to heat and bring to a boil, stirring constantly; boil 1 minute. Add chicken and lemon juice; heat thoroughly. Remove from heat.

To serve the chicken curry, place rice onto individual serving plates and then cover with chicken mixture. Mound on the accompaniments of your choice. Don't be afraid to pile them on. The more accompaniments, the better it tastes!

Makes 4 servings.

CURRY ACCOMPANIMENTS:
Chutney
Tomato wedges
Raisins
Slivered salted almonds
Chopped salted peanuts
Sautéed onion rings
Pineapple chunks
Slivered hard-cooked eggs
Crisp bacon bits
Sweet or sour pickles
Currant jelly
Shredded coconut
India relish
Sliced avocado

Curry Powder

The spices for curry have varied for thousands of years. The word curry comes from the South Indian word "kari," which means sauce.

Curry powder is not one single spice. It actually is a blend of many spices. Curry powder should not be confused with curry leaves, which are obtained from a native tree of India.

Curry powder, as we know it in the United States, simply does not exist in Indian cookery. Spices should be bought whole and ground and blended as needed. This way flavors are truly aromatic and blends are tailor-made to suit individual recipes and personal taste.

There are a lot of variations in curry powder blends. As a general rule, a curry powder blend will contain six or more of the following items: cumin, coriander, fenugreek, turmeric, ginger, pepper, dill, mace, cardamom, and cloves.

Cutting Boards

Did you know that wood cutting boards are the safest to use? For some reason, bacteria have a tougher time surviving on wood boards.

Research has shown that bacteria, such as the salmonella often found on raw chicken, will thrive and multiply if not removed from plastic boards. On wood boards, whether they are new or have been used for years, the bacteria die off within three minutes.

Researchers theorize that the porous surface of the wooden boards deprives the bacteria of water, causing them to die.

IMPORTANT: Whichever kind of cutting board you use, clean it frequently with hot soapy water. Also a quick spray with a solution of water and bleach offers added protection.

Chicken & Shrimp in Marinara Sauce

1/4 cup butter or margarine
1 cup chopped onion
1 clove garlic, minced
6 chicken breasts halves, boneless and skinless
2 teaspoons salt
1/2 teaspoon pepper
1 (8-ounce) can tomato sauce
1/4 cup chopped fresh parsley, divided
1/4 cup port wine
1 teaspoon dried basil, crushed
1 (16-ounce) package frozen shrimp, shelled and deveined

In a large frying pan over medium heat, melt butter or margarine. Add onion and garlic; sauté 5 minutes or until soft. With a slotted spoon, remove mixture to a small bowl.

Rub chicken breasts with salt and pepper. Place chicken in the same frying pan with butter or margarine; cook until golden brown on all sides. Stir in tomato sauce, 3 tablespoons parsley, port wine, basil, and onion mixture; bring to a boil. Reduce heat to low, cover, and simmer 10 minutes or until chicken is fully cooked.

Increase heat to high, add shrimp, and bring just to a boil. Reduce heat to low and simmer 2 to 3 minutes or until shrimp are just pink and tender, stirring often. Remove from heat and transfer into a serving bowl. Sprinkle with remaining parsley and serve immediately.

Makes 6 servings.

Chicken Dijon in Pastry Shells

A lot like a chicken pot pie, but without all the hassle of preparation.

1 (10-ounce) package frozen puff pastry shells
4 whole chicken breasts, boneless and skinless
2 tablespoons butter or margarine, divided
1 1/2 cups broccoli flowerets
1 1/2 cups sliced fresh mushrooms
1 (10 3/4-ounce) can cream of chicken or broccoli soup, undiluted
1/4 cup milk
2 tablespoons Dijon mustard

Prepare pastry shells according to package directions. Cut chicken breasts into 1/4-inch strips.

In a large frying pan over medium-high heat, melt 1 tablespoon butter or margarine. Add half of the chicken and cook until golden brown. Remove chicken to a large plate; set aside. Repeat with remaining half of the chicken.

Reduce heat to medium. In the same frying pan, melt 1 tablespoon butter or margarine; add broccoli flowerets and mushrooms. Cook until tender and liquid is evaporated, stirring often. Stir in chicken soup or broccoli soup, milk, and Dijon mustard; heat to boiling. Return chicken to frying pan and heat thoroughly, stirring occasionally. Remove from heat and spoon over pastry shells. Serve immediately.

Makes 6 servings.

Baked Chicken Dijonnaise

4 chicken breast halves, boneless and skinless
1/4 cup Dijon mustard
1/4 cup finely chopped red onion
1/2 cup shredded swiss cheese

Preheat oven to 350 degrees. Line a baking sheet with aluminum foil and coat with vegetable-oil cooking spray. Place chicken breasts onto prepared baking sheet; brush each with Dijon mustard and sprinkle with onion and swiss cheese.

Bake, uncovered, 30 to 40 minutes or until chicken is fully cooked. Remove from oven, transfer onto a serving platter, and serve immediately.

Makes 4 servings.

Peanutty Pasta With Chicken

Don't judge this recipe until you've tried it. It's absolutely wonderful.

4 chicken breast halves, boneless and skinless
4 tablespoons teriyaki or soy sauce
1 (8-ounce) package uncooked linguine pasta
1 cup fresh or frozen peas, cooked and divided
1 cup sliced carrots, cooked and divided
Peanut Sauce
3 tablespoons sesame seeds (reserve 1 tablespoon for top)

Grill, broil, or microwave chicken brushed with teriyaki or soy sauce.

Cook pasta according to package directions; drain and return to pan. In the pasta pan, toss warm pasta, peas, carrots, Peanut Sauce, and sesame seeds together. Place onto individual serving plates. Cut chicken into strips and lay on top of pasta. Sprinkle reserved sesame seeds over the top. Serve warm or cold.

Makes 8 servings.

PEANUT SAUCE:
1/4 cup creamy peanut butter,
1/4 cup water
1/4 cup soy sauce
1 tablespoon lemon juice
2 tablespoons honey
1/2 cup pineapple juice
1/4 teaspoon ground ginger
Hot chili oil or red (cayenne) pepper to taste

In a small saucepan over low heat, combine peanut butter, water, soy sauce, lemon juice, honey, pineapple juice, ginger, and hot chili oil or cayenne pepper; stir until well blended. Remove from heat and let cool.

VARIATION: This Peanut Sauce is excellent tossed with only cooked pasta and sesame seeds.

Peanuts

1 pound of peanuts in the shell equals 2 cups shelled nuts.

Did you know that peanuts are not nuts, they are legumes?

Peanuts have many names around the world, such as ground nut, earth nut, monkey nut, and goober. They originally came from Brazil and Peru. Peanuts spread to other countries from South America by slave ships, reaching this country from Brazil by way of Africa in the early slave ships. They were first grown in Virginia and North Carolina.

Peanut butter was promoted as a health food at the 1904 St. Louis World's Fair.

TIP: Adding peanut butter to soup is an old southern favorite. Stir one to two tablespoons into the next chicken soup you make and see how good it is.

Southwestern-Style Chicken

2 (2 1/2- to 3-pound) frying chickens, skinned and cut up
Southwestern-Style Sauce
1 cup shredded cheddar cheese
1 (2 1/4-ounce) can sliced black olives, drained

Preheat oven to 350 degrees. Place chicken pieces into two ungreased 13x9-inch baking dishes. Bake, uncovered, 30 minutes.

Remove chicken from oven. Using a spoon, remove most of the pan juices and discard; turn chicken over.

Divide the Southwestern-Style Sauce and pour over chicken in each baking dish. Return to oven; bake, uncovered, another 20 to 30 minutes or until chicken is fully cooked, basting occasionally with sauce. Sprinkle chicken with cheddar cheese. Bake an additional 2 to 3 minutes or until cheese melts. Remove from oven and garnish with black olives. Serve immediately.

Makes 8 to 10 servings.

SOUTHWESTERN-STYLE SAUCE:
1 tablespoon vegetable oil
1 medium onion, thinly sliced
2 cloves garlic, minced
1 (28-ounce) can whole tomatoes, undrained and cut up
1 (11-ounce) can corn kernels
1 (6-ounce) can tomato paste
1 (4-ounce) can chopped green chilies
2 teaspoons chili powder
1 teaspoon paprika
1 teaspoon salt
1/2 teaspoon ground cumin
1/4 teaspoon pepper
1/4 teaspoon hot pepper sauce

In a medium saucepan over medium-high heat, heat vegetable oil. Add onion and garlic; sauté until onion is soft. Stir in tomatoes, corn, tomato paste, green chilies, chili powder, and paprika. Add salt, cumin, pepper, and hot pepper sauce; stir until well blended and thoroughly heated.

Stuffed Cornish Hens

6 Cornish game hens
1/2 lemon
1 tablespoon salt
2 teaspoons pepper
2 tablespoons butter or margarine
6 medium fresh mushrooms, sliced
1/2 cup chopped ham
1/4 cup chopped toasted almonds
2 cups herb stuffing mix
1/4 cup butter or margarine, melted
1/4 cup dry white wine
2 tablespoons red currant jelly

Preheat oven to 350 degrees. Thoroughly wash Cornish game hens inside and out in cold water and pat dry; rub cavities with lemon, salt, and pepper. In a small frying pan over medium heat, melt 2 tablespoons butter or margarine. Add mushrooms and sauté until soft; combine with ham and almonds to use in stuffing (follow directions on herb stuffing mix package).

Stuff hens lightly with herb stuffing mix; skewer the openings and tie legs together. In a small saucepan over low heat, combine 1/4 cup butter or margarine, white wine, and currant jelly; heat thoroughly.

Place hens into an ungreased 13x9-inch baking dish; bake, uncovered, 1 hour or until chicken is fully cooked and tender, basting frequently with jelly mixture. Remove from oven, split in half to serve, and transfer onto a serving platter. Serve immediately.

Makes 6 servings.

Southwestern Chicken Casserole

1 1/2 pounds cooked chicken, torn into bite-sized chunks, divided
1 package (8 to 12) corn tortillas, torn into bite-sized pieces, divided
1 medium onion, chopped and divided
2 cups shredded cheddar cheese, divided
1 (10 3/4-ounce) can cream of mushroom soup, undiluted
1 (10 3/4-ounce) can cream of chicken soup, undiluted
1 (10-ounce) can tomatoes with chilies, undrained
1/2 cup chicken broth
Hot pepper sauce to taste
Unsalted tortilla chips for sprinkling on top

Preheat oven to 350 degrees. In an ungreased 13x9-inch baking dish, layer half of the chicken, half of the corn tortillas, half of the onion, and half of the cheddar cheese.

In a medium bowl, combine mushroom soup, chicken soup, tomatoes with chilies, chicken broth, and hot pepper sauce. Pour half of this mixture evenly over the top. Repeat the layers with the remaining ingredients.

Bake, covered, 30 minutes. Uncover and bake another 30 minutes. Break up the tortilla chips and sprinkle over the casserole 15 minutes before it finishes baking. Remove from oven and cool on a wire rack 10 to 15 minutes before serving.

Makes 8 servings.

Rock Cornish Game Hens

Cornish game hens were originally from England. The name Rock Cornish hen comes from the fact that the bird is a cross between two breeds: Plymouth Rock and Cornish.

They are usually one to two pounds in weight, four to five weeks old, and sport a broad yellow breast for their size. They are best fresh, not frozen. The difference in flavor is well worth finding fresh ones.

Tortillas

Tortillas, plain, buttered, or wrapped around a variety of fillings, are found on Mexican tables at nearly every meal. In the corn-producing regions of the southern states, tortillas are usually made from corn, but in the northern areas where wheat is grown, flour tortillas are favored.

Tortilla factories which sell fresh tortillas are found throughout Mexico and even in some parts of the United States. Since Mexican food has become so popular in the United States, fresh corn and flour tortillas are available in most grocery stores.

Barbecue Sauce

Here's a way to turn odds and ends of molasses, catsup, chili sauce, honey, and/or soy sauce into a useful and wonderful barbecue sauce that will keep well in the refrigerator for about one month.

1 cup molasses
1/2 cup prepared mustard
1/2 cup catsup or chili sauce
1 cup cider or wine vinegar
1 to 4 tablespoons honey
1 to 3 tablespoons soy sauce
1 clove garlic, minced

Place all the ingredients in an one-quart jar with a tight-fitting lid; shake well to combine. Store, tightly covered, in the refrigerator.

Shake well before each use, then brush the food to be broiled, roasted, baked, or braised. If foods require 30 minutes or more to cook, they should be brushed several times during cooking with additional barbecue sauce.

Louisiana Chicken & Sausage Jambalaya

One of the most popular Creole dishes from the southern United States. Serve with crusty bread and a tossed green salad.

6 bacon slices, chopped
1 1/2 cups sliced celery
1 cup long-grain rice
1 cup chopped onion
1 medium-sized green bell pepper, cored, seeded and chopped
1 (14 1/2-ounce) can whole tomatoes, undrained
1/2 pound cooked smoked sausage, cut into 1-inch pieces
1 1/2 cups water
1/2 cup garlic-flavored barbecue sauce
1 teaspoon salt
1/4 teaspoon red (cayenne) pepper
1 1/2 cups diced cooked chicken
Hot cooked rice

In a large pot or a dutch oven over medium-high heat, fry bacon until crisp; drain. Stir in celery, rice, onion, and bell pepper; cook and stir 5 minutes. Add tomatoes, sausage, water, barbecue sauce, salt, and cayenne pepper; stir and bring to a boil. Reduce heat to low, cover, and simmer another 20 minutes, stirring occasionally. Add chicken and simmer an additional 5 minutes. Remove from heat and serve over cooked rice.

Makes 4 servings.

Carbonara (Lowfat)

1 large onion, chopped
1/2 teaspoon fennel seeds
1 3/4 cups chicken broth, divided
Water
1 1/2 pounds cooked chicken, cut into 1-inch pieces
1 sprig fresh parsley, chopped
1 (16-ounce) package uncooked pasta noodles
1 egg
3 egg whites
1 1/2 cups freshly grated parmesan cheese, divided
Salt and pepper to taste

In a large nonstick frying pan over high heat, combine onion, fennel seeds, and 1 cup chicken broth. Bring to a boil and cook until liquid evaporates, stirring occasionally. When browned bits accumulate in pan, add water, 2 tablespoons at a time, to release them; cook until mixture begins to brown again. Repeat deglazing step until onion is golden brown. Add 2 tablespoons more water and chicken pieces; stir often until drippings begin to brown. Deglaze with 2 tablespoons water.

Add 3/4 cup chicken broth and bring to a boil. Add parsley; remove from heat and keep warm. Cook pasta noodles according to package directions; drain and pour into pan with chicken. In a small bowl, combine whole egg and egg whites; pour eggs onto hot pasta and toss immediately to mix well. Stir in 1 cup parmesan cheese. Transfer into a large serving bowl and sprinkle 1/2 cup parmesan cheese over the top. Season with salt and pepper. Serve immediately.

Makes 6 to 7 servings.

Turkey Focaccia Sandwich

1 (1-pound) loaf focaccia bread
4 or 5 marinated artichoke hearts
Mayonnaise and mustard
6 slices salami or thuringer
1/2 pound cooked turkey, sliced
6 slices provolone cheese
Olive oil

Preheat oven to 350 degrees. On an ungreased baking sheet, partially bake focaccia for 7 to 10 minutes. Remove from oven and let cool. Maintain oven temperature.

When focaccia is cool, split it horizontally through center, creating two rounds. Slice artichoke hearts into thin strips. Spread a thin layer of mayonnaise and mustard onto the cut surfaces of the focaccia.

Layer ingredients in this order onto bottom slice of loaf: salami or thuringer, turkey, provolone cheese, and artichoke hearts. Drizzle with a little of the olive oil.

Place onto a baking sheet and bake 10 to 15 minutes or until cheese has melted and the top is brown. Remove from oven and cut into wedges to serve.

Makes 6 servings.

Provolone Cheese

Provolone was first made in southern Italy, but it is now made in the United States, principally in Wisconsin and Michigan. It is a string-like cheese, light golden yellow to golden brown surface with a light ivory interior.

Available in pear, sausage, salami, and other shapes; bound with a cord.

Poultry Stuffing

When you're roasting chicken, game, or turkeys (up to fourteen pounds), allow about three-fourths cup stuffing for each pound of poultry.

For turkeys over fourteen pounds, allow one-half cup stuffing for each pound.

Linda's Turkey Stuffing

Stuffs a 20-pound turkey.

1/4 cup butter or margarine
1 large onion, chopped
2 cups chopped celery
1 pound fresh mushrooms, sliced
1 loaf bread, toasted and cut into cubes
1 egg, beaten
Chicken broth
1 cup chopped nuts
Salt and pepper to taste
Dried crushed sage to taste
Dried crushed thyme to taste

In a large saucepan over medium-high heat, melt butter or margarine. Add onion, celery and mushrooms; sauté until soft. Mix in bread cubes and egg with enough chicken broth to moisten. Add nuts, salt, pepper, sage, and thyme; stir until well blended. Proceed to stuff turkey in your usual way.

Linda's Teriyaki Sauce

Wonderful on grilled chicken.

2 tablespoons vegetable oil
1/4 cup soy sauce
1 1/2 teaspoons cider vinegar
2 tablespoons red wine
Garlic powder to taste
Salt and pepper to taste
1/2 cup water
1 teaspoon freshly grated ginger
2 green onions, chopped

In a medium bowl, combine vegetable oil, soy sauce, cider vinegar, and red wine. Add garlic powder, salt, pepper, water, ginger, and green onions; stir until well blended. Store, covered, in the refrigerator until ready to use.

Salads

White Bean & Seafood Salad

Great for buffets or potlucks.

2 (15-ounce) cans small white or cannellini beans, drained and rinsed
2 (6-ounce) cans water-packed white tuna or shrimp, drained and rinsed
1 red or green bell pepper, cored, seeded, and chopped
3/4 cup chopped green onions
1 cup chopped fresh parsley, divided
Honey-Mustard Dressing
Salt and pepper to taste
1 head lettuce
6 cherry tomatoes for garnish

In a mixing bowl, combine white or cannellini beans, tuna or shrimp, bell pepper, green onions, and 1/2 cup parsley.

Pour Honey-Mustard Dressing over bean mixture, toss gently to blend; season with salt and pepper. Cover and refrigerate until ready to serve.

Before serving, line a serving bowl with lettuce. Using a slotted spoon, place bean mixture onto lettuce bed and garnish with remaining 1/2 cup chopped parsley and cherry tomatoes.

Makes 6 servings.

HONEY-MUSTARD DRESSING:
1/2 cup extra-virgin olive oil
1/4 cup cider vinegar or lemon juice
2 tablespoons water
1 teaspoon sugar
1 teaspoon honey mustard
1 teaspoon dried Italian herbs, crushed
1 clove garlic, minced

In a small jar with a lid, combine olive oil, cider vinegar or lemon juice, water, sugar, honey mustard, Italian herbs, and garlic; cover securely and shake vigorously.

Salads

The word salad comes from the Latin word "sal," meaning salt. Our word salary comes from the same root because salt was once so valuable and rare that it formed part of the pay of Roman soldiers.

We usually think of a salad as a cold dish of greens or other vegetables dressed with oil and vinegar or some other dressing in which oil and vinegar are predominate.

Salads can be made from just about any food material. They can be served in the form of a gelatin or aspic, frozen, cold, or hot. They can include meats, poultry, fish, fruit, or vegetables.

Salads are usually served as an accompaniment to a meal, but they can be a separate course, a complete meal, or even served with a dessert to finish a meal.

Salads

Celery Seeds

Celery seeds are the fruit of a plant related to the parsley family and are not to be confused with the plant we recognize and serve as a vegetable. They are now grown extensively in France, Holland, India, and the United States.

Celery seeds are tiny and brown in color. They taste strongly of the vegetable and are aromatic and slightly bitter. They are sometimes used where celery itself would not be appropriate.

They can be used whole, tossed in salads, over cooked vegetables just before serving, or they can be ground and added to cooked dishes.

Kidney Beans

Kidney beans are also known as french beans, haricot beans, navy beans, pinto beans, common beans, frijoles, and opoca.

Kidney beans have been cultivated by the American Indians since prehistoric times. Remains of vulgaris beans were found at the archaeological sites in the Tehuacan Valley in Mexico. They have been carbon dated as 7,000 years old.

The kidney bean was brought back to Europe in the 16th century. At first it was a luxury, afforded only by the very rich, but its cultivation soon spread throughout Europe.

Three-Bean Salad

Better if made the day before.

1 (14 1/2-ounce) can green beans, drained
1 (14 1/2-ounce) can wax beans, drained
1 (15 1/4-ounce) can red kidney beans, drained and rinsed
1/2 cup chopped green bell pepper
1/2 cup chopped onion
2 pimientos, finely diced
1/2 cup diced celery
Three-Bean Dressing

In a large bowl, combine green beans, wax beans, kidney beans, bell pepper, onion, pimientos, and celery. Pour Three-Bean Dressing over bean mixture; toss gently to blend. Refrigerate at least 1 hour or overnight before serving.

THREE-BEAN DRESSING:
1/2 cup cider vinegar
1/3 cup vegetable oil
1/2 teaspoon pepper
1/2 teaspoon salt
1/2 cup sugar
1/2 teaspoon celery seeds
1/2 teaspoon worcestershire sauce
Garlic salt to taste

In a jar with a lid, combine cider vinegar, vegetable oil, pepper, salt, sugar, celery seeds, worcestershire sauce, and garlic salt; cover securely and shake vigorously.

Makes 6 servings.

Black Bean & Corn Salad

2 (15-ounce) cans black beans, drained and rinsed
1 1/2 cups fresh or frozen corn kernels
1 avocado, peeled, seeded, and cut into 1/2-inch pieces
1 small red bell pepper, cored, seeded, and cut into 1/2-inch pieces
2 medium tomatoes, cut into 1/2-inch cubes
6 green onions, finely chopped
1 jalapeño chile pepper, stemmed, seeded, and minced
1/2 cup coarsely chopped fresh cilantro
Lime Dressing

In a large bowl, combine black beans, corn, avocado, bell pepper, tomatoes, green onions, jalapeño pepper, and cilantro. Pour Lime Dressing over salad; toss gently until blended. Refrigerate at least 1 hour or overnight before serving.

Makes 8 to 10 servings.

LIME DRESSING:
1/2 cup lime juice
1/2 cup extra-virgin olive oil
1 clove garlic, minced
1 teaspoon salt
1/8 teaspoon red (cayenne) pepper

In a jar with a lid, combine lime juice, olive oil, garlic, salt, and cayenne pepper. Cover securely and shake vigorously.

Bell Peppers

1 large bell pepper equals 1 cup diced bell pepper.

Known as "capsicums" in other countries. Familiar to most Americans, these mild sweet bell peppers are used extensively both north and south of the border.

Bell peppers turn red as they ripen, becoming even sweeter. The green ones can be found year-round in grocery stores. There are also yellow, orange, purple, and brown bell peppers.

Select bright, glossy bell peppers that are firm, well shaped, and thick walled; avoid those with soft spots or gashes.

Place unwashed peppers in a plastic bag and refrigerate. Store green bell peppers for up to five days and red bell peppers for up to three days.

It is almost always better to serve sweet bell peppers as fresh from the garden as possible, but if you must freeze them, they will keep well for up to six months.

Layered Salad

1 head lettuce or a combination of different lettuces, washed, torn, and chilled
2/3 cup chopped celery
1 small onion, chopped
1 (8-ounce) can sliced water chestnuts, drained
1 (10-ounce) package frozen peas, uncooked
1 cup mayonnaise
1 cup sour cream
1 tablespoon firmly packed brown sugar
1 1/2 cups shredded cheddar cheese
4 cooked bacon slices, crumbled

In a large glass serving bowl, layer lettuce, celery, onion, water chestnuts, and peas. Cover with mayonnaise and then sour cream; sprinkle with brown sugar. Sprinkle cheddar cheese and bacon over top. Cover with aluminum foil and refrigerate 24 hours before serving.

Makes 6 to 8 servings.

Ginger

Ginger can be used as a fresh root, crystallized, or ground. It has a hot, spicy-sweet flavor that goes well with many foods. It is used in many Asian dishes and is especially good with chicken.

FRESH GREEN GINGER: Look for mature ginger with a smooth skin. If wrinkled or cracked, the root is dry and past its prime. Ginger is at its best when it is very fresh, so it is ideal to buy and use ginger in a matter of a few days. If you must keep it, wrap it in aluminum foil or a paper towel, put into a plastic bag (not tightly closed), and keep it in the refrigerator. It can also be frozen for up to one year.

GROUND GINGER: Has a different flavor than fresh ginger and should not be substituted for fresh ginger. Excellent in soups, curries, meats, fruits, and baked goods.

CRYSTALLIZED GINGER: Has been cooked in a sugar syrup and coated with coarse sugar. To prepare, place the slices in a food processor and whirl until ginger is chopped to the desired consistency. If the ginger begins to stick together, add some granulated sugar and continue to process. Store in an airtight jar at room temperature for up to one year.

Oriental Chicken Salad

A great change for the salad lover. The fresh ginger in this dressing really gives a lot of zip.

Vegetable oil
1 (3 3/4-ounce) package cellophane noodles or 5 cups chow mein noodles
1/2 head lettuce, shredded
3 cups cooked and cubed chicken
1 medium carrot, grated
1/4 cup sliced green onions, green tops included
Ginger Dressing
1 tablespoon toasted sesame seeds

Cellophane Noodles: In a large frying pan over medium-high heat, heat 1-inch of vegetable oil. Add cellophane noodles; fry 1/4 of the noodles at a time, turning once, until puffed, approximately 5 seconds. Remove from heat and drain.

Chow Mein Noodles: Add to salad ingredients without cooking.

In a large bowl, combine lettuce, chicken, carrot, and green onions. Pour Ginger Dressing over greens and toss gently with 1/2 of the cellophane or chow mein noodles. To serve, place remaining noodles onto serving plates; spoon salad over top and sprinkle with sesame seeds.

Makes 6 servings.

GINGER DRESSING:
1/3 cup vegetable oil
1/4 cup white wine vinegar
1 tablespoon sugar
2 teaspoons soy sauce
1/2 teaspoon salt
1/2 teaspoon pepper
1/2 teaspoon freshly grated ginger

In a jar with a lid, combine vegetable oil, wine vinegar, sugar, soy sauce, salt, pepper, and ginger; cover securely and shake vigorously. Refrigerate at least 2 hours.

Rhode Island Red Chicken Salad

2 cups cooked and cubed chicken
1/2 cup finely chopped celery
1/4 cup chopped green onions
1/4 cup chopped walnuts, hazelnuts, or almonds
1/4 cup finely sliced fresh mushrooms
1/4 cup finely chopped water chestnuts
Chicken Salad Dressing
Lettuce
1 hard-cooked egg, sliced
1/4 cup black olives, sliced

In a large bowl, combine chicken, celery, green onions, walnuts, hazelnuts or almonds, mushrooms, and water chestnuts. Pour Chicken Salad Dressing over chicken mixture; mix well and refrigerate. To serve, line individual serving plates with lettuce, and place salad in center; garnish with sliced egg and black olives.

Makes 6 servings.

CHICKEN SALAD DRESSING:
1/4 cup mayonnaise
1 teaspoon lemon juice
Salt and pepper to taste
Garlic powder to taste

In a small bowl, combine mayonnaise, lemon juice, salt, pepper, and garlic power; stir until well blended.

Grape Chicken Salad

Served at bridal showers and luncheons in the classic southern tradition.

3 cups cooked and cubed chicken breasts
1 1/2 cups chopped celery
3 tablespoons lemon juice
1 cup seedless white grapes, cut in halves
2 hard-cooked eggs, chopped
1 cup sliced toasted almonds
1 cup mayonnaise
1 teaspoon ground mustard
1 1/2 teaspoons salt
1/2 teaspoon pepper
1/4 cup light cream
Lettuce

In a large bowl, combine chicken, celery, lemon juice, grapes, eggs, and almonds. In a small bowl, combine mayonnaise, ground mustard, salt, pepper, and light cream; pour over chicken mixture and blend well. To serve, line individual serving plates with lettuce; spoon chicken salad onto lettuce.

Makes 8 servings.

Grapes

The grape grew wild in America as far back as history records. Leif the Lucky, according to legend, was so impressed by the number of wild grapevines growing where he was supposed to have been (Rhode Island or thereabouts), that he named the region "Vineland."

Grapes have been a popular fruit down through the centuries and are raised in large quantities in the United States. Actually, the grape is grown over the greater part of the world except in regions of extreme cold. Grape growing is the world's biggest fruit industry.

When selecting grapes, choose those bunches that are well formed and good looking. The darker varieties should be free of a green tinge, while white grapes should have a decided amber coloring when completely matured.

Fully ripened grapes are fairly soft to the touch. Unlike some other fruits, grapes will not improve in either color, sugar, or quality after they have been harvested.

Since grapes are highly perishable, handle them carefully. They should be stored unwashed in a plastic bag in the refrigerator. Instead of washing them, eat them European style, serving them with a bowl of water into which each grape is dipped before it is eaten.

Salad Ideas

TOMATO: Remove top of a large ripe tomato and scoop out the flesh. Fill with stuffing.

AVOCADO: Split avocado, remove seed, and peel. Use one-half avocado per serving. Sprinkle with lemon juice to keep from darkening. Fill with stuffing.

ARTICHOKE: Trim and cook the normal way; cool. Remove choke with a spoon. Fill with stuffing.

STUFFING MIX:
2 cups cooked crab meat, chopped cooked chicken or cooked shrimp
1 tablespoon lemon juice
1/2 cup finely chopped celery
1/4 cup finely chopped onion
Mayonnaise to moisten
Salt and pepper to taste

In a large bowl, mix all the ingredients together.

Makes 4 servings.

Sliced olives, crumbled bacon, water chestnuts, or hard-cooked eggs may be added or used as a garnish.

Crab Appetizer Salad

CRAB LAYER:
1 pound cooked crab meat or 2 (7 1/2-ounce) cans crab meat
3/4 cup chopped celery
3 tablespoons chopped green onions
1 tablespoon chopped pimiento
1/4 cup mayonnaise
2 teaspoons lemon juice
1/4 teaspoon salt
Pepper to taste

If using fresh cooked crab meat, carefully clean the crab meat of any shells or cartilage. If using canned crab meat, drain and rinse. Reserve a few bite-sized pieces of crab meat for garnish.

In a medium bowl, place remaining crab meat. Add celery, green onions, pimiento, mayonnaise, lemon juice, salt, and pepper; stir gently until blended. Cover and refrigerate 1 1/2 to 2 hours.

On individual serving plates, place Crab Layer and Tomato-Cucumber Layer alternately with Crab Layer on top.

TOMATO-CUCUMBER LAYER:
3 medium tomatoes, diced
1 medium cucumber, peeled and diced
1/4 cup extra-virgin olive oil
1 tablespoon tarragon vinegar
1/8 teaspoon salt
1/8 teaspoon garlic powder
Pepper to taste
Red (cayenne) pepper to taste

In a large bowl, toss tomatoes and cucumber together. In a small bowl, combine olive oil, tarragon vinegar, salt, garlic powder, pepper, and cayenne pepper; stir until well blended and pour over vegetables. Refrigerate 1 1/2 to 2 hours.

Makes 6 servings.

Favorite Potato Salad

6 (2 pounds) medium potatoes
3/4 cup chopped sweet pickles
2 tablespoons chopped onion
3/4 cup chopped celery
2 tablespoons sliced or chopped pimiento
2 teaspoons salt
1 1/4 teaspoons celery seeds
Potato Salad Dressing
6 hard-cooked eggs (5 chopped and 1 sliced)
Fresh parsley
Paprika

Boil potatoes with skins on just until barely done or tender when pierced with a fork; drain and cool slightly. As soon as you can handle them, peel and cut warm potatoes into chunks.

In a large bowl, combine sweet pickles, onion, and celery; add pimiento and potato chunks. Sprinkle with salt and celery seeds; stir until well blended. Pour Potato Salad Dressing over mixture; toss gently. Add 5 chopped hard-cooked eggs, gently mixing into potato salad. Refrigerate salad several hours. If potato salad mixture gets too dry, add additional mayonnaise and 1 teaspoon sweet pickle juice.

Place salad into a serving bowl and garnish with remaining sliced hard-cooked egg. Sprinkle parsley around edge of bowl and sprinkle paprika over sliced eggs. Cover and refrigerate at least 2 hours or overnight before serving.

Makes 10 to 12 servings.

POTATO SALAD DRESSING:
3/4 cup mayonnaise
1 1/2 tablespoons prepared mustard
1 teaspoon sugar
1 tablespoon sweet pickle juice

In a small bowl, combine mayonnaise, prepared mustard, sugar, and sweet pickle juice; stir until well blended.

Hard-Cooked Eggs

Hard-cooked eggs (cooked in the shell in water) should never be boiled. Rather, simmer them in water. If boiled or cooked too long, the protein toughens or becomes rubbery and a greenish or purplish ring forms around the yolk.

TO COOK EGGS IN THE SHELL, SIMMER:
   Soft-cooked eggs:
   3 to 5 minutes

   Medium-cooked eggs:
   7 to 8 minutes

   Hard-cooked eggs:
   about 15 minutes

When eggs are done, plunge into cold water to stop further cooking and to release the pressure inside the egg which brings on the discoloration.

TIP: To keep eggs from cracking when cooking, add some vinegar to the water.

Pimiento

Most people know the pimiento only from the end of a stuffed olive. It is, however, a type of sweet red pepper that is grown largely in California.

Pimientos are roasted sweet red peppers that have been preserved in oil. Use them whole or chopped in salads.

TIP: After opening and using part of a jar of pimientos, to prolong life of remaining pimientos, add a teaspoon of white vinegar and refrigerate.

Salads

Vinegar

The word vinegar comes from the French word "vin aigre," meaning "sour wine."

Any alcoholic liquid under 18 percent alcohol by volume, whether wine, cider, or beer; not to mention fermented juices, can be transformed into vinegar.

Due to vinegar's acetic acid content, vinegar is a natural preservative. When pickling, use a commercial vinegar with a level of at least 4 to 6 percent.

Store vinegars in a cool place away from light; they do not need to be refrigerated. Vinegars can be kept almost indefinitely if stored correctly.

CIDER VINEGAR: Made from fermented apple cider.

DISTILLED WHITE VINEGAR: Made from a grain-alcohol mixture.

WINE VINEGAR: Made from either red or white wine.

RICE VINEGAR: Made from fermented rice.

BALSAMIC VINEGAR: An aged reduction of white sweet grapes (Trebbiano) that are boiled to a syrup.

FRUIT- AND HERB-FLAVORED VINEGARS: Made using fruit or herbs as a flavoring to cider, white or rice vinegar.

Sweet Onion Potato Salad

A very unusual and delicious potato salad. Elevates potato salad to a new plane.

7 (3 pounds) medium red potatoes
1 large sweet onion (Walla Walla, Vidalia, or Maui onion)
1 cup finely chopped celery
1 large Golden Delicious apple, unpeeled, cored, and diced
12 pimiento-stuffed green olives, sliced
1/3 cup chopped sweet pickles
1 1/2 cups mayonnaise
1 teaspoon Dijon mustard
2 tablespoons cider vinegar
1 teaspoon steak sauce or soy sauce
Salt and pepper to taste

Boil potatoes with skins on just until barely done or tender when pierced with a fork; drain and cool slightly. As soon as you can handle them, peel and cut into chunks; place into a large bowl. Cut onion into quarters and slice thin; add to potatoes along with celery, apple, green olives, and sweet pickles.

In a small bowl, combine mayonnaise, Dijon mustard, cider vinegar, and steak sauce or soy sauce. Spoon over potato mixture; mix gently. Season with salt and pepper. Cover and refrigerate at least 2 hours or overnight before serving.

Makes 10 to 12 servings.

Shrimp Salad Dinner

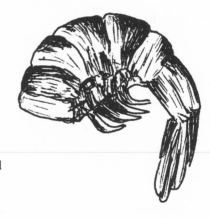

1 (6-ounce) can water-packed tuna, drained
Chopped sweet pickles to taste
Salt to taste
Mayonnaise
2 cups cooked macaroni noodles
Lettuce
1 pound shrimp, deveined, cleaned, and cooked
Carrot sticks
Tomato wedges
2 hard-cooked eggs, peeled and cut in halves
Ritz crackers

In a small bowl, prepare tuna fish salad by combining tuna, sweet pickles, salt, and just enough mayonnaise to moisten. In a medium bowl, prepare macaroni salad by combining macaroni, sweet pickles, salt, and just enough mayonnaise to moisten.

TO ASSEMBLE DISH :
Line individual serving plates with lettuce. Place a scoop of tuna fish salad and a scoop of macaroni salad side by side onto top of the lettuce; place shrimp on top. Arrange carrot sticks, tomato wedges, and hard-cooked eggs around the tuna fish salad and macaroni salad. Serve with Ritz crackers.

Makes 2 servings.

Shrimp Cole Slaw

This is so easy to make and is absolutely wonderful.

1/2 cup mayonnaise
2 teaspoons lemon juice
1 teaspoon sugar
Pepper to taste
1 small head (4 cups) cabbage, finely chopped
1 cup finely chopped celery
1 1/2 tablespoons finely chopped onion
2 cups fresh or frozen small shrimp, deveined and cooked or
    2 cups canned shrimp, drained and rinsed

In a small bowl, combine mayonnaise, lemon juice, sugar, and pepper; stir until well blended. In a large bowl, combine cabbage, celery, onion, and shrimp; add mayonnaise mixture and stir until well blended. Refrigerate until serving time.

Makes 4 servings.

Cilantro Slaw

Cilantro lovers will go crazy over this slaw.

1 medium head cabbage, shredded
1 cucumber, peeled, seeded, and chopped
1 bunch fresh cilantro, chopped
Slaw Dressing

In a large bowl, combine cabbage, cucumber, and cilantro. Pour Slaw Dressing over cabbage mixture and toss gently until blended. For best results, cover and refrigerate several hours or overnight for flavors to blend. Gently toss again before serving.

Makes 6 to 8 servings.

SLAW DRESSING:
1/3 cup lime juice
2 cloves garlic, minced
1/2 teaspoon salt
1/4 cup sugar
Red (cayenne) pepper to taste
1/2 teaspoon coarsely ground pepper
1/2 cup vegetable oil

In a small bowl, combine lime juice, garlic, salt, sugar, cayenne pepper, and pepper; gradually add vegetable oil until well blended.

Using Cabbage

TIPS: A fast and easy way to remove leaves from cabbage is to cut around the core at the base of the cabbage. Remove the core and grasp each individual cabbage leaf at its base, rather than at the leaf's outer edge. Gently lift the cabbage leaf from the cabbage.

To shred the cabbage by hand, quarter and then core the cabbage. Separate the cabbage quarters into stacks so leaves will flatten when pressed lightly. Use a large knife to cut each stack of cabbage diagonally into thin shreds. To chop the cabbage, turn the pile of shredded cabbage widthwise, then cut the cabbage shreds into a fine dice.

For a crisper cabbage for cole slaws, shred the cabbage and soak it in salted ice water for fifteen minutes and then drain.

Cooking Broccoli

Be sure to cook broccoli quickly, since long cooking not only makes it soft and flavorless, but also destroys its rich nutrients.

Salt helps to keep broccoli green. The stalks, when peeled, are good to eat also. Leaves are edible but give a better appearance if cut off.

TIP: To remove the smell of broccoli cooking, throw a couple of thick chunks of bread into the cooking water.

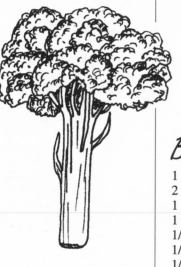

Feta Pasta Primavera

This is always a popular salad at a gathering. Be sure to make plenty because it goes fast.

1 (9-ounce) package refrigerated cheese tortellini
1 cup hot water
2 cups broccoli flowerets
1 cup cherry tomatoes, quartered
1 cup thinly sliced carrots
1 cup crumbled feta cheese with peppercorns
1 cup Italian salad dressing
1/4 cup sliced green onions

Prepare tortellini according to package directions; drain and place in a large bowl, Cover and refrigerate 1 hour.

In a large saucepan (with a steamer rack) over medium-high heat, place water and heat until boiling. Add broccoli flowerets, cover, and steam 2 to 3 minutes or until bright green but still undercooked. Remove from heat and cool.

Remove tortellini from refrigerator. In a large bowl, combine tortellini, broccoli, tomatoes, carrots, feta cheese, salad dressing, and green onions; stir gently until blended. Refrigerate until ready to serve.

Makes 6 servings.

Basil Pasta Salad

1 (16-ounce) package refrigerated filled tortellini
2 cups cherry tomatoes, cut in halves
1 (6-ounce) can black olives, drained and sliced
1 small cucumber, quartered lengthwise, seeded, and thinly sliced
1/2 cup extra-virgin olive oil
1/4 cup white wine vinegar
1/2 cup chopped fresh basil leaves
Salt to taste
1/2 teaspoon pepper

Cook tortellini pasta according to package directions; drain, rinse, and place into a large bowl. Add tomatoes, black olives, and cucumber; toss gently until blended.

In a small bowl, mix olive oil, wine vinegar, basil, salt, and pepper. Pour vinegar mixture over pasta; toss gently. Refrigerate until ready to serve.

Makes 6 to 8 servings.

Italian Pasta Salad

1 (16-ounce) package three-color pasta swirl noodles
1 (15-ounce) can kidney beans, drained and rinsed
4 stalks celery, chopped
1/4 pound mozzarella cheese, cut into small pieces
1 medium red onion, chopped
1 (6-ounce) can black olives, drained and sliced
1 (15-ounce) can corn kernels, drained
1 (4-ounce) jar pimientos, drained and chopped
2 dill pickles, chopped
1 cup mayonnaise
2 hard-cooked eggs, diced
Italian salad dressing
Lettuce
Tomato wedges

Cook pasta according to package directions; drain, rinse, and place into a large bowl. Add kidney beans, celery, mozzarella cheese, red onion, black olives, corn, pimientos, dill pickles, mayonnaise, and eggs; gently toss until mixed.

Pour Italian Dressing over salad and toss gently. Marinate in refrigerator at least 2 hours or overnight. Serve on a bed of lettuce garnished with tomato wedges.

VARIATION: For a super lunch treat, top with cooked crab meat or cooked shrimp. Serve with cocktail sauce and your favorite crackers.

Makes 6 to 8 servings.

ITALIAN DRESSING;
1/4 cup extra-virgin olive oil
2 tablespoons red wine vinegar
1 clove garlic, minced
2 tablespoons chopped fresh parsley
1 teaspoon dried oregano, crushed
1 teaspoon red (cayenne) pepper
Salt and pepper to taste

In a small jar with a lid, combine olive oil, wine vinegar, garlic, parsley, oregano, cayenne pepper, salt, and pepper; cover securely and shake vigorously.

Pasta

Whether buying fresh or dried pasta, read the label and only buy brands made with durum wheat (also called semolina). This is the pasta of preference because it absorbs less water, has a mellow flavor, and retains a pleasant taste when cooked.

How much pasta to use per serving depends on whether it's fresh or dried. Generally, the formula is:

DRIED PASTA:
2 ounces per side-dish serving or 4 ounces per main-dish serving.

FRESH PASTA:
3 ounces per side-dish serving or 5 ounces per main-dish serving.

TIP: Rubbing vegetable oil around the top of the pot you are cooking the pasta in will prevent it from boiling over.

Salads

Cilantro = Fresh Coriander

Cilantro is the Spanish word for coriander leaves. It is also sometimes called Chinese or Mexican parsley. Technically, coriander refers to the entire plant. It is a member of the carrot family.

Chopped fresh leaves are widely used in Mexican and Tex-Mex cooking, where they are combined with chilies and added to salsas, guacamoles, and seasoned rice dishes.

Most people either love it or hate it. Taste experts aren't sure why, but for some people the smell of fresh coriander is fetid and the taste soapy. In other words, while most people love coriander, for some people, coriander just doesn't taste good.

When purchasing, look for leaves that are tender, aromatic, and very green. If it has no aroma, it will have no flavor. Avoid wilted bunches with yellowing leaves.

TIP: Fresh cilantro does not keep well, and the flavor of dried is not comparable. To store fresh coriander, pick out any wilted leaves, and put it in a jar with water like a bunch of flowers. Cover the leaves with a plastic bag and put the whole thing in the refrigerator. Change the water every two days or so, picking out any wilted leaves when you do.

Pasta Salad With Cilantro

1 (16-ounce) package uncooked pasta noodles
Cilantro Dressing
1/4 cup thinly sliced green onions
1/4 cup freshly grated parmesan cheese

Cook pasta according to package directions; drain, and place into a large bowl. Pour Cilantro Dressing over cooked pasta; toss gently. Stir in green onions and parmesan cheese. Serve at room temperature.

Makes 6 to 8 servings.

CILANTRO DRESSING:
1 egg yolk
1 teaspoon freshly grated ginger
1 clove garlic, minced
3 tablespoons lemon juice, divided
1/8 teaspoon red (cayenne) pepper
1/4 teaspoon salt
1/4 cup extra-virgin olive oil
1/4 cup vegetable oil
2 tablespoons water
1 cup firmly packed chopped fresh cilantro

In a food processor or blender, whirl egg yolk, ginger, garlic, 1 tablespoon lemon juice, cayenne pepper, and salt. With motor running add olive oil and vegetable oil in a slow stream; whirl until thick. Add remaining lemon juice, water, and cilantro. Whirl until smooth; set aside.

Spicy Pasta Salad

1 (8-ounce) package uncooked tricolor rotini noodles
8 ounces turkey sausage, diced and cooked
1 (15-ounce) can kidney beans, drained and rinsed
1 (8-ounce) can corn kernels, drained
2 medium tomatoes, chopped
1 small green bell pepper, cored, seeded, and chopped
1/2 cup sliced green onions
1 (2 1/4-ounce) can black olives, drained and sliced
1 cup shredded cheddar cheese
Dressing

Prepare rotini according to package directions; drain and place in a large bowl. Add turkey sausage, kidney beans, corn, tomatoes, bell pepper, green onions, black olives, and cheddar cheese; gently stir until well mixed. Pour Dressing over salad and toss gently. Cover and refrigerate until ready to serve.

Makes 8 servings.

DRESSING:
1 (10-ounce) can diced tomatoes and green chilies, undrained
1/2 cup Italian salad dressing
2 teaspoons Italian herb seasoning
Salt to taste

In a small bowl, combine tomatoes, salad dressing, herb seasoning, and salt.

Greens With Walnut Oil Dressing

5 to 6 cups loosely packed torn mixed lettuce (romaine, watercress, or Boston),
   washed, torn, and chilled
1/2 cup walnut pieces
Walnut Oil Dressing
Edible flowers, if desired

In large salad bowl, combine lettuce and walnuts. Pour Walnut Oil Dressing over salad; toss gently. To serve, garnish with edible flowers.

Makes 4 servings.

WALNUT OIL DRESSING:
3 tablespoons walnut oil
2 tablespoons white wine vinegar
1 clove garlic, minced
1 teaspoon chopped fresh summer savory or 1/4 teaspoon dried
   summer savory, crushed
1/4 teaspoon salt

In a small jar with a lid, combine walnut oil, wine vinegar, garlic, savory, and salt; cover securely and shake vigorously. Store, covered, in refrigerator. Serve at room temperature.

Caesar Salad

2 heads Romaine lettuce, washed, torn, and chilled
1 cup freshly grated parmesan cheese
1 cup fresh garlic croutons
Caesar Dressing

In a large salad bowl, combine lettuce, parmesan cheese, and croutons. Pour Caesar Dressing over salad; toss gently and serve.

Makes 4 servings.

CAESAR DRESSING:
2 anchovies, minced
1 egg yolk
1 clove garlic, minced
2 tablespoons freshly grated parmesan cheese
1 tablespoon red wine vinegar
1 tablespoon lime juice
1 teaspoon Dijon mustard
1/4 teaspoon worcestershire sauce
1/4 teaspoon hot pepper sauce
1/2 teaspoon salt
1/2 teaspoon coarsely ground pepper
1/2 cup extra-virgin olive oil

In a blender or food processor, combine anchovies, egg yolk, garlic, parmesan cheese, wine vinegar, lime juice, Dijon mustard, worcestershire sauce, hot pepper sauce, salt, and pepper; whirl until well blended. With the motor on, add olive oil in a slow steady stream; whirling until dressing is smooth. Store, covered in refrigerator. Serve at room temperature.

Edible Flowers

Edible flowers can add color and an outdoorsy, perfume-like flavor to your cooking. The culinary use of flowers in cooking dates back thousands of years.

EDIBLE FLOWERS:
- *Anise Hyssop*
- *Bachelor's Button*
- *Beebalm*
- *Borage*
- *Chive*
- *English Daisy*
- *Johnny Jump-Up*
- *Forget-Me-Not*
- *Nasturtium*
- *Pansy*
- *Sage*
- *Squash Blossom*
- *Violet*

PICKING & STORING FRESH EDIBLE FLOWERS:
Pick edible flowers in the cool part of the day. Gently wash and separate petals just before use.

DO NOT USE CHEMICALS OR INSECTICIDES ON EDIBLE PLANTS.

TIP: Never add flowers to a salad before tossing. The dressing will spoil the color and fresh appearance of the flower petals.

Salads

Caesar Salad

It is believed that Caesar Salad was named after a restaurant owner in Tijuana, Mexico, named Caesar Cardini, during the 1920s and 1930s.

It is said that he was running out of food in his restaurant, so he used the only ingredients left and invented the Caesar Salad.

Tossed Salad

To impart even more flavor to a tossed salad, a dry piece of bread called a "chapon" is rubbed heavily with garlic and put into the salad until the time the salad is tossed. It is then removed. The "chapon" adds flavor in a manner similar to what is accomplished when the salad bowl is rubbed with garlic.

TIP: Place individual salad plates in the freezer about one hour before placing the tossed salad onto them.

Caesar Margarita Salad

Put your margarita glasses back in the cupboard! Here, the drink's flavors come on a plate.

Lime wedges (optional)
Kosher or margarita salt (optional)
1 large head romaine lettuce, washed, torn, and chilled
1 cup shredded monterey jack cheese
1 red bell pepper, cored, seeded, and cut into thin strips
1/4 cup finely chopped fresh cilantro
Margarita Dressing
Lime wedges

Rub rims of six chilled salad plates with lime wedges and roll edges in salt, if desired. Set aside.

In a large salad bowl, combine lettuce, monterey jack cheese, bell pepper, and cilantro. Pour Margarita Dressing over salad; toss gently. Place salad onto individual serving plates and garnish with lime wedges.

Makes 6 servings.

MARGARITA DRESSING:
1/3 cup vegetable oil
1/4 cup lime juice
2 tablespoons egg substitute
1 1/2 teaspoons tequila
1 1/2 teaspoons orange-flavored liqueur
1 clove garlic, minced
1 chile pepper, cored, seeded, and finely chopped
1/2 teaspoon sugar
1/4 teaspoon salt
1/4 teaspoon ground cumin

In a medium bowl, combine vegetable oil, lime juice, egg substitute, tequila, and orange-flavored liqueur. Add garlic, chili pepper, sugar, salt, and cumin; stir until well blended. Store, covered, in refrigerator. Serve at room temperature.

Yields 1 cup.

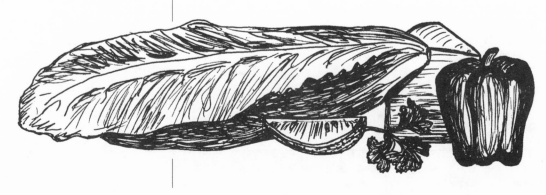

Grilled Chicken Caesar Salad

4 chicken breast halves, boneless and skinless
3/4 cup Caesar Dressing, divided (see page 273)
1 large head romaine lettuce, washed, torn, and chilled
1 (2 1/4-ounce) can black olives, drained and sliced
1 cup garlic croutons
1/4 cup freshly grated parmesan cheese
1 tomato, cut into 8 wedges

In an ungreased 2-quart baking dish or large heavy-duty resealable plastic bag, combine chicken and 1/4 cup salad dressing; turn to coat. Cover dish or seal bag. Refrigerate at least 6 hours or overnight, turning once.

Preheat barbecue grill. Drain chicken, reserving marinade. Place chicken onto hot grill. Cook 20 to 30 minutes or until chicken is fully cooked and tender, turning once and brushing frequently with reserved marinade; discard any remaining marinade. Remove from grill.

In a large salad bowl, combine lettuce, black olives, and remaining 1/2 cup salad dressing; toss gently. Divide evenly onto individual serving plates. Slice chicken breasts into slices; fan chicken slices and place onto lettuce mixture onto each plate. Top each salad with 1/4 cup croutons and 1 tablespoon parmesan cheese. To serve, garnish with tomato wedges.

Makes 4 servings.

Raspberry Blush Pear Salad

This salad would be wonderful served European style, after the main course.

2 pears, peeled and sliced
Raspberry Dressing
1 bunch fresh spinach leaves, washed, dried, and chilled
1 kiwi fruit, peeled and thinly sliced
1/2 cup fresh raspberries

Place pears into a medium bowl. Pour Raspberry Dressing over pears; toss gently. Cover and let stand 15 minutes. Drain; reserve dressing. Cover and refrigerate 30 minutes or until chilled.

Tear spinach into bite-sized pieces. Place spinach onto individual serving plates; top with pears, kiwi fruit, and raspberries. Drizzle salad with half of the Raspberry Dressing. Serve with remaining dressing.

Makes 4 to 6 servings.

RASPBERRY DRESSING:
1/3 cup rice vinegar
1/2 cup seedless raspberry preserves
2 tablespoons vegetable oil

In a small saucepan over medium heat, combine rice vinegar, raspberry preserves, and vegetable oil; cook until preserves are melted and dressing is hot, stirring occasionally. Refrigerate before using.

Washing Lettuce

A quick way to wash the dirt out of "open-ended lettuce," such as red leaf, romaine, and Bibb is to cut a V-shaped wedge from the stem end of the lettuce and remove the wedge. Holding the bottom of the lettuce firmly, run cool water into the cut areas that are now exposed at the base of the lettuce. The water will flow down through the layers of leaves and will gently push the dirt from bottom to top. Because you have cut away the root, the lettuce leaves can be peeled away easily.

To clean other salad greens, remove cores or base of stems and separate leaves. Plunge leaves into a sink of cold water and gently move them around to lift off sand and grit. Drain, rinsing to remove as much grit as possible. Repeat the rinsing process.

Spin greens dry and transfer them to a double thickness of paper towels, or lint-free tea towels. When rolled up in towels and placed in plastic bags, greens can be refrigerated for six to eight hours without losing their crispness.

Spinach & Shrimp Salad

2 oranges
2 bunches fresh spinach leaves, washed, dried, and chilled
1 large avocado, peeled, seeded, and sliced
1 tablespoon fresh orange juice
1 pound shrimp, shelled, deveined, and cooked
Orange Dressing

Grate zest off of one orange and then squeeze for juice; set aside. Peel and section other orange; set aside. Remove stems and veins from spinach and tear into bite-sized pieces; place into a large salad bowl. In a small bowl, sprinkle avocado slices with orange juice. Add avocado, shrimp, and orange sections to spinach. Pour Orange Dressing over mixture; toss gently and serve.

Makes 8 servings.

ORANGE DRESSING:
1 teaspoon grated orange zest
1/3 cup fresh orange juice
1/4 cup honey
1 tablespoon rice vinegar
1/4 teaspoon salt
1/4 teaspoon ground mustard
1/8 teaspoon hot pepper sauce
1/2 cup vegetable oil

In a blender or food processor, combine orange zest, orange juice, honey, rice vinegar, salt, ground mustard, and hot pepper sauce; whirl 1 minute or until well mixed. With the motor on, add vegetable oil in a slow steady stream; whirling until dressing is smooth. Store, covered, in refrigerator. Serve at room temperature.

All-Time-Favorite Spinach Salad

This is one of those salads you can serve as a main course with a bottle of your favorite wine and a fresh loaf of bread.

2 bunches fresh spinach leaves, washed, dried, and chilled
4 to 6 bacon slices, crisply fried and crumbled
1 (8-ounce) can sliced water chestnuts, drained
4 hard-cooked eggs, sliced
5 to 6 green onions, chopped
Sliced almonds
1 cup sliced fresh mushrooms
Italian salad dressing

Remove stems and veins from spinach and tear into bite-sized pieces; place into a large salad bowl. Add bacon, water chestnuts, eggs, green onions, almonds, and mushrooms. Pour salad dressing over salad; toss gently and serve.

Makes 4 servings.

Spinach Salad With Raspberry Vinaigrette

1 bunch fresh spinach leaves, washed, dried, and chilled
1 cup sliced almonds, divided
1/2 cup crumbled blue cheese, divided
1 cup sliced mushrooms, divided
1/3 red onion, thinly sliced and divided
Raspberry Vinaigrette

Remove stems and veins from spinach and tear into bite-sized pieces; place into a large salad bowl. Add half of the almonds, half of the blue cheese, half of the mushrooms, and half of the onion. Pour Raspberry Vinaigrette over salad; toss gently. To serve, top with remaining almonds, blue cheese, mushrooms, and onion.

Makes 6 to 8 servings.

RASPBERRY VINAIGRETTE:
1/4 cup raspberry wine vinegar
1/4 cup fresh or frozen raspberries
1/2 cup honey
2 cloves garlic
1/4 teaspoon ground nutmeg
Salt and coarsely ground pepper to taste
3/4 cup extra-virgin olive oil

In a food processor or blender, combine raspberry wine vinegar, raspberries, honey, garlic, nutmeg, salt, and pepper; whirl at low speed until raspberries are puréed. Slowly add olive oil in a steady stream until dressing is thoroughly blended. Store, covered, in refrigerator. Serve at room temperature.

Spinach Salad With Strawberries

2 bunches fresh spinach leaves, washed, dried, and chilled
Honey Dressing
1 cup thickly sliced fresh strawberries
1 tablespoon sesame seeds, toasted
1 small red onion, thinly sliced (optional)

Remove stems and veins from spinach and tear into bite-sized pieces; place into a large salad bowl. Pour Honey Dressing over spinach; toss gently. Add strawberries, sesame seeds, and onion; toss again and serve.

Makes 6 to 8 servings.

HONEY DRESSING:
2 tablespoons balsamic vinegar
2 tablespoons rice vinegar
1 tablespoon plus 1 teaspoon honey
2 teaspoons Dijon mustard
Salt and pepper to taste

In a small jar with a lid, combine balsamic vinegar, rice vinegar, honey, Dijon mustard, salt, and pepper; cover securely and shake vigorously. Store, covered, in refrigerator. Serve at room temperature.

Sesame Seeds

In ancient Persia, sesame seeds were a precious commodity and no accident that in the popular story of Ali Baba from "The Arabian Nights," the enormous cave full of thieves' treasure could only be entered with the magic words "open sesame." Sesame seeds are also called benne seeds in some parts of the world. African slaves brought sesame seeds to America.

To keep sesame seeds from becoming rancid, store in an airtight container in the refrigerator for up to six months.

TOASTING SESAME SEEDS:
To toast seeds, spread on a baking sheet and cook in a 350-degree oven three to five minutes or until brown, or lightly toast the seeds in a dry pan until they jump.

Packaged Salad Mixes

The quality of the packaged salad mixes depends on maturity at harvest, the mixture's variety, freshness, how the mix is maintained at the market, and how quickly you use it. You can expect to find the freshest and best quality mixes at farmers' markets.

Another kind of fresh salad mix is multiplying rapidly in the produce section. These are mixes sealed in plastic bags. To preserve freshness, some are vacuum packed, some are nitrogen-flushed (the bags are puffed), and some are in bags that breathe.

Even though bulk salad mixes at farmers' markets are rinsed after picking, rinse the leaves again at home to remove dust and any visiting insects, and to refresh the leaves. Packaged salad mixes from the produce department are already pre-washed.

Orange-Spinach Salad

2 medium oranges, peeled
1 bunch fresh spinach leaves, washed, dried, and chilled
1 (6-ounce) can black olives, drained and sliced
1/4 cup Poppy Seed Dressing

Slice oranges widthwise into 1/4-inch thick slices. Cut each slice into 4 pieces.

Remove stems and veins from spinach and tear into bite-sized pieces; place into a large salad bowl. Add black olives, and oranges. Pour Poppy Seed Dressing over salad. Toss gently and serve.

Makes 4 servings.

POPPY SEED DRESSING:
1/2 cup rice or balsamic vinegar
2/3 cup vegetable oil
1/2 cup sugar
1/4 teaspoon ground mustard
1/8 teaspoon salt
1 teaspoon grated onion
2 teaspoons poppy seeds

In a food processor or blender, combine rice or balsamic vinegar, vegetable oil, sugar, ground mustard, salt, onion, and poppy seeds; whirl 1 minute or until well blended. Store, covered, in refrigerator. Serve at room temperature.

Marinated Potatoes With Salad

A very unusual and delicious salad.

1 pound new potatoes, washed and cooked
1 (16-ounce) bottle Italian salad dressing
5 to 6 cups loosely packed torn mixed lettuce (romaine, watercress, or Boston),
    washed, torn and chilled
5 to 6 green onions, chopped
1 cup sliced mushrooms
2 cups sliced cherry tomatoes

Cut cooked potatoes into 1/4-inch slices. Place potatoes into a large bowl with a lid; pour Italian dressing over potatoes, making sure all potatoes are covered (do not mix because you will tear up the potatoes). Cover and refrigerate for 2 hours.

In a large salad bowl, add lettuce, green onions, mushrooms, and tomatoes. Pour potatoes and marinade over salad. Toss gently and serve.

Makes 4 to 6 servings.

Tropical Fruit With Curried Rum Sauce

1 large pineapple
3 cups watermelon balls
3 cups cantaloupe balls
3 cups honeydew balls
3 cups strawberries, rinsed and hulled
Curried Rum Sauce

Lay pineapple on its side. To form a bowl, cut 1/4-inch off top side of pineapple with a knife, cut opening into an oval shape. Do not cut through the bottom. Leave stem intact. Remove cutout section; cut pineapple into cubes. Wrap pineapple bowl in plastic wrap and refrigerate until ready to use.

In a large storage bowl, combine pineapple, watermelon, cantaloupe, honeydew, and strawberries; cover and refrigerate.

To serve, pour Curried Rum Sauce over fruit; toss gently. Spoon a portion of mixture into pineapple bowl; refill bowl as necessary.

Yields 16 cups.

CURRIED RUM SAUCE:
1/2 cup raisins
1 cup hot water
3 tablespoons butter or margarine
1 1/4 cups firmly packed brown sugar
1/2 teaspoon grated orange zest
1/4 cup fresh orange juice
1/4 cup rum
1/4 teaspoon grated lemon zest
1 tablespoon fresh lemon juice
1/2 teaspoon curry powder
1/4 teaspoon ground ginger

In a small bowl, soak raisins in hot water 15 minutes; drain and set aside.

In a medium frying pan over medium heat, melt butter or margarine. Add brown sugar, orange zest, orange juice, rum, lemon zest, lemon juice, curry powder, and ginger; cook 10 minutes, stirring often. Stir in raisins. Remove from heat and cool.

Yields 1 1/2 cups.

How to Buy Melons

A melon should be hard with no soft spots and fully colored. It should be heavy for its size. Weigh a few that look about the same size and choose the heaviest one.

A ripe melon will also give a hollow ring, not a dull thud, when thumped.

*HONEYDEW MELON:
A slightly springy blossom end on a honeydew melon is usually an indication that it is ripe. A honeydew melon will become riper and sweeter if allowed to sit, uncut, at room temperature for a few days.*

*WATERMELON:
The best way to determine if a watermelon is ripe is to thump it and check the flat side of the melon, where it rested on the ground. This spot is yellow when the melon is ripe.*

Salads

Carving Watermelons

Carving a watermelon is very easy and a wonderful way to serve fruit. Best of all, there's no bowl to wash later.

Select and wash a uniformly shaped watermelon. Cut off the top third of the melon. Cut a thin slice from the bottom, avoiding the red pulp (removing the slice from the bottom of the melon will help it sit flat).

Scoop out and save the watermelon pulp, leaving a one-half to one-inch shell. Using a melon scooper will give you bite-sized pieces, or cut melon out of the shell and cut into bite-sized chunks. Reserve melon balls or chunks in refrigerator.

Use your imagination and cut any design you wish. Wrap shell in plastic wrap and refrigerate until ready to use.

Watermelon Boat

Great treat for a hot summer's day.

Whole watermelon
Cantaloupe
Honeydew
Red grapes
Green grapes
Blueberries
Strawberries

Carve watermelon top into whatever shape you like; i.e., basket with handle, boat, zigzag cut, or straight cut. Remove insides of watermelon using a melon scooper, or with a knife cut into 1-inch pieces; set aside. Discard seeds and remove excess memanbrane, leaving a 1-inch shell.

Prepare cantaloupe and honeydew melons by cutting in half and discarding seeds, membrane, and rind; with a knife, cut into 1-inch pieces or use a melon scooper. Wash grapes, blueberries, and strawberries; drain. To assemble, fill carved watermelon with fruits and garnish with strawberries. Store in refrigerator until ready to serve.

Serves many!

Waldorf Salad

If the season is right and you can get different varieties of apples, it makes a wonderful-tasting salad to combine them (be sure to choose apples that are crisp).

VERSION 1:
2 cups unpeeled and diced apples
1 cup diced celery
1/2 cup chopped nuts
1/2 cup mayonnaise

In a large bowl, toss together apples, celery, nuts, and mayonnaise; mix until moistened. Refrigerate before serving.

VERSION 2:
2 cups unpeeled and diced apples
2 cups diced bananas
1/2 cup raisins
1/2 cup chopped nuts (pecans, walnuts, or almonds)
Mayonnaise
Lettuce

In a large bowl, toss together apples, bananas, raisins, nuts, and just enough mayonnaise to moisten. Refrigerate before serving. Serve on a bed of lettuce.

Makes 4 servings.

Northwest Fruit Salad

2 CUPS OF A VARIETY OF FRUITS OF YOUR CHOICE:
Bananas, peeled and sliced
Blueberries
Green or red grapes
Kiwi fruit, peeled and sliced
Pears, peeled and sliced
Peaches, peeled and sliced
Raspberries
Strawberries, sliced
Fruit Dressing

In a large container, combine mixed fruits. Pour Fruit Dressing over fruits; cover and refrigerate for several hours. Serve in chilled cocktail glasses.

Makes 4 servings.

FRUIT DRESSING:
2 tablespoons honey
2 tablespoons lemon or lime juice
2 tablespoons dark rum

In a small bowl, combine honey, lemon or lime juice, and rum.

Apricot Cream Fruit Salad

2 apples, unpeeled, cored, and cut into 1/2-inch cubes
2 peaches, peeled, cored, and cut into 1/2-inch cubes
2 pears, peeled, cored, and cut into 1/2-inch cubes
4 tablespoons concentrated frozen orange juice
1/2 cup golden raisins
1/4 cup toasted chopped walnuts
3/4 cup Apricot Cream

Prepare Apricot Cream. In a large bowl, combine apples, peaches, pears, orange juice, raisins, and walnuts; toss gently until well mixed. Refrigerate until serving time. When ready to serve, toss with Apricot Cream and serve. NOTE: You can also toss the salad with the Apricot Cream several hours before serving and refrigerate until ready to serve.

Makes 6 servings.

APRICOT CREAM:
1/2 cup sour cream
1/4 cup whipping cream
1/2 teaspoon vanilla extract
1 teaspoon sugar
1 tablespoon apricot jam

In a jar with a lid, combine sour cream and whipping cream; stir until well blended. Cover and leave at room temperature for 4 hours.

Add vanilla extract, sugar, and apricot jam; stir to blend well. Cover and store in refrigerate (will keep for approximately one week).

Preparing Fresh Fruits

Always use a stainless-steel knife to cut fruit. The acid in the fruit will cause discoloration on carbon-steel knives, which would then blacken the cut edge of the fruit.

When slicing peaches or nectarines that are not to be eaten within the next few moments, slip the slices into a bowl of water with a little lemon juice in it. This will keep the fruit from turning brown.

Strawberries, raspberries, and blackberries should be rinsed very quickly under running water; never soak them, as they tend to absorb water, which can make them soggy.

Spiking a Watermelon

Some people think that the best thing to do with a watermelon is to spike it. To do so, cut a two-inch plug from the melon and reach in with your knife tip to score the exposed flesh.

Pour in as much vodka, gin, or light rum as the melon will hold. Replace the plug and secure it with tape; refrigerate the melon for eight to twenty-four hours before serving.

Easy Fruit Dressing

Excellent tasting and low in calories. Use either with fresh or canned fruits.

1 ripe banana
Lemon juice
Sugar

Mash banana with fork. Add just enough lemon juice to make it the consistency that you want. Sweeten to taste with sugar.

Yields 1/2 cup.

Kiwi Fruit Salad

This salad is so good that it could also be served for dessert.

1 medium pineapple, peeled, cored, and cut into 1-inch cubes
3 ripe bananas, sliced diagonally
1 cup (1/2-pound) red grapes
6 kiwi fruit, peeled and sliced widthwise
1 cup chopped nuts
Honey-Yogurt Dressing

In a large salad bowl, combine pineapple, bananas, grapes, kiwi fruit, and chopped nuts. Pour Honey-Yogurt Dressing over fruit; toss gently. Cover and refrigerate for at least 30 minutes before serving.

HONEY-YOGURT DRESSING:
1 1/2 tablespoons grated orange zest
1 teaspoon freshly grated ginger
1/4 cup mayonnaise
1/4 cup plain yogurt
2 tablespoons honey
1 tablespoon lemon juice

In a small bowl, combine orange zest, ginger, mayonnaise, yogurt, honey, and lemon juice; stir until well blended. If made ahead, cover and refrigerate.

Makes 4 servings.

Tangy Tomato Aspic

1 1/4 cups boiling water
1 (3-ounce) package lemon-flavored gelatin
1 (8-ounce) can tomato sauce
1 1/2 tablespoons wine vinegar
1/2 teaspoon salt
1 teaspoon finely minced onion
1/8 teaspoon hot pepper sauce
Ground cloves to taste
2 cups diced celery
Lettuce

In a small bowl, pour boiling water over gelatin, stirring until dissolved. Stir in tomato sauce, wine vinegar, salt, onion, hot pepper sauce, and cloves; refrigerate until slightly thickened but not set.

Stir in celery. Pour into a 4-cup mold. Refrigerate until firm. To serve, unmold onto a bed of lettuce.

Makes 4 to 6 servings.

Molded Cranberry Salad

1 (8-ounce) can crushed pineapple, drained (reserve juice)
1 (3-ounce) package raspberry-flavored gelatin
1 (16-ounce) can whole-berry cranberry sauce
1/4 cup chopped celery
1/4 cup chopped nuts
Lettuce

Add enough water to reserved pineapple juice to make 1 1/4 cups of liquid. In a large saucepan over medium-high heat, bring liquid to a boil; remove from heat and stir in gelatin until dissolved. Break up cranberry sauce with a fork; stir into gelatin mixture. Cool until mixture begins to thicken; stir in pineapple, celery, and nuts. Pour into decorative mold. Refrigerate until set. To serve, unmold, and serve on a bed of lettuce.

Makes 8 servings.

Weller Family Cranberry Relish

According to Ben Weller, you MUST use a meat grinder when making this recipe, not a food processor.

2 oranges, unpeeled and sliced into 8 pieces
1 (2-pound) package fresh cranberries
1 cup sugar

Feed the oranges and cranberries through meat grinder (use small grate). In a medium bowl, combine ground oranges, ground cranberries, and sugar. Sprinkle a little sugar over the top. Cover and refrigerator for at least 1 day (the longer you refrigerate, the better the taste).

Makes 8 to 10 servings.

Cranberry Sauce With Raspberry Vinegar

This traditional sauce is enhanced by raspberry vinegar. Very delicious.

1 1/4 cups sugar
1/2 cup raspberry vinegar
1/4 cup water
1 (12-ounce) package fresh cranberries
1 cinnamon stick
1 tablespoon thinly sliced orange peel

In a large saucepan over medium heat, combine sugar, raspberry vinegar, and water; bring to a boil, stirring until sugar dissolves. Mix in cranberries, cinnamon stick, and orange peel. Reduce heat to low, cover partially, and simmer 10 minutes or until cranberries burst. Remove from heat and cool completely (sauce will thicken as it cools). Discard cinnamon stick.

NOTE: Can be made up to one week in advance. Cover and refrigerate.

Yields 2 1/3 cups.

Cranberries

1 (12-ounce) bag of cranberries equals 3 cups whole cranberries, or 2 1/2 cups finely chopped cranberries.

Cranberries got their name from the pilgrims, who called them "craneberries" because their long-necked pink blossoms resembled the heads of cranes.

When buying cranberries, they should appear well colored, plump, firm, and unbruised. Place in a plastic bag and refrigerate for up to one month.

Shortly before using, wash cranberries; pick through them and discard any that are bruised or decaying. Cranberries will freeze beautifully. Wrap them in an airtight bag, squeeze out excess air, and they will keep for almost a year. Do not defrost when adding them to a recipe.

TIPS: Add one teaspoon of butter to each pound of cranberries when cooking to eliminate foam and overboiling.

Cook cranberries just until they pop. Further cooking makes them taste bitter.

How to Cook Asparagus

Snap off and discard tough ends of asparagus. If you desired, scrape off scales. In a large pan over medium-high heat, fill three-fourths full of water; add one teaspoon of salt per quart of water and heat to a boil. Add asparagus, cover just until water begins to boil again, and then remove lid. Reduce heat to medium and cook four minutes.

Test for doneness by piercing spears with a sharp knife. Asparagus is done when just easily pierced. Remove from heat, drain, and cool.

Asparagus Salad

28 fresh or frozen asparagus spears, cooked
2 beefsteak tomatoes, cored and cut into wedges
Blue Cheese Dressing
Salt and coarsely ground pepper to taste
1/2 cup chopped fresh fennel leaves

Place cooked asparagus in the center of chilled individual serving plates and ring with tomato wedges. Drizzle Blue Cheese Dressing over the asparagus. Season with salt and pepper. To serve, garnish with fennel leaves.

Makes 4 to 6 servings.

BLUE CHEESE DRESSING:
1/2 cup plain yogurt
1 tablespoon crumbled blue cheese
1/4 cup fresh lemon juice
1 tablespoon snipped fresh chives
1 clove garlic, minced

In a small saucepan over low heat, combine yogurt and blue cheese; stir until well blended. Cook 1 to 2 minutes, stirring constantly, or until blue cheese has melted. Remove from heat; add lemon juice, chives, and garlic; stir until well blended.

Overnight Marinated Asparagus

1/3 cup warm water
1 tablespoon sugar
1/2 teaspoon dried dill weed, crushed
1/2 teaspoon salt
1/2 cup vegetable oil
1/2 cup white wine vinegar
1 tablespoon finely chopped onion
1 1/2 pounds fresh or frozen asparagus spears, cooked

In a small bowl, make a marinade by combining water, sugar, dill weed, salt, vegetable oil, wine vinegar, and onion. Place asparagus into a large shallow dish; pour marinade over asparagus and refrigerate overnight. To serve, drain asparagus, and transfer onto a serving platter. Serve chilled.

Makes 4 to 6 servings.

Marinated Asparagus With Almonds

2 pounds fresh or frozen asparagus spears, cooked
Almond Marinade
Lettuce leaves

Arrange cooked asparagus in a large shallow dish. Pour Almond Marinade over asparagus. Cover and refrigerate at least 8 hours or overnight. To serve, drain asparagus, place onto a lettuce-leaf-lined platter, and drizzle with additional Almond Marinade.

Makes 8 servings.

ALMOND MARINADE:
1/4 cup sugar
1/4 cup white vinegar
1/4 cup soy sauce
2 tablespoons vegetable oil
1/4 cup finely chopped almonds

In a small bowl, combine sugar, white vinegar, soy sauce, and vegetable oil. Stir in almonds.

Avocados

1 medium avocado equals 1 1/2 cups cubed.

The two most widely marketed avocado varieties are the rough-skinned, almost black Haas and the smooth, thin-skinned green Fuerte. The Haas has a smaller pit and a more buttery texture than the Fuerte.

Avocados do not ripen on the tree and are rarely found ripe in markets. Purchase them two or three days in advance. Avocados will not ripen if placed in the refrigerator. When buying avocados, choose those that yield slightly to gentle palm pressure.

Avocado Stuffed With Crab Meat

3 ripe avocados
Juice of 1 lemon
3/4 pound cooked crab meat
1/2 cup Thousand Island Dressing
1 hard-cooked egg, chopped or slivered
12 black olives

Cut avocados in half, remove seeds, and peel. Dip surfaces in lemon juice. Carefully clean the crab meat of any shells or cartilage.

In a medium bowl, gently combine crab meat and Thousand Island Dressing. Fill the avocado cavities with mounds of crab mixture. Garnish with hard-cooked egg and black olives. Place onto individual serving plates to serve.

Makes 6 servings.

THOUSAND ISLAND DRESSING:
1 cup mayonnaise
1/4 cup chili sauce
2 hard-cooked eggs, finely chopped
1 green onion, finely chopped
2 tablespoons sweet pickle relish
1/8 teaspoon paprika

In a medium bowl, combine mayonnaise, chili sauce, hard-cooked eggs, green onion, pickle relish, and paprika. Cover and refrigerate.

Yields 1 1/2 cups.

To ripen an avocado faster, place in a brown paper bag and set in your oven with only the oven light on.

Do not store in the refrigerator. They'll turn dark and lose flavor.

TIPS: Sprinkle lemon juice over peeled avocados to prevent discoloring.

To remove the seed, cut fruit in half lengthwise; then cup it between palms of hands and gently twist halves apart. Tap seed with sharp edge of knife. Gently lift or pry seed out.

Avocado History

Avocados got their name from the Spanish explorers. They couldn't pronounce the Aztec word for the fruit, known as ahuacatl, "testicle," because of its shape. The Spanish called them aguacate, leading to the guacamole we know today.

The avocado used to be called Alligator Pear. Today, this fruit is grown in Southern California. The first planting of avocados in California was actually recorded in 1848 near what is now called Azusa, a few miles east of Los Angeles.

Did You Know?

That many fresh salad ingredients are living things? A head of lettuce picked from the field and shipped continues to live and breathe. A pear picked from a tree and shipped needs oxygen just as we do.

Do not pack fresh fruits or vegetables together too tightly, since they need oxygen to breathe.

Refrigeration slows the rate of breathing and delays spoiling.

Avocado Salad

2 or 3 ripe avocados
Lemon juice
2 navel oranges
Fresh mushrooms
1 or 2 bunches of seedless grapes
Hot Dressing

Refrigerate all ingredients before starting. Cut avocados in half, remove seeds, and peel. Dip surfaces in lemon juice. Grate zest off of one orange; set aside for Hot Dressing. Peel and separate sections of oranges. Clean and slice fresh mushrooms. Remove seedless grapes from stems; slice avocados into wedges.

In a large salad bowl, combine avocados, oranges, mushrooms, and grapes; toss together lightly. To serve, sprinkle with Hot Dressing.

HOT DRESSING:
3 bacon slices
1 teaspoon sugar
1/4 cup lemon juice
2 tablespoons grated orange zest

In a medium frying pan over medium heat, fry bacon until crisp; remove bacon pieces (reserve for another use). Dissolve sugar in hot bacon fat. Add lemon juice and bring to a boil; add orange zest.

Makes 4 to 6 servings.

Spicy Avocados

A very unusual and tasty way to serve fresh avocados.

6 tablespoons butter or margarine
6 tablespoons catsup
2 1/2 tablespoons cider vinegar
2 1/2 tablespoons water
4 teaspoons sugar
1/2 teaspoon salt
Hot pepper sauce to taste
4 ripe avocados
Lemon juice

In a large saucepan over medium heat, combine butter or margarine, catsup, cider vinegar, water, sugar, salt, and hot pepper sauce; heat until butter or margarine is melted and sauce is smooth. Remove from heat.

Cut avocados in half, remove seeds, and peel. Dip surfaces in lemon juice. Place avocado halves onto individual serving plates, ladle warm sauce onto top, and serve immediately.

Makes 8 servings.

The Ultimate Pea Salad

5 cups frozen peas (two 16-ounce bags), thawed
1 (8-ounce) can sliced water chestnuts, drained
1 cup snow pea pods, stems and strings removed
1/2 cup chopped red onion
1/4 cup mayonnaise
1/4 cup sour cream
1/8 teaspoon pepper
1/8 teaspoon red (cayenne) pepper
1/8 teaspoon salt
1/2 pound bacon, cooked and crumbled
Pea pods (garnish)
8 cherry tomatoes, cut in half

In a large bowl, toss together peas, water chestnuts, pea pods, and red onion. In a small bowl, combine mayonnaise, sour cream, pepper, cayenne pepper, and salt; pour over vegetables and toss gently. Cover and refrigerate.

To serve, fold in crumbled bacon. Garnish with pea pods and tomato wedges.

Makes 8 to 10 servings.

Snow Pea Pods

Snow peas are also known as Chinese pea pods. They are flatter than the sugar snap pea, which is a cross between the snow pea and the English pea (common green pea).

Before using, wash pea pods and snap off the stem ends, using them to pull on and remove the string, if it is necessary.

Store unwashed pea pods in a plastic bag in the refrigerator for up to three days.

Pea pods should either be served raw or cooked only briefly. When using in dishes like stir-frys, add during the last minutes of cooking.

Cauliflower Salad

8 cups (2 medium heads) cauliflower flowerets
2 cups shredded sharp cheddar cheese
1/4 cup sliced green onions
1/4 teaspoon red (cayenne) pepper
Salt and pepper to taste
1 cup mayonnaise

In a large saucepan over medium-high heat, cook cauliflower flowerets, in a small amount of boiling water, 8 to 10 minutes or until tender. Remove from heat and drain well.

In a large salad bowl, combine cauliflower flowerets, cheddar cheese, green onions, cayenne pepper, salt, and pepper; toss gently. Add mayonnaise and toss again.

Makes 8 to 10 servings.

Classic Raspberry Vinaigrette

So easy to make and so absolutely wonderful tasting.

1/2 cup raspberry vinegar
1/4 cup fresh or frozen raspberries
1/4 cup honey
1/2 cup fresh basil leaves
3/4 cup extra-virgin olive oil

In a blender or food processor, combine raspberry vinegar, raspberries, honey, and basil; whirl 1 minute or until well blended. With the motor on, add olive oil in a slow steady stream, whirling until dressing is smooth. Store, covered, in refrigerator. Serve at room temperature.

Yields 1 cup.

Vinaigrettes

Good-quality ingredients must be used in vinaigrette dressings. Making it in the food processor will help keep it emulsified, usually two hours or longer. A clove of garlic, a shallot, mustard, or cream acts as a binder when the oil is slowly processed into the mixture.

SERVING VINAIGRETTES: When a salad is properly tossed with greens, no excess vinaigrette should appear on the bottom of a salad bowl or plates.

A green salad for four will require about one-half cup of dressing. As soon as your salad is mixed, taste a leaf to see if there is sufficient dressing. If not, drizzle vinaigrette over the salad a tablespoon at a time; toss and taste again. Serve salad immediately.

Champagne Cilantro Vinaigrette

1/2 cup chilled champagne
2 tablespoons red wine vinegar
Coarsely ground pepper to taste
1 teaspoon grated lemon zest
1 tablespoon chopped fresh cilantro
1/4 cup extra-virgin olive oil
2 to 3 tablespoons sugar

In a blender or food processor, combine champagne, wine vinegar, pepper, lemon zest, and cilantro; whirl 1 minute or until well blended. With the motor on, add olive oil in a slow steady stream, whirling until dressing is smooth. Add sugar and whirl until well blended. Store, covered, in refrigerator. Serve at room temperature.

Yields 3/4 cup.

Raspberry-Mint Dressing

1/4 cup fresh mint leaves (peppermint is best)
1 egg
1/2 cup raspberry vinegar
3 tablespoons honey
Salt to taste
White pepper to taste
3/4 cup extra-virgin olive oil

In a blender or food processor, combine mint, egg, raspberry vinegar, honey, salt, white pepper, and olive oil; whirl until well blended. Store, covered, in refrigerator. Serve at room temperature.

Yields 1 1/2 cups.

Hazelnut Vinaigrette

1 clove garlic
1/8 teaspoon salt
1/2 teaspoon Dijon mustard
1/4 cup raspberry vinegar
1/4 cup honey
3 tablespoons hazelnut oil
1/2 cup extra-virgin olive oil

In a blender or food processor, mince garlic. Add salt and Dijon mustard; whirl, drizzling in raspberry vinegar, honey, hazelnut oil, and olive oil. Store, covered, in refrigerator. Serve at room temperature.

Yields 1 cup.

Lemon-Basil Vinaigrette Dressing

1 medium lemon
2 cloves garlic
1/2 cup rice vinegar
2 cups loosely packed fresh basil leaves
3 tablespoons honey
1/4 teaspoon salt
1 cup extra-virgin olive oil

Remove the zest from the lemon. Squeeze lemon, reserving juice. In a blender or food processor, add lemon zest and garlic; whirl until minced. Add rice vinegar, basil, honey, and salt; whirl until basil is coarsely chopped.

With motor on, slowly drizzle lemon juice and olive oil into basil mixture. Whirl until vinaigrette has thickened slightly and basil is finely chopped. Store, covered, in refrigerator. Serve at room temperature.

Yields 1 cup.

Hazelnut Tarragon Dressing

1/4 cup rice vinegar
2 tablespoons Dijon mustard
2 small green onions, chopped
2 cloves garlic, minced
1 tablespoon chopped fresh tarragon
1 egg yolk
1/4 cup honey
1/3 cup hazelnut oil
1/2 cup vegetable oil
Salt and pepper to taste

In a blender or food processor, combine rice vinegar, Dijon mustard, onions, garlic, tarragon, egg yolk, and honey; whirl until well blended. With motor on, add hazelnut oil and vegetable oil, one at a time in a slow steady steam; whirling until dressing is smooth. Season with salt and pepper. Store, covered, in refrigerator. Serve at room temperature.

Yields 1 cup.

DO NOT OVERDRESS YOUR SALADS!

Too much salad dressing will weigh down the salad ingredients and mask their flavors. The dressing's role is to highlight, not to overpower the salad ingredients.

Salad Dressings

Honey

TIPS: *Honey should be stored in a tightly covered container in a dark, cool place. Freezing or refrigeration will not harm the honey but may hasten granulation.*

If granules do form, place the jar of honey in a bowl of warm water until all crystals are melted and honey is liquid. Too high a temperature will scorch the honey.

Be sure to wipe the honey bottle well with a damp cloth after each use to avoid attracting ants and roaches. Pay special attention to the cap and screw-top ridges so the cap does not stick in the future.

Vermont Maple Dressing

IMPORTANT: *This salad dressing requires that you use a top-quality Vermont maple syrup. If you use an inferior grade, you'll end up with a thin dressing that doesn't cling to your greens.*

Honey-Mustard Dressing

Honey-mustard dressing lovers will rave about this one.

1/2 cup honey
1/4 cup Dijon mustard
1 clove garlic, minced
2 tablespoons fresh lemon juice
1/4 cup balsamic vinegar
1/2 cup vegetable oil
1/2 teaspoon Oriental sesame oil

In a blender or food processor, combine honey, Dijon mustard, garlic, lemon juice, and balsamic vinegar; whirl 1 minute or until well mixed. With the motor on, add vegetable oil and sesame oil in a slow, steady stream, whirling until dressing is smooth. Store, covered, in refrigerator. Serve at room temperature.

NOTE: For an interesting and delicious taste, add fresh berries (in season) and blend again until smooth.

Yields 1 1/2 cups.

Poppy Seed Dressing

The best poppy seed dressing you have ever tasted.

1 cup sugar
3 teaspoons ground mustard
1 teaspoon salt
2/3 cup rice vinegar
1/4 cup chopped white onion
2 cups vegetable oil
2 tablespoons poppy seeds

In a blender or food processor, combine sugar, ground mustard, salt, rice vinegar, and onion. With the motor on, slowly add vegetable oil in a slow, steady stream; whirling until dressing is smooth and has a creamy texture. Add poppy seeds and blend thoroughly. Store, covered, in refrigerator. Serve at room temperature.

Yields 1 1/2 cups.

Vermont Maple Dressing

This is a wonderful salad dressing. It is one of our favorites and sure to become one of yours.

3/4 cup genuine Vermont maple syrup
1 teaspoon salt
1/2 cup rice vinegar
1 cup vegetable oil
1 1/2 teaspoons ground mustard

In a blender or food processor, combine maple syrup, salt, rice vinegar, vegetable oil, and ground mustard. Whirl 1 minute or until well mixed. Store, covered, in refrigerator. Serve at room temperature.

Yields 2 cups.

Seafoods

Baked Halibut

A simple but delicious way to prepare halibut. Serve with a baked potato and a fresh green salad.

1 (1-pound) halibut fillet, thick cut
4 tablespoons butter or margarine
1/2 cup Ritz crackers, crushed

Preheat oven to 350 degrees. Line the bottom of an ungreased broiling pan with aluminum foil and spray broiler rack with vegetable-oil cooking spray. Wash halibut, pat dry, and place skin side down onto broiler rack.

In a small saucepan over medium heat, melt butter or margarine. Stir in crushed Ritz crackers until mixture is moist. Coat top of halibut with Ritz cracker mixture. Bake, uncovered, 15 to 20 minutes or until halibut is slightly opaque in thickest part (cut to test). Remove from oven, transfer onto a serving platter, and serve immediately.

Makes 2 servings.

WHOLE FISH

STEAKS

Baked Halibut With Cherry Tomatoes

1/2 cup thinly sliced green onions
2 cloves garlic, minced
2 tablespoons chopped fresh dill or 1/2 teaspoon dried dill weed, crushed
2 tablespoons olive oil
1 pound cherry tomatoes, cut in half
4 (8-ounce) halibut steaks
2 tablespoons lemon juice
Salt and pepper to taste

Preheat oven to 425 degrees. In a small bowl, combine onions, garlic, dill, and olive oil. Into an ungreased large baking dish, place tomatoes, cut side up; pour onion mixture evenly over tomatoes. Bake, uncovered, for 25 minutes on the top rack of the oven.

Wash halibut, pat dry, and place into an ungreased 13x9-inch baking dish. Drizzle with lemon juice; cover with aluminum foil. Bake on bottom rack of oven, leaving tomato mixture in oven, 10 to 12 minutes or until halibut is just slightly opaque in thickest part (cut to test). Remove halibut and tomato dishes from oven. Transfer halibut onto a serving platter. Stir halibut juices into tomatoes; spoon mixture over fish. Season with salt and pepper.

Makes 4 servings.

How to Select Fish

Fresh fish is at its very best when in season and plentiful, and the price should be cheaper then. The flesh of fresh fish should always be firm and should adhere firmly to the bone. The odor should be distinctly fresh and mild.

Fresh fish is marketed in a number of ways. They are as follows:

WHOLE, ROUND: Means that the fish are exactly as they came from the water. The eyes should be clear, the gills bright red, and the skin shiny with tightly clinging scales. Allow one pound per serving.

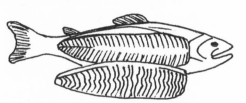

FILLET

DRESSED OR PAN-DRESSED FISH: Fish that have scales and entrails removed, and usually also with head, tail, and fins removed. Allow one-half pound per serving.

STEAKS: Ready-to-cook widthwise slices of large fish. Allow one-third to one-half pound per serving.

FILLETS: Ready-to-cook sides of fish cut lengthwise from the backbone. Allow one-half pound per serving.

Seafood

Halibut

Halibut is a large flatfish, resembling the turbot in appearance, and is the largest in the flatfish group. They sometimes weigh in at over 500 pounds and are six feet in length. The flesh of the halibut is coarser and the flavor is stronger and less refined than the flounder's, and especially the sole's.

Halibut is exclusively a cold-water fish and is found in the North Atlantic and North Pacific oceans. The North Pacific variety is caught along the coast of Oregon, Washington, and Alaska from July to December.

Baked Halibut With Vegetables

1 (3-pound) halibut fillet
1 pound potatoes, peeled and cut into 1-inch pieces
6 carrots, peeled and thinly sliced
1 large onion, sliced
Salt and pepper to taste
Red (cayenne) pepper to taste
Water
1/2 cup butter or margarine

Preheat oven to 350 degrees. Line an ungreased 13x9-inch baking dish with enough aluminum foil to cover and seal in fish and vegetables. Wash halibut, pat dry, and place into prepared baking dish.

Place potatoes, carrots, and onion around fish. Season with salt, pepper, and cayenne pepper. Pour in enough water to measure halfway up sides of halibut. Dot with butter or margarine. Seal aluminum foil so steam does not escape; bake 1 hour or until halibut is just slightly opaque in thickest part (cut to test) and vegetables are cooked. Remove from oven, remove aluminum foil, and transfer onto a serving platter.

Makes 4 servings.

Grilled Halibut With Tropical Fruit Salsa

4 (6- to 8-ounce) halibut fillets or steaks
1/4 cup olive oil
1/3 cup soy sauce
Tropical Fruit Salsa

Preheat barbecue grill. Wash halibut, pat dry, and place onto a large piece of aluminum foil; trim or fold under to fit outline of fish.

In a small bowl, combine olive oil and soy sauce; brush onto halibut fillets or steaks. Place halibut with aluminum foil onto hot grill. Cover barbecue with lid, open any vents, and cook 20 to 30 minutes or until halibut is slightly opaque in thickest part (cut to test). Remove from grill, transfer onto warm serving plates, and top with Tropical Fruit Salsa.

Makes 4 servings.

TROPICAL FRUIT SALSA:
1 papaya, peeled, seeded, and diced
1 mango, peeled, seeded, and diced
1/4 pineapple, peeled, cored, and diced
1/2 medium tomato, chopped
2 jalapeño chilies, cored, seeded, and diced

In a medium bowl, combine papaya, mango, pineapple, tomato and jalapeño chilies; use at room temperature (the salsa will keep in the refrigerator for approximately 6 days).

Grilled Honey-Ginger Halibut

Salmon makes a great substitute in this recipe.

1 (4- to 4 1/2-pound) halibut fillet or steaks
Honey-Ginger Sauce
Lime slices and wedges

Wash halibut, pat dry, and place onto a large piece of aluminum foil; trim or fold under to fit outline of fish. Spoon Honey-Ginger Sauce evenly onto halibut; let stand 15 to 30 minutes, spooning sauce over halibut frequently.

Preheat barbecue grill. Place halibut with aluminum foil onto hot grill. Cover barbecue with lid, open any vents, and cook 20 to 30 minutes or until halibut is slightly opaque in thickest part (cut to test). Remove from grill and transfer onto a serving platter.

May be served hot or cold. If making ahead, cover and refrigerate up to 1 day. To serve, squeeze juice from lime wedges onto halibut and garnish with lime slices.

Makes 10 to 12 servings.

HONEY-GINGER SAUCE:
1 tablespoon butter
1 tablespoon honey
1 tablespoon firmly packed brown sugar
2 tablespoons soy sauce
3 tablespoons Dijon mustard
1 tablespoon olive oil
1 teaspoon freshly grated ginger

In a large frying pan over medium heat, melt butter. Stir in honey and brown sugar until sugar dissolves; remove from heat. Mix in soy sauce, Dijon mustard, olive oil, and ginger. Let sauce cool slightly before serving.

Cooking Fish – The 10-Minute Rule

Regardless of the fish or the cooking method, there is one uncomplicated rule of thumb that can be followed. Measure the fish, whether it be whole, in steaks, or in fillets, at its thickest point. Then cook exactly ten minutes for each measured inch of thickness, fifteen minutes if it is enclosed in aluminum foil or baked in a sauce. For frozen, unthawed fish, double the cooking time.

If you are baking them in an aluminum foil package with the edges sealed, allow a little extra time for the heat to penetrate the foil – five minutes more for fresh fish, ten minutes for frozen fish.

To test for doneness, separate the fish with a fork or tip of a knife.

REMEMBER: FISH WILL CONTINUE TO COOK AFTER IT IS REMOVED FROM THE HEAT SOURCE.

Salmon

To cooks, gourmets, and fishermen alike, the salmon is the king of the waters. The distinctive color of the flesh of a salmon is part of its attraction. It can vary from a very delicate pale pink to a much deeper shade, verging on red.

> The one cardinal rule is: NEVER OVERCOOK SALMON.
>
> Although it is an oily fish, overcooking makes the flesh dry and dense, and it can become quite chewy in texture.

Pacific salmon, of which there are five species, comprise one of the most valuable fishery resources of the United States.

CHINOOK OR KING: Soft in texture, very rich in oil, and separates into large flakes, making it excellent for salads and recipes calling for large pieces.

SOCKEYE: Has deep red meat and considerable oil, is of firm texture, and breaks into smaller flakes, making it attractive for hot dishes and salads.

COHO: Is large flaked, a lighter red than sockeye, and is good in all dishes.

PINK: Is small flaked, ranges from light to deep pink, and is a thrifty buy for main dishes, soups, chowders, and sandwiches.

CHUM: Is large flaked, very light in color, low in oil, and is especially suitable for cooked dishes where color is not important.

Salmon With Grapefruit

A simple but elegant dinner.

1 (2 1/2-pound) salmon fillet, 1-inch thick, cut into 6 equal pieces
2 egg whites
1 cup bread crumbs
2 tablespoons butter, divided
2 large ruby grapefruits
Grapefruit Caper Sauce

Preheat oven to 325 degrees. Wash salmon and pat dry. In a shallow pie plate, beat egg whites until blended. In another shallow pie plate, place bread crumbs. Coat salmon pieces, one at a time, with egg whites; drain briefly, then coat with crumbs. Lay pieces slightly apart onto a sheet of wax paper.

In a large nonstick frying pan over medium heat, melt butter. Add salmon to fill pan. Cook until salmon is brown on bottom, then turn pieces over and brown other side. As pieces are browned, transfer to an ungreased 13x9-inch baking dish.

Bake, uncovered, 5 to 8 minutes or until the pieces are slightly opaque in thickest part (cut to test). Remove salmon from oven and transfer onto a serving platter. Serve with Grapefruit Caper Sauce.

Makes 6 servings.

GRAPEFRUIT CAPER SAUCE:
2 cups ruby grapefruit juice
3/4 cup mayonnaise
3 tablespoons drained capers
2 tablespoons chopped fresh mint leaves

In a medium saucepan over high heat, boil grapefruit juice 30 minutes or until reduced to 1/4 cup; cool. Stir in mayonnaise. Gently stir in capers and mint.

Grilled Washington State Salmon With Onions

16 sweet onions or other young bulb onions with green tops
1 (3-pound) salmon fillet, with skin
3 lemons
2 tablespoons firmly package brown sugar
Olive oil
1 teaspoon dried tarragon, crushed
1/2 cup honey mustard

Preheat barbecue grill. Trim bottoms of onions. In a large frying pan over medium-high heat, bring 1 1/2 inches of water to a boil. Reduce heat to low, place onions into water, and simmer just until wilted. Remove onions from water, immediately immersing into ice water until cold. Remove from ice water and drain. Fold stem tips down onto top of white on each onion; make knot in stems to hold together.

Wash salmon, pat dry, and place skin down on two stacked pieces of foil; trim or fold under to fit the outline of fish. Squeeze juice from half a lemon over salmon. Sift brown sugar over salmon.

Rub onions lightly with oil. Place onto hot grill over direct heat, turning occasionally to brown evenly. After 10 minutes, set salmon on foil in center of grill; sprinkle with tarragon. If stems of onions begin to char, lean onto salmon. Cover barbecue with lid, open any vents, and cook 20 to 25 minutes or until salmon is slightly opaque in thickest part (cut to test). As needed, turn onions to brown evenly. Remove from grill and transfer onto a serving platter.

Cut remaining lemons into wedges. Serve with lemon wedges and honey mustard.

Makes 8 servings.

The Best Baked Salmon

This is one of the easiest ways of cooking fresh salmon. Baking in aluminum foil is particularly recommended for fresh salmon to preserve its delicate flavor. It makes a wonderful party dish, hot or cold.

1 (3- or 4- pound) salmon, dressed
Salt and coarsely ground pepper
6 bacon slices
1 lemon, thinly sliced
1 onion, thinly sliced
1 large tomato, thinly sliced

Preheat oven to 350 degrees. Wash salmon and pat dry; place onto aluminum foil. Salt and pepper the cavity of the salmon. Layer bacon slices, lemon slices, onion slices and tomato slices in the cavity of salmon; wrap in aluminum foil.

Bake 1 to 1 1/2 hours or until fish is slightly opaque in thickest part (cut to test). Remove from oven, remove aluminum foil, and transfer onto a serving platter to serve.

Makes 8 servings.

The Story of Salmon

Everyone throughout the United States knows salmon; but people living far inland or even along the Atlantic Coast do not know salmon as the people of the Pacific states know it.

Salmon is a saltwater fish which spawns in fresh water. The Columbia River and the Puget Sound country are especially noted for their fine salmon, and, of course, Alaska.

The life cycle of the salmon is an interesting one. Spawned in freshwater streams, the young salmon travel to sea early. Here they live and grow for three or four years. In the spring after they reach maturity, the adult salmon return to their native streams to spawn. They will leap over any obstacle in their way, such as braving dams and waterfalls, hurling itself many feet out of the water until it surmounts the obstacle or dies of exhaustion in the attempt; there is no turning back. For some unknown reason, the female always dies after spawning.

Difference Between Fat and Lean Fish

Did you know that the fat content of fish dictates the cooking method?

Lean fish can be poached, deep fried, or baked in a sauce. Fat fish can be baked, broiled, grilled, or pan fried. Both types can be steamed. The fat content of the flesh, much of which is in the form of oil, varies widely according to the species.

Here are the fat contents by weight of a few of the more commonly eaten fish in this country:

Flounder	*.5%*
Swordfish	*4.0%*
Baked Bluefish	*4.2%*
Raw Haddock	*5.2%*
Canned Tuna	*8.2%*
Raw Shad	*9.8%*
Raw Herring	*12.5%*
Caviar	*15.0%*
Salmon	*16.5%*

Generally the more fatty the fish, the more flavorful the fish. The darker the flesh color of a particular species, the higher the fat content is likely to be.

Fat content usually decreases in relation to the depth of a fish's living environment. Bottom-dwelling fish, like sole and cod, are usually leaner than tuna and herring that dwell near the surface. All fish will be leaner after they have spawned.

Baked Salmon Piccata

4 salmon steaks, 1-inch thick
All-purpose flour for dredging
1/4 cup plus 3 tablespoons butter, divided
3 tablespoons finely chopped onion
1 clove garlic, minced
1 heaping tablespoon drained capers
1/8 teaspoon dried Italian seasonings, crushed
1/2 cup white wine
2 tablespoons fresh lemon juice
2 teaspoons beef broth

Preheat oven to 400 degrees. Wash salmon, pat dry, and roll in flour.

In a large ovenproof frying pan or saute pan, heat 1/4 cup butter until it melts. Briefly sauté the salmon, browning both sides.

Bake, covered, 10 to 15 minutes or until salmon is slightly opaque in thickest part (cut to test). Remove from oven. Reserve liquid in the pan and transfer salmon onto a warm serving platter.

Using the same pan over medium heat, stir together onion, garlic, capers, and Italian seasonings into the reserved liquid; simmer for 5 minutes. Add white wine, lemon juice, and beef broth; stir until well blended. Turn off heat, whisk in 3 tablespoons butter until blended. Remove from heat, pour sauce over salmon, and serve immediately.

Makes 4 servings.

Salmon With Dill Mustard Sauce

1 (1-pound) salmon fillet, 1 1/2-inches thick
1/4 cup dill mustard
1/4 cup butter or margarine, melted

Preheat oven to 350 degrees. Line the bottom of an ungreased broiling pan with aluminum foil and spray broiler rack with vegetable-oil cooking spray. Wash salmon, pat dry, and place, skin side down, onto broiler rack.

In a small bowl, combine dill mustard and butter or margarine; brush dill mixture over salmon. Bake, uncovered, 15 to 20 minutes or until salmon is slightly opaque in thickest part (cut to test). Remove from oven and transfer onto a serving platter.

Makes 2 servings.

Salmon Loaf

1 pound cooked salmon or 1 (14 3/4-ounce) can salmon, drained and flaked
1 egg, slightly beaten
1/4 cup evaporated milk or heavy cream
1 cup soft bread crumbs
1/2 teaspoon salt
1 teaspoon lemon pepper
2 teaspoons lemon juice
1 teaspoon worcestershire sauce
1 tablespoon butter or margarine, melted
3 tablespoons chopped fresh parsley
1/4 cup chopped celery
1/4 cup chopped onion
Lemon Mayonnaise

Preheat oven to 350 degrees. Grease a 9x5-inch loaf pan. In a large bowl, combine salmon, egg, evaporated milk or heavy cream, and bread crumbs. Stir in salt, lemon pepper, lemon juice, worcestershire sauce, butter or margarine, parsley, celery, and onion.

Spoon into prepared pan and bake, uncovered, for 30 minutes. Remove from oven and serve with Lemon Mayonnaise.

Makes 4 servings.

LEMON MAYONNAISE
1 cup mayonnaise
1/2 teaspoon grated lemon zest
2 tablespoons fresh lemon juice
1/2 teaspoon lemon-pepper seasoning

In a small bowl, combine mayonnaise, lemon zest, lemon juice, and lemon-pepper seasoning; cover and refrigerate.

Frozen Fish

Did you know that fresh fish, frozen at sea, is usually fresher than so called "fresh fish" bought at your store? Most fish sold frozen is now cleaned, filleted, and frozen right on the boat within a few hours of the catch, preserving its freshness. Frozen fish in our markets come primarily from Alaska, the North Atlantic, and the Orient.

Buy frozen fish where you know the turnover is brisk. See that the packages are fresh looking and unbroken. Once frozen fish is in the distribution chain, the recommended storage life is three months.

To thaw frozen fish, thaw slowly in the refrigerator instead of at room temperature. Try not to thaw frozen fish completely before cooking, or it may make them very dry and mushy.

Factors in Quality Loss

Seafood deteriorates much more quickly than most meats. Bacterial growth is faster and flavor falls off quickly when it is not fresh or when the frozen item is not kept below zero until ready for use. A "fishy" sharp ammonia odor means deterioration.

About five days is the maximum holding time for the top-quality fresh fish, even though it has been cooled quickly after being caught.

Sometimes fish caught at sea are already ten or more days old upon arrival at port, so that the fish has lost "freshness" before it gets to market.

Lemons – The Golden Rule

Lemon juice is perfect for all types of fresh seafood. It counteracts the richness of oily fish and heightens the flavor of white fish.

Make it a golden rule that when buying seafood to buy a lemon at the same time.

Salmon Burgers

Serve these salmon patties with your favorite hamburger-type buns and your favorite toppings. Children love these burgers.

1 (14 3/4-ounce) can salmon, drained and flaked
1 egg, slightly beaten
1 cup bread crumbs
1/2 cup chopped onion
Salt and pepper to taste
3 tablespoons butter or margarine
Lemon-Sour Cream Sauce
Lemon wedges

In a large bowl, combine salmon, egg, bread crumbs, onion, salt, and pepper; shape into six equal-sized patties.

In a large frying pan over medium heat, melt butter or margarine. Add salmon patties and brown on both sides. Remove from heat, transfer onto a serving platter, and serve with Lemon-Sour Cream Sauce and lemon wedges.

Makes 6 servings.

LEMON-SOUR CREAM SAUCE:
1 cup sour cream
1 teaspoon grated lemon zest
2 tablespoons fresh lemon juice
1/2 teaspoon sugar

In a medium bowl, combine sour cream, lemon zest, lemon juice, and sugar; mix until well blended.

Broiled Lemon-Lime Tuna Steaks

1 pound tuna steaks, 1/2-inch thick
1/4 cup fresh lemon juice
1/4 cup fresh lime juice
2 tablespoons olive oil
1 tablespoon finely chopped fresh dill or 1 1/2 teaspoons dried dill weed, crushed
2 cloves garlic, minced
1/8 teaspoon salt
1/8 teaspoon pepper

Wash tuna steaks and pat dry. In a shallow pie plate, mix together lemon juice, lime juice, olive oil, dill, garlic, salt, and pepper. Add tuna steaks; turn to coat. Cover and refrigerate for 30 minutes, turning occasionally.

Preheat broiler. Spray broiler rack with vegetable-oil cooking spray. Remove tuna steaks from marinade and place onto prepared rack of a shallow broiler pan. Broil 6 to 7 inches from heat for 5 minutes, brushing occasionally with marinade. Turn and repeat with other side for another 5 minutes or until tuna steaks are slightly opaque in thickest part (cut to test). Remove from oven and transfer onto a serving platter.

Makes 2 servings.

Oven-Blackened Tuna

1 (1-pound) tuna fillet
1 tablespoon paprika
2 teaspoons onion powder
2 teaspoons garlic powder
1 teaspoon dried thyme, crushed
1 teaspoon dried oregano, crushed
1 teaspoon pepper
1/2 teaspoon red (cayenne) pepper
3 tablespoons butter, melted
Lemon wedges

Preheat broiler. Spray broiler rack with vegetable-oil cooking spray. Wash tuna fillet and pat dry.

In a small bowl, combine paprika, onion powder, garlic powder, thyme, oregano, pepper, and cayenne pepper. Baste tuna with melted butter; roll in herb mixture. Let stand for 5 minutes.

Place tuna onto prepared rack of a shallow broiler pan; broil 10 minutes or until tuna is slightly opaque in thickest part (cut to test). Remove from oven and transfer onto a serving platter. Serve with lemon wedges.

Makes 2 servings.

Marinating Fish

If you marinate fish, fifteen to thirty minutes is all the time you'll need. Any longer immersion in high-acid marinades (lemon juice, wine, or vinegar) cause fish to "cook." The fish will become opaque and firm.

Tuna

Tuna is a member of the mackerel family and can reach a length of five to six feet and weigh anywhere from twenty to as high as 1,500 pounds.

They travel in schools and spend the winter at the bottom of the ocean. When spring comes, they rise to the surface near the shore where there is warmer water to spawn.

The four varieties of tuna used for canning are the albacore tuna, the yellow fin, the blue fin, and the striped tuna. They vary in color, and the flesh may be white, pink, or darkish tan.

Seafood

Substituting One Fish for Another

Never ignore a recipe because you cannot buy the exact fish required. You can always substitute an available fish that has the same characteristics. Here are some guidelines:

FIRM-FLESHED FISH: Shark, swordfish, orange roughy, albacore tuna, sea bass, mackerel, halibut, or mahi mahi.

WHITE FISH FILLETS: Sole, cod, perch, or red snapper.

MILD-FLAVORED WHITE FISH: Halibut, rockfish, cod, catfish, flounder, turbot, or haddock.

OILY FISH: Salmon, mackerel, pollock, black cod, turbot, sturgeon, or tuna.

Light Tuna Burgers

4 tablespoons mayonnaise
2 tablespoons prepared mustard
1 egg white
2 (6-ounce) cans tuna, drained
1/2 cup bread crumbs, divided
1/4 cup chopped green onions

In a medium bowl, combine mayonnaise, prepared mustard, and egg white. Stir in tuna, 1/4 cup bread crumbs, and green onions. Divide mixture into four equal portions, shaping each into patties. Press the remaining bread crumbs evenly onto both sides of tuna patties.

Coat a large frying pan with vegetable-oil cooking spray; place over medium-high heat until hot. Add patties; cover and cook 3 minutes. Carefully turn patties over, cook another 3 minutes or until patties are golden brown. Remove from heat and transfer onto a serving platter.

Makes 4 servings.

Fillets a L'Orange

A light and refreshing way to serve any fish.

1 pound fish fillets
2 tablespoons orange juice
1 teaspoon lemon juice
1 tablespoon butter or margarine, melted
Ground nutmeg to taste
Finely chopped fresh parsley or dried parsley flakes to taste
Lemon-pepper seasoning to taste
Orange slices

Preheat oven to 350 degrees. Wash fish fillets, pat dry, and place into an ungreased 13x9-inch baking dish, dark side down.

In a small bowl, combine orange juice, lemon juice, and butter or margarine; pour over fish fillets. Season with nutmeg, parsley, and lemon-pepper seasoning.

Bake, uncovered, 15 minutes or until fish is slightly opaque in thickest part (cut to test). Remove from oven, transfer onto a serving platter, and garnish with orange slices.

Makes 2 servings.

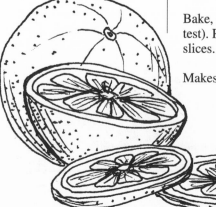

Baked Sole With Almonds

Flounder, trout, or snapper may also be baked this way.

3 pounds fillets of sole
Olive oil
Salt and pepper to taste
3 tablespoons butter
1/3 cup chopped onion
1/2 cup sliced mushrooms
1/4 cup white wine
1 tablespoon light cream
1 egg yolk, beaten
2 tablespoons chopped fresh parsley
1/2 cup toasted sliced almonds

Preheat oven to 350 degrees. Wash fillets, pat dry, and rub with olive oil, salt, and pepper; set aside on wax paper.

In a small saucepan over medium heat, melt butter. Add onion and mushrooms; sauté for 2 to 3 minutes or until onions are soft. Remove from heat and spread onto the bottom of an ungreased 13x9-inch baking dish; place fish fillets on top of the vegetables.

In a small bowl, combine white wine and cream; spread over the fish fillets. Bake, uncovered, 12 to 18 minutes or until fish is slightly opaque in thickest part (cut to test). Remove from oven and transfer onto a serving platter.

Into a small saucepan over medium heat, strain off a little of the sauce from the baked fish; thicken with egg yolk, stirring until it is no thicker than cream. Remove from heat and stir in parsley. To serve, pour sauce over the fish and sprinkle with toasted almonds.

Makes 4 servings.

Oven-Fried Fish

2 pounds fish fillets
1 tablespoon salt
1 cup milk
1 cup bread crumbs
4 tablespoons butter or margarine, melted

Preheat oven to 350 degrees. Butter a 13x9-inch baking dish. Wash fish fillets, pat dry, and cut into serving-sized pieces.

In a large bowl, combine salt and milk; add fillets, soaking for 10 minutes. In a shallow pie plate, place bread crumbs; roll fillets in crumbs, coating well. Place fillets into prepared baking dish. Top with butter or margarine.

Bake on top shelf of oven, uncovered, 10 to 15 minutes or until fish is slightly opaque in thickest part (cut to test). Remove from oven, transfer onto a serving platter, and serve immediately.

Makes 4 servings.

Sole

Sole is a member of the flatfish species that consists of sole, flounder, and halibut.

Sole is significantly superior in flavor and texture to the flounder. This is why much of the flounder sold in America is deceptively called "sole" by the fish markets and restaurants. Gray sole, lemon sole, rex sole, and the Dover sole of the Pacific are all flounders. Genuine sole are the true Dover sole, English sole, and turbot. When these fish are available in the United States, they are usually shipped frozen from Europe.

This lean fish lends itself to dozens of interesting ways of preparation. There are more ways of cooking sole than any other single fish in the world. It is popular with chefs in top restaurants, it is considered, along with the turbot, to be the finest of all white fish. Fried or baked are favorites, served with various sauces ranging from simple to elaborate.

Clams

All clams are mollusks that live in the sediments of bays, estuaries, or the ocean floor. There are three major types of clams.

SOFT-SHELL CLAMS: Known as steamers, manninoses, or squirts, they have brittle shells that break easily.

HARD-SHELL CLAMS: Known as quahog, littleneck, cherrystone, and hard clam.

SURF CLAMS: Make up the bulk of the commercial catch. They are used for preparing chowders, clam sauces, and fried clam strips.

Clams are sold in the shell or shucked. If in the shell, test to see that they are tightly closed. Discard any that float or have broken shells.

All clams are sandy. Before using, they should be scrubbed and washed in several changes of water. To remove sand from the inside of fresh clams, sprinkle them (still in their shells) with cornmeal and then cover them with cold water for thirty minutes. Lift the clams out of the water (do not drain them in a strainer).

Store live clams in an open container covered with a moist cloth for up to two days. Shucked clams, in their liquor, can be stored in the refrigerator for up to three days or in the freezer for up to three months.

Stuffed Fish Mornay

Use either sole, flounder, trout, or snapper fillets.

2 pounds fish fillets
2 tablespoons finely chopped onion
2 tablespoons finely chopped celery
3 bacon slices, cut up
1 1/2 cups bread crumbs
1/2 teaspoon mixed dried herbs of your choice, crushed
Salt and pepper to taste
1 tablespoon hot water
1 tablespoon butter or margarine
1 1/2 tablespoons all-purpose flour
1 cup milk
4 ounces shredded cheddar cheese
1/8 teaspoon ground mustard

Preheat oven to 350 degrees. Butter a 13x9-inch baking dish. Wash fish fillets, pat dry, and place half of the fish fillets into prepared baking dish.

In a medium frying pan over medium-high heat, sauté onion, celery, and bacon pieces until bacon is crisp. Stir in bread crumbs, herbs, salt, pepper, and hot water. Spread stuffing over fish fillets in the baking dish; cover with remainder of fish.

In a small saucepan over medium heat, melt butter or margarine. Add flour and milk; bring to a boil, stirring constantly. Remove from heat and add cheddar cheese, salt, pepper, and ground mustard; stir until cheese is melted. Pour cheese mixture over fish and bake, covered, 35 minutes or until fish is slightly opaque in thickest part (cut to test). Remove from oven and serve immediately.

Makes 4 servings.

Steamed Clams

Thoroughly wash 2 dozen steamer clams in shells.

In a large pot (with a steamer rack) over medium heat, place 1 cup hot water and heat until boiling. Reduce heat to low and bring water to a simmer. Add clams; cover and simmer 5 to 10 minutes or just until clams open (overcooking makes clams tough). Remove from heat and discard any unopened clams. Ladle clams and broth into individual bowls.

Serve with melted butter or cocktail sauce.

Maryland Crab Cakes

You won't believe how wonderful these crab cakes are.
Our husbands think they could win an award. You be the judge.

1 pound cooked blue crab meat or Dungeness crab meat
4 scallions (green part only), minced or 1/4 cup green onions, minced
1 tablespoon chopped fresh herbs (such as cilantro, dill, basil, or parsley)
1 1/2 teaspoons Old Bay seasoning
2 tablespoons or up to 1/4 cup bread crumbs
1/4 cup mayonnaise
Salt and white pepper to taste
1 large egg, slightly beaten
1/4 cup all-purpose flour
4 tablespoons vegetable oil

Carefully clean the crab meat of any shells or cartilage. In a large bowl, gently mix crab meat, scallions or green onions, herbs, Old Bay seasoning, bread crumbs, and mayonnaise. Season with salt and white pepper. Carefully fold in egg with a rubber spatula until mixture just clings together.

Divide crab mixture into four portions and shape each into a flat, round cake about 3 inches across and 1 1/2 inches high. Place onto a baking sheet lined with wax paper; cover with plastic wrap and refrigerate at least 3 hours or overnight (the cold will firm up the cakes so that they will not break up when fried).

Place flour into a shallow pie plate; lightly dredge crab cakes. In a large nonstick frying pan over medium-high heat, heat vegetable oil until hot but not smoking. Gently lay chilled crab cakes onto bottom of the pan; fry 4 to 5 minutes per side or until crisp and browned. Remove from heat, transfer onto a serving platter, and serve hot.

Makes 4 servings.

Angel Hair Pasta With Crab & Pesto

1 (8-ounce) package uncooked angel hair pasta
2 tablespoons extra-virgin olive oil
1/2 pound cooked crab meat
2 tablespoons butter or margarine
1/4 cup sliced fresh mushrooms
1/2 cup prepared pesto sauce
1 large tomato, coarsely chopped
1 teaspoon grated lemon zest
Freshly grated parmesan cheese

Cook pasta according to package directions; drain and return to pan to keep warm. Toss with olive oil. Carefully clean the crab meat of any shells or cartilage.

In a large frying pan over medium heat, melt butter or margarine. Add mushrooms and sauté 3 minutes or until tender. Mix in pesto, tomato, and lemon zest. Add crab meat and gently stir until thoroughly heated. Remove from heat. Transfer pasta onto a serving platter, spoon sauce over pasta, and serve with parmesan cheese.

Makes 4 servings.

Blue Crabs

Crab meat for cakes is traditionally from the blue crab, which can be found in many parts of the world, especially in the Chesapeake Bay and the Gulf of Mexico. Depending on the weather, they can be found from mid-spring to very late fall.

This delicious crab is sold in two forms: hard-shell and soft-shell. These terms describe the growth periods of the crab. A crab is normally hard-shelled. As the crab grows, it outgrows its shell and molts. It then sheds its shell. The blue crab typically undergoes this transformation several times a year.

Hard-shell blue crabs are used in recipes calling for crab meat. Soft-shell crabs are cleaned, cooked, and eaten whole.

Crabs

The Dungeness crab of the Pacific Coast is much larger than the blue crab found along the Atlantic Coast and in the Gulf of Mexico. King and snow crabs are caught in the north off the coast of Canada and Alaska. Stone crabs come from Florida.

Canned crab is usually the meat of the Japanese crab, a giant shellfish sometimes measuring as much as ten feet in leg spread.

TIP: Always use your fingers to pick over crab meat, fresh or canned, to make sure there are no tiny pieces of shells or cartilage.

Crab-Topped English Muffins

Looking for a new luncheon idea? This is it.

3 to 4 tablespoons butter or margarine
6 English muffins, split
1 (8-ounce) package cream cheese, room temperature
1 (8-ounce) can water chestnuts, drained and finely chopped
4 sliced green onions
2 teaspoons Dijon mustard
1/2 teaspoon hot pepper sauce
2 eggs, separated and room temperature
1/2 teaspoon salt
1/2 teaspoon pepper
2 (6-ounce) cans crab meat, drained, rinsed, and flaked
1 teaspoon fresh lemon juice
Paprika
Fresh parsley sprigs

Preheat broiler. Spread butter or margarine onto each English muffin half. Place onto an ungreased baking sheet and broil until light brown. Remove from oven and set aside.

In a medium bowl, combine cream cheese, water chestnuts, onions, Dijon mustard, hot pepper sauce, egg yolks, salt, and pepper. In a small bowl, sprinkle crab meat with lemon juice; gently fold into cream cheese mixture.

In a medium bowl, beat egg whites until stiff peaks form. Gently fold into crab meat mixture. Mound slightly onto toasted English muffins. Broil until golden brown. Remove from oven and sprinkle with paprika. Transfer onto individual serving plates, garnish with fresh parsley sprigs, and serve immediately.

Makes 6 servings.

Boiled Dungeness Crabs

3 Dungeness crabs, dressed
8 quarts water
1/2 cup salt
Butter, melted
Mayonnaise

Have your fish retailer dress the Dungeness crabs for cooking. Wash body cavity of each. In a large pot over high heat, bring water and salt to boiling; drop in crabs. Cover and heat to boiling; reduce heat to low and simmer 15 minutes. Remove from heat and drain.

Crack claws and legs. Serve hot with melted butter, or chill crabs and serve with mayonnaise.

Makes 6 servings.

Boiled Maine Lobster

Nothing tastes quite like a lobster, and nothing is as succulent when properly prepared. Usually, the simpler the preparation, the better. Serve with corn on the cob and barbecue baked beans.

In a large pot over medium-high heat, bring 1 gallon of water and 2/3 cup salt to a boil. Plunge live lobster, head first, into boiling water; reduce heat to low and simmer 10 to 15 minutes for a small-sized lobster (1 to 1 1/4 pounds), 15 to 20 minutes for a medium-sized lobster (1 1/2 pounds), or 20 minutes for a large-sized lobster (2 pounds). Lobsters are cooked when they turn a reddish or bright red color.

Remove lobster from pot and allow to cool, just long enough to be handled. Separate the head from the tail. Cut lobster tail down the center (from the shoulder down toward the tail) with cutlery shears, removing black vein from down the back, small sack in the back of the head, and spongy lungs. Crack the claws with a claw cracker (nut crackers also work).

NOTE: Don't forget to provide a scrap bowl when serving!

Serve with melted butter.

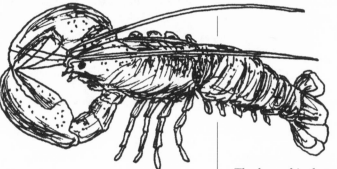

Oregon Baked Oysters

These also make great appetizers.

2 pints extra small oysters, drained
Lemon juice
Seasoned bread crumbs
Red (cayenne) pepper to taste

Preheat oven to 350 degrees and lightly grease a 13x9-inch baking dish. In a medium bowl, sprinkle oysters with lemon juice and stir gently; drain.

In a shallow pie plate, mix seasoned bread crumbs with cayenne pepper. Coat oysters with crumb mixture and place into prepared baking dish.

Bake, uncovered, 15 to 20 minutes or until edges of oysters begin to curl. Remove from oven and serve immediately.

Makes 2 to 3 servings.

Lobster

The American or Northern lobster is caught from Newfoundland to the Carolinas, but lobster is the essence of the Maine seacoast. Lobster and Maine are all but synonymous.

Did you know that for centuries lobsters were so abundant that they were usually considered food for the poor? According to regional legend, John D. Rockefeller Sr. rescued the lobster in 1910.

The legend is that a bowl of lobster stew, meant for the servants' table, was accidently sent upstairs (where it was rapturously received). From then on, it was given a permanent place on his menu. Back in New York, what was good enough for John D. was good enough for the rest of society.

IMPORTANT: When cooking lobster, if they do not move and appear to be dead, discard. Cook only live lobsters.

Oysters

There are four main varieties of oysters in the United States.

EASTERN: Known by many local names, depending on their origin.

OLYMPIA: Very small, from the Pacific coast.

BELON: European oysters now grown in North America.

JAPANESE: Very large, from the Pacific coast.

Oysters in the shell must be alive to be good to eat. If an oyster is open, even slightly, and it doesn't close tightly when handled, discard it. Dead oysters are unfit to eat. Always scrub oyster shells thoroughly before opening.

Open a half dozen oysters at a time by using the microwave. Place the scrubbed oysters in a single layer onto a microwave-proof dish; cover tightly and microwave two minutes.

Live oysters can be refrigerated for two or three days.

Scalloped Oysters

2 cups bread crumbs or salted cracker crumbs
6 tablespoons butter, melted and divided
1 pint oysters, drained (reserve juice)
1/2 cup onions, chopped
2 cups fresh mushrooms, sliced
1 cup light cream
Coarsely ground pepper to taste
2 tablespoons finely chopped fresh parsley

Preheat oven to 375 degrees and grease a 13x9-inch baking dish. In a small bowl, combine bread crumbs or cracker crumbs and 4 tablespoons butter. Spread half the bread crumb mixture onto the bottom of prepared baking dish. Place the oysters over the crumbs.

In a medium frying pan over medium heat, sauté onions in 2 tablespoons butter until onions are soft; add mushrooms and cook for 5 minutes. Cover oysters with mushroom mixture.

In a small bowl, combine 1/4 cup of reserved oyster juice, cream, and pepper; pour onto top of mushroom mixture. Top with the remaining bread crumb mixture and sprinkle with parsley. Bake, uncovered, 20 to 25 minutes or until golden brown on top. Remove from oven and serve immediately.

Makes 4 servings.

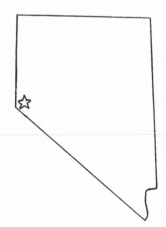

Nevada Oysters Casino

Oyster lovers delight.

1 pint oysters
1/2 cup minced green bell pepper
1/2 cup minced onion
3 bacon slices, minced
1 clove garlic, minced
Pepper to taste
1/2 cup bread crumbs
3 tablespoons lemon juice

Preheat oven to 350 degrees. Drain oysters and place into a 13x9-inch baking dish. Sprinkle with bell pepper, onion, bacon, garlic, and pepper. Sprinkle bread crumbs over all and then sprinkle with lemon juice.

Bake, uncovered, 15 to 20 minutes or until edges of oysters begin to curl. Remove from oven and serve immediately.

Makes 2 servings.

Oysters Rockefeller

You couldn't ask for a more elegant dish.

10 large oysters
1/2 cup cooked fresh spinach, drained and finely chopped
1 teaspoon lemon juice
1 tablespoon worcestershire sauce
1/4 cup minced onion
1/2 teaspoon salt
2 cloves garlic, minced
Cocktail Sauce
2 tablespoons butter
1/4 cup cracker crumbs
5 bacon slices, partially cooked
Lemon wedges

Preheat oven to 350 degrees. Scrub shells thoroughly before opening. Open oysters, leaving them on the half shell. Place shells on top of a thin bed of rock salt in an ungreased baking pan (the salt will keep the shells in place and hold the heat).

In a medium bowl, combine spinach, lemon juice, worcestershire sauce, onion, salt, and garlic; stir in enough Cocktail Sauce to form a paste. Cover each oyster with approximately 1 tablespoon of the mixture.

In a small saucepan over medium heat, melt the butter. Remove from heat and stir in cracker crumbs. Sprinkle each oyster with the crumb mixture. Cut each bacon strip into 8 pieces. Place 4 small pieces of bacon over each oyster.

Bake, uncovered, 10 to 15 minutes or until edges of oysters begin to curl. Remove from heat and transfer onto a serving platter. Serve with Cocktail Sauce and lemon wedges.

NOTE: To make in a casserole dish, arrange shucked oysters in a lightly greased shallow casserole dish. Top with cooked spinach mixture and sprinkle with bread crumbs. Bake, uncovered, at 375 degrees for 25 to 30 minute or until thoroughly heated.

Makes 2 servings.

COCKTAIL SAUCE:
1 cup chili sauce
1/2 cup catsup
2 tablespoons prepared horseradish
1 tablespoon worcestershire sauce
Juice of 1 lemon
1/8 teaspoon hot pepper sauce

In a medium bowl, combine chili sauce, catsup, prepared horseradish, worcestershire sauce, lemon juice, and hot pepper sauce. Refrigerate and use as needed.

Oysters Rockefeller

No other American dish has received so much praise and attention as Oysters Rockefeller. The name Rockefeller once connoted the absolute pinnacle of wealth and position.

The dish was created in 1899 by Jules Alciatore of the famous Antoine Restaurant. It was given the name Rockefeller because it is so gloriously rich and such an elegant food.

The original recipe has never left the restaurant but has been adapted and evolved in a host of ways. Jules Alciatore exacted a promise on his deathbed that the exact proportions be kept forever a secret.

Shucking

Shucking means to remove a natural outer covering from food, such as shells from oysters or husks from corn.

Grilled Oysters

So easy and so delicious.

36 large oysters in the shell
Melted butter
Hot sauce

Preheat barbecue grill. Scrub the oyster shells under cold running water with a brush. Discard any open shells, as the oyster is dead and not edible.

Place oysters on hot grill about 4 inches from hot coals. Cover barbecue with lid, open any vents, and cook 10 to 15 minutes or until shells begin to open. Using a mitt or towel to protect your hand, remove the oysters from the grill, taking care not to spill their juices.

Pry the oysters the rest of the way open with an oyster knife, paring knife, or screwdriver. Sever the muscle that connects the shells, leaving the oyster on the half shell. Transfer onto a serving platter. Serve with melted butter and your favorite hot sauce.

Makes 6 servings.

Broiled Scallops

For simple and extremely delicious scallops, try this recipe:

Preheat broiler. Cut fresh scallops into bite-sized pieces. Place them onto the bottom of a shallow baking dish. Place a teaspoon of butter or margarine on top of each and sprinkle with garlic powder.

Place dish under the broiler and cook for two to three minutes, just enough to brown the top without overcooking the scallops (overcooking will cause the scallops to become tough).

Spectacular Scallop Linguine

1 pound sea or bay scallops
1 (16-ounce) package uncooked linguine pasta
2 tablespoons butter
2 cloves garlic, minced
2 tablespoons finely chopped green onions
1/2 cup dry white wine
1/2 cup half and half cream
1/4 cup sour cream
2 teaspoons Dijon mustard
Salt and white pepper to taste
1 teaspoon lemon juice
Minced fresh parsley

Rinse scallops in cold water to remove any sand; dry on paper towels. Cook pasta according to package directions; drain and return to pan to keep warm.

In a large frying pan over medium heat, melt butter; add scallops and sauté 3 to 4 minutes or just until opaque, stirring and turning gently with a wooden spoon. Do not brown (overcooking will cause the scallops to become tough). Remove from heat and transfer scallops, leaving liquid in the pan, to a bowl.

Return frying pan to medium heat. Add garlic and green onions; cook, stirring constantly, for 30 seconds (do not brown). Add white wine and deglaze the pan, scraping pan to loosen any browned bits clinging to the bottom. Reduce the wine to approximately 2 tablespoons.

Add half and half cream and reduce until thickened. Stir in sour cream, Dijon mustard, salt, white pepper, and lemon juice. Add scallops and toss quickly in sauce to reheat. Remove from heat and pour over pasta; toss to coat thoroughly. Transfer onto individual serving plates and garnish with parsley.

Makes 4 servings.

Noodles With Scallops & Cilantro

3/4 pound sea scallops (cut in fourths) or bay scallops
1 (16-ounce) package uncooked egg noodles
4 tablespoons olive oil, divided
1 clove garlic, minced
1 medium onion, diced
1 small jalapeño chile pepper, cored, seeded, and quartered
1/3 cup dry white wine
1 1/2 cups chicken broth
1 small tomato, chopped
4 tablespoons butter or margarine, room temperature
1/4 teaspoon salt
Coarsely ground pepper to taste
1/4 cup finely minced fresh cilantro

Rinse scallops in cold water to remove any sand. Dry on paper towels.

Cook noodles according to package directions; drain and return to pan to keep warm. Toss with 1 tablespoon of olive oil.

In a large frying pan over medium heat, heat 3 tablespoons olive oil. Reduce heat to low and add garlic, onion, and jalapeño pepper; cook 2 minutes. Add scallops and cook another 2 minutes or just until opaque; remove scallops from pan and place into a small bowl.

Add white wine and chicken stock to frying pan. Reduce heat to low and simmer until mixture measures 2/3 cup. Stir tomato into sauce mixture; add scallops and simmer gently until thoroughly heated. Mix in butter or margarine and season with salt and pepper. Adjust seasoning and stir in the cilantro. Remove from heat.

Spoon scallop mixture over pasta; toss to coat evenly. Transfer onto individual serving plates and serve immediately.

Makes 4 servings.

Scallops

Although hundreds of different species of scallops exist in our oceans worldwide, only a few of these species are harvested commercially on a large scale. The three you're most likely to find at a fish market are Atlantic sea scallops, Atlantic bay scallops, and calicos.

The most expensive are the bay scallops, which are fished in shallow bays of water. They are small in size, about one-half to one inch.

The most common sold and used in recipes are the sea scallops. They can measure up to two inches in diameter and, if very fresh, are spectacular when quickly grilled.

TIPS: Scallops are extremely tender. Bay scallops are even more tender and sweeter than sea scallops. Only three to four minutes are required to cook them in simmering water.

Cut off the small tendon or sinew on the side of each scallop where the meat joins the shell. This piece can be tough.

Shrimp

1 pound of raw shrimp in their shells equals about 1/2 pound peeled and cooked shrimp.

They are found abundantly in America, off the Atlantic and Pacific seaboards in inshore waters, wherever the bottom is sandy.

Shrimp are in season from May to October and 95 percent of the shrimp caught come from the warm waters of the South Atlantic and Gulf states.

Honey-Mustard Shrimp Pasta

A very light and refreshing pasta dish. You'll make this many times.

1 (8-ounce) package uncooked fettuccine pasta
1 (8-ounce) can pineapple chunks, drain juice and reserve
1/4 cup dry sherry
1/4 cup white wine vinegar
1/4 cup honey
1 tablespoon vegetable oil
2 tablespoons Dijon mustard
1 tablespoon finely chopped fresh tarragon or 1 teaspoon dried tarragon, crushed
2 tablespoons butter or margarine
2 cloves garlic, minced
1/4 cup finely chopped onion
Red (cayenne) pepper or to taste
3/4 to 1 pound large shrimp, shelled and deveined

Cook pasta according to package directions; drain and return to pan to keep warm.

In a small saucepan over medium heat, combine reserved pineapple juice, sherry, wine vinegar, honey, vegetable oil, Dijon mustard, and tarragon until thoroughly heated; reduce heat to low and add pineapple chunks.

In a large frying pan over medium heat, melt butter or margarine. Add garlic, onion, and cayenne pepper; cook approximately 5 minutes or until onion is golden brown. Add shrimp and cook 4 to 5 minutes, stirring until opaque in center (cut to test). Add honey-mustard mixture; stir gently until well mixed. Remove from heat and pour over pasta; toss to coat evenly. Transfer onto individual serving plates.

Makes 2 servings.

Sautéed Shrimp

A fantastic shrimp dish.

2 tablespoons vegetable oil
3/4 to 1 pound large shrimp, shelled and deveined, tails still attached
All-purpose flour
1 tablespoon finely minced shallots
2 cloves garlic, minced
1 tablespoon fresh lemon juice
1/4 cup dry white wine
6 tablespoons butter or margarine
Salt and white pepper to taste

In a large frying pan over high heat, heat vegetable oil. In a medium bowl, dust the shrimp with flour. Add to heated oil and sauté 1 minute; turn and cook another 30 seconds. Drain oil from pan.

To the frying pan, add shallots, garlic, lemon juice, white wine, and butter or margarine; reduce heat to low, sauté 5 to 7 minutes or until sauce is reduced and until shrimp are opaque in center (cut to test). Season with salt and pepper. Remove from heat, transfer onto a serving platter, and serve immediately.

Makes 2 servings.

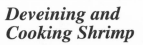

Angel Hair & Shrimp

1 (8-ounce) package uncooked angel hair pasta
2 tablespoons olive oil, divided
2 cloves garlic, minced
2 tablespoons finely chopped fresh basil
1 large tomato, chopped
Salt and coarsely ground pepper to taste
6 large shrimp, shelled and deveined

Cook pasta according to package directions; drain and return to pan to keep warm.

In a large frying pan over medium heat, heat 1 tablespoon olive oil. Add garlic and cook until light brown. Add basil, tomato, salt, and pepper; cook 5 to 7 minutes, stirring occasionally. Remove from heat and set aside.

In a small frying pan over medium heat, heat 1 tablespoon olive oil. Add shrimp and sauté 5 to 7 minutes or until shrimp are opaque in center (cut to test).

Add the pasta to tomato mixture; tossing to coat evenly. Place pasta onto individual serving plates, top with shrimp, and serve immediately.

Makes 2 servings.

Fettuccine & Shrimp in Wine Sauce

This is another one of those absolutely wonderful recipes.

1 (16-ounce) package uncooked fettuccine pasta
6 tablespoons butter or margarine
2 cloves garlic, minced
1 teaspoon all-purpose flour
1 cup white wine
1 cup whipping cream
3/4 cup chopped tomatoes
1/2 cup minced fresh dill
Salt and pepper to taste
3 cups steamed vegetables (asparagus, mushrooms, red bell pepper, or your choice)
3/4 pound cooked medium shrimp, shelled and deveined
Freshly grated parmesan cheese

Cook pasta according to package directions; drain and return to pan to keep warm.

In a medium saucepan over medium heat, melt butter or margarine. Add garlic and sauté until soft. Stir in flour and cook 1 to 2 minutes. Slowly add wine, stirring constantly. Add whipping cream, tomatoes, and fresh dill. Reduce heat to low and simmer another 5 to 10 minutes; season with salt and pepper. Remove from heat.

Stir steamed vegetables into hot pasta. Add sauce and shrimp; toss until mixed well. Transfer onto individual serving plates and top with parmesan cheese.

Makes 4 servings.

Deveining and Cooking Shrimp

Shrimp cook well in or out of their shells, but they're easier to devein before cooking.

DEVEINING SHRIMP:
Run the deveiner or the tip of a small knife down the back of the shrimp. This will allow you to remove the vein. You may remove the shell at this time or boil with shell on and remove after cooking. If frying, shell should be removed first.

COOKING SHRIMP:
Before cooking shrimp, run cold water over shrimp for one to two minutes. This will prevent shrimp from being tough.

They are very quick to cook, and the flavor can easily be ruined by overcooking. To properly cook, place a pound of shrimp in a quart of rapidly boiling water with three tablespoons of salt. Cover and return to a boil, then simmer until the flesh has lost its glossy appearance and is opaque in center (cut to test). Jumbo shrimp take about seven to eight minutes, large shrimp take about five to seven minutes, and medium size are done in about three to four minutes.

Once shrimp are cooked they should be plunged into cold water to stop the cooking process. (Do not let them cool in the cooking liquid. They will continue to cook and get tough.)

Mangoes

The peak season for Florida mangoes is from May to September; however, imported mangoes are available year round.

The color of the mango does not indicate ripeness. They can be yellow, green, and red. When ripe, the skin is soft to the touch. A ripe mango should have a pleasant perfume-like scent and golden yellow flesh.

Store at room temperature until ripe. To ripen quickly, enclose it in a paper bag with other fruit. Refrigerate ripe fruit to prevent spoilage. Mangoes freeze fairly well.

TO SERVE: Mangoes have a flat, oval seed in the center; fruit clings to it. To get the flesh out, stand the mango stem side up on a cutting board. Slice each side along the seed to free it and create three pieces.

Score through the pulp, down to the peel in tic-tac-toe fashion. This makes it easier to get uniform cubes. Hold scored portion with both hands; bend the peel backwards and push center up. Cut cubes along peel and serve or eat as is.

To remove the rest of the fruit, cut around seed at one-inch intervals with a paring knife. Cut cubes off seed on both sides.

TIP: When selecting mangoes, remember one thing: A MANGO THAT SMELLS WONDERFUL, TASTES WONDERFUL.

Grilled Shrimp With Tropical Fruit Salsa

1/2 cup soy sauce
1/4 cup lime juice
2 cloves garlic, minced
1 1/2 pounds large shrimp, shelled and deveined
Vegetable oil
Salt and pepper to taste
Tropical Fruit Salsa

In a shallow glass dish or a large heavy plastic bag, combine soy sauce, lime juice, and garlic. Add shrimp; cover dish or close bag. Marinate in refrigerator 15 to 30 minutes.

Preheat barbecue grill. Remove shrimp from marinade with a slotted spoon; discard marinade. Thread shrimp onto metal skewers. Brush one side of shrimp lightly with vegetable oil; season with salt and pepper.

Oil hot grill to help prevent sticking. Place shrimp, oil side down, onto hot grill. Cover barbecue with lid, open any vents, and cook 5 to 6 minutes. Halfway through cooking time, brush tops of shrimp with oil, season with salt and pepper; turn and continue grilling until shrimp are opaque in center (cut to test). Remove from grill, transfer onto a serving platter, and serve with Tropical Fruit Salsa.

Makes 4 servings.

TROPICAL FRUIT SALSA:
2 mangos, peeled, seeded, and cut into 1/4-inch pieces
2 kiwi fruit, peeled and cut into wedges
3 tablespoons finely chopped red onion
3 tablespoons lime juice
1/4 teaspoon salt
1/3 teaspoon crushed red pepper flakes
1 teaspoon sugar
1 tablespoon finely chopped fresh mint leaves
1 tablespoon finely chopped fresh cilantro

In a medium bowl, combine mangos, kiwi fruit, onion, lime juice, salt, red pepper, sugar, mint leaves, and cilantro; adjust flavors to taste. Cover and refrigerate at least 2 hours or overnight.

VARIATION: Substitute 1 papaya or 2 large or 3 medium peaches for the mangos.

Yields 1 cup.

Shrimp Tex-Mex Stir-Fry

2 tablespoons vegetable oil, divided
1 1/2 cups broccoli flowerets
2 carrots, thinly sliced diagonally
1 red or green bell pepper, cored, seeded, and thinly sliced
1/2 cup thinly sliced celery
1 pound medium shrimp, shelled and deveined
1/3 cup fajita or enchilada sauce
2 tablespoons firmly packed brown sugar
1 teaspoon ground ginger
1 teaspoon ground mustard
3 cups cooked rice, chilled
Sliced almonds, lightly toasted (optional)

In a large frying pan or wok over medium-high heat, heat 1 tablespoon vegetable oil. Add broccoli, carrots, bell pepper, and celery; stir-fry 3 minutes. Remove from pan with slotted spoon, place into a medium bowl, and set aside. Add 1 tablespoon vegetable oil and shrimp to the hot pan; stir-fry 2 minutes. Return vegetables to hot pan; pour in fajita or enchilada sauce, brown sugar, ginger, and ground mustard. Cook another 2 minutes, toss gently to blend. Remove from heat, cover, and set aside.

In a medium frying pan over high heat, place chilled rice; stir-fry 3 to 5 minutes or until slightly crisp and browned. Remove from heat and transfer rice onto a serving platter. Serve shrimp and vegetables over rice; sprinkle with almonds.

Makes 6 servings.

Grilled Teriyaki Shrimp

2 tablespoons vegetable oil
1/4 cup soy sauce
1 1/2 teaspoons cider vinegar
2 tablespoons red wine
Garlic powder to taste
Salt and pepper to taste
1/2 cup water
1 teaspoon freshly grated ginger
2 green onions, chopped
1 1/2 pounds large shrimp, shelled and deveined

In a medium bowl, combine vegetable oil, soy sauce, cider vinegar, and red wine. Add garlic powder, salt, pepper, water, ginger, and green onions; stir until well blended. Add shrimp; cover bowl and marinate in refrigerator 15 to 30 minutes.

Preheat barbecue grill. Remove shrimp from marinade with a slotted spoon, reserving marinade. Thread shrimp onto metal skewers. Oil hot grill to help prevent sticking. Place shrimp onto hot grill.

Cover barbecue with lid, open any vents, and cook 5 to 6 minutes. Halfway through cooking time, brush shrimp with additional marinade; turn and continue grilling until shrimp are opaque in center (cut to test). Remove from grill, transfer onto a serving platter.

Makes 4 servings.

Stir-Frying

Use a vegetable oil with a high smoking point, just as you would for deep-frying. This would include peanut, safflower, or corn oil and rules out the stronger-flavored olive or walnut oils, which have low smoking points.

Choose foods that are tender enough to cook quickly but have enough resilience to withstand constant stirring. White fish and some starchy vegetables tend to break up.

Garlic, onions, and scallions add important flavor to stir-fried food. To extract as much flavor as possible, add them to the oil on low heat at first. Let them cook for a few minutes before turning up the heat and adding other ingredients.

Freshly grated or chopped ginger root adds an unusual and distinctly Oriental flavor to any stir-fry.

Soy sauce is the traditional seasoning for Chinese cuisine. If you use soy, be sparing with the salt, as the sauce itself is very salty. Use fresh-ground black pepper and, for variety, a shake of cayenne pepper, ground ginger, a little curry, or chili paste. Even a little sugar or honey can be added for a hint of sweetness.

TIP: For even cooking in stir-frying, cut foods into equal-sized pieces. Freeze poultry, fish, and meat for fifteen to thirty minutes before cutting, just long enough to firm them.

Sesame Oil

Sesame oil has been used in cooking in Africa and the Far East for many centuries. The main advantage of sesame oil over other oils is that it does not turn rancid, even in hot weather. For this reason, it is very popular in tropical countries.

REGULAR SESAME OIL: This light-colored oil is used in most Chinese cooking. It adds a distinctive nutty flavor to foods and is good for cooking. It is also very good in salad dressings. Purchase in glass rather than plastic bottles.

ASIAN SESAME OIL: This amber-colored oil is pressed from toasted sesame seeds. It is a strong-flavored, aromatic oil that is used in Oriental cooking. This sesame oil is not used as a cooking oil but is added at the last minute for flavor in hot cooked dishes or in marinades. Purchase in glass rather than plastic bottles. Refrigerate after opening.

Thai Shrimp & Noodles

Your family and friends will be delighted with this unusual peanutty pasta dish.

1 pound medium shrimp, shelled and deveined
1/3 cup Italian salad dressing
1 (8-ounce) package uncooked angel hair pasta
2 tablespoons vegetable oil
1 tablespoon sesame oil (regular)
1 cup chopped green onions
2 tablespoons chopped fresh cilantro
Thai Peanut Sauce

In a large bowl, combine shrimp and Italian salad dressing. Cover and refrigerate 30 minutes. Remove shrimp with a slotted spoon, discarding salad dressing.

Cook pasta according to package directions; drain and return to pan to keep warm.

In a large frying pan over medium-high heat, heat vegetable oil and sesame oil until hot; add shrimp and green onions; cook 3 to 4 minutes, stirring constantly, or until shrimp are opaque in center (cut to test). Remove from heat.

Add shrimp mixture, Thai Peanut Sauce, and cilantro to hot pasta; toss until well mixed. Transfer onto individual serving plates to serve.

Makes 4 servings.

THAI PEANUT SAUCE:
2 tablespoons smooth peanut butter, room temperature
1 tablespoon soy sauce
1 tablespoon honey
1 teaspoon freshly grated ginger
1/2 teaspoon red (cayenne) pepper
2/3 cup Italian salad dressing

In a small bowl, combine peanut butter, soy sauce, honey, ginger, cayenne pepper, and salad dressing; set aside.

Paella

Paella, the glory of the Spanish table, is found in many versions, as ingredients vary from region to region. The dish originated in Valencia on the Mediterranean coast. Peasants working in the rice fields would collect snails and eels from the marshes and cook them with saffron and rice. A bottle of wine, salad and bread are all you need to make a terrific dinner.

3 chicken breasts, boneless and skinless
1/4 cup olive oil
2 cloves garlic, chopped
1/3 cup finely chopped onion
1/2 teaspoon pepper
2 teaspoons paprika
1 large green bell pepper, cored, seeded
   and chopped
2 cups uncooked long-grain rice
1 (8-ounce) package frozen peas
2 large tomatoes, peeled and chopped coarsely
4 cups chicken broth
1/4 teaspoon saffron
1 pound shrimp, shelled and deveined
16 steamer clams, washed
1 cup hot water
Chopped fresh parsley
Lemon wedges

Preheat oven to 350 degrees. Cut chicken into small pieces. In a large paella pan, an electric fry pan, or heavy cast-iron pan over medium-high heat, heat olive oil. Add chicken and brown well. Add garlic, onion, pepper, paprika, and bell pepper; stir to blend. Cook 3 minutes. Remove from heat; stir in rice, peas, and tomatoes.

In a large saucepan over medium-high heat, bring chicken stock to a boil, add saffron and stir to dissolve; add to chicken mixture. Return to heat and cook chicken mixture 10 minutes (DO NOT STIR).

Reduce heat to low, cover, and simmer 10 to 15 minutes or until chicken and rice are tender. Uncover pan. Add shrimp, pushing well into liquid; stir lightly with fork. (If using an electric fry pan, transfer into an ungreased 13x9-inch baking dish.) Place in oven and cook, uncovered, 15 minutes or until almost all liquid is absorbed.

Scrub clam shells well with a brush. In a large pot (with a steamer rack) over medium heat, pour 1 cup hot water and heat until boiling. Reduce heat to low and bring water to a simmer. Add clams; cover and simmer 5 to 10 minutes or just until clams open. Remove from heat and discard any unopened clams.

Remove paella from oven. To serve, sprinkle with chopped parsley. Arrange clams and lemon wedges around the top of the paella. Serve immediately. To eat, sprinkle lemon juice over paella.

Makes 8 servings.

Paella

This one-pot dish gets its name from the heavy iron frying pan with two handles in which it is customarily cooked and served. In the absence of a proper paella pan, use a large frying pan, a sauté pan, or a wide-bottomed casserole dish.

Saffron

Saffron, the yellow-orange stigmas from a small purple crocus, is the world's most expensive spice. That's because each flower provides only three stigmas (which must be handpicked and dried), and it takes fourteen thousand of these tiny threads for each ounce of saffron. It is imported from Spain. This spice comes either powdered or in threads (the whole stigmas).

Since heat releases saffron's flavor essence, it's usually steeped in hot water or broth before being added to foods.

TIP: Powdered saffron loses its flavor more rapidly and can easily be adulterated with less-expensive powders like turmeric. Buying cheaper saffron won't save money in the long run, since more will be needed for the same flavor impact.

Northwest Gumbo

This is the northwest version of the famous Creole dish. It is a lighter, simpler version of the Southern gumbo.

1/2 pound cooked Dungeness crab meat
1 cup vegetable oil
1 cup all-purpose flour
1 pound onions, minced
1 pound green bell peppers, cored, seeded, and minced
3 quarts fish broth (can substitute vegetable broth)
2 large (3-pound) cooked Dungeness crabs, cleaned and cracked
1 to 1 1/2 pounds Polish sausage, cut into 1-inch chunks
2 pounds extra large shrimp, shelled and deveined
2 pints fresh shucked small Olympic or Pacific oysters, undrained
2 tablespoons hot pepper sauce
Salt to taste
1/4 cup chopped fresh parsley
12 to 14 cups hot cooked long-grain white rice

Carefully clean the crab meat of any shells or cartilage; set aside.

In a large frying pan on medium-high heat, heat vegetable oil. Add flour all at once; cook 7 to 8 minutes, stirring often until roux is a rich, deep caramel color. Remove from heat and add onions and bell peppers; stir until foaming stops and vegetables are soft.

In a large pot over high heat, bring fish broth to a boil; add hot roux and stir until blended. Add crabs in shell and sausage; reduce heat to low, cover, and simmer 5 to 10 minutes very gently so flavors mingle. Add 1/2 pound of crab meat, shrimp, oysters with liquid, hot pepper sauce, and salt; simmer another 5 to 10 minutes. Remove from heat.

Transfer gumbo into a large serving bowl and sprinkle with parsley. To serve, ladle portions of the gumbo over rice in wide soup bowls.

Makes 12 to 14 servings.

Manhattan-Style Seafood Stew

This delicious and colorful stew lends itself to the ever-popular "Manhattan Clam Chowder," but with a few twists and turns. The addition of shrimp and scallops make it a full hardy meal. Serve it with salad and bread.

3 (28-ounce) cans Italian plum tomatoes, drained
5 bacon slices, chopped
1 1/2 large onions, chopped
5 large shallots or green onions, chopped
3 (8-ounce) bottles clam juice
3/4 cup dry white wine
3 dried bay leaves
1/4 teaspoon red (cayenne) pepper or to taste
1 pound white potatoes, peeled, quartered lengthwise, and thinly sliced
Salt and pepper to taste
24 clams (3 1/2 pounds), washed
1/2 pound scallops, halved widthwise
1/2 pound medium shrimp, shelled, deveined
1/4 cup chopped fresh basil leaves, divided
1 tablespoon thinly sliced lemon peel

In a food processor, chop tomatoes, set aside.

In a large pot or dutch oven over medium heat, cook bacon 5 minutes or until crisp. Add onions and shallots or green onions; sauté 8 minutes or until soft. Add tomatoes, clam juice, white wine, bay leaves and cayenne pepper. Reduce heat to low and simmer another 20 minutes, stirring occasionally.

Add potatoes and simmer an additional 20 minutes or until tender. Season with salt and pepper. (Can be prepared one day ahead. Cover and refrigerate. Return to simmer before continuing.)

Add clams to seafood stew. Cover and simmer 5 minutes longer or until clams begin to open. Add scallops and shrimp, cover and simmer another 3 minutes or until clams open and scallops and shrimp are cooked through. (Discard any clams that do not open.) Mix in 1/2 of basil. Remove from heat and transfer into a large serving bowl. To serve, sprinkle with remaining basil and lemon peel. Serve immediately.

Makes 4 servings.

Seafood Stews

Seafood stews made with fish fresh from the sea are real fishermen's meals. Assorted fish collected in a fisherman's nets and not sold on the dock went into his family's cooking pot.

In the olden days, this was literally one big iron pot on the open fire. The fisherman's wife put everything into it. The assorted fish with locally grown vegetables and herbs made a simmering rich broth.

These one-pot meals are still served from north to south, and in Europe and America. Every coastal community makes its own version. The ingredients and the flavorings vary to some extent in differing climates, but the method does not.

Fish for Stewing

There are several varieties of fish you can use to make a seafood stew. The fish needs to be firm because the large quantity of liquid bubbling around the chunks of fish would break them up if they were soft.

Shellfish are absolutely ideal for use in stews, as they can be put into the hot liquid for the last few minutes of cooking.

Use more than one if you choose, such as flounder, whiting, sole, haddock, perch, salmon, or rock fish. Whatever is on sale that week!

Midwestern Fish Stew

1/2 pound lean bacon, diced
1 cup sliced onion
2 cups fish broth or chicken broth
2 cups dry white wine or water
1 (16-ounce) can tomatoes, undrained, and cut up
1 pound red potatoes, quartered
1/2 cup finely chopped fresh parsley
2 teaspoons minced fresh tarragon or 1/2 teaspoon dried tarragon, crushed
2 teaspoons minced fresh thyme or 1/2 teaspoon dried thyme, crushed
1/4 teaspoon pepper
1 medium-sized green bell pepper, cored, seeded and thinly sliced
1 cup chopped fresh green beans
6 fresh or frozen corn on the cobs
1 1/2 pounds boneless, skinless fish, cut into 1-inch chunks
Salt to taste

In a large pot or dutch oven over medium heat, cook bacon until almost crisp. Add onion and cook until soft; drain off bacon fat and discard. Add fish broth or chicken broth, white wine or water, tomatoes, potatoes, parsley, tarragon, thyme, and pepper; bring to a boil.

Reduce heat to low and simmer, partially covered, 20 to 25 minutes or until potatoes are almost tender. Add bell pepper, green beans, corn, and fish; simmer, covered, another 7 to 9 minutes or until fish flakes easily with a fork. Season with salt. Remove from heat, transfer into a large serving bowl, and serve immediately.

Makes 6 servings.

Cheater's Fish Stock

If you don't have or can't find fish stock, this works great. The important thing to remember about clam juice is that it is extremely salty, so don't add salt to the stock.

1 small onion, minced
1 medium carrot, peeled and minced
2 celery stalks, minced
8 stems fresh parsley, chopped
1 cup dry white wine
3 (8-ounce) bottles clam juice
3 cups water
1 dried hot chile pepper
2 large dried bay leaves
8 whole black peppercorns
1/2 teaspoon dried thyme, crushed
1 tablespoon lemon juice

In a large pot or dutch oven over medium-high heat, combine onion, carrot, celery, parsley, wine, clam juice, and water; bring to a boil. Reduce heat to low and add chile pepper, bay leaves, peppercorns, thyme, and lemon juice; simmer 30 minutes to blend flavors. Remove from heat and strain through cheesecloth, pressing solids with back of a spoon to extract as much liquid as possible. Use in place of regular fish stock.

Yields approximately 1 quart.

Shrimp Cocktail Sauce

1 cup mayonnaise
1/3 cup catsup
1/4 teaspoon prepared horseradish
3 tablespoons worcestershire sauce
Salt and pepper to taste

In a small bowl, combine mayonnaise, catsup, horseradish, worcestershire sauce, salt, and pepper. Transfer into a serving bowl and serve with boiled shrimp.

Yields 1 1/2 cups.

Sauces

A good sauce is the perfect compliment to fish. The more modest the fish and the plainer the method of cooking, the more important the sauce becomes for adding both richness and flavor.

Tartar Sauce

3 tablespoons dill pickles, finely minced
1 tablespoon drained capers, finely minced
1 cup mayonnaise
1 tablespoon lemon juice
2 teaspoons grated onion

In a small bowl, combine pickles and capers; drain through a tea strainer. Return to bowl and add mayonnaise. Add lemon juice and onion; mix well, cover, and refrigerate.

Yields 1 cup.

Herb Mayonnaise

2 cups mayonnaise
1 tablespoon drained capers
1 tablespoon chopped fresh parsley
1 tablespoon chopped scallion greens
1 clove garlic
4 fresh basil leaves, chopped
Salt to taste

In a food processor or blender, combine mayonnaise, capers, parsley, scallion greens, garlic, basil, and salt; whirl until smooth. Refrigerate until serving.

Yields 2 cups.

Herb Butters

Herb butters are great finishes for grilled or broiled fish, adding a touch of fresh flavor.

They are an excellent way of adding both fat and flavoring to fish when baking, broiling, or grilling. Oily fish do not need the extra fat as much as white fish. The herbs or other flavoring in the butter makes the fish more interesting, while the butter provides a little sauce at the same time. Be sure to pour the buttery juices from the pan over the fish just before serving.

Be creative; add a few capers or peppercorns, if you like. Taste as you create!

Lemon Hazelnut Butter

Excellent served over salmon.

1 cup plus 3 tablespoons unsalted butter, divided
2 tablespoons finely chopped shallots or green onions
1/2 cup dry white wine
1/4 cup hazelnut liqueur, divided
3 tablespoons fresh lemon juice
1/2 teaspoon salt
1/8 teaspoon white pepper
1/4 cup toasted hazelnuts, finely chopped

In a medium saucepan over medium heat, melt 2 tablespoons of butter. Add the shallots or green onions and cook, stirring until soft. Add white wine, 3 tablespoons of the hazelnut liqueur, and the lemon juice. Bring to a boil and cook over high heat until reduced to 3 tablespoons. Reduce heat to low and stir in the remaining butter, 1 tablespoon at a time, stirring until the sauce thickens.

Remove from heat and add the remaining hazelnut liqueur, salt, white pepper, and hazelnuts. Transfer into a serving bowl.

Yields 1 1/2 cups.

Fresh Basil Butter

1/2 cup unsalted butter
Juice of 1 lemon
Salt and pepper to taste
Bunch of basil, rinsed and coarsely chopped

In a medium saucepan over medium heat, melt butter; add lemon juice, stirring until well blended. Add salt, pepper, and basil. Heat just enough to wilt basil but not to cook it. Do not brown. Pour basil butter over fish and serve.

Yields 3/4 cup.

VARIATIONS:
HERB BUTTER: Using a food processor, combine 1/2 cup softened butter with several leaves of fresh tarragon, basil, marjoram, or parsley. Whirl until combined.

DILL BUTTER: Combine 3 tablespoons snipped fresh dill, a squeeze of lemon juice, and a dab of mustard; blend with 1/2 cup softened butter.

ORANGE BUTTER: Add 2 teaspoons each of grated orange zest and orange juice to 1/2 cup softened butter.

Soups

Brazilian Black Bean Soup

This soup freezes wonderfully. Serve it with a crisp green salad and hot cornbread.

2 cups dry black beans or 3 (15-ounce) cans black beans, drained and rinsed
4 carrots, chopped
1 medium onion, chopped
3/4 pound cooked ham or chicken, diced
    (NOTE: You can leave out the meat if desired)
4 cloves garlic, minced
2 tablespoons olive oil
2 teaspoons salt
1 teaspoon ground cumin
1/2 teaspoon red (cayenne) pepper
2 whole cloves
1 teaspoon dried coriander, crushed
4 cups water
2 cups beef broth
2 tablespoons lime juice
1/4 cup dry sherry or rum
Green onions, finely chopped
Shredded monterey jack cheese
Sour cream for garnish

If using dry beans, sort, rinse, and drain. In a large soup pot over medium-high heat, place beans and cover with cold water; bring to a boil. Remove from heat; cover and let stand 1 to 2 hours. Drain and rinse beans; set aside.

In the same soup pot over medium heat, combine carrots, onion, ham or chicken, and garlic with olive oil; cook and stir until the vegetables are softened. Stir in salt, cumin, cayenne pepper, cloves, and coriander; cook, stirring for 1 minute. Add beans, water, and beef broth; bring just to a boil. Reduce heat and simmer 1 1/2 to 2 hours or until beans are tender (do not boil or beans will burst).

Remove 2 cups of soup mixture and place into food processor or blender bowl; let cool 5 minutes (if you do not let cool slightly before processing, mixture will explode out of container and make a mess in your kitchen). After cooling, whirl until puréed. Stir puréed mixture into remaining soup.

Remove from heat. Add lime juice. Pour sherry or rum over top of soup. Serve in soup bowls topped with green onions, monterey jack cheese, and sour cream.

Makes 4 to 6 servings.

Soaking Dried Beans

1 pound dried beans equals approximately 2 1/2 cups uncooked beans or 5 1/2 to 6 1/2 cups cooked beans.

Before preparing dried beans, sort through them thoroughly for tiny pebbles or other debris.

Dried beans are often soaked too long. Most recipes say overnight. The best way is to put them in cold water; bring them gently to a boil and then, with saucepan off the heat, allow them to remain in the water for one to two hours only. Do not add salt to the cooking water (it hardens the skins).

If soaked too long, they may ferment, which affects their flavor and makes them difficult to digest.

When cooking beans, always simmer. Boiling can cause the cooking liquid to overflow, as well as the beans to break apart and the skins to separate.

> *IMPORTANT:*
> *To help in the digestion of beans, always discard the water in which they were soaked.*

Beans taste better if cooked a day ahead, but they should be refrigerated to avoid becoming sour. When cooked, they can be frozen.

Soups

TIPS: Refrigerate cooked stews and soups overnight before serving. The fat will rise to the top and you can skim it off before heating and serving.

In a hurry to skim the fat from the soup? An ice cube floated in the soup will help to congeal the fat and make it easier to remove.

A leaf of lettuce dropped in a pot of soup absorbs the grease from the top.

Soups and stews should only simmer (NEVER BOIL) when cooking.

Freeze the liquids from canned mushrooms or vegetables; use it in soups or stews later.

To remove excessive salt from soup, drop in a sliced raw potato.

To thicken your soup, take some of the cooked vegetables out of the soup and purée in the blender. Then return to the original soup mixture.

Southwestern Black Bean Soup

2 1/2 cups dry black beans
1 (14 1/2-ounce) can beef broth
6 cups water
1 large carrot, grated
2 tablespoons taco seasoning mix
1 pound chorizo sausage or hot Italian sausage in casings
2 (14 1/4-ounce) cans stewed tomatoes, undrained
1 (15 1/4-ounce) can corn kernels with green and red sweet peppers, undrained
1 tablespoon lemon juice
Yogurt Topping

Sort, rinse, and drain beans. In a large soup pot over medium-high heat, place beans and cover with cold water; bring to a boil. Remove from heat; cover and let stand 1 to 2 hours. Drain and rinse beans.

In the same soup pot over medium heat, combine beans, beef broth, water, carrot, and taco seasoning mix; bring to a boil. Reduce heat to low, cover, and simmer 1 1/2 to 2 hours or until beans are tender (do not boil or beans will burst). NOTE: Soup can be prepared to this point and frozen up to 1 month.

Pierce sausage several times and brown 15 minutes in a large frying pan over medium heat, turning often. Remove from heat and drain on paper towels. Cut sausage into thin slices. Add to soup along with stewed tomatoes, corn, and lemon juice; stir until well blended. Cover partially and simmer another 30 minutes. Remove from heat.

Serve in soup bowls topped with a dollop of Yogurt Topping.

Makes 8 servings.

YOGURT TOPPING:
4 tablespoons plain yogurt
4 tablespoons sour cream
1 green onion, finely chopped

In small bowl, combine yogurt, sour cream, and green onion; stir until well blended.

Home at Six Soup

With these familiar ingredients on the pantry shelf, this hearty soup can be put on the table in a flash.

1 pound lean ground beef
1 large onion, chopped
1 (28-ounce) can whole tomatoes, cut up and undrained
1 (15 1/2-ounce) can kidney beans, undrained
1 (15 1/4-ounce) can corn kernels, undrained
1 (8-ounce) can tomato sauce
1 tablespoon chili powder
1/2 teaspoon ground cumin
1/2 teaspoon dried basil, crushed
Shredded cheddar cheese

In a large soup pot over medium-high heat, combine ground beef and onion; sauté until beef is brown (drain off fat). Stir in tomatoes, kidney beans, corn, tomato sauce, chili powder, cumin, and basil; bring to a boil. Reduce heat to low, cover, and simmer 1 hour. Remove from heat. Serve in soup bowls and garnish with cheddar cheese.

Makes 6 servings.

Lentil Soup

This delicious soup makes a perfect winter meal. It also freezes very well.

Ham or bacon pieces to taste
2 1/2 cups or 1 (16-ounce) package dried lentils
6 cups chicken broth
1 large onion, chopped
1/2 cup grated carrots
4 tablespoons butter or margarine
1 teaspoon dried thyme, crushed
1/8 teaspoon ground nutmeg
Salt and white pepper to taste

In a large soup pot over medium-high heat, combine ham or bacon pieces, lentils, and chicken broth; bring just to a boil. Reduce heat to low and simmer 1 to 1 1/2 hours or until lentils are soft.

Remove 2 cups of cooked lentils and place into food processor or blender bowl; let cool 5 minutes (if you do not let cool slightly before processing, mixture will explode out of container and make a mess in your kitchen). After cooling, whirl until puréed. Stir puréed lentils into soup mixture.

In a medium frying pan over medium-high heat, sauté onion and carrots in butter or margarine until limp, but do not brown; add to lentils. Add thyme, nutmeg, salt, and white pepper; simmer another 30 minutes. Remove from heat and serve in soup bowls.

Makes 6 servings.

Soup Stock

A stock may be defined as a clear, thin (unthickened) liquid flavored by soluble substances extracted from meat, poultry, and fish; also from their bones, and from vegetables and seasonings.

The very best soups are made with homemade stock, but practically speaking, it may not always be possible to take the time to make stock, and not everyone has freezer space to keep it on hand.

Save all extra bones and store them in the freezer until you are ready to make stock. Keep meat, poultry, and fish bones in separate packages. Uncooked bones are preferable to cooked ones, which tend to make a stock cloudy.

After cooking, let cool and then chill; this will allow you to remove all the fat from the top.

TIP: Never try to make stock in a hurry (use canned broth or water instead). Long slow simmering, from four to six hours, is the essence of good stock.

Lentils

Lentils are like miniature peas except they are flat. They have an outer membrane with the seed inside. The seeds of lentils are split like the seeds of peas. Lentils do not require a soaking period.

Soups

Although soups are not served frequently as a first course today, they are often a principal part of a light meal. Soups are liquids which can be very thin or quite thick, depending upon what they contain, and are classified according to their thickness or to the principle liquid or other ingredients they contain. Here is one system of classification:

STOCKS OR BROTHS: *Bouillons and consommés.*

CREAM SOUPS: *Those thickened with a white sauce.*

BISQUES: *Heavy cream soups usually containing shellfish. The name is now given to any creamed soup, including tomato.*

PURÉES: *Thickened with cooked vegetables or fish passed through a sieve or puréed with a blender or a food processor.*

CHOWDERS: *Thick soups or stews usually containing seafood, potatoes, and milk or cream.*

POTTAGES: *Broths heavy with ingredients such as gumbo, chicken, noodles, or vegetables.*

Minestrone Soup

1 pound lean ground beef
1 cup chopped onion
1 cup chopped celery
1/2 cup chopped green bell pepper
6 cups water
1 (15 1/2-ounce) can kidney beans, drained and rinsed
1 (15-ounce) can tomato sauce
1 cup chopped carrots
4 teaspoons salt
1 tablespoon dried oregano, crushed
1 1/2 teaspoons dried thyme, crushed
1 teaspoon pepper
1 1/2 cups uncooked sea shell pasta noodles

In a large soup pot over medium-high heat, combine ground beef, onion, celery, and bell pepper; sauté until beef is brown (drain off fat). Stir in water, kidney beans, tomato sauce, carrots, salt, oregano, thyme, and pepper. Reduce heat to low, cover, and simmer 1 hour. Add uncooked pasta noodles and simmer another 10 minutes or until noodles are tender. Remove from heat and serve in soup bowls.

Makes 6 servings.

Heartland Beef & Vegetable Soup

Serve with a nice salad and a loaf of fresh bread for a real hearty meal.

1 1/2 pounds ground beef
1 clove garlic, minced
1 medium onion, sliced
1/2 cup uncooked long-grain rice
1 teaspoon salt
1 teaspoon dried basil, crushed
1 teaspoon dried oregano, crushed
1 teaspoon dried rosemary, crushed
1/4 teaspoon dried thyme, crushed
1 teaspoon dried marjoram leaves, crushed
6 cups beef broth
1 teaspoon worcestershire sauce
1 (14 1/2-ounce) can stewed tomatoes, undrained
1 (16-ounce) package frozen broccoli and cauliflower

In a large soup pot over medium-high heat, combine ground beef, garlic, and onion; sauté until beef is brown (drain off fat). Add rice, salt, basil, oregano, rosemary, thyme, marjoram, beef broth, worcestershire sauce, and tomatoes; bring to a boil. Reduce heat to low, cover, and simmer 10 minutes, stirring occasionally.

Add frozen broccoli and cauliflower; cook, covered, another 10 minutes or until vegetables are crisp-tender. Remove from heat and serve in soup bowls.

Makes 8 servings.

Pasta Meatball Minestrone

1/2 pound lean ground beef
1/2 pound sweet Italian sausage
2 tablespoons Italian-seasoned bread crumbs
1 tablespoon freshly grated parmesan cheese
1/4 teaspoon salt
1/4 teaspoon pepper
1 egg
1/4 cup chopped onion
1 clove garlic, minced
1 tablespoon vegetable oil
1/2 cup thinly sliced carrots
1 teaspoon dried Italian seasoning
3 cups beef broth
1 (14 1/2-ounce) can whole tomatoes, undrained and cut up
1/2 cup uncooked rotini noodles (spiral macaroni)
1 small zucchini squash, sliced
Freshly grated parmesan cheese

In a large bowl, combine ground beef, Italian sausage, bread crumbs, parmesan cheese, salt, pepper, and egg; form into meatballs the size of walnuts.

In a large soup pot over medium heat, sauté meatballs, onion, and garlic in hot vegetable oil until meatballs are browned (drain off fat). Add carrots, Italian seasoning, beef broth, tomatoes, and rotini noodles; bring to a boil. Reduce heat to low, cover, and simmer 10 minutes.

Add zucchini and cook, covered, another 5 minutes or until zucchini is crisp-tender and pasta is tender. Remove from heat and serve in soup bowls. Garnish with parmesan cheese.

Makes 4 to 6 servings.

Sausage

Sausage is one of the oldest of processed foods; 3,000 years ago, grinding meat into sausage was an old Mediterranean custom.

Types of sausages fall into three main classes:

FRESHLY GROUND SAUSAGE MEAT or COUNTRY SAUSAGE: Is very perishable and must be cooked and used at once. Since fresh sausages consist largely of pork, you have to cook them well. They must never be served with the inside bright pink.

IMPORTANT: Never taste raw or fresh sausage, whether bought or homemade, because of the danger of trichinosis. After handling raw sausage, always wash your hands and any knife, utensil, or surface you have used.

LIGHTLY CURED SAUSAGES: Often smoked precooked types, such as frankfurters, wieners, Vienna sausage, bologna, and salami; all of which may be eaten as bought unless the label reads to the contrary.

THE PARTIALLY DRY SAUSAGE: Is delicious in sandwiches. Dry sausages include cervelat, salami, pepperoni, chorizo, and thuringer.

Thyme

There is believed to be about 100 species of thyme. All thymes are wonderfully aromatic.

The Persians once nibbled fresh thyme as an appetizer. Some ancients Greeks thought thyme gave one courage.

In the days of chivalry, ladies embroidered a symbolic sprig of thyme and a honey bee on their scarves, which they gave as "favors" to the bravest knights.

The dried flowers of thyme, like lavender, have been used to preserve linen from insects. The leaves and flowering tops are an ingredient in sachets.

Thyme is considered by many herbalists as the very nearly perfect useful herb.

Oktoberfest Soup

2 pounds pork sausage links
1 (28-ounce) can whole tomatoes, undrained and cut up
4 medium potatoes, peeled and diced
2 cups sliced carrots
1 1/2 cups chopped celery
8 cups beef broth
2 cloves garlic, minced
2 teaspoons firmly packed brown sugar
4 cups shredded cabbage
Salt and pepper to taste
Freshly grated parmesan cheese

In a large soup pot over medium-high heat, place sausage links; add water to a depth of approximately 1/2 inch. Bring to a boil; reduce heat to low, cover, and simmer 10 minutes or until sausage is partially cooked. Remove from heat and drain off water. Slice sausage into 1/2-inch slices. Return to soup pot and brown; drain off fat.

Add tomatoes, potatoes, carrots, celery, beef broth, garlic, and brown sugar; bring to a boil. Cover, and simmer 1 hour, stirring occasionally. Add cabbage and simmer another 10 minutes. Season with salt and pepper. Remove from heat. Serve in soup bowls topped with parmesan cheese.

Makes 4 to 6 servings.

Cream of Broccoli Soup

Here's a low-calorie soup that's also rich tasting.

1/4 cup butter or margarine
1/2 cup diced onion
1/2 cup diced celery
1/4 teaspoon dried thyme, crushed
1/4 teaspoon dried oregano, crushed
1/4 teaspoon dried basil, crushed
2 cloves garlic, minced
1/4 cup all-purpose flour
10 cups chicken broth
1 small bunch (approximately 1 1/2 pounds) broccoli, chopped
2 cups powdered dairy creamer
Salt to taste

In a large soup pot over medium-high heat, melt butter or margarine. Add onion, celery, thyme, oregano, basil, and garlic; sauté 10 minutes or until vegetables are soft. Reduce heat to low; add flour and cook, stirring constantly, until flour is absorbed and rolls easily from edge of pan.

Add chicken broth to vegetables and stir until all flour is dissolved. Simmer for at least 30 minutes. Add broccoli and simmer another 20 minutes; stir in dairy creamer and salt. Remove from heat and serve in soup bowls.

Makes 6 to 8 servings.

Beer Cheese Soup

Beer adds a wonderful tang to this delicious cheese soup. This soup will remind you of a cold, snowy winter day in front of a fireplace.

1 cup butter or margarine
1 cup finely chopped celery
1 cup finely chopped carrots
1 cup finely chopped onion
1 cup all-purpose flour
1 teaspoon prepared mustard
8 cups chicken broth
1 (12-ounce) can beer (preferably flat)
2 cups shredded sharp cheddar cheese
3 tablespoons freshly grated parmesan cheese
Chopped fresh parsley

In a large soup pot over medium heat, melt butter or margarine. Add celery, carrots, and onion; sauté until tender but not brown. Remove vegetables with a slotted spoon, reserving butter in soup pot. Place vegetables into a food processor or blender; whirl until smooth; set aside.

In the soup pot over medium heat, make a roux with reserved butter or margarine, flour, and prepared mustard. Gradually add chicken broth, stirring constantly. Reduce heat to medium-low and cook 10 to 15 minutes, stirring constantly, until mixture just comes to a gentle boil and is thickened.

Reduce heat to low. Add beer and stir to combine. Mix in puréed vegetables and cheddar cheese; simmer another 20 minutes, stirring occasionally, until cheese is melted. Remove from heat. Serve in soup bowls topped with parmesan cheese and parsley.

Makes 8 servings.

Roux

Roux is an equal mixture of flour and fat cooked together at the very start of the recipe before any liquid is added. A good roux should be stiff, not runny or pourable. A roux with too much fat is called a slack roux.

A roux must be cooked so that the finished sauce does not have the raw, starchy taste of the flour. The time allowed for the cooking of brown roux cannot be precisely determined, as it depends upon the degree of heat employed. It is very important that brown roux should not be cooked too rapidly.

When adding flour to butter or oil in making a roux, remove the pan from the heat and mix the flour in well before returning the pan to the heat. This will prevent lumping.

Simmer, stirring from time to time, until all the starchy taste of the flour has been cooked out. This will take at least ten to twenty minutes.

Use a heavy saucepan to prevent scorching. Slowly pour in the liquid, all the while beating vigorously with a wire whip to prevent lumps from forming. Bring the liquid to a boil, continuing to beat well. The roux does not reach its full thickening power until near the boiling point.

Tarragon

The plant's name is derived from the French word "esdragon," meaning "little dragon." The plant's dragon-like roots may strangle the plant if it is not divided often. In medicinal lore, any plant with a serpentine root system is given credit for treating snakebites.

In the Middle Ages, the Romans put sprigs of it in their shoes before beginning a long trip on foot. They said it could prevent fatigue.

It is used in sauces and butters for fish and eggs, in mayonnaise and salad dressings, and to flavor mustards and vinegar.

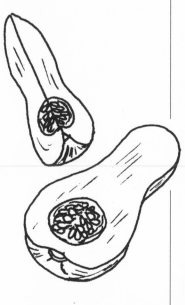

Cream of Cauliflower Soup

1/4 cup butter
2 tablespoons lemon juice
2 (10-ounce) packages frozen cauliflower
1 large potato, peeled and coarsely chopped
1 medium onion, chopped
2 cloves garlic, chopped
3 1/2 cups chicken broth
Salt and white pepper to taste
1 teaspoon chopped fresh tarragon
1 (10 3/4-ounce) can cream of mushroom soup, undiluted
1/2 cup milk
1 cup sour cream

In a large soup pot over medium heat, combine butter and lemon juice; heat until butter is melted. Add cauliflower, potato, onion, and garlic; sauté until vegetables are soft (do not allow the vegetables to brown). Remove from heat and cool 15 to 20 minutes.

In a food processor or a blender, in small batches, purée cauliflower mixture with some of the chicken broth. Pour blended soup back into the soup pot. Add remaining chicken broth, salt, white pepper, and tarragon; bring to a gentle boil and simmer 2 to 3 minutes. Add mushroom soup and milk; stir until well blended and thoroughly heated. Add sour cream and stir until well blended. Remove from heat and serve in soup bowls.

Makes 6 servings.

Curried Butternut Squash Soup

2 tablespoons vegetable oil
1 cup chopped onion
4 cloves garlic, minced
1 tablespoon curry powder
1 teaspoon ground cumin
Red (cayenne) pepper to taste
2 1/2 pounds butternut squash, peeled, seeded, halved lengthwise, and sliced thin
3 cups chicken broth
3 cups water
1 pound tart apples, peeled, cored, and chopped
Salt and pepper to taste

In a large heavy soup pot over medium heat, heat vegetable oil. Add onion and sauté until golden brown. Add garlic, curry powder, cumin, and cayenne pepper; cook, stirring constantly, 30 seconds. Add squash, chicken broth, water, and apples. Bring liquid to a boil; reduce heat to low and simmer, covered, 25 minutes or until squash is tender. Remove from heat and cool 15 to 20 minutes.

Purée mixture in a blender or food processor, in batches, and transfer back into soup pot. Season with salt and pepper; heat over low heat, stirring until hot. Remove from heat and serve in soup bowls.

Makes 6 servings.

Dill Pickle Soup

This soup tastes fantastic. Excellent for a dinner party to give your meal a spectacular start.

3 tablespoons butter
1/4 cup finely chopped onion
1/2 cup white wine
1/2 cup plus 1 tablespoon all-purpose flour
5 cups water
1 1/2 cups dill pickle juice
2 teaspoons dried dill weed, crushed
1/2 cup whipping cream or milk
Salt and white pepper to taste
1 large dill pickle, cut julienne

In a large soup pot over medium heat, melt butter. Add onion and sauté until soft. Add white wine and continue cooking until almost all liquid evaporates. Reduce heat to low and stir in flour (do not brown).

In a large bowl, combine water and pickle juice; add and whisk in all at once to onion mixture. Bring to a boil, stirring constantly, until soup slightly thickens. Add dill weed. Stir in whipping cream or milk to desired consistency. Season with salt and white pepper. Remove from heat. Serve in soup bowls and garnish with julienne dill pickle.

Makes 4 servings.

Helen's Dutch Potato Soup

4 medium potatoes, peeled and sliced
2 tablespoons butter or margarine
1 small onion, diced
2 tablespoons all-purpose flour
1 cup milk
1 (10 3/4-ounce) can cream of mushroom or celery soup, undiluted
1 teaspoon salt
2 cups water
1 1/2 cups cottage cheese (small curd)

In a large saucepan over medium-high heat, cover potatoes with water and simmer 15 minutes or until tender; drain and set aside.

In a large frying pan over medium-high heat, melt butter or margarine. Add onion and sauté until soft. Add flour, stirring constantly until mixture is smooth and bubbly. Add milk and bring to a boil, stirring constantly; reduce heat to low. Add mushroom or celery soup, potatoes, salt, and water; gently stir in cottage cheese. Remove from heat. Serve in soup bowls.

VARIATION: Add 1 cup shredded zucchini and 1 tablespoon green bell pepper to potatoes while cooking. Also add diced tomatoes, as desired, with cottage cheese.

Makes 6 servings.

Garnishing Soup

Thin soups can be garnished with small herb sprigs or a sprinkling of fresh-snipped or minced herbs, which will float on the surface.

Thick soups will often support a dollop of whipped cream, a spoonful of sour cream, crème fraîche, or yogurt.

Some suggested garnishing ideas are as follows:

- *Chopped chives, parsley, watercress, or green onions*
- *Slivered almonds*
- *Croutons*
- *Whipped cream seasoned with horseradish*
- *Browned onion slices or rings*
- *Frankfurter slices*
- *Cooked bacon bits*
- *Grated or shredded cheese*
- *Sliced stuffed olives*
- *Thin lemon slices*
- *Sour cream*
- *Carrot or radish slices*
- *Diced fresh tomato*

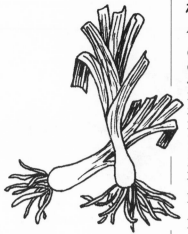

Leeks

Did you know that the leek is the national emblem of Wales? It is said that the victorious 6th-century Welsh army wore them on their helmets to distinguish themselves from the enemy.

The leek is an onion-like plant which is used much like the mature onion, but which is milder in flavor. Leeks are a cold-weather crop. They can be harvested in the fall when they are mature, or left in the ground and dug as needed during the winter.

They are served cooked, and may be prepared in the same ways suitable for asparagus. They are often called the poor man's asparagus.

Store them in a plastic bag in the refrigerator for up to five days.

TIPS: Leeks should be prepared by stripping off the outside leaves, cutting the green part down to five or six inches in length, and cutting off the root.

Austrian Cream Cheese Soup

A very delicate-tasting soup. You'll love this one.

6 tablespoons butter or margarine
6 leeks (white part only), chopped
4 celery stalks, chopped
3 to 4 tablespoons all-purpose flour
5 cups chicken broth, divided
3 cups water
1 (8-ounce) packages cream cheese, room temperature
1 cup sour cream
3 egg yolks, beaten
White pepper to taste
Fresh chives or fresh parsley, chopped

In a large soup pot over medium-high heat, melt butter or margarine. Add leeks and celery; sauté until leeks are transparent. Remove from heat and let cool 10 to 15 minutes.

In a food processor or a blender, whirl leek mixture and 1 1/2 cups chicken broth until smooth; return to soup pot. Stir in flour; cook until mixture is thickened and smooth. Add 3 1/2 cups chicken broth; bring to a boil, stirring occasionally. Reduce heat to low and simmer an additional 15 minutes.

In a medium bowl, whisk cream cheese, sour cream, and egg yolks until smooth. Gradually add 2 cups of soup mixture; blending thoroughly. Reduce heat to low, stir cream cheese mixture into soup until thoroughly heated. Season with white pepper. Remove from heat. Serve in soup bowls with chives or parsley sprinkled on top.

Makes 4 to 6 servings.

Chilled Georgia Peach Soup

2 1/2 pounds frozen peaches, defrosted and undrained
1 large ripe banana, peeled
1 cup water
1/2 cup sugar
1 teaspoon whole cloves
1 cinnamon stick
1 1/2 tablespoons cornstarch
2 cups dry white wine
1/2 teaspoon lemon juice
1/2 cup half and half cream

In a food processor or a blender, add peaches and banana; whirl until pureed. Set aside. In a medium saucepan over medium-high heat. Combine water, sugar, cloves, and cinnamon stick; bring to a boil. Reduce heat to medium low, cover, and simmer 30 minutes. Remove from heat; strain and return to saucepan.

In a medium bowl, add cornstarch and white wine; stir until cornstarch is dissolved. Add to syrup; stirring until well blended. Increase heat to medium-high and bring to a boil, stirring occasionally. Remove from heat and let cool. Add puréed peaches, lemon juice, and half and half cream; stir until well blended. Refrigerate until well chilled. Serve in chilled soup bowls.

Makes 8 to 10 servings.

Chilled Cherry-Cream Soup

Nothing could be more refreshing on a hot summer day than a cup of this wonderful creamy soup.

2 cups fresh or canned pitted sour cherries, reserving juice
3 cups water for fresh cherries or 2 cups for canned cherries
3/4 cup sugar
1/2 lemon, thinly sliced
1/2 teaspoon cinnamon
1/2 cup water
3 tablespoons cornstarch
1/2 teaspoon almond extract
1 cup heavy cream
1/4 to 1/2 cup milk

In a blender or a food processor, purée cherries and their juices slightly. In a large saucepan over medium-low heat, combine puréed cherries, water, sugar, lemon slices, and cinnamon. Reduce heat to low, cover, and simmer 30 minutes.

In a small bowl, dissolve cornstarch in 1/2 cup water; add to cherry mixture. Stir in almond extract; cook, stirring constantly, until soup just begins to thicken. Remove from heat and remove lemon pieces. Add heavy cream and 1/4 cup milk; stir until well blended (if too thick, add additional milk).

Cool, then refrigerate until well chilled. To serve, pour into chilled soup bowls.

Makes 4 to 6 servings.

Chilled Strawberry-Mint Soup

This soup is not only delicious, but the color is lovely.

1 1/2 cups sliced fresh strawberries
3/4 cup sour cream
3/4 cup heavy cream
2 tablespoons orange juice
2 tablespoons honey
1 1/2 teaspoons finely chopped fresh mint leaves
Fresh strawberry slices, kiwi fruit slices, or fresh mint sprigs

In a food processor or blender, place the strawberries, sour cream, heavy cream, orange juice, and honey; whirl until smooth. Stir in mint. Taste for sweetness; if necessary, add more honey. Refrigerate until well chilled. To serve, put into chilled soup bowls and top with strawberry slices, kiwi fruit slices, or mint sprigs.

Makes 2 servings.

Chilled Soups

We usually think of soups as being served hot, but there are many cold ones as well.

Vichyssoise is a cream of potato soup which is served cold and garnished with some chopped chives. Scandinavians love a cold fruit soup which contains a quantity of cooked dried fruits. The Spanish gazpacho is a refreshing chopped tomato soup served chilled.

FRUIT SOUPS: Made from dried or fresh fruit. Fruit soups originate in the Scandinavian countries, where they are served either as the main course of a luncheon or supper, or for dessert with whipped cream.

TIPS: A cold soup should always be thoroughly chilled. Prepare and refrigerate the day before, if you can. When serving a cold soup, chill the bowls or cups you are going to serve it in. The soup will remain cold longer.

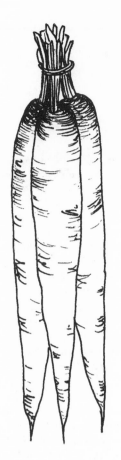

Gingered Carrot Soup

This soup is good served either hot or cold. If reheating, do not boil.

1 teaspoon vegetable oil
1/4 cup chopped onion
2 teaspoons freshly grated ginger
2 cups chicken broth
1 medium potato, peeled and cubed
2 medium carrots, peeled and sliced
1 cup milk
1/4 teaspoon salt
White pepper to taste
1/4 teaspoon ground cinnamon

In a large frying pan over medium-high heat, heat vegetable oil. Add onion and ginger and cook 5 minutes or until onion is tender. Add chicken broth, potato, and carrots; bring to a boil. Reduce heat to low, cover, and simmer 30 minutes. Remove from heat and let cool 10 to 15 minutes.

In a food processor or a blender, add vegetable mixture, milk, salt, white pepper, and cinnamon; whirl until very smooth. Serve in soup bowls.

Makes 4 servings.

Caraway Seeds

Caraway seeds have been used as a spice for about 5,000 years; there is evidence of its culinary use in the Stone Age.

They are available whole; if desired, grind or pound before using. Caraway seeds can become bitter during long cooking. When preparing soups and stews, add the crushed or whole seed only fifteen minutes before you take the pot off the stove.

Store in airtight containers away from light.

Carrot & Cream Cheese Soup

2 1/2 cups chicken broth
3 cups peeled and sliced carrots
1/2 cup chopped onion
3/4 teaspoon caraway seeds, divided
1/2 cup chicken broth
1 (8-ounce) package cream cheese, room temperature
1/3 cup shredded carrots

In a large soup pot over medium-high heat, bring 2 1/2 cups chicken broth, carrots, onion, and 1/2 teaspoon caraway seeds to a boil. Reduce heat to low, cover, and simmer 15 minutes or until carrots are tender when pierced. Remove from heat and let cool 10 to 15 minutes.

Pour chicken broth mixture into a food processor or a blender; whirl 3 to 5 minutes. Return to soup pot and add 1/2 cup chicken broth; cook and stir until thoroughly heated.

Cut cream cheese into small pieces; add to soup and whisk until smooth. Remove from heat. Serve in soup bowls. To garnish, sprinkle with shredded carrot and 1/4 teaspoon caraway seeds.

Makes 3 to 5 servings.

Summer Gazpacho

A light, cool, refreshing soup from Spain. The Spanish call Gazpacho "salad." However, to an American it is a soup. This soup is perfect for those hot summer days.

3 large tomatoes, finely chopped
1 cucumber, peeled and finely chopped
1 green bell pepper, cored, seeded, and finely chopped
1/2 medium white or sweet onion, minced
3 cups vegetable cocktail juice
1 (14 1/2-ounce) can beef broth
1 cup prepared tomato salsa
5 tablespoons wine vinegar
1/4 cup vegetable oil (added for flavor, but can be omitted)
2 teaspoons worcestershire sauce
1 teaspoon dried dill weed, crushed
1 teaspoon dried basil, crushed
1/2 teaspoon salt
1/4 teaspoon hot pepper sauce
1 clove garlic, minced
Garnishes

In a large bowl, combine tomatoes, cucumber, bell pepper, onion, vegetable cocktail juice, beef broth, tomato salsa, wine vinegar, and vegetable oil. Add worcestershire sauce, dill weed, basil, salt, hot pepper sauce, and garlic; stir until blended.

Refrigerate at least 4 hours or overnight before serving. Serve in chilled soup bowls with small bowls of garnishes.

Makes 8 servings.

GARNISHES:
Sour cream
Avocado chunks
Tortilla chips

Easy Patio Soup

Serve as an appetizer with crackers before the main dinner.

3 cups canned tomato juice
1 thick slice onion, chopped
1 stalk celery, sliced
1 dried bay leaf
4 whole cloves
1 (14 1/2-ounce) can vegetable broth
1/2 cup red wine
Salt and pepper to taste
Thin lemon slices

In a medium saucepan over medium-high heat, combine tomato juice, onion, celery, bay leaf, and cloves; bring to a boil. Reduce heat to low, cover, and simmer 20 minutes; strain. Add broth, red wine, salt, and pepper. Remove from heat. Serve in chilled soup bowls. Float a slice of lemon in each bowl.

Makes 5 to 6 servings.

Zucchini Soup

Here's what to do with all those giant zucchini you can't get rid of.

3 tablespoons butter or margarine
2 medium onions, chopped
4 cups sliced zucchini
1 cup water
1 (10 3/4-ounce) can cream of chicken soup, undiluted
1 cup milk
1 cup light cream
1 teaspoon dried basil, crushed
Salt and pepper to taste

In a large soup pot over medium heat, melt butter or margarine. Add onions and sauté until soft. Add zucchini and water; reduce heat to low and simmer 30 minutes. Remove from heat; cool slightly.

In a food processor or a blender at high speed, whirl vegetables until puréed; return to soup pot. Add the chicken soup, milk, light cream, basil, salt, and pepper; heat to simmering. Remove from heat. Serve in soup bowls.

Makes 4 servings.

Cutting Terms

CHOP:
Cut food into irregular pieces.

CUBE OR DICE:
Cut into small, straight-sided cubes, or into very fine cubes to dice.

GRATE:
Rub hard-textured food against a grater to reduce to fine particles. Grating works best with firm foods.

JULIENNE:
Cut food into fine matchstick-sized strips.

MINCE:
Chop food into tiny bits.

SHRED:
Use a knife or a shredder to cut food into long, thin strands.

SLICE:
Cut food into flat-sided pieces. Some recipes call for food to be cut on the diagonal, which simply means cutting it at an angle.

Maine Corn Chowder

This is quick to make with ingredients that can easily be kept on hand.

1 large onion, chopped
3 large potatoes, peeled and diced
1 (15-ounce) can cream-style corn
1 (12-ounce) can evaporated skim milk
2 tablespoons butter or margarine
Salt and coarsely ground pepper to taste

In a large saucepan over medium-high heat, place onion and potatoes, cover with water, and cook until soft but not mushy; drain off excess water. Add corn and evaporated milk; reduce heat to low and heat thoroughly. Stir in butter or margarine; season with salt and pepper. Remove from heat and serve in soup bowls.

Makes 4 servings.

Egg Drop Soup

This soup has a very delicate flavor yet is very simple to make. The egg will form thin ribbons, attractive as a garnish but also an appealing taste accent.

3 tablespoons cornstarch
1/4 cup water
7 cups chicken broth, fat removed
1/2 teaspoon sugar
1 teaspoon salt
Sherry to taste (optional)
2 eggs, beaten
1/4 teaspoon freshly grated ginger
1/4 cup chopped green onions

In a small bowl, make a paste of cornstarch and water. In a large soup pot over medium-high heat, heat chicken broth to boiling; stir cornstarch mixture into broth until smooth. Add sugar and salt; return broth to boiling, stirring constantly (mixture should thicken slightly). If desired, a little sherry may be added at this time.

Reduce heat to low. Add eggs gradually, mixing well to separate into shreds. Remove from heat; add ginger and green onions. Serve immediately in soup bowls.

Makes 6 servings.

Serving Soup

A liner plate placed under each bowl allows you to serve bowls filled with hot liquid gracefully. Use a salad plate beneath rimless bowls, and a ten-inch dinner plate beneath rimmed bowls.

The plate also gives your guests a place to put the spoon when they have finished eating, and helps to protect the table.

Chilled Avocado Soup

What could be simpler? So easy to make and serve at the last minute.

1 large ripe avocado, peeled, seeded, and halved
3/4 cup half and half, light cream, sour cream, or whipping cream
1/2 cup dry white wine
1 cup chicken broth
1 tablespoon lemon juice
Salt to taste
Red (cayenne) pepper to taste
Chopped fresh chives or fresh dill
Sour cream

Place avocado halves, cream, white wine, chicken broth, and lemon juice in a food processor or a blender; whirl until smooth. Season with salt and cayenne pepper. Cover and refrigerate several hours. To serve, place into chilled soup bowls and sprinkle with chives or dill and a spoonful of sour cream.

Makes 4 to 6 servings.

Mushroom Bisque

1/2 cup butter or margarine
3 cups sliced mushrooms
4 tablespoons all-purpose flour
1/2 teaspoon ground mustard
1 teaspoon salt
2 1/2 cups chicken broth
2 cups light cream
1/4 cup chopped fresh chives
1/4 cup sherry
Sour cream
Fresh parsley

In a large soup pot over medium heat, melt butter or margarine. Add mushrooms and sauté until tender. Add flour, ground mustard, and salt; cook another 1 minute, stirring constantly (flour should not brown). Add chicken broth; cook, uncovered, until mixture thickens. Gradually stir in light cream. Add chives; heat thoroughly but do not boil. Add sherry just before serving. Remove from heat. Serve in soup bowls and garnish with sour cream and top with a sprig of parsley.

Makes 4 to 6 servings.

Oyster & Brie Champagne Soup

1 cup unsalted butter
1/2 cup all-purpose flour
2 quarts oyster liquid, bottled clam juice, or fish broth
5 cups heavy cream
1 1/2 teaspoons red (cayenne) pepper
1 1/2 pounds brie cheese, rind removed and cut into small pieces
2 cups dry champagne
3 dozen fresh oysters, shucked
1 cup finely minced green onion stems
Salt to taste

In a large soup pot over low heat, melt butter. Add flour and cook 3 minutes, stirring constantly. Add oyster liquid, clam juice, or fish broth and cook another 3 to 4 minutes or until flour is absorbed. Increase heat to medium and bring just to a boil; reduce heat to low and simmer an additional 10 minutes, stirring occasionally. Add heavy cream; simmer 5 minutes longer, stirring constantly. Add cayenne pepper and brie cheese, stirring until cheese is melted completely.

Stir in champagne, oysters, and green onion stems. Remove from heat, cover and let stand 10 minutes. Season with salt. Serve in soup bowls.

Makes 8 servings.

Champagne

Champagne was once called devil wine "vin diable." Not because of what it did to people, but for what it did to its casks. The wine would "blow out the barrels" in the monasteries when warm weather got fermentation well under way.

They say the best part about cooking with champagnes is that recipes rarely, if ever, call for a whole bottle. This means that the goings-on in the kitchen can turn festive!

The secret to opening champagne successfully is to ease the cork out until it is forced from the bottle by the internal pressure.

One method is to hold the cork still while slowly twisting the bottle, and another is to hold the bottle still while maneuvering the cork.

Brie Cheese Bisque

A very rich and flavorful bisque.

4 tablespoons butter or margarine, divided
1 medium onion, chopped
8 cups chicken broth
4 tart apples, unpeeled, cored, and sliced
1 clove garlic, minced
2 tablespoons cider vinegar
1 pound brie cheese, rind removed and cut into small pieces
1 cup half and half cream
Salt and white pepper to taste
Freshly grated nutmeg

In a large soup pot over medium-high heat, melt 2 tablespoons butter or margarine. Add onion and sauté until soft. Add chicken broth; bring to a boil. Add apples, garlic, and cider vinegar; return to a boil. Reduce heat to low, cover, and simmer 30 minutes.

Add brie cheese and half and half cream; cook, stirring constantly, for another 5 minutes until brie cheese is melted. Remove from heat and let cool 10 to 15 minutes.

In a food processor or a blender, purée soup in small batches. Pour soup through a medium strainer back into soup pot. Season to taste with salt and pepper.

Serve in soup bowls and sprinkle lightly with nutmeg.

Makes 8 servings.

Bisque

A thick, rich, smooth soup, usually made with a shellfish base.

Modern quick cookery gives this name to a soup made with a white sauce base to which is added a purée of fish, vegetables, or fruits.

At one time bisques were thickened with rice, but today they are more frequently thickened with roux.

Chives

This close relative of the onion and garlic has been known since earliest times but was probably not cultivated until the Middle Ages.

Chives have been added to foods for nearly 5,000 years. Native to the Orient, they were probably first used by the Chinese and then the ancient Greeks.

Chives, one of the most popular of all culinary seasonings, looks like slender green onions but has a more refined flavor. The plants, with their lovely little lavender pompon flowers, are ornamental as well as tasty.

TIP: Snip chives with scissors for best results. Any other method crushes out their juices.

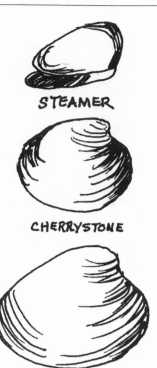

STEAMER

CHERRYSTONE

CHOWDER

Chowder

Chowder comes from the French word "cauldron," meaning cooking kettle. Vegetables or fish stewed in a cauldron thus became known as chowder in English-speaking nations, a corruption of the name of the pot or kettle in which they were cooked. The first chowders on this continent were brought by French fishermen to Canada.

A true chowder is a matter of debate between New Englanders and those further down the coast. New Englanders say that milk must be used, while New Yorkers and Philadelphians maintain just as stoutly that a chowder is not a chowder unless the stock is made from fish and contains tomatoes. In other parts of the country the subject is academic, and both are acceptable.

Pacific Coast Clam Chowder

5 bacon slices, cut into 1/4-inch pieces
1/4 cup butter or margarine
1 medium onion, chopped
1/4 cup all-purpose flour
Salt and pepper to taste
4 cups milk
Potatoes, peeled and cut into 1/4-inch pieces (as many potatoes as you prefer)
2 (6 1/2-ounce) cans minced clams, undrained
Crackers

In a large soup pot over medium heat, sauté bacon until crisp and golden brown. Remove bacon with a slotted spoon; drain bacon on paper towels (drain off fat from soup pot). Set aside.

Reduce heat to low and add butter or margarine and stir until melted. Add onion and sauté until soft. Add flour, salt, and pepper, stirring constantly until well blended. Gradually add milk, stirring constantly until sauce comes to a boil and thickens.

Add potatoes and simmer 10 to 15 minutes or until potatoes are soft. Add bacon, clams, and clam liquid; simmer until thoroughly heated. Season to taste with additional salt and pepper. Remove from heat and serve in soup bowls. Serve with crackers.

Makes 8 servings.

Clam Bisque Florentine

1 (10-ounce) package frozen chopped spinach
1 (6 1/2-ounce) can minced clams, undrained
2 tablespoons butter or margarine
2 tablespoons all-purpose flour
2 cups milk, divided
1/2 teaspoon Beau Monde seasoning
1 teaspoon dried oregano, crushed
1/4 teaspoon ground nutmeg
1 clove garlic, minced
Salt and coarsely ground pepper to taste

In a medium saucepan over medium-high heat, steam spinach in water just until tender; drain and set aside.

In a large saucepan over medium heat, heat clams and clam liquid with butter or margarine; blend in flour until smooth. Add 1 1/2 cups milk, Beau Monde seasoning, oregano, nutmeg, and garlic.

In a food processor or blender, combine spinach and 1/2 cup milk; whirl until smooth. Add spinach mixture to clam mixture. Season with salt and pepper. Simmer 15 minutes to blend flavors. Remove from heat. Serve in soup bowls.

Makes 6 servings.

Seafood Soup

Great meal. Serve with bread and salad.

1 pound fresh mussels
2 cups water
2 cups dry vermouth
1 dried bay leaf
1/2 cube fish bouillon
5 tablespoons butter or margarine, divided
1/2 pound fresh scallops
2 scallions, chopped (include green part)
3 tablespoons all-purpose flour
2 (8-ounce) bottles clam juice
1 cup light cream
1/2 pound cooked shrimp
Coarsely ground pepper to taste
Fresh parsley

Scrub the mussels and remove the beards. In a large soup pot over high heat, place mussels, water, vermouth and bay leaf; cover, and cook for a few minutes or until all mussels have opened (watch the pot carefully so you can turn down the heat just as the liquid comes to a boil). Lift them from the pot with a slotted spoon; set aside. Reserve the cooking liquid and stir in the fish bouillon cube; drain through cheese-cloth and set aside.

In a small bowl, reserve four mussels for garnishing. Pull the remaining mussels from their shells and set aside.

In a medium frying pan over medium heat, melt 1 tablespoon butter or margarine. Add scallops and sauté 4 to 5 minutes; remove from heat and set aside.

In a medium saucepan over medium heat, melt remaining butter or margarine; sauté scallions until soft but not brown. Stir in the flour and cook 2 minutes. Add clam juice, stirring constantly until it comes to a boil and thickens; reduce heat to low and add cream, reserved liquid, mussels, scallops, and shrimp. Season with pepper. Remove from heat.

Serve in soup bowls and float reserved mussels in their shells and a sprig of parsley on each serving.

Makes 4 servings.

Mussels

Like clams and oysters, mussels should be used only if they're tightly closed. Discard opened ones which won't close on handling or which float when placed in water. Scrub under cold water with a stiff brush.

Sea mussels are found in great masses, closely crowded together, adhering to rocks. The entire beds of mussels are practically bound together.

When young, the mussels move about, but they soon anchor themselves to rocks and remain there throughout their life.

The shell, black on the outside and blue inside, is oblong and generally about three inches long by one and one-half inches wide. They are at their best from October until the end of April, after which they spawn and are indigestible.

Quick Peeling Method for Garlic

For peeling of large amounts of garlic, the following methods work well:

STOVE TOP METHOD: Separate head of garlic into individual, unpeeled cloves. Drop cloves into boiling water to cover; cook two minutes. Turn into colander; rinse with cold water. Let stand until cool enough to handle, then peel.

MICROWAVE METHOD: Place whole head of garlic on a paper plate. Microwave on high for about one minute, rotating plate at thirty seconds. (Time will vary according to the size of the head.) Let rest in microwave oven one minute. Remove; let stand until cool enough to handle, then peel.

HIT THE KNIFE METHOD: Place clove of garlic on cutting board and place the flat side of a chef's knife on top of the clove and rap the blade sharply with your fist to break the skin for easy removal. This is a good method for peeling a few cloves at a time. Don't apply too much pressure because the clove can easily be smashed.

Poached Garlic Soup

Your guests will never believe how much garlic there is in this soup. After the garlic has been cooked slowly for a certain length of time, it loses its harsh rawness and becomes delicate and refined. It's hard to say exactly how or at what stage this happens – it is one of those mysteries which makes cooking so fascinating. THIS WILL BE ONE OF YOUR FAVORITE RECIPES.

30 cloves garlic, peeled
7 cups chicken broth, divided
1/2 cup butter or margarine
1/2 cup chopped onion
8 small new potatoes, peeled, diced, and reserved in cold water
Salt and pepper to taste
1 cup heavy cream
1 cup milk
Salt and coarsely ground pepper to taste
Freshly grated parmesan cheese
Toasted Garlic-Butter Bread

In a medium saucepan over medium-high heat, combine garlic cloves and 3 cups of chicken broth; bring to a boil and poach 15 minutes or until soft. Remove garlic cloves to a small bowl and mash with a fork; set aside for use in making Toasted Garlic-Butter Bread. Cook and reduce chicken broth to a glaze; remove from heat and set aside.

In a large soup pot over low heat, melt butter or margarine. Add onion and saute until soft. Drain potatoes; stir into butter and onion. Season with salt and pepper. Add 4 cups chicken broth. Increase heat to medium-high; simmer, uncovered, 25 minutes or until the potatoes are softened. Remove from heat and let cool 10 to 15 minutes.

In a food processor or blender, purée soup; return to soup pot. Add garlic-chicken glaze; stir until well blended. Stir in heavy cream, milk, salt, and pepper; cook, over low heat, another 10 minutes. Remove from heat. Serve in soup bowls and garnish with parmesan cheese. Serve with Toasted Garlic-Butter Bread.

Makes 6 servings.

TOASTED GARLIC-BUTTER BREAD:
6 slices sour dough bread, thinly sliced and lightly toasted
6 tablespoons butter, room temperature
Poached garlic cloves

Preheat broiler. In a small bowl, combine butter and mashed garlic cloves; mash until well blended. Spread garlic mixture evenly over the top of the bread slices. When ready to serve, broil bread for a few seconds or until top is lightly browned and bubbly.

NOTE: Bread can be assembled earlier in the day and placed in a pan. Cover well with plastic wrap.

Tomato Bisque

1/4 pound sliced bacon
4 cloves garlic, minced
2 onions, finely chopped and divided
6 celery stalks, finely chopped
1 dried bay leaf
1 teaspoon dried thyme, crushed
1 (28-ounce) can whole tomatoes, undrained and diced
1 (6-ounce) can tomato paste
2 tablespoons butter or margarine
3 tablespoons all-purpose flour
1 quart whipping cream, room temperature
2 whole cloves
Salt and pepper to taste

In a large frying pan over medium heat, cook bacon until crisp and golden; remove bacon (save for another use). Add garlic to bacon fat and saute until lightly browned. Add 3/4 of the onions, celery, bay leaf, and thyme; sauté until onion is translucent. Add tomatoes with juice and tomato paste; bring to a boil, stirring occasionally. Reduce heat to low, cover, and simmer 30 minutes.

In a large frying pan over medium heat, melt butter or margarine. Stir in flour and bring to a boil, stirring constantly. Remove from heat and slowly add whipping cream. Stir in remaining onions and cloves; return to heat and cook, uncovered, 45 minutes, stirring occasionally.

Remove from heat and strain through fine strainer into tomato mixture. Season with salt and pepper. Cover and simmer, stirring occasionally, 15 minutes. Stir in a little milk if thinner consistency is preferred.

Makes 6 to 8 servings.

Bay Leaf

Bay or laurel, a symbol of glory and reward, is a romantic herb.

Apollo, the Greek god of the sun, was in love with the nymph Daphne. He pursued her relentlessly. Daphne wanted nothing to do with Apollo. (This was all Cupid's doing. He shot an arrow into Daphne that made her hate Apollo.) To help her escape Apollo's pursuit, Daphne's father changed her into a laurel tree. Apollo fell upon his knees before the laurel tree and declared it eternally sacred. From then on he wore a wreath of laurel leaves upon his head.

Thus the tree became a sign of glory, honor, and greatness. In Greece and Rome, men and women wove wreaths to crown the heads of great people. At the first Olympics in 776 B.C., laurel garlands were presented to the champions.

Bay leaves are used to add pungent, woodsy flavor to long-cooking dishes like soups, stews, and meats. Leaving them in food too long can turn a dish bitter.

TIP: Never crumble a bay leaf before adding it to a dish. Removing the pieces will be impossible.

Basil

The Greek name for basil means "king," which shows how highly it has been regarded throughout the ages.

Italian cooks love this easy-to-grow herb and use it generously in their sauces. In Italy this plant is a symbol of love; a sprig of it presented to your lover bespeaks fidelity. When a woman puts a pot of basil on the balcony outside her room, it means that she is ready to receive her suitor.

Basil has become one of the most popular herbs in the garden today.

EASY PESTO SAUCE:
1 cup fresh basil leaves
3 tablespoons pine nuts or walnuts
3 tablespoons freshly grated parmesan cheese
2 or 3 cloves garlic
Olive oil

In a food processor, purée basil leaves, pine nuts or walnuts, parmesan cheese and garlic. Add enough olive oil to make a smooth paste.

Use pesto sauce with pasta, rice, fish, vegetables, or in soups.

Summer Tomato Soup

This delicate tomato soup is perfect for August and September when tomatoes are plentiful and wonderful tasting. Serve lukewarm or chilled.

4 tablespoons butter or margarine
1 medium onion, thinly sliced
2 teaspoons salt or to taste
3 pounds tomatoes, peeled, seeded, and coarsely chopped
2 cups chicken broth
2 cups milk
Salt and white pepper to taste
1/2 cup loosely packed fresh basil leaves, finely chopped
Small basil leaves for garnish (optional)

In a large saucepan over medium heat, melt butter or margarine. Add onion and sauté 7 to 8 minutes or until wilted and very lightly colored. Stir in salt and tomatoes; reduce heat to low, cover tightly, and simmer another 12 minutes or until the tomatoes are soft.

Transfer mixture into bowl of a food processor and whirl until smooth. Return puree to saucepan, stir in chicken broth, milk, salt, and white pepper. Heat gently for a few minutes. Remove from heat and set aside to cool. Stir in basil.

Serve in soup bowls and place a couple of basil leaves in the center.

Makes 4 servings.

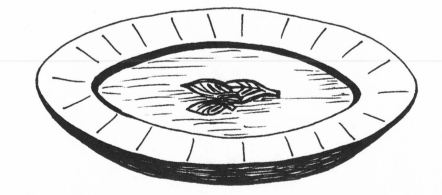

Vegetables

Shrimp-Avocado Cocktail in Artichokes

1 medium avocado, peeled, seeded, and diced
2 tablespoons lemon juice
4 medium artichokes, cooked, choke removed, and chilled
Cocktail Sauce
3/4 cup cleaned and cooked small fresh shrimp, or 1 (6-ounce) package
    frozen small shrimp
Fresh parsley

In a large bowl, toss avocado with lemon juice until well coated; drain. Gently spread center leaves of chilled artichoke and spoon 1 tablespoon Cocktail Sauce into each artichoke center. Stuff artichoke evenly with avocado and shrimp; top each with 1 tablespoon Cocktail Sauce. Transfer onto individual serving plates and garnish with parsley.

Makes 4 servings.

COCKTAIL SAUCE:
2/3 cup chili sauce
2/3 cup catsup
4 teaspoons prepared horseradish
3 tablespoons lemon juice

In a medium bowl, combine chili sauce, catsup, prepared horseradish, and lemon juice.

Stuffed Artichokes

1/4 cup butter or margarine
3 tablespoons lemon juice
1/2 cup water
2 cups herb-seasoned bread stuffing
1 tablespoon finely chopped onion
1/4 cup finely chopped fresh parsley
2 tablespoons freshly grated parmesan cheese
1 clove garlic, minced
1 tablespoon pine nuts
1/2 teaspoon dried oregano, crushed
6 medium artichokes, cooked, choke removed, and chilled

Preheat oven to 350 degrees. In a large saucepan over medium heat, melt butter or margarine. Stir in lemon juice, water, and herb stuffing. Add onion, parsley, parmesan cheese, garlic, pine nuts, and oregano; stir until well blended. Remove from heat.

Gently spread center leaves of chilled artichoke and spoon stuffing into each artichoke center; place close together into an ungreased 13x9-inch baking dish. Add 1/2-inch boiling water around the artichokes and bake, uncovered, 20 minutes. Remove from oven and transfer onto individual serving plates.

Makes 6 servings.

Cooking Artichokes

When cooking artichokes, check for doneness by pulling on the top of an interior leaf. If the leaf comes free under the artichoke's weight, then it's done. If it needs more coercion to break loose, then it needs more cooking. Artichokes usually take approximately thirty minutes to cook.

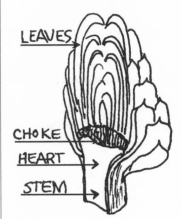

How to Eat a Whole Artichoke

Pull the leaves off one at a time, dip the base of each leaf in the sauce of your choice, and nibble off the fleshy end. Discard the rest of the leaf (use your fingers for this operation).

When all the outer leaves are removed, you come to the tiny undeveloped leaves growing out of the bottom. Pull these off and discard them, and with a knife cut out the fluffy choke underneath. This exposes the most delectable part of the artichoke – the heart or bottom. Cut this into bite-sized pieces and dip into sauce of your choice.

Artichokes

The globe artichoke is a member of the thistle family. The "choke" in the center is actually an immature flower, enclosed in leaf scales.

For best flavor, purchase March through May.

Choose compact, tightly closed heads with green, clean-looking leaves. The artichoke is a flower bud; if it has started to open, it is too old and will be tough and bitter. Avoid any that feel spongy when squeezed. Their size is not related to quality. Avoid ones that have brown leaves or show signs of mold.

To prepare for cooking, wash and cut one inch off top. Cut off stem and lower leaves. Scrape out choke or fuzzy center (removal of choke can be done before or after cooking). Dip in lemon juice immediately to prevent cut leaves from browning.

To store fresh artichokes, put them, unwashed, into a plastic bag and refrigerate. They will keep about two to three weeks.

TIPS: Cook artichokes with the heart side up. This keeps the heart from overcooking.

When cooking, you can obtain a better flavor if you add a small amount of sugar and salt to the water. They will be sweeter and will retain their color better.

Sombrero Artichokes

1 tablespoon vegetable oil
1/2 cup chopped onion
2 cloves garlic, minced
1 pound lean ground beef
1 (15-ounce) can tomato sauce
2 tablespoons chopped fresh parsley
1 1/2 teaspoons chili powder
1/4 teaspoon salt
1/8 teaspoon pepper
1/8 teaspoon red (cayenne) pepper
Hot pepper sauce to taste
4 large artichokes, cooked, choke removed, and chilled
Toppings
Diablo Dip

In a large frying pan over medium-high heat, heat vegetable oil. Add onion, garlic, and ground beef; sauté until beef is brown. Reduce heat to low. Add tomato sauce, parsley, chili powder, salt, pepper, cayenne pepper, and hot pepper sauce; simmer, uncovered, 15 to 20 minutes. Remove from heat.

Gently spread center leaves of chilled artichoke and spoon mixture into each artichoke center. To serve, garnish with desired toppings and Diablo Dip.

Makes 4 servings.

TOPPINGS:
Sour cream
Shredded cheddar cheese
Shredded lettuce
Chopped onion

DIABLO DIP:
1 (8-ounce) can tomato sauce
1/2 teaspoon lemon juice
1 clove garlic, minced
1/8 teaspoon pepper
1/8 hot pepper sauce or to taste

In a small bowl, combine tomato sauce, lemon juice, garlic, pepper, and hot pepper sauce.

Yields 1 cup.

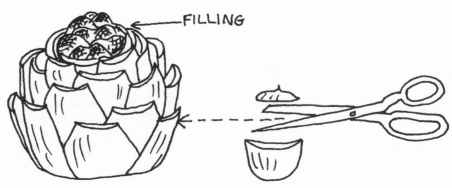

FILLING

Pepper Pesto Asparagus

1 pound fresh asparagus spears
Pepper Pesto
Pesto Vinaigrette

Snap off and discard tough ends of asparagus. If desired, scrape off scales. In a large pan over medium-high heat, fill 3/4 full of water; add a teaspoon of salt per quart of water and bring to a boil. Add asparagus, cover, and heat just until water begins to boil again, then remove the lid. Reduce heat to medium and cook 4 minutes. Test for doneness by piercing spears with a sharp knife. Asparagus is done when just easily pierced.

Remove from heat, drain, and cool; arrange asparagus spears onto individual serving plates. Spread Pepper Pesto on top of the asparagus spears. Spoon a small mound of Pesto Vinaigrette onto top of asparagus spears.

Makes 4 servings.

PEPPER PESTO:
1 large clove garlic
1/2 cup toasted pine nuts
1/2 cup fresh parsley
1/2 cup fresh cilantro
1 1/2 teaspoons coarsely ground pepper
3/4 cup virgin olive oil

In a food processor, place garlic, pine nuts, parsley, cilantro, and pepper; whirl a few times. With machine running, slowly pour in olive oil. Pesto should be slightly coarse. Reserve 1/4 cup pesto for Pesto Vinaigrette; set aside.

PESTO VINAIGRETTE:
1 cup extra-virgin olive oil
1/4 cup red wine vinegar
1/4 cup Pepper Pesto

In a small bowl, combine olive oil, wine vinegar, and Pepper Pesto.

Asparagus

Stalks should be green with compact, closed, and tender tips. Avoid flat stalks or stalks that have a lot of white to them.

Wait to clean until you are ready to use. Otherwise, they will dry out. Break off woody lower ends where each spear snaps naturally. Remove lower scales, which may harbor sand, or peel lower part of stalk.

To make thick asparagus stalks tender, peel lower parts up to tender part with a vegetable peeler. Stalks taste as good as the tips this way.

If you must keep asparagus for a day or two, stand spears upright in a container with about an inch of water or wrap bottoms with wet paper towels. Cover with plastic to maintain moisture.

TIP: To revive limp asparagus, try placing them in a tall container with ice water in the refrigerator for thirty minutes.

Cooking Vegetables

As a cook, you have a choice of many different kinds of vegetables and many different cooking methods.

A vegetable is said to be done when it has reached the desired degree of tenderness. This stage varies from vegetable to vegetable. Most vegetables, however, are best cooked very briefly or until they are crisp-tender or al dente (firm to the bite). At this stage of tenderness, they not only have the most pleasing texture, but they retain maximum flavor, color, and nutrients.

GENERAL RULES FOR COOKING VEGETABLES:

- *Don't overcook.*
- *Cook as close to serving time as possible.*
- *If cooking ahead of time, undercook slightly and chill. Reheat at serving time.*
- *Cut vegetables as uniform in size as possible.*

Asparagus With Orange-Basil Hollandaise Sauce

1 pound fresh asparagus spears
Orange-Basil Hollandaise Sauce

Snap off and discard tough ends of asparagus. If desired, scrape off scales. In a large pan, fill 3/4 full of water; add a teaspoon of salt per quart of water and bring to a boil. Add asparagus, cover, and heat just until water begins to boil again, then remove the lid. Reduce heat to medium and cook 4 minutes. Test for doneness by piercing spears with a sharp knife. Asparagus is done when just easily pierced.

Remove from heat, drain, and transfer onto a serving platter. Spoon Orange-Basil Hollandaise Sauce over asparagus. Serve immediately.

Makes 4 servings.

ORANGE-BASIL HOLLANDAISE SAUCE:
3 egg yolks, beaten
1/4 cup fresh orange juice, divided
1 teaspoon chopped basil leaves or 1/4 teaspoon dried basil, crushed
Salt to taste
Coarsely ground pepper to taste
1/2 cup butter or margarine, room temperature
1 1/2 teaspoons grated orange zest

In top of a double boiler, combine egg yolks, 2 tablespoons orange juice, basil, salt, and pepper. Divide butter or margarine into three equal portions; add one portion of butter or margarine to egg mixture.

Place over boiling water (upper pan should not touch water). Cook, stirring rapidly with a wire whisk, until butter or margarine melts and sauce begins to thicken. Add remaining butter or margarine, one portion at a time, stirring constantly. Cook and stir 1 to 2 minutes or until sauce thickens.

Immediately remove from heat. Stir in 2 tablespoons orange juice and orange zest. (If sauce is too thick or curdles, immediately beat in 1 to 2 tablespoons hot water.)

Green Beans Supreme

Can be done early in the day.

3 (14.5-ounce) cans french-style green beans, undrained
4 bacon slices, chopped
2 tablespoons chopped onion
1 green bell pepper, cored, seeded, and chopped
1/2 cup chopped pimiento, drained
2 tablespoons butter or margarine
1 (10 3/4-ounce) can cream of mushroom soup, undiluted
1 (2-ounce) can mushrooms, undrained
1/2 pound processed American cheese, cut into cubes
1/4 teaspoon worcestershire sauce
1 cup crushed Ritz crackers
Butter

Preheat oven to 350 degrees. In a large saucepan over medium-high heat, cook green beans with bacon pieces and onion long enough to cook bacon and season beans; remove from heat. Drain bean mixture and place into an ungreased 2-quart casserole dish.

In the same saucepan over medium heat, sauté bell pepper and pimiento in butter or margarine. Add mushroom soup, mushrooms, American cheese, and worcestershire sauce. Cook, stirring occasionally, until cheese is melted and mixture is thick. Remove from heat and pour over beans. Sprinkle with crushed Ritz crackers and dot with butter.

Bake, uncovered, 30 minutes or until top is golden brown and thoroughly heated. Remove from oven and serve.

Makes 8 servings.

Green Beans

Green beans are available year round, with a peak season of May to October. Green beans are also called string beans and snap beans.

Choose slender beans that are crisp, bright-colored, and free of blemishes.

Green beans were once called string beans. Today they are stringless; just break off the ends as you wash them. Leave whole or cut into desired lengths.

Store green beans in the refrigerator, tightly wrapped in a plastic bag, for up to five days. Before cooking, wash beans and trim stem ends.

TIP: The fewer beans in the pan, the quicker they cook and the better they taste. If cooking more than one pound at a time, use separate pans.

Green Beans With Dill

1 1/2 pounds fresh green beans, ends trimmed
1/4 cup butter or margarine
1 medium onion, minced
1 tablespoon minced fresh dill
1/4 teaspoon salt
Coarsely ground pepper to taste
2 hard-cooked eggs, peeled and coarsely chopped

In a large saucepan over medium-high heat, bring 3 quarts of water to a boil. Add green beans and cook, uncovered, 10 to 15 minutes or until crisp-tender (taste one to see if it is done; it should still be very crunchy). Remove from heat, drain, and rinse under cold water to stop cooking.

In the same saucepan over medium heat, melt butter or margarine; add onion and sauté until tender. Stir in green beans, dill, salt, and pepper. Cook and stir until thoroughly heated. Remove from heat and transfer into a serving dish. To serve, garnish with hard-cooked eggs.

Makes 6 servings.

Green Beans

Suggested Serving Ideas for Green Beans

SEASONINGS:
Dill, basil, tarragon, oregano, garlic, or soy sauce.

FLAVORINGS AND COMBINATIONS:
Almonds, sesame seeds, onion, tomato, celery, mushrooms, or bacon.

Cooking Green Beans and Other Green Vegetables

Green coloring, or chlorophyll, is present in all green plants. Acids are enemies of green vegetables. Both acid and long cooking turn green vegetables drab olive-green.

Always cook uncovered to allow plant acids to escape. Do not overcook fresh beans, they should be crisp-tender when done.

TIP: A pinch of sugar in the cooking water will bring out the flavor of fresh beans.

Green Bean Casserole

1 (10 3/4-ounce) can cream of mushroom soup, undiluted
1/2 cup milk
1 teaspoon soy sauce
Pepper to taste
2 (6-ounce) cans green beans, undrained
1 (2.8-ounce) can french-fried onions

Preheat oven to 350 degrees. In an ungreased 1 1/2-quart casserole dish, combine mushroom soup, milk, soy sauce, and pepper; stir in green beans and 1/2 can french-fried onions. Bake, uncovered, 25 minutes or until thoroughly heated. Top with remaining onions. Bake another 5 minutes or until onions are golden brown. Remove from oven and serve.

VARIATION:
Use one (16 to 20 ounces) bag frozen green beans or two packages (9 ounces each) frozen green beans or about 1 1/2 pounds fresh green beans for this recipe. Precook beans before adding to recipe.

Makes 6 servings.

Forget the Diet Beans

There are certain recipes where things like bacon fat cannot be substituted.

1 1/2 pounds fresh green beans, ends trimmed
10 bacon slices
6 tablespoons sugar
6 tablespoons cider vinegar
1/4 cup slivered almonds

Preheat oven to 350 degrees. Leave green beans whole or cut into 1-inch pieces. In a large saucepan over medium-high heat, bring 3 quarts of water to a boil. Add green beans and cook, uncovered, 10 to 15 minutes or until crisp-tender (taste one to see if it is done; it should still be very crunchy). Remove from heat, drain, and rinse under cold water to stop cooking. Set aside.

In the same saucepan over medium-high heat, cook bacon until crisp. Remove bacon and crumble; reserving drippings in pan. Stir sugar and cider vinegar into drippings.

In an ungreased 1 1/2-quart casserole dish, layer half of the beans, half of the crumbled bacon, and half of the almonds. Repeat layering. Pour prepared drippings over all. Bake 35 to 45 minutes or until thoroughly heated. Remove from oven and serve.

Makes 6 to 8 servings.

Marinated Green Beans

1 pound fresh green beans, ends trimmed
1 small onion, thinly sliced
1/2 cup vegetable oil
1/2 cup rice vinegar
1 tablespoon chopped fresh dill or 1 teaspoon dried dill weed, crushed
1 clove garlic, minced
1/2 teaspoon ground mustard
1/2 teaspoon sugar
1/2 teaspoon salt
1/8 teaspoon pepper

In a large saucepan over medium-high heat, bring 3 quarts of water to a boil. Add green beans and cook, uncovered, 10 to 15 minutes or until crisp-tender (taste one to see if it is done; it should still be very crunchy). Remove from heat, drain, and rinse under cold water to stop cooking. Put beans and onion slices into an airtight container.

In a jar with a lid, combine vegetable oil, rice vinegar, dill, garlic, ground mustard, sugar, salt, and pepper; cover securely and shake vigorously. Pour over vegetables. Cover and refrigerate several hours or overnight. Drain before serving.

Makes 8 servings.

Pickled Green Beans With Dill

These pickled green beans will keep in the refrigerator for up to two weeks.

1 pound fresh green beans, ends trimmed
8 sprigs fresh dill
1 teaspoon mustard seeds
2 cloves garlic, minced
1 small hot red chile pepper
Pickling Liquid

In a large saucepan over medium-high, bring 3 quarts water to a boil. Add green beans and blanch 2 to 3 minutes. Remove from heat, drain, and transfer to a large bowl. Stir in dill, mustard seeds, garlic, and chile pepper. Pour Pickling Liquid over bean mixture. Cool to room temperature and refrigerate overnight before serving.

Yields 4 cups.

PICKLING LIQUID:
1 cup rice vinegar
1 cup water
1/3 cup white wine vinegar
3 tablespoons sugar
2 teaspoons kosher salt

In a medium saucepan over medium-high heat, combine rice vinegar, water, wine vinegar, sugar, and kosher salt; bring to simmer and remove from heat.

Blanching

The word "blanch" comes from the French word "blanchir," which means to whiten.

Blanch means to partially cook food in either hot fat, steam, or boiling water. Blanching in deep fat is usually done to precook foods so that they may be finish-cooked later when time is at a premium.

Vegetables, fruits, and nuts are blanched in boiling water to remove their skins, to remove off flavors, to inactivate enzymes, and to shrink the foods prior to canning or freezing.

Beans

Molasses

Molasses is made from sugar cane, which goes through a complex process which removes all of the nutrients, resulting in a white sugar. When the natural sugar crystallizes, the molasses is drawn off or "spun out."

Molasses from the first boiling is the finest grade, from which only a small part of the sugar has been removed. First-boil molasses is mostly for table use.

When the molasses is boiled again, it takes on a darker color, is less sweet, and has a more pronounced flavor. This second-boil molasses is used for the making of candies and cakes.

Today molasses is used more for flavoring than for sweetening. A cupful of molasses is comparable to about three-fourths of a cup of granulated sugar.

TIP: To aid in pouring molasses from a measuring cup, oil the inside of the cup first.

Easy Crock Pot Baked Beans

1 pound bacon, diced
1 cup chopped onion
4 (16-ounce) cans pork and beans, undrained
1/2 cup molasses
1/4 cup firmly packed brown sugar
1 cup strong coffee
1/2 cup catsup
1/4 teaspoon ground mustard

In a medium frying pan over medium-high heat, fry bacon until crisp; remove and drain on paper towels. Sauté onion in bacon grease; remove with slotted spoon and drain on paper towels.

In the crock pot, combine bacon, onion, and pork and beans; mix in molasses, brown sugar, coffee, catsup and ground mustard. Simmer, covered, on low in crock pot for several hours before serving.

Serves 6 to 8.

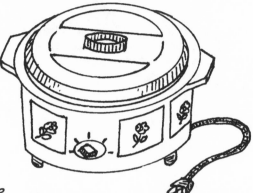

Andra's Barbecue Beans

Andra is famous for her delicious North Carolina barbecue bean recipe. It is always a favorite at any gathering she brings it to.

1 medium onion, finely chopped
1 clove garlic, minced
1/2 cup butter or margarine
1/4 cup cider vinegar
1/2 cup sugar
1 tablespoon prepared mustard
1 teaspoon worcestershire sauce
3/4 cup catsup
Salt to taste
1 (16-ounce) can pork and beans, drained and rinsed
1 (15 1/4-ounce) can red kidney beans, drained and rinsed
1 (14 1/4-ounce) can lima beans, drained and rinsed

Preheat oven to 350 degrees. In a large frying pan, sauté onion and garlic in butter or margarine. Stir in cider vinegar, sugar, prepared mustard, worcestershire sauce, catsup, and salt; cook and stir 1 to 2 minutes or until well blended. Remove from heat.

In an ungreased 2-quart casserole dish, combine pork and beans, kidney beans, and lima beans. Pour catsup mixture over top and mix well. Bake, uncovered, 1 hour. Remove from oven and serve.

Serves 6 to 8.

Boston Baked Beans

While Boston gets the credit for this dish, it was actually popular throughout all the colonies of America. Since Boston Baked Beans could be made a day ahead, this dish was a favorite with those whose religion restricted work on the Sabbath.

1 (16-ounce) package navy or pea beans
6 cups water
1/2 teaspoon baking soda
1/2 pound bacon, diced
1 small onion, chopped
1/3 cup molasses
1 teaspoon salt
5 tablespoons firmly packed brown sugar
1 teaspoon ground mustard
1/2 teaspoon pepper

In a large pot, soak navy or pea beans overnight in 6 cups water. Next day, drain beans and return to pot. Add another 6 cups water and baking soda; bring to a boil. Reduce heat to low and simmer 10 minutes. Remove from heat and drain in a colander over a large bowl; reserve liquid.

Preheat oven to 300 degrees. In an ungreased bean pot or large casserole dish, combine beans, bacon, and onion. Add molasses, salt, brown sugar, ground mustard, pepper, and a cup of reserved liquid; stir until well blended. Cover bean pot or casserole dish.

Bake, covered, 2 1/2 to 3 hours. Add remaining liquid and stir again. Bake another 1 1/2 hours or until beans are tender. Uncover last 30 minutes of baking. Remove from oven and serve.

Makes 8 servings.

Baked Beans as a Dip

Don't discard leftover baked beans. How about making a delicious dip?

It is very simple to do – just purée in the food processor or blender until desired texture is reached. Then serve with corn chips and enjoy!

Chehalem Mountain Baked Beans

1 1/2 pounds ground beef or ground turkey
1/4 cup chopped onion
1 tablespoon lemon-pepper seasoning
1 teaspoon garlic powder
1 1/4 cups catsup
1/2 cup firmly packed brown sugar
1 tablespoon worcestershire sauce
1 tablespoon ground mustard
1 teaspoon coarsely ground pepper
1 (16-ounce) can pork and beans, undrained

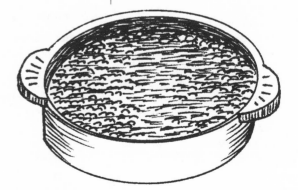

Preheat oven to 350 degrees. In a large frying pan over medium-high heat, cook ground beef or ground turkey and onion until meat is brown, sprinkling with lemon-pepper seasoning and garlic powder after meat has started to brown.

Remove from heat and drain; transfer into an ungreased 3-quart casserole dish. Mix in catsup, brown sugar, worcestershire sauce, ground mustard, and pepper. Carefully stir in pork and beans until well mixed. Bake, uncovered, 30 minutes or until bubbly. Remove from oven and serve.

Makes 10 to 12 servings.

Beets

Beets

1 pound trimmed beets equals 2 cups chopped cooked beets.

Fresh beets are available year round, with a peak season from June to late September. Choose firm, smooth-skinned beets without any soft spots or blemishes. Buy only small- or medium-sized beets. Large beets are usually not very tender.

Beet greens should be removed as soon as you get them home because they leach moisture. Leave about one inch of the stem and the root attached to prevent loss of nutrients, color, and flavor during cooking. Beet greens are very flavorful and can be used in salads or cooked as a substitute for spinach.

Store beets in a plastic bag in the refrigerator for three to four weeks. Greens can be stored in a sealed plastic bag for up to one week. Just before cooking, wash beets gently.

Beets should be cooked whole to retain their red color. Peel after cooking.

Pickled Beets

4 bunches small beets (about 4 pounds)
2 cups sugar
2 cups water
2 cups cider vinegar
1 tablespoon ground cloves
1 tablespoon ground allspice
1 tablespoon ground cinnamon

Cut off beet tops (reserve greens for another use), leaving a 1-inch stem attached. Leave roots on. Wash thoroughly.

In a large pot over medium-high heat, pour 1 cup hot water and heat until boiling. Add beets, cover, and cook 30 to 45 minutes or until beets can be easily pierced with a thin knife. Remove from heat, drain, cool slightly, and remove skins.

In a large saucepan over medium heat, combine sugar, water, and cider vinegar. Stir in cloves, allspice, and cinnamon. Add beets and simmer 15 minutes. Remove from heat and transfer beets and liquid into a serving bowl.

Makes 8 servings.

Harvard Beets

2 bunches beets (about 4 pounds)
1 tablespoon cornstarch
1 tablespoon plus 1 teaspoon sugar
3/4 teaspoon salt
2/3 cup liquid (beet juice from cooked beets and water)
1/4 cup cider vinegar

Cut off beet tops (reserve greens for another use), leaving a 1-inch stem attached. Leave roots on. Wash thoroughly.

In a large pot over medium-high heat, pour 1 cup hot water and heat until boiling. Add beets, cover, and cook 30 to 45 minutes or until beets can be easily pierced with a thin knife. Remove from heat, drain, cool slightly, and remove skins; cut into cubes or slices.

In a medium saucepan over medium-high heat, combine cornstarch, sugar, and salt; stir until well blended. Blend beet liquid and cider vinegar into cornstarch mixture. Bring to a boil; boil 1 minute. Add beets; reduce heat to low and simmer 15 minutes. Remove from heat and transfer into a serving bowl.

Makes 4 servings.

Pickled Beets With Orange & Rosemary

2 bunches beets (about 2 pounds)
Orange & Rosemary Vinaigrette

Cut off beet tops (reserve greens for another use), leaving a 1-inch stem attached. Leave roots on. Wash thoroughly.

In a large pot over medium-high heat, pour 1 cup hot water and heat until boiling. Add beets, cover, and cook 30 to 45 minutes or until beets can be easily pierced with a thin knife. Remove from heat, drain, cool slightly, and remove skins.

Place beets into a medium bowl. Pour Orange & Rosemary Vinaigrette over beets. Cool to room temperature. Refrigerate, covered, until ready to serve.

NOTE: Can be refrigerated up to 1 month.

Makes 4 servings.

ORANGE & ROSEMARY VINAIGRETTE:
1/2 cup sweet vermouth
2/3 cup red wine
1/2 cup cider vinegar
1/4 cup honey or firmly packed brown sugar
1 teaspoon whole cloves
1 cinnamon stick
1 medium sprig fresh rosemary
1 teaspoon grated orange zest
1 orange, peeled and sliced 1/4-inch thick
Salt and coarsely ground pepper to taste

In a large saucepan over medium heat, combine sweet vermouth, red wine, cider vinegar, and honey or brown sugar. Stir in cloves, cinnamon stick, rosemary, orange zest, and orange slices; bring to a boil.

Reduce heat to low and simmer 10 minutes to blend flavors; add salt and pepper. Remove from heat and strain.

Steamed Beets

Be careful not to let the pan run out of water during this long steaming process.

Remove greens (reserve for another use), leaving a one-inch top; wash thoroughly. In a large saucepan (with a steamer rack) place one cup hot water and heat until boiling.

Place beets in steamer basket. Cover, and steam approximately forty to sixty minutes or until beets can be easily pierced with thin knife. Remove from heat, drain, cool slightly, and remove skins.

Baked Beets

This is the perfect bake-along when you're already roasting meat or cooking a casserole. It is also the easiest way to cook beets and very delicious.

Preheat oven to 300 degrees. Remove greens (reserve for another use), leaving a one-inch top; wash thoroughly. Leave beets whole.

Place into an ungreased casserole or baking dish (do not add water) and cover securely. Bake one hour or until beets are just tender. Remove from oven and cool slightly; remove skins and slice. Serve immediately.

Broccoli & Brussels Sprouts

Broccoli

Broccoli is available all year, with a peak season from October through April.

Select a bunch that is dark green with tightly closed flowerets. The stalks should be firm, without leggy branches. The buds should be tightly closed and the leaves crisp. Also the stronger broccoli smells, the older it is. Refrigerate, unwashed, in a plastic bag, for up to four days.

If you peel the tough fibrous outer layer off broccoli stems, it cooks faster, makes it easier to digest, and is more attractive.

Broccoli stems can be cooked in the same length of time as the flowerets if you make "X" incisions from top to bottom through stems.

Brussels Sprouts

Brussels sprouts are available from late August through March. Buy small bright green sprouts with compact heads; with no sign of yellowing on the leaves.

Store unwashed sprouts in a plastic bag in the refrigerator for up to three days. Longer than that, sprouts will develop a strong flavor.

Before cooking, remove any loose leaves. Wash sprouts, then lightly trim the stem.

Broccoli Cheese Casserole

5 eggs, beaten
2 1/4 cups cracker crumbs
1/4 pound butter or margarine, melted
4 cups hot milk or a combination of cream of mushroom soup or celery soup
    mixed with milk to equal 4 cups
1/4 cup grated onion
1 1/3 cups shredded cheddar cheese
1 1/3 cups shredded swiss cheese
1 1/3 cups shredded mozzarella cheese
Salt and pepper to taste
1 1/2 pounds chopped broccoli

Preheat oven to 325 degrees. In a large bowl, combine eggs, cracker crumbs, butter or margarine, and hot milk or milk and soup combination; stir until well blended. Stir in onion, cheddar cheese, swiss cheese, and mozzarella cheese. Season with salt and pepper and gently fold in broccoli. Pour into an ungreased 2-quart casserole dish and bake, uncovered, 45 minutes. Remove from oven and serve immediately.

Makes 10 to 12 servings.

Brussels Sprouts With Mustard Glaze

If you weren't a brussels sprouts lover before, you'll definitely be one after enjoying this recipe.

1/4 cup slivered almonds
4 cups Brussels sprouts
2 tablespoons cider vinegar
3 tablespoons firmly packed brown sugar
1 tablespoon Dijon mustard
1 tablespoon butter or margarine
Salt to taste

In a small frying pan over medium-high heat, cook and stir almonds 2 minutes or until golden brown. Remove from heat and set aside.

Discard coarse outer leaves of brussels sprouts; rinse and drain. In a large pan (with a steamer rack) over medium-high heat, cook, covered, 15 to 20 minutes or until tender when pierced.

In a large frying pan over medium-high heat, combine cider vinegar, brown sugar, Dijon mustard, and butter or margarine; stir until boiling vigorously. Add brussels sprouts and almonds; stir until well blended. Season with salt. Transfer into a serving bowl and serve immediately.

Makes 4 servings.

Cabbage With Caraway & Bacon

Serve with a pork roast for a delicious dinner.

4 bacon slices
1 small head cabbage, cored, halved, and shredded
1 tablespoon caraway seeds
3 tablespoons cider vinegar
Salt and coarsely ground pepper to taste

In a large frying pan over medium-high heat, cook bacon until crisp; remove from heat and drain on paper towels. Pour off all but 2 tablespoons of bacon fat. Heat the 2 tablespoons bacon fat until hot; add cabbage and toss to coat. Cover and reduce heat to medium. Cook, stirring occasionally, 10 to 15 minutes or until tender.

Sprinkle with caraway seeds, cider vinegar, salt, and pepper; toss until mixed. Remove from heat and transfer into a serving bowl. To serve, crumble bacon over the top.

Makes 4 to 6 servings.

Braised Red Cabbage

This dish may be stored, covered, in the refrigerator for up to 3 days.

1 large red cabbage (about 2 1/2 pounds), cored, halved, and tough outer
   leaves discarded
2 tablespoons butter or margarine
1 cup dried sour cherries
1/4 cup red wine vinegar
1/4 cup apple juice
1/4 cup red currant jelly
1 tablespoon sugar
Salt and pepper to taste

Preheat oven to 325 degrees. Cut cabbage into thin slices and set aside.

In a large ungreased cast-iron pan over medium heat, melt butter or margarine. Stir in cherries and cook 2 minutes or until they begin to soften. Reduce heat to low; add cabbage, wine vinegar, apple juice, red currant jelly, sugar, salt, and pepper. Cook, stirring occasionally, another 5 minutes or until cabbage begins to wilt.

Cover and bake in oven 1 hour. (Cabbage will be tender and the liquid slightly thickened.) Remove from oven and serve immediately.

Makes 6 to 8 servings.

Cabbage

*1 pound cabbage equals
4 cups shredded or
2 cups cooked cabbage.*

Choose firm heads that feel heavy for their size. Outer leaves should look fresh, have good color, and be free of blemishes.

Cabbage should be boiled just until it is tender. Overcooking it will turn it limp and, because cabbage contains some sulfurous compounds, will produce an unpleasant odor. Try steaming cabbage wedges. They will hold together better than if they are boiled.

TIPS: To reduce odor while cooking cabbage, place a small cup of vinegar on the range or add a wedge of lemon to the pot.

When cooking red cabbage, add one-half tablespoon lemon juice or vinegar for each cup of cooking water. This will preserve its color and keep it from turning purple.

Carrots

Carrots

1 pound carrots equals 3 cups sliced carrots or 2 1/2 cups shredded carrots.

Did you know that when carrots were first brought to England from Holland, stylish ladies used the feathery leaves to decorate their hair?

The early Indians liked carrots so much that they would steal them from the early settlers' gardens, when they stole nothing else.

The best carrots are young and slender. When buying, look for ones that are firm and smooth; avoid any with cracks. If buying with greenery, make sure the leaves are moist and bright green. Avoid topped carrots that have green shoots and bunched carrots that have yellow tops – they are too old and have not been stored properly.

To prepare for eating or cooking, trim top and bottom ends. Peel with a vegetable peeler.

TIP: Remove the greens of carrots before storing in the refrigerator. Greens drain the carrots of moisture, making them limp and dry. Store carrots in a plastic bag in the refrigerator for up to two weeks.

Baby Carrots With Curry Sauce

1/2 pound (4-inch size) baby carrots
2 tablespoons mayonnaise
1 tablespoon sour cream
1/2 teaspoon curry powder
1 teaspoon skim milk
1/2 teaspoon fresh lemon juice
1/2 teaspoon honey

In a large saucepan over medium heat, boil carrots in water 8 to 10 minutes or just until crisp-tender (taste one to see if it is done; it should still be very crunchy). Remove from heat and drain.

In a small saucepan over medium-low heat, combine mayonnaise, sour cream, curry powder, milk, lemon juice, and honey; cook, stirring occasionally, until thoroughly heated. Remove from heat and pour sauce over carrots to serve.

Makes 2 servings.

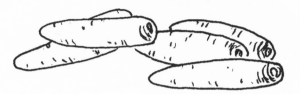

Mom's Marinated Carrots

This is a wonderful dish for potlucks. It is always well received.

5 cups sliced carrots
1 onion, sliced
1 green bell pepper, cored, seeded, and coarsely chopped
Tomato Marinade

In a large saucepan over medium heat, boil carrots in water 5 minutes only; remove from heat and drain. Stir in onion and bell pepper. Transfer into a large serving bowl and stir in Tomato Marinade. Cover and refrigerate 1 to 2 days before serving.

Makes 10 to 12 servings.

TOMATO MARINADE:
1 (10 3/4-ounce) can tomato soup, undiluted
1/2 cup vegetable oil
3/4 cup sugar
1/4 cup firmly packed brown sugar
1/2 cup cider vinegar
1 teaspoon salt
1/2 teaspoon pepper
1 teaspoon ground mustard
1 teaspoon worcestershire sauce

In a small bowl, combine tomato soup, vegetable oil, sugar, brown sugar, and cider vinegar; stir until well blended. Stir in salt, pepper, ground mustard, and worcestershire sauce.

Roasted Carrots & Parsnips

2 tablespoons cumin seeds
1 pound carrots, peeled and sliced 1/4-inch on the diagonal
1 pound parsnips, peeled and sliced 1/4-inch on the diagonal
3 cloves garlic, thinly sliced
3 tablespoons honey
1/4 cup olive oil
1/3 cup water
Salt to taste
1/2 tablespoon pepper
Juice of 2 limes
1/2 cup chopped fresh mint leaves

Preheat oven to 350 degrees. In a medium saucepan over medium heat, place cumin seeds; shake and toss seeds in the pan until their aroma is released, no more than 1 minute. Remove from heat and set aside.

In a medium ungreased baking dish, combine carrots, parsnips, garlic, and cumin seeds. Stir in honey, olive oil, water, salt, and pepper.

Cover and bake 30 minutes. Remove cover and bake another 30 minutes or until the carrots begin to caramelize (there should be no liquid remaining in the dish). Remove from oven and sprinkle with lime juice and mint leaves; serve hot or cold.

Makes 6 to 8 servings.

Gingered Carrots

10 carrots, peeled, halved widthwise, and quartered lengthwise
6 tablespoons butter or margarine
1/2 cup sugar
1/2 teaspoon ground ginger

In a medium saucepan over medium heat, boil carrots in water 8 to 10 minutes or just until crisp-tender (taste one to see if it is done; it should still be very crunchy). Remove from heat and drain well.

In a medium frying pan over medium heat, combine butter or margarine, sugar, and ginger, stirring frequently until butter or margarine is melted. Reduce heat to low, add carrots and toss thoroughly until well glazed. Remove from heat and transfer into a serving bowl.

Makes 6 to 8 servings.

Parsnips

Parsnips are one of the hardiest vegetables on the market and hold up well under either warm or quite cold temperatures. Some authorities state that the parsnip's flavor is not really brought out until it has been stored for some time at a temperature close to thirty-two degrees.

Select firm, well-shaped parsnips. Avoid those that are limp, shriveled or spotted. Place unwashed parsnips in a plastic bag and store them in the refrigerator.

Parsnips, which have a naturally sweet flavor, can be used as you would carrots.

TIP: They quickly turn mushy when overcooked, so be sure to add them to soups and stews toward the end of cooking time.

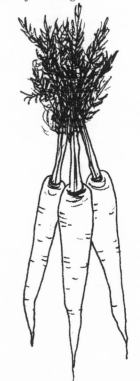

Cauliflower

Cleaning and Cooking Cauliflower

Remove leaves and trim tough part of stalk. Cut away any discolored parts. Soak in salted water thirty minutes to remove insects. Separate into flowerets, leaving a portion of center stalk attached to each one. If cooking whole, cut out center of stalk for more even cooking.

TIPS: If you add a little milk to water in which cauliflower is cooking, the cauliflower will remain attractively white. This way of cooking will also sweeten the flavor. Use this milk for soups or sauces.

Also adding a little lemon juice or cream of tartar (don't add too much, as this may toughen it) to the cooking water will help keep it white.

Crusty Herbed Cauliflower

These would also make good appetizers.

1 medium head cauliflower, stem and leaves removed
1 cup hot water
1 tablespoon lemon juice
2 eggs
1/2 teaspoon salt
1/4 teaspoon pepper
1 cup bread crumbs
1/2 cup chopped fresh basil leaves, or 1 tablespoon dried basil, crushed
1/4 teaspoon chopped fresh parsley
1 tablespoon butter or margarine, melted

Preheat oven to 400 degrees. Coat a baking sheet with vegetable-oil cooking spray. Cut cauliflower into bite-sized flowerets. In a large pan (with a steamer rack) over medium-high heat, pour water and lemon juice; heat until boiling. Add cauliflower and cook 7 to 10 minutes or until tender. Remove from heat.

In a small bowl, combine eggs, salt, and pepper; stir until well blended. In a shallow pie pan, toss together bread crumbs, basil, and parsley. Dip flowerets into egg mixture and then into crumb mixture, turning to coat all sides.

Place onto prepared baking sheet. Drizzle with butter or margarine. Bake 20 minutes or until golden brown and crispy. Remove from oven and transfer into a serving bowl. Serve immediately.

Makes 4 servings.

Crazy Cauliflower

1 cup hot water
1 tablespoon lemon juice
1 medium head cauliflower, stem and leaves removed
3/4 cup mayonnaise
1 tablespoon prepared mustard
1 teaspoon ground mustard
1/2 to 1 teaspoon curry powder
1 cup shredded sharp cheddar cheese

Preheat oven to 350 degrees. In a large pan (with a steamer rack) over medium-high heat, pour water and lemon juice; heat until boiling. Add cauliflower head, floweret side down; return water to a boil. Reduce heat to medium, cover, and cook 25 minutes or until tender. Remove from heat and drain. Transfer cauliflower, floweret side up, into an ungreased 3-quart casserole dish.

In a small bowl, combine mayonnaise, prepared mustard, ground mustard, and curry powder; stir until well blended. Spread mayonnaise mixture over cauliflower and sprinkle with cheddar cheese. Bake 15 to 20 minutes or until cheese is melted. Remove from oven and serve immediately.

Makes 4 servings.

Cauliflower With Toasted Mustard Seeds

3 tablespoons mustard seeds, divided
1 cup hot water
1 tablespoon lemon juice
1 large head cauliflower, stem and leaves removed
1 1/2 cups plain yogurt
1/4 cup minced fresh mint leaves or 2 tablespoons crumbled dry mint leaves
2 teaspoons sugar
1 teaspoon ground cumin

In a small frying pan over medium heat, place mustard seeds; shake and toss about 5 minutes or until seeds turn gray. Remove from heat and set aside.

In a large pan (with a steamer rack) over medium-high heat, pour water and lemon juice; heat until boiling. Add cauliflower, floweret side down. Return water to a boil. Reduce heat to medium, cover, and cook 25 minutes or until tender. Remove from heat, drain, and immerse in ice water; let stand until cold. Drain well on paper towels and transfer into a serving bowl.

In a large bowl, stir together yogurt, mint, sugar, cumin, and 2 tablespoons mustard seeds. To serve, spread yogurt mixture over cauliflower head and sprinkle with remaining mustard seeds.

Makes 4 servings.

Cheesy Cauliflower

1 cup hot water
1 tablespoon lemon juice
1 medium head cauliflower, stem and leaves removed
1/2 pound processed American cheese

In a large pan (with a steamer rack) over medium-high heat, pour water and lemon juice; heat until boiling. Add cauliflower head, floweret side down; return water to a boil. Reduce heat to medium, cover, and cook 25 minutes or until tender. Remove from heat, drain, and transfer cauliflower, floweret side up, onto a serving platter.

In a small saucepan over low heat, melt American cheese; pour over cauliflower and serve immediately.

Makes 4 servings.

Cauliflower

1 pound cauliflower equals 1 1/2 cups chopped or sliced cauliflower.

1 (10-ounce) package frozen cauliflower equals about 2 cups chopped or sliced cauliflower.

The word "cauliflower" comes from two Latin terms and literally means cabbage flower or stalk flower. Cauliflower is a cultivated descendant of the common cabbage.

Choose firm, compact, creamy white heads. A yellow tinge and spreading flowerets indicate over maturity. Any leaves should be crisp and bright green.

The size of the head does not affect quality, nor do the tiny leaves you occasionally find growing through the curds.

Store unwashed cauliflower, tightly wrapped, in the refrigerator for up to five days. Do not wash until you are ready to use.

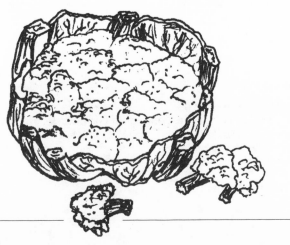

How to Cook Fresh Corn – The Right Way

IN WATER:
Choose a pot large enough to hold the amount of corn you want to cook, with room for water to cover the corn. Cover pot and bring water to a boil on high heat. Add husked corn ears and continue to cook on high heat (covered or not) three or four minutes or until kernels are very hot.

TIP: If you're having a party, borrow this trick from markets in Mexico. Vendors selling ears of corn for snacks keep them ready and waiting for several hours in tubs of lukewarm water. Instead of butter, ears are rubbed with lime wedges and sprinkled with salt. This nonfat alternative is very good.

IN THE HUSK – GRILLED OR BAKED:
Corn cooked this way is steamed and does not taste very different from boiled corn. It is handy to serve in the husk because you can season or butter the corn before it is cooked.

To prepare, pull husk back from each ear of corn, but leave attached at base of cob. Pull off and discard silk; trim off any insect damage, and rinse ears. If you want to butter them, pat ears dry and rub with soft butter. Pull husks back up around corn.

If you want the husk to stay snugly against the ear, pull off one or two of the outer husk layers, tear lengthwise into thin strips, and tie them around ear in several places. Just before cooking, immerse the ears in cool water (this keeps husks from burning).

TO GRILL:
Husk corn and discard silk; wrap each ear loosely with aluminum foil. Over gas or hot coals, place corn onto a hot grill over medium heat. Cover barbecue with lid, open any vents, and cook fifteen to twenty minutes; turn occasionally.

TO BAKE:
Preheat oven to 375 degrees. Prepare corn as directed for grilling, but put ears in a single layer, separating them slightly, directly onto the oven rack or onto a baking pan. Bake twenty to twenty-five minutes or until corn is tender when pierced and very hot.

MICROWAVING:
Perfect for cooking just one ear of corn. Husk corn and discard silk. Rinse and wrap each ear loosely in a paper towel. Cook on full power one to two minutes or until ears are very hot to touch.

Grandma Myers' Corn Tip

Grandma Myers always said to put a pot of water on the stove, and while it comes to a boil, pick your corn and husk it. Drop the corn into the boiling water, when the water starts to boil again, remove the corn. IT'S DONE!

Iowa Corn Au Gratin

A wonderful way to serve corn. Try it – you'll like it.

6 ears of corn or 1 (12-ounce) can corn kernels, drained
3 tablespoons butter or margarine
1 small onion, finely chopped
1 green bell pepper, cored, seeded, and finely chopped
3 tablespoons all-purpose flour
2 cups milk
1 cup shredded cheddar cheese
2 eggs, well beaten
1 teaspoon sugar
Salt and pepper to taste
1/2 cup bread crumbs

Preheat oven to 350 degrees. Grease a 2-quart casserole dish. If fresh corn is used, remove husk and silk, and cut kernels from cob.

In a large frying pan over medium heat, melt butter or margarine. Add onion and bell pepper and sauté until tender; stir in flour and then add milk. Cook, stirring constantly, until mixture has thickened and is smooth. Remove from heat; add corn, cheddar cheese, eggs, sugar, salt, and pepper.

Pour into prepared casserole dish and top with bread crumbs. Set into a shallow pan of hot water and bake 45 minutes. Remove from oven and serve immediately.

Makes 6 servings.

Baked Corn on the Cob

1 tablespoon prepared mustard
1 teaspoon salt
1 teaspoon prepared horseradish
Pepper to taste
1/2 cup butter or margarine, room temperature
6 ears of corn, husk and silk removed

Preheat oven to 375 degrees. In a small bowl, combine prepared mustard, salt, prepared horseradish, pepper, and butter or margarine; spread onto corn. Wrap each piece of corn loosely in aluminum foil.

Bake 20 to 25 minutes or until corn is very hot. Remove from oven, remove aluminum foil, and serve.

Makes 4 to 6 servings.

Corn

2 medium ears of corn equals 1 cup corn kernels.

1 (10-ounce) package frozen corn kernels equals 1 3/4 cups corn kernels.

To prepare corn for cooking, strip off husks, remove silk, and cut off bottom stump.

IMPORTANT: Fresh corn should be cooked and served the day it is picked or purchased.

As soon as corn is picked, its sugar begins its gradual conversion to starch, which reduces the corn's natural sweetness. Corn will lose 25 percent or more of its sugar within twenty-four hours after harvesting it. If for some reason corn is not being used immediately or has been purchased from the supermarket, add sugar to replace that which has been lost. Add one teaspoon sugar for each quart of water.

Removing Corn from the Cob

In a shallow bowl, hold ears of corn upright and, with a sharp knife, cut kernels from cobs. Then with blunt edge of the knife, scrape juice from cobs.

Chile Peppers

Be careful when you handle any kind of chile peppers. They contain oils which can burn your skin and especially your eyes. Avoid direct contact as much as possible. Many cooks wear rubber gloves while handling chilies. In any case, after you have worked with them, be sure to wash your hands and nails thoroughly with soap and water.

TYPES OF CHILIES:

ANAHEIM: Very mild. Six to eight inches in size and deep, shiny green. Often stuffed or added to salsas.

CAYENNE: From four to twelve inches in length. Deep green, yellow, orange, or red. Long, skinny, and wrinkled in appearance. Hot in taste.

JALAPEÑO: Range from dark green to red. Use whenever recipe simply calls for hot chile peppers. They can be fresh or canned.

POBLANO: Dark green, shiny and large in size. Mild to medium on the hotness scale. They can be fresh or canned.

SERRANO: Fairly high on the hotness scale. Can be found canned, pickled, or packed in oil with vegetables. Often served in Thai or Mexican dishes.

Quick Tamale-Corn Casserole

3 vegetarian tamales
1 (15-ounce) can cream-style corn
1 (15 1/4-ounce) can corn kernels, undrained
1 (15-ounce) can vegetarian chili con carne
1 cup chopped onion
1 (6-ounce) can black olives, drained
1/2 pound cheddar cheese, cut into cubes

Preheat oven to 350 degrees. Cook tamales according to package directions. In a large bowl, combine cooked tamales, cream corn, corn kernels, chili con carne, onion, black olives, and cheddar cheese. Place into a 2-quart casserole dish and bake 40 to 45 minutes. Remove from oven and serve.

Makes 8 to 10 servings.

Creamed Corn

This is the best creamed corn you'll ever eat.

1 (16-ounce) package frozen corn kernels
1/2 cup whipping cream
1/2 cup milk
1/2 teaspoon salt
1 tablespoon sugar
Red (cayenne) pepper to taste
1 tablespoon butter or margarine, melted
1 tablespoon all-purpose flour

In a large saucepan over medium-low heat, combine corn, whipping cream, milk, salt, sugar, and cayenne pepper; bring to a boil. Reduce heat to low and simmer 5 minutes. In a small bowl, combine butter or margarine with flour; stir into the corn mixture. Transfer into a serving bowl and serve.

Makes 4 to 6 servings.

Avocado-Corn Salsa

2 small to medium ripe avocados, peeled, seeded, and finely diced
1 cup fresh or frozen corn kernels
2 medium tomatoes, seeded, and finely diced
2 to 3 tablespoons lime juice
1 tablespoon finely chopped fresh cilantro
1/2 to 1 teaspoon minced hot green chile peppers
1/2 teaspoon salt

In a medium bowl, gently combine avocado, corn, tomatoes, lime juice, cilantro, chile peppers, and salt. Cover and refrigerate until ready to be served.

Yields 1 1/2 cups.

Fresh Corn Relish

10 cups fresh corn kernels
3 cups chopped cabbage
1 1/2 cups chopped onion
3/4 cup chopped green bell pepper
3/4 cup chopped red bell pepper
2 tablespoons ground mustard
1 1/2 teaspoons all-purpose flour
1/2 teaspoon ground turmeric
1/2 teaspoon ground cloves
1/2 teaspoon mustard seeds
1 tablespoon celery seeds
2 1/2 cups sugar
4 cups cider vinegar, divided
1/2 cup firmly packed brown sugar
2 tablespoons salt

In a large saucepan, combine corn, cabbage, onion, green bell pepper, and red bell pepper; set aside.

In a small bowl, combine ground mustard, flour, turmeric, cloves, mustard seeds, celery seeds, and 1/4 cup cider vinegar; add to vegetables in saucepan. Add sugar, 3 3/4 cups cider vinegar, brown sugar, and salt; stir until well blended. Bring to a boil over medium-high heat; reduce heat to low and simmer, uncovered, 15 minutes. Ladle into hot jars and seal.

Yields 8 pints.

Sweet Corn Risotto

2 cups finely chopped sweet onion, divided
1 to 3 teaspoons butter or margarine
2 tablespoons water
1 cup arborio rice or short-grain white rice
1/4 cup lime juice, divided
4 cups vegetable or chicken broth, divided
1 cup fresh or frozen corn kernels
1 to 2 tablespoons thinly sliced green onion tops or chives
Freshly grated parmesan cheese
Salt and coarsely ground pepper to taste

In a large frying pan over medium-high heat, combine 1 cup onion, butter or margarine, and water; cook, stirring constantly, 5 minutes or until liquid has evaporated and onion is limp. Stir in rice; cook another 3 minutes or until onion turns opaque. Stir in 2 tablespoons lime juice and 3 cups vegetable or chicken broth; cook an additional 10 minutes or until liquid is absorbed. Add 1 cup broth, corn, and remaining onion; cook, stirring often, 6 to 7 minutes longer or until rice is firm but not mushy and mixture is creamy.

Remove from heat and spoon risotto into soup bowls; sprinkle with green onion tops or chives, and parmesan cheese. Season to taste with remaining lime juice, salt, and pepper.

Makes 2 servings.

Turmeric

Turmeric, like dill, has been too long banished to the pickle jar. This spice, which is popular in East Indian cookery, can complement the natural taste of many flavors.

During Biblical times, turmeric was used not only as a flavoring but as a perfume and dye as well.

Turmeric has a bittersweet flavor and a brilliant yellow color. It is a member of the ginger family.

It is used principally in commercial preparation of mustard, curry powder, and certain pickles.

TIP: Although turmeric lacks the exquisite aromatic flavor of saffron, it can be used as a substitute. The taste will be milder and musky, but the color will be a brilliant golden-yellow.

Cucumbers

Cucumbers are always available, but are at their peak in the summer months.

Choose firm deep green cucumbers with no signs of mushiness, yellowing, or withering that indicate age.

Store whole cucumbers, unwashed, in a plastic bag in the refrigerator for up to five days.

Most cucumbers sold in supermarkets are waxed to protect against spoiling. Peel or wash well to remove this wax.

TIPS: To make fast and easy homemade cucumber pickles, cut crisp peeled cucumbers into one-half inch slices and soak in pickle juice for four days.

Thai Marinated Cucumbers

4 medium cucumbers
1/2 cup rice vinegar
1/2 cup water
2 tablespoons sugar
1/2 teaspoon salt
2 to 4 small hot red chile peppers, cored, seeded, and thinly sliced
1/3 cup sliced green onions
1/4 cup chopped fresh cilantro

Peel and halve cucumbers lengthwise and remove seeds; cut in half lengthwise again; cut widthwise into 1-inch thick pieces.

In a medium bowl, combine rice vinegar, water, sugar, salt, and red chile peppers. Add cucumbers and green onions; toss to coat. Stir in cilantro. Cover and refrigerate at least 1 hour or overnight before serving, stirring occasionally.

Makes 4 to 6 servings.

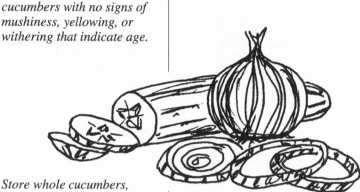

Sweet & Sour Cucumbers With Red Onion

2 large cucumbers
1 teaspoon olive oil
1 small red onion, chopped
2 tablespoons red wine vinegar
2 teaspoons sugar
1 tablespoon snipped fresh chives or finely chopped green onion tops
1 to 2 teaspoons grated orange zest
1 teaspoon butter or margarine
Salt to taste
1/8 teaspoon pepper

Peel and halve cucumbers lengthwise and remove seeds; cut in half lengthwise again; cut widthwise into 1-inch thick pieces.

In a medium frying pan over medium heat, heat olive oil. Add onion and sauté 2 minutes. Add cucumbers, wine vinegar, and sugar; cook another 3 minutes or until cucumbers are tender but still crisp. Stir in chives or green onion tops, orange zest, butter or margarine, salt, and pepper. Remove from heat and serve immediately.

Makes 4 servings.

Craven County Sweet Pickles

Cucumbers, washed and cut into 1/4-inch slices
Water
Pickling salt
Alum
Cider vinegar
Pickling spices
Sugar

DAY 1 – Place cucumbers in a large container and cover with boiling water.

DAY 2 – Drain off water and cover with fresh boiling water and pickling salt mixture (1 1/2 cups pickling salt to 1 gallon boiling water).

DAY 3 – Drain off water and cover with boiling water and alum mixture (1 tablespoon alum to 1 gallon boiling water).

DAY 4 – Drain off alum water. Boil together enough cider vinegar and pickling spices to cover cucumber slices (1 gallon cider vinegar and 3 tablespoons pickling spices wrapped in cheese cloth). Pour cider vinegar and spices over cucumbers.

DAYS 5, 6 and 7 – Let stand.

DAY 8 – Take cucumbers out of cider vinegar and pack in jars. Keep cucumbers covered with sugar (layer cucumber slices and sugar as you pack jars). A sweet syrup will form from sugar as time passes.

> *NOTE: Don't worry if you cannot get back to them after four days!*
>
> *Cucumbers can stay in the vinegar solution for an indefinite period of time.*

Grandmammy's Carolina Sharps

Cucumbers, washed and cut into 1/2-inch slices
Water
Pickling salt
Alum
Cider vinegar
Sugar
Pickling spices

DAY 1 – Place cucumbers into a large container and cover with boiling water and pickling salt mixture (1 1/2 cups pickling salt to 1 gallon water).

DAYS 2 and 3 – Repeat the day one process by pouring off the salt water and recovering with fresh salt water.

DAY 4 – Pour off water. Cover cucumbers with fresh boiling water with alum (1 tablespoon alum to 1 gallon water).

DAYS 5 and 6 – Repeat the Day 4 process by pouring off the alum water and recovering with fresh alum water.

DAY 7 – Pour off water. Cover with equal parts cider vinegar and water. This mixture should be boiling.

DAY 8 – Pour off vinegar solution. Pack cucumbers in jars and fill with equal parts cider vinegar and sugar. Add 1 tablespoon pickling spices and 1 extra tablespoon sugar in each jar before sealing.

Pickling Salt

When making pickles, use pickling or plain salt (not iodized salt, or you will get an unpleasant flavor).

Pickling salt is preferable to table salt. It is a superfine, fast-dissolving salt that contains no additives to cloud the brine in a pickling recipe.

Eggplant

Aubergine (Eggplant)

1 pound of eggplant equals 3 to 4 cups chopped eggplant.

1 average-sized eggplant will serve 3 people.

The eggplant is a member of the potato family, and it is known worldwide as aubergine, eggplant, brinjal, melanzana, garden egg, and patlican.

There are many varieties of aubergines, which range from dark purple to pale mauve, and from yellow to white. The long purple variety is the most commonly eaten.

It is one of the more popular vegetables in the world, and it is a staple of Italian cooking throughout Italy.

For hundreds of years, it was grown only in Sicily and southern Italy.

Tomato, Basil & Eggplant Casserole

12 small Italian or baby eggplants
Coarse salt
6 large tomatoes
4 cloves garlic, cut into slivers
1 bunch fresh basil, stems discarded and divided
1/2 cup olive oil, divided
Salt and coarsely ground pepper to taste
2 tablespoons lemon juice, divided
1 cup freshly grated parmesan cheese, divided
6 tablespoons fresh thyme or 2 tablespoons dried thyme, divided
1/4 cup coarsely chopped parsley, divided

Remove stems and cut eggplants in half lengthwise. Sprinkle with salt and let rest on paper towels for 30 minutes to release moisture; pat dry. Cut tomatoes into 1/2-inch slices. Sprinkle with salt and let rest on paper towels 30 minutes to release moisture; pat dry.

Preheat oven to 425 degrees. Make a 2-inch slit lengthwise on the cut side of each eggplant half. Into the slits, insert garlic slivers and a basil leaf. Place prepared eggplants, skin side down, onto an ungreased cookie sheet. Drizzle with 1/4 cup olive oil and sprinkle with pepper. Cover tightly with aluminum foil and bake 20 minutes. Remove eggplants from oven and reduce heat to 350 degrees.

Place 12 eggplant halves and half of the tomato slices in rows onto the bottom of a large ungreased baking dish. Drizzle with 1 tablespoon lemon juice; sprinkle with salt and pepper. Cover with 1/2 cup parmesan cheese and half of the thyme. Cover with a layer of whole basil leaves; drizzle with 2 tablespoons olive oil. Repeat with another layer, so that tomatoes cover eggplants. Sprinkle top with 2 tablespoons parsley.

Cover dish with aluminum foil and bake 1 hour. Remove aluminum foil and bake another 10 minutes or until eggplants and tomatoes are tender. Remove from oven and garnish with remaining chopped parsley. Serve hot or at room temperature.

Makes 8 servings.

Baked Sweet Onions

This is so simple and so good.

4 large sweet onions (Vidalia, Walla Walla, or Maui), peeled
Salt and pepper
4 teaspoons butter

Preheat oven to 250 degrees. Place onions into a baking dish with approximately 1 inch of water. Bake, uncovered, 2 hours or until onions are soft when you squeeze them.

Remove from oven and place onto a cutting board; pull back brown skins and cut them off at the roots. Transfer onto a serving platter and season each with salt, pepper, and 1 teaspoon of butter.

Makes 4 servings.

Blooming Onion Flowers

These onion flowers are almost as much fun to watch as they come out of their foil packets with petals unfolding as they are to eat. They are especially pretty if you use red onions.

6 medium onions (about 3 inches in diameter), peeled
3 teaspoons balsamic vinegar, divided
6 tablespoons olive oil, divided
6 teaspoons chutney (your favorite), divided
Salt and coarsely ground pepper to taste

Trim the root end of each onion carefully so that the onion is still intact. Standing each onion on its end, cut parallel vertical slices at 1/4-inch intervals into, but not through, the onion, stopping about 1/2 inch above the root end. Turn each onion 90 degrees and cut parallel vertical slices in the same manner to form a crosshatch pattern, keeping the onions intact.

In a large bowl of cold water and ice cubes, place onions; let soak for 3 to 4 hours or until they have opened into flowers. Carefully remove from ice water; drain, root end up, for 10 minutes.

Place each onion, root end down, onto the center of a square of aluminum foil. Drizzle with 1 teaspoon balsamic vinegar, 1 tablespoon olive oil, and 1 teaspoon chutney. Season with salt and pepper. Bring the edges of the foil together to enclose the onions, crimping the edges to seal them.

To bake, preheat oven to 375 degrees. Bake 60 to 70 minutes. Remove from oven, remove aluminum foil, and transfer onto individual serving plates.

To barbecue, preheat barbecue grill. Place the packets on hot grill over direct heat. Cover barbecue with lid, open any vents, and cook 60 to 70 minutes. Remove from barbecue, remove aluminum foil, and transfer onto individual serving plates.

Makes 6 servings.

Sweet Onions

How about eating a raw onion that is almost as sweet as an apple? Certain fresh onions, called sweet onions, are known for their mild, even sugary, taste. These onions contain more sugars and fewer sulfur-containing compounds than other onions do.

They are often named by geographic origin and described as being sweet. The best known are Vidalia from Georgia, Walla Walla from Washington, Maui from Hawaii, Imperial from California, Carzalia from New Mexico, and the Texas Spring or Supersweet from Texas.

They are available from February to August. Because their individual seasons are short, they often command premium prices.

Onions

When buying onions, choose those that are heavy for their size with dry, papery skins, and that show no signs of spotting or moistness. Avoid onions that are soft or sprouting. Store onions in a cool, dry place with good air circulation for up to three months.

TIP: To get rid of "onion breath," eat several sprigs of vinegar- or salt-dipped parsley. You can also chew on fennel seeds or coffee beans. You now have a "different" breath!

Onion Myths & Facts

To keep your automobile windshield from frosting at night, slice an onion and rub the windshield with the onion. The juice will keep it frost-free.

To cure baldness, rub head with the onion. The onion juice was supposed to cause hair to grow "thick as thistles." Note: You may have to sleep alone, but at least you'll have hair!

To select your husband-to-be from among suitors, it is said that if the name of each suitor is written on an onion and then placed in a cool dark storeroom, the first onion that sprouts will be the man she should marry!

During the Civil War, General Grant believed that onions would prevent dysentery and other ills of warm climates. He sent the following wire to the War Department: "I will not move my army without onions." The next day, three trainloads of onions were dispatched to the front.

Roasted Balsamic Onions

So simple and so elegant – you eat it right in the skin.

2 medium yellow onions, unpeeled
Salt and coarsely ground pepper to taste
4 teaspoons butter
8 teaspoons balsamic vinegar

Preheat oven to 350 degrees. Butter a baking dish just large enough to hold the onions. Cut the unpeeled onions in half lengthwise through the root and stem ends. Cut a thin slice off the rounded side of each half so that it will sit upright in the baking dish. Arrange the onion halves, cut side up, in the prepared baking dish. Season with salt and pepper, and place 1 teaspoon of butter on each half.

Cover and bake 45 to 50 minutes or until onions give slightly when the edges are squeezed together between your fingers. Uncover and sprinkle each onion half with 2 teaspoons of balsamic vinegar (use a fork to spread the onion layers apart so that the vinegar can dribble down between the layers). Bake, uncovered, another 15 minutes. Remove from oven and serve hot or at room temperature.

Makes 4 servings.

Stuffed Baked Onion

6 medium onions
1/4 cup butter or margarine
2 tablespoons chopped fresh parsley
1/2 teaspoon dried thyme, crushed
1/2 teaspoon Beau Monde seasoning
1/4 teaspoon salt
Pepper to taste
3/4 cup bread crumbs
3 tablespoon half and half cream

Preheat oven to 350 degrees. Grease a large casserole dish. Make onion shells by peeling the onions and gently cutting out centers. Chop onion centers; set aside.

In a large pot over medium heat, boil onion shells in salted water 7 to 10 minutes or until only slightly done. Remove from heat, gently drain, and set aside.

In a medium frying pan over medium high heat, melt butter or margarine. Add chopped onion centers and sauté 5 to 8 minute or until soft and translucent; stir in parsley, thyme, Beau Monde seasoning, salt, pepper, and bread crumbs. Mix in half and half cream until mixture is soft and moist like a stuffing.

Stuff filling into onion shells. Place into prepared casserole dish and bake, uncovered, 20 minutes. Remove from oven and serve immediately.

Makes 6 servings.

Kahlua Candied Yams

4 medium (1 3/4-pounds) yams
1/4 cup butter or margarine
1/3 cup firmly packed brown sugar
1/4 cup kahlua liqueur

In a medium saucepan over medium-high heat, boil yams in water until tender but still firm. Remove from heat, peel, and cut in half lengthwise. Set aside.

In a large frying pan over medium heat, melt butter or margarine. Add sugar and liqueur; stir and cook 1 minute. Add yams; cook until brown on both sides. Reduce heat to low and simmer another 15 minutes, turning yams several times. Remove from heat and transfer into a serving bowl. Serve immediately.

NOTE: Sweet potatoes may be substituted for the yams.

Makes 4 servings.

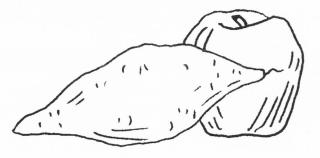

Sweet Potatoes & Apples

4 medium (1 3/4-pounds) sweet potatoes, cooked, peeled, and sliced 1/2-inch thick
Maple Sauce
2 cups thinly sliced tart apples

Preheat oven to 350 degrees. Butter a medium casserole dish. Place half of the sweet potato slices onto the bottom of prepared casserole dish; pour half of the Maple Sauce over the top. Layer apple slices over potatoes and then layer with remaining sweet potatoes; pour remaining Maple Sauce on top.

Bake, covered, 40 minutes. Remove cover and bake another 10 to 15 minutes. Remove from oven and serve immediately.

Makes 4 servings.

MAPLE SAUCE:
1/2 cup firmly packed brown sugar
Grated orange zest
1 teaspoon ground cinnamon
1/2 teaspoon freshly grated nutmeg
4 tablespoons butter or margarine
1/2 cup apple juice
1/2 cup genuine maple syrup

In a small saucepan over medium-low heat, combine brown sugar, orange zest, cinnamon, nutmeg, and butter or margarine. Mix in apple juice, and maple syrup; stir until well blended. Heat until sugar is dissolved.

Yams

Yam is the name of a cultivated climbing plant which grows in tropical areas, of which only the root or tuber is eaten. They vary in color from red to brown and the moist flesh from white to yellow.

Store yams in a cool, dry, well-ventilated place.

TIP: Yams may be substituted for sweet potatoes in most recipes.

Sweet Potatoes

Sweet potatoes should be uniformly light-tan-colored. Do not purchase if they have white areas or are damaged; this probably means decay.

Sweet potatoes store well. If you grow your own, they will be sweeter when allowed to age for a month or so (the very minute they are harvested, sugar starts to form).

To peel sweet potatoes easily, take them from boiling water and immerse immediately in very cold water. The skins will almost fall off by themselves.

TIP: To keep raw sweet potatoes from turning dark when peeling, place them in one quart water mixed with three tablespoons lemon juice for a few minutes. Drain well before using.

Sweet Potatoes

Marshmallows

When we think of traditional holiday meals, sweet potatoes with marshmallows always comes to mind.

As a candy, marshmallows date back at least to the late nineteenth century. They were originally made from the sticky root of the marshmallow plant. Today they are generally made of gelatin, water, sugar, egg whites or corn syrup, and vanilla extract.

In the 1920s, marshmallows were introduced as a topper for sweet potatoes. While sweet potatoes and marshmallows were not originally created for the holiday meal, it has become a tradition.

TIP: Store marshmallows in a tightly sealed plastic bag in the freezer and you won't have to worry about them drying out.

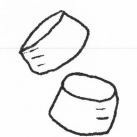

Grandma Gertie's Sweet Potatoes

6 medium (2 1/2 pounds) sweet potatoes, cooked, peeled, and sliced 1/2-inch thick
1/2 cup firmly packed brown sugar, divided
Salt and pepper to taste
3 tart apples, peeled and sliced 1/2-inch thick
Syrup
Marshmallows

Preheat oven to 350 degrees. Grease a 13x9-inch baking dish. Place a layer of sweet potato slices into prepared baking dish. Sprinkle 2 tablespoons brown sugar over the top. Season with salt and pepper.

Place a layer of sliced apples over the top of the sweet potatoes. Sprinkle with 2 tablespoons brown sugar. Make another layer each of sweet potatoes and apples. Sprinkle 2 tablespoons brown sugar over each layer. Pour Syrup over the top of the sweet potatoes and apple mixture. Bake, uncovered, 20 minutes; during the last 5 minutes of cooking, place whole marshmallows onto the top of each slice and let brown. Remove from oven and serve immediately.

Makes 8 servings.

SYRUP:
1 2/3 cups firmly packed brown sugar
1 cup water

In a medium saucepan over low heat, combine brown sugar and water; stir until sugar is dissolved.

Pear & Sweet Potato Gratin

2 medium sweet potatoes, cooked, peeled, and sliced 1/4-inch thick
2 Anjou or Bartlett pears, peeled, cored, and sliced 1/4-inch thick
2 tablespoons lemon juice
2 tablespoons butter, melted and divided
1 tablespoon firmly packed brown sugar
2 teaspoons all-purpose flour
1/8 teaspoon ground cinnamon
1/8 teaspoon ground ginger
1/8 teaspoon ground mace
Salt and pepper to taste
1/2 cup freshly grated parmesan cheese
1/2 cup bread crumbs

Preheat oven to 400 degrees. Butter a 1 1/2-quart gratin or casserole dish. In a large bowl, combine sweet potatoes and pears. Add lemon juice, 1 tablespoon butter, brown sugar, flour, cinnamon, ginger, mace, salt, and pepper; stir until well blended. Place mixture in prepared baking dish, packing it down firmly. Bake, uncovered, 45 mintutes or until thoroughly heated. Remove from oven.

Increase oven temperature to broil. In a small bowl combine parmesan cheese, bread crumbs, and 1 tablespoon butter; sprinkle mixture over the top and broil 4 inches from heat until topping is crisp and golden. Remove from oven and serve immediately.

Makes 4 servings.

Roast Potato Duo

2 large (1 pound) baking potatoes, peeled
2 small (3/4 pound) sweet potatoes, peeled
1 tablespoon vegetable oil
3/4 teaspoon salt
1/4 teaspoon dried rosemary, crushed

Preheat oven to 350 degrees. Spray a baking sheet with vegetable-oil cooking spray. Cut each potato lengthwise into 6 wedges; arrange in prepared pan. Sprinkle with vegetable oil, salt, and rosemary.

Bake, uncovered, 50 to 60 minutes, stirring occasionally, or until potatoes are tender when pierced with a fork. Remove from oven and transfer onto a serving platter to serve.

Makes 4 servings.

French Fries

Try french frying sweet potatoes for an interesting flavor.

Sprinkle with flour before frying and they will be deliciously golden brown.

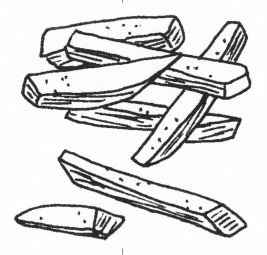

Two-Potato Gratin

This is great for a buffet-style meal or to take to a potluck.

2 cloves garlic, minced
1 small bunch fresh basil, coarsely chopped
3 jalapeño chile peppers, cored, seeded, and thinly sliced
1/2 cup toasted pine nuts
1/2 small red onion, thinly sliced
3 eggs, lightly beaten
4 cups heavy cream
5 medium (2 1/4 pounds) sweet potatoes, peeled and very thinly sliced
5 medium (2 1/4 pounds) baking potatoes, peeled and very thinly sliced
Salt and pepper to taste

Preheat oven to 350 degrees. On the bottom of an ungreased 13x9-inch casserole dish, mix together garlic, basil, chile peppers, pine nuts, and onion.

In a small bowl, combine eggs and heavy cream; stir until well blended. Alternate layers of sweet and baking potatoes and some of the egg mixture over the pine nut mixture in the baking dish. Season with salt and pepper. Push down evenly to send egg mixture into layers.

Bake, covered, 1 hour or until potatoes are tender when pierced with a fork. Remove aluminum foil and brown for a few minutes. Remove from oven and serve immediately.

Makes 12 servings.

Cooking Potatoes

BOILED POTATOES:
Boiled potatoes should be started in cold water rather than in hot water. This allows for a more even cooking and heat penetration from outside to inside during the relatively long cooking time required.

Potatoes are never cooled in cold water, unlike most vegetables. This would make them soggy.

BAKED POTATOES:
Scrub well and pierce the ends with a fork or skewer so steam can escape.

For crisp skins, rub lightly with oil. For more tender skins, leave dry.

Place onto an oven rack in a preheated 400-degree oven and bake until done, approximately one hour. To test doneness, squeeze gently. Done potatoes will yield to gentle pressure.

Aluminum-foil-wrapped potatoes are not baked but steamed in their own moisture. The texture of a steamed potato is entirely different from that of a baked potato. Save yourself the trouble and expense of wrapping in aluminum foil and serve a better product.

Two-Potato Casserole

A lovely melange of three root vegetables and a little milk sauce.

1 tablespoon vegetable oil
2 medium onions, thinly sliced
5 medium (2 1/4 pounds) baking potatoes, cooked and peeled
3 medium (1 1/4 pounds) sweet potatoes, cooked and peeled
Two-Potato Sauce, divided

Preheat oven to 350 degrees. In a large frying pan over medium heat, heat vegetable oil. Add onions and sauté until tender and golden brown, stirring occasionally; set aside.

Cut both kinds of potatoes into 1/4-inch thick slices. In an ungreased 13x9-inch casserole dish, alternately layer a third of both kinds of potatoes; top with half of the onions, then a third of the Two-Potato Sauce. Top with half of the remaining potatoes, all the remaining onions, and half the remaining sauce. Arrange remaining potatoes in casserole dish; top with remaining sauce.

Bake, uncovered, 45 minutes or until gently bubbling and mixture is thoroughly heated. If you prefer, broil 1 to 2 minutes to brown top of potatoes slightly. Remove from oven and serve immediately.

Makes 10 servings.

TWO-POTATO SAUCE:
3 tablespoons all-purpose flour
1 1/4 teaspoons salt
1/4 teaspoon pepper
3 tablespoons vegetable oil
2 3/4 cups milk

In medium saucepan over medium heat, cook flour, salt, and pepper in vegetable oil for 1 minute. Gradually stir in milk; cook another 10 to 15 minutes, stirring constantly, until sauce thickens and just comes to a boil.

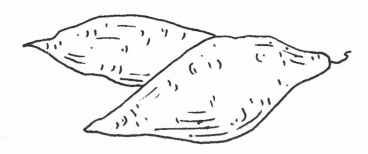

Idaho Baked Potatoes With Onions

1 large onion, sliced
2 large baking potatoes
Salt and pepper to taste
Butter or margarine

Preheat oven to 350 degrees. Slice potatoes into 1/4-inch slices (it is not necessary to cut all the way through potatoes). Wedge onion slices between slits. Generously season with salt and pepper. Dot with butter or margarine. Wrap aluminum foil securely around the potatoes and onions.

Bake 45 to 50 minutes or until potatoes are tender when pierced with a fork. Remove from oven and remove aluminum foil to serve.

Makes 2 servings.

Sliced Baked Potatoes

Always a family favorite.

4 medium (1 3/4 pounds) baking potatoes, peeled
1 teaspoon salt
2 to 3 tablespoons butter or margarine, melted
2 to 3 tablespoons chopped fresh herbs (such as parsley, chives, thyme or sage)
4 tablespoons shredded cheddar cheese
1 1/2 tablespoons freshly grated parmesan cheese

Preheat oven to 350 degrees. Cut potatoes into quarters lengthwise. Put potatoes into an ungreased baking dish. Sprinkle with salt and drizzle with butter or margarine. Sprinkle with fresh herbs.

Bake, uncovered, 50 minutes or until potatoes are tender when pierced with a fork; remove from oven. Sprinkle with cheddar cheese and parmesan cheese. Bake another 10 to 15 minutes or until lightly browned and cheeses are melted. Remove from oven and serve immediately.

Makes 4 servings.

Potatoes

1 1/4 pounds (3 medium potatoes) equals 3 cups chopped or sliced raw potatoes, or 2 to 3 cups cooked mashed potatoes.

Potatoes should be smooth, well shaped, and unbruised. Do not buy if they have sprouted or have a green tint to the skin.

When selecting potatoes, choose new potatoes for boiling and salads. They have thinner skins and are firmer.

Store at room temperature in a dark area. Do not refrigerate.

Rub butter over potatoes before baking to prevent skin from cracking and to improve the taste.

Potatoes will bake in a hurry if they are boiled in salted water for ten minutes before putting them into a very hot oven.

For fluffier boiled potatoes, simply pour off all the water after they are boiled and cover the pot with a double thickness of paper towels, then cover with the saucepan lid. In ten minutes, steam will be absorbed by the towels and your potatoes will be dry and fluffy.

TIP: Never attempt to bake a mature potato without puncturing the skin – it might explode.

Make-Ahead Mashed Potatoes

Wonderful recipe – use this dish at your Thanksgiving or Christmas dinner. Saves the last-minute hassle of mashing potatoes.

15 medium (5 pounds) potatoes, peeled and quartered
6 ounces cream cheese, room temperature
1 cup sour cream
2 teaspoons onion powder
1 teaspoon salt
1/2 teaspoon pepper
2 egg whites, slightly beaten
1 tablespoon butter or margarine

Spray a large casserole dish with vegetable-oil cooking spray. In a large pot of boiling water over medium-high heat, cook potatoes until tender when pierced with a fork; remove from heat and drain. Mash potatoes until there are no lumps. Add cream cheese, sour cream, onion powder, salt, pepper, and egg whites; blend well. Dot with butter or margarine. Cool slightly, cover, and refrigerate.

Preheat oven to 350 degrees. Take potatoes out of the refrigerator 30 minutes before baking. Bake, covered, 40 minutes or until steaming hot in center. Remove from oven and serve immediately.

NOTE: This can be made up to a week ahead. If preparing ahead, place in an ovenproof baking dish, allow to cool slightly, cover, and refrigerate.

Makes 12 to 25 servings.

Mashed Potatoes

Russet potatoes make the best mashed potatoes. Peel them and cut into equal-sized pieces. Boil and drain.

Dry over low heat for a few minutes. Mash with a potato masher, or electric beaters. Do this very quickly so the potatoes remain hot.

Add one tablespoon butter (more or less if you like) for each two potatoes, and salt to your taste. Beat until the butter is melted. Then add milk or light cream that has been heated but not brought to the boil (if you add cold liquid, the potatoes will be cold and gummy). Beat the liquid into the potatoes to make a smooth, fluffy mixture. Add only enough liquid to make the mixture smooth, about one tablespoon for each potato. Do not overbeat. They should be soft and moist, but firm enough to hold their shape.

All this should be done as QUICKLY AS POSSIBLE so the potatoes never have a chance to get cold – that is the secret of delicious mashed potatoes!

Garlic Mashed Potatoes

Excellent served with pork chops.

Follow recipe for Mashed Potatoes except lightly brown 1 clove of minced garlic in 3 tablespoons of butter. Add to mashed potatoes; stir to blend.

Baked French Fries

5 large (2 1/4 pounds) baking potatoes
2 egg whites
2 teaspoons Cajun spice

Preheat oven to 350 degrees. Spray a baking sheet heavily with vegetable-oil cooking spray.

Peel and slice each potato lengthwise into 1/4-inch slices, then slice each slice lengthwise into matchsticks.

In a large bowl, combine egg whites and Cajun spice; add the potatoes and stir to coat. Pour onto prepared baking sheet and spread out into a single layer, leaving a little space between each piece.

Place baking sheet onto bottom shelf of oven. Bake, uncovered, 20 to 25 minutes or until fries are crispy, turning them every 6 to 8 minutes with a spatula so that they brown evenly. Remove from oven and transfer onto a serving platter. Serve immediately.

Makes 4 servings.

Northwestern Potatoes Au Gratin

Excellent dish for a dinner party.

4 medium (1 3/4 pounds) potatoes, cooked and peeled
2 tablespoons butter or margarine
2 tablespoons all-purpose flour
1 1/2 cups hot milk
1/2 cup shredded sharp cheddar cheese
1 teaspoon freshly grated parmesan cheese
1 clove garlic, minced
Salt and coarsely ground pepper to taste
Shredded cheddar cheese
Freshly grated parmesan cheese
Paprika

Preheat oven to 350 degrees. Butter a large casserole dish. Cut potatoes into 1/4-inch slices. Layer slices onto bottom of prepared casserole dish.

In a medium saucepan over medium heat, melt butter or margarine; stir in flour until mixture is smooth. Gradually add hot milk, stirring constantly. Stir in cheddar cheese, parmesan cheese, and garlic; continue cooking until cheese is melted. Season with salt and pepper. Remove from heat.

Pour cheese sauce over potatoes and sprinkle with additional cheddar cheese, parmesan cheese, and paprika. Bake, uncovered, 20 minutes. Place under broiler and broil just until brown and bubbly. Remove from oven and serve immediately.

Makes 6 servings.

Potato Sprouts

Did you know that potato sprouts are poisonous? There's no problem with the potato; just cut off the sprouts, and it's fine for eating. A sprout of any size can be toxic, but you'd have to eat many sprouts to get sick.

The same is true for potatoes that turn a greenish hue. A potato in this condition is called "light-struck," and it happens when a chemical just beneath the potato's skin reacts to light. The green part will taste a little bitter, but if you peel it off, the rest of the potato will taste fine.

Both conditions can be retarded by storing the potatoes in a cool, very dark place.

Clay Pot Potatoes With Pine Nuts

21 small (2 pounds) red potatoes, scrubbed
2 small red onions, thinly sliced
2 tablespoons currants
3 tablespoons pine nuts
2 tablespoons olive oil
2 cloves garlic, minced
12 black olives, pitted and sliced
1 dried bay leaf
Salt and pepper to taste
1/2 cup red vermouth
2 tablespoons chopped fresh basil

Place potatoes into soaked clay pot. Mix in onion slices, currants, pine nuts, and olive oil. Add garlic, olives, and bay leaf with a generous sprinkling of salt and pepper. Pour in vermouth.

Cover the clay pot and place into a COLD oven. Cook 1 hour at 450 degrees or until potatoes are tender. Remove from oven and set on a wire rack. Let potatoes stand in pot 10 minutes without removing lid. Before serving, mix in basil.

Makes 4 to 6 servings.

Dried Currants

1 pound of currants equals about 3 cups.

SUBSTITUTION:
1 cup currants may be substituted with 1 cup raisins or 1 cup soft prunes or dates (finely chopped).

This fruit gets its name from Corinth, a once-famous city of ancient Greece, where currants were cultivated and exported in considerable quantities.

Dried currants are the dried fruit of a practically seedless grape, smaller, darker, and much more tart than the seedless raisin.

The word "currant" is a corruption of Corinth, Greece, which is the principal source of supply, although California furnishes a lot.

They are sometimes called Zante currants or Corinth currants to distinguish them from the Sultana raisins, which are also called currants in certain localities.

Roasted Mustard Potatoes

4 tablespoons Dijon mustard
1 egg white
2 teaspoons paprika
1 teaspoon ground cumin
1 teaspoon chili powder
1/8 teaspoon red (cayenne) pepper
16 small (1 1/4 pounds) red potatoes

Preheat oven to 400 degrees. Spray a baking sheet heavily with vegetable-oil cooking spray.

In a large bowl, combine Dijon mustard, egg white, paprika, cumin, chili powder, and cayenne pepper. Prick potatoes several times with a fork; add to mustard mixture and toss to coat potatoes evenly. Pour coated potatoes onto baking sheet, leaving a little space in between.

Bake, uncovered, 30 to 35 minutes or until potatoes are tender when pierced with a fork, turning them every 6 to 8 minutes with a spatula so that they brown evenly. Remove from oven and serve immediately.

Makes 4 servings.

Potato Delight Casserole

3 large baking potatoes, peeled
1 large onion, thinly sliced
1/2 medium green bell pepper, cored, seeded, and chopped
8 to 10 bacon slices cut in half
Salt and coarsely ground pepper to taste
1/2 cup shredded swiss cheese
1/2 cup freshly grated parmesan cheese
4 to 6 tablespoons butter
3/4 cup heavy cream

Preheat oven to 350 degrees. Grease a large baking dish. Thinly slice the potatoes and place into a bowl of cold water; set aside.

Layer half of the bacon slices onto bottom of prepared baking dish. Drain and dry the potato slices thoroughly with paper towels. Place a layer of potato slices (slightly overlapping) over the top of the bacon. Place a layer of onion slices over the top of the potatoes and sprinkle with bell pepper. Season with salt and pepper, sprinkle with half of the swiss cheese and half of the parmesan cheese, and dot with butter.

Repeat the layers of bacon, potatoes, onions, and bell pepper. Season with salt and pepper and sprinkle with the remaining swiss cheese and parmesan cheese. Pour the heavy cream onto the top of the cheese. Cover and place the baking dish in the center of the oven.

Bake 1 hour and 15 minutes. Uncover, and bake another 30 minutes or until the potatoes are very tender and the top is browned. Remove from oven and serve immediately.

Makes 6 to 8 servings.

Seeding Bell Peppers

To quickly remove the stem and meaty bulb of seeds from a bell pepper, slice the pepper from the tip or bottom towards the stem, stopping just short of the stem.

Pull the two pieces of peppers apart. They'll break off from the stem, leaving most of the seeds and the stem behind.

German Creamed Spinach

This dish is absolutely wonderful. If your children won't eat spinach, try this.

2 to 3 large bunches (2 pounds) fresh spinach leaves
Cream Sauce
Salt and pepper to taste

Wash spinach leaves thoroughly. In a large saucepan, cook spinach in as little water as possible until tender. As soon as spinach is thoroughly wilted, remove from heat, and drain in a colander, pressing with the back of a kitchen spoon to squeeze out excess liquid. Place on a cutting board; cut spinach very fine.

In a medium bowl, mix together Cream Sauce and spinach. Season with salt and pepper. Serve immediately.

NOTE: If spinach bunches are extra large, you probably will need to double the Cream Sauce recipe.

Makes 6 to 8 servings.

CREAM SAUCE:
2 tablespoons butter or margarine
2 tablespoons finely chopped onion
2 tablespoons all-purpose flour
Salt and pepper to taste
1 cup milk

In a large frying pan over medium heat, melt butter or margarine. Add onion and sauté until soft; add flour and blend thoroughly. When perfectly smooth and free from lumps but not in the least browned, add salt and pepper. Gradually add milk; reduce heat to low and cook, stirring constantly, until sauce boils (may use some spinach juice in place of milk).

Washing Spinach

Like all greens, spinach should be washed as soon as you buy it. Loose spinach can be very gritty, so it must be thoroughly rinsed (it can't be washed enough). It grows in sandy soils that seem to cling to the growing leaves.

The easiest way to wash spinach is to put it into a sink or large container full of cold water. Remove stems by twisting or cutting spinach leaves off just above stem line and immerse in water. Swish leaves around, then let them stand for a few minutes while dirt sinks to the bottom.

Thoroughly dry by using a salad spinner or by blotting with paper towels. Wrap in dry paper towels and seal in a plastic bag.

Wilted Spinach

2 bunches (1 1/2 pounds) fresh spinach leaves
Sweet and Sour Dressing
3 bacon slices, cooked and crumbled

Wash spinach leaves thoroughly and tear into bite-sized pieces. Place into a large bowl. To serve, pour desired amount of hot Sweet and Sour Dressing over spinach; toss to mix well. Garnish with bacon and serve immediately.

Makes 4 to 6 servings.

SWEET AND SOUR DRESSING:
1 tablespoon vegetable oil
4 tablespoons sesame seeds
2 tablespoons sugar
4 tablespoons cider vinegar
1 tablespoon soy sauce

In a large frying pan over medium heat, heat vegetable oil. Add sesame seeds and brown lightly. Remove from heat and add sugar, cider vinegar, and soy sauce. Return to heat and cook until almost boiling.

Simple Supper Spinach Pie

For a lazy weekend brunch or a simple evening meal, this quiche-like dish can be put together in minutes with delicious results.

2 bunches (1 1/2 pounds) fresh spinach leaves
3 eggs
3 tablespoons all-purpose flour
2 cups (1 pint) cottage cheese
1 small onion, minced
12 fresh mushrooms, coarsely chopped
1 cup coarsely shredded cheddar cheese
1/2 cup freshly grated parmesan cheese
1 teaspoon ground cumin
Salt and pepper to taste

Preheat oven to 350 degrees. Spray a deep-dish pie pan or shallow casserole dish with vegetable-oil cooking spray.

Wash spinach leaves thoroughly and cut into large pieces. In a large saucepan over medium heat, place the spinach leaves with a small amount of water. Cover and steam 2 to 3 minutes or until leaves are just wilted. Remove from heat, drain, and set aside to cool.

In a large bowl, lightly beat eggs. Slowly beat in flour. Fold in cottage cheese, onion, mushrooms, spinach, cheddar cheese, and parmesan cheese. Add cumin, salt, and pepper. Mix well and pour into prepared pan or dish.

Bake, uncovered, 50 minutes or until lightly browned on top (mixture will bubble while it is baking). Remove from oven and let cool 15 minutes before serving.

Makes 6 servings.

Spinach

1 pound of fresh spinach equals about 1 cup of cooked spinach.

According to historical records, spinach was cultivated by the Greeks and Romans even before the Christian era. Today spinach is one of our most commonly used vegetables.

Choose leaves that are crisp and dark green with a nice fresh fragrance. Avoid those that are limp, damaged, or spotted.

Winter Squash

TYPES OF WINTER SQUASH:

- *Acorn*
- *Butternut*
- *Delicata*
- *Hubbard*
- *Turban*
- *Pumpkin*
- *Spaghetti*

Winter squash have hard, thick skins. Store in a cool, dark, well-ventilated place for up to one month.

Winter squash can be cut in halves or pieces. To cook them, first remove fibers and seeds; then bake, steam, or boil the squash. When water is used in cooking, the quantity of water should be kept small to avoid losing flavor and nutrients.

Acorn and butternut squash are frequently cut in half, baked, and served in the shell. Squash pulp is also used for pies and may be prepared in casseroles, soufflés, pancakes, and custards.

TIP: The easiest way to prepare winter squash is to halve it, scoop out the seeds, and bake the pulp in the rind until tender. Serve with butter, maple syrup, brown sugar, or honey.

Baked Butternut Squash

1 (2 to 3 pounds) butternut squash
1 to 2 tablespoons lime juice
Salt and pepper to taste

Preheat oven to 375 degrees. Place squash onto an ungreased baking sheet, and prick in a few places with a sharp knife. Bake, uncovered, 1 hour or until tender. Remove from oven. Cut squash in half lengthwise and remove fibers and seeds. Season each half with lime juice, salt, and pepper. Cut each half in half again and serve.

VARIATION: In a small frying pan over low heat, melt 2 tablespoons butter or margarine; stir in 1/2 teaspoon ground cinnamon. Add 1 tablespoon brown sugar; stir until well blended. Brush the butter mixture over each portion of squash before serving.

Makes 2 to 4 servings.

Baked Squash With Blueberries

This squash is so delicious that it could be served for dessert.

3 acorn squash
1 1/2 cups fresh or frozen blueberries
1/2 tart apple, peeled and diced
6 tablespoons firmly packed brown sugar
6 teaspoons butter or margarine

Preheat oven to 350 degrees. Cut squash in half lengthwise and remove fibers and seeds. In a medium bowl, mix together blueberries, apple, brown sugar, and butter or margarine. Fill squash halves with topping mixture.

Place into an ungreased casserole dish, add 1/2 cup water around the squash; cover and bake 50 to 60 minutes. Remove cover and bake another 10 minutes or until squash is tender. Remove from oven and serve immediately.

Makes 6 servings.

Baked Delicata Squash With Lime Butter

2 (3/4 pound each) delicata squash
3 tablespoon butter, softened
1 tablespoon lime juice
1 teaspoon chili powder
Salt and coarsely ground pepper to taste

Preheat oven to 350 degrees. Cut each squash in half lengthwise and remove fibers and seeds. Place cut side down in a glass baking dish and add water to the dish to a depth of 1/4 inch. Bake 30 minutes or until squash is soft but not mushy. Remove from oven.

In a small bowl, combine butter, lime juice, and chili powder; stir until well blended. Season with salt and pepper. Spoon the butter mixture into baked squash cavities and serve hot.

Makes 4 servings.

Winter Squash Treat

2 acorn squash
1/2 pound sharp cheddar cheese, cut into 8 slices
1 small onion, cut into rings
Salt and pepper to taste

Preheat oven to 350 degrees. Bake the whole squash 35 to 50 minutes or until soft (depending on size). Remove from oven and slice lengthwise into quarters; remove fibers and seeds. Place cheese and onion onto meat side of squash.

Preheat broiler. Place prepared squash onto rack of a broiler pan and broil for a few minutes to melt cheese (watch carefully). Remove from oven, transfer onto a serving platter, and serve immediately with salt and pepper.

Makes 8 servings.

Mashed Winter Squash

2 pounds winter squash, any kind
4 tablespoons butter or margarine
1/4 teaspoon ground nutmeg
1/2 cup light cream or milk
Salt to taste

Cut squash in half lengthwise and remove fibers and seeds; cut into large chunks. In a large saucepan over medium-high heat, boil squash in salted water until tender.

Remove from heat and drain well. Scoop pulp from skin and place into a large bowl with butter or margarine, nutmeg, light cream or milk, and salt. Stir until smooth and well blended. Transfer into a serving bowl and serve immediately.

Makes 4 to 6 servings.

Delicata Squash

Delicata squash are small (weighing a little more than a pound). These slender, oval squash are cream colored with dark green stripes on the outside and deep orange-yellow inside.

They are sweet tasting and evoke the flavor of corn. Their sweet flesh or skin also makes fine eating. They are best simply baked and buttered, but can also be stuffed.

They are available late July through October. In larger cities, they are available year round in most supermarkets.

BAKED WHOLE DELICATA SQUASH: Preheat oven to 400 degrees. Wash squash thoroughly, pierce a few holes in the skin, and bake whole thirty to forty minutes or until squash is soft but not mushy. Remove from oven, slice, and remove seeds and membrane.

Cutting Squash

To cut a small winter squash, first knock off the dried stem by pressing it firmly against the counter. Then, with a whack, sink the blade (not the tip) of a large chef's knife or cleaver into the squash and press down on it heavily or tap it with a mallet, using a rocking motion to help the knife work its way through.

Parmesan Cheese

Parmesan is a very ancient cheese. There are claims that it has been made for over 2,000 years. In Italy, it is made under very controlled conditions only from April to November in great wheels weighing from fifty to sixty pounds. The cheese is then aged for at least two years.

The quality of a cheese can easily determine the flavor of a dish, and no cheese proves to be more of a critical element than parmesan, particularly in pasta, risotto, bread, or soup.

Good parmesan cheese is hard and pungent, and has a sharp, slightly salty taste. Buy imported parmesan in small amounts, store tightly wrapped, and grate just before serving.

Parmesan cheese can be grated in the food processor. Before processing, bring it to room temperature, then chip off one-inch cubes with the point of a sharp knife.

Since parmesan cheese is an aged cheese, it is a misnomer to call it "fresh." "Freshly cut or grated" is a better way to describe it.

TIP: To store parmesan cheese, wrap with a single sheet of plastic wrap and place it in a plastic bag (zipper-lock bag) lined with a paper towel to trap excess moisture.

Fried Summer Squash

1/2 pound summer squash
3 tablespoons all-purpose flour
5 tablespoons water
1/2 teaspoon salt
1/2 teaspoon pepper
4 tablespoons vegetable oil

Cut squash into 1/4-inch thick slices. With a paper towel, pat excess moisture off the squash. In a small bowl, combine flour, water, salt, and pepper to form a batter.

In a large frying pan over medium heat, heat vegetable oil. Dip squash slices into batter and drain excess batter from slices. Add squash slices to hot vegetable oil and cook until lightly browned (turn to brown other side). Remove from heat and drain on paper towels. Transfer onto a serving platter and serve immediately.

Makes 2 servings.

Zucchini Parmesan

These can be served hot as a side dish or at room temperature as an appetizer.

4 small zucchini squash
1 tablespoons olive oil
1/4 cup bread crumbs
1/3 cup freshly grated parmesan cheese
1/2 teaspoon dried rosemary, crushed
2 to 3 dashes red (cayenne) pepper
1/2 teaspoon salt
1/4 teaspoon coarsely ground pepper
1 egg

Preheat oven to 400 degrees. Lightly oil a heavy baking sheet. Trim the ends of the squash. Cut each squash in half lengthwise. Lay the halves flat and cut in half lengthwise again. Cut the strips in half widthwise.

In a shallow dish, combine bread crumbs, parmesan cheese, rosemary, cayenne pepper, salt, and pepper; stir until well blended. In another shallow dish, lightly beat the egg. Dredge each squash piece first in the egg and then in the cheese mixture, coating evenly.

Arrange in a single layer on the prepared baking sheet. Bake 5 to 7 minutes, turn the squash over and bake another 5 to 7 minutes or until crisp and lightly browned. Remove from oven and serve hot or at room temperature.

Makes 4 servings.

Zucchini Puff

4 cups shredded zucchini squash
4 eggs, slightly beaten
1/4 cup baking mix (Bisquick)
1 cup shredded cheddar cheese
1 tablespoon chopped fresh parsley
1 tablespoon dried onion flakes
2 tablespoons freshly grated parmesan cheese
1/4 teaspoon garlic salt
Salt and pepper to taste

Preheat oven to 350 degrees. Drain zucchini in a colander for 1 hour; press out all juice.

In a large bowl, combine eggs and zucchini. Gradually add baking mix, cheddar cheese, parsley, onion flakes, and parmesan cheese. Stir in garlic salt, salt, and pepper. Pour mixture into an ungreased 2-quart casserole dish; bake, uncovered, 25 to 30 minutes. Remove from oven and serve immediately.

Makes 6 to 8 servings.

Zucchini With Lemon

May also be grilled on your barbecue.

1 1/4 pounds zucchini squash
2 tablespoons olive oil
2 cloves garlic, minced
1 teaspoon finely chopped fresh rosemary or 1/2 teaspoon
   dried rosemary, crushed
1/2 teaspoon coarsely ground pepper
1/4 teaspoon salt
Lemon wedges

Preheat broiler. Trim and cut zucchini lengthwise into 1/4-inch thick slices. Arrange zucchini slices in single layer onto a large ungreased baking sheet; overlapping slices to fit if necessary.

In a small bowl, combine olive oil, garlic, rosemary, and pepper. Brush zucchini slices with olive-oil mixture.

Broil 6 inches from heat 5 to 6 minutes or until tender. Remove from heat and transfer to a serving bowl. Season with salt. To serve, garnish with lemon wedges.

Makes 4 to 6 servings.

Rosemary

Rosemary is native to the Mediterranean area. It is a slender leaf resembling pine needles and has a distinctive fresh flavor.

Italian cooks are devoted to rosemary, which is said to grow only in the gardens of the righteous.

One of the many legends about this herb declares that sleeping with a sprig of it under your pillow would ward off demons and prevent bad dreams.

In ancient Greece, students believed this herb would improve their memory, so they wore rosemary garlands while studying for exams.

At one time, rosemary was used in almost every wedding ceremony. Brides wore wreaths woven with sprigs of rosemary dipped in scented water or they carried rosemary in their bouquets.

TIPS: A rosemary bath can refresh and stimulate a worn and sluggish body.

Make a strong tea from the leaves and add it to the bath water, or make a steam facial with an infusion of rosemary leaves to perk up your face.

Squash

Squash Blossoms

Do as the Italians have done for generations. Enjoy the prolific production of a squash vine by eating the blossoms as well as the fruit.

The flowers from both summer and winter squash are edible and delicious. Zucchini and pumpkin flowers make a colorful dish. They are both used extensively in Italian cooking.

Pick blossoms soon after they open. They need to be handled gently but are more durable than you might expect.

Use the blossoms right away or, if you want to save them until you have more to use at one time, refrigerate them for up to three days in a sealed container.

Before refrigerating, lay washed and drained blossoms cut side down or on their sides in a single layer on a pan lined with paper towels; cover lightly, but airtight, with plastic wrap.

TIP: Use only the male blossoms or you won't have any squash to eat later. Don't use all your male blossoms. Leave about half of them on the vine for pollinating female blossoms.

Deep-Fried Squash Blossoms

This recipe may be used with any squash blossom.

18 large or 36 small squash blossoms
Vegetable oil
Blossom Batter
1 clove garlic, minced
2 tablespoons finely chopped fresh Italian parsley or cilantro
Salt
Lemon juice

Reach into the well of the squash blossom and pinch out the stem in the middle, then rinse thoroughly with gentle running water to wash them; drain flowers, cup down on paper towels or pat dry.

In a large, heavy saucepan over medium heat, heat 1 inch of vegetable oil. Just before immersing blossoms, add garlic and Italian parsley or cilantro to batter; stirring well.

Hold each blossom by the stem and dip it completely into Blossom Batter (coating it inside and out). Lift blossom out and let any excess batter drip back into bowl.

Carefully place each blossom into hot vegetable oil and fry until golden brown on the first side, then turn and continue cooking until the second side is well colored (total cooking time 2 to 3 minutes). Only fry as many blossoms as will fit comfortably in the frying pan at a time.

Remove from heat and drain on paper towels; sprinkle with salt. Sprinkle a few drops of lemon juice over the deep-fried blossoms for flavor. Transfer onto a serving platter and serve at once or place the fried blossoms into a 275-degree oven until serving time (lay them on paper towels).

Makes 6 servings.

BLOSSOM BATTER:
1 1/2 cups all-purpose flour
1 teaspoon salt
2 cups cold water
1 tablespoon olive oil
1 egg, lightly beaten

In a medium bowl, sift flour and salt; whisk in water, olive oil, and egg. Batter should be smooth and the consistency of light cream.

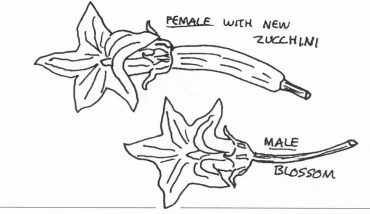

FEMALE WITH NEW ZUCCHINI

MALE BLOSSOM

Enchiladas de Zucchini

You will be pleasantly surprised with this delicious dish. Great last-minute dinner dish.

5 tablespoons butter or margarine, divided
3 tablespoons vegetable oil
12 corn tortillas
1 yellow onion, finely chopped
1 pound lean ground beef
3 cups grated unpeeled zucchini squash
1/4 cup chopped black olives
1 teaspoon garlic powder
Salt and pepper to taste
2 cups shredded monterey jack cheese
2 (10-ounce) cans enchilada sauce
1 to 1 1/2 cups shredded cheddar cheese

Preheat oven to 350 degrees. In a large frying pan over medium heat, melt 3 tablespoons butter or margarine and vegetable oil. Fry tortillas, one or two at a time, 5 seconds each, turning once. Remove from heat as soon as they become limp; drain well on paper towels.

In same frying pan, melt 2 tablespoons butter or margarine. Add onion and sauté until soft. Add ground beef and cook until all pink is gone; drain off fat. Add zucchini, olives, garlic powder, salt, and pepper. Sauté another 5 minutes; stirring from time to time. Remove from heat.

To form enchiladas, place a fried tortilla onto a plate. Heap a rounded 1/4 cup of zucchini mixture onto center of tortilla and top with a heaping tablespoon of monterey jack cheese. Roll tortilla and place seam side down into an ungreased shallow baking dish. When all tortillas are filled, pour enchilada sauce over top and sprinkle with cheddar cheese.

Bake, uncovered, 15 minutes. (If enchiladas have been made ahead and refrigerated, bake 30 minutes.) Remove from oven and serve immediately.

Makes 6 servings (2 enchiladas each).

Summer Squash

The term "summer" and "winter" for squash are only based on current usage, not on actuality. "Summer" types are on the market all winter; and "winter" types are on the market in the late summer and fall, as well as winter. Thus, the terms "summer" and "winter" are deceptive and confusing.

TYPES OF SUMMER SQUASH:

- *Chayote*
- *Straightneck*
- *White pattypan*
- *Yellow crookneck*
- *Zucchini*

Summer squash have thin, edible skins. Store summer squash in a plastic bag in the refrigerator for no more than five days.

Summer squash may be prepared in any of the usual ways for boiling and baking vegetables and may also be fried.

Grilling Vegetables

Almost any vegetable will work when grilling. Just pick what looks best in your garden or at the farm stand. Tender, quick-cooking vegetables are the easiest to work with. Some suggested vegetables for grilling are asparagus, bell pepper slices, corn, mushrooms, onion slices or baby onions, scallions, summer squash, eggplant slices, and small new potatoes.

Preheat barbecue grill. Cook vegetables over direct heat, but don't crowd them or they'll cook unevenly.

Skewering vegetables makes it much easier to move them around and turn them on the grill. If skewered, small vegetables won't fall through the grill bars and into the fire.

Cooking times will vary, depending on your grill, the weather, and the size of the vegetables – so watch carefully. Vegetables are cooked properly when they're soft enough to be pierced easily with a fork or the tip of a knife (but they still have some "bite" to them).

TIP: You can use crowding to your advantage if the vegetables are done too soon. Push them off to the side and bunch them together. This slows the cooking but keeps the vegetables moist and warm.

Grilled Vegetables With Balsamic Vinaigrette

1 medium eggplant (about 1 1/4 pounds)
1 1/4 pounds zucchini squash
1 1/4 pounds yellow summer squash
2 medium red bell peppers, cored and seeded
Balsamic Vinaigrette

Trim and slice eggplant, zucchini, and yellow squash lengthwise into 1/4- to 1/2-inch thick slices. Cut peppers into 1-inch wide strips.

Place all the vegetables into a large casserole dish. Pour Balsamic Vinaigrette over vegetables; turn to coat. Let stand 30 minutes or longer. Lift vegetables from vinaigrette, reserving vinaigrette.

Preheat barbecue grill. Place vegetables onto hot grill and cook 8 to 16 minutes or until fork tender, turning once or twice (time will depend on the vegetables; eggplant takes the longest). As vegetables are done, transfer into a casserole dish, then turn to coat with Balsamic Vinaigrette.

Makes 6 servings.

BALSAMIC VINAIGRETTE:
3/4 cup olive oil
1/4 cup balsamic vinegar
1 teaspoon salt
1/4 teaspoon pepper
1 clove garlic, minced
2 to 3 tablespoons finely chopped mixed fresh herbs (basil, tarragon, chives, and/or rosemary)

In a small bowl, combine olive oil, balsamic vinegar, salt, pepper, garlic, and chopped herbs.

Blue Baked Tomatoes

4 medium tomatoes, peeled
1 cup thick blue cheese salad dressing
1/4 cup sliced green onions
4 bacon slices, cooked crisp and crumbled
4 teaspoons chopped fresh parsley

Slice stem end from tomatoes. With a sharp knife make 3 or 4 vertical cuts onto top of tomato, cutting about halfway through tomato. Place, cut side up, into an ungreased 8-inch square baking dish. Pour 1/4 inch of water into baking dish.

Preheat broiler. In a small bowl, combine blue cheese salad dressing and green onions; spoon a heaping tablespoon of mixture over each tomato. Broil 4 minutes or until bubbly and lightly browned. Remove from oven and garnish with crumbled bacon and parsley to serve.

Makes 4 servings.

The Terrific Tomato

4 large tomatoes
Salt and pepper to taste
Mayonnaise Dressing
Paprika

Cut tomatoes in half, widthwise. Place into a microwave-safe dish. Sprinkle with salt and pepper. Spread Mayonnaise Dressing on tomatoes; sprinkle lightly with paprika.

Cook, uncovered, in microwave oven 2 1/2 to 3 minutes at full power. When mixture starts to bubble, remove from microwave and serve. Tomatoes will finish cooking in their own heat.

Makes 4 servings.

MAYONNAISE DRESSING:
1/2 cup mayonnaise
2 teaspoons minced onion
2 tablespoons prepared mustard

In a small bowl, combine mayonnaise, onion, and prepared mustard.

History of Tomatoes

Contrary to popular belief, tomatoes have been grown as a food since the 16th century, though they have in various times and places been regarded as both poisonous and decorative plants.

The Italian name for the tomato is pomodoro, meaning "apple of love" or "golden apple," because the first to reach Europe were yellow varieties.

Tomatoes were not cultivated in North America until the 1700s, and then only in home gardens. Thomas Jefferson was raising tomatoes by 1782. Most people of that century paid little attention to tomatoes. Only in the next century did they make their way into American cookbooks, always with instructions that they be cooked for at least three hours or else they "will not lose their raw taste."

Stuffed or Baked Tomatoes

To keep baked or stuffed tomatoes from collapsing, bake in greased muffin tins. The tins will give them some support as they cook. The same trick can be used when making stuffed onions.

Tomatoes

How to Peel Tomatoes

Bring a large pot of water to a boil. With a paring knife, cut an "X" through the skin on bottom of each tomato. Drop tomatoes, a few at a time, into water for thirty seconds. Remove tomatoes with a slotted spoon to a bowl filled with ice water to cool them down. The skin will easily slip off each tomato.

If you have a gas stove, tomatoes can be peeled easily and quickly. Pierce a tomato with a long-handled fork and rotate the tomato over the flame until the skin darkens and blisters. It's then ready to peel.

Tomatoes Equivalents

FRESH PEELED PLUM TOMATOES: 2 1/2 pounds tomatoes equals 3 cups chopped and drained fresh tomatoes, or 2 1/2 cups chopped and cooked tomatoes, or 2 1/2 cups canned tomatoes in purée or juice.

1 (35-ounce) can equals 4 cups undrained or 2 1/2 to 3 cups drained tomatoes.

1 (28-ounce) can equals 3 cups undrained or 2 to 2 1/2 cups drained tomatoes.

1 (16-ounce) can equals 2 cups drained tomatoes or 1 cup undrained tomatoes.

CANNED CRUSHED OR CHOPPED TOMATOES: 1 (28-ounce can) equals 3 cups tomatoes.

Baked Tomatoes in Cream

This is one of the most delicious ways to serve garden-ripe tomatoes. This seems to be a favorite of most men.

6 to 8 large tomatoes
Sugar
6 to 8 tablespoons butter, divided
Salt to taste
2 cups heavy cream
3 tablespoons chopped fresh chives
1 teaspoon salt

Preheat oven to 350 degrees. Peel tomatoes by immersing in boiling water for 10 seconds or until skins are loosened. Cut out a cone-shaped piece, about 1-inch long, from each stem-end. Place the tomatoes in a shallow glass baking dish.

Fill the tomato hollows with sugar. Top each with 1 tablespoon butter and sprinkle with salt. Fill baking dish with 1/4-inch of warm water. Bake, uncovered, 20 to 25 minutes or until tomatoes are tender (do not bake too long or they will lose their shape).

In a large saucepan over medium-low heat, combine cream, chives, and salt; heat but do not allow to boil. To serve, place the tomatoes in individual serving dishes. Spoon equal amounts of tomato broth and hot cream mixture over tomatoes.

Makes 6 to 8 servings.

Fried Green Tomatoes

3 tablespoons all-purpose flour
5 tablespoons water
1/2 teaspoon salt
1/2 teaspoon pepper
4 tablespoons vegetable oil
4 firm green tomatoes, sliced 1/4-inch thick

In a medium bowl, combine flour, water, salt, and pepper to form a batter to coat the tomatoes.

In a medium frying pan over medium heat, heat vegetable oil. Dip tomatoes into batter; drain excess batter from slices and cook 5 minutes in hot vegetable oil. Turn to brown other side. Remove from heat and drain on paper towels. Transfer onto a serving platter and serve immediately.

Makes 4 servings.

Tomato Pie With Potato Crust

When tomatoes are in season, you must make this tomato pie. It's absolutely wonderful.

Potato Crust
3 or 4 medium tomatoes, sliced, drained, and patted dry
Salt and pepper to taste
8 bacon slices, cooked crisp and crumbled
4 tablespoons coarsely chopped fresh basil, divided
3/4 cup freshly grated parmesan cheese
3/4 cup mayonnaise
1/3 cup crushed saltine crackers

Make Potato Crust and bake while you are preparing tomato mixture.

Layer half of the tomato slices onto the bottom of baked Potato Crust; lightly season tomatoes with salt and pepper. Sprinkle with half of the bacon and 3 tablespoons basil. Repeat layer, using remaining tomato slices, salt, pepper, bacon, and basil.

In a small bowl, combine parmesan cheese and mayonnaise; carefully spread over tomato mixture. Sprinkle with crushed crackers and 1 tablespoon basil. Bake, uncovered, 30 minutes or until crumbs begin to brown. Remove from oven and serve immediately.

NOTE: A 9-inch unbaked deep-dish pie crust may be substituted for the Potato Crust (see page 122).

Makes 4 servings.

POTATO CRUST:
2 firmly packed cups grated raw potatoes
1/2 teaspoon salt
1 egg, beaten
1/4 cup grated onion
Vegetable oil

Preheat oven to 400 degrees. Oil a 9-inch pie pan. Place raw potatoes in a colander. Salt potatoes and let set for 10 minutes. Squeeze out the excess water.

In a medium bowl combine potatoes, egg, and onion. Pat potato mixture into prepared pie pan, building up the sides of the crust with lightly floured fingers. Bake 35 to 40 minutes or until golden brown (after the first 20 minutes brush the crust with vegetable oil to crispen it). Remove from oven. Reduce oven temperature to 350 degrees.

Tomatoes

Tomatoes don't develop adequate flavor unless allowed to ripen on the vine. Seek out locally grown tomatoes whenever possible. They may not be as "pretty" as store bought, but beauty, of course, is only skin deep.

Since fresh tomatoes are summer fare and off-season tomatoes are rarely flavorful, substitute canned Italian plum tomatoes in cooked dishes. Cook for ten minutes to reduce the liquid and enhance the taste.

Never refrigerate fresh tomatoes! Cold temperatures make the flesh of a tomato pulpy and destroys the flavor.

To ripen, place green or unripened tomatoes in a brown paper bag and place in a dark spot for three or four days, depending on the degree of greenness. Do not put tomatoes in the sun to ripen – this softens them.

TIP: Always add a pinch of sugar to tomatoes when cooking them. It enhances the flavor.

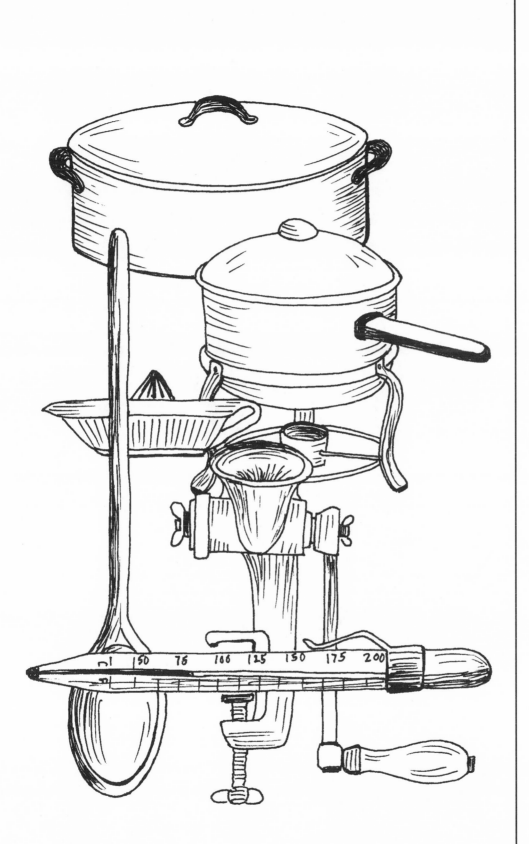

Cooking Basics

Equivalent Measurements

This table is to help you translate amounts stated in terms of one measuring device into those of another.

TEASPOONS:

1/8 teaspoon	a pinch
1/2 teaspoon	30 drops
1 teaspoon	1/3 tablespoon
3 teaspoons	1 tablespoon

TABLESPOONS:

1/2 tablespoon	1 1/2 teaspoons
1 tablespoon	3 teaspoons or 1/2 ounce
2 tablespoons	1/8 cup or 1 ounce
3 tablespoons	1 1/2 ounces
3 tablespoons	1 jigger
4 tablespoons	1/4 cup or 2 ounces
5 tablespoons + 1 teaspoon	1/3 cup
8 tablespoons	1/2 cup or 4 ounces
10 tablespoons + 2 teaspoons	2/3 cup
12 tablespoons	3/4 cup or 6 ounces
16 tablespoons	1 cup
16 tablespoons	1/2 pint or 8 ounces
64 tablespoons	1 quart

CUPS:

1/8 cup	2 tablespoons or 1 ounce
1/4 cup	4 tablespoons or 2 ounces
1/3 cup	5 tablespoons + 1 teaspoon
3/8 cup	6 tablespoons
1/2 cup	8 tablespoons or 4 ounces
1/2 cup	1 tea cup
1/2 cup	1/4 pint
2/3 cup	10 tablespoons + 2 teaspoons
3/4 cup	12 tablespoons or 6 ounces
1 cup	16 tablespoons or 8 ounces or 1/2 pound
1 cup	1/2 pint
2 cups	1 pint or 16 ounces or 1 pound
4 cups	2 pints or 1 quart or 32 ounces
16 cups	1 gallon

Approximate Common Food Equivalents

Ingredient	Weight or Amount	Approximate Measure or Yield
Apples	1 pound (3 medium)	3 cups sliced
Bananas	1 pound (3 medium)	2 1/2 cups sliced, 2 cups mashed
Beans, dried	1 pound (2 1/2 cups)	6 cups cooked
Bell Pepper	1 large (6 ounces)	1 cup diced
Butter or Margarine	1 pound	2 cups
1 stick or cube	1/2 cup	
Celery	2 ribs	1 cup sliced
Cheese, American	1 pound	4 to 5 cups shredded
Cottage	1 pound	2 cups
Cream	3-ounce package	6 tablespoons
Hard Cheese	1/4 pound	1 cup grated or shredded
Chicken	3 1/2-pound fryer	3 cups cooked, diced
Chocolate	1 ounce (1 square)	5 tablespoons
Cocoa	1 pound	4 cups
Coconut, shredded	1 pound	5 cups
Corn	2 medium ears	1 cup, cut off cob
Cream, whipping	1 cup or 1/2 pint	2 cups whipped
Crumbs, fine		
Bread	1 slice dried bread	1/3 cup fine crumbs
Chocolate wafers	18 wafers	1 cup fine crumbs
Graham crackers	16 squares	1 cup fine crumbs
Saltine crackers	28 squares	1 cup fine crumbs
Vanilla wafers	22 wafers	1 cup fine crumbs
Lemon Juice	1 medium sized	2 tablespoons
Zest	1 medium sized	1 tablespoon
Milk		
Evaporated	6-ounce can	3/4 cup
Evaporated	14.5-ounce can	1 2/3 cups
Powdered	1 pound	3 cups
Sweetened Condensed	14.5-ounce can	1 1/4 cups
Onion	1 small	1/4 cup chopped
	1 medium	3/4 cup chopped
	1 large	1 cup chopped
Orange Juice	1 medium sized	1/4 to 1/3 cup
Zest	1 medium sized	1 to 2 tablespoons
Peaches	1 pound (4 to 5 peaches)	2 1/2 cups sliced
Potatoes	1 1/4 pounds (3 medium)	3 cups chopped
Raisins, seedless	1 pound	3 cups
Rice, uncooked	1 cup	3 cups cooked
Strawberries	1 pint	2 1/4 cups sliced
Sugar		
Brown	1 pound	2 1/4 cups firmly packed
Powdered	1 pound	4 to 4 1/2 cups unsifted
Granulated	1 pound	2 cups
Tomatoes	2 1/2 pounds	3 cups chopped and drained

Emergency Ingredient Substitutions

No substitution will yield a product exactly like that made by the item it's replacing. But for baking and cooking purposes, recipes will work with substitutes. This guide is handy to have when your supplies run short.

Ingredient	Substitute
Baking powder – 1 teaspoon	= 1/4 teaspoon baking soda + 5/8 teaspoon cream of tartar
	= 1/4 teaspoon baking soda + 1/2 cup sour milk or buttermilk (reduce liquid in recipe by 1/2 cup)
Bread crumbs – 1 cup	= 3/4 cup cracker crumbs
Broth, chicken or beef – 1 cup	= 1 chicken or beef bouillon cube + 1 cup hot water
Butter – 1 cup	= Same amount of margarine
	= 7/8 cups vegetable oil, lard, or vegetable shortening
	= 3/4 cup chicken or bacon fat
Buttermilk or sour milk – 1 cup	= 1 cup plain yogurt
	= 1 tablespoon vinegar or lemon juice + enough milk to equal 1 cup
Chocolate, semisweet – 1 ounce	= 1/2 ounce unsweetened chocolate + 1 tablespoon granulated sugar
Chocolate, unsweetened – 1 ounce	= 3 tablespoons unsweetened cocoa + 1 tablespoon butter or margarine
	= 3 tablespoons carob powder + 2 tablespoons water
Cornstarch – 1 tablespoon	= 2 tablespoons all-purpose flour or 2 teaspoons arrowroot
Corn syrup, light or dark – 1 cup	= 1 1/4 cups granulated or packed brown sugar + 1/4 cup liquid
	= 3/4 cup maple syrup or honey or 1 1/4 cups molasses
Cream, light – 1 cup	= 3 tablespoon butter + enough whole milk to equal 1 cup
Cream, whipping – 1 cup	= 3/4 cup whole milk + 1/3 cup butter (for baking or cooking only)
Eggs, whole – 1 large egg	= 2 large egg yolks + 1 tablespoon cold water
Eggs, whole – 2 large eggs	= 3 small eggs
Flour, sifted all-purpose – 1 cup	= 1 cup minus 2 tablespoons unsifted all-purpose flour
Flour, cake – 1 cup	= 1 cup all-purpose flour minus 2 tablespoons or all-purpose flour sifted 3 times and then measured to make 1 cup
Flour (thickening) – 2 tablespoons	= 1 tablespoon cornstarch, potato starch, or rice starch
	= 4 teaspoons arrowroot or 2 tablespoons quick-cooking tapioca
Garlic, fresh – 1 clove	= 1 teaspoon garlic salt or 1/8 teaspoon garlic powder
Ginger, ground – 1/8 teaspoon	= 1 tablespoon fresh ginger root, finely chopped
Herbs, fresh – 1 tablespoon	= 1 teaspoon dried crumbled or 1/4 heaping teaspoon ground herbs
Honey – 1 cup	= 1 1/4 cups granulated sugar + 1/4 cup liquid in recipe
Lemon juice – 1 fresh lemon	= 2 tablespoons bottled lemon juice
Lemon juice – 1 teaspoon	= 1/2 teaspoon vinegar
Milk, nonfat – 1 cup	= 1/3 cup powdered nonfat milk + 3/4 cup water
Milk, whole – 1 cup	= 1 cup water + 1 1/2 teaspoons butter
	= 1/2 cup evaporated milk + 1/2 cup water
Mustard, prepared – 1 teaspoon	= 1 teaspoon powdered mustard + 1 teaspoon water
Onion, minced – 1/4 cup	= 1 tablespoon instant minced onion, rehydrated
Orange juice – 1 fresh orange	= 1/4 cup reconstituted frozen orange juice
Sugar, powdered – 1 cup	= 1/2 cup + 1 tablespoon granulated sugar
Sugar, brown – 1/2 cup	= 2 tablespoons molasses + 1/2 cup granulated sugar
Tomato sauce – 1 cup	= 3/8 cup tomato paste + 1/2 cup water
Yeast, active dry – 1 envelope (1 tbs)	= 1 compressed yeast cake, crumbled
Yogurt – 1 cup	= 1 cup buttermilk

Metric Conversions

By making a few conversions, cooks in Australia, Canada, and Europe can use the recipes in this book. To figure the approximate conversion for metric values, see the following simple table. THERE IS NO EXACT CONVERSION. Most recipes with metric equivalents of imperial weights and measures have been rounded off to the closest convenient figure. NOTE: When converting to or from metric, be sure to convert ALL measurements. Otherwise, the proportions of the ingredients could be critically unbalanced.

When You Know	Multiply By	To Find
Ounces (oz)	28.35	Grams (g)
Pounds (lb)	0.454	Kilograms (kg)
Teaspoons (tsp)	4.93	Milliliters (ml)
Tablespoons (tbs)	14.79	Milliliters (ml)
Fluid Ounces (fl oz)	30.0	Milliliters (ml)
Cups (c)	236.59	Milliliters (ml)
Cups (c)	0.236	Liters (l)
Pints (pt)	473.18	Milliliters (ml)
Pints (pt)	0.473	Liters (l)
Quarts (qt)	946.36	Milliliters (ml)
Quarts (qt)	0.946	Liters (l)
Gallons (gal)	3.785	Liters (l)

PRODUCT DIFFERENCES GUIDE

Most products and ingredients used in the recipes in this book are available in English-speaking countries. However, some are known by different names. Here are some common American ingredients and their possible counterparts.

American Name	Counterpart Name
All-purpose flour	Plain household flour or white flour
Slice of bacon	Rasher of bacon
Baking soda	Bicarbonate of soda
Beet	Beetroot
Bell pepper	Capsicum
Cornstarch	Cornflour
Light corn syrup	Golden syrup
Powdered sugar	Icing sugar
Green Beans	Runner beans
Sugar	Granulated or caster sugar
Vanilla extract	Vanilla essence
Yogurt	Yoghurt

OVEN TEMPERATURE GUIDE
Oven temperature in Fahrenheit and Celsius (formerly Centrigrade) are:

Oven	Degrees F	Degrees C
Cool	200	100
Very Slow	250	120
Slow	300	150
Moderately Slow	325	160
Moderate	350	180
Moderately Hot	375	190
Hot	400	200
Very Hot	450	230
Extremely Hot	500	260

Legumes Cooking Chart

Most dried legumes should be soaked before they are cooked. Either soak overnight in water to cover or use the quick-soak method.

QUICK SOAKING: For each pound of dry legumes, bring eight cups water to a boil. Add washed and sorted legumes and boil for two minutes. Remove from heat, cover pan, and let stand for one hour. Drain and rinse legumes, discarding water.

OVERNIGHT SOAKING: For each pound of dry legumes, add six cups water. Add washed and sorted legumes; soak until next day. Drain and rinse legumes, discarding water.

The following chart gives boiling time and quantities to serve three to four persons, depending on whether vegetable is an accompaniment or a main course. NOTE: Always pick over dried beans, careful to remove stones, etc.

Vegetable	Soaking	Water (in cups)	Cooking Time (hours)	Yield (in cups)
1 1/4 cups black beans	Yes	3	2	2 1/2
1 cup blackeyed peas	Yes	2 1/2	1/2	2 1/2
1 cup garbanzo beans or chick peas	Yes	2 1/2	2	2 1/2
1 cup great northern beans (white beans)	Yes	2 1/2	1 1/4	2 1/2
1 cup kidney beans	Yes	3	2	2 3/4
1 cup lentils	No	2 1/2	1/2	2 1/2
1 cup lima beans, large	Yes	2 1/2	1	2 1/2
1 1/4 cups lima beans, small	Yes	2 1/2	3/4	2 1/2
1 cup navy beans (small white beans)	Yes	3	1 3/4	2 1/2
1 cup pea beans	Yes	3	1 3/4	2 1/2
1 cup peas, whole	Yes	2 1/2	1	2 1/2
1 cup pink pinto & red beans	Yes	3	2	2 1/2
1 cup split peas (green & yellow)	No	3	1/2	2 1/2
1 cup soybeans	Yes	3	3	2 1/2

Broiling & Grilling Steaks

Always thaw meat in the refrigerator. Bring meat to room temperature before cooking. For juicier and more flavorful steaks, tongs should be used when handling or turning meat (do not puncture meat when cooking).

Cooking units vary, and it is always advisable to run your own tests when cooking steaks. The chart below is a guide. The cooking times below are for fully thawed steaks.

You can successfully cook frozen steaks. Start by searing both sides to seal in juices. Then reduce heat for slow cooking to allow the inside to thaw. Follow the chart below, but allow about twice the cooking time for frozen steaks.

Cooking Instructions		Charcoal or Gas Barbecue 2 3/4" from heat source		Pre-Heated Oven Broiler 2" from heat source	
Thickness	*Doneness*	*First Side*	*After Turning*	*First Side*	*After Turning*
3/4"	Rare	4 Minutes	2 Minutes	5 Minutes	4 Minutes
3/4"	Medium	5 Minutes	3 Minutes	7 Minutes	5 Minutes
3/4"	Well	7 Minutes	5 Minutes	10 Minutes	8 Minutes
1"	Rare	5 Minutes	3 Minutes	6 Minutes	5 Minutes
1"	Medium	6 Minutes	4 Minutes	8 Minutes	6 Minutes
1"	Well	8 Minutes	6 Minutes	11 Minutes	9 Minutes
1 1/4"	Rare	5 Minutes	4 Minutes	7 Minutes	5 Minutes
1 1/4"	Medium	7 Minutes	5 Minutes	8 Minutes	7 Minutes
1 1/4"	Well	9 Minutes	7 Minutes	12 Minutes	10 Minutes
1 1/2"	Rare	6 Minutes	4 Minutes	7 Minutes	6 Minutes
1 1/2"	Medium	7 Minutes	6 Minutes	9 Minutes	7 Minutes
1 1/2"	Well	10 Minutes	8 Minutes	13 Minutes	11 Minutes
1 3/4"	Rare	7 Minutes	5 Minutes	8 Minutes	7 Minutes
1 3/4"	Medium	8 Minutes	7 Minutes	9 Minutes	8 Minutes
1 3/4"	Well	11 Minutes	9 Minutes	14 Minutes	12 Minutes

Vegetable Cooking Time Table

Vegetable	Baking (minutes)	Boiling (minutes)	Grilling (minutes)	Steaming (minutes)	Test for Doneness
Artichokes, whole		25 to 40		30 to 45	Tender when pierced
Asparagus spears		5 to 8		8 to 12	Tender when pierced
Beans, green		10 to 20		20 to 30	Tender-crisp to bite
Beets, whole	50 to 60	30 to 45		40 to 60	Tender when pierced
Broccoli flowerets	20 to 25	7 to 12		15 to 20	Stalk tender when pierced
Brussels sprouts		8 to 10		15 to 20	Tender when pierced
Cabbage					Tender when pierced
chopped	25 to 30	5 to 10		8 to 12	
wedges	15 to 30	10 to 15		15 to 20	
Carrots					Tender when pierced
whole, baby	35 to 45	8 to 10	25 to 30	15 to 20	
whole, large	60	20 to 30		40 to 50	
1/4" - 1" slices	30 to 40	10 to 15	25 to 30	15 to 20	
Cauliflower					Tender when pierced
whole	30	15 to 20		25 to 30	
flowerets	25	7 to 14		10 to 20	
Corn on the cob	20 to 25	3 to 5	15 to 20	8 to 10	Tender when pierced
Garlic, large heads	60				Tender when pierced
Onions					Tender when pierced
small boiling	20	15 to 20	20	20 to 25	
medium sized	30 to 45	20 to 30	30 to 45	35 to 40	
Parsnips, whole	35 to 45	8 to 10		10 to 20	Tender when pierced
Peas, green (shelled)		8 to 15		10 to 20	Tender to bite
Potatoes, red or white					Tender when pierced
whole	50 to 60	20 to 30	50 to 55	30 to 35	
1/2" slices		8 to 10		8 to 10	
Potatoes, sweet or yams					
whole	45 to 50	20 to 30		30 to 40	Tender when pierced
Spinach, leaves		3 to 7		5 to 10	Wilted appearance
Squash – summer					
1/4" - 1" slices	20 to 30	3 to 6	10 to 15	4 to 7	Tender when pierced
Squash – winter					
1/2" - 1" slices		7 to 9	15 to 25	9 to 12	Tender when pierced
cut in half	30 to 40				

Baking Dish and Pan Sizes

The following table will help determine substitutions of pans and dishes of similar approximate sizes if you do not have the specific-sized baking pan, dish, or mold called for in a recipe.

IMPORTANT TIPS TO REMEMBER:

- To substitute with glass pan, reduce the baking temperature by 25 degrees.

- To substitute a pan that is shallower than the pan in the recipe, reduce the baking time by one-fourth.

- To substitute a pan that is deeper than the pan in the recipe, increase the baking time by one-fourth.

3-CUP BAKING DISH OR PAN:

8" x 1 1/4" round pie pan

4-CUP BAKING DISH OR PAN:

8" x 1 1/2" round layer cake pan

8" x 4" x 2 1/2" loaf pan

9" x 1 1/2" round pie pan

11" x 1" round tart pan

6-CUP BAKING DISH OR PAN:

7 1/2" x 3" bundt tube pan

8" x 8" x 2" square pan

8 1/2" x 4 1/2" x 2 1/2" loaf pan

9" x 1 1/2" round layer cake pan

9" x 2" round pie plate (deep dish)

9" x 9" x 1 1/2" rectangular pan

10" x 1 1/2" round pie plate

11" x 7" x 2" rectangular pan

7-CUP BAKING DISH OR PAN:

8" x 2" round cake pan

9" x 9" x 2" rectangular pan

8-CUP BAKING DISH OR PAN:

8" x 8" x 2" square pan

9" x 2" round cake pan

9" x 5" x 3" loaf pan

9" x 9" x 1 1/2" square pan

9 1/4" x 2 3/4" ring mold

9 1/2" x 3 1/4" brioche pan

11" x 7" x 1 1/2" baking pan

9-CUP BAKING DISH OR PAN:

8" x 3" bundt pan

9" x 3" tube pan

10-CUP BAKING DISH OR PAN:

8" x 2 1/2" springform pan

9" x 9" x 2" square pan

11 3/4" x 7 1/2" x 1 3/4" baking pan

13" x 9" x 2" rectangular pan

15 1/2" x 10 1/2" x 1" jelly-roll pan

11-CUP BAKING DISH OR PAN:

9" x 3" springform pan

10" x 2" round cake pan

12-CUP BAKING DISH OR PAN:

9" x 3" angel-cake pan or tube pan

10" x 2 1/2" springform pan

10" x 3 1/2" bundt pan

13" x 9" x 2" metal baking pan

14" x 10 1/2" x 2 1/2" roasting pan

15-CUP BAKING DISH OR PAN:

13" x 9" x 2" rectangular pan

16-CUP BAKING DISH OR PAN:

9" x 3 1/2" springform pan

10" x 4" fancy tube mold

18-CUP BAKING DISH OR PAN:

10" x 4" angel-cake or tube pan

Index

A

Index

Index

Index

Index

D

Index

Index

Index

Index

P

Pacific Coast Clam Chowder, 342
Paella, 317
  about, 317

Index

Q

R

Index

S

Index

X-Y-Z